Kant's Deontological Eudaemonism

Kant's Deontological Eudaemonism

The Dutiful Pursuit of Virtue and Happiness

JEANINE M. GRENBERG

OXFORD
UNIVERSITY PRESS

Great Clarendon Street, Oxford, OX2 6DP,
United Kingdom

Oxford University Press is a department of the University of Oxford.
It furthers the University's objective of excellence in research, scholarship,
and education by publishing worldwide. Oxford is a registered trade mark of
Oxford University Press in the UK and in certain other countries

© Jeanine M. Grenberg 2022

The moral rights of the author have been asserted

First Edition published in 2022

All rights reserved. No part of this publication may be reproduced, stored in
a retrieval system, or transmitted, in any form or by any means, without the
prior permission in writing of Oxford University Press, or as expressly permitted
by law, by licence or under terms agreed with the appropriate reprographics
rights organization. Enquiries concerning reproduction outside the scope of the
above should be sent to the Rights Department, Oxford University Press, at the
address above

You must not circulate this work in any other form
and you must impose this same condition on any acquirer

Published in the United States of America by Oxford University Press
198 Madison Avenue, New York, NY 10016, United States of America

British Library Cataloguing in Publication Data

Data available

Library of Congress Control Number: 2022934424

ISBN 978–0–19–286438–3

DOI: 10.1093/oso/9780192864383.001.0001

Printed and bound in the UK by
Clays Ltd, Elcograf S.p.A.

Links to third party websites are provided by Oxford in good faith and
for information only. Oxford disclaims any responsibility for the materials
contained in any third party website referenced in this work.

To Anthony, once again, for everything.

Cicero, De officiis I.117: "In primis autem constituendum est, quos nos et quales esse velimus et in quo genere vitae, quae deliberatio est omnium difficillima"

"Most importantly, however, we must decide who we want to be, what kind of people we want to be, and what kind of life we want to live. This is the most difficult decision of all."

translation by Professor Hilary Bouxsein,
Classics Department, St. Olaf College

Contents

Acknowledgments   xi

Introductory Thoughts   1
  Introduction   1
    I. A History of Philosophical Blunders   2
    II. Toward a Positive Conception of Kant's Deontological Eudaemonism   9
    III. Summary of Chapters   17
    IV. A Note on Phenomenological Method   28

I. DEONTOLOGICAL TELEOLOGY: THE OBJECTIVE TELOS OF VIRTUE

I.i In Search of the Objective Telos of Self-Governance   33
  Introduction   33
    I. The Contours and Limits of Naturalistic reasoning   34
    II. Seeking a More Satisfactory Objective Telos for Self-Governance of Desire   60
  Conclusion   71

I.ii Deontological Teleology: An Objective and End-Based Approach to the Virtuous Self-Governance of Desire   73
  Introduction   73
    I. Interpretive Work on Kant, Ends, and the Formula of Humanity   76
    II. Kant's Early Thoughts on Ends   97
    III. The Freedom of End-Setting   106
  Conclusion   130

I.iii The Proper Objective Telos of Deontological Teleology: Making Persons as Such One's End   135
  Introduction   135
    I. Preliminary Thoughts on the Deduction of Respect for Persons as the Material, Objective Telos of Virtue   137
    II. The Deduction of Respect for Persons as the Material, Objective Telos of Virtue   147
  Concluding Thoughts   165

I.iv A Deontological Deduction of the Obligatory Ends of Virtue   172
  Introduction: The Establishment of an End as a Telos via Desire-Governance and End-Setting   172

	I. Desire-Governance via a Moral-Feeling-Expressed Experience of Conscience	175
	II. A Dedication of Obligatory Ends	185
I.v	Objections to Deontological Teleology Considered	219
	Introduction	219
	I. Objections	220
	II. A Further Objection: A Persons-Centered Telos Fails to Respect Non-Human Beings?	225
	Conclusion of Part I	240

II. DEONTOLOGICAL EUDAEMONISM: THE SUBJECTIVE TELOS OF VIRTUE

II.i	Apathy, Moderation, Excitement: The Herculean Work of Virtue	245
	Introduction: The Subjective Telos of Virtue	245
	I. Step One: Moral Apathetic Toleration of Sacrifice	248
	II. Step Two: Governing One's Felt Attachments in the Herculean Pursuit of the Subjective Telos of Virtue	257
	Conclusion	279
II.ii	Happiness, Rationally Conceived: Pleasure in the Virtually Unimpeded Activity of a Free Aptitude for Virtue	280
	Introduction	280
	I. Review of Secondary Literature	282
	II. A Kantian Story of the Pleasure of Unimpeded Activity in the Free Aptitude for Virtue	289
	III. A Transcendentally Ideal Defense of the Nature of the Pleasure One Takes in the Unimpeded Activity of Virtue	300
	IV. Caveat #1 to Happiness: Virtually Unimpeded Activity	331
	V. Caveat #2 to Happiness: A Postscript on Suffering in the Life of Virtue	341
	Conclusion	347
II.iii	Happiness, Empirically Conceived: The Virtuous, Non-Self-Absorbed Pursuit of Desire-Fulfillment	349
	Introduction	349
	I. Recent Literature on the Relationship of Morality and Happiness, Empirically Conceived	353
	II. An Obligatory End with a Pragmatic Purpose: The Virtuous Pursuit of Happiness	358
	III. A Picture of the Virtuous Pursuit of Happiness	372
	Conclusion	403

Bibliography	405
Index	411

Acknowledgments

This is the book I always meant to write. That it took me thirty years, and two other books, to find my way to this one is simply an indication of the head-clearing I needed to do to create a space within myself from which I could confidently express these thoughts which I take to be best descriptive both of my understanding of Kant and of my understanding of what a well-lived life guided by his insights can look like. That I found my way here is due in part to a great number of persons who have provided thoughts, encouragement, or simply just existed and acted unbeknownst to themselves as inspiration to me. A regrettably incomplete list of those persons includes: Julia Annas, Anne Margaret Baxley, Jens Timmermann, Keith Ward, Gary Watson, Victoria Wike, as well as two of my most talented former students, Bjorn Wastvedt and Matt Vinton. Most crucially, though, I once again thank the great love of my life and the great philosopher, Anthony Rudd, for his constant intellectual companionship. I look forward to establishing with him, in our retirement, a thriving Swanage Institute for Advanced Studies.

Introductory Thoughts

Introduction

Immanuel Kant's so-called "deontological" moral theory is often thought to be the direct opponent of eudaemonism. But this assumption has a hold on us only because of a series of philosophical blunders. On the one hand, we've swallowed a flawed conception of what "deontology" means, one which unnecessarily distinguishes moral theories concerned with duty from those thought of as eudaemonistic. On the other, Kant himself construed of "eudaemonism" so narrowly as to conflate it with hedonism and utilitarianism, leading many wrongly to assume that he is an enemy of eudaemonistic and happiness-related ideas which are in fact entirely compatible with and supportive of his own concern to identify a moral theory grounded in autonomously legislated principles of duty. And then, for the past 200 years, we Kant interpreters have just made things worse by focusing narrowly on a few action-focused arguments in Kant's *Groundwork*, ignoring his more mature character-based virtue theory in the *Metaphysics of Morals*, a virtue theory which (contrary to assumptions about it) encompasses elements exceedingly sympathetic to eudaemonist theories of virtue.

In the past thirty years or so, Kant scholars have begun to correct for these errors and omissions. Since the 1990s, when thinkers like Onora O'Neill (1996, 1998a) and Robert Louden (1986) started to think about Kant and virtue—and many after them followed suit—things have begun to look much better for a more accurate interpretation of Kant as a virtue theorist. But for all this excellent work, and although one can find in the literature intermittent references to Kant as a eudaemonist,[1] there has been no sustained reflection upon and defense of the notion that Kant's virtue theory is essentially a theory of virtue eudaemonism. In this book, I thus explore and defend the idea that Kant's virtue theory is best

---

[1] Watson (1983) and Wood (2000) both started discussions about Kant and eudaemonism, but neither of these reflections led to any sustained discussion of the topic in the literature. Only very recently, Forman (2016) and Holberg (2018) have revived the discussion in some interesting ways, bringing Watson's and Wood's earlier ideas into conversation with more recent interpreters, including Kohl (2017). I will engage all these thinkers at various points later in this work. In the interim between Wood's account and these later discussions, the excellent work by Engstrom (2000) and Baxley (2010) played an important role in pursuing thoughts of the connection between Kantian virtue and a well-lived life. Both Baxley and Engstrom distinguish Kantian virtue from mere Aristotelian continence and defend the idea that the life of virtue can be a pleasant one. I consider my work here to be in sympathy with and a continuation of their thoughts.

understood as a system of eudaemonism, indeed, as a distinctive form of eudaemonism that makes it preferable to other forms of it: a system of what I call Deontological Eudaemonism.

That I describe Kant's account of virtue as a system of Deonotological Eudaemonism may be surprising to some. We tend to think of deontology and eudaemonism as contradictory terms: deontology is concerned with right, but eudaemonism with the good. Deontology is concerned with duty, but eudaemonism with happiness. Deontology constrains desire, but eudaemonism welcomes it as the vehicle for realizing one's flourishing. And so on. This historical opposition is, however, predicated upon a long series of philosophical mistakes related to how we understand both "deontology" and "eudaemonism." To set the record straight on our understanding of and the relationship between these terms, I will thus begin by reflecting upon the history of the meaning and use of the term "deontology," and then turn to reflections upon Kant's own at times vague, at other times overly narrow, but in all cases inevitably confusing conceptions of the meaning of the term "eudaemonism." I will then steer us in the more positive direction of making sense in general terms of what Kant's Deontological Eudaemonism is. I conclude these introductory thoughts by providing an overview of the entire book.

I. A History of Philosophical Blunders

A History of Philosophical Blunders: Deontology

If, as we shall shortly see, Kant himself is to blame for confusions about the relationship of his moral theory to eudaemonism, he can at least blame others for confusions arising from the use of the language of "deontology" to describe his system. After all, we can hardly blame Kant for confusions about a word he himself never knew or used! "Deontology" is a term that was invented in the early 19th century, and only came into fashion specifically for describing Kant's moral theory in the 20th century, as a way of distinguishing his moral theory from teleological and utilitarian forms of moral theory. Jens Timmermann did all Kant scholars a particular favor when he traced for us both this history of the word and all the problems it has created for those genuinely interested in understanding Kant's moral theory.[2] In short, deontology is an invented word used first by Bentham to describe duty-based utilitarianism, then co-opted by Broad to introduce his preferred philosophical taxonomy of moral systems as either consequentialist or non-consequentialist.

---

[2] See Timmermann (2015).

I am exceedingly sympathetic to Timmermann's suggestion that we should discard the language of deontology as a means for distinguishing between consequentialist and non-consequentialist moral theories. I am convinced that he is right that such a taxonomy of moral theories is too murky and confusing, obscuring both differences and similarities among moral theories that are important not to obscure. Timmermann makes the point nicely:

> The textbook dichotomy between two types of ethical theory must…be discarded. It lumps together wildly different theories; it excludes 'mixed' theories of the type envisaged by Broad; and it imposes upon non-consequentialist theories the consequentialist assumption that "right" is the basic category of ethical evaluation. Introducing "virtue ethics" as a third category does not help. If anything, it makes things worse because it obscures the fact that there are assumptions sensible non-consequentialists share. As with Aristotle, Kant's ethics is primarily about character (the "good will"), not about right or wrong action. Like Kant, Aristotle maintains that there are strict ethical requirements: there is no right way to go about adultery, theft or murder (*NE* 1107a8–12). Arguably, neither Aristotle nor Kant would advocate committing a crime for the sake of the deed's alleged good overall consequences.   (Timmermann, 89)

For all these reasons, and more, I stand with Timmermann in rejecting the idea that deontology should be understood as a word distinguishing consequentialist and non-consequentialist theories of morality, and then as attributing a central concern for "right" to the latter but not the former sort of theory.

But I am less convinced by Timmermann's suggestion that we should abandon the language of deontology altogether, including its sense of being "the study or science of duty," the sense originally intended by Jeremy Bentham when he invented the word in the early 19th century.[3] Timmermann worries that "it is difficult to see how a new 'deontology' could enhance ethics as a discipline. It does not help us say anything we cannot say well already" (Timmermann 2015, 90). But I disagree. In the 21st century, Kant has indeed become firmly associated with an approach to ethics which emphasizes duty, and this—unlike the further, problematic associations Broad brought to the term a century later—is an entirely fair characterization of Kant's ideas. Ironically, had Broad stuck with Bentham's understanding of the word "deontology" when he attached it to Kant's moral theory in the early 20th century, he would have been doing a meaningful and helpful thing for genuine interpretation of Kant. Indeed, properly construed, this emphasis on duty—and especially upon duties that hold categorically—is a distinctive and defining characteristic of Kantian ethics. So it makes good sense to call Kant

---

[3] See Timmermann (2015), 76.

a deontologist in this sense, thereby highlighting something that is genuinely characteristic of his approach to morality. In the proper context, and with a proper definition, this word can indeed allow us to say well and distinctly something that couldn't easily be said otherwise.

So, Timmermann thinks we should entirely dispose of the term "deontology": "[t]he word 'deontology' should be banished from the classroom. It may be best to abandon it altogether."[4] But I am more sanguine than Timmermann about rehabilitating instead of abandoning this term, especially if we take refuge in its *etymological* instead of its sordid *historical* roots.

A History of Philosophical Blunders: Eudaemonism

If Kant can blame others for the creation and use of the term "deontology," I fear he has only himself to blame for confusion in his understanding and use of the term "eudaemonism." Kant rarely uses the word "eudaemonism" explicitly. But when he does, it is always negatively, as an approach to moral theorizing that should be avoided. And yet, when we look at these conceptions of eudaemonism which Kant rejects, a contemporary philosopher—or a defender of Aristotle's ethical theory—would understandably be perplexed by the meanings he attributes to the word. In all cases of its usage, Kant is consistent in associating eudaemonism with a moral theory somehow concerned with and grounded in the realization of happiness, empirically conceived as desire fulfillment. But a review of his explicit uses of the term makes clear that Kant has, at best, thought in only the most general and vague of ways about what exactly eudaemonism is and, at worst, has simply misunderstood what this word means.

The only two explicit uses of the word in his mature moral works both come from the *Metaphysics of Morals*, one from the Doctrine of Right and the other from the Doctrine of Virtue.[5] In the first, Kant reflects upon and rejects what he takes to be "eudaemonis[tic]" theories of punishment:

> The law of punishment is a categorical imperative, and woe to him who crawls through the windings of eudaemonism in order to discover something that releases the criminal from punishment or even reduces its amount by the advantage it promises, in accordance with the pharisaical saying, "It is better for one man to die than for an entire people to perish"...What, therefore, should one think of the proposal to preserve the life of a criminal sentenced to death if he agrees to let dangerous experiments be made on him and is lucky enough to

---

[4] See Timmermann (2015), 75.
[5] Kant also argues against eudaemonism in *The Conflict of the Faculties*. But his discussion there is similar in form and content to what I describe below, so I set the *Conflict* references aside.

survive them, so that in this way physicians learn something new of benefit to the commonwealth? A court would reject with contempt such a proposal from a medical college, for justice ceases to be justice f it can be bought for any price whatsoever. (6:331–332/105)

Kant here understands the "eudaemonism" he is rejecting as a would-be system of justice whereby appeal to the greater happiness of persons overall justifies the lessening of a punishment for an individual criminal: the eudaemonist would see the commutation of a death sentence for an individual criminal and then the submission of that individual to "dangerous experiments" as a justified form of punishment as long as such experiments would lead to greater happiness for persons overall. "Eudaemonism" as Kant presents it here is thus certainly a moral theory concerned with happiness; but, in this case at least, this appeal to happiness is not an Aristotelian appeal to a principled and qualitatively defined happiness as pleasure in the proper functioning of one's being through the pursuit of that organizing telos most appropriate to one's being. Rather, we see here a quantitative concern for increasing happiness (implicitly understood as maximal increase in pleasure) in persons overall as a moral goal which justifies a simultaneous lessening of happiness (implicitly understood as a decrease in pleasure) and commuting of an otherwise just punishment for some. This "eudaemonism" is thus really more a form of act utilitarianism concerned with maximizing pleasure for the greatest number of persons than anything Aristotle would recognize as a telos of human activity.

In Kant's Doctrine of Virtue appeal to eudaemonism, we get a rather different sense of what Kant means by the term. There, once again in very condemnatory language, he reflects not upon a moral theory seeking the greatest happiness for the greatest number, but instead upon one that would claim happiness as desire fulfillment as the only possible motive for fulfilling one's duties:

When a thoughtful human being has overcome incentives to vice and is aware of having done his often bitter duty, he finds himself in a state that could well be called happiness, a state of contentment and peace of soul in which virtue is its own reward.—Now a *eudaemonist* says: this delight, this happiness is really his motive for acting virtuously. The concept of duty does not determine his will *directly*; he is moved to do his duty only by means of the happiness he anticipates... A eudaemonist's *etiology* involves him in a circle; that is to say, he can hope to be happy (or inwardly blessed) only if he is conscious of having fulfilled his duty, but he can be moved to fulfill his duty only if he foresees that he will be made happy by it. (6:377/142–143)

Here, a "eudaemonist" is one who takes the assurance of his happiness as the only possible motive for doing his duty. Eudaemonism is thus no longer a rule whereby one justifies various actions through appeal to an overall increase of happiness for all, but instead a hedonistic theory of moral motivation whereby humans are understood to be that kind of being who can only be moved by the prospect of an increase of one's pleasures: all one's acts must be motivated by a concern to increase those pleasures which constitute one's own happiness.

It is clear in these two explicit references to eudaemonism that Kant fails to have a consistent sense of what the term means. On the one hand, eudaemonism is a form of utilitarianism; on the other, it is a rather flat-footed hedonistic theory of the proper motivation for dutiful actions. In neither case does Kant exhibit any genuine understanding of or serious engagement with a eudaemonist of Aristotelian stature, viz. a eudaemonist for whom happiness is construed not as a quantitatively measured pursuit of pleasure and desire fulfillment, but instead as a pleasurable realization of one's qualitatively defined and principle-led notion of proper functioning.

These conflations of eudaemonism with utilitarian and hedonistic appeals to happiness should not surprise us, though. Rather, they should remind us of Kant's more general admonitions against reliance upon empirical notions of happiness as a ground for moral theorizing. Furthermore, when placed against that background, we can better understand what Kant is doing when he so briefly and inadequately both considers and condemns eudaemonism. In essence, what Kant is really doing when he apparently condemns eudaemonism is to condemn any moral theory based on empirical and quantitatively definable conceptions of happiness. And we can best understand his concerns about this issue by reflecting on his more substantive criticisms of this nature, criticisms which do not explicitly refer to "eudaemonism" as such, but which more accurately and completely articulate some of Kant's more justifiable concerns about any moral theory grounded in empirical and quantitatively defined conceptions of happiness.

The most familiar of these discussions can be found near the end of section two of the *Groundwork*. Here, Kant is summarizing his defense of the Categorical Imperative as the only viable principle of morality by arguing that every other approach to morality is heteronomous while the Categorical Imperative is the only genuine and reliable autonomous approach to morality. One of the heteronomous and therefore "spurious" approaches to morality he rejects here is the "empirical" approach grounded in "the principle of happiness" (4:442/53):

> *Empirical principles* are not fit to be the foundation of moral laws at all... Yet the principle of one's own happiness is the most objectionable [of empirical principles], not merely because it is false, and [because] experience contradicts the pretense that being well always tallies with behaving well, ... but [more centrally] because it underpins morality with incentives that rather undermine it and annihilate all its sublimity, since they put motives to virtue and those to vice in

the same class and only teach us to improve our calculations, but totally and entirely extinguish the specific difference between the two.

(4:442/53, translation slightly modified)

Here, Kant provides two arguments against grounding morality in the pursuit of one's happiness. The first is itself a simple empirical claim: experience has shown and continues to show us that being moral and being happy do not always coincide; sometime the two come apart. We thus need to reject the idea that morality could be defined through and grounded upon happiness, and need instead to seek a principle of morality which respects the idea that sometimes doing the moral thing will cause injury to our happiness. Second, when we try to ground morality in happiness, we end up being unable really to determine what distinguishes good from bad (i.e., what distinguishes "virtue" and "vice"), especially in terms of our motives. Relying upon happiness, an empirical notion, as a guide for moral motives may help us to "improve our calculations" about what will increase and what will decrease our pleasure. But such empirical, pleasure-based calculations will do nothing to identify for us the specific difference between what is virtuous and what is vicious in our motives.

Ultimately, though, neither of these arguments is intended to stand on its own; rather, they are both pointed toward and dependent upon another larger and more central argument Kant makes not only against any moral theory grounded in happiness but against any moral theory grounded in anything other than the nature of one's own rational will: all such appeals to the grounding of morality will be heteronomous and thus illicit. Here, then, is Kant's most central concern about grounding morality through appeal to one's happiness:

> Wherever an object of the will has to be made the foundation for prescribing the rule that determines it, there the rule is nothing other than heteronomy; the imperative is conditional, namely: *if* or *because* one wills this object, one ought to act in such or such a way; hence it can never command morally, i.e., categorically. Whether the object determines the will by means of inclination, as with the principle of one's own happiness, or by means of reason directed to objects of our possible willing as such, in the case of the principle of perfection, the will never determines itself *immediately*, by the representation of the action, but only by an incentive that the anticipated effect of the action has on the will: *I ought to do something because I want something else.* (4:444/54–55)

Kant's point here is that the principles of a rational will should be determined only by that will itself; but appeal to happiness—and especially appeal to a conception of happiness that is empirical and quantifiable—involves appeal to something outside that rational will, making any justification of adherence to a principle grounded in it merely conditional upon concern for that external thing (here, the satisfaction of one's happiness). But we already know that for a principle to hold as a moral principle, it needs to hold unconditionally. As such, one cannot appeal to *anything* outside one's rational will (including happiness) to ground one's most basic and unconditionally valid moral principles.

Happiness-grounded moral theories are heteronomous in a particularly interesting way, though, in a way that, for example, moralities grounded in the principle of perfection are not: appeals to happiness to ground morality are both heteronomous *and* empirical. Kant's rejection of any *heteronomous* grounding of morality is thus here also a rejection of any *empirical* grounding of morality. And, of course, the two are linked: a rational will, to be determined by itself, needs (by definition) to be determined by something rational, not empirical. And happiness (at least in the sense of pleasure in desire fulfillment), because it is an empirical concept, is also (by definition) something that cannot autonomously determine a rational will. Happiness thusly conceived is a *heteronomous* ground for morality precisely because it is a would-be *empirical* ground for morality.

At the heart of Kant's worries about the relationship of happiness and morality is thus the idea that happiness is a merely empirical and quantitative notion of the greatest pleasure possible. As Kant puts it elsewhere in the *Groundwork*, happiness is the concept of a state in which the satisfaction of "all inclinations unite in one sum" (4:399/14). It is, in other words, a quantifiable state composed of the collection of the maximum sum of one's pleasures realized through the fulfillment of one's inclinations or desires. Kant thus, essentially, defines happiness quantitatively; it is the sum of the realization of our inclinations through the experience of pleasures of various sorts. Kant grants that humans inevitably pursue this state (4:415/26), and he even welcomes the idea that one should pursue it as an indirect means to support one's moral goals (4:399/12). But he emphatically rejects any effort, by whatever means, to take this quantitative and empirical conception of happiness as the ground of autonomous moral principles.[6]

One can perhaps question whether Kant's arguments here are conclusive. It is not my intention, though, to provide an ultimate defense of these arguments but only to clarify the nature of Kant's commitments which inform his confused rejection of eudaemonism. Because he is committed to discovering autonomously grounded principles of morality, Kant has a deep and abiding concern to accomplish the grounding of such principles without any appeal to quantitative or

---

[6] I suspect this grounding distinction between one's will being determined either by itself or by something external to itself is what inspires Kohl's (2017) recent claim that the pursuit of maximal pleasure is not technically a pursuit of goodness or value and thus technically not an example of practical judgment as such. In order to speak of practical judgments, we need to appeal to notions of value intrinsic to the will. Although I take that point, I find his conclusion—that the pursuit of happiness empirically conceived is not a project of practical reasoning—too extreme. I will discuss Kohl at greater length later in this work, especially in my II.iii affirmation of Holberg's (2018) rejection of his extreme position.

empirical conceptions of happiness. And Kant's confused assumption, which informs his condemnations of eudaemonism, is that eudaemonism is an approach to morality that seeks to ground moral principles in the pursuit of such a quantitative and empirically defined conception of happiness.

And so, when Kant utilizes the language of "eudaemonism," we should take it as a sort of catch-all term to refer to conceptions of morality grounded in quantitative and empirical conceptions of happiness, all of which are illicit because heteronomous. Whether he rejects appeal to the greatest happiness for the greatest number as a sufficient ground of justifiable moral claims, or condemns those who would assert that concern for increasing one's pleasures is the only possible and sufficient motive for doing one's duty, Kant's use of the word "eudaemonism" is meant to flag for us readers any would-be moral system that involves illicit heteronomous appeal to a quantitative and empirical conception of happiness. The shared link amongst these otherwise multi-various condemnations of eudaemonism is that eudaemonism is a moral theory grounded in empirical conceptions of happiness as desire fulfillment and, by that very empirical association, unfit for prescribing truly moral principles. We can thus understand Kant's rejection of eudaemonism as a rejection of accounts of morality grounded in empirical conceptions of happiness: a rejection of hedonistic accounts of motivation or utilitarian accounts of action.

II. Toward a Positive Conception of Kant's Deontological Eudaemonism

Aristotelian Moments in Kant's Deontological Eudaemonism

One has to admit though, when Kant rejects eudaemonism in this way, that he has done little to reject eudaemonism as Aristotle conceived of it. Kant's rejections of eudaemonism are rejections of the use of empirical conceptions of happiness to ground morality in either a utilitarian or a hedonist motivational fashion. But eudaemonism, most centrally and definitionally, is an approach to virtue concerned with assuring the pleasurable proper functioning of a certain kind of being, guided by pursuit of the proper and substantive telos of one's being. A eudaemonist thus needn't espouse *any* of the claims which Kant rejects in its name: utilitarian principles of action, or a morality which accepts only in an empirical, desire-based conception of motivation. Furthermore, and conversely, Kantian virtue theorists can affirm Kant's rejections of hedonistic motivation or of any morality grounded in assuring a quantitative increase in pleasure while simultaneously welcoming a generally eudaemonistic approach to virtue which makes the notion of pleasurable proper functioning central to the ordering of the virtuous person's choices, activities, and life.

In fact, the Aristotelian notion of proper functioning has the potential to be particularly helpful in articulating and supporting Kant's conception of virtue, since it is not an empirically based but a more principle-informed notion: one does not pursue one's functioning simply by seeking quantitatively to increase one's pleasures. Instead, one must articulate some qualitative function or principle "proper" to one's being which guides one's activity overall.[7] As Aristotle notes:

> [I]t may be held that the good of man resides in the function of man, if he has a function. Are we then to suppose that, while the carpenter and the shoemaker have definite functions or businesses belonging to them, man as such has none, and is not designed by nature to fulfil any function? Must we not rather assume that, just as the eye, the hand, the foot and each of the various members of the body manifestly has a certain function of its own, so a human being also has a certain function over and above all the functions of his particular members?
> (*NE* I.7, 11–12)

Aristotle's notion of a function proper to being human as such thus, instead of appealing to a quantitative conception of happiness, points us toward that function which would be proper to the being in question and then takes that notion of proper function as a principled teleological guide both for how that being should act and for how that being realizes well-being.

Furthermore, later in the *Nicomachean Ethics*, Aristotle associates the exercise or activity of one's proper function with a distinctive sort of pleasure and happiness. According to him, "*pleasure* is ... called *activity* of the natural state, and ... [is called] 'unimpeded'" (1153a13, emphases added). In other words, Aristotle suggests that any activity that is proper to one's being, precisely because it expresses the "natural" and proper state of that being, is best described as an intrinsically *pleasurable* activity, as long as that activity can move forward without any external obstruction or impediment to its exercise.

We will have much more to say (in II.ii) about how a parallel to this notion of pleasurable unimpeded activity proper and natural to oneself can be found in Kant's corpus, particularly in his notion of a contentment of self which pervades the exercise of one's free aptitude for virtue, an aptitude that is established through the repeated exercise of one's inner freedom, and which thereby expels or moderates all would-be external impediments to the natural exercise of one's rational will.

---

[7] The only hint I have seen in the literature of the suggestion that something similar to this Aristotelian notion of proper functioning could be found in Kant's works is in Elizondo (2014). I will consider his thoughts in some detail in II.ii, when I reject his particular reading of how to ground an Aristotelian notion of pleasure in unimpeded activity in Kant's writings in favor of my own account of the same which I argue is more attentive to the limits imposed upon sensibly affected rational beings by Kant's Transcendental Idealism commitments.

For now, we simply more generally welcome the idea that this notion of the pleasurable exercise of that activity or function most proper or natural to oneself seems—once one backs away from the idea of that principle being in accordance with a mean—a particularly, even distinctively or characteristically, Kantian concern. After all, to function in a way proper to one's being is to function in a way guided by the principles of one's own being. To put the same point in Kantian terms: the "proper" functioning of a certain kind of being is just the "autonomous" functioning of that being. Essentially, *proper* functioning just is, by definition, *autonomous* functioning!

Kantians can thus welcome the notion of proper functioning as a means for articulating the virtuous internalization of principles of morality. And by defining the telos or goal of eudaemonism via appeal to proper functioning instead of via appeal to empirical conceptions of happiness, the Kantian can thus (while moving away from the connection of morality to happiness as quantitative desire fulfillment) rely instead upon a notion of pleasure which pervades the unimpeded exercise of one's proper function (instead of upon the empirical notion of pleasure as the fulfillment of a desire) to articulate a meaningful notion of Kant's Deontological Eudaemonism. The pleasurable proper functioning of one's state as guided by the proper telos or goal of one's being, a telos or goal which guides one's own rational will and indeed one's being overall as a sensibly affected rational being toward a state of well-being: this is precisely what we assert and investigate in this account of Deontological Eudaemonism.

It may be odd and unexpected to think that Kant could welcome eudaemonism as proper functioning into his moral theory. We are so accustomed to thinking of deontological theories as concerned with right and eudaemonistic theories as concerned with realization of the good that it is odd to consider introducing so eudaemonistic a conception as proper function (i.e, the pleasurable realization of a good proper to our being) into a deontological theory of ethics.[8] But, in fact, there is nothing about Kant's rationalist system of morality as grounded in an autonomously determined categorical imperative that prevents us from welcoming the pleasurable proper functioning of oneself as a sensibly affected rational being as being central to his conceptions of both virtue and happiness. A Kantian

---

[8] There has in fact been at least some discussion of Kantian eudaemonism in the literature, but consideration of it has been sporadic at best. Watson (1983) was the first to introduce some ideas about this relation in some really helpful ways. But the notion wasn't taken up seriously again until Wood (2000). And since Wood's reflections, there has been a similar dearth of discussions of Kantian eudaemonism until Forman (2016) and Holberg (2018) re-invigorated the debate. Interestingly, though, while Forman and Holberg both engage directly and deeply in questions of how to resolve Kant's ethics to some form of eudaemonism, neither appeals explicitly to Aristotle's notion of "proper function," nor to the related notion of pleasure as unimpeded activity, to investigate connections between Kant and eudaemonism. The appeals I make to these two notions thus distinguish my work from the current state of the debate. I will discuss both Forman and Holberg's work in more detail in Part II.

will, of course, rightly reject the idea that this proper functioning and ultimate telos of a sensibly affected rational being should be understood as "happiness" in any empirical or quantitative conception of that word. Indeed, as we shall see, one's ultimate telos must have explicitly moral content, a content which we shall identify in Part I as the telos of making persons as such one's end. But to insist upon a telos of the sensibly affected rational being that is higher than happiness empirically conceived does not mean that the proper functioning of that being is entirely unconcerned with a more qualitatively construed and principle-guided conception of pleasurable flourishing and well-being for that kind of being. Indeed, as we shall see in II.ii, we can identify for Kant a notion of happiness conceived non-empirically, a notion of happiness parallel to the Aristotelian notion of pleasure in unimpeded activity, thereby assuring that the virtuous realization of one's objective telos through proper functioning is something that will be experienced pleasurably in this new sense of pleasure, non-empirically conceived.

To think of happiness as consisting not simply in the sum of all one's pleasures accomplished through desire-satisfaction, but also as constituted by the experience of acting unimpededly in a way consistent with one's being, introduces an idea that is indeed implicit in Kant's thought but has not been identified as "happiness" as such, so has not yet been thought through as clearly as it could. We will, in II.ii, see that happiness in this rationally conceived sense of it is not distinct from being moral or virtuous, but instead part and parcel of the exercise of the free aptitude for virtue. It is in affirming a parallel between what Kant calls this "free aptitude" and what Aristotle calls "unimpeded activity," that we will bring our reading of Kant into sympathetic connection with Annas' interpretation of Aristotle's notion of happiness as pleasure in the unimpeded activity of virtue.

This central move I make in defining Deontological Eudaemonism—viz., that I affirm pleasurable unimpeded activity of one's proper functioning as a central notion for articulating Kant's eudaemonism—is, furthermore, a move that pushes both recent and less-recent considerations of the relationship of Kant to eudaemonism in some new directions. None of the interpreters who consider the relationship of Kant and eudaemonism[9] focus centrally on proper functioning or unimpeded activity.[10] Instead, all are (reasonably) concerned to make sense of how, for Kant, the notion of happiness, empirically conceived, is or is not related to virtue. This is not an unimportant concern, and indeed, is one we will take up

---

[9] See Watson (1983); Wood (2000); Forman (2016); and Holberg (2018).

[10] The only exception I know of are Herman (2010) and Elizondo (2014). Herman, without argument, dismisses the idea that Kant's ethics involves any notion of "function": "There are some ideas associated with virtue ethics—noncodifiability, practical wisdom, function, teleology of the Good, the holism of the practical—that are not found in Kantian moral theory." (Herman [2010], 92) I will discuss Herman at greater length in Part I when I address the question of the role obligatory ends play in Kant's moral theory. And Elizondo (2014) defends the notion of pleasure in proper function, but in ways that I will find problematic in II.ii.

ourselves in II.iii. But it will be in first claiming this notion of happiness as pleasurable unimpeded activity (in II.ii) that I most emphatically distinguish my account of eudaemonism from Forman's (2016) "Moderate Cynical" reading of Kant and Holberg's (2018) quasi-eudaemonistic reading, both of which assume that a more strict and thorough distinction must be made for Kant between virtue and happiness. Both are right that such a strict distinction must be made between virtue and empirical conceptions of happiness as desire-satisfaction; the refusal to conflate virtue and happiness empirically conceived in a quasi-Stoic fashion is something that clearly distinguishes Kant from Stoicism. But once we accept a notion of happiness as the pleasurable unimpeded activity of those dispositions most proper to one's being, it is no longer necessary for Kant to maintain a separation between happiness thusly conceived and virtuous activity. Indeed, the happiness identified here simply is the subjective experience of the exercise of virtue itself. The only distinction we will need to make between Kant and Aristotle on this point is that, for Kant, we must accept that such exercise can be only virtually and not completely unimpeded.

Furthermore, in II.iii, even happiness empirically conceived, though it cannot be affirmed as identical with this pleasurable exercise of virtue, will nonetheless be welcomed as a state most satisfactorily realized via this pleasurable exercise of virtue for itself, thereby affirming Watson's (1983) suggestion of the same, a suggestion he makes precisely because he (like I) affirm a meaningful conception of non-moral value for Kant but also see any pursuit of such value utterly distinct from the pursuit of virtue futile. As such, though happiness empirically conceived remains distinct from the exercise of virtue, it is able to be best realized through a deep connection to that exercise. Or as we will put the point in II.iii: the obligatory end of cultivating one's natural capacities with a pragmatic purpose provides the best model for organizing one's pragmatic end-setting generally under the purview of one's virtuous telos of respecting persons. We shall discuss all such things at greater length in Part II.

At the heart of my understanding of Deontological Eudaemonism is thus the idea that one can be eu-daemon (i.e., can be a spirit in good order, can have a life well-lived, or can realize a pleasurable state of virtually unimpeded activity) without being guided by an ultimate telos of happiness, empirically conceived. Instead the ultimate guiding telos of one's being is a demand intrinsic and thus proper to one's rational nature: the demand to respect persons. The "eu-" or well-being, of a rational being will thus be found first in being true to that rational nature, finding the pleasure of acting toward that goal in an unimpeded manner, and, simultaneously, in elevating one's sensible nature toward that goal beyond itself in a way that allows us to introduce pleasure and cheerfulness into one's subjective experience of the virtually unimpeded activity of a free aptitude for virtue. And then, from this height of the pleasurable exercise of virtue, even happiness empirically conceived, though not part and parcel of one's exercise of one's aptitude for virtue, is revealed as something best achieved through adherence to virtue. My account thus claims a eudaemonism that is specifically deontological: viz., a pursuit of pleasurable well-being ordered by realization of those principles which affirm what is demanded of us as sensibly affected rational beings.[11]

An Objection Considered

One might raise an objection at this point: isn't the distinctive thing about Kant's moral philosophy the fact that it emphasizes the conflicts we encounter between happiness and morality, thereby affirming the centrality of such conflicts in a human life? We have already seen, above, that Kant himself takes it to be obvious from experience that morality and happiness are distinct from and often in opposition to each other, so distinct and opposed as to make it impossible to ground the former in the latter.[12] If all this is true, then isn't it counter-productive to what is really valuable in Kant to seek to smooth over the ineradicable conflict between happiness and morality in the way that a eudaemonistic interpretation of his writings would do? Wouldn't it be better to take up his appreciation for the inevitable conflicts in human life as a more helpful guide to the living of that life?[13]

There is something about this objector's concerns with which I am deeply sympathetic. Kant is indeed very aware of conflict in living a human life, and especially of the conflict between happiness and morality. Indeed, in a previous book, I dwelt at length upon how attention to the moral consciousness of the conflict between happiness and morality is the way that one comes, phenomenologically, to an appreciation of Kant's most basic notion of a categorical imperative.[14]

But conflict is not the end of the story in Kant's ethics. And now, we have a different task at hand: instead of simply understanding the nature and grounding of a categorical demand, we are here drawing the picture of the fully virtuous person who makes this command the center of her life. This is the person who will have done as much as is humanly possible to *relieve* the existential conflict between happiness and morality. As such, it shouldn't surprise readers that I will focus in this book less on those passages where Kant emphasizes that conflict and more on those where he investigates what humans can do about resolving that conflict.

---

[11] One might argue that this is not a completely eudaemonistic position, since we must still admit that virtue is not *identical* with happiness empirically conceived. But, given the history of Kant interpretation which emphasizes an exceedingly harsh contrast and conflict between happiness and morality, the introduction of even one conception of happiness that is in indeed identical with the pursuit of virtue, and then of this intimate connection between the exercise of virtue and happiness empirically conceived, is sufficient to give the name of "eudaemonism" to this reading of Kant's texts.

[12] "The principle of one's own happiness is the most objectionable [of would-be empirical principles grounding morality]...because it is false, and [because] experience contradicts the pretense that being well always tallies with behaving well." We thus need a principle of morality which respects the idea that sometimes doing the moral thing will cause *injury* to our happiness (4:442/53).

[13] I'd like to thank an anonymous reader at Oxford University Press for raising this concern.

[14] See Grenberg (2013a).

The potential for conflict will, of course, remain to a certain extent; for, even the fully virtuous person will not possess that perfect tranquility of character that might be attributed to, e.g., the Aristotelian fully virtuous person. As we shall see in Part II, even this fully virtuous person does not entirely remove herself from the possibility of internal conflict. Instead, she maintains a vigilance about the bare possibility of succumbing to her propensity for radical evil; and also faces the possibility that tragic circumstances (like one's prince demanding that one do immoral things or die) will indeed affirm that, at least sometimes in life, doing the moral thing *will* cause injury to our happiness.

On the other hand, we need to remember that most of us will not achieve these heights of virtue! And there is plenty to be found in Kant's writings which affirms this very human experience of the conflict between happiness and morality. But nothing in our current emphasis on the life of the fully virtuous person prevents us from agreeing that the less-than-fully virtuous—i.e., the great majority of us!— still face that basic conflict between happiness and morality of which Kant speaks with some regularity. Indeed, our affirmation of the possibility of the eudaemonistic unity of happiness and virtue is entirely compatible with a robust simultaneous affirmation that the less-than-fully virtuous have *lots* of unsatisfied desires, thus leaving lots of room for Kant's virtue ethics still to speak to the challenges of a conflicted and disunified self.

One might raise a different objection at this point:[15] it is well-known that Kant has a commitment to the equality of all persons. But isn't there something very non-egalitarian about the thought that only the fully virtuous person will experience the exercise of virtue pleasurably? Why should the fully virtuous be entitled to a different kind of pleasure than the rest of us could ever have?

Frankly, I do not find this inequality of pleasures a disturbing thing. It seems right to me that someone who has successfully completed the hard work of virtue is entitled to the fruits of her work, including the new experience of the pleasurable exercise of virtue. We can, furthermore, confirm such an idea in Kant's texts. In the *Groundwork* and the second *Critique*, Kant rarely speaks in terms of degrees of virtue, freedom, or pleasure. But once we enter the realm of virtue, viz. that arena for freedom in which freedom becomes not just a capacity shared equally by all but also a chosen aptitude accomplished more successfully by some and less successfully by others, then we also enter a realm within which it does indeed make sense to say that one can be more or less free and virtuous—and therefore can have more or less an experience of pleasure—than another. Indeed, these individuals will have more freedom because they have acquired more virtue as strength. As Kant notes: "The less a human being can be constrained by natural means and the more he can be constrained morally (through the mere representation of duty), so much the more free he is" (382n/147n). If some people are

---

[15] An objection for which I thank another anonymous reader from Oxford University Press.

more free than others, it shouldn't surprise us that some will also have a greater experience of pleasure than others, a pleasure that tracks one's virtue and freedom. The very fact that the more fully virtuous person will be "less...constrained by natural means" means that person will have less internal conflict. And, as we'll see in II.ii, that lowering of conflicts is replaced by a distinctive pleasure in the virtually unimpeded exercise of one's aptitude for virtue.

Given all this, we can therefore welcome the idea that the virtuous person's experience of pleasure is not an either/or, but instead a sliding scale proposition. That is: the closer one gets to full virtue and freedom, the less conflicts and the more pleasure one will experience in its exercise. It is certainly true that some may do the hard work of virtue and then, because of tragic circumstances outside one's control (like an authoritarian prince imposing unjust demands), end up not being able to experience as much pleasure in its exercise as one not tragically submitted to such circumstances. But that doesn't seem non-egalitarian to me; rather, it is simply an inescapable fact of life. Finally, Kant's interest in egalitarianism is preserved in the already noted need for even for the fully virtuous person (along with all her less-than-fully virtuous compatriots) to be vigilant about the possibility of succumbing to her propensity for radical evil.

Summing Up

We have now completed our account of the history of errors that has led us to believe that deontology and eudaemonism are inherently opposed terms. To reclaim the value of eudaemonism for Kantians, all we need do is lose the link between eudaemonism and empirical conceptions of happiness, affirming instead the more plausible and rational link between eudaemonism and pleasurable proper functioning. And to reclaim deontology, we need only go back to its etymological roots as the study or science of duty, rejecting false and un-Kantian historical associations of the term with the notion of right.

Once we do both these things, what we discover is that deontology and eudaemonism are rather good companions to each other. Indeed, we find no essential conflict in the etymologies of these words. "Eu-daemonism" refers to my "daemon"—my soul, spirit, or being—functioning *well*, or being in its proper order. And "deont-ology" refers to the *study* of what is *necessary* or *dutiful*. We've *assumed* that the *proper* functioning of eudaemonism must be related to *happiness, empirically conceived*, and that the *necessity* of deontology must be related to *rights* (conceived as prior to *goodness*). But neither of these assumptions need be made: pleasurable proper functioning needn't mean realization of all one's empirical desires. And what is *necessary* needn't be limited to necessary *rights*. What is *necessary* for the pleasurable exercise of *virtue* is, in other words, not a contradiction in terms. What all this means is that Deontological Eudaemonism is not only not a contradiction in terms but is in fact a meaningful association of moral ideas which, because of earlier historical confusions, has been understudied and now sorely needs to be explored.

So, to conclude these general remarks: Deontological Eudaemonism asserts that it is only in being guided by a strictly necessary principle of duty that sensibly affected rational beings like us humans can govern themselves properly and thus flourish. Deontological Eudaemonism introduces a telos more self-encompassing than happiness, empirically conceived, to define this flourishing; but it thereby promises a more satisfying life than what any merely naturalistic pursuit of desire-satisfaction could offer. In Deontological Eudaemonism, we do not abandon—or even constrain and stifle—but instead elevate and enhance the empirical world of desire. It will be by admitting, within the world of empirical desire, one quasi-desire with a non-desire-based cause which tracks the strictly necessary demand to respect persons (viz., the moral feeling of respect) that Deontological Eudaemonism will reveal how a strictly necessary principle of duty enters into, informs, and elevates the otherwise unwieldy and self-absorbed naturalistic and empirical world of pleasure and desire. The result is the pleasurable proper functioning of a *sensibly* affected *rational* being: all parts of this being realize their proper function once put into proper relationship with each other via this necessary principle which acts as a guiding telos of one's person.

III. Summary of Chapters

And so, in this book, I articulate and defend this account of Deontological Eudaemonism. I provide here a summary of the structure of the book and the arguments to come.

Part I. Deontological Teleology: The Objective Telos of Virtue

Given all of what I have just said, one might reasonably expect this book to begin with an account of pleasurable proper functioning. But we instead begin with some orienting thoughts on the essentially teleological, or goal-driven, nature of Kant's deontological ethics. In other words, our account of Kant's Deontological Eudaemonism will need to be preceded by an account of his Deontological Teleology. It is in this first part of the book that we make sense of the very notion of an objective telos for virtue within a deontological system of morality, and then understand this objective telos of virtue specifically as respect for persons in the thick, beyond-permissibility-constraints sense of making persons as such one's end. The book thus breaks into two large parts—one about Kant's Deontological Teleology and one about his Deontological Eudaemonism—each of which is essentially readable on its own.

Part I on Deontological Teleology shall proceed as follows. I.i, is focused on providing a general outline of the teleological structure of the process of self-governance of desire which is the work of virtue. We begin by arguing, despite our ultimate goal of affirming a eudaemonistic Kant, that complete happiness, empirically conceived, is *not* the proper telos for guiding the process of self-governance for sensibly affected rational beings. In short, the unavoidable incompleteness of empirical series assures that happiness empirically conceived would be an utterly inadequate goal to assert as the telos of the self-governance of desire. To find a telos with the adequate axiological oomph to play the role of governor of desire for a sensibly affected rational being, we must look beyond desires themselves to a necessary rational goal. We thus find Kant's non-naturalistic account of the self-governance of desire—one in which the governance of one's affects and passions is guided by the quasi-desire or moral feeling of respect, a feeling with a rational provenance which situates itself within the empirical world of desire—to be preferable to any would-be naturalistic account of the same.

We then turn to an initial articulation of respect for persons as the proper objective telos or goal of self-governance, a goal which reveals the activity of governance as having the specifically moral goal of the attainment of virtue. To make sense of what it means to call this telos "objective," we then explore it in comparison and contrast with its supervening "subjective" telos of virtue (which itself will not be explored in full depth until Part II of the book). In short, an objective telos is the material, objective end at which all desire-governance aims, the reason explaining every end one sets, and that end which orders all end-setting. The subjective telos is the supervening subjective flip-side of the pursuit of the realization of the objective end of respecting persons, that subjective state of person at which one aims for the sake of realizing this objective telos. The virtuous person thus simultaneously aims at her objective telos of making persons as such her end and also at a subjective state correlative to that objective end-setting activity, a state which, when achieved, concretizes her commitment to respecting persons within her subjective states. She aims, in other words, at becoming the kind of person capable of virtuous end-setting, and capable of controlling herself such that she always respects persons no matter what else she wants, feels, or desires.

In affirming the subjective telos of virtue as "supervening" upon the exercise of the pursuit of the objective telos in this way, I distinguish myself from Forman (2016) who is satisfied to defend a merely contingent relation between virtue and happiness, empirically conceived. As Forman notes: "an account of a merely *contingent* harmony [between virtue and happiness] is sufficient for an effective response" (Forman 2016, 78) to the question of how virtue and happiness are related. Although the supervenience relation I assert between the objective and subjective teloi of virtue is not, in contrast to Forman, a strictly necessary relation, I do nonetheless assert a relationship of conditional necessity between virtue and happiness: all other things being equal (i.e., as long as there is no tragic set of circumstances present, like Priam's fate as Aristotle discusses), a greater happiness, empirically conceived, will necessarily supervene on the exercise of virtue. The limits of this supervenience relation in specifically tragic circumstances are something I will revisit in Part II.

In I.ii, we then turn to an extensive review of the state of the secondary literature on a variety of topics within the broad theme of Kant and teleology. Having shown that there is (despite a wealth of literature on the centrality of notions like end, purpose, or vocation in current interpretive work in Kant's ideas of history, religion, and politics) a curious lacuna in the literature specifically on the topic of teleology and Kant's moral theory, I turn to consideration of those few but influential interpreters who have defended a teleological reading of Kant,[16] arguing that my account of the overall telos of making persons as such one's end is a preferable way of conceiving of the ultimate end and source of value for Kant. We then begin our positive account[17] by considering and responding to an objector who insists that deontological morality is concerned only with principles of action, and not with an objective telos, goal, or end as such. Our response to this objector—viz., that a careful review of some central *Groundwork* passages alongside consideration of Kant's most mature account of the Categorical Imperative in the Doctrine of Virtue reveals that his wavering in the former work on whether pure practical reason is an inherently end-, goal-, or vocation-based capacity is robustly asserted and unambiguously defended and confirmed in the latter work, and that Kant's most mature understanding of such practical reason is thus that it operates in reciprocally deontological and teleological modes—completes our initial defense of Kant's account of Deontological Teleology, viz. our defense of the idea that deontology and teleology are not opposed to each other but rather reciprocally related notions. In so doing we affirm, despite his earlier *Groundwork* and second *Critique* suggestions to the contrary, Kant's ultimate *Metaphysics of Morals* claim that end-setting is consistent with an *a priori* and free grounding of morality. Indeed, the free setting of not just pragmatic but now also of obligatory ends—a new notion introduced in the Doctrine of Virtue and not previously unambiguously present in his earlier moral works—is simply the complete realization of the practicality of pure reason and a continuation of the notion of freedom as incorporation which Kant introduced in the *Religion*, bringing that freedom not only to the determination of maxims but now also to the determination of specific matters of choice, that is, to the setting of particular ends of virtue. I thereby clarify and defend what has been, at best, an implicit distinction in the literature between incorporation of maxims and ends,[18] and conclude the chapter

---

[16] Especially Herman (1993a); Wood (1999, 2008); Guyer (2000, 2002).
[17] One in which I take inspiration from Ward (1971), Watson (1983), and Wike (1994), interpreters whose teleological visions of Kant's ethics have, I think, been sadly neglected in the literature.
[18] See, e.g., Allison (1990); Potter (1994); and McCarty (2009).

by affirming, counter to our original objector, the reciprocal relationship of the deontological determination of maxims of action with the teleological pursuit of ends of action.

We continue our articulation and defense of Deontological Teleology in I.iii and I.iv. First, in I.iii, we deduce the precise substantive, organizing, and obligatory telos of all end-setting: respect for persons understood as a thick, positive moral command to make persons as such one's end. The deduction of this materialized, end-based version of the Second Formulation in the Doctrine of Virtue affirms Kant's own resolution of a point that remained ambiguous by the end of *Groundwork II*, viz. the question of whether, because all ends are based in inclination, one must reject the Second Formulation as a basis for the positive command to make persons as such one's end, and instead accept it merely as the negative command to assure that, whatever your end is, you will make sure never to treat persons merely as means. What we discover in the Doctrine of Virtue is a wholehearted rejection of the latter, merely negative reading of this principle in favor of the positive claim that we must positively make persons as such one's end. Kant's argument for this is grounded both in the affirmation of the very category of non-empirical obligatory ends we confirmed in I.ii combined with a new deduction of a materialized version of the Second Formulation which rejects indifference toward persons as incompatible with the absolute value of persons.

The work of this chapter thus furthers discussions in the existing literature on a variety of issues about the Formula of Humanity. Most centrally, it takes up and pushes further recent literature on the especially important category of non-empirical obligatory ends. Herman (2010) affirms obligatory ends as central to an "end-anchored" conception of Kantian morality, and Formosa (2014) helpfully distinguishes and characterizes how the Formula of Humanity grounds not only perfect but also imperfect duties (a distinction roughly though not thoroughly identical to the distinction between duties of right and duties of virtue). But neither takes up the previous and urgent question noted in the previous chapter (I.ii): in light of Kant's initial *Groundwork* identification of ends of action as all inevitably empirical, how can one even defend the very notion of an end or matter of choice that has rational and obligatory instead of empirical and contingent grounding? It is that question with which this chapter is centrally concerned. On the other side of answering it, we also, in light of Kant's insistence that we understand ends-in-themselves as individual, independently *existing* ends,[19] reject any would-be constructivist reading of his moral theory in favor of a realist reading thereof and, with that, insist upon a reading of the Second Formulation of the Categorical Imperative that, through appeal to a distinct matter of the law inherent to the formula, affirms its normative distinctness from the First Formulation.

---

[19] My thoughts on which were improved by and are indebted to discussions and co-writing with my student, Matt Vinton.

We continue our articulation and defense of Deontological Teleology in I.iv, wherein this objective end of making persons as such one's end, in conjunction with the experience of the moral feeling of respect which tracks the value of persons within the world of desire, is shown to act as the substantive, organizational, material, and objective telos for the deontological deduction of all more precise obligatory ends which constitute its realization. Self-constraint, or the governance of desire, is thus now understood as what occurs through the establishment of obligatory ends set through one's capacity for inner freedom via the voice of one's moral-feeling-expressed experience of conscience. The result is that this telos of making persons as such one's end establishes itself as that value with governing authority over all one's desires. This chapter thus clarifies one important meaning of our assertion that there is a "reciprocal" relationship between deontological principles and a teleological goal in Deontological Teleology: with the telos of making persons as such one's end in place (a telos affirmed via appeal to the value of the presence of humanity in individually existing persons), the traditional deontological Second Formulation of the Categorical Imperative, with subsidiary assistance from the First Formulation of the same, becomes the means by which to affirm all those more precise obligatory ends which constitute the realization of this guiding telos.

Taking the notion of rejection of indifference to persons that was highlighted in our I.iii deduction of the materialized version of the Second Formulation of the Categorical Imperative as our guide, we thus consider some of the obligatory ends which emerge through application of that formula. First, we reconsider the role that the First Formulation of the Categorical Imperative plays in conjunction with the Second to deduce that obligatory end toward others called the duty of beneficence, showing that although the First Formulation is unable on its own to generate the needed contradictions of one's maxim via a universalization test, more general reflection upon the importance of universalizability as one aspect of the nature of any end in which one makes persons as such one's end proves to be an important moral psychological tool of attentiveness, one which allows a more perspicuous appreciation of the nature of obligatory ends to others, including more clarity about the obligatory end of beneficence. As such, I place myself in a middle position between, on the one hand, interpreters like Herman (2010) who assert a strict equivalency between the First and Second Formulations and, on the other hand, interpreters like Wood (2008) who reject any usefulness at all for the First Formulation specifically on the matter of deducing obligatory ends. Instead, I find myself in general sympathy with Timmons' (2017) take on the First Formulation, an account which rejects equivalency claims and prioritizes the Second Formulation, but finds nonetheless a secondary role for the First Formulation.

We then turn to consideration of two aspects of Kant's person-centered catalog of duties—the very category of duties to self and the interesting duty to cultivate the feeling of sympathy—to anticipate the usefulness of just these moral tools in our forthcoming Part II discussion of Deontological Eudaemonism proper, that is, the usefulness of these tools for the pursuit of pleasurable proper functioning. In reflecting upon the very category of duties to self as well as on the priority which Kant asserts for such duties over duties to others, I anticipate the usefulness of the objective telos of making persons as such one's end in the pursuit of self-governance, and also affirm and expand upon Paton's (1990) consideration of such matters. And in reviewing the unique duty to cultivate the feeling of sympathy, we further anticipate the usefulness of reflection from a perspective of objective value for the purposes of governing oneself and cultivating one's emotional life toward the realization of both virtue and happiness, both rationally and empirically conceived.

In I.v we conclude all of Part I by considering a series of objections to this model of Deontological Teleology, all of which in one way or another challenge the idea that making persons as such one's end could be the proper telos of all end-setting: those who claim happiness empirically conceived is the only possible telos of a eudaemonistic morality, those who fear a rational governor of empirical desires is a foreign invader instead of an authoritative governor, and those who fear that so person-centered a morality disregards the value of non-person valuable existences like animals and the environment. We focus particularly on this last question of whether so person-centered an approach to virtue can do anything to ground meaningful obligations in relation to non-human beings, like animals and the environment. Through appeal to a new account of what Kant means by having only "indirect" obligations in regard to non-human beings, an account which rejects a merely instrumental appeal to the usefulness of non-human nature and appeals instead "indirectly" to our capacity for self-obligation to ground an appreciation for the intrinsic value of such nature, we defend a robust Kantian approach to understanding our obligations to non-human beings from an unapologetically persons-centered point of view, revealing new possibilities for a Kantian understanding of the obligations persons have in regard to non-persons. I engage, in particular Broadie and Pybus (1974), Wood (1998b), and O'Neill (1998b), pushing them toward a new understanding of what it means to say one has a duty "in regard to" animals, one that does not reduce that relationship to what Kant elsewhere calls an "indirect" duty. I thereby provide new ground from which to reject critics like Skidmore (2001), but in a way different than interpreters like Rocha (2015) or Korsgaard (2018), both of whom seek to affirm some full or limited status for some animals as rational beings. We instead embrace Kant's notion that our duties in regard to non-human beings are accessed indirectly via appeal to a robust duty to oneself.

In rejecting all the claims of these objectors, we thereby affirm Deontological Teleology as an approach to the virtuous self-governance of desire which elevates the world of desire beyond itself through appeal to a rational principle of respect for persons which orders the governance of desires and thereby introduces an absolute value which provides the proper evaluative perspective from which to assess all desires, values, and ends.

Part II. Deontological Eudaemonism: The Subjective Telos of Virtue

Part I has provided us with an understanding of that objective telos which guides the development of virtue. But, as noted briefly in I.i, in the realization of this objective and material telos, one also has the subjective experience of being a person guided by this telos, a state of person at which the would-be virtuous person aims, the realization of which constitutes the proper subjective functioning of a sensibly affected rational being. This state is, in other words, the *subjective telos* of virtue, that state which constitutes the subjective experience of the properly functioning person of virtue, and Part II provides a complete articulation of this subjective telos of virtue. In so doing, we provide a story of how the deontological teleology we've just introduced is also a deontological eudaemonism, viz. an account of the dutiful governance of desire that assures not only the realization of virtue but also the most satisfying pursuit and realization of that happiness and proper functioning possible for sensibly affected rational beings.

Consideration of the details of the subjective side of virtuous self-governance is a crucial and central piece of our articulation of Deontological Eudaemonism, because it is in his articulation of the subjective experience of virtue that Kant is most often thought to be distinctively *non*-eudaemonistic: he is thought to envision not a virtuous life of pleasurable well-being, but instead one of conflict and constraint. What we shall discover in exploring the contours of the subjective telos of virtue, though, is that the proper functioning of the person of virtue is in fact a pleasurable state of well-being. Indeed, the attainment of virtue is the realization of the pleasurable proper functioning of one's person overall, the proper state of one's whole person, a distinctive pleasure that is not just pleasure in the realization of narrow, self-absorbed desires.

First, in II.i, we see that Kant's familiar appeals to the need of the virtuous person to sacrifice her happiness (as, for example, in the well-known Gallows Man example), while central to what a virtuous person is capable of, is not in fact a description of the subjective telos of virtue. The goal of virtue is not to suffer! A moral apathetic ability to regulate one's felt attachments in light of the absolute value of persons and as guided by one's experience of the moral feeling of respect, an ability which the Gallows Man has in spades, provides us, however, with a model for how to think of the virtuous governance of felt attachments generally. We thereby, in a move that stands in sympathy with Forman's (2016) account of Kant's moderate cynicism, understand especially the virtuous person's capacity to manage such sacrifice and suffering as what we shall call morally apathetic toleration of sacrifice, a capacity via which one moderates one's felt attachments through appeal to one's experience of moral feeling and the absolute value of persons toward which that feeling points. In such apathetic moderation, one is now able to take a proper evaluative distance upon one's felt attachments and recognize the objects of them as the merely relatively valuable things they are, making the toleration of the loss of those objects to which one is affectively attached that much more manageable.[20]

We then turn to an expansion of this point, arguing that the very same tools for apathetic moderation of one's affects are also tools for their governance generally, including not only their constraint and moderation but also their excitement and invigoration in line with virtue. In so doing, we return to and expand upon the ideas, first raised in I.i and I.iv, about how to govern one's felt attachments via the exercise of inner freedom, a process in which one relies upon contemplation of the power of one's moral feeling of respect and also upon the repeated practice of virtue to accomplish such control and governance. In exploring the nature of this governance work, we appeal to Kant's reference to Hercules at the crossroads as an image helping us appreciate the challenges of coming to terms with things about oneself that need to be changed: this is difficult work that constitutes a genuine battle within oneself between the lure of a life of easy desire-satisfaction and a life in which one authentically chooses and integrates into her person the demands of virtue. The fruits of all this hard labor will be shown in the next chapter when we describe the victorious acquisition of a free aptitude for virtue, a notion which constitutes a conception of happiness, rationally conceived.

II.ii is, in many ways, the real heart of this entire exploration of Kant's Deontological Eudaemonism. In this chapter, we defend the notion that there exists for Kant a notion of contentment of self in the exercise of the free aptitude for virtue, a notion that is essentially identical with the Aristotelian claim that one takes intrinsic pleasure in the unimpeded activity of a function most proper to oneself, and which constitutes a practical version of the formal aesthetic pleasure one takes in the harmony of one's intellectual faculties. This subjective state which supervenes immediately upon the exercise of a free aptitude for virtue is

---

[20] As Forman puts the point: "the best chance we have for approximating happiness in this life lies in our willingness to do without (but not in actively denying ourselves) all the luxuries that have come to seem like necessities in our corrupt era...[T]his moderate Cynic prescription for happiness stands in harmony with virtue as Kant depicts it" (Forman 2016, 78). And: "[P]rudence itself—when understood in the proper, moderate Cynic way—limits my ambitions in a way that allows the end of happiness to be in harmony with the end of virtue" (Forman 2016, 103). Forman thus relates this cynicism specifically to the pursuit of happiness, empirically conceived. That is a topic we'll consider explicitly in II.ii. Later in this chapter, though, I will distinguish myself from Forman when I suggest that although I agree with him that "any authentic moral demands are wholly distinct from the demands of prudence" as such (Forman 2016, 75), there is one sense of "happiness"—as unimpeded activity—which is indeed identical with the exercise of virtue.

furthermore best understood as happiness, rationally—instead of empirically—conceived, a state which constitutes the heart of Kant's Deontological Eudaemonism. We begin with a review of the current state of the literature on the relationship of morality, eudaemonism, and happiness for Kant, a discussion wherein we identify a range of interpreters with whom we engage for the rest of Part II, taking the work of Watson (1983), Forman (2016), and Holberg (2018) as sympathetic companions in the effort to reject interpreters like Wood (2000) and Kohl (2017), both of whom in their own distinctive ways insist upon a more fractured conception of the life of a sensibly affected rational being than what we accept. We then rely on Annas' (2011) gloss on Aristotle's notion of pleasure as unimpeded activity as an interpretive lens through which to understand and interpret Kant's ideas about the pleasurable exercise of a free aptitude for virtue, and affirm, in sympathy with Zuckert (2002), that this pleasure in the harmony of one's practical faculties of will and choice is a practical version of the formal aesthetic pleasure one takes in the harmony of one's intellectual faculties. We focus in particular on a careful reading and consideration of Kant's notion of "aptitude," understanding the facility or ease of this state as essentially an experience of non-felt formal pleasure in the virtually unimpeded activity of virtue.

In so doing, we, on the one hand, appeal to a connection between Kant and Annas' reading of Aristotle and, on the other, distinguish ourselves from Forman's reading of Kant as a "moderate cynic" who must entirely eschew the identity of virtue and happiness. While (as we shall see in II.iii) happiness empirically conceived must be distinguished from virtue, pleasure in the unimpeded exercise of virtue cannot and should not be so distinguished. We also consider and reject Elizondo's (2014) version of the idea that there is a purely intellectual felt pleasure for Kant, akin to Aristotle's notion of pleasure in unimpeded action. Although we agree with him that a rational pleasure exists for Kant, we reject his suggestion that such pleasure consists in a purely active feeling. Because feeling as such for Kant definitionally involves a moment of passivity, we instead, following Zuckert's (2002) articulation of a non-felt and formal experience of pleasure, understand the rational pleasure that is equivalent with the exercise of virtue to be a non-felt pleasurable experience of the harmony, facility, and ease with which one experiences the alignment of one's rational will with one's choice. And because this is pleasure in not just any activity but in that activity which defines the very essence of a sensibly affected rational being, we call that pleasure not just intellectual *contentment*, but intellectual or rational *happiness* as such.

We conclude this chapter by addressing an objector who would assert that such pleasure in rational activity undermines the very notion of the moral law expressing itself as an imperative, and then by noting two important caveats to the assertion of a pleasurable experience of virtue: on the one hand, because of the inextirpable propensity to evil, even the fully virtuous agent must experience her pleasure alongside an attitude of humble vigilance which she brings to her exercise of virtue; and, on the other, we grant that extreme experiences of suffering outside of one's control have the potential to undermine the otherwise necessary coincidence of virtue and rational happiness. And so, although, in all this, Kant must admit something less than the full perfection of the virtuous person, and although he must also admit that extreme external circumstances can destroy the supervenience of pleasure upon the exercise of virtue, his account is no worse off than Aristotle's on these points. Indeed, Deontological Eudaemonism is preferable to the Aristotelian account of virtue precisely in that it holds out a model for how the virtuous person can thrive, experiencing the virtually unimpeded activity of virtue, even in the midst of unavoidable suffering (a point to which we shall return in II.iii, especially in relation to happiness empirically conceived).

We then, in II.iii, expand this story of the subjective telos of virtue as happiness rationally conceived to the virtuous pursuit of happiness now empirically conceived, revealing a harmonious marriage of virtue and the non-self-absorbed pursuit of such happiness. First Watson (1983), and then, more recently, both Forman (2016) and Holberg (2018) have made progress in this direction, challenging Kohl's (2017) overly harsh distinction between the functioning of moral and prudential reasoning, and we take our own efforts here as a continuation of their projects. Telling a story of the marriage of virtue with happiness, empirically conceived is crucial; for, indeed, if Kant thought that the pleasure one takes in the unimpeded exercise of virtue were the only kind of pleasure for which the virtuous person could hope, then he wouldn't be anything more than a Stoic Eudaemonist, i.e. someone whose conception of value is construed so narrowly that the pleasure one takes in being moral is sufficient to constitute one's happiness, full stop. But Kant's conception of human flourishing is more expansive than this: in addition to the pleasure one takes in being virtuous, the virtuous person has the hope, through use of the same tools she uses to realize her subjective telos of virtue, of also maximizing her pleasure, empirically conceived, overall, in all sorts of valuable non-moral activities like bird-watching, cello-playing, good joke-telling, relationships, travel, and more. There is, in other words, a meaningful conception of non-moral value for Kant, and, with Watson (1983), I agree that affirmation of such value through the pursuit of happiness empirically conceived is a crucial piece of a well-lived life, Kantian style.[21] That same reorientation of

---

[21] As Watson puts the point: "Kant's position is that human beings necessarily will care significantly about the fulfillment of their natural needs and desires. Even if we were perfect in virtue, our contentment with our lives on the whole would depend upon fortune. When things go very badly (and virtue does not preclude this), we will not be happy. While self-contentment is not irrelevant to happiness—not excluded by definition—it is simply insufficient to provide us with contentment with our lives on the whole" (Watson 1983, 93). And again: "A good life for us as human beings—as finite, rational creatures with needs—simply could not be a life that failed to meet our basic needs and interests. As [Kant] puts it in one place, that 'could not be in accordance with the complete volition of an omnipotent rational being' (2, 115, [110]). Given his doctrine of moral contentment, and of the unconditional goodness of the moral life, the virtuous could not be rendered morose or totally cheerless even by

desire via one's objective telos of making persons as such one's end which was utilized in II.i to guide the process of desire-*governance* is thus now applied to the process of desire-*satisfaction*, with particular attention to how the obligatory end of cultivating one's natural capacities with a pragmatic purpose provides a model for organizing one's pragmatic end-setting generally under the purview of one's virtuous telos of respecting persons.

As such, even as we grant that the realization of happiness empirically conceived becomes a secondary goal of governance, we also ultimately achieve on this model of Deontological Eudaemonism a more satisfying fulfillment of desires than any non-naturalistic effort at the same (viz., than any effort at desire fulfillment solely from within the realm of desire itself, without any appeal to a non-contingent, non-desire-based guide) could accomplish: the non-negotiable and exception-less way in which the goal of making persons as such one's end is introduced as the guide for seeking happiness empirically conceived brings a new order and stability to the subjective experience of the pursuit of desire fulfillment, introducing an objective goal for the organization and realization of that desire fulfillment which is more proper to the kind of being one is overall. In this virtuous pursuit of happiness, we discover a marriage both of non-moral relative and moral absolute value on the one hand, and a thoroughgoing intertwining of one's pragmatic and moral felt attachments on the other.

We conclude by affirming that, in fact, the pursuit of virtue is the *best* way to pursue happiness successfully, since the very tools of virtue, considered both objectively and subjectively act also as the best tools for the pursuit of happiness: virtue helps both objectively to heighten and focus one's capacity for good judgment about the relative ordering of things of value, and subjectively to provide an evaluative perspective, akin to the one which assured moral apathy and moral excitement in the pursuit of virtue, which allows one to shape and guide one's feelings in relation to that pragmatic end-setting meant to encourage the best development of happiness. In so doing, even as we admit the bare possibility that one's commitment to virtue can under extreme circumstances cause injury to one's happiness empirically conceived, we nonetheless affirm the hope of a being whose satisfactions both rational and empirical are reliably unified and in harmony with one's pursuit of virtue. As such, we again place ourselves in sympathy with Watson's (1983) suggestion that "[o]ne's contentment with one's life on the whole will properly depend upon both" the virtuous discipline of practical reason and on the hope of "far[ing] well" (Watson 1983, 94); and, further, that the latter will be accomplished most successfully from the perspective of the former.[22]

---

serious misfortune. But such a fate would prompt the judgment that their existence as finite rational beings is lacking in something significantly good. They would say of such troubles: 'It's only pain, not evil, for it leaves my moral worth untouched' (2,62 [601])."

[22] His statement of the point is powerful: "the life devoted [only] to inclination will he devoid of meaning and at least dimly discerned as such by those who live it. Such a life finally creates a great

We also affirm sympathy with Holberg's (2018) suggestion that "virtue is the best, and maybe the only, way to pursue happiness" (Holberg 2018, 23), and seek only to challenge Holberg to drop the "quasi" from her account of Kant's "quasi-eudaemonism." Ultimately, by affirming that the tools of virtue are simultaneously the tools of happiness, empirically conceived, and that the pursuit of happiness rationally conceived and happiness empirically conceived are both guided by a singular life-guiding telos of making persons as such one's end, our story of Deontological Eudaemonism is complete.

IV. A Note on Phenomenological Method

Before turning to our discussion, I want to emphasize a point about the methods I am using as I make my interpretive arguments. This work is, clearly, an interpretation of Kant's texts; but the ways in which one can interpret texts is myriad. One can take a rigorously historical perspective, investigating the history of the interpretation of these texts. One can take a rigorously textual perspective, investigating exactly how a particular excerpt fits into the larger arguments of the text from which it comes. One can also take what I would call a "phenomenological" approach to interpreting historical texts, seeking to enter into the point of view of the text through appeal to first-personal and literary examples which illustrate and bring to life the meaning implicit in the underlying text.

In this work, I take great care to ensure that the textual excepts upon which I rely are not read out of context (viz., not read in a way that is in conflict with or contrary to the original context of that excerpt). But I will not always dwell at length on the details of the context from which an excerpt comes. Instead of such "extensive" interpretation, I sometimes opt for what I would call "intensive" interpretation: in order really to appreciate what Kant is saying in what are often very terse excerpts, I first investigate the precise language of the excerpt, and then clarify the sense of his central ideas through appeal to illustrative examples drawn from literature or my own first-personal experiences. Some might worry that doing so takes us away from the original text and even places us on merely exploratory or speculative grounds. But I suggest, to the contrary, that such, what I would call "phenomenological," appeals to illustrative examples actually take us more deeply into an understanding of the original texts and ideas of which they are illustrative. These examples are simply helping us to pay attention, in more depth, to the moral or practical point at issue.

"'void,' an emptiness that leads us on a futile search for significance among the various ends of inclinations. Even those who satisfy their inclinations are not likely to be satisfied" (Watson 1983, 90).

In using examples in this way, I am in fact following Kant's own advice about paying attention to one's own moral consciousness, advice he gives both in the *Groundwork* and the *Critique of Practical Reason*. Consider the following excerpts:

> [Common human reason] is very well informed in all cases that occur, to distinguish what is good, what is evil, what conforms with duty or is contrary to it, if—without in the least teaching it anything new—if one only, as Socrates did, *makes it aware of its own principle*; and that there is thus no need of science and philosophy to know what one has to do in order to be honest and good, indeed even to be wise and virtuous. (4:404/19, emphasis added)

> [H]ow is consciousness of that moral law possible? We can become aware of pure practical laws just as we are aware of pure theoretical principles, *by attending to the necessity with which reason prescribes them to us*. (5:30/27, emphasis added)

In both these passages, we see Kant admonishing us to focus our minds on the principles to be discovered in one's moral consciousness. The further implication of both these passages is that it would be very easy for us to do otherwise: to ignore, or obscure, the true meaning of the principle under consideration. But when we "attend" carefully to that principle, paying particular attention to the way it imposes its "necessity" upon us, we become more "aware" of that principle and its import, pointing us not only toward "honest[y] and good[ness]" but also toward "wis[dom] and virtu[e]." The phenomenological method of attentiveness is, in other words, a means not only to understand ideas intellectually but also to gain attentive appreciation of the practical import and worth of those ideas in one's life.

I shall not expand on the exact nature of this method here. That is something I have done more fully in a previous book.[23] What I do in this book is to exercise that method to draw a detailed picture of Deontological Eudaemonism, one intended to inspire attentiveness in the reader's own moral consciousness. In II.ii and II.iii, wherein I articulate what I take to be the real heart of this work on Kant's Deontological Eudaemonism, you will find particularly distinctive examples of the use of this method.

Let us turn, then, to this account of Deontological Teleology and Deontological Eudaemonism.

---

[23] See Grenberg (2013a).

PART I
DEONTOLOGICAL TELEOLOGY
The Objective Telos of Virtue

I.i
In Search of the Objective Telos of Self-Governance

Introduction

Deontological Eudaemonism asserts that it is only in being guided by a strictly necessary principle of duty to respect persons that sensibly affected rational beings like us humans can govern themselves properly and therefore flourish. Deontological Eudaemonism thus introduces a telos and principle of governance more self-encompassing than desire-fulfillment, or happiness empirically conceived, to define this flourishing. We will eventually, in this section of the book, affirm respect for persons as this non-relative, non-contingent, strictly necessary principle-cum-telos which is the only principle with legitimate governing authority for sensibly affected rational beings. It is the objective principle which defines the ultimate goal or telos of the virtuous self-governance of desires, a telos which, unlike any would-be self-elevated desire-cum-passions, is in fact capable of introducing that evaluative distance necessary for the proper ordering and governing of one's world of desire overall.

The result of the admission of this rational and strictly necessary telos for the governance of desire is the hope for the proper functioning of a *sensibly* affected *rational* being: all parts of this being realize their proper function once put into proper relationship with each other via this necessary principle which acts as a guiding telos of one's person, a telos which finds its objective ground in reason but which also, through the establishment of virtue, situates itself subjectively within the self-governing person as that affective-rational subjective state most appropriate to the realization of this objective end. As a result, sensibly affected rational beings have the hope of achieving the most pleasurable, virtually unimpeded, proper functioning of their being.

We are not yet ready, however, to articulate the contours of Deontological Eudaemonism as such, because there is a previous task to accomplish: in this Part I, we focus first on making sense of the very notion of an objective teleological (that is, end-based) focus for virtue within a deontological system of morality, and then on understanding this objective telos of virtue specifically as respect for persons. We shall thereby affirm Kant's moral theory as essentially teleological or end-based. In so doing we affirm, despite his earlier *Groundwork* and second *Critique* suggestions to the contrary, Kant's ultimate *Metaphysics of Morals* claim that end-setting is consistent with the affirmation of an *a priori* and free grounding of morality. Indeed, the free setting of obligatory ends—a new notion introduced in the Doctrine of Virtue and not previously explicitly present in his earlier moral works—is simply a continuation of the notion of freedom as incorporation which Kant introduced in the *Religion*, bringing that freedom not only to the *a priori* determination of maxims but now also to the *a priori* determination of specific matters of choice, that is, to the setting of particular ends of virtue. What we ultimately discover in Part I is that in the Doctrine of Virtue Kant explicitly affirms a robust reading of the Formula of Humanity, defending it not only as a principle which limits our interactions with persons but which also positively demands of us that we make persons as such our end, that is, our guiding telos in the pursuit of virtuous self-governance. By introducing this telos for virtue, I am, essentially, understanding Kant's account of virtue as grounded in what I call Deontological Teleology, a model of virtue grounded in a reciprocal relationship between a deontological principle of action and an objective end of virtue which acts as an organizing telos for all end-setting.

In this chapter, we prepare ourselves for our Part I investigation of Deontological Teleology with some initial reflections upon why happiness, empirically conceived, is not the proper telos for sensibly affected rational beings, and upon how we are pointed toward a more satisfying telos for the self-governance of desires by the distinctive quasi-desire of the moral feeling of respect. We turn then, to an initial articulation of that telos toward which this feeling points us: respect for persons as the proper objective telos or goal of self-governance, a goal which defines the pursuit of governance as the specifically moral one of the attainment of virtue. To make sense of what it means to call this telos objective, we then explore it in comparison and contrast with its supervening subjective telos of virtue (a notion which itself will not be explored fully until Part II of the book).

I. The Contours and Limits of Naturalistic reasoning

The Limits of Naturalistically Grounded Reasoning

How, then, can we make sense of the proper and authoritative telos for the governance of desires? One might think, since our goal is a eudaemonistic one of pleasurable well-being, that the proper goal for the governance of desires would be the goal of exception-less and complete fulfillment of one's desires, that is, *complete happiness*, conceived empirically as the satisfaction of all one's desires or lacks.

But happiness empirically conceived cannot be the proper guiding telos for desire-governance in the life of a sensibly affected rational being. The short explanation for why this is the case for Kant is that a merely sensible, natural, or empirical goal like this could not be the proper telos of a being who is both sensible and rational. We shall, eventually, have more to say about what kind of telos would be proper to a complex being like this.

But there is, first, another explanation for why, even on its own terms, the complete satisfaction of one's empirical desires cannot be an adequate telos or guide in the governance of desire: for Kant, it is simply the case that nothing in the empirical world can realize perfect completeness. And so, in an empirical world full of incompleteness, one cannot set the perfect fulfillment of desires as a meaningful goal. Rather, something approaching such completeness is only to be found in the categorical necessitation we will encounter in the realm of the rational. But first, to appreciate in more detail why the empirical goal of complete desire-fulfillment is an inadequate guide for the governance of desire, let us explore both the contours and the limits of what one can hope for in a pursuit of completeness in the fulfillment of desire merely on the natural or empirical level so as to appreciate the inadequacy of the realization of happiness, empirically conceived, as the proper telos of a sensibly affected rational being.

The first thing to say about such governance of desire is that it would be governance *of* desire *by* desire. We would, in other words, have nothing other than the tools of desires themselves to make sense of the structure of one's self-governance. The most obvious disadvantage of any would-be governance of desire by desire is that such ordering is limited by the constraints of that sort of rational order or governance permissible within the natural world. Before turning to the question of desire-governance as such, some initial reflections upon how to construe the powers of and constraints upon rationality within a merely naturalistic framework are thus in order. Kant makes at least two points about the natural world of reason that will help us here: a distinction between claims which hold only contingently or with empirical generality versus those that hold with strict universality and necessity, and a claim about the impossibility of completing an empirical series. Let us consider each point in turn.

In the *Critique of Pure Reason*, Kant makes a helpful distinction between pure and empirical cognitions, the former of which hold with universality and necessity and the latter of which hold only with empirical generality. As he notes:

> At issue here is a mark by means of which we can securely distinguish a pure cognition from an empirical one. Experience teaches us [first], to be sure, that something is constituted thus and so, but not that it could not be otherwise... Second: Experience never gives its judgments true or strict but only assumed and comparative universality (through induction), so properly it must be said: as far as we have yet perceived, there is no exception to this or that rule... Empirical universality is therefore only an arbitrary increase in validity from that which holds in most cases to that which holds in all... whereas strict universality belongs to a judgment essentially.   (B3–4/137, emphases removed)

In short, empirical judgments, precisely because they are grounded in experience, cannot hold with strict universality or necessity, but only with what he calls "empirical universality." That is: because we cannot say with confidence that the judgment could not be other than it is (viz., that it is necessary), we also cannot say with confidence that every example of the event in question under the auspices of this judgment holds in a similar way (viz., that it is universal). Instead, one can say only that such judgments hold generally and reliably, or "in most cases," but it would be entirely "arbitrary" and unjustified to move from such general reliability to the assertion of any "strict universality" or necessity for such judgments. As such, all empirical judgments hold only contingently (viz., things could always be other than they are) and only with empirical generality instead of strict universality.

Kant goes on to rely on this distinction between empirical and pure cognitions for his argument grounding the existence of pure concepts of the understanding. If the most basic and grounding claims in the natural world of experience—laws of nature and even more basic claims like "every event has a cause"—are in fact to hold with strict universality and necessity, we must seek rules for the ordering of such claims from somewhere other than empirical, inductive experience. It is only in appeal to *pure a priori* rational principles undergirding nature and empirical experience that we transcend merely contingent claims and thereby properly ground the strict universality and necessity of those relations which we in fact discover as constituting the order of nature. As Kant summarizes the point later, in the *Prolegomena*:

> [T]he highest legislation of nature must lie in our self, i.e., in our understanding, and...we must not seek the universal laws of nature from nature by means of experience, but, conversely, must seek nature, as regards its universal conformity to law, solely in the conditions of the possibility of experience that lie in our sensibility and understanding.   (4:319/71)

In short, one cannot hope for strict universality or necessity to adhere to any merely empirically grounded rational judgment or principle. Those aspects of the world of nature that do hold with strict universality and necessity—claims like "every event has a cause"—hold thusly only because we can tell an *a priori* story of their origin. But more basic empirical claims that depend only on repeated experience—like determining whether a flame will cause pain to my hand when I touch it—will never reach that exulted status of holding with strict universality and necessity. These empirical claims—and, indeed, even the empirical "laws" one might establish on their basis—will always be subject to exceptions, moments when the expected relation does not hold. Merely empirical laws thus cannot be truly necessary laws (or even true "laws" as such), since, despite the general reliability in causal relations they assure, a certain contingency will always cling to them: instead of deriving from that strict necessity which would require an *a priori* origin, empirical laws might not necessarily obtain as expected. Things could always be different.

The failure of strict universality and necessity in principles emerging from the empirical world of experience is not the only limit of empirical knowledge claims. Later in the first *Critique*, at the heart of his worries in the so-called Antinomies, Kant presents a series of arguments which show that for an empirical world governed only by natural causality, beyond the failure of strict universality and necessity for any knowledge claim grounded in that experience just noted, one could also never adequately *complete* any series of events in that world. Here is the way he makes this point in relation to the Thesis of the Third Antinomy, a point at which Kant provides an argument against the idea that natural causality is the only kind of causality. If we assume only natural causality, then:

> the causality of the cause through which something happens is always something **that has happened**, which according to the law of nature presupposes once again a previous state and its causality, and this in the same way a still earlier state, and so on. If, therefore, everything happens according to mere laws of nature, then at every time there is only a subordinate but never a first beginning, and thus no completeness of the series on the side of the causes descending one from another. (A445–446/B473–474)

If we can appeal only to empirical and natural laws to explain events, one's search for a complete cause of any single event can never come to rest or completion. There is no natural principle adequate for explaining completely the order and ground of any series of events. An empirical series of events is, in other words, by its very nature an incomplete series. If every event has only a natural cause, that series of causes must inevitably go back to infinity, never finding a complete causal story to ground and explain the entire series. As such, the series of natural causes is open-ended, stretching toward some incompletable, never reachable infinity.

It is not my intention here to defend at length the arguments Kant makes for either of these claims (viz., the distinction between empirical generality and strict universality on the one hand, or the incompleteness of a natural series on the other). One can, however, with these ideas draw a picture of the contours of naturalistic rational reflection: naturalistic knowledge claims are contingent and subject to exceptions; and any series of empirical events can never be fully explained, grounded, or completed. Furthermore, empirical knowledge claims hold contingently and with mere generality precisely *because* they emerge from such incompletable series of empirical events. Lacking a grounding principle which would tell a complete rational story of the series' existence, any knowledge claim grounded in that series will inevitably sometimes misfire (i.e., will hold contingently, with only empirical generality, and not with rigorous rational necessity).

Natural Limits Applied to the Practical Realm: Incompleteness in the Pursuit of Happiness

Let's return now to the practical world of self-governance with this general picture of naturally based reasoning in hand. What would it be like to be a self-governing agent guided only by a telos within the natural world, and taking only naturalistically based rational reflections on her desires as her tools for governance? Kant himself does in fact apply both these theoretical ideas (exceptions to general rules and the incompleteness of a series) in the practical realm: when he commits himself to the Categorical Imperative in the moral realm, Kant does so with a concern to distinguish strictly universal moral claims from merely contingent and empirically general practical claims, thereby highlighting the limits of the latter; and when he expresses skepticism about the possibility of determining perfect happiness for oneself, it is with an appreciation for the inevitable incompleteness of any series within the empirical world (including that series which would be the whole of one's desires). Let us investigate each of these points in turn.

First, Kant defends a rational principle for action more strictly universal and necessary than any contingent rule grounded only in empirical generality could provide. This is a familiar and grounding point about Kant's ethics. Kant considers it to be "of the utmost necessity to work out...a pure moral philosophy, completely cleansed of everything that might be in some way empirical," thereby confirming our "common conception of moral laws as holding with '*absolute* necessity,'" and not merely with that empirical generality adequate for merely anthropological (i.e., not genuinely moral) studies (4:390/4–5, emphasis added). This quest for strict universality and necessity in moral laws is, indeed, the whole point and purpose of his emphasis upon the *categorical* nature of moral imperatives: "if the action is represented as good in itself, hence as necessary in a will that *in itself* conforms to reason, as its principle, then it is *categorical*" (4:414/28). In order truly to have a principle which orders one's actions in an exception-less and non-contingent way, without any rough edges (that is, without any exceptions to that rule or principle), we must forego any would-be empirical grounding of morality centered in the self-ordering of desires, and instead seek a rule of action grounded in reason and freedom, distinct from nature. Were we to rely only on empirical principles to ground morality, we would discover only contingent rules which hold with empirical generality, and not a genuine "law" as such: "[A] law, if it is to hold morally, i.e., as the ground of an obligation, must carry with it *absolute* necessity" (4:389/5, emphasis added).

I have argued elsewhere[1] that Kant is committed to the application of strictly universal and necessary principles in the moral realm because it is only such

---

[1] See Grenberg (2013a) where I defend the idea that Kant grounds these universal and necessary principles of morality through appeal to common, felt, first-personal phenomenological experience of morality.

principles that do justice to our common experience of moral demands. Any merely contingent and empirically based rule thus cannot be called a "law" as such, because a principle holding with mere empirical generality cannot aspire to that true hallmark of complete universality and necessity that is found in our own felt phenomenological experience of moral demands like "Do not lie" and "Do not cause injury to persons." Rules that held only with empirical generality could not, that is, hold with the strict necessity that is in fact already found in one's common understanding of dutiful action. We will discuss such strictly universal and necessary principles in much more depth later in Part I. For now, we appeal to them to provide a contrast which highlights just what merely empirical practical principles lack: strict, or categorical, necessity.

Second, even setting moral concerns aside and looking only at the question of how best to order one's desires so as to assure happiness, we once again encounter the limits of naturalistic principles of order. First, and importantly, in the pursuit of happiness, we are indeed seeking a complete whole, not unlike that would-be completion of a series Kant sought in making sense of natural causality. Happiness would be "the *entire* well-being and contentment with one's condition" (4:393/9, emphasis added), a state in which "*all* inclinations unite in one sum" (4:399/14, emphasis added). Happiness would, in other words, be that ordering of oneself which assures the satisfaction of *all* one's desires. When we pursue happiness, we thus want to find that rule whereby *all* our desires—present and future—are satisfied. Otherwise stated: happiness would be the completion of that empirical series which is the series of the realization of our desires. Were such completion realized, all one's desires would be realized, that is, satisfied. One would be perfectly content.

As soon as we define happiness this way, we see the problem: an empirical pursuit of completeness is, by definition, a futile pursuit. Empirical desires are inherently incapable of complete self-organization. As Kant puts it, "happiness is not an ideal of reason, but of the imagination, which rests merely on empirical grounds, of which it is futile to expect that they should determine an action by which the totality of an infinite series of consequences would be attained" (4:418–419/32). One can put the point more generally: it is futile to try to realize a complete causal series by relying only on a principle of natural causality. But the series of our desires that would make up happiness just is an example of this sort of complete causal series. It is therefore equally futile to try to realize or satisfy a complete series of our desires by relying only on that ideal of the imagination called the principle of happiness.

The reason for the incompleteness in the realization of one's desires is thus the very same as for the failure of completion of any empirical series: these series are merely empirical and so not merely incomplete but also, by their very nature, incomplete-able:

> The cause of this [indeterminacy of the concept of happiness, and thus also of the futility of the pursuit of a completion of all one's desires] is: that the elements

that belong to the concept of happiness are one and all empirical, i.e., must be borrowed from experience and that, even so, for the idea of happiness an absolute whole is required, a maximum of well-being, in my present and every future condition. (4:418/31)

As such, attainment of happiness, defined as the complete fulfillment of one's desires, is simply impossible by empirical means. An empirical ordering of one's desires will always be inadequate for the complete ordering of one's infinite set of desires. This is true even apart from the question of whether such order properly integrates moral demands. Even on its own empirical and non-moral terms, desires and the empirical reasoning grounded in them can order themselves only so far.

Happiness is thus an empirical ideal struggling against its own empirical limits. It seeks a perfection it cannot attain simply in virtue of the kind of things by which it is constituted. An empirical, that is, a sensibly affected, rational being is unable to realize its own goal of completeness, that is, to complete, satisfy or fulfill *all* its desires. The pursuit of happiness is thus, at best, rough around the edges. One can pursue a goal of empirical generality in the ordering of one's desires. But this is a pursuit in which one must expect exceptions, misfires, and incompleteness. That is, one must expect unfulfilled desires, individual desires which do not find complete satisfaction, and satisfied desires which prove to be not as satisfying overall as one originally envisioned they would be. If we are looking for a telos completely to guide and order the governance of our desires, looking to the merely empirical telos of the fulfillment of all one's desires is not going to be a promising candidate.

A Frankfurtian Objection: Good Enough Governance by Rules of Thumb?

One might object at this point, though: couldn't a merely empirical ordering of one's desires, despite its incompleteness, still be considered a *success* in the governance of one's desires? It might, after all, be that although one cannot hope, naturalistically, for an utterly exception-less realization of the satisfaction of one's desires, one could nonetheless achieve some tolerably organized unity of them with few exceptions. And, so, one might argue that one can manage the fact that the state of one's desires is not perfectly satisfied and yet still claim to acquire something very reasonably called "happiness" via what could also very reasonably be called "self-governance." This exception-filled, rough-around-the-edges ordering of one's desires might just be entirely adequate for living a human life.

Such a claim makes a certain amount of sense.[2] Kant himself suggests that empirical principles of action based upon a choice about how to realize a desire

---

[2] Indeed, it is a sort of practical equivalent to criticisms that have been made of Kant's Third Antinomy argument. Some have argued that the proponent of natural causality needn't worry about

one has—what he calls counsels of reason—although they can never be non-contingent and strictly necessary, "commands" pointed toward a perfect satisfaction of all one's desires can nonetheless offer themselves as general rules of thumb to guide one's pursuit of happiness:

> To be happy, one cannot therefore act on determinate principles, but only according to empirical counsels, e.g., of diet, or thrift, of politeness, of restraint, and so on, which experience teaches on average advance well-being most. From this it follows that the imperative of prudence cannot, to be precise, *command* at all, i.e. present actions objectively as practically *necessary*; that they are to be taken rather as counsels (consilia) than as commands (praecepta) of reason.
> (4:418/32, emphases added)

Counsels of reason can thus be applied with empirical generality, and can thereby provide some order to one's person. Indeed, this is an order that is often even consistent not only with an impressive amount of self-control over particular desires but even with a certain adherence to moral principles, like a general willingness to respect and love persons. Someone who orders her life by such counsels of reason has, to a certain extent, risen above the simple bumper-car-style wantonness about which, say, Frankfurt would worry, and is in the process of moving toward governance and establishment of personhood via what Frankfurt would again call a second-order desire.[3] Kant would still refuse the accolade of "personhood" to someone ordered only by such principles; for him, personhood demands appeal to the ability to act in accordance with categorical reasons. But, granting this, we could still say that someone guided only by counsels of reason is not just tossed about by her desires. Instead, she finds some rules of thumb within the realm of desire itself to organize the satisfaction of her desires. She might even identify what Frankfurt would call a ruling second-order desire which guides the pursuit of her field of desires generally.

As such, even if one only has the set of tools to which someone like Frankfurt is committed—that is, even if one insists that the principles upon which one relies to order oneself can only emerge from the world of nature—one can thus articulate what initially seems a rather attractive way of governing oneself. It might even be quite satisfying to discover—given the initial appearance of boundlessness, volatility, and unpredictability that a life guided by nature might first appear to promise—that nature could bring as much order to a life as these merely empirical precepts would allow. The order that emerges in the Frankfurtian account of self-governance is what Kant would describe as a not-entirely-ordered and merely

---

the contradiction Kant asserts within a world of merely natural causality because formation of that contradiction assumes a commitment—viz., a concern for the completeness of the series of natural causes—which a proponent of natural causality would not hold. See Allison (1990) for an excellent discussion of this point.

[3] See especially Frankfurt (1971).

empirical ordering of the self via the imagination; nonetheless, one might argue that this could be a tolerably well-ordered life, and at the very least, a life that rises above the erratic and random life of the wanton.

And so: if one seeks to order one's empirical desires only through appeal to rational principles which are themselves grounded in empirical desires (that is, if we seek to order our lives only by these rules of counsel leading to rule by a second-order desire which acts as our governing telos), we seem to have the tools for a limited order to our desires. The empirical pursuit of happiness can never be perfectly completed; it can never achieve that complete ordering of desires that would avoid exceptions (viz., unsatisfied desires). But it would appear that it can realize its own version of empirical generality, giving us those rules which "on average advance well-being most" (4:418/32). There will always be failures in our pursuit of the satisfaction of our desires, but one can develop some pretty good counsels or rules of thumb that apparently allow one to muck along in the world tolerably well.

The Volatility of Boundless Desires

And yet, worries immediately arise. There are various failures or misfires to which a merely empirical ordering of desire by desire is subject which raise serious concerns about whether a self-governance guided only by a desire-based telos could really assure a life that is tolerably happy or tolerably well-governed. The series of our desires is, like any empirical series, a boundless one. That is just what it means for a series to be incomplete, as affirmed above. But there is a particular pressure to note in this failed completion of the series that is our pursuit of happiness: this is a particularly *volatile* boundless series seeking completion. Even as one admits to oneself that perfect resolution of one's desires is not possible, desires are just not the sort of thing easily to submit to failure of satisfaction and go away. Instead, desires do just the opposite: they vigorously, persistently, and relentlessly *seek* completion, especially when there is no non-desire restraint to be placed on them. When the volatility of desire is added to the boundlessness of one's series of desires, with no promise of any solid space of peacefulness either within or outside this boundless and volatile realm of desire, the hope of achieving happiness through the empirically based governance of desires moves further and further from one's grasp.

Kant has a particular appreciation for how governance of volatile desires pursued only by desire-based rules can get out of hand. This passage from *Groundwork II* is particularly familiar to Kantians, but can also be read, anachronistically, as a sort of Kantian response to Frankfurtians who would confidently assert the successful establishment of happiness through a self-governance grounded only in naturalistic second-order desires-cum-volitions:

> [U]nfortunately, the concept of happiness is so indeterminate a concept that, even though every human being wishes to achieve it, yet he can never say determinately and in agreement with himself what he actually wishes and wants... [I]t is impossible that the most insightful and at the same time singularly able, but still *finite* being should make for himself a determinate concept of what he actually wants here. If he wants riches, how much worry, envy and intrigue might he not by this bring down upon his shoulders! If he wants much cognition and insight, that might perhaps only sharpen his eyes all the more, to show him as all the more terrible the ills that are still concealed from him now and yet cannot be avoided, or to burden his desires, which already give him enough trouble, with more needs still. If he wants a long life, who will guarantee him that it would not be a long misery? If at least he wants health, how often has not bodily discomfort kept someone from excess into which unlimited health would have plunged him, and so on. *In short, he is not able to determine with complete certainty, according to any principle, what will make him truly happy, because **omniscience** would be required for this.* (4:418/31, emphases added)

It is true that Kant is reflecting here on happiness, and Frankfurt himself does not often speak of happiness as such, but instead simply of the governance of desires. Nonetheless, in reflecting on happiness here, Kant essentially reflects on just the same project of desire-governance which is the center of Frankfurt's concerns. That is, he reflects on the establishment of a variety of what Frankfurt would call second-order desires intended to allow persons to achieve that overall state of governance Kant calls happiness but Frankfurt would call whole-heartedness. But in every case of would-be desire-governance, Kant notes how something important escapes one's governance: if I seek wealth, I get worries; if I seek knowledge I only become more acutely aware of the miseries of the world; if I seek a long life, I might only get a temporal increase in my miseries. Neither happiness empirically conceived nor whole-heartedness is forthcoming from the application of merely empirical rules of counsel, that is, from desire-based principles of governance.

Indeed, on the basis of this passage, we can identify two distinct ways in which governance of desire by desire fails us: both quantitatively and axiologically. In reflection upon these two kinds of failure, what we shall discover is not only that a complete realization of one's desires is impossible but, further, that desire-based governance is no *governance* at all. Both quantitatively and axiologically, one encounters so many failures of ordering of one's person via desire that the resulting states are better understood as dysfunctional failures of governance than as any successful realization of it.[4]

---

[4] In emphasizing the futility of a life governed only by the search for happiness, I seek to further here a project first introduced by Watson (1983), who notes that "the life devoted to inclination" promises only "a futile search for significance among the various ends of inclinations" (Watson 1983, 90). I am deeply sympathetic with Watson's approach to these matters, and will return to discussion of him in Part II.

To prepare for those reflections, let us first reflect in general terms upon what it is that a desire needs to accomplish when it plays this role of being a second-order desire aiming at complete happiness. Any desire that is elevated into a ruling position is still itself, first and foremost, a *desire*, that is, an inclination for getting something that one lacks. A desire is a state, then, of need: there is something that I want that I do not yet have, and this quality of a desire does not go away when one elevates that desire to a governing role. To the contrary, it is precisely this quality of wanting something that provides the energy, oomph, and structure for one's governance: the object of one's desire—what one is seeking—is established as the ultimate goal of one's person, a goal in accordance with which all one's other desires are organized. In addition to being a desire in need of fulfillment itself, this second-order desire thus also takes responsibility for the ordering and guidance of other desires. To govern successfully, this second-order desire must not only fulfill itself but must also organize maximal fulfillment of all one's other desires which agree with this governing desire, and then manage, control and constrain all the rest of one's desires which are in opposition to and would be destructive of this guiding second-order desire. A second-order desire is thus simultaneously a state of need and a perspective from which to organize oneself. It is an empirically grounded principle which holds only with empirical generality and which, furthermore, takes as its empirical ground that particularly needy and unstable empirical thing called desire.

But, furthermore, this desire's efforts at governance go on within that volatile and boundless world of desire of which we have spoken, a world in which we are guaranteed that there will be not only multitudinous but also mutually contradictory desires. And the only guide one has is itself this finite and empirical desire or state of need which has boot-strapped itself into a governing position as a rule of counsel, an empirically grounded rule which thus holds (or can be applied) only with empirical generality. This is a recipe for disaster! The scope, boundlessness, and volatility of one's desires, combined with one's merely finite, empirical, and inherently unstable tool for corralling them, will assure a whole series of misfires in governance, efforts which result not in a gently imperfect and tolerably happy order, but instead in a state of person that is not ordered or governed at all. One envisions, in fact, the emergence of just the sorts of problems for self-governance for which Frankfurt's appeal to second-order-desires-cum-volitions was meant to correct in the first place: addiction, self-deception, internal revolutions of governance, and reversion to wantonness. Let us, then, taking the above-quoted passage from Kant as our guide, explore how governance by second-order desires leads to these disordered, ungoverned outcomes, appreciating first the quantitative and then the axiological failures which inevitably attend upon empirical efforts at governance.

Quantitative Failures of Governance of Desire by Desire

First, we can see that the misfires of would-be desire-based governance which Kant considers in this passage find their ground in the fact of the *incompleteness* of any empirical series which we considered previously, now combined with the relentless *volatility* of the desires which make up this particular empirical series of desires. This incompleteness of realization of one's series of desires can thus, in the first instance, be understood as what one might call the "quantitative" challenge of governance of desires by desire: there are just too many desires to govern, and any merely empirical, desire-based rule of governance will fail to contain and control all of them. In Kant's language, we are "finite" beings trying to accomplish an infinite calculation which would be possible only for a perfectly "omniscien[t]" being (4:418/31). Whenever one thinks one has found the thing that will make one happy—whenever, that is, one determines what Frankfurt would call a second-order and governing desire—immediately things start to slip through the cracks or net of one's governance. Getting a good hold on the object of *this* desire, I make it more difficult or impossible to realize *that* desire. One wants, fervently, to believe that there is a stable desire-based point of view from which one could pull absolutely everything together—one wants, in other words, to hope for what Frankfurt has called the possibility of whole-hearted governance via one's chosen second-order desire that holds with the strength of volitional necessity—but the boundless scope of our volatile desires just won't submit to such governance, and the very tool meant to order this boundless scope is itself a potentially unstable state of need which, *qua* principle, can hold with only empirical generality. Our desires are too numerous, too mutually incompatible, and too volatile to order themselves by the principles of a merely finite and desire-needy mind. Desire-based self-governance is thus the futile effort of a finite being to corral an infinite—or at least a multifarious and mutually incompatible—series of volatile desires via a contingently chosen desire-based governor using mere rules of thumb.[5]

This quantitative incompleteness, which becomes more urgent through the additional pressure of the relentlessness of volatile desires (i.e., their insistence upon being satisfied), expresses itself in the pursuit of the self-governance of desires on at least two levels: macro- and micro-levels. First, as we've already seen, one simply cannot achieve a complete whole that would be happiness because no

---

[5] This is a point that has a certain similarity with a point that has already been made by O'Neill (2007), in slightly different terms, in relation to would-be utilitarian grounds of morality: we sensibly affected human beings are simply not very good rational calculators of what would make us happy. We are not good at calculating the consequences of our actions so as to aim at those actions that would increase our happiness. Although I do not emphasize the consequentialist point here, the idea is similar: it is impossible to calculate how to organize, encourage, and constrain our desires so as to assure an overall state of self-governance.

such complete whole is possible for any empirical series. True *"whole*-heartedness" is, in other words, not possible within an empirical series. Let's call this incompleteness in a series the macro-level of incompleteness. But we can also take the incompleteness of an empirical series to the micro-level: no individual desire—including that desire which is elevated into a ruling position—is capable of complete fulfillment. The fulfillment of desire is, instead, a process extended out over a boundless timeline: every fulfillment of a desire will be followed in time by a further loss of one's object of desire and thus a further need to re-seek its fulfillment. This too is a continual, never-ending process with no finite end-point, in other words, a perpetually *incomplete* process.

Axiological Failures of Desire-Governance: The Passionate Failure of Evaluative Distance

There is, however, yet another reason that we should be wary of a naturalistic desires-governed-only-by-desire model of governance, a reason we can uncover this time by focusing on another limit of natural things: their incapacity to provide an adequate basis for *valuing*. Desire, on its own, is not the sort of thing capable of establishing that *evaluative distance* on one's desires overall that would be necessary for successful governance of those desires. The failure of desire-based governance is thus both quantitative and axiological. Indeed, one can read the very same guiding passage from Kant which we utilized to support our understanding of the quantitative failures of naturalistic governance to gird also our understanding of these new axiological failures in governance. Incompleteness, in other words, can be understood as incompleteness not only quantitatively but also in the proper awareness and ordering of the values related to one's series of desires. And when one fails to satisfy and order one's series of desires in a way that would genuinely understand and integrate those things of value related to those desires, one's governance once again is a failure. Naturalistic principles, in addition to being unstable and merely finite, also lack the value perspective that would allow them to organize one's desires overall into a satisfying evaluative whole.

It is important to note at the outset of this argument that we are not, at least at this point, introducing explicitly moral concerns here. That is, in saying that naturalistic governance fails on the axiological level, we are not (yet) saying that it fails to realize morality or virtue in its governance. Instead, we are making a previous point: morality aside, any naturalistic model of governance cannot achieve a unified evaluative whole in the satisfaction of one's desires. The values of those desires brought under governance by one guiding second-order desire cannot resolve themselves into one *coherent* unity of values, whether moral, immoral, or ammoral. In short, desire cannot provide that evaluative distance on all one's desires overall that could provide that governing principle that would be successful in providing that axiological unity which Frankfurt would call whole-heartedness.

At the heart of our inquiry here is the need to interrogate the very nature of desire-based governance: what *is* desire such that it either is or is not capable of governance? Are desire-based principles the sort of thing that actually can *govern* a whole self, placing all of one's values in a coherent order? Or should the nature of desire in general make us suspicious about whether such principles *could* or *should* be placed in such a governing role? What we shall discover in answering these questions is that desire simply is not the sort of thing made to govern. To the contrary, desire-based principles emerge from and further encourage a lack of attentiveness to one's self overall, a lack of attentiveness which results in the failure to gain proper evaluative distance upon those desires it is meant to govern, and results ultimately in a self-absorption that Kant very reasonably calls vicious and evil (even apart from any previous commitment to the idea of there being something like an autonomous rational self who provides a more adequate perspective from which to evaluate and thus govern oneself). Once we articulate this axiological inadequacy of governance by desire on its own terms, we will, I hope, be that much more tempted to admit, with Kant, a moral premise in the story of self-governance.

The story of the axiological failure of second-order desires as governors is grounded textually in the very same passage from which we were able to identify the quantitative limits of naturalistic self-governance. Here, once again, is that same passage:

> [U]nfortunately, the concept of happiness is so indeterminate a concept that, even though every human being wishes to achieve it, yet he can never say determinately and in agreement with himself what he actually wishes and wants... [I]t is impossible that the most insightful and at the same time singularly able, but still finite being should make for himself a determinate concept of what he actually wants here. If he wants riches, how much worry, envy and intrigue might he not by this bring down upon his shoulders! If he wants much cognition and insight, that might perhaps only sharpen his eyes all the more, to show him as all the more terrible the ills that are still concealed from him now and yet cannot be avoided, or to burden his desires, which already give him enough trouble, with more needs still. If he wants a long life, who will guarantee him that it would not be a long misery? If at least he wants health, how often has not bodily discomfort kept someone from excess into which unlimited health would have plunged him, and so on. In short, he is not able to determine with complete certainty, according to any principle, what will make him truly happy, because omniscience would be required for this. (4:418/31)

In reviewing this passage previously, we focused upon the quantitative slant one can bring to it in light of language about a "finite being" subject to an infinite task requiring "omniscience." But one can see in this passage—especially in the long list of would-be second-order desires gone wrong—another, more evaluative worry: whatever value you make the ruling value of your life, there is something else in your evaluative life that will get lost, fall short, mess things up, or just generally create trouble for the would-be governed person. If I get wealth, I've got too much intrigue to worry about in my life; but in addition to money, I value a life without intrigue. If I get knowledge, I only know too intensely just how many problems there are in the world; but in addition to knowledge, I value peacefulness of mind. If I get a long life, maybe it will just be a long miserable life; but in addition to the length of my life, I value its quality as well. And so on. In short, Kant suggests here that no inclination, when elevated to a ruling role, is capable of ordering one's values overall so as to assure that most all the things one values get a hearing and are realized.

There is another important point to make about this passage: the elevated desires noted in this litany of governance failures are just what Kant elsewhere calls passions. Let us briefly review Kant's account of affects and passions so as to appreciate this point. This account of affects and passions arises within the context of Kant's pursuit of understanding the virtuous governance of the self via what he calls inner freedom: "[T]wo things are required for inner freedom: being one's own master in a given case (*animus sui compos*) and ruling oneself (*imperium in semetipsum*), that is, subduing one's affects and governing one's passions" (6:407/166). When seeking to acquire freedom in one's person via the governance of one's inclinations, we can, thus more precisely, say that we need to subdue our affects and govern our passions. An affect is previous to and more fleeting than an inclination, whereas a passion establishes an already existing inclination more firmly as a lasting principle of action. An affect "belong[s] to feeling" and "precede[s] reflection," making such reflection "impossible or more difficult" (6:407/166). It comes upon a person unexpectedly, confusing her reflection, but then departs, "a tempest [that] quickly subsides" (6:408/166). A passion, however, is "a *lasting* inclination" (6:408/166, emphasis added), one which *does* "permit reflection," and even "allow[s] ... the mind to form principles upon it" (6:408/166).

The difference in these psychological states helps clarify precisely what kind of control is required to achieve inner freedom. With an affect, one loses one's composure; the goal is thus to regain composure, precisely what is suggested in Kant's parenthetical Latin gloss, "animus sui *compos*." Such composure of person is best understood as both the infrequency of experiencing surprise affects but also the ability to manage unavoidable surprise affects when they do arise. For the composed person experiencing an affect, "reason says, through the concept of virtue, that one should *get hold of* oneself" (6:408/166) while the flutter of the affect passes.[6]

---

[6] Jeeves, from P.G. Wodehouse's *Jeeves and Wooster*, is perhaps the paradigmatic example of a person of composure. Jeeves experiences very strong affects when he observes various indiscretions in his lord, Bertie. But the only evidence we observe of those affects is the slightest raising of an eyebrow

When I manage myself in the face of affects, I thus exhibit a certain level of self-*control*. But it is in the management of passions that we discover the real heart of virtue specifically as self-*governance*. Affects come and go, but passions are something I myself have chosen to give ordering power in my soul and person. They are thus much more firmly entrenched in my person than affects. Passions "permit...reflection" and "allow the mind to form principles upon [one's inclinations]." Such rationally chosen passions thus become something "to brood upon," and "to get...rooted deeply" in one's mind. In establishing a passion, I thus order my soul through the rationally chosen prioritization, encouragement, and cultivation of a particular affect or inclination. Kant's passions are thus roughly equivalent to what Frankfurt calls second-order desires: they are, in other words, desires which we identify and elevate as having governing status within the realm of one's desires generally.[7]

It turns out, though, that Kant takes the establishment of such passions to be the very heart of vice or vicious self-governance, and thus the true opponent in one's battle for virtue. Here is Kant's most explicit statement of what a passion is:

> A passion is a sensible desire that has become a lasting inclination (e.g., *hatred*, as opposed to anger). The calm with which one gives oneself up to it permits reflection and allows the mind to form principles upon it and so, if inclination lights upon something contrary to the law, to brood upon it, to get it rooted deeply, and so to take up what is evil (as something premeditated) into its maxim. And the evil is then *properly* evil, that is, a true *vice*. (6:408/166)

Interestingly, one thing that needs to be said about this passage is that the formation of a passion is simply an example of an inclination being incorporated into a principle or maxim of action. For, as this passage notes, a passion is simply a "lasting"—that is, a regular and characteristic—expression of an inclination or desire, now taken up as a chosen principle or maxim of action. Furthermore, in the formation of a passion, one "form[s] *principles*" (emphasis added) on the basis of one's inclination or desire. Passion formation is, thus, simply a particular example of choosing or "incorporating" an inclination as the ground of one's principle or maxim of action.[8] Instead of the inclination swooping upon me unexpectedly, I welcome and choose that inclination as the basis of a reason for my actions. The inclination does not determine my will directly, naturally, or unexpectedly, but instead is turned into a calm reason which guides my action. When an inclination becomes a passion in this way, it thus has, calmly and freely, been turned into a reason. Indeed, one could even say (at least in this early stage of passion formation)

---

followed by a clever plan for extricating Bertie from the troubles which inevitably ensue based upon his indiscretions. See Wodehouse (1991).

[7] See Frankfurt (1971 and 2006).

[8] See Allison (1990) for an explanation and discussion of "incorporation."

that what is in charge (or "governing") here in the process of passion-production is reason, not inclination: one has looked at an inclination and its object, and said "yes, I welcome regular expression of that inclination into my life."

But the rhetoric of this passage forces us to move things beyond these *prima facie* considerations. Kant says not only that "the mind...form[s] principles upon" this inclination, but, further, that one "*gives oneself up to*" (emphases added) the inclination in question. What we see going on here is thus something more than the simple incorporation of an inclination into a maxim, but more radically, a sort of reversal in the governance of one's soul. In simple incorporation, I freely choose to make this inclination the basis of a maxim or rational principle of action. But in the establishment of a passion, I now "give [my]self up to" that inclination. In other words, I am no longer guiding or controlling my inclination; instead, I allow it to take over control of my choice.

Passion is, in short, a *failure* of attentiveness, a turning of the mind's eye so insistently and obsessively toward one thing that the desire for this one thing takes over one's person, and one is no longer able to view one's full range of moral objects and concerns even-handedly. Let's explore this state more.

The first thing to say, then, about what it means to say that I have *given myself over* to the passion is that I am so fascinated by this inclination-cum-principle, so taken with it as the object of my attentiveness, that I grant it pride of place in the field of my attentiveness. Kant's language for this attentiveness gone awry is to say that I "brood" upon this inclination and "get it rooted deeply" within me (6:408/166). I can't think about anything else! I wake up at 3 o'clock in the morning thinking about it. I can't get it out of my mind.

It is this brooding, or obsessive attentiveness to a particular inclination, the giving over of ourselves to it, that provides fertile ground, then, for turning this inclination-cum-principle into the subversive thing that it is, into a passion proper. But, as we've already noted, this does not mean that we completely abandon choice or maxim-making; instead, we *corrupt* the process of choice or maxim-making. Kant notes that this inclination, now that it has become the center of one's attention is fully "take[n] up...into its *maxim*," and thereby given a *governing* role in one's person. But when a passion obtains this governing position in the soul, we have to say that this is no longer a simple garden-variety maxim; it is, rather, a rational maxim that has given itself over to its grounding inclination and thereby become a governing maxim for one's entire person. That inclination upon which one broods and obsesses is now in charge and has become the governing principle of one's person, mutinously replacing any would-be autonomously legislated rational demand as the center of one's self-governance. What began as a rational or principled welcoming or acceptance of an inclination thus becomes a passion-guided point of view from which I seek to govern or rule my entire self. A passion, in the fullest sense of that term, is thus not just an incorporated inclination, but, more fully, an incorporated inclination-cum-principle which, through obsessive attentiveness to its grounding inclination, is elevated into a governing or ruling position amongst my desires and which thereby becomes the point of view from which I organize and control not only this favored inclination but also all *other* desires and inclinations.

But in Kant's world, this established ordering of oneself via passions is a quasi-rational mutiny of the legitimate rule of one's autonomous self, an attempt to give ruling order of oneself over to that affect or inclination. By their very nature, passions thus encourage us to reason in ways "contrary to the law," that is, contrary to the authoritative governance of that law over one's person which demands always that I place respect for persons at the heart of my self-governance. One must, therefore, not simply subdue and tolerate the passing of, but instead more firmly "*govern* [, such] passions" (6:407/166, emphasis added). Such governance is glossed in Latin as an "*imperium in semetipsum*," an *absolute* power over oneself.[9] When passions are around, the task of *governing* oneself thus comes into its own: one of my inclinations has become actualized as a would-be ruling principle in my soul. This mutinous passion must therefore be defeated by reason much as a seditious plotter intending to overthrow a legitimate government would be defeated.

The Passionate Failure of the Pursuit of Happiness

Let's bring all of this back, then, to Kant's discussion of the failure of the pursuit of happiness. Another way of reading the above passage on happiness is to say that passions, established as second-order desires, are inept governors, axiological failures. We will, ultimately, want to defend Kant's stronger claim that these ruling passions are not only inept but also vicious governors; but we shall begin with consideration and defense of this weaker claim that such passionate second-order desires are simply inept evaluative governors. Passionate second-order desires do not have the evaluative strength or power to bring axiological unity to one's person through their governance of inclinations overall.

So, to begin: one reason to be suspicious of the capacity of passions to play a ruling role in the evaluation of one's desires overall is the fact that the *strength* of feeling connected with the original inclination grounding the passion informs both the process of passion formation and then the evaluative order and structure of the resulting self-governance of other desires and inclinations. Kant tells us that a passion is calm. But to say that a passion is calm, or calmly chosen, is entirely compatible with the idea that this same passion is a very strong one. Indeed, it is the strong inclinations that are more likely to become passions in the first place. I am not saying that the felt strength of an inclination determines one's

---

[9] Indeed, the Latin phrase "imperium," referred, in ancient Rome, to "the supreme power held by consuls or emperors to command and administer...in *military* affairs." See www.dictionary.com.

choice of a passion directly, for I accept instead what Allison has identified as the Incorporation Thesis, a claim that no inclination influences choice until it is incorporated into a maxim.[10] But when the candidates for choice (that is, our range of inclinations) present themselves, some make themselves heard in our agential consciousness more than others. Some are quiet, and some are raging. As a result, the choosing person assessing her field of desires is more likely to focus her attention on the parts of her soul screaming for that attention. The very formation of this passion rather than that one is thus attributable, in part, simply to the strength of the underlying inclination and the weakness of the others in comparison: the range of one's choice is limited by one's attentiveness as itself influenced by the varying weaknesses and strengths of present inclinations.[11] Desire-based governance will thus be even more susceptible than other choice-making processes to the indirect influence of the underlying strength of one's inclinations, and the resulting tendency to pay most attention to those inclinations that are strongest.

But once this strength-informed scope of one's attentiveness is in place, and one's passion is chosen, one's capacity for rational reflection upon one's desires is already warped, even previous to any actual establishment of macro-level governance on the basis of that passionately claimed inclination. My rational reflection on how to realize this passion might be very calm, engaged, and intense, but it is not—and here is the evaluative point—appropriately informed or balanced. If the proposals for what to think about come always and only from where I have been focusing my attention, and I've already let a strong inclination warp the focus of my attention, then the proposals for choice and governance emerging from passionate guidance are going to be rather lopsided in their evaluation of other desires. Worse, once I place my attention upon the object of this passionately chosen inclination, I only further encourage my attentiveness to and the strength of the original inclination, making it even more likely in the future that my attention will remain thusly riveted. By letting a strong inclination-cum-passion determine my objects of attentiveness, my emerging capacity for choice and governance is thus egregiously both narrowed and intensified, not broadened or made more balanced and capable of evaluation of all parts of myself equally.[12]

What results is the promise of a failure of proper evaluative distance on those very desires which this ruling passionate desire is meant to govern. That is: no one desire can provide an evaluative point of view capable of putting one's desires

---

[10] See Allison (1990).

[11] See Grenberg (2013a) for more detail on this story of the import of attentiveness in relation to choice.

[12] It should be noted that it is this very same intensity of attention to one thing that yields the firmness of virtue when that one thing to which one attends is the "dignity of the pure rational law" (6:397/170), viz. when that one thing is something in fact capable of providing proper axiological and reflective distance upon one's desires. We shall consider this point in more detail later in Part I.

overall into a coherent axiological order. To the contrary, Kant's point in this central *Groundwork* passage is that my passionate second-order desire will highlight some things but will inevitably cloud, obscure, and misconstrue others, either failing to see them at all or failing to see them as they are. Beyond assuring a quantitative failure in virtue of holding with merely empirical generality, my empirical and desire-based governing rule or passion will thus also fail axiologically. Let's look more carefully at how this evaluative failure of self-governance by passionate second-order desires occurs.

The Obfuscating Relativity of Evaluation by Passion

First, one has to admit, whatever its eventual failures, that a would-be governing passion makes the person possessing it very *good* at a couple things: at understanding the central interest one has in the object of one's passion, and then at determining how to understand the value of every other desire and thing in life *in terms of the value of that guiding passion*. By its very nature, a desire or inclination focuses on one thing. So a life governed by a passionate second-order desire makes that one thing central. If my passion is wealth and power, I am thus very good at appreciating how valuable money can be for getting the powerful life I want, and I'm also good at evaluating everything else in my decision-making process in terms of whether and to what extent it contributes to my passion for money and what it can get me. A passion is thus an excellent tool or lens by which to evaluate all other things, as long as the express purpose of one's evaluation is to determine another thing's worth *relative to* this ruling passion.

But this singular focus of a passion is not a good point of view from which to view, assess, or govern other things in one's field of desires even-handedly, or perhaps even at all, for what those things are in themselves. Indeed, one can even say that, by definition, in passion-ruled governance, I *cannot* see my other desires, or the values connected with them, for what *they* really are. To the contrary, I can only see them for what they are and are worth *relative to* the interests of my singular, narrowly focused guiding passion. This is true whether the thing I am looking at and seeking to evaluate is another desire, another object of desire, or, indeed, something else about me entirely unrelated to desire. Essentially, a passionate second-order desire-governed life is a life in which I am, by definition, incapable of attending properly to anything else within my realm of desires for what it truly is in itself. In other words, passionate second-order desires do not provide proper *evaluative distance* upon these other desires that would allow one to see those desires and their objects as they really are. Instead, they can only, at best, determine what those other things are good for relative to the concern of the ruling desire. But this is not just relativistic; it is obfuscating. That is, by using an intense desire-cum-passion as one's evaluative lens, the nature, intensity, and import of one's actual desires are obscured from one's view: one cannot see the other desire and any values connected with it on its own terms for what it really is. Empirical, desire-based rules of counsel are thus not only quantitative but also axiological failures.[13]

These failures of attentiveness which assure the evaluative failure of the perspective of the person of passion are of various sorts. In the first instance, I may not even properly *see* other desires I have: these are the quiet, whimpering desires of which we spoke in the previous section. If I am not able to *see* what desires I have, then, clearly, I am not able to *govern* them properly. It is indeed even possible that I will not look at desires which, *objectively* construed, might be very important in terms of the value structure built by this very passion. That is, the subjective focus of my attention may not jive well with what in fact would, objectively speaking, further the realization of my central passion.

One might object that at least talented persons in the sway of a passion could become particularly good at identifying those things relevant to the pursuit of her passion: someone who guides her life by her passion, e.g. for money, would have a heightened sensitivity to how anything in the world might contribute to or detract from the realization of her central passions.

I grant, however, that certain passionately governed persons would acquire this heightened sensitivity that would allow them to identify an awful lot of other desires relevant to the pursuit of their passions. But even when she is successful in this way, this does not mean that the passionate governor is at all good in seeing these other desires and their objects *for what they really are*. If my passion is money, and I look, for example, at a work of art or a bottle of wine, I cannot judge the value of that art or wine on its own merits, but only in terms of how much money I could get for it or would have to pay for it. This same sort of biased judgment can be brought not just to objects external to me but to my very desires themselves: I look at desires that I have for art, wine, or for being nice to people or for relaxing or for cello-playing, and govern or corral them all in light of the demands of my ruling desire. I thus *shape*—one might say "warp" or even "pervert"— my desires from the perspective of the governing desire. What started as a genuine interest in the qualities of different kinds of wine morphs into an interest in those wines that will increase in price over the years. But someone who only cares about wine for how much money they can make from it doesn't really care about *wine* at all! There is thus, at the bottom of such governance and ordering of desires and their objects, a misconstrual, a failure in one's ability to judge the value of that desire or object in terms of what it is in itself. Even when I see it, I cannot see it for

---

[13] What we are doing here is taking Iris Murdoch's (1970) point about failure of attentiveness to persons and things outside of oneself and bringing it into the internal dynamics of one's moral psychology. That is, just as I can fail to attend properly to what is of value *outside* of me, I can fail to attend properly to what is of value *inside* of me: my own desires!

what it is in itself, but only for what it can be for my ruling passion. As such, I cannot value it or its realization for what it is in itself, but only for how valuable it is relative to my ruling passion. The result is an arena of one's desire in which certain desires are coaxed so much in one direction (toward the desire in relation to which they are made relative) that they are not able to be what they really are. Alternatively, some stubborn desires might refuse such shaping, and are thus either constrained or ignored, becoming what we might now call the axiological remainder of one's governance.

Now, to say that one necessarily gets one's judgments about other desires "wrong" in this way does imply that there is some "right" way to see them. That is, I recognize the commitment to some sort of *axiological realism* underlying my argument here. But the commitment to realism one needs for the sake of this argument is a rather meagre one: all one needs to admit is that some second-order desire-cum-passion might not be the most important thing in the world to ground the idea that evaluating everything else in light of that one thing results in improper and mistaken valuing of other things. Indeed, the singular focus or narrowness of the value structure in a passion-governed life that we have already identified only encourages us to beg for a bit more realism in the world of value than what this one-trick pony of a passion can provide.

The very narrowness of the value perspective of a person of passion, just on its own (even before admitting the misconstrual of other desires and their objects), raises immediate worries: how can *one* thing in this finite world, contingently chosen by me, be so valuable that it *deserves* to be the point of view from which I value *absolutely everything else* in my person? In order to govern one's entire field of desires, one needs a point of view with a certain axiological oomph and generosity as it were, something capable of knowing its own value but also of appreciating the true value of other desires and their objects. But this is exactly what could not be forthcoming from a contingently chosen desire plucked out from among the whole series of my desires. It makes no sense to point to one random and contingently chosen part of a series and say: "here is the point of this series that will organize and order all the rest!" The best one could do by such an approach is, as we've noted, to provide a sense of how everything else is related to that point. This might be enough to order, e.g., a merely temporal series (as Kant himself does in his argument for the Second Analogy, saying that the way to assure a necessary order within a temporal series is to seek the rule whereby members of that series relate to, or "date," each other in time[14]). But such loose ordering of the elements of a series is inadequate to order an empirical series of desires. The well-governed person wants not only to know that this comes before (or after) that but also to have some value perspective from which to make sense of the qualitative

---

[14] See, e.g., A198/B243.

nature of each of the members of that series. But a passion accomplishes such ordering only by warping or misconstruing the other members of the series. No adequate, coherent ordering of the series as a whole is thus possible.

The axiological limits of a desire-governed life thus begin to emerge. Kant says that one can never realize that perfect whole which would be complete happiness. But one can put the same point in Frankfurtian terms: by definition, a passionately governed life can never be *whole*-hearted, not just quantitatively but axiologically. When governing myself via passion, I am guaranteed to ignore the value of some desires and misconstrue others, resulting inevitably in axiological remainders in my governance. But with axiological remainders, I can never acquire that wholeness or integrity that would be the mark of the *whole*-hearted person. To the contrary, there is much about my heart that is slipping through my net of governance. My heart is not whole; it is in pieces. There will always be parts of one's heart—things that one really values—that the passion-governed person cannot understand properly because one either is mistaken about their true nature, ignores them, or actively deceives oneself about what they are. And when one does not understand a desire properly, one cannot satisfy it properly. There are important things in one's person and, correlatively, in the world, objectively speaking, concern for which is never integrated into one's net of governance. Passionate governance is thus, inevitably, an axiologically incomplete governance.

This failure of completeness is a point we've already seen simply in virtue of the quantitative limits on empirical desire-governance. But we now have further understanding of how quantitative incompleteness comes hand-in-hand with axiological incompleteness: when one takes one point from within this empirical series which is our world of desire as the privileged point from which to view all other points within that world, we find that this point does not provide the proper perspective from which to govern so multifarious a world and, to the contrary, in virtue of its singular insistence on being itself (viz., on being a desire *for this*) establishes a definitionally narrow model of governance, both quantitatively and axiologically. Desire is, in other words, incapable of a self-governance that would realize itself in whole-hearted integrity of person. This is not only an incompleteness in the realization of desires but an incompleteness in the proper valuing of the worthiness of one's desires. The person ordering her desires by a passion is, beyond the natural quantitative incompleteness of that ordering process, also incapable of properly valuing her individual desires and her desires overall. Passionate second-order desires fail as governors because they fail to provide that point of view which would provide proper evaluative distance and perspective on the things being governed.[15]

---

[15] My position here is thus in sympathetic agreement with Watson's (1983) claim that who notes that "the life devoted to inclination" promises only "a futile search for significance among the various ends of inclinations" (Watson 1983, 90).

This account of the failure of evaluative distance in one's governance of desires is, thus, like what we saw in the earlier naturalistic story of incompleteness, a sort of incompleteness, but now on the level of value. Incompleteness on the axiological level is, however, best called a lack of integrity or whole-heartedness, because incompleteness on the axiological level is just what one means by a failure of whole-heartedness. To be whole-hearted is a claim about values: one's values are in order precisely because one's entire heart is committed to the goal identified in one's second-order desire; when that goal faces challenges from other desires and their objects, I need to be able to stand firmly with my central goal. But when the values connected to my desires are not being identified or realized through my governance because they are not being understood for what they really are, then it is impossible for my whole "heart" to be in my governance.[16]

The Self-Absorption of Desire

We can, however, take the evaluative failure of passionate self-governance even further. Once we understand the axiological incompleteness of passionate self-governance—that is, once we understand it as a failure of proper evaluative distance on one's desires which assures the failure of integrity in one's person—it also makes most sense to understand this failure as a vicious, because self-absorbed, failure. Indeed, we needn't go very far in order to make this further claim.

We have already noted that a desire is, by definition, focused on one thing: its object and the satisfaction of that desire through attainment of that object. One might put the point more strongly: by definition, all a desire can care about is itself. There is thus a certain self-focus built into the very structure of a desire: what it is to have a desire is to be concerned with satisfying the need at the basis of that desire. But it is just exactly this self-focus of *desire* that gets built into one's *person* when a desire is made the governing principle of one's person. If the only tools for self-governance I have are the tools of desire (and the rules of counsel grounded in desires), then the self-absorption of the structure of desire replicates itself in a self-absorption of the structure of my person. When I govern myself by a desire, I build a world in which the ultimate goal of my life is to satisfy all my

---

[16] Despite all these problems for self-governance, one's model of self-governance may still succeed—at least in fits and spurts—in keeping most of one's desires somehow ordered within the net of one's second-order desire. One can even, from the perspective of other persons, appear quite calm and ordered. The subterranean unsatisfied desires of all the types mentioned might very often simply not come to the surface to be recognized either because I am actively controlling them or because the ignored ones have not (yet) risen to the level of revolt. And because such disorder sits at the ground of one's order, one's *partial* governance is also never a calm, peaceful, or *settled* governance. Despite the appearance of peacefulness, it is *not* stable and peaceful but instead precariously grounded. And one's apparent order will always—to a perceptive observer—eventually be revealed for the fraught and disordered mess that it is.

desires in light of and in guidance from my passionate governing desire. We thus reveal another—and perhaps almost tautological!—axiological limit in a world governed only by desire: in a desire-governed world, the only way to determine value is to determine whether something satisfies my desires. The result is a rather self-centered mode of self-governance. Desires are full of themselves, and a life governed by desire is and can only be about the satisfaction of the person experiencing and ordering these desires. Our just completed account of the failure and obfuscation of desires by one's ruling desire is, in fact, simply a description of what one might call the self-centeredness or self-absorption of rule by desire. If my rule is guided only by my strong desires, I am also guaranteed that my governance will only be about *me*, about what *I* want, and about how to satisfy myself (in the most limited and egregious sense of satisfaction or self-fulfillment). Rule by desire thus assures a government entirely absorbed with itself.

One might object that it is entirely possible to have a ruling desire whose content is not about oneself at all. For example, one's strongest desire might be to help other people. This is fair enough, but even such desires with other-oriented content would still have the self-focused structure of desire just described: that is, *qua* desire, the oomph they would provide for action would be the oomph to satisfy that state of need. By definition, a desire seeks *its* fulfillment. And a person guided even by this second-order desire is still, axiologically, guided by the value of desire-fulfillment as such, because seeking to fulfill desire is the only method one has for the guidance of choice and governance. This is true even if my guiding desire is to help other people. If I understand the increase in others' happiness as something I desire, then the most important thing to me is not that others become more happy as such but, more precisely, that my desire to see them more happy is satisfied (a desire that might be satisfied perhaps only if I end up being the source or cause of their increase in happiness).

Indeed, this self-absorption is simply a continuation of the narrow, singular passion-focused point of view already described. Not only am I focused only on one desire at the expense of all others. I am, at heart, focused on desire-fulfillment as such, full stop: my determination of value is based only in a concern for the satisfaction of my desires. The central concern in this governance structure to fulfill a desire means that the person so governed is centrally focused on herself and her desire-fulfillment. She *can't* value anything except some sort of fulfillment of her desires. The singular and narrow point of view of passionate self-governance is thus also a self-absorbed point of view.[17]

---

[17] We shall, furthermore, with little urging, envision in the following section how this inherent self-focus on a desire-governed life turns one's inadvertent failure of attentiveness into an *active* obfuscation in the evaluation of other desires and their objects. I would, that is, be very easily tempted, even in those rare moments when they revealed themselves to me clearly, to refuse to admit to see my other desires and their objects for what they really are. Instead, I begin *actively* to warp and disfigure what I

It thus shouldn't surprise us not only that Kant thinks passions are inept governors, but also that, by definition, he takes them to be both *evil* and *vicious*.[18] He will, furthermore, also see a passion-governed life as a *mutinous* one, since he (unlike Frankfurt) accepts the idea that there is another non-desire-based part of us more capable of and authorized to govern ourselves which is overthrown by the establishment of a passion-based government. But even apart from any other such deep commitments, one already can see that a passion-governed life is self-centered enough on its own so as to deserve the moniker of "viciousness," even without reference to the plausibility of other sources of governance. Apart from the fact that it undermines proper ruling authority, a passion-governed life is vicious in that a passion-governed life is guaranteed to involve the self-absorption we have just described. Kant will eventually tell a larger story about the nature of evil generally that, at its heart, involves an excessive valuing of the self over everything else in the world. Ultimately, to call that state "evil," we will need, in Kantian terms, also to talk about how one rationally *chooses* not just to make this passion central to one's person but also explicitly chooses to prefer oneself (in the sense of preferring the satisfaction of one's desires) to all else. But from the story of the hapless adventures in the pursuit of a passion-governed life we've just completed, we can see that the natural realm of desire very happily sets us up, and indeed prompts us to be tempted toward, just such a rational claiming of explicitly evil self-centeredness. The self-absorption distinctive of Kant's account of rationally chosen radical evil finds its natural ground in the self-absorption natural to the world of desire.[19]

We can thus, even apart from any explicit commitment to an autonomously legislating self, defend Kant's claim that any true governor is entitled to "scorn" the use of the paltry intermediaries of the inclinations as a means of self-governance (6:396/158). Perhaps Kant himself simply assumes that one must reject the idea of governing one's desires by other desires. But when we study Kant's own reflections on desire-based governance, we discover a series of claims which, taken as a whole, robustly defend the idea that naturalistic models of self-governance will, in all cases, be failed models of self-governance. Empirically grounded desires or inclinations are simply incapable, both quantitatively and axiologically, of providing an adequate order to one's soul. Passionate second-order desires, on their own, fail as governors because they fail to provide that point of view which would provide proper evaluative distance on the things being governed (viz., my desires and

---

see so as to remain committed to my governing desire. Such tendency toward self-deception only increases the vicious nature of passionate self-governance.

[18] See especially 6:408.

[19] In this account, I am thus not making radical evil an *assumption* of the tale of the natural imbalance and incompleteness of desire. That is, the imbalance and failure of evaluative distance does not occur *because* I am radically evil. Rather, radical evil is one possible *result* of that imbalance. The imbalance is a natural imbalance of desire, but one has to rationally claim and choose this self-absorbed imbalance to become radically evil.

their objects) and, furthermore, base their governance only on an egregiously self-centered concern to satisfy one's desires. Passionate, second-order self-governance is thus a recipe for vicious self-absorption at the basis of self-governance. Kant brings this language of viciousness and radical evil to our understanding of this self-absorption; but one needn't take that route to appreciate the problems inherent in desire-based governance. Whatever you call it, such governance is incomplete both quantitatively and axiologically. It is neither whole-hearted nor grounded in a coherent set of values. Rather, it promises false, incomplete, obfuscatory, and self-absorbed government. As such, it is incumbent upon us to seek the proper guiding telos for self-governance and well-being elsewhere.

II. Seeking a More Satisfactory Objective Telos for Self-Governance of Desire

Introduction

We can conclude from all these reflections on the quantitative and axiological limits of the governance of desire by desire that the attainment of the perfect and complete satisfaction of empirical desires is impossible. Attainment of such completeness would require an utter removal of oneself from the natural and empirical world. Indeed, the dream of complete satisfaction of one's empirical desires as the guiding telos of one's life is in fact merely a dream to become something other than a sensibly affected rational being. The pursuit of completeness in self-governance by merely empirical means promises failure. Ultimately, we seek not to escape the limits of the natural world within which sensibly affected rational beings operate, nor to settle for passionate failures of self-governance, but instead to govern our desires by placing our natural selves within a higher, non-natural order. And this means we must reject the notion that happiness, empirically conceived as the sum of the fulfillment of all our desires, could be the proper guiding telos for sensibly affect rational beings.

We must instead seek a goal of the self-governance of desire more appropriate to sensibly affected rational beings, a goal which transcends happiness as desire-satisfaction and thereby places that merely empirical pursuit (and its limits) in a larger perspective. With such a goal in place, we can, furthermore, speak of a governance of desires that does not collapse into simple self-absorption or a desire-fulfillment fetish. Rather, to *govern* one's desires is to acquire *virtue*.[20]

---

[20] In so doing, we once again place ourselves in agreement with Watson (1983), who, through appeal to a notion of "contentment" (*Zufriedenheit*) distinct from "happiness" (*Glu(e)ckseeligkeit*) appreciates that desire-fulfillment is not the be-all and end-all of explaining what self-satisfaction is for the sensibly affected rational being: "[I]nclination in Kant's sense is not the sole source of contentment or discontentment. Moral concern is another. Therefore, as Kant knew, one might be discontent,

Where, then, to look for a proper telos for these beings? These sensibly affected rational beings are complex beings. They are not just natural, empirical beings, and they are not just rational beings; they are a combination of the two. And so it shouldn't surprise us that the proper goal of their governance demands appeal to a goal beyond mere fulfillment of natural, empirical desires. But this goal must also not simply be a rational goal, a goal appropriate, that is, to a being like God who is fully and only rational. Instead, we need a goal that is an expression of our deepest rational selves, but which does not abandon or ignore the empirical, desiring self. We need, in other words, a goal that lifts our empirical selves to meet the demands and possibilities of our rational selves. Ironically, what this means is that the proper governance of desire involves appeal to a goal beyond desire-fulfillment. If we were only empirical beings, and if only happiness empirically conceived were an achievable thing, complete desire-fulfillment could be a proper ultimate telos of our being. But sensibly affected rational beings need a deeper goal than this. The ultimate goal of one's desiring self must, ironically, be pointed beyond that desiring self. The desiring self must seek its ultimate goal in one's rational self and, more specifically, in the principles of morality which are to be found in one's own rational self. But that rational goal must situate itself firmly within one's sensible, desire self. The result of accepting these principles as establishing the contours of the self-governance of desires is to introduce the *virtuous* self-governance of desires.

This virtuous governance of desire by a goal beyond desire-fulfillment is what I would describe as the *elevation* of desire: the raising of one's empirical desiring self to a goal beyond itself. We can now explore how such elevation of the governance of desire is best understood through appeal to Kant's distinctive moral feeling of respect. In short, to affirm this non-naturalistic governance of desire, Kant introduces, within the realm of desire, a special feeling, a feeling which acts as a quasi-desire. This quasi-desire exists within one's empirical desiring self, but has a distinctive rational causal provenance which tracks, within the empirical world of desire, the strictly rational and necessary demand to respect persons. This feeling thereby establishes this rational and necessary demand of respect for persons as the proper goal of the self-governance of empirical desires. Indeed, by expressing this rational demand of respecting persons as a quasi-desire or feeling, our rational selves find a way to express this rational demand *within* the empirical world of desire, as a quasi-desire which meets desires, as it were, on their own terms.

---

even though one satisfied all one's inclinations, because one lacked self-respect. But, second, even a purely inclusive notion of happiness would not be equivalent to the contentment-conception. Even the realization of all of one's ends could leave one discontent. (My desires are "satisfied" but I am not.) Finally, it seems conceptually, if not humanly, possible that a person who fails to realize her system of inclinations might be content overall just the same [17]" (Watson 1983, 82). Although I will, in II.ii, take Kant's notions of *Zufriedenheit*—and especially of *Selbstzufriedenheit*—in different directions than Watson does, I nonetheless remain in deep sympathy with this large-picture appreciation he has that, for sensibly affected rational beings, desire-satisfaction is not the highest goal for self-satisfaction overall.

One's rational self thereby establishes itself as the non-natural goal for all empirical desires, a goal which we can now properly call the *telos* of the self-governance of desire. Self-governance of desire is now pointed toward the realization of that order, integrity, and proper functioning of person possible in accordance with what is necessary, in accordance, that is, with what we shall in the rest of Part I identify as the material and objectively valid telos of respect for persons which the moral feeling of respect tracks.

With this provenance, the moral feeling of respect becomes an importantly distinctive feeling or quasi-desire: it is the only feeling within our world of desire which points us beyond and above that world of desire to something more deeply true about ourselves.[21] I call it a "quasi-desire" because, although it is a feeling that operates on the same level with empirical desires, it is not a desire in the sense of marking or identifying to one's consciousness a lack of something that needs to be fulfilled. To the contrary, it points one toward a capacity for reason-giving one has that resides in a part of the self distinct from but related to one's empirical self. By providing a representative of that rational self within the world of empirical desires, it also thereby provides the would-be self-governing person with enhanced tools for the pursuit of self-governance of desire, tools with more potential for that governance than those provided by merely contingently elevated second-order desires.[22] It points us, that is, toward that objectively true fact about oneself and all persons—the absolute value of persons—which establishes a point of view that is both axiologically capable of and authorized to play a governing role in one's world of desires.

There are, of course, disagreements amongst Kant interpreters about how best to understand both the nature and the role of this moral feeling of respect. Some interpreters accept the rational demand to respect persons but don't think there is or needs to be a desire or feeling which tracks this moral demand. These are what Richard McCarty has called the Intellectualist (as opposed to the Affectivist) interpreters of moral feeling.[23] Andrews Reath[24] is the primary representative of the Intellectualist school. McCarty, Patrick Frierson,[25] Owen Ware,[26] and myself[27] (amongst others) represent the Affectivist school, viz. those who assert that one's awareness of and/or motivation to act upon the moral law involves some sort of appeal to the moral feeling of respect *qua* affect. I have, more precisely, argued previously that the moral feeling of respect is a feeling which plays a practical epistemic role in helping one become aware of the categorical nature of moral

---

[21] I am choosing here to use the language of feeling and desire loosely, though I recognize the technical need to make a distinction between the two in Kant's writings. I accept the looser usage in order to maintain a means of communication and connection between this forthcoming Kantian version of self-governance and more naturalistic accounts of the same, as for example in the work of Frankfurt (1971, 2002, 2006).

[22] As, e.g., Frankfurt (1971, 2002, 2006) would seek to do.   [23] See McCarty (2009).
[24] See Reath (1989).   [25] See Frierson (2014).   [26] See Ware (2014).
[27] See Grenberg (2005, 2013a, and 2018).

demands and which has a distinctive causal provenance that allows it to play this role successfully: it is caused by our free, rational, autonomous, and moral selves. I point you to my discussion of such things in my most recent writing for the metaphysical and technical details of this story.[28]

But what I suggest now is that this feeling goes beyond playing a practical epistemic role and becomes a crucial practical tool in the establishment of that self-governance of desire required for the pursuit of virtue. Kant suggests as much when, in the introduction to the Doctrine of Virtue, he describes what is necessary to acquire virtue. Noting that "the capacity to overcome all sensible impulses [i.e., self-governance]...is something [the human being] must acquire" (6:397/169–70), he goes on to say that such acquisition of virtue demands that the would-be virtuous person "contemplate...the dignity of the pure rational law in us" (6:397/170).

The means of such contemplation is, however, simply a process of the experience and cultivation of the moral feeling of respect:

> Obligation with regard to moral feeling can be only to cultivate it and to strengthen it through wonder at its inscrutable source. This comes about by its being shown how it is set apart from any pathological stimulus and is induced most intensely in its purity by a merely rational representation. (6:399–400/171)

In short, because the moral feeling of respect, although itself feeling, is, unlike other feelings, "induced...by a merely rational representation," this feeling gains particular stature in the moral consciousness of the would-be virtuous person. By reminding herself, through experience of this feeling, that she has rational capacities to control and guide her desires toward moral ends, and by relying on that same feeling to contemplate—that is, pay careful attention—to the dignity of that rational heritage we have and especially to the dignity of rational persons themselves, the would-be virtuous person discovers a guiding end-point for her self-governance: in all governance of her desires, she must seek to respect persons.

What I seek to explore in this book, then, is the moral psychological story of the pursuit of virtue which emerges from the admission of this quasi-desire tracking and thereby establishing as one's objective telos for self-governance the non-negotiable demand to respect the absolute value of persons.

The Material, Objective Telos of Virtuous Self-Governance

Our first goal, however, must be to explore and defend this objective telos of virtue toward which the experience of moral feeling points a person. In this opening

---

[28] See Grenberg (2013a and 2018).

discussion of such things, I first provide an overview of this objective telos of virtue, contrasting it briefly with its correlative subjective telos. I will then turn, in Part II, to a complete philosophical defense of the idea of Kant's deontological system of morality as being simultaneously deeply teleological, to a defense, that is, of Kant's Deontological Teleology.

And so, I call this telos of respect for persons the *objective* or *material* telos of self-governance because this telos is the proper *end*—that is, the proper *object* or *matter*—of my choice, one which is objectively valid for all sensibly affected rational beings and which therefore guides the setting of all subsidiary ends of action. This telos is thus the aim of, and is realized in, the setting of those more precise *material ends* of action brought about *through* the governing of my desires: in all choice, I act such that I respect persons. My desire-governance is thus oriented toward those obligatory "ends that are also duties" which constitute the concern of the person of virtue. With this moral marker in the world of desire, Kant can thus, unlike more naturalistic accounts of self-governance like Frankfurt's, tell a story of the self-governance of desire that is also a story of *virtuous self-governance of, by, and for persons*.

In speaking of this end as a material end, I refer indirectly to what I would call "materialized" versions of both the First and Second Formulations of the Categorical Imperative which Kant introduces in the Doctrine of Virtue to guide the pursuit of virtue. The pursuit of virtue is about the pursuit of specific ends of action. But to be a principle which guides successfully toward the pursuit of these specific ends, the Categorical Imperative must move beyond the merely formal versions of it articulated in the *Groundwork*. The concern of the virtuous person must, that is, be not only to act on those maxims which can be universalized without contradiction but also to pursue those material ends demanded by reason. The material or ends of these formulations thus constitute what I am here calling the objective, material, and end-based telos of the person of virtue. We shall dwell on this point at greater length later in Part I.

With this non-desire-based quasi-desire now situated within the realm of desire, the ordering of desires becomes a more complex thing; now, no mere garden-variety desire could be contingently or naturalistically elevated into the role of desire-governance (Frankfurt's so-called "second-order desires"). There is already one amongst the throng of desires that, through its connection to the absolute, non-relative value of persons, has an authoritative governing status and cannot legitimately be ejected as ruler. A new, necessary, and organizing goal for the governance of our desires—a goal beyond the mere satisfaction of desire—is thus established. I thereby acquire a capacity for evaluative distance from these other—now merely relativistically valuable—desires, a distance that promises more success in governing them. I must, that is, assure that all my choices governing the constraint and cultivation of my desires are in agreement with this non-negotiable, absolute, and exception-less demand to respect persons. The absolute value of persons becomes the end-point for all my desires and the reason that explains why I govern them as I do: in everything that I do, I must respect persons.

One can even think of the moral feeling of respect which tracks this objective telos of respect for persons as the means by which one's *conscience* expresses itself.[29] Experience of this feeling is that point at which one encounters something recalcitrant in one's desires that refuses to bow to the would-be governance of desires by any of one's contingently chosen self-elevated desires. To *elevate* one's world of desire is thus, simply, to introduce this guiding *telos* to it.

One might worry that guiding absolutely *all* my desires and *all* my end-setting activity through reference to the moral demand to respect persons is just too heavy-handed and moralistic a way of thinking of the governance of desire. Do we really want to accept the idea that the goal of *all* one's desires is to respect persons? Don't I have goals beyond, before, or just separate from my need to respect persons? What about cello playing, or downhill skiing? I recognize these worries and yet, ultimately, remain committed to the idea that *all* our goals are indeed "moralized" to a certain extent through appeal to and guidance by this objective telos. We shall consider this objector more completely in Part II, and also, most thoroughly in our consideration of how happiness, empirically conceived, supervenes upon a life of virtue in II.iii.

The Subjective Telos of Virtuous Self-Governance

There is more that needs to be said about this objective telos of virtue; and, indeed, we shall do just that in the rest of Part I. But to fully appreciate how the objective telos of respecting persons fits into the complete story of the virtuous self-governance of desire and, ultimately, the story of Deontological Eudaemonism, we must first, at least briefly, consider how this objective telos of virtue also grounds a subjective telos of virtue. That is: in the realization of this objective and material telos of respect for persons, one also encounters the subjective experience of being a person guided by this telos, a state of person which constitutes the proper functioning of a sensibly affected rational being. This subjective state is the *subjective telos* of virtue, and itself constitutes a further goal at which the would-be virtuous person aims and in which the fully virtuous person finds herself.

And so: we will not consider the complete nature of this subjective telos of virtue until Part II of this book; but let us now briefly consider it so as to understand better in contrast what the objective telos of virtue ultimately does for the person seeking to govern her desires virtuously. We have said that this subjective state is

---

[29] See 6:400/160 where conscience is described as something "not directed to an object but merely to the subject (to affect moral feeling by its act)." We will discuss this conscience/moral feeling connection in more depth in I.iv and II.ii.

indeed itself a telos or goal, something at which the would-be virtuous person aims. But the would-be virtuous person does not "aim" at this subjective telos in the sense of taking it as the *reason* she chooses the life of virtue. Rather, this subjective state is a telos in another sense: the virtuous person takes the objective telos of respecting persons as a guide for making her *entire* person whole; that is, she aims at respect for persons as the guiding activity of her life, the reason that she does what she does. But, in so doing, she thus also simultaneously aims at a subjective state correlative to her objective end-setting activity, aiming to concretize her commitment to respecting persons *in* her subjective states. In other words, she aims at acquiring just those subjective states appropriate to the realization of that objective telos. She aims at becoming the kind of person capable of end-setting in accordance with the objective end of respect for persons, capable of controlling herself such that she always respects persons no matter what else she wants, feels, or desires.

So, although the realization of this subjective state is not what explains why the virtuous person does what she does, it is nonetheless a telos: something at which she aims. In fulfilling her objective telos of respecting persons, the would-be virtuous person also aims at developing subjective states appropriate to her end-setting. And, once in place, those states act as tools for the enhanced pursuit of virtue. We will not consider in what exactly this subjective state consists until Part II of the book. For now, though, we can summarize that this state will be the jewel of Kant's Deontological Eudaemonism: it consists in a strong, healthy state in which I gain the proper evaluative distance upon my felt attachments generally. This is a state consisting of a capacity for moral apathetic toleration of suffering and loss on the one hand, but also, simultaneously, a capacity to morally excite and enliven those felt attachments supportive of virtue, leading to the characteristic pleasurable experience of the virtually unimpeded exercise of the life of virtue in which I am able to love the life of virtue I have chosen, being cheerful in the exercise of the duties to which I am obligated, and even finding myself thereby most able to achieve and maintain that happiness empirically conceived that is possible for finite sensibly affected beings. The story of Deontological Eudaemonism—that is, the story of how one's well-being, flourishing, or happiness is best pursued through adherence to those necessary principles or imperatives which define our being—thus becomes a more complex story in that happiness empirically conceived is no longer the only notion of happiness with which to be concerned in the pursuit of well-being or flourishing. To the contrary, a higher, non-desire-fulfillment-based and guiding notion of happiness as pleasure in the virtually unimpeded activity of one's proper functioning (a state in which one is cheerful and loving in the exercise of one's proper function of virtue) provides the larger context within which one also continues (now more successfully!) to pursue happiness, empirically conceived (that is, happiness as desire-fulfillment).

Furthermore, we assert a quasi-*necessary* supervenience relation between successful realization of the objective and material telos of respecting persons and this subjective telos of realizing this moral psychological state appropriate to virtue: when I accomplish the former, the latter emerges as the subjective flip-side of my objective realization of virtue.

I want to be very careful as I introduce this language of supervenience, as I am using it in a very particular and idiosyncratic way. In the hopes of avoiding the assumption of any precise extant interpreter's use of the term, I've sought out as neutral a definition as I could find: from Wikipedia. According to Wikipedia, a relationship of supervenience is one in which "a system's upper-level properties are determined by its lower level properties."

Now, usually, this relation is asserted between physical properties and mental properties, where, e.g., consciousness, supervenes upon a collection of physical states. Here the "lower level" properties are physical states and the "upper level" properties are mental states. But I am appropriating this relationship for a different purpose with different kinds of properties in relation to each other, and so the language of "lower" and "upper" is not apropos for us. The "system" in question is the overall system of a sensibly affected rational being. And, on my account, the properties standing in as the "lower level" properties of a system—let's call them, instead, the "bedrock" or "objective" properties of the system—are the objective activities associated with the exercise of virtue (reason-giving and end-setting). These bedrock properties thus "determine" the other set of "higher level" properties of the system—but let's just call these the "subjective properties constituting proper-functioning" (virtually unimpeded activity as expressed in one's state of health / apathy / cheerfulness / enhanced capacity to pursue happiness / etc., as will be discussed in Part II). The objective, bedrock properties of the exercise of virtue (viz., the successful realization of respect for persons as the ordering principle of my end-setting generally) thus *determine* the highest subjective proper functioning (of pleasure/health/cheerfulness/happiness/etc.) possible in the "system" of the sensibly affected rational being overall. That is what I mean when I say that realization of the subjective telos of virtue "supervenes" upon realization of the objective telos of virtue.

One might be tempted to take more than this from my use of the language of supervenience. One might assume, for example, that, in claiming a supervenience relationship between the objective and subjective teloi of virtue, I am making an *empirical* claim about their relation. That is, one might assume that one could prove the claim that apathy, cheerfulness, etc., supervene on a life of virtue by going out into the world and surveying virtuous people to find out whether a high proportion of them are apathetic, cheerful, and happy. I do not, however, accept the idea that this could be an empirically verifiable claim. In order to be empirically verifiable, one would need to understand the relationship between the objective and subjective aspects of one's person as being connected by an empirical causal relationship; but this is not the case.

To appreciate that this is not an empirical causal relation, let's think more about how to conceive of the idea that the "bedrock" objective qualities "*determine*" the subjective proper functioning qualities: what is the nature of this "determination"? If it were *natural* causal determinism, then one might be able to argue that the supervenience relationship here would be subject to empirical verifiability. But because the tools of virtue have a non-natural source (and hence an ultimately *inscrutable* and *noumenal* causal force upon our sensible selves), it would be too simple to say that the relationship between these objective and subjective poles is just an empirical relation. It is instead a noumenal-phenomenal relation. I am not, however, going to explore that knotty metaphysical problem here in any detail. It is something I have already considered at length; and, for those interested, I point you to that discussion wherein I consider how the moral feeling of respect—a sensible feeling with a noumenal cause—expresses itself in phenomenological, not empirical, time.[30] When we speak of the subjective telos of virtue supervening upon the objective telos of virtue, it is thus this metaphysical background that is assumed as the context within which such moral psychological activity occurs.

It turns out, though, once we assume this metaphysical background, that the question of causal relations amongst these objective and subjective teloi of the exercise of virtue is a more complex thing than just the movement of the causal arrow from the noumenal to the phenomenological world of experience. In the pursuit of a virtue one does not yet have, that is indeed the direction of the causal arrow: from the objectively valid noumenal law towards the production of one's phenomenological subjective state. But once one has acquired this subjective state, we can speak in some quasi-causal way of how the subjective state at least facilitates or upholds the ongoing setting and pursuit of those ends which constitute the realization of one's objective telos. That is, having become cheerful and loving in my exercise of duty, I become that much more capable of just that virtuous exercise of my duties. One can add a third relation of objective and subjective states such that these two merge into one: once this subjective state is well-ensconced in my person, I can begin to say that the exercise of virtue just *is* this objective pursuit of ends via these subjective states, or that there is one virtue overall, with its objective and subjective poles.

---

[30] For more discussion of this, and also for more reflection on the grounding metaphysical story of how this supervenience relation is not an empirical relation, but rather an ultimately inscrutable causal (not merely correlational) relation obtaining between noumenal and phenomenal self, best construed as a schematism of Moral Law found within our (sensible) experience of moral feeling, see Grenberg (2018).

These varying articulations of causal relations amongst one's objective and subjective teloi might seem contradictory, but they are not. Interestingly, in fact, they mirror what Aristotle would say in Book II of the *Nicomachean Ethics* about the development of virtue. One can become a virtuous person only by engaging in the setting of virtuous ends and the completion of virtuous acts. But through repeated engagement in those virtuous ends and acts, one builds up a subjective state appropriate to the realization of those ends and acts. But once that state is built, it becomes the perspective from which one engages in those ends and acts, or that subjective point of view which facilitates further engagement in virtuous end-setting. The perfection of virtue is when one's subjective states so perfectly mirror what is required for one's objective end-setting that it makes sense to see one's subjective state as identical with one's objective telos, a state which, in II.ii, we shall see Kant describe as an "aptitude" for virtue, a state essentially identical with what Aristotle calls "happiness," now not as desire-fulfillment but as pleasure in unimpeded activity.

One can raise the question at this point about whether in asserting a *supervenience* relationship, we are asserting a *necessary* relationship between these objective and subjective teloi, that is, whether once one has the objective requirements of virtue in place that the attendant subjective elements, including happiness, would necessarily follow without exception. Were such a necessary relationship to obtain, it would be akin to saying that, for Kant, there is a necessary relationship between virtue and flourishing, well-being and happiness.

The full answer to this question is something we will not complete until Part II of this work, but it behooves us at this point to lay out the broad contours of our approach, situating it in relation to current interpretive work on the question. Recently, David Forman, in taking on a similar version of the question we raise here, suggests the following:

> [W]hereas Kant's own early attempt to answer this challenge [of how to assure the virtuous person the hope of happiness] appeals to a *necessary* connection between virtue and happiness (in the concept of the highest good), an account of a merely *contingent* harmony is sufficient for an effective response.
> (Forman 2016, 78)

There is something right about Forman's move of at least setting aside for now the question of whether Kant's appeal to the Highest Good (i.e., to the promise of happiness consistent with virtue in an afterlife as underwritten by the existence of God and the assurance of immortality) can answer this question of the relationship of virtue and happiness. Really to connect Kant's virtue ethics with eudaemonism as such, we need to investigate the relationship of virtue and happiness in *this* world and not only in another one. And when he turns to that this-worldly question of the relationship of virtue and happiness, Forman suggests that there is something un-Kantian about asserting a necessary connection between the two. To do so would make him more of a Stoic, someone who thought that virtue and happiness were virtually identical. But, according to Forman, we must grant more of a distinction than this between virtue and happiness for Kant. Hence, although he finds it very important to reject the too common assumption that "Kantian moral demands are incompatible with our human nature as happiness-seekers" (Forman 2016, 75), he will be satisfied if the compatible relationship between virtue and happiness is a merely contingent instead of a necessary one; that is, even granting that he (I think successfully) defends the notion that Kantians needn't "abandon our hope for happiness in this life" (Forman 2016, 75), he accepts the possibility that things could be otherwise, that one might be fully virtuous but unhappy. He thus describes Kant as a "moderate Cynic" instead of as a Stoic, since Kant insists upon more of a distinction between virtue and happiness than a Stoic would tolerate whereas a "Cynic," at least as described by Rousseau and adopted by Kant, is someone who learns how to moderate the demands of nature (i.e., in my language, the demands of happiness, empirically conceived) so as to assure their compatibility with virtue. So, according to Forman: "[Kant's view] would not be the Stoic view that morality itself makes us happy, but rather the Cynic view that the virtuous disposition is the one in which our non-moral needs can be easily satisfied since they are the simple needs of nature" (Forman 2016, 103). And for this moderate Cynic, "the best chance we have for approximating happiness in this life lies in our willingness to do without (but not in actively denying ourselves) all the luxuries that have come to seem like necessities in our corrupt era" (Forman 2016, 78).

Although I am very sympathetic with his characterization here of the moderation that visits upon a life of virtue, my account of the relationship of the objective and subjective teloi of virtue—an account that will not come to completion until Part II of this book—challenges Forman to consider something more than a merely contingent relationship between virtue and happiness. As we shall see in Part II, the question of how virtue and "happiness" are related becomes more complicated on my account when I distinguish two different forms of happiness as part of the subjective telos of virtue: happiness empirically conceived as desire-fulfillment, and happiness conceived as pleasure in the virtually unimpeded exercise of one's proper function. Once we admit these two distinct forms of happiness, a more complex story of the relationship of virtue and "happiness" emerges. Essentially, we assert, contra Forman, a necessary relationship (approaching identity) between one's aptitude for virtue and happiness conceived as pleasure in virtually unimpeded activity. This is because the experience of such unimpeded activity simply is the subjective experience of exercising one's aptitude for virtue.

But the relationship between virtue and happiness empirically conceived is closer to Forman's story of a merely contingent relationship. But when I assert a supervenience relationship between pursuit of the objective telos of virtue and that specific aspect of the subjective teloi of virtue that is happiness empirically conceived, although I admit contingency in this relationship, I also emphasize that, *ceteris paribus*, the latter *will* follow upon the former. I'm not sure whether this is a substantive difference from Forman or more a shift in rhetorical emphasis. Whichever it is, though, I think it is a distinction with a difference. There seems to me something too weak about settling for a "sufficient" (Forman 2016, 78) answer to this problem as opposed to a truly satisfying one.

So whereas Forman tolerates a merely contingent relation between virtue and happiness empirically conceived, I assert something subtly nestled between necessity and contingency: all other things being equal (i.e., as long as there is no tragic set of circumstances present, like Priam's fate of which Aristotle speaks), a greater happiness empirically conceived will "necessarily" supervene on the exercise of virtue. Taking the *ceteris paribus* clause into consideration, one might then call this a position of "conditional necessity."

Conclusion

We can thus now more clearly understand and distinguish the objective and subjective teloi of virtuous self-governance. The objective telos is the material, objective end at which all desire-governance aims, the reason explaining every end one sets, and that end which orders all end-setting. The subjective telos is that subjective state of person which emerges in the pursuit of one's objective telos and at which one aims for the sake of realizing this objective telos. It is the supervening subjective flip-side of the pursuit of the realization of the objective end of respecting persons. As such, it is not something at which one aims in and for itself, but only for the sake of one's objective telos. Indeed, the state could not be pursued or exist in and for itself precisely because it is a state that emerges only when a person has committed, in and for itself, to guiding and ordering her end-setting by the objective telos of respecting persons: it is only when one pursues that objective telos well and for itself that one ends up becoming this sort of person. To understand the overall telos of the sensibly affected rational being, we must thus welcome both these objective and subjective poles of it.

We have thereby asserted Kant as a teleological thinker, but now need to defend this distinctive claim. We shall thus spend the rest of Part I providing a complete defense of Deontological Teleology, starting in I.ii by considering and responding to an objector who would insist that deontology is concerned with principles of action, not with a telos, goal, or end as such. Our response to this objector—viz., that Kant's account of virtue is inherently end-based and that it thus makes perfect sense to introduce the eudaemonistic language of telos to deontology—completes our initial defense of Kant's account of Deontological Teleology, viz. the idea that deontology and teleology are not opposed to each other but rather that deontological principles of action are the basis upon which one affirms an objective telos of virtue.

I.ii
Deontological Teleology
An Objective and End-Based Approach to the Virtuous Self-Governance of Desire

Introduction

We need now to spend some extended time defending the assertion of this objective telos for virtue that I have only briefly reviewed in the previous chapter.

To defend Kant as a Deontological Teleologist, we must begin by responding to a central objection that will inevitably arise to my articulation of this telos-guided conception of Kantian virtue: is deontological morality really about realizing a telos? Isn't deontology centrally concerned to determine principles meant to constrain our action, and not at all concerned with goals or ends that would guide it toward well-being?

Herman (2010) states the voice of this objector well, an objector who assumes a generally accepted and strong contrast between teleological virtue theory and Kantian deontological moral theory:

> Teleological ends are substantive, objective, and regulative. Whether they are one or many, they should be able to play an organizing role in a complete human life (if they are many, they should also cohere). Kantian theory is not end-anchored in this way... Especially in the contrast with virtue theories, it is regarded as a principle- or rule-based theory whose normative elements are specific duties—duties whose role is to constrain, not to organize or transform, activities that have their source elsewhere. (Herman 2010, 95–96)[1]

According to objectors like this, we should thus think of Kant's deontological moral theory as essentially different from any teleologically based approach to virtue like, e.g., Aristotle's. Whereas the latter is concerned with a substantive objective telos which organizes one's entire life, the former is concerned not with a positive end or telos but only with principles which act to constrain one from prohibited actions.

---

[1] I find Herman's language of ends that are "substantive, objective and regulative" helpful and precise. I will thus regularly use that language in speaking of ends which have the proper weight attributable to truly "teleological" ends.

We have already briefly addressed assumptions about the apparent opposition of Kant's ethics and virtue ethics from a slightly different angle in our Introductory Thoughts. There, we did not raise the issue of *teleology* as such, but instead showed that deontology and *eudaemonism* (understood as the pursuit of well-being through the attainment of pleasurable proper functioning) are in fact not mutually contradictory approaches to morality: the science of necessary duties and the pursuit of well-being through proper functioning can be brought together. But now, having explicitly identified an objective telos toward which Deontological Eudaemonism points, this same tension re-emerges more explicitly as a tension between deontology and teleology: can an *a priori*, principle-based, deontological approach to morality really be compatible with an approach to virtue which accepts a guiding end or telos as the organizing goal of all one's end-setting?

This movement from eudaemonism generally to the more precise question of teleology is natural, since eudaemonist systems of ethics are generally thought to be teleologically oriented. That is, a life of well-being assured by proper functioning finds that "proper" function via appeal to an end or telos which affirms that at which this kind of being should properly aim. If we are to affirm Kant as a Deontological Eudaemonist, we must therefore affirm some guiding telos compatible with deontology and compatible particularly with the *a priori* grounding of principles of that deontological morality. That is, we must affirm Deontological Teleology.

The response to our objector who would assert that deontology and teleology are mutually opposed approaches to morality will occur in numerous discussions which will occupy us for the rest of Part I. First, in this chapter, we'll defend the very notion of teleology being compatible with Kant's *a priori* and deontological morality, a claim that needs to be defended especially in light of Kant's early *Groundwork* and *Critique of Practical Reason* claims which seem to eschew a meaningful role for material ends of any sort in making sense of morality.

In the following chapters (I.iii and I.iv), we shall deduce these obligatory ends of virtue, first defending Kant's privileging of a materialized (that is, end-based) version of the Second Formulation of the Categorical Imperative, grounded in that ultimate objective end of persons as ends-in-themselves, as the proper deontological, principle-based tool for orienting one's governance of desire now understood as free end-setting; and then, finally, in I.iv, considering how this objective telos of virtue acts as a guide for that virtuous setting of a whole range of obligatory ends which constitutes proper self-governance of one's desires. In so doing, we confirm, through attentive reflection upon the objective telos of respect for persons, those obligatory ends which constitute both duties to self and duties to others.

Once we appreciate the centrality of all these ideas for Kant's theory of virtue, it will be clear that Kant's deontological story of morality is indeed simultaneously a teleological story of virtue. Respect for personhood simply is the proper substantive, organizing, and objective end, goal, or telos toward which all our desire-governance (now understood as end-setting) is pointed. But even as we welcome this telos, we do not abandon concern for formal, deontological principles of action. To the contrary, as we shall see especially in I.iv, we appeal to these principles as so many tools for assuring the realization of this ultimate end. In appreciating all these ideas, we thus complete our account of what we have been calling the objective, material telos of virtue as respect for persons.

This current chapter is organized as follows. I begin with reflections on the current state of the interpretive literature on deontology and teleology in Kant with the purpose of situating my own forthcoming account amongst these extant thoughts on the matter. After noting, despite the clear presence of teleological concern in Kant's ethical texts, the vexed relationship interpreters have had to such teleological ideas in recent years, I defend persons as such—as opposed to moral principles, freedom as autonomy, or humanity abstractly conceived—as the preferable way of characterizing the value which forms the basis Kant's teleology. I also review recent interpretive literature on the specific topic of obligatory ends, noting that, although some have taken up this notion in helpful ways sympathetic to our forthcoming project, none have adequately identified or addressed the question of how Kant can defend so robust a notion of ends (i.e., of *matters* of choice) while maintaining his commitment to an *a priori* morality. I then turn to my own positive defense of *a priori* grounded ends, first by examining Kant's early claims in the *Groundwork* and in the *Critique of Practical Reason* that would reasonably lead his readers to assume that his moral system must reject such a notion and must therefore be inherently *non*-teleological.[2] I then set those claims against the intent of Kant's project in the Doctrine of Virtue, showing that precisely what he eschewed in his earlier works (viz., the very possibility of the free, *a priori* setting of ends as the matter of choice) is exactly what he now needs to embrace in order to make sense of virtue. We turn then, in Section II, to the defense of Kant's teleologically oriented conception of virtue, beginning with an articulation of the expanded conception of ends he introduces, then turning to a defense of the idea that each of these types of ends—pragmatic and obligatory— can be set freely, and that the latter sort can also be set *a priori*, autonomously, and virtuously. We thereby extend and clarify how the notion of incorporation extends not only to maxims but also to ends and action.

What we shall discover by the end of this chapter is that Kant's deontologically informed virtue theory is, at its heart, also an end- or telos-based one. Having set aside appeal to ends in his *Groundwork* pursuit of the grounding of the supreme formal and *a priori* principle of morality, and having understood all ends then as

---

[2] These are just the claims to which defenders of a strict deontological reading of Kant's ethics will appeal and, indeed, have appealed. See, for example, Reath 1994; Schneewind 1996; and Johnson (2007, 2008).

inevitably material, unfree, subjective, and relative, the Kant of the Doctrine of Virtue expands his definition of ends so as to ground the possibility of the free setting of both pragmatic and objectively valid obligatory ends. It is especially in his confidence that one can deduce these latter objective obligatory ends from a single deontological principle of respect for persons (a task we will take on in the next chapter, I.iii) that Kant essentially establishes not only individual *ends* of virtue but also a singular guiding *telos* for virtue generally, that is, a substantive, organizing, and objective end shared by all sensibly affected rational beings that should be taken as one's guide in the governance of one's desires, now understood as the virtuous setting of obligatory ends. In short, a careful review of the Doctrine of Virtue reveals Kant's welcoming of a reciprocal relationship between *a priori* grounded deontological principles of action and an objective end of virtue which acts as a telos for all end-setting. We thus defend Kant's Deontological Teleology.

I. Interpretive Work on Kant, Ends, and the Formula of Humanity

Teleology in Kant Interpretation

As we prepare to dwell at length on the relationship between deontology and ends/teleology in Kant's moral theory—with a particular focus on interpretations of the Second Formulation, or the so-called Formula of Humanity (henceforward, FH), which centers on that crucial Kantian notion of rational nature as existing as an end-it-itself—it will behoove us to review current interpretive work on these notions so as to situate our forthcoming account of Deontological Teleology in relation to this body of literature.

Despite what I described above as a "generally accepted" division between deontological and teleological approaches to morality, there has indeed been some discussion of teleological dimensions of Kant's ethics. These concerns about ends and teleology are approached in the literature on Kant's moral theory in a variety of ways. I begin with some general reflections on both the presence and absence of such themes in Kant interpretation generally, then turn to the specific interpretive question of the relationship of teleology to deontology in interpretations of Kant's ethics, with the purpose of carving out reasons to follow our own person-based account of the central value which informs Kant's teleology.

One very precise question about the inclusion of teleology in the interpretation of Kant's ethics arises when one asks how best to interpret the First Formulation of the Categorical Imperative (or Formula of Universal Law; henceforward, FUL). Paton (1948) has famously defended the Teleological Contradiction interpretation of the Categorical Imperative, a procedure which assumes some purpose apropos of rational agents so as to generate a contradiction of one's maxim with this purpose.[3]

This is not, however, a very popular interpretation of FUL right now. More recent interpreters take their lead from Korsgaard (1996c) who criticizes Paton, and teleological readings of the Categorical Imperative generally, in this way:

> On... Paton's... view, teleological analysis requires a commitment to specific purposes, either purposes of nature (like the preservation of life in the suicide example) or purposes required for the systematic harmony of human purposes. The trouble with bringing in teleological considerations in order to assign these purposes to natural as well as conventional actions is that such purposes may have nothing to do with what the agent wants, or ought rationally to want, or even with what any human being wants. Unless we can show that the agent is committed to the purpose, it is possible to say that the system can do without the teleological arrangement because it can do without the purpose.
> (Korsgaard 1996c, 91–92)

The reason that the Teleological Contradiction Interpretation cannot work on Korsgaard's account is that she believes Kantians have no appeal to a view of human nature from which one could make meaningful assertions about purposes that persons actually share, *qua person*. Instead, we can appeal only to subjective purposes which individual persons actually and consciously identify. If we accept that assumption, then Korsgaard's rejection of Paton makes sense. And with this criticism of the teleological interpretation of FUL complete, Korsgaard turns to her own preferred Practical Contradiction interpretation of the First Formulation, an interpretation focused on precisely what she claims the Teleological Contradiction Interpretation lacks, viz. appeal to purposes that individual agents actually have.

Korsgaard's rejection of Paton is informative for us, though, beyond just the question of how best to interpret FUL. What she reveals in her analysis of Paton is a willingness to reject without argument the possibility that Kant might in fact actually hold a thick notion of human nature, one which could be entirely adequate for establishing those purposes proper to humanity as such from which one could generate a contradiction in one's maxim in Paton-esque style.

---

[3] See especially Paton (1948, chapter XV), wherein Paton reveals himself as a strong proponent of the teleological interpretation of the First Formulation. Beck (1960, 159–163) also considers and signs on to a certain version of Paton's account. And Ward (1972) forcefully defends the need for a teleological reading of FUL, arguing that "one could not discard the notion of a generally purposive constitution of human nature;... for it is essential to Kant's use of the principle of universalizability that it assumes the existence of essential ends of human nature—the ends, in general, of perfection and happiness—by reference to which the criteria of consistency and contradiction can be formulated" (Ward 1972, 112).

This is a curious confidence to have as a Kant interpreter. If one looks at Kant's corpus more broadly, it is obvious that he is more than willing to entertain the notion of purposes for humanity *qua* humanity: an end for reason itself late in the *Critique of Pure Reason*; the Kingdom of Ends in *Groundwork II*; teleological ends of nature in the *Critique of Judgment*; the end of history in *Perpetual Peace*; and the religious end of the ethical commonwealth of the Church in the *Religion*. Such regular appeal to ends has, furthermore, led a variety of more teleologically inclined interpreters of Kant to explore teleologically oriented readings of Kant from a variety of perspectives.[4]

Why then are interpreters of Kant's ethics loathe to take up such purposes?[5] Indeed, why are they happy, like Korsgaard, to set aside appeal to them without argument? There is, I think, an interpretive pressure operating in recent discussions of Kant's ethics that is not as present in other areas of Kant studies, and it is that pressure that explains this lacuna. The hope amongst some interpreters of Kant's moral theory is that one could claim the spoils of pure practical reason without committing oneself to metaphysically robust and, for these interpreters, metaphysically onerous notions that would come with it. The hope, especially amongst Rawlsian-inspired interpreters of Kant's ethics, is to defend a self-standing notion of practical reason without these religious, aesthetic, historical, or political buttresses for it. Appeals to robust teleological notions are thus clearly present in Kant's ethical works, but many interpreters consider these commitments things to set aside or work around in pursuit of a self-standing—and therefore more strictly deontological and non-teleological—conception of practical reason.

Ward (1972) noted just exactly this tendency in Kant scholarship not in relation to Rawlsian-inspired interpreters but in connection with what one might call an earlier generation of such metaphysically lite readings of Kant's ethics:

> [I]s it not the case that Kant's ethical system is well able to survive the abandonment of its metaphysical context, however true it may be to say that it originated in such a context? One can, for instance, construct a purely descriptive account of the logic of moral discourse, bringing out perhaps the features of universalizability,

---

[4] See, for example: Velkley (1989) for an extended defense of the end of reason itself; Rossi (2019) for a defense of peace-making as the moral vocation of reason; Wood (1998a, 2009, 2020) for a variety of reflections on and commitments to religious, historical, and political teleology; and Makkreel (1995) for teleological commitments in aesthetics.

[5] Wood (2020) also notes this curious lacuna in recent interpretations of Kant's ethics. He even explicitly notes in his preface that a variety of themes specifically in Kant's ethics and with a teleological flavor to them are "underrepresented" in the literature: "We will also have to appreciate some themes in Kant's ethics that have been underemphasized or even badly distorted, such as... the vital importance of community in Kant's ethics and of the hope for moral progress of the human species in history" (p. xiii). Ward (1972) too, is astounded by similar failures in the work of earlier 20th-century interpreters of Kant: "The extraordinary fact that a great many able Anglo-Saxon critics of Kant have failed to see [his assumption of the existence of essential ends in human nature] has no doubt led them to be more scathing about the emptiness and inadequacy of the principle of universalisability than they might otherwise have been" (Ward 1972, 112).

impartiality and autonomy which it contains and the substantive rule of respect for persons which it embodies, rather as R.M. Hare and R.S. Downie have done. (Ward 1972, 96)

Ward goes on to admit that "such views can be developed from and are expressed in Kant's writings on ethics" (Ward 1972, 96). But he adds: "it is equally certain that [such views] do not give the whole Kantian story, and even that they omit consideration of what was most central to Kant's ethical concern, the notion of human flourishing" (Ward 1972, 96). Ward himself goes on to provide an account of such flourishing that is guided ultimately by a religious telos.[6]

And some scattered, generally teleologically informed interpretations of Kant are to be found in a few more recent historical, political, aesthetic, and religious interpretations of his works, interpreters who, with Ward, reject the notion that one could get to what is most central in Kant's ethics without dipping one's toe in some sort of metaphysical waters. It is from such interpreters that we can expect exactly the opposite of Korsgaard's approach, viz. an interpretive approach committed to a thicker notion of the human being such that one can make meaningful assertions about ends or purposes that all persons share, *qua* person.

Clearly, though, this is the same "Kant" about whose works we are talking here! The Kant who wrote about the FUL is the same Kant who is willing to entertain a notion of humanity thick enough to sustain ends or purposes that obtain *qua* humanity. My forthcoming account of Deontological Teleology clearly stakes its claim with Ward and others who find that what is most central in Kant's ethics cannot be accessed without commitment to metaphysically informed notions of human flourishing. We thus reject any effort to expunge teleological commitments from Kant's ethics. Unlike Ward (1972), Rossi (2019), and others, it is not my intention, however, to explore in depth the religious, historical, aesthetic, and political context within which this metaphysically robust reading of Kant's ethical theory situates itself. Instead, I accept that background, articulated well by these interpreters, as the context within which I interpret Kant's ethical theory as one committed to a deep, metaphysically informed notion of human purposes, and take the forthcoming account as congenial to and sympathetic with such interpreters.

How to Construe the Value at the Heart of Kant's Teleology?

We return, then, to the historical fact that Kant has traditionally been interpreted as presenting a "deontological" instead of a "teleological" approach to ethics. Traditionally, this distinction is drawn by appealing to an underlying distinction

---

[6] And to that extent, is a helpful precursor to Rossi's (2019) more recent work on Kant's ethical commonwealth.

between the right and the good: whereas deontological theories of morality are concerned to constrain action in accordance with what is right or wrong, teleological theories of ethics are concerned to draw persons toward their highest level of fulfillment or self-realization through appeal to a notion of the good which acts as a value-laden teleological pull upon one's action and person. A strict deontologist would thus be one who derives moral duties entirely independently of any claims of goodness or value, relying instead upon the constraining notion of right to do the derivation work, and a strict teleologist would be precisely the opposite, viz. one who appeals only to an objectively existent notion of value or goodness to provide the context for one's pursuit of a pleasurable life in accordance with that value.

While some Kant scholars hold firmly to understanding Kant as a deontologist along some version of these lines,[7] a minority group of scholars has, mostly since the mid-1990s, been pushing in a more teleological direction.[8] I focus in this section on those thinkers.

Herman (1993a) challenges the idea that Kant is a deontologist, suggesting instead that one must appeal to a conception of what is good or valuable in order to make sense of our duties. According to Herman, although appeal only to formal notions of right succeeds in constraining our actions, it "fails to give a *reason* or *rationale* for [such] moral constraint" (Herman 1993a, 216). As such, we must turn to a conception of value in order to find such reason. It is important to Herman, though, when seeking that grounding value, to stick close to the rational principle of the Categorical Imperative. Instead, then, of appealing to some value independent of the principles of practical reason, Herman argues that these principles of practical rationality themselves are regulative only because they *themselves* are valuable. And so it is the value of these principles themselves that provides the reason or rationale for moral constraint that pure deontology is lacking.[9] She thus suggests that we should no longer speak of Kant's ethics as "deontological" as such, but should (as the title of her chapter suggests), move "beyond deontology" in our understanding of Kantian ethics.

Although some would say that in welcoming a notion of the value of rational agency to ground the principle of the Categorical Imperative (a principle which then itself goes on to determine what is "right"), Herman's position should now be described as a "teleological" one, I am less willing to grant that moniker to her account simply on that basis. In one sense of what one might mean by "deontology" and "teleology," her account is obviously teleological: if deontologists ground

---

[7] See especially Reath (1994); Korsgaard (1996a); Schneewind (1996); and Johnson (2007, 2008).

[8] As we shall see in the forthcoming discussion, this includes (in the order I discuss them): Herman (1993a); Guyer (2000, 2002); Wood (1999, 2008); Wike (1994); and Ward (1971).

[9] Wood (1999) and Guyer (2000) also affirm teleological explanations of the Categorical Imperative, but they appeal to different notions of value to do so: Guyer appeals autonomy as the value of rational agency and Wood to humanity itself. I will, shortly, discuss their ideas at greater length.

morality in right, and teleologists ground morality in value, then Herman is clearly a teleological interpreter of Kant. But even in admitting appeal to value as she does, I would suggest that Herman is not thereby a "teleological" thinker more robustly construed. This is because the just described opposition of teleology to deontology does not, ultimately, provide a complete notion of what teleological ethical thought is. Beyond grounding morality in a notion of value, teleological thinkers also envision that value to be acting as a singular, substantive, and organizational end, goal, or telos of all one's end-setting. Further, a teleological thinker would envision the moral task generally as one of becoming most fully who or what one is in accordance with that telos, realizing thereby that function which is most proper to one's being. In this chapter at least, Herman does not address these larger issues, and so the spot at which she ends up is in a sort of no-man's land in between a strict deontological reading of Kant on the one hand and a robust teleological reading on the other. In more recent work,[10] Herman does begin to explore these more robust notions of teleology, but we will reserve discussion of that work for later in this section.

But I have a further, and deeper, concern to note about Herman's account of value: there is something not quite right about describing rational principles themselves as what is of ultimate value for Kant. I understand why she does so: with some concern for the deontological nature of Kant's ethics still in the background for her, she wants to avoid appeal to value distinct from these principles themselves. But claiming principles as the most basic value for Kant makes Herman's account more susceptible to familiar criticisms of him that he cares more about the principles of duty than he does about persons. Think, for example, of Williams' (1985) complaint that the motive of duty is "one thought too many" for a truly responsible moral agent, since the real focus of one's concern when, e.g., I go to visit my friend in the hospital, is to care about my *friend*, and not about *duty* as such. If what is most deeply valuable for him is a moral principle itself, then I believe Kant would be susceptible to Williams' criticism. But I think we can tell a more person-centered story of value for Kant than what Herman provides, one not susceptible to such criticisms.

Indeed, it is just this point about how best to conceive of the most basic value for Kant that moves us into productive discussion with other teleological interpreters of Kant. Later, more extensive and, for our purposes, more helpful teleological interpretations of Kant can be found in the work of Wood (1999, 2008) and Guyer (2000, 2002). Both appeal to notions of value: Guyer to freedom as autonomy and Wood to humanity. But, as we shall see, although such appeals are in general sympathy with my own forthcoming account of the value of persons as such as the most basic guiding value for Kant, we have reasons to prefer that

---

[10] Herman (2010).

language of "persons" to either the language of "freedom as autonomy" or "humanity" to describe that most basic valuable and orienting thing.[11] I should emphasize, though, that I find the textual evidence for answering this question ambiguous at best: there are points in Kant's texts at which he appeals to each of these things as describing that most basic value. When faced with such ambiguity, it is best to follow whatever makes most sense philosophically, and that is what I seek to do here.

So, first, in Guyer (2000), in the chapter titled, "Kant's Morality of Law and Morality of Freedom," Guyer argues that the absolute value of the free and autonomous will is the grounding value of all moral requirements, and this means Kantian ethics is fundamentally teleological. I am sympathetic to this teleological move, but I fear taking freedom as autonomy—essentially a capacity or an activity—as the most valuable thing for Kant threatens to make Guyer's point susceptible, like Herman's, to the Williams criticism. To avoid admitting that Kant cares more about a capacity than he does about persons, it makes most sense to emphasize simply that it is *persons*—particular sorts of existing *beings*, and not just a capacity abstractly conceived—who are the ultimate source of value for his ethics, and that it is to the value of such persons that we appeal to deduce our fundamental moral demands. This is a fine, but I think important, difference between me and Guyer. The point at issue is this: do we value the beings who have this capacity, or do we value the capacity such beings have? When one pushes the Williams criticism, though, clinging firmly to the language of persons as beings to describe the most basic value for Kant is our best move. For me, then, as opposed to Guyer, the value of freedom as autonomy must be based on the deeper fact that it is *persons*—particular sorts of *beings*—who have this distinctive capacity.

The only other strong point of disagreement with Guyer which I would note is his suggestion that Kant's ethics is straightforwardly and unambiguously teleological even in the *Groundwork*. As we shall see in this forthcoming account, I agree heartily that we find distinctive appeals to teleology in the *Groundwork*. But his appeal there to things teleological is not unequivocal: Kant wavers in his *Groundwork* teleological commitments because of his uncertainty there about the very possibility of *a priori* obligatory ends, and he does not provide an unwavering commitment to his end-based deduction of the Categorical Imperative until the Doctrine of Virtue.[12]

---

[11] There is a closely related but distinct interpretive issue recently discussed in a debate in the literature between Denis (2007, 2010) and Dean (2009). The question at issue in these discussions is one of how best to conceive of what Kant means by "humanity": does it refer to rational nature generally? To the moral capacity for autonomous legislation of the will specifically? Or to the value of a will which has fully realized itself as a free will? Dean (2009) argues for the good will reading, but Denis (2010) challenges that, arguing that humanity needs to be something attributable to all humans. I am asking a slightly different question here: how can we best conceive of the most basic value that grounds Kant's ethics?

[12] This is one point with which I am in agreement with Dean's (2009) interpretation, since he claims that the Kant of the *Groundwork* can ground only negative and not positive duties.

Beyond these distinctions, I take my forthcoming account to be in general sympathy with much of Guyer's account. This is particularly the case when, later, in Guyer (2002), Guyer connects freedom with the crucial capacity for end-setting which is described as a capacity to impose both negative and positive duties upon us. This move is in general sympathy with the story I go on to tell in this book, viz. that end-setting is the crucial human capacity and that Kant's account of virtue demands of us that we understand the value of persons as imposing robust—both negative constraints and positive commands—expectations upon the sensibly affected rational being. Guyer's further points that our status as end-setters needs to be something the virtuous person realizes within nature, and that such realization needs to be complemented as well by a happiness achieved within nature also sit well with our own forthcoming story of Deontological Eudaemonism. For, as I go on to argue in both Parts I and II of this book, the story of virtue is a story of the elevation of nature and one's sensible self toward one's rational self, one in which we emphasize the possibility of the pleasurable exercise of virtue in this natural life and the possibility of thereby of realizing happiness, both rationally and empirically conceived, again in this life.

I turn now to Wood. First, for Wood (1999), at least the Kant of the *Metaphysics of Morals* is essentially teleological, indeed, as he puts it, "overwhelmingly teleological" (Wood 1999, 327). In Wood (2008), he reaffirms this point in the chapter titled "Duties." There, Wood argues, based again on passages from the *Metaphysics of Morals*, that everyday moral reasoning about positive duties does not depend at all upon the FUL's permissibility requirement. Positive duties simply cannot arise from the FUL since such duties involve an appeal to ends, but the FUL is entirely formal, lacking reference to, or any ability to produce, such material ends. Based on this reasoning, Wood thus explicitly restates his 1999 point that "the foundations of a Kantian theory of ethical duties are teleological" (Wood, 2008, 166), now with the clarification that these obligatory ends will be derived from the FH rather than FUL, and that the value of humanity implicit in FH is thus the fundamental value which grounds moral obligation.

In this appeal to humanity as the ultimate value for Kant, Wood comes the closest of any current interpreters to my own claim that it is persons—and not principles or capacities—which is the best way to conceive of the value grounding moral obligations. But his appeal to "humanity" as the guiding telos for the establishment of obligations is not perfectly equivalent to my own appeal to "persons" as the objective telos of virtue. The problem is that Kant sometimes speaks of "the humanity in one's person" implying that there is a distinction to be drawn here: "humanity" is an abstract quality applied to and found in the being of all persons. But the "person" herself is the individual entity or being in whom this quality resides.[13] Once we draw this distinction, I would assert that it is crucial to appeal

---

[13] See, for example, 5:87/74 (second emphasis added): "The moral law is holy (inviolable). A human being is indeed unholy enough but the *humanity* in his *person* must be holy to him." The

to the concrete, individual entities of "persons," and not only to the abstract language of "humanity," in order fully to characterize just what Kant is asserting as the ultimate basis of value. The best way to describe this ultimate value is thus the value of "*humanity in* one's own or another's *person*."

There are multiple reasons to prefer such locution. First, it is the prevalent—perhaps ever the dominant—language Kant uses in his famous description of the FH itself: "So act that you use *humanity*, in your own *person* as well as in the person of any other, always at the same time as an end, never merely as a means"(4:429/41, emphases removed and added). The language surrounding this description of the formula itself similarly emphasizes that Kant is concerned to speak of the "beings" or even the "entities" who have this feature of humanity or rationality, and who therefore "exist," and not just to a conception of "humanity," abstractly or universally conceived: "rational *beings* are called *persons*, because their nature already marks them out as ends in themselves. These are therefore... objective ends, i.e., *entities* whose *existence* in itself is an end" (4:428/40–41, all emphases added).[14]

Later, in the *Critique of Practical Reason*, when he returns to reflection upon such things, we discover a similar emphasis upon persons: "The moral law is holy (inviolable). A human being is indeed unholy enough but the *humanity* in his *person* must be holy to him" (5:87/74, emphases removed and added). And, once again, even this larger passage taken as a whole reveals that it is the person—i.e., the existent entity or being–who has this quality of humanity who is to be respected:

> [A] *human being* alone, and with him every rational creature, is an end in itself... [S]uch a *being* is not to be subjected to any purpose that is not possible in accordance with a law that could arise from the will of the affected subject himself... We rightly attribute this condition even to the divine will with respect to the rational *beings* in the world as its creatures, inasmuch as it rests on their personality, by which alone they are ends in themselves. (5:87/74, emphases removed and added)[15]

---

language is also prominent in Kant's most famous statement of the Second Formulation of the Categorical Imperative itself: "So act that you use *humanity*, in your own *person* as well as in the person of any other, always at the same time as an end, never merely as a means"(4:429/41, emphases removed and added).

[14] Kant's use of the word *Ding* (here translated as "entity") is unusual, especially since, just previous to this passage, he had distinguished persons from "things" (*Dingen*). I am thus sympathetic with this translation of *Ding* as "entity" since such language preserves the very special meaning Kant intends here: *Ding* does not always refer to non-human beings, but can, more broadly, be understood as a term to describe something that *exists*, whatever its nature. Kant's point here, then, is to emphasize that what has value is not an abstract notion, but instead a concrete particular existing entity.

[15] Cf. also 5:131/109–110.

Kant's texts thus encourage us to emphasize the notion that it is "humanity in one's person"—i.e., a valuable universal quality as instantiated in a valuable particular, individual being—to which we should refer in speaking of the most basic value in his moral system. By insisting upon this locution, we affirm that what is *most* valuable for Kant is not simply an abstract universal notion, or even a kind of being, but instead the concrete individual beings in whom such a distinctive abstract rational capacity resides. And such dual appeal to an abstract notion and to individual beings makes sense. It would, after all, be odd to suggest that when a particular instantiation of humanity or rational nature ceases to exist, there is no loss. But this is the odd point to which we would be pushed if we clung to the idea that it is only the notion of humanity, abstractly conceived, that has value. After all, this abstract notion would still exist in some sense even when some or most instantiations of it no longer do.[16] So if it were only the abstract notion that had value, the loss of individuals possessing that valuable thing would not be problematic. But it is problematic when persons who have this feature cease to exist! Hence our insistence upon this more concrete universal way of describing this value.

A further advantage to this locution is that, through appeal to it, we can thereby avoid not only the Williams-type criticisms already noted but also Dillon's (1992, 1995) criticisms that affirming the value of rational nature or humanity is not really a valuing of particular individuals as such but only the valuing of an abstract entity. But in appealing to the humanity in one's person as the full way of describing this valuable entity, we simultaneously affirm the universally shared quality of "humanity" and the singularity of this universal quality as instantiated in particular individuals, a sort of concrete universal at the ground of value: it is the "humanity" (universal quality) in *this* person (concrete individual) who has value![17] On such a reading, we once again reject the idea that the most basic unit of value is something only universal or abstract. Rather, it is individual beings—albeit ones who instantiate a universal quality—who have value.[18]

And so, when I go on to explore, later in this chapter and, indeed, in the entirety of Part I, the notion that making persons as such one's end is the ultimate telos of virtuous end-setting, it is with this notion of the humanity in one's person as the most basic value in Kant's system in the background that we make that move. The entity of value is this individual entity with this distinctive universal

---

[16] It is an interesting question (that I will not explore here) whether and to what extent we could even speak of a universal notion "existing" if there were absolutely no instantiations of it. Kant's Transcendental Ideal commitments encourage us to be suspicious of such free-floating rational entities.

[17] Denis (2007) considers a similar point when she dwells on the question of whether it is individual rational choice or rational choice generally that is the source of value for Kant, but it is not clear to me that Denis comes to a firm answer to this question. My answer would be: it is both!

[18] For further reflection upon the import of this particular reading of how best to understand the humanity at the basis of FH, see Grenberg and Vinton (2021).

quality which leads us to describe that entity as a "person." And the way that we shall see it makes best sense to understand to what we are all obligated in light of the admission of this value is that we must all make it our singular, substantial, and life-guiding end or telos to make persons as such our end.

To return to my comparison of my forthcoming account with Wood's: first, as we shall see in I.iii, I agree with Wood that appeal to FUL alone cannot deduce obligatory ends. There is, however, one main point in relation to this claim upon which I distinguish my account from his.[19] The point of disagreement comes out most clearly, though, in Wood (2008). Although I agree with Wood that obligatory ends cannot be directly derived from FUL, and are instead successfully derived by appeal to the value of humanity (or, for me, persons) implicit in FH, as we shall see in I.iii, I depart from his thought that FUL is entirely useless in the deduction of obligatory ends and, instead, appeal to an indirect way in which this formulation can be helpful, in tandem with the telos of making persons as such one's end, in establishing specific obligatory ends meant to be constitutive of one's telos.

The Reciprocity of Deontology and Teleology

Let us step back from all this discussion of the secondary literature for a moment so as to emphasize in contrast my own forthcoming account. Insistence especially upon the need to appeal to the First (as well as the Second) Formulation(s) of the Categorical Imperative in the establishment of more precise obligatory ends as I just have helps explain what I mean in saying that, even as I defend a robustly teleological reading of Kant, when it comes to the derivation of precise obligatory ends the setting of which constitute a realization of one's overall objective telos of making persons as such my end, I affirm simultaneously a *reciprocal* relationship between that valuable and guiding telos on the one hand and deontological principles of action on the other. This assertion of reciprocity distinguishes myself

---

[19] In fact, there is a second point of disagreement as well, though a less crucial one: Wood insists also on describing Kant's teleology as "consequentialist," but I don't find that language helpful. According to Wood, "Kant's theory of ethical duties is consequentialist in its style of reasoning [viz., more means-ends related?], but not in its fundamental principle" (Wood 1999, 414). That is: within the "style of reasoning" which grounds Kant's system of duties, Kant is a consequentialist not a deontologist because the good (ends) has priority over the right. Even perfect ethical duties are grounded teleologically in the Doctrine of Virtue since violating them involves refusing to set an obligatory end or setting an end that conflicts with an obligatory end. Wood is careful, though, to note that this Doctrine of Virtue consequentialism breaks with common consequentialist theories in that it does not utilize consequentialist tools such as averaging, maximizing, or satisficing. And, in this respect, he asserts that Kant's consequentialism avoids the typical self-defeating charges levied against consequentialism based on these tools. It is not that I disagree as such with anything Wood says here. But I find the distinction he draws between Kant's consequentialism and common conceptions of consequentialism distinctive enough to abandon the language of consequentialism for Kant. Use of the word just comes with too much baggage to be a helpful way of making the point he makes here.

further from Wood, who reads Kant in a more *thoroughly* teleological (and hence non-deontological) way, at least for the purposes of such derivation of obligatory ends. Recall, after all, that he describes Kant as "overwhelmingly teleological" (Wood 1999, 327), and that we cannot appeal at all to FUL to guide us in the establishment of obligatory ends. We, to the contrary, consider the telos of making persons as such one's end to act hand-in-hand with deontological principles which help to make the meaning of the realization of that telos more precise.[20]

It is right to say that Wood thoroughly rejects usefulness at least of FUL for the purposes of establishing obligatory ends. To that extent, his account of the determination of these ends is thoroughly teleological (i.e., based in a value or end), without any appeal to the work of a deontological principle. Versus Wood, I claim a reciprocal relationship of a guiding teleological value and a determining deontological principle, even in the establishment of obligatory ends. On my account, "deontological" principles are not principles of "right" as such, but, more broadly, are formal principles of action which work in tandem with the guiding telos of making persons as such one's end to establish precise obligatory ends which constitute the realization of that telos.

Briefly, the account we will defend in this and upcoming chapters looks like this: duties which aren't merely formal duties of right—that is, duties which involve "obligatory ends"—emerge in the first instance from teleological appeal to the value of persons. But this value of persons is intimately related with the deontological principles of FUL, and especially FH. As such, once we affirm the telos of all practical reasoning as the concern to make persons as such one's end, we then rely on the deontologically articulated principles of FUL and FH, in tandem with the affirmed and orienting value of persons as such, to identify the details of specific duties as obligatory ends which realize this telos. These principles thus work reciprocally with affirmation of the value of persons to establish one coherent theory of virtue. On my account, we must thus understand the exercise of pure practical reason as involving a reciprocal relationship between deontological principles (now understood more broadly as principles which identify necessary duties with obligatory ends) and a teleologically guiding end of making persons as such one's end.

In affirming the reciprocal relationship of teleology and deontology, I thus place myself in general agreement with another at least implicitly teleological interpreter of Kant, Wike (1994).[21]

---

[20] I will, however, consider myself *more* teleologically concerned than Wood when we turn to issues of eudaemonism. Although I am generally sympathetic with Wood's approach to teleology as discussed here, I am in sharp disagreement with him about the non-eudaemonistic conclusions to which he comes in other works, especially Wood (2000). I will discuss such matters at length in I.iii and, indeed, through much of Part II.

[21] Wike's thoughts on what is essentially teleology have not been discussed as much as her thoughts on happiness. This may be because her reflections on ends are bound up within a larger work on the

According to her, appeal to ends as such is part and parcel of Kant's principle-led conception of deontology and, indeed, of his notion of practical reason itself. Although she does not dwell upon underlying tensions in the very notion of welcoming ends (the matter of choice) into a story of pure practical reason (a tension upon which I shall dwell at length in the forthcoming chapter), her conviction that a rational faculty of principles can simultaneously be a volitional faculty of ends is very much in line with my own understanding of such matters:

> What can be spoken about in terms of ends can also be spoken about in terms of principles. A faculty of ends is also a faculty of principles. Presumably, the reverse is also true. A faculty of principles (reason) is also a faculty of ends (will). While laws and principles can be treated separately from objects and ends, the separation is only an abstraction. In fact, the principles of ethics (the form) are useless, without an application, apart from the ends or objects whose pursuit they direct. Similarly, the ends of ethics (the matter) are useless, unable to morally direct the will, apart from principles. This is perhaps analogous to the way in which concepts are empty without intuitions and intuitions are blind without concepts. (A51/B75)   (Wike 1994, 30–31)

But the extant teleological reading of Kant's ethics with which I am in deepest sympathy is Ward's somewhat neglected 1971 account of such matters. Ward appeals to "human perfection" as the telos of the deontological principle of the Categorical Imperative, a notion of value which I would suggest is just another way of describing what I will go on to describe as the telos of making persons as such one's end.[22] In my forthcoming account, my appeal to persons as such as a guiding telos for the pursuit of virtue will play a role similar to what his appeal to human perfection does.

As part of his overall defense of Kant's Teleological Ethics, Ward also appeals, briefly, to just the notion of materialized versions of the Categorical Imperative in the Doctrine of Virtue on which I will be focusing my own upcoming account, noting (as I do too) that this reading of the Categorical Imperative, though generally overlooked in the literature, is perhaps the most satisfying one for making sense of Kant's ethics overall:

---

nature of happiness for Kant; for, indeed, her reflections on happiness as such have been meaningfully integrated in recent literature. I will return, in Part II, to some of her ideas specifically on happiness.

[22] "My thesis is that Kant's main ethical concern was with human perfection; while he rejected the Wolffian claim that one could define perfection independently of moral considerations, the categorical obligations of the moral law are, he believed, motiveless, arbitrary and absurd if they are not conceived as determining human perfection" (Ward 1971, p.337). Ward also notes: "It should be clear that Kant's ultimate concern in ethics was with human fulfilment in a harmonious and constantly developing community; his religious doctrines are attempts to establish the possibility of such fulfilment, which is uncertain in this life; and, without appreciation of that concern, the *Groundwork* must remain largely unintelligible" (Ward 1971, 351).

In the *Metaphysic of Morals*, [Kant] provides, as a new formula of the Categorical Imperative: "Act according to a maxim of ends which it can be a universal law for everyone to have" (The Doctrine of Virtue) (Pt. 2 of Metaphysic of Morals), trans. M. J. Gregor (New York, 1964), p. 55.) It is ironic that this formula, which, inferring explicitly to ends of action, is perhaps the most adequate formulation of Kant's fundamental principle of ethics, does not appear in the Fundamental Principles [i.e., the *Groundwork*]. But it does make it quite clear that Kant was fundamentally concerned with ends of action; and, indeed, that "were there no such ends [which were also duties] a categorical imperative would be impossible. (ibid, p.43)". (Ward 1971, 341)[23]

In my own forthcoming account, I take these thoughts from both Wike and Ward as inspiration for exploring more fully the reciprocally related deontological and teleological aspects of practical reason.[24]

Interpretations of the Formula of Humanity

I conclude my review of recent literature related to Kant and teleology by reflecting on the state of interpretation for the second Formulation of the Categorical Imperative (the FH), an aspect of Kant's thought particularly important for our purposes because of its appeal to an objective and apparently teleological notion of rational nature as an end-in-itself.

Most recent discussion of FH in the literature has focused on three questions: (a) how best to understand the "humanity" that is at the basis of the FH;[25] (b)

---

[23] I do, however, reject Ward's conclusion that Kant's teleological ethics "suffers from a radical internal incoherence" (Ward 1971, 350). I suspect Ward's claim of overall incoherence rests on his own overemphasis upon formalistic *Groundwork* readings of the Categorical Imperative, because once he emphasizes the ideas of the Doctrine of Virtue, worries about incoherence seem to evaporate for him: "Moral effort is of supreme worth; but it would be senseless, on Kant's view, if it were not aimed at the realization of one's natural perfections in a harmonious community. This is the doctrine implicit in the Fundamental Principles [i.e., the *Groundwork*]; and it is unfortunate that Kant's attempt to provide just one supreme principle of morality, and a purely formal one at that, has helped to conceal it from those critics who have failed to take into account the Metaphysic of Morals, to which the Fundamental Principles was meant to be a propaedeutic" (Ward 1971, 341). My own forthcoming account will balance what Ward calls this "Rationalistic" formalism of the *Groundwork* with a careful reading of Kant's more "materialistic" reading of the Categorical Imperative which emerges in the Doctrine of Virtue, a notion to which (as I've already noted) Ward himself briefly appeals.

[24] And although I shall not engage it here, Ward (1972) provides perhaps the most thorough historical background for and defense of a teleological and metaphysical reading of Kant's ethics, one which also highlights the neglected centrality of happiness for that account.

[25] See especially an ongoing debate between Dean (2009, 2013) and Denis (2010). Dean (2009) argues that "humanity" consists in having acquired fully developed moral capacities, essentially having acquired a good will. Both Denis (2010) and Formosa (2017) argue—I think successfully—against that position, suggesting that accepting such a reading would undermine the universal attribution of "humanity" to all human agents.

how best to understand the relationship of FH to FUL;[26] and (c) how best to understand the argument Kant gives at 4:427–429 for grounding the validity of FH.[27] I am not unconcerned with these questions. On the one hand, I accept the argument of interpreters who claim that the notion that humanity is best conceived as the rational capacity for moral legislation[28] (and point readers to Grenberg 2013a for my own reflections on that point); and, on the other, I will, later in Part I, offer a new, middle-of-the-road reading of the FH/FUL relation which sits in between current equivalency and non-equivalency readings of that relation.

There is, however, a previous question I take to be crucial for making sense of how best to interpret FH, a question that has not been directly or fully addressed in the literature to date. The question is this: given that, in the *Groundwork*, Kant must set aside all ends, or matters of choice, as he seeks to defend a formal and universal grounding of morality, how and to what extent can we defend Kant's turn in the Doctrine of Virtue to a robust reading of FH as grounding a demand to limit or constrain our actions in relation to persons but also positively to command certain ends, or *matters* of choice, as obligatory?

Kant himself states the problem well in Section VI of the Doctrine of Virtue:

Maxims are here regarded as subjective principles which merely qualify for a giving of universal law, and the requirement that they so qualify is only a negative principle (not to come into conflict with a law as such).—How can

---

[26] One group of scholars believe the FUL and FH are in some sense equivalent. Engstrom (2009, see especially pp. 98–118), Herman (2010), Reath (2013), Allison (2013), and Cureton (2013) all hold some version of this view. Allison (2013) argues for a thick version of FUL in which universalizability is grounded in a conception of rational agency being an end-in-itself (EII): a maxim which did not treat rational agency as an EII would not be endorsable by all agents and thus not universalizable. Herman (2010) argues that treating another human as an EII requires the possibility of fully reciprocal practical reasoning, viz. a principle that can be co-willed because of its rational validity. According to her, only principles that can be universalized are capable of this reciprocity or co-willing, and thus, the formulas have different foci but are equivalent in outcome. Reath (2013), following Engstrom (2009) to a certain extent, argues that FUL and FH are equivalent formal principles: FUL implicitly contains FH in that the requirement of universality is the requirement to use practical reason in a way that all subjects can support. Cureton (2013) reads a thin version of FH into FUL by arguing that FUL holds that rational agents can only act on maxims capable of being universally willed by self-regarding rational agents, and since FH states that these agents conceive of their *own* nature as an EII, a maxim could only be universalized if it treated *everyone else* as an EII.

A second group of scholars believe FUL and FH are not equivalent. Korsgaard (1986), Wood (2008), and Formosa (2017) all hold some version this view. Wood (2008) argues that FUL and FH differ in abstraction and content and only FH is capable of deriving positive duties. Formosa (2014) argues that FUL produces false negatives that FH does not due to a difference in focus between the principles: FUL is a principle of *consistency* while FH is a principle of *dignity*.

[27] Interpreters on this issue break down generally into realist and constructivist readings of the argument. The main proponents of the realist reading are Guyer (2000, see especially pp. 96–171) and Wood (2008), but they are challenged in interesting ways by Kerstein (2013, especially chapters 1 and 2), Cureton (2013), and Formosa (2017). Amongst the constructivist interpreters, see Korsgaard (1986), Dean (2009), Herman (2010), Reath (2013), and Formosa (2017).

[28] Viz., Denis (2010), Formosa (2017), and especially Hill (1980).

there be, beyond this principle, a law for the maxims of actions? Only the concept of an end that is also a duty, a concept that belongs exclusively to ethics, establishes a law for maxims of actions by subordinating the subjective end (that everyone has) to the objective end (that everyone ought to make his end). The imperative "You ought to make this or that (e.g., the happiness of others) your end" has to do with the matter of choice (an object). (6:389/162–163)

It is not that there has been no discussion of this important category of obligatory ends (i.e., "ends that are also duties") for Kant. To the contrary, especially Herman (2010) and Formosa (2014, 2017) have recently provided excellent and helpful reflections on this notion, as well as on the related notion of imperfect duties with which these obligatory ends are integrally related.[29] As I prepare to take on the question I've just articulated, I will thus briefly consider each of their thoughts in turn so as to situate my thoughts in relation to theirs.

First, although she eschews the idea of identifying Kant's ethics explicitly as a teleological system of ethics, Herman (2010) nonetheless, in an effort to put Kant's ethics in productive conversation with virtue theory, pursues the general outlines of what she calls an "end-anchored interpretation of Kant's ethics" (p. 114), with particular concern for the anchoring role of obligatory ends. Indeed, for her, his notion of obligatory ends is precisely what puts Kant in the most "congenial" relation to virtue ethics: "Especially once we factor in obligatory ends, differences [between Kant's ethics and virtue ethics] at the level of practice, and even of moral self-conception, are not likely to be great" (Herman 2010, 114–115). But although Herman identifies obligatory ends as central to Kant's Doctrine of Virtue, she explicitly rejects the notion that that end-of-all-ends for Kant, viz. rational nature as an end-in-itself, could act as an overall guiding telos which would guide the establishment of individual obligatory ends of virtue. Since this is exactly the task to which we will be turning in this part of the book, it is thus crucial for us to reflect upon and challenge Herman's account.

So, having articulated well the traditional distinction most commonly made between Kant and teleological approaches to ethics (as we saw at the opening of this chapter), Herman goes on to suggest, in contrast to this generally accepted view, that it is precisely the notion of "rational nature as an end in itself [which will] prove…to be a useful focal point if our aim is to deepen the comparison between Kantian and virtue theory" (p. 97). But she insists simultaneously upon limiting the role this notion of an end-in-itself can play for Kant's ethics. We should not accept rational nature as an end-in-itself as "a separate normative

---

[29] Such work is to be contrasted with, e.g., Kerstein (2013) who focuses centrally on how the FH demands that persons not be treated as mere means. It is in such works that we find the most robust commitment to the strictly deontological notion that a principle like FH must act as a constraining or limiting principle instead of as a positive teleological guide to one's life overall.

principle [viz., separate from FUL], but [merely] as the gateway concept to Kant's view of moral action and agency" (p. 97). Herman's worry, then, is that, were we to grant rational nature as an end-it-itself a robustly teleological role, we'd have to admit that it is a principle distinct from (perhaps in competition with?) FUL (or perhaps even a source of value distinct from the Categorical Imperative entirely?), and she is not willing to admit such a distinction. To the contrary, for Herman, whatever role rational nature as an end-in-itself plays in making sense of "moral action and agency," it must do so simply as a principle equivalent in general terms with FUL:

> Once we have the theoretical elements of the argument in place, it is clear that the formula of humanity is, as Kant says it is, just another formulation of the one moral law, equivalent in its normative import to the formula of universal law...For those who find in the formula of humanity Kant's deepest moral insight, this austere conclusion will seem to come at a great cost. I think that, to the contrary, the austere conclusion makes sense of the formula and secures its place as a distinctive source of moral insight. (Herman 2010, 109)

Now is not the time to investigate the question of the relationship of FH and FUL, nor the reasons why it is fact makes more sense to conceive of all formulations of the Categorical Imperative, and indeed, practical reason itself, as inherently teleological; I will do so in I.iv and I.iii, respectively. For now, we bring up her assertion of this "austere" equivalency only to note Herman's motivation for rejecting a broadly teleological role for the notion of rational nature as an end-in-itself. She *is* committed to an "end-anchored" conception of Kant's ethics (and, indeed, in concert with Herman 1993a, a conception of Kant's ethics that takes it beyond deontology), but also to a conception of it with only an "austere" instead of a robustly teleological appeal to such ends, an austerity which apparently also includes the rejection (as best I can tell, without argument) of the Aristotelian notion of "function" (and, with that, the central Aristotelian idea of *proper* function): "There are some ideas associated with virtue ethics—noncodifiability, practical wisdom, function, teleology of the Good, the holism of the practical— that are not found in Kantian moral theory" (Herman 2010, 92).

Ultimately, I struggle to understand entirely why Herman eschews an explicit teleological role for the notion of humanity as an end-in-itself.[30] I will thus try to

---

[30] I suspect, in addition to the interpretive analysis I go on to provide of Herman's ideas here, that Herman's background commitment to a constructivist as opposed to a realist interpretation of Kant practical philosophy implicitly informs her aversion to welcoming a robustly teleological reading of rational nature as an end-in-itself. Were one to welcome rational nature as an end in this way, one would be that much closer to asserting a metaphysical claim about the existence of rational nature as such instead of relying upon the constructivist affirmation of value which starts its story from the actual exercise of practical reason and not from some previous metaphysical assertion of the status of rational nature. I discuss such matters at greater length in I.iii.

trace as best I can what I take her argument to be. Herman suggests that the problem for any would-be complete reconciliation of Kantian and more teleologically grounded virtue ethics is a "theoretical" one. As she puts the point: "once we have the theoretical elements of the argument in place, it is clear that the formula of humanity is, as Kant says it is, just another formulation of the one moral law, equivalent in its normative import to the formula of universal law" (Herman 2010, 109). And she states later that "[w]ithout [this theoretical principle of] rational nature as an end in itself, final and authoritative for us as free agents, there could be no doctrine of virtue [for Kant]. Whether theories of virtue can get along without some such [theoretical] foundations is, I think, an important question to ask" (Herman 2010, 115).

In putting her "theoretical" point this way, Herman seems to suggest the following contrast between Kant's moral theory and virtue ethics: Kant's moral theory is *based* in principle (and any virtue that might emerge for it emerges only in the application of this previous principle), but the virtue ethics has no "basis" as such for its appeal to virtue, only a foundationless reliance upon virtue as somehow self-standing with its own telos or end, a telos that while organizational and substantive, plays a role somehow different than any principled normative foundation. Herman thus implies that many (most? all?) virtue theories, unlike Kant's, *avoid* reliance upon a previous principled foundation for the particular virtues expounded and defended. Kant, in contrast, begins with the rational principle of the Categorical Imperative,[31] and virtue as such can emerge only after this principle is asserted as the more fundamental ground of morality. Furthermore, because Herman accepts a strict equivalency between FUL and FH versions of the Categorical Imperative, it seems she also accepts the notion that what might *look* like a robust telos of virtue (viz., rational nature as an end-in-itself) is in fact simply another way of describing that foundational, rational principle of action, the Categorical Imperative. As such, we must not think of this end as a substantive, objective, and organization telos of one's life, but instead as just another way of describing a formal principle of action.

In suggesting all this, Herman's thoughts remind me of what I asserted in Grenberg (2005). There, I suggested that not all approaches to virtue ethics are un-principled in the way Herman assumes. To the contrary, one can, for example, find the "principle" of acting for the sake of the noble in Aristotle's virtue ethics.[32] This principle would thus, for Aristotle, play the principled, grounding foundational role for individual virtues which Herman implies are lacking in virtue theory as such. Herman's suggestion that there is harsh theoretical distinction between Kantian and virtue ethics should thus be rejected. It could hold only for

---

[31] A principle which we can say, in virtue of Herman (1993a) is a value-laden one, i.e. one which affirms itself on the basis of the value of the very rational agency this principle expresses.

[32] See also Korsgaard (1996b) who was the first to suggest such links between Kant and Aristotle.

what I[33] (and others[34]) have described as "radical" virtue ethics, an approach to virtue which explicitly eschews appeal to grounding principles. And as long as we reject any such "radical" virtue ethics, Kant's ethics and "virtue" ethics actually seem pretty similar, both practically and "theoretically" (as Herman would put the point).

Furthermore, once we grant this *rapprochement*, we can also reject Herman's related inference that, because of this theoretical distinction, we must reject a robust teleological role for the notion of humanity as an end-in-itself in favor of a weaker, more "austere" appeal to an end-anchored ethics grounded only in a formal principle, and not in an orienting telos. Her insistence that rational nature as an end-in-itself does not play a teleological role seems grounded in the assumption that, because this end is essentially another version of FUL,[35] because that means it is more a "principle" than it is a robust telos of end-setting, and because a telos is something different from such grounding principles (since virtue theorists for her do not have principles, so a telos couldn't be a principle as such)—because of all these things, we must reject the idea that rational nature as an end-in-itself is a telos. But if we reject a crucial assumption Herman makes here—the assumption that a telos is something radically distinct from a rational principle—then the conclusion that rational nature is not a telos does not hold. To the contrary, as I go on to argue in this and forthcoming chapters of Part I, deontological principle and substantive organization telos are not mutually opposed but instead reciprocally related notions, and it is precisely in Kant's Doctrine of Virtue account of materialized—that is, end-based—notions of both FUL and FH that we shall encounter that happy reciprocity.

Interestingly though, although I reject Herman's "theoretical" argument, the practical conclusions to which she comes even on her "austere" reading of the role of rational nature are conclusions very much in agreement with the picture of Deontological Teleology and Deontological Euadaemonism forthcoming in this book. Indeed, having claimed this more austere, end-anchored interpretation of Kant's ethics, it is a difficult thing to say what exactly is "austere" about the practical conclusions Herman draws from it. For, once she begins to articulate what the notion of obligatory ends, and the related notion of imperfect duties, can do for

---

[33] See Grenberg (2005). Look especially to chapter 2 (pp. 49–79), "Constraints on Any Possible Kantian Account of Virtue."

[34] See Baier (1988).

[35] The idea here seems to be that, given this equivalence, FH is subject to the same austere, merely formal constraints in its content that FUL is. To assure the a priority of his moral law, Kant appeals, especially in his discussion of FUL, only to the formal condition of "conformity with law as such" and not to any specific effect or end to determine one's will. By "rob[bing] the will of all impulses that could arise for it" (4:402/17), Kant has removed all material concerns of the will (viz., any specific matter, object, or end which the will might will) and appealed only to the mere *form* of one's willing (i.e., universalizability) to ground the proper *law* of one's willing. And so, if, for Herman, FH is essentially equivalent to FUL, then the removal of all material—i.e., end-based or teleological—concerns for the will needs also to hold for FH.

Kantian morality (Herman 2010, 112ff), she seems to re-welcome just exactly those notions—an organizing telos, proper function, holism, and more—which she warned us we'd need to reject. For Herman, reason "must have its own object; it cannot be merely regulative," and this object "can only be reason or rational nature as an end in itself" (Herman 2010, 112). She then goes on to consider how "rational nature as an end in itself" guides reasoning beings in the adoption of a wide range of obligatory ends related to oneself and also to other rational agents.[36] She even suggests that "obligatory ends set a complete framework within which we are to adopt discretionary ends and activities," and that "the full account of obligatory ends frames a doctrine (a *Lehre* or teaching) of virtue" rooted in a "holism of the moral," a holism which finds its source precisely in what is good for rational nature: "the source of the holism of the moral lies in the object of pure practical reason—the good—as specified in ends and principles of action suited for the condition of human rational beings" (Herman 2010, 113).

Similarly, the notion that in adopting these ends, we realize our proper function as rational beings is also something she seems surreptitiously to re-welcome: "Rather than talking about rule-following or obedience to duty, action that is morally motivated—having its causal source in an agent's self-conception as a rational and active being—is better described in the language of self-expression or self-realization for our kind of rational being" (Herman 2010, 114). To "realize" oneself for the "kind of rational being" one is just sounds to me like successfully finding one's proper function.

If all of this is the case, can Herman really say that rational nature as an end-in-itself is not playing a "substantive, objective and organizing" (Herman 2010, 96) teleological role in guiding one's end-setting generally? Indeed, why would she *want* to say such a thing? She would tell us that this rational nature is nothing other than FUL in other clothing. But even if that is the case, can we not say that, once we get to the details of the pursuit of virtue, rational nature as an end itself, taken as a whole, does indeed play a "teleological" role in guiding end-setting, i.e. a role that is, in Herman's own language "substantive, objective and regulative" and which "play[s] an organizing role in a complete human life" (Herman 2010, 96)?

I thus admit perplexity about why Herman feels the need explicitly to reject the notions of "teleology" and "function" as out of order in Kantian ethics. She insists upon a "theoretical" difference between Kant's ethics and virtue ethics and, I

---

[36] Consider the following snippets from her positive account of obligatory ends: "Obligatory ends set norms (further specified by imperfect duties) responsive to the conditions of human rational agency... [I]t is an interest of reason that we develop and refine our rational abilities..., discipline our desires so that they become reason-responsive, and pursue projects and activities, work and relationship, in ways that enhance rather than detract from realizing sound practical judgment" (Herman 2010, 112). "It is equally in reason's interest, in each human being's interest as a reasoning being, that others not reason badly" (Herman 2010, 112).

suppose, considers that theoretical difference to also drive a wedge between Kantian principle and teleology. But the theoretical difference she notes does not apply to all virtue theories (as, for example, Aristotle's) and she seems simply to assume that a "principle" cannot do double-duty as a "telos."

In short, I wish Herman would have said more about this lamentably brief series of rejections of teleological and Aristotelian notions as inapplicable to Kant's ethics. And despite the fact that her account of obligatory ends rejects these notions that will be central to our own forthcoming account, we ironically take Herman's initial forays into the world of obligatory ends and her flirtation with articulating Kant's ethics "in terms congenial to the ambitions of virtue theory" (p. 114) as supportive of and sympathetic to our own forthcoming project, even helping to point us in the direction we want to go to make sense of Deontological Teleology, now explicitly, consciously, and happily pursued as such.

My thoughts on Formosa (2014) are more brief than those on Herman. Unlike Herman, he is willing to reject the equivalency of FUL and FH, especially when trying to make sense of how best to apply the Categorical Imperative. This task of application is indeed his stated goal in this work: "[W]e shall focus on a different set of issues: How do we apply or use this formula [viz., the Categorical Imperative] in practice, that is, how does this principle work as a moral guide to what duties and obligations we have in particular cases?" (Formosa 2014, 49). Given that this is his task, his work is particularly congenial to our own forthcoming project. Indeed, his language of appeal to the Categorical Imperative as "a moral guide" for determining our "duties and obligations" is one way I go on to describe what it would mean to take that principle (and especially that principle as FH) as a "telos" for one's life.

Furthermore, Formosa, helpfully and at some length, argues convincingly that the best way to apply FH so as to make practical progress with it is to accept that this formula both limits our actions in accordance with perfect duties and commands positive material obligatory end-setting in accordance with imperfect duties.[37] Although he does not use the language of "telos" or "teleology" to cash out his thoughts, what he is doing here—viz., taking the Categorical Imperative as the ground for determining all one's end-setting—is exactly the project I will go on in this Part I of the book to describe in teleological terms.

Having described Formosa's and Herman's projects, though, the most crucial thing to note to situate my project relative to theirs is an issue that never hits the radar for either of them, an issue the resolution of which is previous to the very acceptance of the category of "obligatory ends" as central for Kant. That issue is to identify and address an underlying tension in Kant's texts which, at least on the face of it, gives the impression that appeal to obligatory ends would undermine

---

[37] See Formosa (2014), 57–68. In Herman's language, Formosa thus shows that FH plays a "substantive, objective and regulative role in a complete human life" (Herman 2010, 96).

the *a priori* basis of Kant's moral principles. It is upon this tension that we shall centrally focus for the rest of this chapter. In so doing, and in defending the very notion of material ends not only as not in contradiction with but in fact as central to and definitional of Kant's *a priori* morality, I present and defend Kant's moral theory generally not only as deeply end-anchored *à la* Herman but also as explicitly teleological, and thus more in sympathy with Ward's account of "Kant's Teleological Ethics" (1971). What emerges is a story of what I call Kant's Deontological Teleology. Let us turn to that story.

II. Kant's Early Thoughts on Ends

Relative, Subjective, and Unfree Ends in the *Groundwork* and second *Critique*

One can understand why readers familiar only with Kant's *Groundwork* and *Critique of Practical Reason* might assume that deontology must be essentially opposed to teleology. This is because two central concerns of both these works—viz., the determination of an *a priori* and purely formal grounding of the supreme principle of morality, and the assurance of the reciprocity of that moral law with free determination of the will—demand of Kant that he set aside any appeal to the so-called "matter" of one's maxim, that is, any appeal to the actual ends toward which a maxim is directed. Let's review some of his concerns in these earlier works so as to appreciate the attitude toward ends that develops in them.

First, most generally, what Kant is seeking in both the *Groundwork* and the second *Critique*, as is well-known, is "a pure moral philosophy, completely cleansed of everything that might be in some way empirical," and thus a conception of a moral law grounded "a priori solely in concepts of pure reason" (4:389/4–5). Kant is emphatic that this project of finding a pure, *a priori* moral law is a fundamental and grounding concern for moral theory, one that must be separated from any further moral concerns: "the identification and corroboration of *the supreme principle of morality*... by itself constitutes a business that is complete in its purpose and [is] to be separated from every other moral investigation" (4:392/7).

Furthermore, when engaged in this fundamental and grounding task, Kant must be particularly concerned to cleanse his arguments of appeal to anything empirical, anything that would sully the pure a priority of his project. Toward that end, he does a few things which require the expunging of any appeal to the ends of action in his arguments, favoring instead appeal to the mere form of maxims of action. First, and famously, he insists that a truly *a priori* law of the will would be grounded only in the mere form of that law and its maxim, not in any appeal to the matter or end of one's action:

[W]hat kind of law can that possibly be, the representation of which—even without regard for the effect expected from it—must determine the will for it to be called good absolutely and without limitation? Since I have robbed the will of all impulses that could arise for it from following some particular law, nothing remains but the universal conformity of actions with law as such, which alone is to serve the will as its principle, i.e., I ought never to proceed except in such a way *that I could also will that my maxim should become a universal law.* Here, then, mere conformity with law as such (not founded on any law determined with a view to certain actions) is what serves the will as its principle.

(4:402/17, translation slightly modified)

To assure the a priority of his moral law, Kant here appeals only to the formal condition of "conformity with law as such" and not to any specific effect or end to determine one's will. By "robb[ing] the will of all impulses that could arise for it," Kant has removed all material concerns of the will (viz., any specific matter, object, or end which the will might will) and appealed only to the mere *form* of one's willing (i.e., universalizability) to ground the proper *law* of one's willing.

In so doing, Kant thus places the heart of deontological, duty-focused morality—the determination of one's "moral worth"—not in the intending of any specific purpose, end, object, or effect of willing but only in the *principle* of one's will:

[A]n action from duty has its moral worth *not in the purpose* that is to be attained by it, but in the maxim according to which it is resolved upon, and thus it does not depend on the actuality of the object of the action, but merely on the *principle* of *willing* according to which—regardless of any object of the desiderative faculty—the action is done... [Moral worth] can lie nowhere else *than in the principle of the will*, **regardless of the ends that can be effected by such action**; for the will stands halfway between its a priori principle, which is formal, and its a posteriori incentive, which is material, as it were at a crossroads, and since it must after all be determined by something, it will have to be determined by the formal principle of willing as such when an action is done from duty, as every material principle has been taken away from it.

(4:399–400/15–16, bolded emphases added)

Kant makes a similar point in the *Critique of Practical Reason*:

If a rational being is to think of his maxims as practical universal laws, he can think of them only as principles that contain the determining ground of the will not by their matter but only by their form... Now, all that remains of a law if one separates from it everything material, that is, every object of the will (as its determining ground), is the mere form of giving universal law. (5:27/24)

In short, according to the Kant of the *Groundwork* and second *Critique*, both the ground of one's willing and the moral worthiness for which one can hope are to be found only in the mere form or principle of one's willing and not at all in any matter, object, or end of one's willing. Were one to appeal to such material grounds, one would compromise the *a priori* purity, universality, and necessity of the law one was trying to ground.[38]

Because any will bound by this pure, *a priori* law must also ultimately be shown to be a thoroughly free will, Kant has further grounds—affirmed again both in the *Groundwork* and in the second *Critique*—to distance himself from appeal to material ends or objects of willing. To show that a law-bound will is simultaneously a free will, he must find a determining ground of that will that does not rely at all upon inclinations connecting that will to material ends of action which would undermine the free determination of that will. He must thus rely, once again, only upon the mere form of the law that would determine the will, and not upon anything about the matter or end toward which that will would direct itself. Here is one way he describes both the reciprocal relation of a law-bound will and a free will and the resulting need for the expungement of any material source of the will's determination:

> Supposing that the mere lawgiving form of maxims is the only sufficient determining ground of a will: to find the constitution of a will that is determinable by it alone. Since the mere form of a law can be represented only by reason and is therefore not an object of the senses..., the representation of this form as the determining ground of the will is distinct from all determining grounds of events in nature in accordance with the law of causality... [S]uch a will must be thought as altogether independent of the natural law of appearances in their relations to one another, namely the law of causality. But such independence is called freedom in the strictest, that is, in the transcendental sense. Therefore, a will for which the mere lawgiving form of a maxim can alone serve as a law is a free will. (5:28–29/26)

Kant's point here is to affirm that if a will is determinable by a merely formal law of reason, without any appeal to the matter of one's willing, then by that very fact the same will is free. This is because, in being determined by the mere form of a law which emerges from one's own reason, the will escapes determination by nature's "law of causality." A will bound only by the merely formal law of reason is thus free, first, in the sense that it is not determined by some alien, physical "event...in nature" outside of itself. This includes avoidance of determination by

---

[38] It is upon just these passages that many strict deontological interpreters of Kant depend, either explicitly or implicitly, to defend that strict reading. See, for example, Reath 1994; Schneewind 1996; and Johnson 2007, 2008.

natural events both outside of us and within us as well. That is, we avoid being determined by some force outside of us; but we also avoid being determined by merely sensible forces within oneself, viz. one's own sensible inclinations. In the *Groundwork*, Kant calls this the avoidance of determination by "alien causes" (4:446/56). Second, this will is free in the sense that it *is* determined positively by the form of a law that can "be represented only by reason," indeed only by its *own* reason. In *Groundwork* language, this determination of the will by its formal law is "the property of the will of being a law to itself" (4:446/56). This avoidance of determination from alien causes and the resulting self-determination by reason are thus, essentially, what Kant has described earlier, in the *Groundwork*, as "negative freedom" and "positive freedom," respectively.[39] But to affirm both of these notions of freedom as applying to one's will, it is, once again, necessary that this will be determined only by "the mere lawgiving form of maxims," and not at all by any appeal to any "object of the senses" or any "events in nature in accordance with the law of causality," that is, to any matter or end of willing.

Kant's project of affirming an *a priori* principle which determines a free will thus demands of him that he set aside any appeal to material ends of action. As a result, in both the *Groundwork* and the second *Critique*, Kant treats ends (that is, the material of one's maxims) as entirely subjective and relative, things that must be set aside so as to identify that quality of maxims that is not subjective and relative but instead objective, absolute, necessary, universalizable, and free:

> Practical principles are formal if they abstract from all subjective ends; they are material if they have these, and hence certain incentives, at their foundation. *The ends that a rational being intends at its discretion as effects of its actions (material ends) are one and all only relative*; for merely their relation to a particular kind of desiderative faculty of the subject gives them their worth, which can therefore furnish no universal principles that are valid as well as necessary for all rational beings, or for all willing, i.e., practical laws. That is why all these relative ends are the ground of hypothetical imperatives only.   (4:427–428/40, emphases added)

For the Kant of the *Groundwork*, all ends that an agent sets are material, and therefore subjective and relative. Kant's commitment to an *a priori* morality leads him to equate all ends, or matters of choice, with empirically determined ends.[40]

---

[39] First, when thinking about the will as "a kind of causality," he defines negative freedom of that will as "that property of such a causality, as it can be efficient independently of alien causes determining it" (4:446/56). He then explains that this negative conception of freedom is also related to a "positive concept of freedom, which is so much the richer and more fruitful," one in which we realize that "the concept of causality carries with it that of laws," and that, in the case of the rational will, these laws of causality "must...be a causality according to immutable laws, but of a special kind," namely, "the property of the will of being a law to itself" (4:446/56).

[40] There is one caveat to admit here: Kant does of course speak of persons as "ends in themselves," and such ends do have both objective and absolute value. Crucially, though, ends in themselves are

The principle of one's will is successfully "formal" and plausibly "free" only if it abstracts from all these empirical, material ends.

We find a similar claim in the second *Critique*: "All practical principles that presuppose an object (matter) of the faculty of desire as the determining ground of the will are, *without exception*, empirical and can furnish no practical laws" (5:21/19, emphasis added). To affirm an *a priori* project of freely determined moral laws, Kant thus rejects any end-based approach to the grounding of moral principles.

Virtue's Need for Ends

And so, again, one can understand why a reader only of the *Groundwork* and the second *Critique* would assume that deontology must be strictly distinguished from teleology. In deontology, one focuses on pure, formal principles of the will, not on messy empirical, material ends of action. To assure one's moral worth, one must be concerned only to assure that the formal principle guiding one's maxim of action is universalizable. Deontology seems thoroughly to reject any appeal to ends, goals, or the matter of one's willing as such. How, then, could such a *deontological* moral theory—that is, one concerned to identify pure dutiful principles of action exclusive of any appeal to an end—ever be concerned with *teleology*—that is, with an approach to morality that takes an ultimate and material end, goal, or telos as the organizing principle of one's pursuit of virtue?

An actual answer to this rhetorical question emerges in a careful review of Kant's virtue theory, and it is the goal of the rest of this chapter and, indeed, the rest of Part I, to tell that story. It makes sense, after all, that once he has settled the foundational and grounding question of the nature of the supreme principle of morality, Kant would need to find his way back to concern for ends. He wants, that is, among other things, to consider what a life of virtue guided by this pure, *a priori*, supreme principle of morality would look like. But it is hard to imagine the articulation of a life of virtue without any appeal to the matter or ends of one's actions.

We can even affirm Kant's concern for appeal to such ends in the Doctrine of Virtue well before he considers the nature of virtue as such. Even just his new Doctrine of Virtue focus on making sense of *action* as such (as opposed to his

---

not ends that one sets, but instead ends which already exist and which therefore place constraints on an agent's choice and end-setting. It is not until I.iii that we will discuss this broader appeal to existent ends and, indeed, to a whole variety of objectively existing ends of reason in the *Groundwork*. For the present, we simply emphasize, more precisely, that in the *Groundwork* all ends *as matters of choice* or *as ends to be set* are merely empirical, subjective, and relative. Kant also describes these ends as ends *to be effected* or *attained*. I thank an anonymous reader from Oxford University Press for seeking clarity on this point.

Groundwork concern for the formal qualities of one's *maxims*) requires of Kant that he be concerned with ends. As Kant notes, "the law...prescribes only *the maxim of the action*...and hence not the *action itself*" (6:392/155). But in moving toward making sense of virtue, we need to bring maxims *to* "action itself," and this means also that we must reintroduce concern for ends. After all, as he also notes, "*every* action...has its end" (6:385/149, emphasis added). And so, if one is concerned with actions as such (virtuous or otherwise), and not just with the maxims of one's will, one must also inevitably be concerned with ends. To set and have an end is, simply, part and parcel of any action: every time I in fact act on a maxim that I have willed, that act is pointed toward accomplishing something; and this matter or object toward which my maxim-guided action is pointed is, simply, the end of my action.

It is clear, though, that not just action, but also virtue is centrally concerned with ends. Indeed, it is through appeal to material ends which go beyond a merely formal concern for morality that Kant defines the realm of virtue he wants to explore in the Doctrine of Virtue. That is, when we are discussing virtue, we need "to have, besides the formal determining ground of choice (such as right contains), a material one as well, an end" (6:381/146). To be concerned with virtue is thus to move from the merely "formal" world of the Doctrine of Right to a concern for the "end[s]" one sets as the material determining ground or "the matter of choice" (6:375/141). Here is perhaps his best articulation of how a doctrine of virtue needs to pursue ends and, more specifically, "ends that are also duties," or obligatory ends:

> Maxims are here regarded as subjective principles which merely qualify for a giving of universal law, and the requirement that they so qualify is only a negative principle (not to come into conflict with a law as such).—How can there be, beyond this principle, a law for the maxims of actions? Only the concept of an end that is also a duty, a concept that belongs exclusively to ethics, establishes a law for maxims of actions by subordinating the subjective end (that everyone has) to the objective end (that everyone ought to make his end). The imperative "You ought to make this or that (e.g., the happiness of others) your end" has to do with the matter of choice (an object). (6:389/162–163)

Kant even asserts at one point that the very nature of the pursuit of these ends that are also duties is guided by some singular "moral end." When speaking of the "perfection" the virtuous person is meant to realize, he notes that "as having to do with one's entire moral end, such perfection consists objectively in fulfilling all one's duties and in attaining completely one's moral end with regard to oneself" (6:446/196).

It is, thus, clear that Kant cannot avoid appeal to ends in his consideration of the pursuit of virtue in accordance with the supreme principle of morality he defined and defended in both the *Groundwork* and the second *Critique*. Indeed, it is clear that he has no interest in avoiding such appeal. To the contrary, a clearly stated central concern of the Doctrine of Virtue, and of Kant's virtue theory generally, is to make sure that the *a priori* rubber of formal laws of the will hits the material road of action. That is, he is concerned to assure that his project of determining an *a priori*, formal principle of maxims of the will has its impact in the determination of specific ends of action, ends that he ultimately identifies as obligatory ends, or "ends that are also duties." Indeed, it is his conviction in the Doctrine of Virtue that if such extension of the practicality of pure reason to end-setting is not successful, then pure reason is not really practical at all:

> [P]ure practical reason is a faculty of ends generally, and for it to be indifferent to ends, that is, to take no interest in them, would therefore be a contradiction, since then it would not determine maxims for actions either (because every maxim of action contains an end) and so would not be practical reason.
> (6:395/157)

One might even say, from this quote, that Kant is not so much seeking to extend the practicality of pure reason to some new goal beyond itself, but, rather, finally, to affirm what such practical pure reason has been all along, since the *Groundwork*: "a faculty of *ends* generally" (emphasis added).

But, given everything that Kant has said about ends in the *Groundwork* and in the second *Critique*, this new project of determining obligatory ends of virtue puts him in a difficult situation. The Kant of the *Groundwork*, tells us that we need to avoid appeal to ends, because all end-setting is subjective, relative, and empirical; as such, such appeal would undermine both the a priority and the freedom of any determination of one's will. But the Kant of the Doctrine of Virtue welcomes not just the possibility but the very necessity of material ends of action that are objective, absolute, free, and rationally chosen, that is, ends that somehow can be integrated within an *a priori* story of morality.

This is a desirable goal, but it seems also an impossible one. Here is the heart of the problem: if my will is determined toward the fulfillment of an end, even an objective and obligatory one, this means that the will is determined to some specific matter of willing. But this means also that my will is determined not only by the mere form of the law but also by some material object. And such appeal seems to undermine both the *a priori* basis for the determination of one's will and, with that, the freedom of the will choosing that end. That is, as we've seen above, determination by the mere form of the law was what assured both a truly law-bound will and a free will: if my will is bound by the mere form of the rational law that is my own, it avoids determination by any material object or "event in nature" (5:28–29/26). But now that we are talking about the will being determined not only *by* the mere form of the law but also being determined *to* particular obligatory matters or ends tied to that law, aren't we undermining both the a priority of the determination of one's will and that happy freedom that would come with the will being determined only by a mere form?

It is worth re-emphasizing the precise language Kant used back in the second *Critique* and the *Groundwork* so as to emphasize the conundrum Kant now faces as he seeks to welcome determination of the will by material ends of action. In the second *Critique*, he asserted quite emphatically that "the matter of a practical law, that is, an object of a maxim can *never* be given otherwise than empirically" (5:29/26, emphasis added), and that a free will needs to be "*independent* of empirical conditions" (5:29/26, emphasis added). As such, "a free will must find a determining ground in the law but *independently* of the *matter* of the law" (5:29/26, first emphasis added), that is, independent of ends.

This same insistence that every matter or object of action must be an empirical one and must thus be avoided in determination of the would-be moral will is emphasized in the *Groundwork* as well. There, Kant insists that ends, as material, are entirely subjective and relative. That is, they have this subjectivity and relativity precisely *because* they are empirically or materially grounded, that is, grounded in an inclination or desire for some particular material thing:

> Practical principles are formal if they abstract from all subjective ends; they are material if they have these, and hence certain incentives, at their foundation. *The ends that a rational being intends at its discretion as effects of its actions (material ends) are one and all only relative; for merely their relation to a particular kind of desiderative faculty of the subject gives them their worth*, which can therefore furnish no universal principles that are valid as well as necessary for all rational beings, or for all willing, i.e., practical laws. That is why all these relative ends are the ground of hypothetical imperatives only.
>
> (4:427–428/40, emphases added)

We thus see the challenge Kant faces in the Doctrine of Virtue. His new claim that we can appeal to ends to determine the virtuous person to action is directly at odds with his earlier claims that all ends are empirical and thus inappropriate for moral determination of the will. His willingness to introduce ends into morality seems to toll the death knell of his *a priori* project of morality. How can he re-welcome ends into his story of morality and virtue without abandoning the a priority of that story and, with that, his affirmation of a law-bound will as a free will? Maybe one can determine the mere *form* of one's willing on *a priori* grounds. But how could one possibly determine precise *material* ends as *a priori* obligatory? Is there any way to assure now, in the Doctrine of Virtue, that, when I am determined to certain ends or matters of action, that I am *not* thereby determined by something empirical and external to me, via the law of causality and/or an event in nature?

Kant himself, however, does not see this as an impossible task. The Kant of the Doctrine of Virtue is so convinced that ends can be integrated into an *a priori* story of the free realization of virtue that he now insists that such ends, far from being an obstacle to free choice, are in fact a characteristic, definitional, and integral aspect of that free choice: "An end is an *object* of free choice, the representation of which determines it to an action (by which the object is brought about)" (6:384–385/149). And the actual choice or setting of an end is taken to be the ultimate and characteristic act of a free agent: "[T]o have any end of action whatsoever is an act of *freedom* on the part of the acting subject, not an effect of *nature*" (6:385/149). And: "To have an end that I have not myself made an end is self-contradictory, an act of freedom which is yet not free" (6:381/147).

But how can we possibly claim as the ultimate act of freedom the very notion that needed to be expunged in the *Groundwork* and the second *Critique* in order to assure freedom? Clearly, Kant has changed his mind. And the change comes in the form of having a broader conception of what it means to set and have ends. For the Kant of the Doctrine of Virtue, if one were unable to determine a realm of freely set, non-empirical, obligatory ends then, as he puts the point, reason "would not be practical reason" (6:395/157). That is, if we really want to affirm that reason is practical, we need to accept not just that it is capable of determining the pure, *a priori* form of one's maxims but also that "pure practical reason is a faculty of ends generally" (6:395/157). Without admitting that practical reason is capable of determining ends *a priori*, reason would not be able to realize itself in the ultimate realm of the practical, viz. in the realm of virtuous action. To complete his account of practical reason, then, Kant simply *must* abandon his previous stance that *all* ends are merely empirical and therefore subjective and relative. He thus needs to go beyond his *Groundwork* and second *Critique* claims about the nature of ends of actions. He needs, that is, to tell a story of the free setting of objective, absolute, rational, and obligatory ends via pure practical reason to complement his earlier story of merely empirical, and therefore relative and subjective, ends.

In order to understand Kant's new position on ends, we must first defend the new notion of free end-setting, and introduce Kant's new claim that, while all ends remain material (viz., constitute the matter or object of choice), not all ends are thereby empirical (nor therefore also relative and subjective). We shall then explore the differences in the freedom of the setting of empirical (what he now calls "pragmatic") ends and the freedom in the setting of moral (what he now calls "obligatory") ends. What we shall see, ultimately, is that although every setting or adoption of an end is indeed a free act (itself a new claim for Kant), some free acts are more free than others.[41] That is, the freedom (or "free self-constraint")

---

[41] Kant rarely speaks in terms of degrees of freedom. But once we enter the realm of virtue, viz. that arena for freedom in which freedom becomes not just a capacity shared equally by all but also a

associated with virtue, that free self-constraint by which I constrain myself to certain obligatory ends, is in fact *more* free than just any free setting of ends.

We thus need to confirm virtue as *free* virtue via the setting (and, ultimately, the realization) not of just any end, but more precisely of objectively valid, *a priori* grounded, obligatory ends (a.k.a., ends that are also duties) but ends which (by definition) I also most fully and freely choose for myself. In defending this story of the free—and, ultimately, the autonomous—setting of ends, we will thereby simultaneously defend the teleological nature of Kant's account of virtue: free virtue is about the realization of objectively valid and obligatory ends which are determined by one's objective telos as a rational being, the telos of respect for persons. In affirming the existence of these freely and virtuously chosen objective ends of action, we shall thus, in this and in the following chapters of Part I, affirm Kant's Deontological Teleology, that is, his commitment to guiding the virtuous governance of desire (now understood as the virtuous setting of ends) via appeal to an orienting objective end or telos of action, that end which we have already identified as respect for persons. Let us begin this story by devoting the rest of this chapter to understanding Kant's new understanding of the free setting of ends as central to the pursuit of virtue.

III. The Freedom of End-Setting

Introduction: The Basics of Ends in the Doctrine of Virtue

In what sense can we say, then, despite Kant's *Groundwork* and second *Critique* worries to the contrary, that the integration of material ends to determine one's maxims to action needn't undermine the freedom and a priority of one's will? To answer this question, we need first simply to review Kant's new and clarified sense of what an end is, as compared to his previous *Groundwork* and second *Critique* accounts of the term.

First, in the Doctrine of Virtue, like in his earlier writings, Kant identifies ends as the "matter" or "object" of one's choice (6:380/146). That is, they are the object or state of affairs toward which one's choice is aimed. Furthermore, such matter of choice is something found in absolutely every action. As Kant notes: "[t]here can

---

chosen aptitude accomplished more successfully by some and less successfully by others, then we also enter a realm within which it does indeed make sense to say that one can be more, or less, free than another. As will emerge below, the setting of an obligatory end is more free an act than the setting of a pragmatic end. As such, those individuals who succeed in guiding their end-setting by obligatory ends will, by that very fact, be more free than those who do not. Indeed, these individuals will have more freedom because, through attending to their obligatory end-setting, they have acquired more virtue as strength than others. See, e.g., 382n/147n: "The less a human being can be constrained by natural means and the more he can be constrained morally (through the mere representation of duty), so much the more free he is."

be no action without an end" (6:385/149), and "every maxim *of action* contains an end" (6:395/157).

Some reflection on this point is in order. When Kant says that every action has an end, he is making a point about a theory of action which was, perhaps, implicit in his earlier discussions of ends, but upon which he did not reflect then. Kant emphasizes here in a way he did not earlier that, just as one's choice is determined formally by a maxim, that same choice, in order to realize itself in action, needs to be determined materially *by* and *to* an end. In short, one can *never* actually *act* only on the mere form of a maxim. *Every* action has its end, and every end is a matter or object of choice. So when I act, my act is determined toward the realization of an end, that is, toward the realization of some matter or object which determines the precise nature of the action that expresses the maxim. Every act thus has an end, because every act, in addition to being guided by a formal maxim, needs also to be pointed toward bringing about some specific material object, thing, or state of affairs. It may be that one can *speak* of maxims without speaking of ends; that was Kant's *Groundwork* project, to discover the mere form of a maxim without appeal to any matter. And so one can speak of the merely formal maxim of intending to act only on universalizable maxims without thereby appealing to any material end. But once we are concerned with the *actions* that would emerge from application of a maxim, we cannot similarly eschew concern for ends. In short, "[t]here can be no action without an end" (6:385/149), and "every maxim *of action* contains an end" (6:395/157). As such, to be concerned with actions, we must concern ourselves with ends. Indeed, an end is a rather *common* thing: every time we act, we have an end.

So far, everything we note here about ends in the Doctrine of Virtue is in general agreement with Kant's *Groundwork* and second *Critique* discussions of such things. But our next point in the definition of ends is something new: instead of suggesting, as he did earlier, that any appeal to an end of action would undermine the a priority and freedom of one's law of action, he suggests instead (apparently precisely to the contrary) that ends are a part of free choice and even that the setting of an end is constitutive of one's free choice: "An **end** is an *object* of free choice, the representation of which determines it to an action (by which the object is brought about)" (6:384–385/149). And: "To have an end that I have not myself made an end is self-contradictory, an act of freedom which is yet not free" (6:381/147). Kant thus suggests that, instead of ends undermining the freedom of an act, they in fact facilitate it: "no free action is possible unless the agent also intends an end (which is the matter of choice)" (6:389/152).[42]

---

[42] See also 6:389/152: "[N]o *free* action is possible unless the agent also intends an end (which is the matter of choice)" (6:389/152, emphasis added). That is, not only would appeal to ends not undermine the freedom of one's *choice*, further, if I do not appeal to an end, no free *action* is possible at all! It may be that mere "*maxims* of actions can be arbitrarily chosen [willkurlich]" without appeal to ends. But once we get to the notion of a free *action*, we must appeal to an end.

Furthermore, because the setting of such ends is now itself taken to be an act of freedom, this capacity must also be seen as a capacity that is distinctive of and defining of what humans are and do as practical reasoners: "The capacity to set oneself an end—any end whatsoever—is what characterizes humanity (as distinguished from animality)" (6:392/154). Other beings may react or be caused to move by things external to them. But humans are different from animals. Humans are the kind of beings they are precisely because they are able freely to set and pursue ends—the object or matter of choice.

One has to find these new claims about the freedom of end-setting rather surprising, given Kant's strong claims, especially in the second *Critique*, that any matter of choice is precisely what *undermines* freedom. Indeed, given those earlier claims, it is incumbent upon Kant (and us) to do some serious philosophical footwork to show that end-setting can be this characteristically free human act that Kant asserts it to be, and also to show what exact sort(s) of freedom is/are operative in this account of end-setting. What this means is that, because we need first to affirm the freedom of end-setting as the first stage of defending Deontological Teleology, complete affirmation of our main point that deontological principles are inherently and simultaneously end-based or teleological will have to wait until the next chapter (I.iii). Let us turn, then, for the rest of this chapter to this first question of the freedom of end-setting, both pragmatic and moral.

A. Pragmatic Ends

Pragmatic versus Moral (Obligatory) Ends

The first thing we need to do to defend the freedom of end-setting is to make a distinction in the kinds of ends that are possible (so as to then distinguish different types of freedom that are operative in the setting of these different kinds of ends). For, although every act of end-setting is a free act and every action has an end, not every end is an obligatory end. Rather, Kant now makes a distinction in kinds of ends one can set. All ends, according to Kant, are either "pragmatic" or "moral" (that is, obligatory) ends. Pragmatic ends are "the ends the human being *adopts* according to sensuous impulses of his nature" (6:385/149). That is, these are ends I make through reference to my inclinations and desires: I find something that would satisfy my desires and thus set that thing as the matter, object, or end which I seek to achieve in action. Moral (or obligatory) ends, in contrast, are "the objects of the free faculty of choice under its laws, which [one] *ought to make* his ends" (6:385/149). That is, they are ends set without reference to inclination but, instead, with reference only to the will's own rational laws. The matter or object that I seek here is not determined by my desires or my pursuit of happiness but instead is determined through my own law-giving reason. Or, as Kant puts the point: "[a] law...takes away from action what is arbitrarily chosen" (6:389/153, translation modified). Such a law, in other words, "subordinat[es] the subjective end (that everyone has) to the objective end (that everyone ought to make his end)" (6:389/152).

According to Kant's new Doctrine of Virtue categorization of ends, then, pragmatic ends are similar to the ends we considered in the *Groundwork* and second *Critique*; they are, that is, "subjective" and "contain...the rules of prudence in the choice of one's ends" (6:385/149). But "the latter [obligatory ends] must be called the moral (objective) doctrine of ends" (6:385/149). In short, Kant is distinguishing here between ends I set simply through my desire for them in relation to my overall pursuit of happiness, and the ends I set because *a priori* laws of reason demand I set them. The former are subjective in the sense that they are grounded on things (inclinations) specific to a particular subject; but the latter are objective in the sense that they are grounded in a law of reason shared by all rational beings. Whereas pragmatic ends are the "ends the human being does adopt in keeping with the sensible impulses of his nature," moral ends are this person's ends which are "objects of free choice under its laws which he ought to make his ends" (6:385/149). They are, in other words, *obligatory* ends or "an end that, as far as human beings are concerned, it is a *duty* to have" (6:380/146, emphasis added).

We need to be careful here, though, as we draw this distinction between pragmatic and moral ends. On the face of it, it seems that Kant is drawing a distinction between ends that are determined by "sensuous impulses" and ends that are determined by "the free faculty of choice under its laws." If we accepted this distinction rigorously, though, we would have to admit that the former determination of ends is unfree and the latter is free. Yet Kant has already told us that the setting of an end—"*any* end whatsoever" (6:392/154, emphasis added)—is an act of freedom characteristic of humanity. Our first goal, then, is to make sense of how it is that, even in the adoption of these pragmatic ends related to inclination or "sensuous impulses," the actual setting of the end is free. Only after we accomplish that task will we turn to consideration of those ends most distinctive of rational beings, moral obligatory ends.

In the first instance, the freedom of all ends, including pragmatic ends, is guaranteed by a new notion that Kant introduces in the Doctrine of Virtue: the act of end-setting is an act thoroughly internal to an agent, accomplishable only by oneself, and thus free in the sense of being free from external coercion by other agents. As Kant puts the point: "I can indeed be constrained by others to perform actions that are directed as means to an end, but I can never be constrained by others to have an end; only I myself can make something my end" (6:381/146). The adoption of *any* end (pragmatic or moral) is thus something accomplished internally, only by oneself, not something that can be ordered, coerced, or enforced by persons or forces external to me.

Let's dwell on this notion of freedom for a moment. Kant's point here is that someone can indeed coerce me to *act* in a whole variety of ways and for a whole variety of reasons. I can, that is, be forced to act in ways that do not relate to my own setting of ends. Think of a mother saying to her child "Be nice to your sister!" The child can be made to engage in these acts, but she cannot be forced to adopt an end of concern for the welfare of her sister. Being forced to act in such ways is what Kant calls "coercion": "Another can indeed *coerce* me *to do* something that is not my end (but only a means to another's end)" (6:381/146). But even under such coercion, I have not been coerced into adopting an end; I have only been coerced into doing something supporting someone else's adopted end. One might say that the "matter" of my action here (since every action has a matter or end) is not "to be nice to my sister," but, at best, only "to do what my mother wants."[43] In other cases, it might be that I will eventually also claim the end associated with the action I do (e.g., the welfare of my sister) as my own end. But Kant's point is that only I can decide whether to claim this end as something that I want, as the object of my choice, and the act of end-setting is thus free in this sense of not being externally coerce-able. This is the most internal, the most intimate, of free acts for a rational, choosing being.[44]

In what sense, then, is such capacity for the setting of ends a specifically *free* act? The notion of freedom in play here is one version of what we have already called "negative freedom." That is, when I set an end, I am free from alien influence on my will, with the "alien" influence in question here being the would-be influence of the wills and intentions of other persons external to me. When I enter the realm of end-setting, it is as if I situate myself in a hermetically sealed space where no one else can find or influence me. Setting ends is entirely up to me: the ends I set are the ends *I* set, and even if others would want to influence

---

[43] It may in fact be that some or all examples of coercion are cases in which there is no end of the coerced person as such and, thus, by definition, no action as such. It is an interesting question: if there might be at least some cases of coercion in which one has to admit that the person being coerced is not "acting" as such, that is, that the person being coerced, because she has *no* end as such, is, in effect, doing nothing, then we need to admit that no "action" as such is going on here. She is only having someone else move her around. It thus might be that, in cases of coercion, it isn't entirely proper to speak of there being an end to the action at all, and, thus, by definition, of there being an "*action*" at all.

[44] The claims Kant makes here also raise interesting questions about what exactly it means to have or set an end, especially once we remember that this capacity to set ends extends beyond the realm of obligatory to "any end whatsoever": "The capacity to set oneself an end—any end whatsoever—is what characterizes humanity (as distinguished from animality)" (6:392/154). It is clear enough that having an end is something more than externally acting in a way that brings about a future state of affairs. I can be coerced into such actions, so this is not the definition of having an end. But what exactly beyond engaging in such actions is required for having an end is unclear. It seems that having an end is a more long-term state of one's will (e.g., the "welfare of my sister" is something that might be realized in a series of actions over a long period of time, and not just in one action). But even appeal to a series of actions extended in time does not itself complete the idea of having an end, since a series of actions could be compelled or coerced as easily as a single action. Having an end thus needs to involve appeal to something entirely internal, something about the state of one's will, perhaps also the state of one's desires, inclinations, and person overall. For excellent discussion of such matters, see Fahmy (2015).

me in my end-setting, they are not capable of doing so. My choices of ends are inevitably and truly my own.

Kant's main concern in introducing this particular notion of freedom to end-setting is to distinguish end-setting from other sorts of things to which I *can* be externally coerced. That is, he is distinguishing the realm of virtue from the realm of right. In the realm of right, there *are* constraints on my actions that can be imposed upon me from persons external to me. If I don't repay a debt, I can have my paycheck garnished. If I try to kill someone, others can intervene to stop me. These are matters for the realm of right, duties I have that can be externally enforced if I fail internally to enforce them. But Kant is preparing here for the realm of virtue, a realm defined by the setting of ends, and thus a realm wherein no one else can force me to do anything. As such, he emphasizes an act—the setting of ends—which *cannot* be externally enforced. And so: someone can indeed coerce me into doing something, but no one can coerce me into that act of will by which I choose to set something as my end. And to claim this sort of negative freedom in end-setting is at least a partial response to the earlier Kant who worried that all end-setting was empirical and therefore unfree. The freedom from coercion from others is at least avoiding the determination of one's will from one set of would-be external empirical determinants: viz., the will and/or resulting physical force imposed on us by others.

But appeal to freedom in this sense does not yet resolve what was at the heart of the earlier Kant's worries about how ends undermine freedom. After all, his bigger worry there, when he insisted that empirical ends were unfree, was that empirical ends were, one and all, grounded in some inclination or desire; and it was this relationship to inclination (and not the presence of some external force in the form of another person) that was really compromising the would-be freedom of one's end-setting. There are even points in the Doctrine of Virtue which make it seem that Kant is resigned to the idea that at least some ends, because they are grounded in one's inclinations, continue to have this problematically empirical and unfree nature. As we have already seen, he describes pragmatic ends as ones "adopt[ed] in keeping with the sensible impulses of [one's] nature" (6:385/149); that is, they are adopted on the basis of whatever inclination or desire one might have. If I have a strong desire for cheesecake, I might, with reference to that desire, set an end to eat cheesecake once a week. But, problematically, Kant, at times, right in the middle of asserting one's choice of ends as free, seems simultaneously to suggest that such an end of my action (here, the cheesecake) in fact *determines* my action: "An **end** is an *object* of free choice, the representation of which *determines* it to an action (by which the object is brought about)" (6:384/149, last emphasis added).[45] As such, even if my pragmatic end-setting

---

[45] See also 6:381/146: "An *end* is an object of the choice (of a rational being), through the representation of which choice is determined to an action to bring this object about."

cannot be coerced by persons external to me, it seems one might still be coerced or forced to end-setting by the object or matter of that end to which I am connected by inclination (here, the cheesecake).

Furthermore, Kant does not, in the Doctrine of Virtue, reflect upon just that idea that would help him avoid such a problematic conclusion: incorporation. That discussion, as is well-known, is found in the *Religion*.[46] But Kant does reflect in the Doctrine of Virtue on the crucial relation of maxims to ends. It is in these discussions that we can connect the *Religion* discussion of incorporation of maxims to the just suggested Doctrine of Virtue determination of ends. In so doing, we can find reasonable textual support for extending freedom as incorporation to the act of end-setting. Indeed, the Kant of the Doctrine of Virtue, in league with the Kant of the *Religion*, can overcome these fears that ends remain irreducibly empirical and unfree.

The Free Incorporation of Ends

Let us thus consider Kant's recognition of the freedom in the setting of *all* ends ("any end whatsoever" (6:392/154)) in light of the Incorporation Thesis. First, as has been much discussed in the literature, according to the Incorporation Thesis, when I act on an empirical maxim involving appeal to my inclinations, I am in fact not determined directly by my inclination for, e.g., cheesecake, but am instead freely incorporating my inclination for cheesecake into a reason or maxim for action. In this process of incorporation, I essentially turn my inclination or desire into a reason by deciding that there is good reason to accept its sway upon me. So much has been repeatedly argued and affirmed in recent literature.

What has been less noted in this famously quoted passage is that Kant speaks of incorporation as extending not just to the determination of a *maxim* but also to the realization of that maxim in *action*. As he notes, one's "power of choice...cannot be determined *to action* through any incentive except so far as the human being has incorporated it into his maxim" (6:23–24/49, emphases removed and added). That is, free incorporation of an incentive into one's maxim is not limited to the choice of a maxim. Such free incorporation, in order to be successfully free (and, as we've noted above, fully practical), needs to realize itself not only in the choosing of a general maxim or policy but also in the realization of that maxim in specific *actions* associated with the chosen maxim. As such, we find ourselves in the territory of ends; for, as we recall, "*every*...action has its end" (6:385/149, emphasis added). To claim the spoils of victory for freedom in the act of incorporation, we must thus broaden our conception of what incorporation involves. First, one incorporates one's inclinations into the choice of a maxim; but then one incorporates that same inclination within the free setting of an end of action, the pursuit of which realizes that freely chosen maxim *in action*.

---

[46] See *Religion*, 6:23–24/49.

The Kant of the *Religion* does not make a clear distinction between maxim adoption and action. But, as we've already noted, the Kant of the Doctrine of Virtue, regularly affirms just such a distinction, a sort of movement from maxim choice to action that goes via end-setting. An end "determines [choice] *to* an action" (6:385/149, emphasis added); and, again, "*choice* is determined *to* an *action* to bring this object [viz., the end] about" (6:381/146, emphases added). He even later suggests, in passing, that "the law...prescribes only *the maxim of the action*...and hence not the *action itself*" (6:392/155), implying that the action itself needs to be determined by some further free act (now, of end-setting).

If all of this is the case, then, by bringing Kant's *Religion* discussion of incorporation together with his Doctrine of Virtue distinction between choice and action, we can affirm a two-stage process of incorporation, first in the choice of one's maxim and second in the setting of one's end which realizes that maxim in action. And, when we do affirm this two-step incorporation, even the setting of pragmatic ends, which appeal to inclinations, is thus free in the sense that (like any chosen thing) I have *chosen* to incorporate that inclination at the ground of my maxim and now also have freely set the corresponding end for action in relation to that inclination as so incorporated. The freedom of the choosing of my maxim extends itself into the freedom of the setting of my end and, ultimately, into free action. I am thus, in both maxim choosing and end-setting, never directly determined by inclinations or their external objects; I only always freely choose to place myself under their sway first in the choosing of my maxim and then in the setting of an end related to that maxim. In virtue of the Incorporation Thesis, both maxim-setting and end-setting which leads to action are free. A freely chosen maxim of choice thus flows naturally into a freely chosen matter of choice, or end.[47]

Interestingly, it is difficult to assess the extent to which recent interpreters have focused on the possibility of incorporating ends of actions as well as maxims. I suspect this ambiguity is traceable ultimately to Allison (1990) himself, the first person to put emphasis on the notion of incorporation. In reviewing his groundbreaking discussion of incorporation, it is not evident to me that he makes any explicit distinction between incorporation in maxim adoption as compared to incorporation in end-setting based on a maxim, this despite the fact that his most important grounding text—Kant's lamentably brief discussion of incorporation in the *Religion* just quoted above—does explicitly appeal to the need for incorporation to extend to actions and, thus, as we have just argued, to ends.

When, for example, Allison initially details the Incorporation Thesis, he describes incentives as incorporated into a reason for action generally, suggesting

---

[47] It is worth nothing that it is precisely this natural connection or flow from maxim to end that Kant needed, unnaturally, to interrupt or separate when, in the *Groundwork*, he sought a maxim that could be determined thoroughly *a priori* and without any reference to the material of choice.

perhaps that such incorporation would presumably include both maxim adoption and end-setting: "to the extent to which such [desire-based] actions are taken as genuine expressions of agency [...] they are thought to involve an act of spontaneity on the part of the agent, through which the inclination or desire is deemed or taken as an *appropriate basis of action*" (Allison 1990, 39; emphasis added). And Allison does affirm that ends are implicitly constitutive of maxims, an idea implying perhaps that end-setting is part and parcel of maxim adoption rather than a separate internal choice as I've suggested:

> every maxim reflects an underlying *interest* of the agent [...] a reference to this interest is implicit in every maxim [...] implicit in every *maxim* is the assumption that the selected action type is, under the particular circumstances (the existence of an S-type situation), the best available means for the attainment of the chosen *end*. (Allison 1990, 90–91; emphasis added)

Allison also clearly holds that free end-setting is a constitutive part of rational agency:

> I cannot conceive of myself as such an [rational] agent without regarding myself as pursuing *ends that I frame for myself* [...] I cannot conceive of myself as such an agent without assuming that I have a certain control over my inclinations, that I am capable of deciding which of them *are to be acted upon*.
> (Allison 1990, 41, emphasis added)

But despite all these implicit appeals to ends in his discussion, Allison's clearest articulation of what incorporation is makes clear that it is specifically *maxims* into which incentives are incorporated: "incentives do not motivate by themselves causing action but rather by being taken as reasons and incorporated *into maxims*" (Allison 1990, 51, emphasis added). In short, Allison fails to make an explicit distinction between incorporation of maxim adoption and incorporation of end-setting necessary for the realization of such maxims in action; instead, he holds that ends are implicitly a part of maxims generally and thus that incorporation applies to a reason for action generally. In other words, Allison is, at best, ambiguous on the question of whether one incorporates inclinations into ends as well as into maxims, and whether this is a singular or a two-step process.

This ambiguity haunts later literature on the topic as well. For example, Potter (1994) clearly asserts that the freedom of incorporation extends to end-setting:

> The "standard account" of maxims is going to be incorrect insofar as it is offered as a complete interpretation, because it fails to take account of Kant's view that we not only choose and hence are responsible for our own actions, but that we also choose our ends of action and our own underlying character. (Potter 1994, 63)

Here, we at least have reference to two distinct acts of choice, one of "action" and one of "ends of action" (as well as, actually, of a third choice of "character"). Nonetheless, this account also seems to collapse the act of end-setting into the act of maxim adoption, or at minimum fails to make a truly clear distinction between them (note, for example, in the above quote that the language of "maxim" never actually appears).

We thus offer our own just completed account as at least a clarification of what is only implicit in current literature. A full understanding of incorporation demands that we understand that act in two parts: first, an incorporation of inclinations into maxims; and then a further incorporation into chosen ends of action. It may be that, as Allison suggest, incorporation into an end can occur simultaneously with incorporation into a maxim. But, for clarity, we emphasize this as a two-part process.

And this expansion of incorporation to ends makes perfect sense, and is, indeed, necessary in order to defend the idea that actions as well as wills can be free. Every action on a maxim has an end. So, when I seek in fact to *act* on that maxim (e.g., of eating cheesecake once a week), I *have* to claim an end to my action: the actual achievement of eating the cheesecake (or, perhaps, the management of my cheesecake desires in light of my overall interest in health and weight management). If my free reason-making only went as far as my maxim and didn't extend to the pursuit of the actual end itself, we would be in the odd situation of freely choosing a reason for action, but then, in the would-be action itself, finding ourselves empirically determined either by an entirely nonrational object external to my will or by the sensible inclination associated with that object. This is, perhaps, the worry that Kant had in mind previously when, in the second *Critique*, he called all ends "empirical." Ends thusly construed do indeed seem thoroughly to undermine the freedom of one's action. And yet, with appeal to the incorporation Thesis, now as extended to the incorporation of one's inclinations into the free setting of pragmatic ends, we can resolve this dilemma.

In fact, if we revisit those Doctrine of Virtue passages that seemed to imply an unfree, sensible determination of one's ends, we discover, with the help of Incorporation Thesis thoughts, a more complex story. Consider the two most relevant passages in which it seemed that even the Kant of the Doctrine of Virtue was accepting that our will is determined by that object external to our will that constitutes an end:

> An *end* is an object of the choice (of a rational being), through the representation of which choice is determined to an action to bring this object about.
> (6:381/146)

> An **end** is an *object* of free choice, the representation of which determines it to an action (by which the object is brought about). (6:384–385/149)

In both these passages, we find the language of the "representation" of an end. It is not an *end* (i.e., some material thing separate from me) as such but, more precisely, the *representation* of an end (i.e., my taking up of this material thing) that does the work of determining the movement from choice to action. Kant offers no hints about how he construes the exact nature of this representation. But it is not unreasonable to construe "representation" here as a conscious rational act,[48] one whereby one incorporates the object of one's inclination into a rationally set end. Indeed, it is not unreasonable to surmise that Kant's thinking about incorporation from the *Religion* (1793) informed his thinking about end-setting as a rational act in the Doctrine of Virtue (1797). Even if it did not, acceding to just this reading of the representation of ends via the language of incorporation is precisely what Kant needs so as to confirm his strong and unwavering claim that the setting of an end—any end whatsoever—is an ultimate act of freedom.

Once we accept this extended version of the Incorporation Thesis so as to include the free incorporation of the object of one's inclination in the setting of an end, we can thus confidently speak of the setting of even empirical ends as free at least in the minimal sense of having negative freedom. That is, when I choose to incorporate my inclination for cheesecake into a maxim of action and thus set the end of my action of eating cheesecake when I actually act on the maxim, I am not determined by something alien to me. It is not that the merely physical, natural object external to my will (the cheesecake) determines my will, or even that my desire for that external object determines my will. My will is, rather, determined first through my rational choice to incorporate my desire for cheesecake into my maxim and then through my rational incorporation of the object of that inclination into the setting of an end of action.

I thus claim a pragmatic end without being determined by an empirical object external to me, or even by a sensible impulse internal to me but external to my rational, choosing self. Avoiding such determination by inclination is, ultimately, just another account (next to the avoidance of being determined by some other person external to me) of how I avoid being determined by something "external" to me, since both the object of the inclination and the inclination itself are things external to me in the sense that neither is an aspect of my rational will. Without this intervening act of representation or incorporation, either or both this object and my inclination for it would influence my will (either directly via the object or indirectly via that inclination I have for the object). But with this rational act of representing to myself (and thereby incorporating) the object of my end-setting, we can welcome even such pragmatic end-setting as negatively free.

It is, however, important to note that while pragmatic ends will thus be at least negatively free in just this sense, these freely set ends will still (like the empirical

---

[48] As opposed to that implicit transcendental occurrence of representation by which we represent to ourselves the thing-in-itself, now ordered by intuitions and concepts, as an object of experience.

ends of the *Groundwork* and second *Critique*) be both *subjective* (viz., not applicable to all rational beings but instead only to those individual persons who possess the relevant inclination) and *relative* (viz., not claiming the end as absolutely and non-contingently valuable, but only as valuable as the desire grounding it, relative to other desires). It is not until later in this chapter, when we affirm the category of obligatory ends, that we fully welcome ends into Kant's project of grounding an *a priori* morality and virtue, since the ends of virtue we will discover will be both objective (not merely subjective) and absolute (not relative).

"The Dutiful Maxim Test" for Pragmatic Ends

There is a final sense in which pragmatic ends can be said to be freely set. To appreciate this further sense of the freedom of pragmatic ends, we need however to take a small detour into Kant's Doctrine of Virtue discussion of the relationship of pragmatic ends to dutiful maxims of action, that is, into the question of the agreement of one's pragmatic ends with maxims approved by the moral law.

Here, then, is how Kant explains the relationship of the setting of pragmatic ends to the claiming of dutiful maxims. When we speak of the setting of pragmatic ends, we are not beginning with a concern for duty in our end-setting. To the contrary, we are, at best, placing any concern for the dutifulness of one's maxims *after* both the claiming of a maxim and the setting of the end. That is, I set a pragmatic end on the basis of my freely chosen maxim which incorporates an inclination, and only then raise the question of what moral constraints there might be on the proposed maxim, end, and action. As Kant puts the point: "one can begin with the end and seek out the maxim of actions in conformity with duty" (6:382/147).

This is not, however, an understanding of the order of ends and dutiful maxims appropriate to the pursuit of virtue. Rather, it is the order of ends and dutiful maxims most appropriate to the pursuit of the fulfillment of those duties identified in the Doctrine of Right. As Kant notes, in the realm of right, "[w]hat *end* anyone wants to set for his action is left to his free choice. The *maxim* of his action, however, is determined a priori, namely, that the freedom of the agent could coexist with the freedom of every other in accordance with a universal law" (6:382/147, emphasis added). That is, when we are concerned only with those duties that are externally enforceable, we are concerned only to assure that one's free pursuit of one's pragmatic ends is not in conflict with other persons' free pursuit of their pragmatic ends.

And yet, in so doing, we can, even when beginning only with an empirical, pragmatic end, bring a moral concern for the mere form of one's maxim related to that end to the table so as to assure that both one's freely chosen maxim and one's freely set end can pass what one might call the Dutiful Maxim Test: one's pragmatic ends are deemed permissible only if the maxim from which they emerge is such that it does not interfere with other persons' free setting of ends. Duties of right thus determine the moral constraints upon what pragmatic ends I can set. Of course, not all pragmatic ends will meet this constraint. It is just wrong to do certain things, and if I try to do them, I will be externally constrained. But there are also pragmatic ends that will pass this dutiful maxim test.

But in relating pragmatic end-setting to duties of right in this way, we have simultaneously introduced another sense in which the setting of at least some of these ends can be said to be free: in addition to all pragmatic ends (and indeed all ends as such) being negatively free in that I freely choose the matter of that end as the realization of my maxim, those pragmatic ends which also pass the Dutiful Maxim Test can be said to be free in the sense that they define the realm of what I can freely set for myself without interfering with the similar free choice of other agents around me. I am not coercing them, and they are not coercing me.

Conclusion and Caveat

We can thus, despite Kant's earlier worries to the contrary, indeed appreciate end-setting—the setting of *any* end whatsoever, pragmatic or moral/obligatory—as a free act:

> [D]etermination to an end is the only determination of choice the very concept of which excludes the possibility of constraint *through natural means* by the choice of another. Another can indeed *coerce* me *to do* something that is not my end (but only a means to another's end), but not to *make this my end*; and yet I can have no end without making it an end for myself. To have an end that I have not myself made an end is self-contradictory, an act of freedom which is yet not free. (6:381/146–147)

Kant's heart-felt claiming of the freedom of end-setting articulated here focuses on not being coerced by others to set an end. But, in fact, we have affirmed the freedom of end-setting in three distinct senses. First, in the setting of any end, I am not coerced by anyone external to me. Second, in virtue of the incorporation of my end, I am not determined by any object or material external to me, nor by any inclination internal to me which connects me to that object or material. This is true even when that end-setting occurs in relation to the empirical or sensuous impulses of my nature because the very act of end-setting, like that of the incorporation of incentives into one's maxim, assures that the ground of my setting this end is a reason based upon that object of inclination and not a direct empirical determination by the sensible inclination (or by the object which constitutes the end) itself. Finally, for those pragmatic ends which pass the Dutiful Maxim Test, my setting of ends can be said to be free in the sense that it does not interfere with the free end-setting of other rational agents.

The earlier *Groundwork* and second *Critique* worries of Kant are thus resolved. Even if one had to admit that all of our ends are empirical in the limited sense that they all appeal to inclinations in their setting, they would all still nonetheless be free in the sense that they were freely *set* in these three ways. In the setting of an end—"any end whatsoever" (6:392/154)—objects of my empirical inclinations do not directly determine my end-setting, but are taken up as rationally chosen ends.

We thus accept pragmatic end-setting as a negatively free act. We need, however, to introduce a caveat to this claim: the possibility for such freedom piggybacks necessarily upon the assumption of a deeper sense of positive freedom yet to be discussed. In short, I am sympathetic with Iain Morrisson's (2008) argument in relation to Allison's account of the Incorporation Thesis, that merely negative freedom cannot be self-sustaining because, in the pursuit of pragmatic ends, we have nothing but desire "all the way down" to guide that rational distancing we seek in our relationship to our inclinations, that distance from them that would assure they are freely chosen in maxims and freely set as ends. Morrison's worry is that reasons grounded only in a merely Hypothetical Imperatives aren't really reasons, not true transformations of one's inclination into a "reason," but only desires all the way down, and he argues as much in relation to the incorporation of inclinations into maxim. But this is a problem for incorporation of the object of one's inclinations into ends as well: to assure the freedom of pragmatic end-setting, we need at least indirectly to refer to the Categorical Imperative (and either its acceptance or its rejection in the form of either the moral disposition or a radically evil disposition) as the rule under which such incorporation ultimately occurs. The freedom we have here affirmed for pragmatic ends thus depends, ultimately, upon the deeper sense of freedom we're going to consider in the next section.[49]

B. Moral or Obligatory Ends

Introduction

Having affirmed the freedom of all end-setting, we can now finally consider the nature of those freely set ends which are also obligatory ends, or ends that are also duties. The setting of such ends is, furthermore, not only the height of freedom for sensibly affected rational beings but also a *freedom* which constitutes *virtue*. That is, in the setting of obligatory ends via appeal only to one's own rational principles and without any appeal to one's inclinations, free end-setting is brought

---

[49] This more "moralized" understanding of freedom will, furthermore, undergird my forthcoming more moralized understanding of virtuous end-setting generally. As we shall see in Part II, I defend a strongly moralized conception of end-setting in which everything I choose—including those things I choose in hopes of realizing my happiness empirically conceived—needs to be evaluated in light of the moral demand to respect persons.

to the level of what Kant calls "inner freedom" (or "internal freedom"),[50] a free capacity to constrain oneself to obligatory ends that is constitutive of virtue. Such virtuous constraint is not coercion, nor determination of one's will by anything alien to it, but instead a free self-constraint to obligatory ends in accordance with one's own rational law which demands at all times that one respect persons. In affirming this broadening of the category of the kinds of end-setting possible for sensibly affected rational beings, and in pointing toward the ground of all such objectively valid obligatory ends in the rational and strictly necessary demand to respect persons, we simultaneously conclude our first defense of Kant's theory of virtue as one of Deontological Teleology.

Obligatory Ends

Let us turn then, to consideration of the realm of obligatory ends. We have already seen an end is the matter of one's choice and, further, that all ends, pragmatic or obligatory, are negatively free in several senses. In affirming this negative freedom for end-setting generally, we thus accomplish one response to the Kant of the *Groundwork* and second *Critique* who worried that appeal to any material end would undermine the freedom of that action within which such end was involved.

There is, however, a further response to provide to the worries of our earlier Kant. Recall that, previously, he had said that all ends are empirical ends: "the matter of a practical law, that is, an object of maxim can never be given otherwise than empirically" (5:29/26). As such, even though pragmatic ends are free in the senses just described above, we still have to grant to the earlier Kant the point that these ends remain "empirical" at least in the sense that they require reference to one's inclinations in order to be set. Furthermore, if inclination-based ends are the only ends that exist, then we would need to admit that all ends, despite being freely set in the ways we've just discussed, are still, as Kant originally asserted in the *Groundwork*, only subjective and relative, that is, dependent upon arbitrarily chosen coincidental quirks or desires of individual persons. There would be no ends that all persons share, objectively.

But the Kant of the Doctrine of Virtue, by introducing the new category of moral, or obligatory, ends—a.k.a. ends that are also duties—presents an even further challenge to his earlier self who claimed that all ends were only empirical, subjective, and relative:

> The doctrine of right dealt only with the *formal* condition of outer freedom (the consistency of outer freedom with itself if its maxim were made universal law), that is, with **Right**. But ethics goes beyond this and provides a *matter* (an object of free choice), and **end** of pure reason which it represents as an end that is also

---

[50] See especially 6:380–381/155–156, 6:394–395/167–168, and 6:405–408/175–178.

objectively necessary, that is, an end that, as far as human beings are concerned, it is a duty to have. (6:380/146)

By introducing these obligatory ends that are also duties, Kant thus now suggests that there are indeed ends that all persons share, objectively, and which therefore are not contingently and empirically determined through whatever a person happens to like, but instead are absolutely and rationally demanded of all rational agents. That is, he asserts we must welcome a realm of "objective end[s] (that everyone ought to make his end)" (6:389/152). We now have not only an objective and rationally determined *a priori form* of moral maxims but also objective, rationally determined, and *a priori matters*, objects, or ends of those maxims. We have, that is, obligatory or moral ends.

Let's reflect more on the process of the free determination of such obligatory ends.

Back in the *Groundwork*, Kant had made a problem for himself for the very possibility of such ends when he insisted that moral maxims could be determined without any reference at all to the matter or object of the maxim. As such, when we speak of adopting a maxim which is universalizable without contradiction, we are speaking of a maxim that in fact has no reference at all to an end. That is what made such maxims universalizable and distinguished them as specifically moral maxims, distinct from empirical maxims. But with the introduction of obligatory ends, we are now seeking to reintroduce ends to *a priori* morality. We are, that is, seeking a deduction of those ends that are also duties, a deduction not only of the form but also of the matter of one's obligatory maxims through appeal only to pure reason, not inclinations. Indeed, if we are actually going to speak of actions that need to occur in accordance with this merely formal maxim, we need *some* matter, object, or end toward which to act. For (to repeat) *every* action has its end. So, in order to move from the choice of that maxim to action, I need some matter upon which to act. I need, in other words, an end. But with a moral maxim, all we have is the mere form of the maxim, but (as Hegel reminds us) we have no idea on what matter exactly to act until we get that matter or end from somewhere.

How, then, does one freely determine these specific obligatory matters (or ends) for moral maxims? That is, how can we freely determine *material* but *a priori* ends of action? One could seek to review one's various inclinations to identify various would-be matters of choice. But this, of course, would undermine the *a priori* purity of one's process of end-setting. At best, in this case, one could, as in the case of pragmatic ends, after identifying one's inclination and its object, revisit the Categorical Imperative to determine whether its pursuit is permissible (not in conflict with others' pursuit of freedom, as in the Doctrine of Right). But in the obligatory case, instead of appealing to inclination to identify one's end or matter so as to move to action, one needs something else, another way of identifying that matter. Obligatory ends, or ends that are also duties—that new "matter" being added to the previously merely formal articulation of our duties—must, in order for them to be affirmed as *a priori* ends, be determined without *any* appeal to inclination. Instead, such ends are determined only through appeal to pure reason. In so doing, one determines ends which hold for all rational beings, that is, which hold objectively (and not merely subjectively, dependent upon what inclinations one might or might not have): "ethics...provides a *matter* (an object of free choice), and **end** of pure reason which it represents as an end that is also objectively necessary, that is, an end that, as far as human beings are concerned, it is a duty to have" (6:380/146).

To assure the free setting of an objective, obligatory, and *a priori* end or matter of choice, I thus simply cannot turn to my inclinations to "fill in the blanks" of my formal choice, depending on them to determine the precise ends I seek. And in rejecting inclination as the basis upon which I freely set my ends of action, I take my capacity for free end-setting to a new, higher level. This is because, when I determine my ends solely by reason, I can now assure that my ends are *not* empirical, at least in the sense that they are not determined with reference to inclinations. As such, while these ends introduce specific matter of choice and make one's formal maxims more precise, material, and prepared for the experiential world of action thereby, they nonetheless escape the relativity and subjectivity of ends grounded only in idiosyncratic inclinations, grounding themselves instead in an objective and *a priori* notion of reason shared by all persons. We thus have what has to be admitted is an empirical *matter* of choice that is not empirically *grounded*. As Kant puts the point: "[E]thics...provides a matter (an object of free choice), an end of pure reason which it represents as an end that is also objectively necessary" (6:380/146). We finally have a matter of choice adequate for putting my maxims into action that finds its ground somewhere other than in our inclinations and pursuit of happiness. We have, that is, ends—m*atters* of choice— that are *a priori* objectively valid for all sensibly affected rational beings because they are grounded not in any passing, subjective, or relative inclinations of such beings, but only in the reason which defines those beings as rational beings.

When we are concerned with the free setting of these objective and *a priori* obligatory ends, we must thus understand their relation to maxims of duty differently than we did with pragmatic ends. Whereas with pragmatic ends, we begin with the end we want (determined through appeal to our inclinations) and then ask what constraints are placed on my action by morality, with moral or obligatory ends, "one can begin with the *maxim* of actions in conformity with duty and [then] seek out the end that is also a duty...Hence in ethics the concept of duty will lead to ends and will have to establish maxims with respect to ends we ought to set ourselves, grounding them [viz., these ends] in accordance with moral principles" (6:382/147, emphasis added). That is, in the setting of obligatory ends, one starts with those maxims which affirm our duty in formal terms, and *then* seeks out specific objects or matters of choice that are incumbent upon us in virtue of the demands of the moral law itself.

When I set an end in this way, I thus do so without any empirical influence; that is, I set an end, or matter of choice, without needing to appeal to any inclination or object of desire that would determine the content of my end. We have, in other words, determined *a priori* a set of objectively valid obligatory ends, or ends that are also duties. As Kant puts it, such objective ends are "*given* a priori, independently of inclinations" (6:381/146, emphases added and removed). That is, although they are indeed matters of choice—specific material goals of action—we do not determine them via any appeal to experience. Rather, once again, they are determined only via appeal to reason, previous to experience, i.e. *a priori*.

Some reflection on this interesting category of *a priori* matters of choice is, however, in order. After all, these ends contain what one might call an ironic structure. When I identify obligatory ends only on the basis of what is demanded by an *a priori* law of reason, I am, in effect, identifying a *matter* of choice that in fact *is* an empirical thing in one sense: it is a matter of choice, some material thing in the world that I seek to accomplish. But this empirical thing in the world is not empirically *determined*. That is, it is not chosen on the basis of any would-be empirical inclination for that end. One might thus say that an obligatory end is a little bit like *a priori* intuition. That is, in the Transcendental Aesthetic, Kant worried about the question of how one could speak at all of *a priori* intuition, i.e. an intuition that is, by definition, something "given" (present in experience) and yet still somehow *a priori*, or *previous* to experience. The notion of an obligatory end shares this same commitment to the idea that we can identify *a priori* conditions or structures in empirical entities: while pursuing understanding of an actual material thing in the world of experience, one appeals to *a priori* laws previous to experience (either a notion of pure intuition as a transcendental condition for the possibility of claims of geometry and arithmetic, or a notion of the laws of practical pure reason as a ground for actual empirical but still obligatory ends).

Such a matter of choice that is not empirically determined is, of course, exactly what Kant thought one could not accomplish in the *Groundwork*. There, as we have seen, he took every end to be empirical in the latter, problematic sense of being determined through reference to inclination, and thus sought *a priori* laws of morality only in the mere form of our maxims, not in our ends:

> The ends that a rational being intends at its discretion as effects of its actions (material ends) are one and all only relative; *for merely their relation to a particular kind of desiderative faculty of the subject gives them their worth*, which can therefore furnish no universal principles that are valid as well as necessary for

all rational beings, or for all willing, i.e., practical laws. That is why all these relative ends are the ground of hypothetical imperatives only.

(4:427–428/40, emphases added)[51]

But now we are genuinely able to speak of a material end that, despite being a material and empirical component of action, is not empirically determined and, indeed, is *set a priori*, involving no appeal to one's inclinations. The *Groundwork* limitation on all ends being merely empirical is thus overcome through this new notion of obligatory ends. We can, that is, welcome material ends that are objective, *a* priori, and obligatory, and not just subjective, relative, and arbitrary. Amongst our subjective and relative ends there are also objective, obligatory, and necessary ones, ends which, as he says, "everyone ought to make his end" (6:389/152).

And in introducing this new category of objective and obligatory ends, we put our finger on that aspect of Kant's virtue theory that really moves it into the realm of the teleological. If inclination-based ends were the only ends that existed, then we would need to admit Kant's *Groundwork* claim that all ends, despite being freely set, are only subjective and relative, that is, dependent upon coincidental quirks or desires of individual persons. There would be no ends that all persons share, objectively. Tragically, of course, we would also have to admit that pure reason could not be practical at all, since, although it could determine maxims *a priori*, it could not carry that practical reasoning further into the realm of ends and action.[52]

But the introduction of obligatory ends is the introduction of ends that all persons share, objectively, and the basis upon which we can claim the victory of pure reason as practical. As such, focusing upon them gives us the potential to tell a story about what ends can be demanded of persons as moral beings and, ultimately, a story about that ultimate telos or end which guides (or "deduces") all these individual objective ends of a virtuous life. That is, because we can now focus not only upon that form of maxim that is obligatory but also, and more centrally, upon those matters or objects of our choosing that are obligatory, we have the potential to speak more specifically, concretely, and materially about exactly what sorts of actions are demanded by duty. We can, that is, seek to identify that realm of ends that are also duties. Ultimately, by showing (as we will in

---

[51] One could, more generously, suggest that Kant assumes the possibility of this non-empirical set of ends in the *Groundwork* but does not explicitly discuss it. After all, he states, more precisely, that "all ends that a rational being intends at its discretion" are material, subjective, and relative. Does this mean that, even here in the *Groundwork*, although Kant himself does not speak of them, one could make room for obligatory ends (viz., ends that a rational being does not intend at its discretion but is instead obligated to via its very nature) that could be understood as material, but objective and absolute (instead of subjective and relative)?

[52] In I.iv, we shall consider at much greater length Kant's argument for the inherent contradiction in any would-be practical reason that cannot carry its determinations into the realm of ends and, correspondingly, his positive deduction of an objective end and telos for end-setting generally.

I.iii and I.iv) that such objective and obligatory ends are all guided by appeal to one overarching objective end of respecting persons, we'll be able, finally, to affirm Kant's commitment to what can now reasonably be called an objective telos of virtue: to say Kant deduces a range of obligatory ends guided by one existing end of personhood is just another way of saying that Kant affirms an *a priori* telos or organizing end or goal of respecting persons that guides the free development of that governance of desire that is virtue. Such *desire-governance* is, furthermore, better understood at this point as *end-setting*, i.e. desire is successfully governed when we tie the encouragement of some desires and the discouragement or control of others with the setting of those ends that are obligatory.

There is, ultimately, much that we need to say about the deduction of these obligatory ends. Most importantly, we still need to consider exactly *how* reason determines them, thereby affirming their objectivity and, simultaneously, reason's practicality. This is, however, a task we will not take on until I.iii and I.iv. What we shall see there is that, in order to deduce these ends, the formal law of reason itself needs to take on material clothing; that is, it needs itself to push toward material expression of itself. It will be in such "materialized" versions of both FUL and FH—and, ultimately, in a privileging of the materialized version of FH—that we will, finally affirm the substantive, objective, and materialized but still *a priori* telos of virtue, respect for persons. The ultimate objective end of respect for persons—an end which we can now identify as the telos of sensibly affected rational beings—is thus that means by which one determines that more lengthy list of obligatory ends that are also duties. In short, every obligatory end that is also a duty is thusly obligatory precisely because it is one example of an objectively valid end of action through which one seeks to affirm respect for persons, both oneself and others. Ultimately, what emerges is affirmation that pure reason is both deontological in the sense of determining those maxims which are moral and teleological in the sense of guiding would-be virtuous persons toward those ends obligatory and incumbent upon them so as to realize the value of persons as rational beings. All this, however, will be the task of the next chapter.

But our next goal, one which will bring to a conclusion this chapter's concern to make sense of the freedom of end-setting, is to make sense of the precise sense in which the setting of such obligatory ends (whatever their precise content) is free, over and above that freedom we have already affirmed for end-setting generally. How, then, can we make sense of the freedom of a will which has not only an obligatory form of its maxims but also an obligatory *end*, viz. an end that is objectively and absolutely required of that will but is not externally or empirically given? Otherwise stated: how is it that I have an obligatory matter of choice which I nonetheless adopt freely, and in what new sense(s) of the term can we say that this will is "free"? In answering this question we shall, finally, affirm that special and virtuous "inner freedom" via which one sets these obligatory ends which are also duties.

Free, Obligatory Ends are the Heart of Virtuous Inner Freedom

What, then, is distinctively free about the setting of this special category of obligatory ends? Most centrally, a freedom is assured for these ends that goes beyond that freedom already affirmed for pragmatic ends. This further freedom (and, along with that, removal from the subjectivity and relativity to which merely pragmatic ends are still subject) is assured because the adoption of moral, or obligatory, ends has this further removal or "independence from inclination" (6:381/146) beyond that already articulated for pragmatic ends. Whereas pragmatic end-setting is free in that I freely act in a way not constrainable by other acting agents external to me, and I freely choose to incorporate an inclination instead of being directly determined by it or its object, the setting of obligatory ends, beyond all this, simply involves no appeal whatsoever to inclination. It is this *complete* independence from inclination which identifies these ends as not only freely *adopted* ends (in the above-given senses) but also as ends freely "*given a priori, independently of inclinations*" (6:381/146, emphases added and removed). In effect, because these ends are set without reference to what I desire, they are determined only by my law-giving reason. As such, the setting of them expresses not only negative freedom (by which I avoid determination by something external to me) but also that positive freedom by which I identify myself and my own reason as the sole source of the determination of my will. In the setting of these obligatory ends, reason thus freely and *a priori* determines not only the form but also the matter of that to which I am obligated.

We can thus affirm that the freedom involved in the setting of obligatory ends goes beyond that which is accomplished in merely pragmatic end-setting. In pragmatic end-setting, as we have seen, we can only speak of ourselves as negatively free. When I set an end, I avoid any external constraint by the very nature of the act of end-setting, and I avoid the empirical constraint by my inclinations by freely choosing to incorporate my desires into reasons and then ends instead of them determining my will directly. But in the setting of obligatory ends, we go beyond these two senses of merely negative freedom. We can now speak also of end-setting also as being positively free, or autonomous.

That is, just as the mere *form* of the law of one's will is autonomously legislated, so too is any obligatory *matter* or end of the will also autonomously determined always and only by one's own will, via the self-constraint of end-setting, that is, via that end-setting by which I choose for myself ends of action determined by my own formal rational law. Like that constraint on my will found in the legislation of the mere form of its maxims, this constraint in the adoption of an obligatory end is a constraint to set an "end that must...be given *a priori, independently* of inclinations" (6:381/146, emphasis added). And this independence from inclination is an independence beyond what was accomplished in the setting of pragmatic ends. There, we acquired a certain distance from our inclinations by considering them as the basis of reasons instead of as the direct determinants of our wills. But here, we do not even need to appeal to our inclinations at all in order to determine our ends. It is not only that I bring external forces under the control of my free choice. Beyond that, I act entirely independently of *any* external or internal physical or natural constraint. Obligatory end-setting is thus an act that is free from causation by natural means in just the same way that the mere form of one's lawful maxim is free from such causation. The setting of an obligatory end is, in other words, something that is caused "*only* by oneself" in the most rigorous sense of that phrase: I am relying only upon my rational self to determine the ground of my end. As such, Kant is confident in asserting that "it is no contradiction to set an end for myself that is also a duty, since I constrain myself to it and this is altogether consistent with freedom" (6:381–382/147), and indeed with that positive freedom that goes beyond independence from external influence and relies only on the positive determination of one's will by one's own reason.[53]

It is with just such thoughts of negative and positive freedom as connected to a will determined only by the form of the law in mind that Kant, now concerned to provide a definition of *virtue*, insists that this state is one that must be accomplished with an "inner freedom" that replicates this structure of both negative and positive freedom.[54] We've already seen, in the second *Critique* and the *Groundwork*, these two senses of freedom as negative and positive: a morally obligated will, to be a morally obligated will, must find its law in its own rational, formal law of universalizability; and the freedom of this same law-bound will is found in its ability, positively, to claim that very law (and, negatively, not by appeal to anything alien to it) as what determines it. But now, in the Doctrine of Virtue, for virtue to be virtue, we must re-establish such negative and positive freedom not simply on the level of *legislation* of one's own laws but in their *realization*, or what Kant calls their "execution": "Virtue is...a moral constraint through his own lawgiving reason, insofar as this constitutes itself an authority *executing* the law...[Virtue] commands and accompanies its command with a moral constraint (a constraint possible in accordance with laws of inner freedom)" (6:405/175, emphasis added). Virtue must, that is, be a state of *person* in accordance with this same law-bound and (negatively and positively) free *will*: just as any *legislation* of a law, to be authoritative, needs to be self-legislation, now any actual *constraint* of a will to *execute* (or realize) this legislation in the setting of particular ends, to be a proper constraint, needs to be *self*-constraint in accordance with that same law,

---

[53] This is the sense of freedom to which I appealed briefly when noting the caveat we must admit for welcoming the freedom of pragmatic end-setting. The negative freedom of pragmatic end-setting—that "distance" I get from the objects of my inclinations by turning them into reason-based ends—is, really, parasitical upon this fuller sense of free end-setting which is thoroughly independent of any appeal at all to inclination. It is only when the determination of my will can be reason all-the-way-down that we can speak of my choosing self as having acquired that complete distance from determination by inclination necessary to understand oneself as truly free.

[54] See especially 6:380–381/155–156, 6:394–395/167–168, and 6:405–408/175–178.

a constraint which thereby assures the positive freedom of the person since this self-constraint avoids constraint from alien causes and thus is accomplished only through itself.

As such, to say that I constrain myself to set obligatory ends in accordance with my own law of reason is simply another way of saying that I freely and autonomously constrain myself to virtue. Indeed, to affirm the freedom of that same virtuous will which is constrained, we must assert for virtue a particularly strong notion of *free self-constraint*, a self-constraint in accordance with one's own autonomously legislated law: "[V]irtue is not merely a self-constraint (for then one natural inclination could strive to overcome another), but also a self-constraint in accordance with a principle of inner freedom, and so through the mere representation of one's duty in accordance with its formal law" (6:394/167). Here, Kant clarifies that any constraint of one's will, inclinations, and person, to be virtuous, needs not only to come from oneself but also to come from that very precise part of oneself that freely legislates a law to oneself independently of one's inclinations. It cannot simply be that one stronger inclination in oneself constrains another weaker inclination. That would indeed be "*self*-constraint," but it would not be the autonomous and free self-constraint that avoided determination by natural means and was in accordance with one's own law. This autonomous, free, and lawful constraint is exactly the constraint one needs in order to confirm that constraint is *virtuous* constraint: that constraint constituted by virtue as strength, to be "virtue," must also be this more thoroughly free self-constraint in accordance with a law, a constraint accomplished via one's own law which deserves thereby to be called "inner freedom."[55]

It is worth noting here that in affirming that self-governance needs to occur not by one inclination controlling another but only by a law which is entirely independent of inclination, we return ourselves to the territory whereby, in Part I, we distinguished Kantian self-governance from Frankfurt's story of

---

[55] It is difficult to determine in his Doctrine of Virtue discussion of such things, whether Kant now prefers the *Groundwork* or the second *Critique* line of argument for proving both a law-bound and a free will. The only spots I note wherein he suggests some sort of movement from one to the other are in these quotes just provided: "virtue is... a self-constraint in accordance with a principle of inner freedom, *and so* through the mere representation of one's duty in accordance with its formal law" (6:394/156, emphases added); and: "Virtue is... a moral constraint through his own lawgiving reason, insofar as this constitutes itself an authority executing the law... [virtue] commands and accompanies its command with a moral constraint (a constraint possible in accordance with laws of inner freedom)" (6:405/164). We see in both these quotes a connection between a law-bound will and a free will, but the order of that connection is obscure. On the one hand, one might say here that we first understand the notion of free self-constraint of the will and *therefore* the notion of lawful constraint of the will follows. But one could also read these passages as suggesting that the whole notion of "constraint" is the original notion and that Kant is therefore in fact starting from the notion of a law-bound will, and then affirming the freedom of that same will. I am most tempted by this latter reading, as it suggests that the phenomenological experience of obligatedness is primary, and that one must infer from that an underlying state of freedom. But we simply do not have sufficient text to confirm that reading. It may simply be that, having considered such questions in the *Groundwork* and second *Critique*, Kant sets them aside here.

self-governance. But we can now affirm that distinction with even further defense of Kant's insistence that desire cannot be self-governing. Because determination of the will via inclinations can assure (at best) only negative and not positive freedom, such determination is inadequate for fully virtuous determination of the will. Virtue must be determined by one's own law-giving reason and not at all by appeal to anything external to me, and so governance of the self and its inclinations/desires must emerge from one's reason and not at all from one's inclinations (and hence not from the Frankfurtian self-elevated second-order desires).

End-setting—the ultimate act of freedom—is thus precisely that notion which girds the true inner freedom constitutive of virtue. This is the true freedom to be found in "virtue as strength" because it is a manner of constraining oneself that is clearly distinguished from mere coercion. To be *coerced* would be to be caused to act by some force external to me, either other persons or some aspect of myself grounded in the natural world. But I can *constrain* myself toward an end—indeed this is just what it is to have obligatory ends or ends that are also duties—without being *coerced* by anything external to me and without being determined by anything sensible within me. It is certainly the case that when I claim an obligatory end, I am simultaneously constraining (or limiting/preventing) the effect that certain of my inclinations would pursue, left to their own devices. But in such *constraint* of myself, I am not *coercing* myself. Indeed, the very notion of self-coercion would make no sense, since coercion of the will is influence upon the will from something external to the will; and when I constrain my inclinations I am not doing so via any external force or any internal but sensible/non-rational force, but only via my own rational law which belongs to the will itself. I cannot coerce myself *or* be coerced by another human or another "natural" cause to have an end. Instead, the constraint implicit in virtue as strength is always only *self*-constraint to (*a priori*) ends. Kant's insistence upon a constraint of one's will that is self-constraint in accordance with one's own formal, rational law thus assures that we can speak of a *constraint* of one's will and person that does not collapse into non-virtuous *coercion* of that will and person.

With this account of freely set obligatory ends, we thus affirm the precise nature of that free self-constraint which constitutes virtue as strength: when I constrain myself in accordance with the law to respect persons, I set a variety of ends for myself (e.g., to treat others beneficently or to treat myself respectfully). But this choice of ends is a matter of my choice to which I am not constrained by any persons external to me and to which I am not determined by any of my inclinations or their objects. When I set these ends, *I*, and I alone, am setting the ends. It is not that some natural means in the world is causing me so to choose. I am not, for example, pushed through my inclinations of sympathy to help another person. To the contrary, these obligatory ends are "end[s] that must...be given *a priori*, independently of inclinations*" (6:381/148, cf. 6:385/149), and indeed, independent of any external, natural means or causation. The choice of an end may indeed be a constraint on my will but it is an autonomously chosen self-constraint of my will: the will constraining itself. The very fact that end-setting is an act of freedom which only I can do for myself, combined with the fact that I can set certain ends without reference to my sensible nature, assures that I am indeed able to constrain myself to adopt obligatory ends—the *matter* of choice—freely and autonomously. Fully *free* constraint must always be nothing but this utterly *self*-constraint. Or as Kant concludes the point: "That ethics contains duties that one cannot be constrained by others (through natural means) to fulfill follows merely from its being a doctrine of *ends*, since coercion to ends (to have them) is self-contradictory" (6:381/146).

Conclusion
Deontological Teleology Affirmed

We thus complete our initial defense of the integration of ends within a free, *a priori*, and deontological morality. Indeed, any suggestion that deontology and teleology are intrinsically opposed to each other has now been eliminated. Early in his moral writings, Kant does indeed introduce a narrow conception of ends that would make one believe he was opposed to teleological conceptions of pure practical reason and the virtue obtained through it: admission of material ends, as defined there, into deontological morality would indeed undermine both the freedom and a priority of such morality. But through his more mature Doctrine of Virtue reflections on ends, end-setting, and especially the new category of obligatory ends determined by reason not inclination, we discover a broader notion of ends, one which does not eliminate but instead elevates Kant's initial deontological commitments to maxims toward their teleological realization in ends of action. Were end-setting always inevitably only relative and empirical end-setting, ends could have no place in a deontology concerned to affirm strictly formal and necessary maxims of action. But such restriction of practical pure reason to the merely formal qualities of one's choice would also mean, tragically, that pure reason could *not* be fully practical: having brought us pure *a priori* principles to determine our maxims, it would have fallen short in giving us pure *a priori* grounds to determine our ends and actions. But once we affirm the free setting of both pragmatic and especially obligatory ends, all guided by an objective end determined by reason alone (an end which we will identify in I.iii as the end of making persons as such our end), the would-be incompatibility of deontology and teleology dissolves, and we reveal Kant's deontological moral theory simultaneously as teleological.

Kant's commitment especially to the establishment of objectively valid obligatory ends for sensibly affected rational beings determined through appeal to reason, not inclination, is what assures the coherence and, indeed, the very ground and possibility of Deontological Teleology. Through this category of obligatory end, not only can we admit a broader conception of ends above and beyond the empirical, subjective, and relative ends which Kant identified in the *Groundwork* and second *Critique*; further, we can affirm that this new category of free, *a* priori, and autonomously set obligatory ends constitutes the heart of free virtue: to pursue virtue simply is to pursue the setting of a series of objectively obligatory ends which (as we shall see in I.iii and I.iv) are deduced and defined through appeal to one overall guiding telos determined by our reason, the telos of respect for persons. In accepting this new understanding of the centrality of freely set and *a priori* grounded obligatory ends for Kantian virtue, we thus simultaneously accept a more general claim about it: Kant's deontological approach to virtue is simultaneously a teleological one.

At this point, we have not yet completed the details of this Deontological Teleology, but we have laid the groundwork for it in the nature of practical pure reason itself. Most centrally, we have seen that, once we consider the nature of practical pure reason as it is articulated in both the *Groundwork* and in the Doctrine of Virtue, it is a broader, more encompassing thing than traditional conceptions of merely deontological approaches to ethics would admit. Practical reason is certainly concerned with the mere form of maxims, with relying only upon itself to identify those formal qualities of maxims which affirm the morality of one's maxim-setting and with determining thereby what constitutes "right" action. But, once seen in light of the Doctrine of Virtue consideration of pure practical reason as, definitionally, "a faculty of *ends*" (6:395/157, emphasis added), we need to place this vision of practical reason as articulated in the *Groundwork*— one wherein practical reason is concerned merely with the formal determination of maxims—within a larger context. Affirming the formal qualities of one's maxims is, in fact, only a preparatory stage in affirming the practicality of pure reason. If that reason could not continue to apply itself in the determination of ends and, ultimately, action, it would not be pure *practical* reason. But when it does so apply itself, we discover what, all along, has been the goal, or even the vocation, of practical pure reason: to determine and set ends in accordance with an ultimate end of reason itself.[56] Furthermore, we have welcomed this broader mandate for practical pure reason while maintaining its "purity," that is, while maintaining the free and *a priori* grounding of its determinations. We thus affirm that pure practical

---

[56] I do not mean to suggest that I am unsympathetic to conceiving of the end of practical reason in even larger, more social, and communal terms. To the contrary, I am deeply sympathetic with, e.g., Rossi (2019) who sees the end or vocation of reason in the communal pursuit of peace-making. My goal in this book is, however, to focus on Kant's ethics as they are best articulated from an individual perspective and in this life. And it is my hope that this individual focus could be shown to be complementary to, and not in opposition with, more social, historical, and religious accounts which pursue those larger ends.

reason is, at its heart, a teleological faculty, that is, a faculty concerned with and guided by a substantive, objective, and life-organizing end.

A strict deontologist might object at this point: true teleological theories of virtue need to be guided *fundamentally* by a telos, whereas on our just-completed story, the ultimate guide is a formal, rational principle of the will which determines the telos, and thus is previous to that telos. So, this objector would assert, whatever teleological language can be introduced to deontological principles, such teleology is founded most basically on those formal deontological principles and thus is *not* most centrally or basically teleological. This isn't teleology; it is deontology.

We grant to this objector that it is "pure reason," in the form of a rational principle of the will, which is here still claimed as the "*supreme* principle of morality" (4:392/7), that is, as its most basic ground. And so, yes, we grant that the account we have provided is indeed a deontological one in this limited sense: it is a theory centrally concerned to identify rational formal principles of action which ground one's duties in the nature of one's maxims. We do not, however, accept the further traditional deontological claim that Kant's theory is concerned only with right.

But our objector also misses the main point to be asserted here: once we reject the notion that deontology can be concerned only with right, we can grant that a genuinely deontological system of morality is *simultaneously* a genuinely teleological system. Indeed, the goals of a pure reason seeking to be practical could not be accomplished simply through its ability to determine formal principles of reason which restrain maxims of action. Otherwise stated: Kant's deontology *is* deontology, but it is not *just* deontology. It is, most fully, an affirmation of the reciprocal relationship of deontology and teleology within the overall functioning of the practicality of pure reason: being committed to a formal and supreme rational principle of the will to determine one's duties is not at odds with taking a particular objective end as the proper, organizing telos for the virtuous realization of one's telos. To the contrary, pure reason cannot be practical unless both of these goals are realized, hence, Deontological Teleology.[57]

There is, furthermore, an underlying assumption this objector makes about the nature of virtue ethics which we also reject. The assumption (one which, earlier in this chapter, we saw Herman 2010 make) is that, were virtue ethics to be grounded in merely formal principles of pure reason, it would not really be *virtue* ethics. True virtue theory, so this objector continues, would be principle-less. Such an assumption of all virtue ethics as "radical" virtue ethics is, however, something we already rejected earlier in this chapter in relation to Herman's (2010) assumption

---

[57] Questions do remain, though, about whether, within the world of Deontological Teleology, one should grant priority in some sense to deontology or to teleology. These are, however, questions best answered once we have a clearer sense of the precise content of the telos of virtue, so we shall turn to them as part of our discussion in I.iii.

of the same. We thus also reject Herman's (2010) suggestion that Kant's appeal to even the more material formulation of the Categorical Imperative, a formulation which appeals to rational nature as an *end*-in-itself, is only a deontological principle of action, not a substantive, objective organizing "telos" as such. We now assert, to the contrary, because pure reason will not be practical unless and until it affirms obligatory ends, and because those obligatory ends are articulated only via the singular governing end determined by pure practical reason (a governing end which we shall identify in I.iii as a demand to make persons as such one's end), that Kant's notion of rational nature as an end-in-itself acts simultaneously as a deontological principle of action and a telos which substantively guides and structures the end-setting of the would-be virtuous person.

We thus affirm not only that deontology and teleology are not mutually contradictory but also that they are mutually enhancing. One begins with an *a priori* principle of action that eschews appeal to ends to determine its validity. But Kant's insistence that pure practical reason is a faculty of ends, and his simultaneous welcoming of the notion of freely set *a priori* obligatory ends at the heart of virtue, move that deontological principle into the realm of teleology. The practicality of pure reason is, in other words, as much a teleological project (viz., one concerned to be guided by the realization of an objective end shared by all rational beings) as it is a deontological project (viz., one concerned to determine formal principles of the will that establish those precise obligatory ends which would constitute the realization of this telos). Furthermore, were one not able to tell a story of how a rational principle of action realizes itself in obligatory ends, we could not say that pure reason was practical at all; that is, Kant's project for the practicality of pure reason would have failed. Despite Kant's *Groundwork* tendency to reject ends so as to assure free determination of an *a priori* formal principle of morality, he is thus able, in the Doctrine of Virtue, to introduce and defend the notion of reason-grounded obligatory ends, bringing formal maxims into the world of material ends. Indeed, as we shall explore at greater length in I.iii, Kant's willingness to move, in the Doctrine of Virtue, to this more expanded understanding of the whole notion of obligatory ends as guided by an overall end of making persons as such one's end is what really affirms his virtue theory as a distinctively teleological one: this appeal to an overall or general end of respect for persons—an end which is shared objectively by all rational beings—is simply Kant's appeal to a substantive, objective, and organizing telos of virtue.

What we have done thus far, though, is only a bare framework: we have welcomed the setting of ends into the free and *a priori* activity of pure practical reason and thereby affirmed the teleological nature of that reason. But we have much, much more to say about the details of this Deontological Teleology. We thus turn, in I.iii, to further details about the deduction and establishment of the precise objective telos for virtue—that single overarching end most proper to one's being—and about how this singular telos, in concert with deontological principles, is the very means by which one rationally deduces all those ends which are also duties. Essentially, what we still need to consider is exactly how reason affirms this singular telos and then determines these objective ends, thereby affirming their objectivity and, simultaneously, reason's practicality. What we shall see is that, in order to deduce these ends, the formal law of reason itself needs to take on material clothing; that is, it needs itself to push toward material expression of itself. It will be in such "materialized" versions of both FUL and FH—and, ultimately, in a privileging of the materialized version of FH—that we will finally affirm the objective and materialized telos of virtue, the concern to make persons as such one's end. The ultimate objective end of respect for persons—an end which we can now identify as the substantive and organizing telos of sensibly affected rational beings—is thus that means by which one determines that more lengthy list of obligatory ends that are also duties. In short, every obligatory end that is also a duty is thusly obligatory precisely because it is one example of an objectively valid end of action through which one seeks to affirm respect for persons, both oneself and others. In so doing, we shall complete our story of Kant's Deontological Teleology, that is, his commitment to guiding the virtuous governance of desire (now understood as the virtuous setting of ends) via appeal to an orienting objective end or telos of action, viz. respect for persons. Let us turn to this discussion.

I.iii
The Proper Objective Telos of Deontological Teleology
Making Persons as Such One's End

Introduction

We have, in the previous chapter, through showing that the setting of objective and obligatory ends is consistent with the free and autonomous grounding of an *a priori* morality, affirmed our most basic claim that deontological virtue is inherently end-based or teleological. We need now to complete our account of Deontological Teleology, first by showing that reason affirms a precise obligatory end or telos of all end-setting: making persons as such one's end, as commanded by a new, materialized version of the Second Formulation of the Categorical Imperative. That is the concern of this chapter. Second, we must articulate how this telos of making persons as such one's end, in conjunction with one's experience of the moral feeling of respect which tracks the value of persons within the world of desire, acts as the guiding material and objective telos for the deduction of all other more precise obligatory ends which provide organizing shape and structure to the project of virtuous self-governance, a self-governance guided by this teleologically informed notion of reason; that will be the task of the next chapter, I.iv.

The main goal of this chapter, then, is to consider how Kant grounds the pursuit of virtue through a deduction of a new materialized version of the Second Formulation of the Categorical Imperative, a materialized *principle* which becomes the objective *telos* of all one's virtuous end-setting. In so doing, we take up a hint that was suggested by Ward (1971), but never fully explored then.[1]

---

[1] It is to just this idea of a materialized notion of the Categorical Imperative in the Doctrine of Virtue that Ward (1971) tantalizingly appealed to suggest that Kant's ethics is indeed intrinsically a "teleological ethics": "In the Metaphysic of Morals, [Kant] provides, as a new formula of the Categorical Imperative: 'Act according to a maxim of ends which it can be a universal law for everyone to have' (The Doctrine of Virtue (Pt. 2 of Metaphysic of Morals), trans. M. J. Gregor (New York, 1964), p. 55.) It is ironic that this formula, which, inferring explicitly to ends of action, is perhaps the most adequate formulation of Kant's fundamental principle of ethics, does not appear in the Fundamental Principles [i.e., the *Groundwork*]. But it does make it quite clear that Kant was fundamentally concerned with ends of action; and, indeed, that 'were there no such ends [which were also duties] a categorical imperative would be impossible'. (ibid, p.43)" (Ward 1971, 341) Sadly, Ward's point has not been taken up by other interpreters since it was made. I consider the forthcoming account to be an effort to fill that lacuna, viz. an effort to affirm, continue, and expand upon just that point from Ward's article.

Although Kant confirmed a strong version of the Second Formulation of the Categorical Imperative in the *Groundwork*, and although he establishes there a conception of practical reason which is already purpose-driven and teleological in nature, we shall see that the narrow conception of ends with which he was working there prevented him from accepting the Second Formulation as grounding persons explicitly as the matter of one's choice, choosing instead to emphasize this Formulation's role in establishing a limiting condition upon all choice. In the Doctrine of Virtue, however, with a broader conception of obligatory ends to hand, Kant is able to realize the teleological nature of practical reason first introduced in the *Groundwork* by unambiguously deducing and defending a materialized version of the Humanity Formula, one which affirms not simply that the value of persons *limits* (or sets permissibility constraints on) our end-setting generally but that, more strongly, positively affirms persons as such as the central end-setting content, concern, and governing guide of the virtuous person. What emerges is a particularly person-centered conception of that telos which guides the rational pursuit of virtue: the Humanity Formulation of the Categorical Imperative reveals itself both as a deontological principle of action and the objective telos of virtuous end-setting generally, all centered upon loving and respecting persons.

This chapter is organized into three main sections: first, a variety of preliminary thoughts on any would-be deduction of an end for virtue, then the actual deduction itself, and finally some concluding thoughts on Deontological Teleology.

In the first section, I begin by reviewing Kant's general thoughts on the need for practical reason to determine ends and not just maxims, and then offer some preliminary thoughts about how any such practical deduction of ends must occur. We then introduce and reflect upon Kant's new end-based and materialized versions of both the First and Second Formulations of the Categorical Imperative, taking these materialized formulations as indicative of the objective telos of the virtuous life of a sensibly affected rational being. It will turn out, however, in the exploration of these ideas, that once we privilege end-setting (and not just the form of one's maxims) as the thing to be deduced, we must also privilege the Second Formulation of the Categorical Imperative—a formulation of the Categorical Imperative which is already a matter or end-informed version of that principle—as the most appropriate basis for deducing the ultimate telos of virtuous end-setting.

So, after briefly considering and setting aside the materialized First Formulation as inadequate to the task of confirming the material telos of virtue, and affirming a non-equivalence of the First and Second Formulations by asserting a more robust "intuition" of normative demands through the Second Formulation, we turn, in the second section of this chapter, to the deduction of this materialized version of the Second Formulation itself, beginning by considering what exactly it is that Kant needs to deduce in this new version of the Second Formulation. Doing so returns us to reflection on the Kant of the *Groundwork* and the question of what exactly he had and had not asserted of this same formulation then: although Kant had flirted there with the idea of relying upon the Second Formulation to ground a positive demand to make persons as such one's end, he backs away from unequivocal support for such a claim in light of a narrow conception of ends which prevents him from welcoming this positive demand to make persons our end while preserving his *a priori* grounding of morality. This narrow conception of ends is, however, precisely what we saw Kant correct and expand in the Doctrine of Virtue, as we saw in I.ii, We can thus reclaim the more robust reading of the Second Formulation with which Kant had flirted in the *Groundwork* by turning to the actual deduction of the materialized version of the Second Formulation he provides in the Doctrine of Virtue, emphasizing Kant's new appeal to rejection of indifference toward persons as the heart of the deduction leading to affirmation of the demand to make persons as such our end.

We conclude the chapter with a final section wherein we provide some general reflections on the model of Deontological Teleology that has emerged, affirming and clarifying the reciprocal relationship between deontological principles and teleological goals which was introduced in I.ii. We thus, by affirming a reciprocal relationship between a deontological principle of action and a teleological end of virtue corresponding to it, affirm making persons as such one's end as the ultimate end or telos of all virtuous end-setting. In identifying this corresponding or reciprocal end associated with one's supreme formal principle of morality, we thereby affirm the proper end of virtuous activity, an end which constitutes the telos of all one's virtuous end-setting, and which, in the next chapter (I.iv), will serve as the ground of deduction of one's more particular obligatory ends.

I. Preliminary Thoughts on the Deduction of Respect for Persons as the Material, Objective Telos of Virtue

Introduction

How, then, can we determine the proper, obligatory end of virtue? If virtue is about end-setting, and we cannot appeal to our inclinations or arbitrary preferences to determine our ends, on what basis can and should we go about setting an end? It is here that deontology proper (viz., a concern for maxim-guiding principles determining one's duties) informs the end of virtue. To determine the objective end or telos of virtue—and, ultimately, to determine what Kant calls the more precise individual obligatory ends of virtue—we need to appeal to principles which determine what is obligatory not only in terms of the mere form of one's maxim but now also in terms of the actual matter, or end, of one's choice. And, as we saw in I.ii, it is Kant's conviction that pure reason itself is weighty enough to determine not only the mere form of our maxims but also these more precise and material, but still *a priori*, ends of action that are duties.

One might worry, to the contrary, that such *a priori* ends simply cannot exist and that, to determine specific ends of virtue, we need more than just "pure reason." That is, one might argue that we need more than just the mere form of the law as expressed in either the First or Second Formulations of the Categorical Imperative to determine the ends of virtue. The temptation to appeal to inclinations sensibly affected rational beings tend to have is tempting here: doesn't one need to know something *experientially* about the nature of such beings and their desires, and not just something formal about rational beings as such, in order to know, materially, what ends such beings are obligated to set?

There is something that Kant will accept about this objector's worries. He will, after all, as we will go on to discuss, seek to appeal to versions of the Categorical Imperative which are themselves inherently more material than his previous versions thereof. As such, he implicitly admits that merely formal principles of reason, as they were presented in the *Groundwork*, *qua* formal, are inadequate, in themselves, to determine the *a priori* obligatory matter or end of virtue. But he will reject this objector's suggestion that there can be no such thing as *a priori* matter of virtue. To the contrary, as we saw in the previous chapter, the very notion of obligatory ends affirms the existence of *a priori*, strictly necessary matters or ends of virtue. Just as in the first *Critique*, when Kant introduced us to a pure form of the matter of sensible intuition, he now wants to introduce us to the pure *a priori* form or structure of material ends of action.

We need, however, to show that Kant's confidence in the existence of these rationally grounded obligatory ends is justified. What does pure reason need to be in order to play this role of deducing *a priori* both an objective telos of virtue and those individual material obligatory ends which follow from it? Kant notes the problem himself: having just affirmed that we can at least speak, without contradiction, about the very notion of obligatory ends in an *a priori* morality, he goes on to ask: "But how is such an end possible? That is the question now. For that the concept of a thing is possible (not self-contradictory) is not yet sufficient for assuming the possibility of the thing itself (the objective reality of the concept)" (6:382/147). In other words, though we can accept that the notion of a freely set, *a priori*, material, and obligatory end of virtue is not impossible, we still need to figure out exactly what this end is, viz. to affirm, beyond its mere possibility, the "objective reality" of an obligatory end.

Most immediately, Kant answers this question by providing a general deduction of obligatory ends of virtue:

Now, there must be such an end and a categorical imperative corresponding to it. For since there are free actions there must also be ends to which, as their objects, these actions are directed. But among these ends there must be some that are also (i.e., by their concept) duties.—For were there no such ends, then all ends would hold for practical reason only as means to other ends; and since there can be no action without an end, a categorical imperative would be impossible. This would do away with any doctrine of morals. (6:385/149)

What we see here, is Kant confirming that, for pure reason to be practical, it *must* establish obligatory ends. Every action has an end, and if pure reason could not realize itself in that end-setting which is integral to all action, then it would fall short as practical reason. At best, reason would be able to establish only merely relatively valuable instrumental ends, but no categorical ends. The categorical demand of morality could not, that is, realize itself in categorically required end-setting.

Kant later suggests, as part of his official deduction of obligatory ends, that such a failure of pure reason in the setting of categorically required ends would be the failure of practical reason itself:

[F]or pure practical reason is a faculty of ends generally, and for it to be indifferent to ends, that is, to take no interest in them, would therefore be a contradiction, since then it would not determine maxims for actions either (because every maxim of action contains an end) and so would not be practical reason. But pure reason can prescribe no ends a priori without setting them forth as also duties, and such duties are then called duties of virtue. (6:395/157)

Kant affirms here that pure reason could not be said to be "practical" as such unless it is able to prescribe ends which, by their very nature of being determined necessarily by reason itself, would have to be ends that are "also duties," that is, obligatory ends. His suggestion is that, were such ends not to be determinable, then the Categorical Imperative—already proved in the *Groundwork* to be capable of determining *maxims* of actions—would not really be able to determine even those maxims of actions (since even maxims, considered most completely, also involve ends). It would be meaningless, in other words, were a principle successfully to determine a maxim but then falter in the determination of an end: every maxim is, after all, a maxim of action and, *qua* action, must have its correlative end.

This deduction, however, at least on the face of it, is a rather formal and, on its own, not an entirely adequate deduction of obligatory ends. We understand that the very notion of pure practical reason must extend itself to the determination of ends in order to be practical reason. But this, in itself, does little to help the person trying to become virtuous! *How* must I act? *What* must I do? To answer these questions, we need a more concrete understanding of what it means to say that "pure practical reason is a faculty of ends generally" (6:395/157) and, with that, how to deduce both an overall telos of virtue and then more particular and precise obligatory ends of virtue which can be derived from that telos. We can, that is, make sense of how the Categorical Imperative really is "a faculty of ends generally" (6:395/157) and how it therefore provides direction not only for the form of one's maxim but also, even most characteristically and centrally, for the precise matter, end, or telos of one's virtuous choices. It is the point, then, of the rest of this chapter to affirm the practicality of pure reason by establishing the objective telos or end of virtue through appeal to a materialized version of the Second Formulation of the Categorical Imperative.

A Note on Practical Deductions

We should, before we engage in this deduction, reflect a bit on what exactly to expect from it. First, we are not here seeking to deduce or prove the Categorical Imperative itself. That was the task of the *Groundwork* and second *Critique*, and is something we take for granted here. Indeed, what we take for granted is a very particular reading of that previous practical deduction and, with that, a particular understanding of what practical deductions, in general, are. I have argued previously that deductions in the practical realm are different beasts than those we find in the theoretical realm.[2] There, I argued we can make sense of the nature of practical deductions most successfully by understanding them not as starting from ground zero as it were (viz., from a point where we make no initial assumptions about morality), but instead as finding their starting point in a commonly felt, first-personal, phenomenologically experienced encounter with moral demands. In virtue of this common basis for morality, practical deductions do not begin from some non-moral starting point and deduce their way to things moral. Rather, practical deductions allow one to explore with more philosophical rigor and precision what is already discovered in one's felt phenomenological experience of morality. As such, they are not a direct or rigorous proof of morality that would be convincing to one who did not have access to these felt, phenomenological starting points. But once one grants these grounding felt experiences, one can deduce further things about one's moral status and obligations through attentiveness to these felt experiences. Deductions do, thus, allow for deeper philosophical exploration of one's felt phenomenological experience of being morally obligated.

And so, in my previous book, I argued that we could deduce the various formulations of the Categorical Imperative through appeal to and attentive consideration of the first-personal, felt phenomenological experience of the conflict between happiness and morality. I consider this current pursuit of the deduction

---

[2] See Grenberg (2013a), especially part one.

of the objective telos and resulting obligatory ends of virtue to be a continuation of this same attentive consideration of this grounding felt phenomenological experience and of the principles (viz., the formulations of the Categorical Imperative) we have already derived from that grounding felt experience.[3]

Kant himself also considers the forthcoming Doctrine of Virtue deduction to be something different than a strict, start-from-ground-zero rational proof. Just after introducing his materialized versions of the Categorical Imperative, he notes that "[t]his basic principle of the doctrine of virtue [viz., what he has just described as 'the supreme principle of the doctrine of virtue'], as a categorical imperative, cannot be proved, but it can be given a deduction from pure practical reason" (6:395/157). One would usually think of a deduction simply *as* a proof. But Kant is drawing a distinction between the two here, saying that although a deduction of the supreme principle of the Doctrine of Virtue is possible, this deduction is also going to be something short of a rigorous, complete proof.

What we understand this deduction of the materialized principles of virtue to be, then, is a continuing effort to unpack the import of what we discover in our felt phenomenological experience of practical reason. The deduction of a materialized version of the Categorical Imperative, and the later deduction of specific obligatory ends on the basis of this materialized Categorical Imperative will both simply be further attentive philosophical explorations of our felt phenomenological experience of categorical obligation, now with the objective telos of respect for persons (as guided by one's continuing experience of the moral feeling of respect which tracks this principle in one's world of desire) leading the way for our attentive reflection. We already assume that we have affirmed the Categorical Imperative in its First and Second Formulations, as explorations of our common phenomenological experience of obligation. And we are now seeking, with these principles and attentive reflection upon them, to deduce the obligatory matter or end of virtue. What will emerge, in short, is a principle *of virtue*, that is, a principle which not only affirms an obligatory form of one's maxims but which also determines the obligatory content, matter, end, or telos of one's choice and action.

Materialized Imperatives: The Birth of Deontological Teleology

Let us look, then, at the central text that will guide the deduction proper. In this text, Kant introduces a new and important tool for the deduction of obligatory

---

[3] It is not insignificant that a book moving toward claiming Kant as a eudaemonist begins with affirmation of this felt phenomenal experience of the conflict between happiness and morality. The unity of happiness and morality we shall assert in Part II is not something to be taken for granted but is the prize of the hard work in which one engages to become virtuous. The virtual unity of virtue and happiness is thus something to be attained by addressing and responding to this essential conflict between happiness and morality that all sensibly affected rational beings discover.

ends: materialized versions of these previously only formal formulations of the Categorical Imperative. Here is this brief but important moment of his Doctrine of Virtue discussion:

> The supreme principle of the doctrine of virtue is: act in accordance with a maxim of ends that it can be a universal law for everyone to have.—In accordance with this principle a human being is an end for himself as well as for others, and it is not enough that he is not authorized to use either himself or others merely as means (since he could then still be indifferent to them); it is in itself his duty to make human beings as such his end.
> (6:395/157, translation slightly modified)

A close reading of this passage reveals that we find here new versions of both the First and Second Formulations of the Categorical Imperative. Now, first, instead of merely saying that one is obligated to adopt only on those maxims that are universalizable without contradiction, Kant says further that one must act only on a "maxim of *ends*" (emphasis added) which can be universally required of all persons: "act in accordance with a maxim of ends that it can be a universal law for everyone to have" (6:395/157). And, instead of saying merely that one is obligated to adopt only on those maxims wherein one treats persons not simply as means but also always as ends, he says further that one must, more precisely, set a very particular end: one must act so as actually to "make human beings as such [one's] end" (6:395/157). We have here, in other words, *end*-focused versions of both the First and Second Formulations, versions which seek to bring the setting of ends and the matter of choice under the purview or constraint of deontological principles.

This moment, when Kant *materializes* his formal principles, is, in fact, a very important one, and I want to dwell for a moment upon it. To "materialize" any formal principle of the will would be to affirm an obligation not only to maxims with a proper form but also, simultaneously, to that formal principle's corresponding or reciprocal matter or end. But, these principles—the First and Second Formulations—are very important principles of the will. They are not just any maxim that a rational will might or might not choose. Rather, they are the most basic and most generally conceived principles of a sensibly affected rational will which constitute that will as a rational will. These principles thus establish the most basic rules and requirements of rationality as such. So, when we understand the proper reciprocal matter or end of so basic, constitutive, and generally conceived a principle, we have alighted upon something very important: we have found that matter of choice—that most general purpose, goal, or end—which is proper to and constitutive of sensibly affected rational beings as such. By affirming the reciprocal *matter* for one's most basic *formal* principles of actions, one understands that objective, material state of affairs toward which one's choice should be aimed.[4]

Furthermore, if Kant is successful in affirming these materialized versions of the Categorical Imperative, then this deontological principle we call the Categorical Imperative is no longer just a deontological principle. It is a deontological principle that has affirmed its reciprocal or corresponding material, teleological end, or telos. When Kant materializes deontological principles, he essentially affirms that deontological principles are the kinds of things which have corresponding teleological ends, finally realizing his original *Groundwork* suggestion[5] that practical reason, at its heart, is aimed at a purpose or vocation.[6] The matter or end corresponding with these principles is simply that at which one aims in realizing virtuous action through end-setting. And to say that we have materialized versions of these principles is thus to say that one is just as obligated to these corresponding ends of action as one is to the proper form of one's maxims. The reciprocal matter of one's most basic formal principle is, in other words, the objective telos or end of the proper functioning of one's rational will. To affirm these ends is, essentially, to affirm the practicality of pure reason itself, the ability of that reason not only to determine maxims of action but further to determine those obligatory ends which will allow virtuous agents actually to act in accordance with pure reason.

But to call this end a "telos" says something not just about the setting of that end corresponding to one's most general rational principle, but about end-setting generally. A telos is something meant to guide one's end-setting generally: all one's ends are pointed toward and constitutive of a telos. As such, if Kant is successful in establishing these material ends of the deontological principles of the Categorical Imperative, he will have established the ultimate end or ends that guide(s) and order(s) one's end-setting generally. These materialized versions of

---

[4] Herman (2010) seems to want to avoid just this sort of claim when, on her "austere" reading of the formulations of the Categorical Imperative, she insists that FH is just another way of saying what is already said in FUL: "Once we have the theoretical elements of the argument in place, it is clear that the formula of humanity is, as Kant says it is, just another formulation of the one moral law, equivalent in its normative import to the formula of universal law" (Herman 2010, 109). But in her effort to affirm this strict equivalency between FUL and FH, Herman seems simultaneously to contradict Kant's own *Groundwork* point that there is a *distinction* to be made between the normative claim of FUL and the normative claim of FH: "The above three ways of representing the principle of morality are at bottom only so many formulae of the very same law... There is nevertheless a difference among them" (4:436/43). What is this difference? According to Kant, FUL presents "a form, which consists in universality" and FH presents "a matter, namely an end" (4:436/43). As such, there *is* normative content we learn from FH that is in principle not possible to access merely from FUL. They are indeed aspects, or formulae, of the very same law, but to be a different aspect or formulation of a law is to be something distinctive in its own right even as it claims its provenance in a common law.

[5] At 4:394–395/10–11, as discussed in I.ii.

[6] This is just the point that a strict deontologist would reject: a true deontologist must eschew any appeal to ends, goods, or values in the articulation of her principles. It will be clear, though, from our forthcoming discussion, that Kant never was that strict deontologist that many have taken him to be.

the Categorical Imperative are thus the assertion of an objective end corresponding to one's most basic rational principles, objective ends which, in virtue of this correspondence not just to any principle/maxim, but to these most basic objective principles or imperatives which define oneself as a rational being, can thus be understood as the proper objective end to guide any and all further end-setting and action. They are, in other words, the establishment of a proper telos for the pursuit of virtue.

And so, if Kant is successful in affirming these corresponding ends for either or both the First and Second Formulations of the Categorical Imperative, he will have been successful in establishing a reciprocal relationship between a deontological principle and a teleological end as the proper ground of virtue and, with that, a guiding telos for all one's virtuous end-setting. It is thus these ends-focused versions of the Categorical Imperative we need to interrogate and, ultimately, defend in order to affirm Kant's system of Deontological Teleology.

Perplexities about a Materialized Version of a Formal Formulation

I want to pause at this point. Kant has provided us with two new, end-based formulations of the Categorical Imperative. But anyone familiar with his *Groundwork* discussions of the Categorical Imperative will find something funny about this move. After all, one will recall that in his *Groundwork* discussion of such things, the First and Second Formulations were presented, respectively, as different expressions—one the formal and the other the material expression—of the same underlying principle. As Kant noted there, in reflecting upon his just-completed articulation of three formulations of the Categorical Imperative: "The above three ways of representing the principle of morality are at bottom only so many formulae of the very same law... There is nevertheless a difference among them" (4:436/43). He then went on to distinguish the First Formulation as presenting "a form, which consists in universality" and the Second Formulation as presenting "a matter, namely an end" (4:436/43).

It is thus odd at this point in the Doctrine of Virtue to say that *both* these formulations will take on a new, materialized, end-based form. Such a claim seems, in fact, to threaten to obliterate the distinction he drew earlier in the *Groundwork*: if we say that both formulations have a material reference to ends, can we really say that one formulation is the more formal and the other the more material expression of the same principle? It seems we would have to say now that both formulations are material formulations of the same principle, but then it becomes difficult to draw a distinction between them. There is, in particular, something very awkward about encouraging a materialized version specifically of the First Formulation of the Categorical Imperative. Kant does, as we have just seen, assert such a formulation. But in so doing, he introduces the matter of ends to the very heart of his most formal formulation of the Categorical Imperative, a move that seems to go against its very nature as a formula meant to affirm the mere *form* of moral maxims.

One can resolve this tension to a certain extent by understanding the material version of the formal First Formulation as Kant's effort to extend the usefulness of this formula to reflection upon the proper and mere *form* not just of moral *maxims*, but also of moral *ends*, generally. We are, he says, "to act in accordance with a maxim of ends that it can be a universal law for everyone to have" (6: 395/157), and there will be something to be gained in reflecting on the idea that the formal requirement of universalization extends to ends in this way. Merely formal reflection on what must be true of any matter or ends generally thus does give at least some guidance: set that material end that all persons, universally, could set.

But knowing only this formal criterion for ends generally does little, in itself, to introduce a *specific* obligatory end of virtue. This merely formal statement of the nature of ends generally does not obviously help us answer the question of "*what* would an end-setter set?" or "What would be important to or constitutive of value specifically for end-setting beings?" And, interestingly, Kant does not help us at this point by making any appeal to the familiar language of contradiction as a means to help us think about how to seek these more precise universalized ends. Perhaps he intends for the contradiction test to extend to the setting of ends and not just to the choice of maxims, but he does not state as much.[7]

Furthermore, the limits of universalization as a moral practice are pushed quite a bit when we are asking it to become a procedure which determines not just maxims but now also material ends of action. The limits of universalizability as a test for maxims is a familiar theme and problem in Kant interpretation. Even those who would give credence to the centrality of this formula over others admit the challenges and limits in so doing.[8] But now we are setting the bar even higher: we are, after all, now asking this formulation to deduce *material* ends of virtue. And it is from this perspective of concern for the identification and realization of material ends that we should evaluate the usefulness of both these new end-centered versions of both the First and Second Formulations. The value of any

---

[7] Kant does use the explicit language of "contradiction" (*Widerspruch*) quite a bit elsewhere in the Doctrine of Virtue, though not with specific concern for that contradiction associated with universalization of one's maxims (see 6:381/156–157, 6:401/172, and 6:417/185 amongst others). And he does more precisely (as we will see below) seek a First-Formulation-style contradiction for the establishment of the particular obligatory end of beneficence toward others (see 6:452–454/216–218). Interestingly though, there he does not succeed in revealing contradictions without explicit appeal to the substance of ends which he gets not from the First but from the Second Formulation. We will consider this interesting twist later in this chapter.

[8] See, for example, Korsgaard (1996c) who helpfully reviews the standard objections to the formality of the First Formulation; and also Timmons (2017), who argues we must reject the validity of the First Formulation on its own but open up the possibility of relying on it successfully for other moral psychological purposes. I will later, in I.iv, claim a position in sympathy with Timmons by considering other indirect but still morally important uses of the First Formulation.

would-be principle of virtue needs to depend upon its ability to bring the merely formal Categorical Imperative into the material world of ends, that world of free end-setting which Kant describes as the realm of virtue. We are, that is, finally putting the formal rubber of the Categorical Imperative to the material road of ends of virtue.

But when we affirm this as the perspective from which to evaluate these principles, it becomes clear that the universalizability formula, even in its materialized version, is not the best formula for our purposes. Indeed, it is difficult to envision a way in which we *could* rely on the formal criterion of universalizability as such to reveal anything beyond the mere form of what a material end of virtue must be. That is, it does not seem possible for this formal formulation to issue in the precise content or matter of the end of virtue. We can indeed speak of *some* generally conceived end or matter corresponding with universalizability: set that end that all persons, universally, could set. But at this point, we are stopped short: the very appeal to universalizability as such assures that, for all our appeal to ends, we remain on essentially formal, non-material territory. A formal principle struggles to produce anything more than a formal conception of a material end. The more material we get in the demands of virtue, the less apt this most formal and abstract version of the supreme principle of morality is for our purposes. The Hegelian critique of the excessive formality of Kant's ethics looms here, but now extends itself to ends.[9]

And so, perhaps obviously, it doesn't really make sense to begin our search for the obligatory matter of virtue with a consideration of a materialized First Formulation. The correlative end of the First Formulation has at least given us, in formal terms, the constraint any fully material end needs to respect: this end, whatever it is, must be one which all rational beings could, universally, set. But it is only through appeal to the Second Formulation that we can bring content to this formal description of the end. Given our concern to affirm the ultimate end of virtue, it thus makes sense to start with the Second, more obviously material, version of the Categorical Imperative. We will, however, after deducing the telos of virtue from this more materialized version of the Categorical Imperative, return, in I.iv, to the question of whether and to what extent this odd materialized version of Kant's formal First Formulation can help us in conceiving most fully of the nature of our more precise obligatory ends. First, though, let us turn to a deduction of the telos or ultimate obligatory end of virtue through consideration of Kant's materialized version of the Second Formulation.

---

[9] I thus reject Herman's (2010) claim that different formulae of the Categorical Imperative do not introduce new "normative import": "[I]t is clear that the formula of humanity is, as Kant says it is, just another formulation of the one moral law, equivalent in its normative import to the formula of universal law" (p. 109). To the contrary, there is a kind of normative import or force to FH that cannot be seen as a simple derivation of FUL.

II. The Deduction of Respect for Persons as the Material, Objective Telos of Virtue

Introduction: What is Being Deduced Here?

What, then, to make of the materialized version of the Second Formulation? Here, again, is Kant's statement of it:

> In accordance with this principle [viz., in accordance with "the supreme principle of the doctrine of virtue"] a human being is an end for himself as well as for others, and it is not enough that he is not authorized to use either himself or others merely as means (since he could then still be indifferent to them); it is in itself his duty to make the human being as such his end.
> (6:395/157, translation slightly modified)

It is in this materialized version of the Second Formulation that we begin to gain insight into how to think in concrete terms about the details of obligatory end-setting. In short, beyond any virtuous concern for what is formal in maxims or ends, the fully virtuous person (that is, the person who has virtue as strength to constrain her inclinations freely so as to set ends properly) needs to be concerned with "mak[ing] the human being *as such* his end" (6:394/157, emphasis added).

One might be perplexed in a new way at this point: if it was odd, above, to welcome the very notion of a materialized version of the most formal First Formulation of the Categorical Imperative, it might now seem simply redundant to present the notion of "making human beings as such [one's] end" as some new matter or end that needs to be *deduced* from the Second Formulation. Isn't such a demand already part and parcel of what that principle itself is? Is there any more deducing to be done here?

This is a fair concern. In responding to this worry that we really have nothing in our Doctrine of Virtue discussion of the Second Formulation to deduce beyond the *Groundwork* presentation of that same principle, we are really asking the question of what it is that Kant did and did not prove about the Second Formulation back in the *Groundwork*. We thus need to return to reflection upon the *Groundwork* not only to assess the status of the Second Formulation there but also to revisit the question of the extent to which concern for ends generally is and is not present there. We have already argued in I.ii, that Kant focused more centrally on ends in the Doctrine of Virtue than he did in the *Groundwork* and, further, that he *needed* to set aside appeal to ends in the *Groundwork* specifically to get to a free and *a priori* basis of morality, the main concern of the *Groundwork*. But it would be wrong to suggest that Kant's discussions in the *Groundwork* of the Categorical Imperative, and of practical reason generally, eschew any and all reference to ends or even to the teleological nature of practical reason. To the contrary, we see him regularly appealing to them. But because, at this point in the *Groundwork*, Kant is taking all ends to be effected to be inclination-based ends, he also needs to maintain a certain distance from them in his articulation of the formulations of the Categorical Imperative, and this complicates and confuses things.

The question of what exactly it is that Kant proved in his *Groundwork* discussion of the Second Formulation of the Categorical Imperative—and hence our current question of whether it is redundant to claim to "deduce" something in the Doctrine of Virtue materialized version of this imperative—is, indeed, one of the interpretive difficulties that emerges within this larger context of Kant's regular appeal to the import of ends and the teleological nature of reason in the *Groundwork*. We must thus, at this point, reflect on a few of these moments in the *Groundwork* with an eye to resolving the question of whether and to what extent Kant's *Groundwork* discussion of the Second Formulation can be understood as identical with this new, Doctrine of Virtue materialized version of it within which we are enjoined to make human beings as such one's end. In so doing, we shall affirm that there is indeed a deduction to be made in the Doctrine of Virtue, or at least a new affirmation, not unambiguously present in the *Groundwork*, which affirms the need for the strong, materialized version of this principle we see presented in the Doctrine of Virtue. In the course of this argument, we'll also be able to appreciate how, even as early as in the *Groundwork*, Kant's deontological approach to morality is introduced within a teleological context. But, not having yet completely worked out for himself the nature of obligatory ends as expressed in the Doctrine of Virtue, the appeals Kant makes in the *Groundwork* to teleology and ends end up complicating and confusing matters as much as they further them: indeed we are left there with an inherent tension between teleology and the *a priori* grounding of morality, a tension that will need to seek its resolution in the Doctrine of Virtue. Let us turn to consideration and disambiguation of such things from the heights and clarity of vision his later confirmation of the very possibility of obligatory ends of virtue provides us.

Revisiting the *Groundwork*

Where then do we see Kant appeal to ends in the *Groundwork*? In the first instance, we should note that when providing examples of the application of First Formulations of the Categorical Imperative, Kant appeals not just to the deontological principle being applied, but also to some end or purpose of reason to which one must appeal in order properly to apply that principle. For example, in Example 3 of the First Formulation, where he seeks to prove that it is a duty to oneself to develop one's capacities, he claims as part of the argument that a rational being's "capacities...are given to him for all sorts of possible *purposes*"

(4:423/33, emphasis added). That is, one must understand one's capacities, including one's rational capacities, as having ends and purposes of their own. Without appeal to this assumed end or purpose of our capacities, one cannot find a contradiction in any maxim that would, instead of realizing these capacities, simply "let [one's] talents rust and be concerned with devoting [one's] life merely to idleness, amusement, procreation—in a word, to enjoyment" (4:423/33). We see, then, that appeal to the non-universalization of one's maxim is indeed a central aspect of realizing the First Formulation, but that such appeal works for this example best when the rational will being assessed is understood robustly as a will whose capacities are purposive.[10]

A careful reader of the *Groundwork* wouldn't be surprised by such a move, for the purposive nature of reason was something introduced very early in the *Groundwork*, during Kant's opening discussion of the nature of a good will. There, Kant notes the following: "In the natural constitution of an organized being, that is, one constituted purposively for life, we assume as a principle that there will be found in it no instrument for some end other than what is also most appropriate to that end and best adapted to it" (4:395/8). Kant suggests here that every capacity of an intelligent, "organized" being like a human being—every capacity including this being's capacity for reason—is going to have an "end" and, further, that such capacities can and should be assumed to be "best adapted to"—that is, most appropriate for the realization of—that correlative end. Capacity and end thus stand in reciprocal relation to each other: one's capacity is pointed toward the realization of an end, and that end is the point or purpose which structures the capacity as the kind of thing that it is and is meant to be. So too, then, with our capacity for reason. Kant goes on to suggest in this section that the proper end or purpose to which our capacity for reason is adapted, or what he now calls "the true *vocation* of reason must be to produce a will that is good" (4:396/10, emphasis added).

But this is not the end of Kant's presentation of the inherently teleological nature of reason in the *Groundwork*. Indeed, as is well-known, Kant later suggests that this vocation of reason to produce a good will is most fully realized not just individually, in one rational being, but in concert with all rational beings or "a whole of all ends in systematic connection (a whole both of rational beings as ends in themselves and of the ends of his own that each may set himself), that is, a kingdom of ends" (4:433/41). In his discussion of this kingdom, Kant even suggests that the "objective laws" which govern the kingdom—essentially, all the versions of the Categorical Imperative he has just articulated—all these laws "have as their *purpose*... just the relation of these beings to one another as ends and means"

---

[10] This is just the sort of example upon which Paton (1948) relies for his Teleological Contradiction reading of the First Formulation, and which, in I.ii, we saw Korsgaard reject precisely because of what she takes to be its ungrounded appeal to purposes.

(4:433/41, emphasis added). In other words, not only is reason itself aimed at a goal or purpose; its rational laws of action are also themselves purposively guided. That is, there is an end toward which these principles themselves are oriented. What is this purpose of the laws of morality? Through these laws, through guiding our lives and action by them, we seek to "bring...about, in conformity with this very idea [viz., the idea of the kingdom of ends], that which does not exist but which can become real by means of our conduct" (4:436n/44n). In other words, the vocation of reason becomes the vocation of humanity: through the application of laws of reason to our actions—all our actions—we seek to bring about a state of affairs in which all rational beings treat each other "as ends and means" (4:433/41).

One can thus think about the end or vocation of reason on two distinct but related levels. On the one hand, reason has a vocation internal to the individual who possesses it: an individual is built such that her own use of reason is meant to guide her toward the establishment of a good will within her own person. On the other, reason has a vocation beyond that of any particular individual rational being: the very same laws of reason which are adapted to help individuals achieve the end of a good will are also adapted to move all rational beings together toward a community, society, or "kingdom" whose laws are the very realization of one's own rational laws, a kingdom of persons bound together by the laws of rationality and in which everyone therefore treats each other with the respect demanded by those laws, the so-called Kingdom of Ends.[11]

So, once again, just as reason itself is purposive (that is, pointed toward the realization of a purpose), so too are reason's laws inherently purposive; and, ultimately, so too is the very existence of rational beings purposive. One thus does not understand the true nature of a deontological principle guiding maxims of action unless and until one understands that principle as being pointed toward a purpose. And one does not understand a being guided by such a principle unless one thinks of all that being's actions as pointed toward this meaningful goal or purpose which brings her together with all such rational beings. The thought that

---

[11] We shall, as this chapter develops, need also to affirm a third sense in which the notion of purpose, vocation, or telos is operative in Kant's thought: in addition to the good will as the purpose of practical reason and the kingdom of ends as the purpose of reason's laws, persons as such are identified as the purpose or telos of individual end-setting generally. So, practical reason in general has its telos (the good will), its laws have a telos (the kingdom of ends), and my own individual end-setting also has a telos (bringing about the kingdom of ends by taking persons as such to be my end). How to clarify, then, what brings all these (only apparently distinct) ends together as one? When we speak of the laws of practical reason having an end or vocation, that vocation is the kingdom of ends. When we speak of individual persons having an end or vocation as rational beings, it is making persons as such my end, the realization of which is, essentially equivalent to realization of the good will that is my vocation. But this individual pursuit of the good will through the activity of making persons as such my end is itself pointed toward the larger, communal telos of realizing the kingdom of ends, an end that is in principle beyond the capacity of my individual end-setting and yet remains the ultimate end toward which all individual virtuous end-setting is pointed.

deontology and teleology are inherently opposed to each other as different means for expressing morality is thus once again firmly rejected. To the contrary, in order really to understand what a so-called deontological principle is, we need to ask what its purpose is. Even in the *Groundwork*, then, Kant unequivocally confirms a notion of practical reason used to affirm deontological principles of action which is itself simultaneously a teleologically oriented conception of reason. Practical reason, to be itself, must be oriented toward the realization of a goal. Kant's claim, in the Doctrine of Virtue, that practical reason is a "faculty of ends" (6:395/157) is thus, really, not a new claim at all for Kant. The very same notion is firmly located within the very opening pages of the *Groundwork*.

As we have seen in I.ii, for some Kant interpreters, this is just too thick a conception of reason and its laws to tolerate, too thick because too beholden to unproved premises about the nature, order, and purpose of the world within which reason operates. Kant himself is quite willing to accept such a thick premise (he notes, for example, when first introducing the purposiveness of reason that this is something "we assume as a principle" (4:395/8)). But many Kant interpreters have not, preferring instead to defend, e.g., interpretations of the First Formulation of the Categorical Imperative which do not require so robust a teleological premise,[12] or an understanding of deontology generally that is stripped of any appeal to teleological purposes and thus becomes a method of morality concerned only with right and thus with no appeal to goodness or value.[13] And, yet, simply to abandon this teleological context for deontological principles and to try to utilize the deontological principles abstracted from this context is a project that promises to go awry. For Kant, rational principles of action are not self-standing rational constructs; rather, they are meant to be understood and applied within a larger context which provides these principles with their purpose and meaning. And we cannot speak of the purpose and meaning of principles without appeal to ends. From the very beginning then, the Categorical Imperative, in all its formulations, is meant to be not just a principle constraining maxims of action, but a principle constraining maxims of action in accordance with an end, vocation, or purpose in mind. Deontological principles constrain action for the overall purpose of moving toward something positive that is to be realized. Otherwise stated: deontological principles are simultaneously teleologically oriented. It shouldn't surprise us, then, when Kant turns to consideration of a life of virtue guided by the principle of the Categorical Imperative in the Doctrine of Virtue, that this pursuit of virtue would itself have a teleological goal in relation to which the process of virtuous end-setting would be structured, a vocation toward which the virtuous person aims, an end which Kant describes at various points within the

---

[12] See especially Korsgaard (1996c), who we discussed at greater length in I.ii.
[13] See Reath (1994), Schneewind (1996), and Johnson (2007, 2008), amongst others, again, as previously discussed in I.ii.

Doctrine of Virtue as "one's entire moral end" (6:446/196), that end, in other words, which encompasses all other ends, and organizes them toward their proper goal. Such a structure is firmly grounded in the nature of practical reason itself. As we carry on with this work, we will, with Kant, assume this purpose-driven conception of practical reason as our background. Although I am sympathetic to conceiving of this purpose or vocation of reason on both the individual and communal levels that I described above, I will focus my own reflections on the context of the individual and the ethical demands the individual seeks to realize in herself.[14]

The Second Formulation in the *Groundwork*

All of this discussion of the inherently purposive nature of reason and its principles is, however, only the prolegomena to our main concern, viz. the question of how best to interpret the Second Formulation of the Categorical Imperative as it is presented in the *Groundwork* so as to be able to appreciate the extent to which the materialized version of that principle, as presented in the Doctrine of Virtue, is something in need of a deduction. Let us turn to this central task.

When we continue to explore, then, the extent to which the Second Formulation, as it is presented in the *Groundwork*, continues this teleological concern with an orienting end or purpose for reason, the ground begins to shift a bit under our feet. When we saw ends and purposes introduced as part of one's application of the First Formulation, that was something surprising and in need of explanation. But when one appeals to ends or purposes in one's application of the Second Formulation, it should seem just part and parcel of what one does with this formulation: the Second Formulation is centrally concerned with persons as ends and what this means for our choices. But there is a particular tension for Kant to confront in his presentation of this principle, a tension about how best to construe the teleological structure of this specific articulation of the Categorical Imperative. Essentially, the question becomes whether we should think of the Second Formulation as a principle which simply limits our choice, determining what is and is not permissible in our relations with persons; or whether, beyond that, this principle also positively commands us toward a certain end or telos of respect for persons which structures and orients our choice more positively. Let's explore the text to reveal the tensions therein.

When Kant first introduces his discussion of the Second Formulation, it is clear that he wants, on the basis of an assumption about the absolute value of rational beings, to determine some sort of law:

---

[14] And I point the reader toward Rossi (2019) for an excellent work focusing on the more communal teleological perspective, a work with the tenets of which I am in deep sympathy.

But suppose there were something the existence of which in itself has an absolute worth, something which as an end in itself could be a ground of determinate laws; then in it, and in it alone, would lie the ground of a possible categorical imperative, that is, of a practical law. (4:428/36, emphases removed)

Kant begins his argument here by telling us that he is going to move *from* the assumption of something that possesses "worth" or value *to* the grounding of a "determinate law." Such a structure for his argument indicates already to us that—to use later language not current in Kant's time—he is doing something more than strict "deontology" here. A strict deontologist, as we have seen in I.ii, would appeal only to some notion of right, and not to any notion of value, worth, or goodness, to ground her laws. But, clearly, that is not what Kant intends here.

It is not my intention here, though, to assess the success of the complete argument of this section.[15] I note this initial structuring of it only for the purposes of highlighting, at least to this extent, the continuation of Kant's teleological, as opposed to strict deontological, mien. The question at this point, though, is of what exactly this law is that emerges from a ground of absolute value. Kant's first articulation of the law that emerges at least implies a two-pronged answer to this question, encouraging a reading wherein one sees this law both as a limiting condition upon choice and as one which positively commands respect for persons as the goal or purpose of one's choice: "[R]ational beings are called persons because their nature already marks them out as an end in itself, that is, as something that may not be used merely as a means, and hence so far limits all choice (and is an object of respect)" (4:428/37). Kant suggests here both that the worth of persons "limits all choice" *and* "is an object of respect." That is, we can take this value as a guide for determining what is permissible and impermissible in our choosing of discretionary ends we determine ourselves; but it is also a direct object of our concern, a matter of concern we must take up positively ourselves as an object or end.[16]

Such a two-pronged reading is also encouraged by the nature of the examples Kant presents in applying this principle. The first two examples present cases of actions that would "conflict with humanity in our person" (4:430/38), namely, suicide and lying. We are thus instructed by this principle about what is and is not permissible in our actions: it is impermissible to kill oneself or to lie, because such actions would be in direct conflict with the worth of humanity in one's person.

---

[15] There is a large body of literature on this question of how best to interpret this argument at 4:427–429. Interpreters on this issue break down generally into realist and constructivist readings of the argument. The main proponents of the realist reading are Guyer (2000, see especially pp. 96–171) and Wood (2008), but they are challenged in interesting ways by Cureton (2013), Kerstein (2013, especially chapters 1 and 2), and Formosa (2017). Amongst the constructivist interpreters, see Korsgaard (1996c); Dean (2009); Herman (2010); Reath (2013); and Formosa (2017).

[16] I point readers toward Formosa (2014) for an excellent extended discussion of how this distinction marks, ultimately, the distinction between perfect and imperfect duties.

But when Kant turns to the third and fourth examples, he broadens his interpretation of the principle: "it is not enough that the action does not conflict with humanity in our person as an end in itself; it must also *harmonize with it*" (4:430/38–39). This idea that one must not only assure that one's actions do not conflict with persons' worth but must also, beyond that, harmonize (that is, enhance, further, support or be in agreement) with it is simply another way of drawing the same distinction we've been considering between a permissibility constraint and a positive command. An action that does not conflict with one's worth is permissible. This is a negative constraint on one's choice, generally. But an action that harmonizes with one's worth is more than that; it is the commanding of an action in which one positively makes persons as such one's end. Kant himself makes the point: if one were to stay out of peoples' way but, beyond that, do nothing positively for other persons, then, in one's actions, "there is still only a negative and not a positive agreement with humanity as an end in itself" (4:431/39). But, as he has said, we need to be concerned not only with negative constraints upon our choice but also with this positive agreement with humanity.

Kant even provides at least a partial defense for why we should envision the principle more broadly in this way: "For, the ends of a subject who is an end in itself must as far as possible be also *my* ends, if that representation [of humanity as an end-in-itself] is to have its *full* effect in me" (4:430/39). That is: in order for the absolute value of persons to be something that truly—fully, and completely—guides my life and actions, I need not simply to take that value as a limiting condition upon my choice but also actively to take another's ends as my own, in other words, to be beneficent toward them by seeking to increase their happiness. If I don't, I'm not really understanding what it means for persons to have absolute value.[17]

We are, clearly, in this example moving in the direction of seeing the absolute value of persons as something that acts as a guiding telos for one's choices. But we aren't quite there yet. Interestingly, for example, we still don't have here in the *Groundwork* the same robust statement of this positive demand as we see later in the Doctrine of Virtue. There, Kant will speak of taking *persons as such* as my end, but here he speaks only of taking *another's ends* as my own end. The *Groundwork*'s positive command is thus essentially equivalent to affirming a duty of beneficence whereas the positive command in the Doctrine of Virtue is a broader construal of what is demanded of us: we mustn't just make other persons' ends our own ends; more generally than that, and indeed, as a general context for that duty of

---

[17] Formosa (2014) states the point well: "Even if we do not use others (or ourselves) as mere means (or even means at all), we still fail to also treat them as ends in themselves if we do not make these obligatory ends our own by actually adopting effective means to these obligatory ends…Imperfect duties…demand that we also perfect, develop and cultivate our rational capacities, and support and further the proper exercise of the rational capacities in others" (pp. 65–66). See also Fahmy (2015) for an excellent extended discussion especially of the challenges of taking up others' ends as our own.

beneficence, we must make that *person* herself my end. It is, furthermore, only with this broader Doctrine of Virtue construal of things that we can begin to envision the strong telos-style role that appeal to the absolute value of persons will play. We thus do not yet, in the *Groundwork*, have the full recognition of the teleological potential of this positive demand of the Second Formulation. And yet, despite all this, we are still essentially able to realize the Second Formulation as demanding both negative constraint on choice and as enjoining us to make persons' concerns a positive content of my choice.

Backing Away from Positive Commands of Virtue

Were his account of things to end here, it would seem that we could defend a robust reading of the Second Formulation in the *Groundwork*, one which demands taking it both as a permissibility constraint on choice and also as a positive basis for making persons' ends my own ends. But his later discussion of the same Second Formulation reveals that Kant himself is less confident about taking the principle in this fullest sense. When, upon completion of all the formulations of the Categorical Imperative, Kant returns to summarize what he has argued, his articulation of the Second Formulation reverts decidedly back to being a mere limiting condition. Here is the text:

> Rational nature is distinguished from the rest of nature by this, that it sets itself an end. This end would be the matter of every good will. But since, in the idea of a will absolutely good without any limiting condition (attainment of this or that end) abstraction must be made altogether from every end to be *effected* (this would make every will only relatively good), the end must here be thought not as an end to be effected but as an *independently existing* end, and hence thought only negatively, that is, as that which must never be acted against and which must therefore in every volition be estimated never merely as a means but always at the same time as an end. (4:437/44–45)

What we see here is Kant retreating from his previous, more expansive reading of the Second Formulation. Having previously asserted that the Second Formulation acts both as a limiting condition of choice and as a positive basis for end-setting, here he insists quite explicitly that we must think of the end-status of persons as something that is "thought *only* negatively" (emphasis added), that is, thought only as something that constrains our choice. What has happened here? The problem is exactly the issue with which we first began our discussion of the *Groundwork*, in I.ii: the worry that any and all ends for action that could be set would be merely subjective and relative. Let's explore this important text in more depth to appreciate how Kant's narrow conception of ends in the *Groundwork* prevents him from unambiguously defending the Second Formulation as enjoining us to the positive settings of ends.

In this excerpt, Kant seems to conflate two questions: the question of how to think of persons as ends and the question of how to think of the activity of end-setting in a person with a good will. First, and unproblematically, Kant says that when we think of a person as an end, "the end must here be thought not as an end to be effected but as an *independently existing* end" (4:437/44). This, of course, makes sense. When I think of a person as an end, I am not thinking of them as something that does not yet exist which I intend to bring into existence through my action. Instead, we accept that, independent of any end-setting of my own, the person simply exists as an end, that is, as a being of absolute value who constrains my choice. Kant thus establishes a distinction between existent ends and effected ends: humans are existent ends, but when they choose, they seek to effect, or bring about, an end that does not yet exist.[18]

Why, though, wouldn't Kant go on to say that this existent end is also something to be supported positively and not just be seen as a negative constraint upon my other actions? That is, why does he not now say that this independently existing end is also something for the sake of which I act directly and positively, seeking not to bring it into existence, but to support, further, and enhance its existence through explicit and positive choices wherein the concerns of this person become my own ends? The answer seems to be that he is worried that if he were to introduce so material an object as this to the good will, the goodness of that will would be compromised: it would be made merely relatively instead of absolutely good. Hence, to avoid this, in our conception of the realization of a good will, "abstraction must be made altogether from every end to be effected" (emphasis removed) since, were we to make such appeal to material ends of action to be effected (even if this end were rational nature itself as a good), "this would make every will only relatively good." We thus abstract from *all* material ends when we understand the Second Formulation. But without *any* material end of action at all to which to appeal, we cannot speak of the material end of persons as such—nor (even more clearly) any specific ends they themselves seek to effect—as an end of the good will.

In an effort to avoid relativizing of the goodness of the good will, Kant thus abandons the more robust positive command to make persons' ends my own ends, and reverts instead to a merely negative reading of the Second Formulation. But in so doing, he abandons just what he said, previously, was necessary in order for the representation of a person as an end-in-itself "to have its full effect in me" (4:430/39), and what would allow us to interpret the Second Formulation as the

---

[18] Wood (2015) draws this distinction nicely, noting also that the best way to characterize ends generally (viz., in a way that encompasses these two different notions of existent and not-yet-existent ends) is to say that every end is "that for the sake of which one acts."

complete realization of practical reason moving toward its teleological purpose or vocation, as suggested early in *Groundwork I*. Without claiming the positive command to make persons as such my end (or at least positively making the ends of others my own end), Kant cannot present the absolute value of persons as something that becomes the direct object of my choice or that teleologically structures my end-setting generally. It is obvious that what Kant needs here is a conception of a *material* end that is not a *relative* end, just that conception of a freely and autonomously chosen obligatory end which we confirmed in I.ii as the fruit of Kant's change of heart on end-setting in the Doctrine of Virtue. What we see here, though, is the effect in the *Groundwork* of not having that broader notion of ends: without it, the Second Formulation cannot become the principle it is meant to be without simultaneously descending into being a merely relativistically valuable principle of action.

There is thus an inherent tension in the *Groundwork* between the realization of the teleological dimension of practical reason and Kant's commitment to an *a priori* grounding of morality that comes to a head in his presentation of the Second Formulation. There is, in other words, a tension between realizing most fully the telos of taking persons as ends on the one hand and the need, on the other, in the establishment of a free and *a priori* grounding of morality, to set aside all appeal to material ends. Indeed, it is just this tension that makes for a certain ambiguity in Kant's presentation of the Second Formulation in the *Groundwork* and thus for intense interpretive disagreement about how really to understand that formula, disagreements that have been the fodder for much discussion in the literature. Because Kant himself goes back and forth about whether to take that principle as a mere permissibility constraint or, more robustly, as a positive demand to make persons as such one's end, one must also expect his interpreters to follow suit.[19]

It is clear, though, given our present project, how best to resolve this interpretive question of how to understand the Second Formulation: once we get to the Doctrine of Virtue, with Kant's new and firm commitment to the existence of material ends with an *a priori* rational ground, we can affirm unwaveringly that Kant himself commits to the stronger reading of the Second Formulation, and with good reason. Once we are able (as we saw in I.ii) to integrate ends which are not merely subjective and relative but which, far from undermining, instead

---

[19] I point the reader back to all the literature we considered in I.ii, especially those wrestling with whether and to what extent Kant is either a deontological or teleological thinker. Further, although I will not explore the issue at length here, I would assert that all three of the main topics of interpretive concern about the Second Formulation in recent literature—viz., the question of whether and how the First and Second Formulations are equivalent, the question of how to interpret 4:427–429, and the question of whether Kant is best interpreted in realist or constructivist terms—are influenced, either implicitly or explicitly, by how one deals with this question of how to welcome ends robustly into the fulfillment of one's duties without thereby falling into a merely relativistic and *a posteriori* setting of ends.

affirm and enhance the power of Kant's *a priori* grounding of a free and autonomously exercised morality, there is no need to "abstract entirely" from ends to be effected in our understanding of the application of the Second Formulation. Let us return to our deduction of the materialized version of the Second Formulation in the Doctrine of Virtue with this new understanding of Kant's consideration of the Second Formulation in the *Groundwork* firmly in hand.

Deduction of a Materialized Version of the Second Formulation

So, in response to our earlier perplexity about the nature of this deduction: there *is* more to be done here! In the *Groundwork*, one can argue about whether Kant goes beyond a mere permissibility-constraint reading of the Second Formulation: at some points in the text, he flirts with such a possibility, but at others rejects it. But when we move to the level of virtue and the pursuit of obligatory ends, it is clear we are no longer looking simply for a principle which places permissibility constraints upon our action. Beyond that, virtue will demand that we make persons as such our end, and a mere permissibility reading of the Second Formulation would be inadequate to this task. We must thus affirm that the fact that persons exist as ends grounds not only a negative constraint on choice but also a positive demand that we make persons as such our end. *This* is what needs to be deduced. Let us turn to that deduction.

In the central passage from the Doctrine of Virtue with which we are concerned for this deduction, the tension between these two roles that we want the Second Formulation to play is clear in Kant's own language. To repeat it:

> In accordance with this principle [viz., in accordance with "the supreme principle of the doctrine of virtue"] a human being is an end for himself as well as for others, and it is not enough that he is not authorized to use either himself or others merely as means (since he could then still be indifferent to them); it is in itself his duty to make the human being as such his end.
>
> (6:395/157, translation slightly modified)

When Kant notes here that "a human being is an end for himself as well as for others," he goes on immediately to distinguish two senses of what that could mean. First, this means that one "is not authorized to use either himself or others merely as means." That is, the fact that humans exist as ends-in-themselves imposes a permissibility constraint on one's choosing: *whatever* you do (the content of which is pretty much up to you to decide), you must always assure that you do not simultaneously treat persons merely as a means.

Back in the *Groundwork*, Kant was happy to assert this Formulation as imposing the above permissibility constraint upon action through appeal to the notion intrinsic to this formulation of an independently existing end: "in this respect the formula says that a rational being, as an end by its nature and hence as an end in itself, must in every maxim serve as the limiting condition of all merely relative and arbitrary ends" (4:436/43–44). But now, when we ask how to *set* ends virtuously—that is, not just how we should approach our "relative and arbitrary ends" (all of which would be set via appeal to inclination) but also what ends we should claim as obligatory (all of which would need to be set entirely independently of inclination and only via appeal to reason)—this imperative (viz., the Second Formulation) has more to say. Beyond acting as a limiting condition, this imperative now also asserts: "make the human being as such [your] end." This is a stronger claim than the permissibility-constraint claim because to make human beings or persons one's end is a directive about what the content of your end-setting should be, not just a claim about how you need to restrain other contents of your end-setting by some other rule: your end of action—indeed, as we shall eventually see, your ultimate end of all end-setting generally—must be to *respect* persons, recognizing their absolute value for what it is, and seeking to affirm, protect, further, enhance, and uphold that value in the myriad ways possible through your end-setting. Respect for persons as such becomes a positive end to be set and not just a negative constraint upon our other actions.

Furthermore, and importantly, Kant then provides an argument for why we should accept this stronger conclusion based upon the fact of humanity's status as an existent end. He suggests that, were we only to take the weaker reading of this imperative, seeing it only as demanding of us that we never treat persons as mere means, then we would be in an odd, contradictory state: we would both accept the absolute value of persons and, simultaneously "be indifferent to them." That is, because I would not be obligated positively to make persons as such the explicit matter or content of my end-setting, there would be no rational demand for me to be concerned with them. I'd have to avoid injuring them in whatever else I do, but could consistently be utterly indifferent to their welfare. But this indifference is problematic: such indifference is not an appropriate response to beings of absolute value! Indifference toward persons must be rejected because it would, essentially, violate the worth of persons to be indifferent toward them. It makes no sense—is not reasonable—to be indifferent toward a being of such stature. We must thus reject the weaker, permissibility-constraint-only reading of the Second Formulation which Kant himself had accepted in the *Groundwork*. So limited a reading of it would put us in a state of contradiction in relation to our obligations to persons.

This appeal to the threat of indifference toward persons as a reason for making persons as such my end is a new and important move. Kant had not said this previously in the *Groundwork* when he briefly defended a weaker version of the positive command to make persons' ends one's own end. Then, he simply suggested that without accepting the duty of beneficence as a genuine duty, we would not "fully" realize the effect of the absolute value of persons in our choices.[20] But what exactly would be missing or incomplete without such beneficence was left unclear there. What he is saying now, though, is that, were one not to make persons as such one's end through beneficence, or through the setting of a variety of other to-be-determined obligatory ends of action whereby I make persons as such my end, one would, essentially, be indifferent to persons, thereby putting oneself into an unstable state of contradiction in relation to them. This indifference argument is thus a furthering and completion of the incompleteness argument in the *Groundwork*. Then, he had said there would be something missing in my attitude toward persons were I not to be beneficent toward them, but he didn't say what exactly would be missing. Now we know what would be missing: actual concern for persons. A mere permissibility-constraint reading of the Second Formulation would tolerate indifference toward persons, but such indifference is in fact intolerable because inconsistent with the absolute worth of persons. We now, finally, have a genuine argument for why we should prefer the stronger reading of the Second Formulation: reason, in order to avoid undermining itself, must reject mere indifference to persons, and this means that reason itself presents a higher moral demand than what Kant asserted in the *Groundwork*, viz. active respectful concern for persons, or making persons as such my end. This version of the Second Formulation thus takes up the vaguer affirmation of the need for making the ends of others my own end from the *Groundwork*, and wholeheartedly and unambiguously affirms this more material version of it through an explicit argument, or deduction.

And, once again, it is important to re-emphasize at this point that the reason Kant can offer this argument unambiguously here is that he no longer needs to worry that the affirmation of this material end of persons would be relativized by its materiality. For, clearly, this argument *does* establish a specific material end as obligatory: persons. But as our I.ii discussion of obligatory ends has shown us, some material ends can be determined entirely independently of inclination, and thus absolutely and freely instead of relativisitically. Through the deduction of making persons as such my end through a rational argument about the need to avoid indifference, Kant establishes just such an obligatory end independently of inclination.

The deduction we are making here, then, is to move *from* the idea that persons as such exist as sources of absolute value and thus impose a limiting condition upon all end-setting *to* the stronger claim that this fact of their absolute value— this fact, that is, that persons exist *as ends*—enjoins upon all persons that we make persons as such a positive end that we set. In other words, it is obligatory that we make respect for persons an explicit *content* of our end-setting (i.e., persons as

---

[20] "For, the ends of a subject who is an end in itself must as far as possible be also *my* ends, if that representation [of humanity as an end-in-itself] is to have its *full* effect in me" (4:430/39).

such is the explicit end I set; it is not just that I must make sure that I do nothing to injure them).

In accepting this materialized version of the Second Formulation, we thus realize the first step in Kant's pursuit of the free setting of obligatory ends. We surely have a whole slew of specific obligatory material ends yet to affirm, but in materializing the most basic rational principle of one's will so as to affirm a concrete end which is demanded by reason itself without appeal to inclination, we now have an indication of the guiding telos or structure in accordance with which such more precise determination of ends will be made. That is, we have deduced the most general obligatory end of virtue, an end which Kant describes at one point as "one's entire moral end" (6:446/196), or that end at which all other ends aim. In so doing, we affirm Kant's earlier insistence that, from the perspective of the Doctrine of Virtue, we must begin with maxims and proceed to ends: that is, in the realm of virtue:

> one can begin with the maxim of actions in conformity with duty and [then] seek out the end that is also a duty... —Hence in ethics the concept of duty will lead to ends and will have to establish maxims with respect to ends we ought to set ourselves, grounding them [viz., these ends] in accordance with moral principles. (6:382/147)

In light of Kant's broader conception of ends—and especially his defense of ends that can be set independently of inclination—which he welcomes in the Doctrine of Virtue, Kant is now also going to be able to understand the Second Formulation of the Categorical imperative not only as a deontological constraint on action but also, and more basically, as the ultimate orienting end of all end-setting: an objective demand to respect the absolute value of persons, to make persons as such my end, will be established as the telos of rational choice.[21]

This is a good point at which to summarize the course of the arguments of I.ii and I.iii that have led us to this point. We noted first that we need to interpret the deontological principle of the Second Formulation in light of Kant's teleological conception of reason. But we then noted that, in the *Groundwork*, once we move to the precise question of what kind of ends to set, Kant's general commitment to a teleologically conceived notion of practical reason comes into conflict with his commitment to abstracting from ends to get to free *a priori* basis of morality. And so, even though he flirts there with a version of the Second Formulation that

---

[21] We shall explore and defend this claim that making persons as such one's end must be accepted not only as one content amongst others in our end-setting but, further, as the ultimate guiding *telos* of all end-setting at much greater length, in both the rest of Part I and in all of Part II of this work. The ultimate story we shall tell is that, in determining what content to bring to my end-setting, I must take the value of persons as such as the guide in accordance with which I determine the content of *all* my other ends, both moral and pragmatic.

commands something positively and is not just a negative constraint, his overly narrow conception of ends at that point, combined with his abiding commitment to the *a priori* establishment of morality leads him, ultimately, to favoring a narrow permissibility-only conception of the Second Formulation. It is only when, in the Doctrine of Virtue, he broadens his conception of what an end can be—and especially clarification of the category of obligatory ends set entirely independently of inclination—that Kant is able to make intellectual space for the stronger claim that the Second Formulation demands we make persons as such our end without thereby undermining the *a priori* basis of morality. As such, this new "materialized" version of the formulation affirms a reciprocal relationship between deontological demands and the teleological purpose or vocation of reason, a concrete realization of the teleological conception of practical reason first introduced early in the *Groundwork*.

Which is Prior: The Deontological Principle or the Teleological Purpose?

Once we affirm the reciprocal deontological and teleological status of the Second Formulations of the Categorical Imperative, one can, however, raise a further question: what exactly is the relation between the deontological principle on the one hand, and the teleological purpose on the other? In other words: in what exactly does this "reciprocity" consist? Does the Second Formulation, *qua* deontological principle determine, or deduce, the teleological purpose? Or do we discover that this deontological principle was, all along, really guided, urged, or undergirded by an existent end or purpose which is now more simply revealed than deduced? This is an important question: in asking it, we are essentially asking whether Kant's system of virtue is most basically deontological or teleological.

There is a passage from the Doctrine of Virtue, earlier than the official deduction section we've been interpreting, but still very much in the spirit of the deduction, that will help us see this matter in its full light:

> [T]his act which determines an end is a practical principle that prescribes the end itself (and so prescribes unconditionally), not the means (hence not conditionally). [This act which determines an end] is a categorical imperative of pure practical reason, and therefore an imperative which connects a concept of duty with that of an end in general. Now there must be such an end and a categorical imperative corresponding to it. (6:385/149)

What's interesting about this passage is that, on the one hand, Kant speaks of an "act" (and, indeed, just previously, of a "free" act) of pure reason that "determines an end," suggesting that this act (which is affirmed as the activity of the categorical imperative itself) precedes the end: the activity of the principle/imperative determines, or deduces, the end or telos. Reading this passage in this way essentially affirms the order of how we have just considered things: in reflecting on the "act" of the Categorical Imperative, we discover an "end in general," viz. the demand to make human beings as such my end.

But at the very end of this above-quoted passage, Kant speaks more generally about how an end and a categorical imperative relate to each other: they simply "correspond" to each other: "Now, there must be such an end and a categorical imperative corresponding to it" (6:385/149). Here, it seems that Kant is, more simply, saying that where one finds an end in general, one also finds a corresponding Categorical Imperative, and vice versa. Indeed, there are moments in the Doctrine of Virtue at which it seems that ends are the more basic and grounding aspect of practical reason, not a secondarily deduced thing from some more basic and grounding deontological principle. He suggests, for example, that, most basically and definitionally, "pure practical reason is a faculty of *ends* generally" (6:395/157, emphasis added), not that it is, e.g., a faculty of principles of action which determine ends. Ends thus seem, from this perspective, more basic than principles for our capacity for practical reasoning, and not derivative of them. One could, thus, envision doing the just-completed deduction backwards, as it were: starting from the assumption of an objective end in general or telos to respect persons and working toward a more formal and deontological principle which provides a permissibility constraint for action.

Which, then, to prioritize: principle/imperative or end/telos? In the end, we do best to reject the idea that one or the other approach is more basic and, instead, simply to say that there is a "corresponding" or "reciprocal" relationship between the deontological principle of practical reason and the teleological purpose, telos, or vocation of practical reason. To appreciate this reciprocity of deontology and teleology in Kant's moral theory, I appeal to a medieval distinction between the order of knowing and the order of being.

First, when Kant, back in the *Groundwork*, determined the supreme principle of morality, the proper order of knowing demanded that, by appeal to maxims which have been separated from their empirical matter or ends, we could affirm categorical and deontological principles of action. But now, in the Doctrine of Virtue, we discover that, all along, in the order of being, this principle which we were able to access through *a priori*, non-materialized reasoning had a corresponding already-and-always existent, material, and teleological end at its ground: persons as existent ends. In other words, this was not an end that did not yet exist and thus needed to be brought into existence or produced by some (conscious) rational activity of an individually existing rational being. Of course, given that, epistemically, we had to begin by proving *a priori* the existence of the Categorical Imperative, it makes sense that we then had to go on to deduce its proper, corresponding end from this original deontological and *a priori* principle.

It was only via this principle (and via the grounding felt phenomenological experience of obligatedness by which that principle was revealed to one's moral consciousness) that we had any access at all to awareness of this reciprocal objective end or telos. So, from the perspective of the order of knowing, we thus say that the deontological principle has priority: the deontological principle is what determines, or deduces, our knowledge of this end in general as a telos for our end-setting, and so is prior to it in that sense.

But in the order of being, it is exactly the reverse: the metaphysical claim of the existence of persons as absolutely valuable ends-in-themselves (that always existing fact which provides the ground for all our end-setting) existed long before anyone ever thought to deduce it deontologically. Indeed, it is only because this deontological principle is grounded in this ultimate, objectively existing end of the absolute value of persons as ends that our deduction from deontological principle to objective end-in-general or telos was successful in the first place. Without this metaphysical grounding or objectively existing telos, we could not say that this deontological principle had any moral punch to it in the first place. That is, the power of the deontological principle is grounded in or finds its source in a metaphysical fact of the ultimate objective existence of beings with absolute value, a metaphysical fact which also affirms the proper teleological end toward which all rational end-setting must be pointed. From the perspective of the order of being, we thus say that this objectively existing end which provides a telos for end-setting has priority: the existence of this objectively existing end is what gives the principle of the Categorical Imperative its moral weight by grounding the deontological principle in the objective reality of an absolute value.

There is a further point to clarify: from this perspective of the order of being, how exactly are the already-existing end which has absolute value and the not-yet-realized telos of all end-setting related? In short, it is by appeal to the former that the latter is affirmed and the process of choosing/end-setting is organized thereby. The particular individual's actual achievement of the telos of one's person is what does not yet exist: she has not yet accomplished this in her end-setting. But that she already exists as an end-in-itself or source of absolute value—*and* that this already existent end sets and makes real the proper telos or guiding structure of her choosing and end-setting—is already true, and was true even "before" she started choosing anything at all. So this already existent end exists also as an already existent telos, even though that telos is not yet realized in the actual choice and character of any particular agent/existent end-in-itself.

And, indeed, Kant's original presentation of such ideas in the *Groundwork* affirms this order. As he prepares to defend the Formula of Humanity, he begins by noting: "[S]uppose there were something the existence of which in itself has an absolute worth, something which as an end in itself could be a ground of determinate laws; then in it, and in it alone, would lie the ground of a possible categorical imperative, that is, of a practical law" (4:428/36). In other words, if only we *could*, epistemically, start from the metaphysical claim of the existence of something with absolute value, then we could, both in the order of knowing and the order of being, simply take the existence of ends, and teleology, as our moral point of view and starting point. But because the demands of practical epistemology require of us that we begin with our felt experience of obligation that is revealed in the conflict between happiness and morality, we cannot begin with this metaphysical fact of the existence of absolute value. Instead, we must work our way to it and to the deduction of what this fact means for the pursuit of virtuous end-setting.

One might say, in the end, that it is only the limits of reason that prevent us from thinking of Kant's moral theory as being as fully teleological as, say, Aristotle's. Both Kant and Aristotle claim an ultimate objective end-in-general or telos toward which all one's end-setting must be pointed and by which all one's end-setting must be guided. One might even say that both Kant and Aristotle are also equally deontological, since while Kant emphasizes the principle that emerges from this telos—viz., the principle of always treating persons as ends and never simply as means, Aristotle emphasizes the principle that emerges from his telos—viz., the principle of always acting for the sake of the noble.[22] One might even wonder at this point why it is that deontology and teleology have been distinguished in the history of moral philosophy as two distinct and opposed ways of approaching morality! Are they not simply the flip sides of the same coin?[23]

Concluding Thoughts

A New Prominence for the Second Formulation in Grounding Duties of Virtue

Before turning to our next main task—viz., affirming that this positive end of virtue acts also as a substantive organizing telos for all one's end-setting, the task of the next chapter—I will first conclude this chapter with a few further reflections upon the import of this just-completed deduction for our forthcoming account of Kant's account of the virtuous governance of desire leading to the pleasurable exercise of the free aptitude for virtue.

First, let's situate this new obligatory end of making human beings as such one's end in the context of the new distinction Kant makes in the *Metaphysics of Morals* between duties of right and duties of virtue. This obligatory end of making human beings as such my end is, clearly, a demand that goes beyond concerns of what

---

[22] A point first made by Korsgaard (1996b).
[23] The notion of virtue being guided by proper function, i.e. the idea that to act virtuously is akin to functioning properly for the kind of being one is, is another idea that Kant and Aristotle share, one which will be explored in more depth in Part II.

Kant now calls Duties of Right and is, indeed, a demand distinctive of the new realm of Duties of Virtue. This distinction between two large categories of duties is a new distinction in the *Metaphysics of Morals*, one to which Kant did not explicitly appeal in the *Groundwork*. Something *roughly* akin to the distinction is suggested when considering the examples to which Kant appealed in the *Groundwork* when illustrating the formulae of the Categorical Imperative (viz., prohibitions on suicide and on lying, on the one hand; and the demands to cultivate one's talents and be beneficent, on the other). But the distinction between Duties of Right and Duties of Virtue only roughly parallels that distinction As Kant now, in the Doctrine of Virtue, draws this distinction, "duties of right" do indeed, like all duties as articulated in the *Groundwork*, "involve a concept of constraint through a law." But now, because Kant needs to expand the notion of "constraint" beyond mere permissibility constraints (as would be appropriate to what he now calls duties of right), he also introduces beyond that notion of constraint (a notion generally in line with the first two examples of perfect duties as articulated in the *Groundwork*), a distinction in *kinds* of constraint. Essentially, now duties of right "involve a constraint for which *external* lawgiving is also possible" (6:394/156, emphasis added), but the new duties of virtue, conversely, "involve a constraint for which only *internal* lawgiving is possible" (6:394/156, emphasis added).

And so, when we are in the realm of externally enforceable duties (e.g., a duty to pay my debts), we are not yet in the territory of virtue. Here, it makes sense to think of the Second Formulation as operating in only a permissibility constraining way: however I handle my incurring and paying of my debts, make sure not to treat anyone as a mere means. This is a demand of the Doctrine of Right.

Kant does, however, suggest that although fulfilling such demands of right is not an accomplishment of virtue as such, we can nonetheless *take up* even these duties of right in a virtuous *way*, "for it is the doctrine of *virtue* that commands us to hold the *right* of human beings sacred" (6:395/157, emphases added). One can, that is, *positively* make it one's end to respect the rights of all persons—taking this as one way in which I make persons as such my end—and this is thus a "virtuous" thing to do. That is, when I make the formal rights of persons my end (when I make all persons' right to be treated fairly in financial transactions a positive object of my respect for persons), I am taking a non-externally enforceable *attitude* toward things I need to do for persons that are themselves externally enforceable. I am not introducing anything new about what I am obligated to do for persons, but I am taking a new, virtuous attitude in relation to what right already demands that I do (e.g., pay back a debt).

But when I make "the human being as such" my end (that is, when I make persons the direct content of my end and thus the direct object of my respect), I am taking a non-externally enforceable attitude toward things I need to do for persons that are also themselves not externally enforceable. That is, I discover, in taking persons as such as my end, that there are a whole range of new things I am obligated to do for persons, things that cannot be *externally* demanded of me, but things that still remain *obligatory* for me. I thus discover the realm of "ends that are also duties," that is, obligatory ends which define the terrain of virtue.[24]

In granting all this, we can now also say that the Humanity Formula—in both its original *Groundwork* version and now in its new materialized ends-centered version—acquires a new prominence in the Doctrine of Virtue's pursuit of virtue: it is a more apt sort of principle than the First Formulation for pursuing the content of those obligatory ends the person of virtue must freely set. In the *Groundwork*, one might argue the opposite: because Kant was centrally concerned to ground a supreme principle of morality purely and *a priori*, the setting aside of all matter of choice—that is, the setting aside of concern for *ends*—was of paramount concern. As such, in the *Groundwork*, the First Formulation had a particular prominence, in virtue of its utter formality. One might even suggest that the philosophical high point of the *Groundwork* was the ability to say something grounding and meaningful about morality *without* appeal to anything material in one's pursuit of it.

But if the First Formulation isn't really made for ends, or the matter of choice, the situation is precisely the opposite when one looks at the Second Formulation. Indeed, this Formula of Humanity is already more material from the start, even before the deduction of a materialized version of it that we have seen above. It is a formula which includes the very notion of that end of all ends—viz., the existent end of a person as an end-in-itself—within the formula itself, even in the most austere permissibility reading of it we find in the *Groundwork*. That is: when I am constrained to treat persons not merely as means but always also as ends in themselves, I am *not* simply admitting another *formal* constraint upon action (that is, I am not being constrained in the mere form of my choosing) but am instead being constrained by what Kant describes as an "independently existing end" (as

---

[24] It is, thus, curious that Kant claims that in taking the proper, respectful attitude toward right, I am making the rights of persons my "end." It is certainly the case that ends, generally, for Kant *do* refer to the "matter" of maxims. But there *is* no new *matter* of duty as such to be found in the acquisition of a new *attitude* toward right. And yet there is *something* introduced that cannot be externally legislated. The fact that this attitude is something I can only do for myself and that cannot (like the actual repayment of a debt) be forced upon me by someone else is why Kant will insist that the language of ends does make sense here. For, as we recall, the other defining quality of making an end, beyond identifying the matter of a maxim, is that setting that end is the ultimate act of freedom, something that I can only do for myself. In all other cases of end-setting, this free internal legislation of the end goes hand-in-hand with that end itself being a new matter of choice (and not just something formal). But in this one case of end-setting these two criteria come apart. That is, I freely, internally choose an end that is itself not a matter of choice. I choose an end (a freely chosen attitude of respect) that is an attitude toward what is merely formal in maxims and in persons. So, at the end of the day, is my virtuous attitude toward the right of humanity itself a "formal" thing or a "material" thing? The question is whether my incentive to do what is right out of respect for right is itself a material or formal thing. It seems material in that it is identified as an "end" (I make the right of humanity my end, and an end is "the matter of choice"). But it seems formal in that it does not yet introduce things that I do for other people that are not externally legislatable. The end I make is related only to what is formally required of me.

opposed to an end that is to be "effected") (4:437/44). Because the constraint of the Second Formulation is a constraint determined by an end (viz., by an actually existing end-in-itself, and not merely by a would-be end-to-be-effected), it is a *material* constraint. One might even say that Kant, by making this distinction between existing ends and effected ends, then affirming the power of the former end to constrain choice, asserts for the first time an *a priori* end or matter of choice: independently existing ends-in-themselves are that matter. This principle does not constrain me just in the mere form of my choosing, but also by this most basic *a priori* matter of ends: persons.[25]

In light of all this, we thus affirm some big-picture conclusions. First of all, we affirm a realist instead of a constructivist reading of the Second Formulation. The end which introduces the normative constraint upon one's actions is an "independently existing end," "independent" in the sense that it exists independent of the process of any particular rational being who would or would not choose to "effect" it. It is thus not an end to be constructed by choice, but an end that exists independently of the process of choice.[26] We thus reject any constructivist account of normativity for Kant[27] and place our account instead within a realist assumption of the actual existence of persons as ends-in-themselves.

Furthermore, since these same claims undermine any would-be rigorous equivalency between the First and Second Formulations, I thus reject any such assertion of equivalency.[28] In so doing, I underscore interpretively Kant's claim that, even though these formulae are indeed just different versions of the same law (viz., the Categorical Imperative), there is nonetheless an important distinction to be drawn between them in terms of how they operate upon the will: the First Formulation introduces a formal normative constraint, but the Second Formulation introduces a material normative constraint, thereby bringing one's encounter with the law to a more intuitive, content-ful, complete—and even *felt*—state:

---

[25] This appeal to an *a priori* existent end is thus the precursor to Kant's more extensive discussion of what he will call obligatory ends (or ends that are also duties) in the Doctrine of Virtue.

[26] Of course, in his equivocal *Groundwork* consideration of this point, he hedges and suggests that this actually independently existing end "must here be thought...only negatively, i.e., that which must never be contravened in action" (4:437/49). But we have already understood his equivocations there, and know now, with the affirmation of *a priori* ends of reason, that this end can play a positive commanding role as well as a negative constraining role.

[27] As, for example, Korsgaard (1996a, 1996c); Dean (2009); Herman (2010); Reath (2013); and, to a certain limited extent, Formosa (2017).

[28] As, for example, Engstrom (2009, see especially pp. 98–118); Herman (2010); Reath (2013); Allison (2013); and Cureton (2013). And I place myself more in agreement with a second group of scholars who believe the First and Second Formulations are not equivalent. Korsgaard (1986), Wood (2008), and Formosa (2017) all hold some version this view. I am in particular agreement with Wood (2008), who argues that the formulations differ in both abstraction and content, and that only the Second Formulation is capable of deriving positive duties; and with Formosa (2017), who argues that the Second Formulation has an importantly different focus than the First Formulation (whereas the first formulation is a principle of *consistency*, the Second Formulation is a principle of *dignity*), making it more apropos to actual application of the Categorical Imperative.

The above three ways of representing the principle of morality are fundamentally only so many formulae of the selfsame law... However, there is yet a dissimilarity among them, namely to bring an idea of reason closer to intuition (according to a certain analogy) and thereby to feeling... For all maxims have 1) a *form*, which consists in universality... [and] 2) a *matter*, namely an end.

(4:436/48)[29]

And yet, as far as the Kant of the *Groundwork* is concerned, this material constraint is not yet being made the matter of choice in the sense of making it the *content* of what I choose. This was exactly Kant's point when he insisted that the person of good will must *entirely* abstract from all ends to be effected so as not to fall into mere relativity in her end-effecting.[30] Persons as existent ends-in-themselves thus provide that most primary and central matter of choice by which all subsequent and particular choices must be constrained; but, in the *Groundwork*, these *existent* ends are not yet affirmed *also* as ends to be effected. That is, persons as such are not yet made the obligatory content, object, or matter of my actual choices in the *Groundwork*. But even with this *Groundwork* constraint that we now know we can set aside, we are not thereby prevented from welcoming existent ends as an *a priori and material* constraint on choice generally. Even Kant's *Groundwork* appeal to persons as independently existing ends is indeed a "material", not formal constraint on my choice.

Kant's *Groundwork* establishment of the distinction between existent ends and effected ends thus, essentially, does for him the same work that a distinction between obligatory and pragmatic ends will do more robustly and completely for him in the Doctrine of Virtue: both distinctions allow him to say that some ends are determined via inclinations and others not. But this distinction in the *Groundwork* is limited to ends that are not effected whereas, in the Doctrine of Virtue, he extends it also to ends that can be effected. That is, with the introduction of obligatory ends that we saw in I.ii, we can now speak of ends that can be effected—or, to use the new Doctrine of Virtue language, "set"—without any appeal to inclination, something that, even with the distinction between existent and effected ends in the *Groundwork*, was not possible there.

---

[29] This reading of the Second Formulation is thus in accord with my (Grenberg 2013a) claim that the normative content of the moral law is something accessed through felt, first-personal, phenomenological experience. See also 4:437/48: "If, however, one wants at the same time to obtain access for the moral law, it is very useful to lead one and the same action through the said three concepts and thereby, as far as can be done, bring it closer to intuition." This is a text particularly supportive of Formosa's (2017) claim that the Second Formulation is more reliable specifically for applying the Categorical Imperative to actions.

[30] There is a powerful irony here for constructivist interpreters of Kant: precisely the thing that Kant needs to *reject* in the *Groundwork* (viz., appeal to any end-to-be-effected, or an end that is chosen) is precisely the thing to which constructivist interpreters want to *appeal* to ground morality (viz., a value constructed through choice of ends to be effected.

So, now, in the Doctrine of Virtue, Kant's *Groundwork* appeal to persons as an *a priori* matter which constrains choice is no longer a hindrance to Kant's project (as it might have been in the purely *a priori* pursuit of the supreme principle of morality in the *Groundwork*). To the contrary, it is in fact an aid. In the *Groundwork*, one might have worried (as scores of interpreters have) that the introduction of the absolute value of persons was a thick moral notion that compromised Kant's *a priori* pursuit of morality. Indeed, this is the problem interpreters have historically had with the Second Formulation: that a purportedly formal moral principle in fact begs the question by surreptitiously sneaking in some sort of moral content or matter without proving it.[31] And, as we have seen, even the Kant of the *Groundwork* decides that a strong appeal to persons as the end or matter of choice—that is, as ends to be effected—is out of place. But now, in the Doctrine of Virtue, the very same material content of morality is what assures Kant is able, through appeal to a new category of obligatory ends (viz., effected ends that are not effected or set through inclination but instead through pure reason) to realize his goal of bringing the *a priori* principles of morality to the material world of virtue: appeal to a materialized version of the Second Formulation is the idea that provides the necessary link from pure *a priori* morality to those more material but still *a priori*-set matters of choice, obligatory ends. Now, the existent ends of the *Groundwork* can be appealed to as a basis upon which to determine ends to be effected.

So, although the language of a material formulation of the Categorical Imperative, and the notion of something existing as an end were both already central in Kant's *Groundwork* discussion of the Formula of Humanity, the precise language of end-setting and the precise question of how to understand the free setting of obligatory ends were not. But once we introduce these concerns and then make the interesting move from understanding persons as ends (i.e., as sources of absolute value) to the demand of virtue that "it is in itself [one's] duty to make the human being *as such* his end" (6:395/157, translation slightly modified, emphasis added), we finally realize the centrality of the Second Formulation for any deontological account of action seeking its virtuous and organizing telos. A materialized and virtue-focused version of the Second Formulation affirms most emphatically to my felt moral experience that I must take up and *make* the concerns of others my own end: I must, that is, set ends the content of which actively seeks the welfare of persons through respecting and loving them. And this is the proper material end of virtue precisely *because* persons *are* or *exist as*

---

[31] I should note in passing that, because on my reading (Grenberg 2013a), the Categorical Imperative finds its *a priori* ground in a phenomenological experience of the conflict between happiness and morality, I needn't worry that appeal to the ends formulation would undermine an *a priori* argument for proving necessity of the moral law. On my reading, this necessity is something I encounter directly in felt, first-personal, phenomenological experience instead of something that is deduced through argument.

ends. The Second Formulation, in this materialized version, is thus, simultaneously, a rational, deontological principle which affirms the absolute value of persons and places constraints on our behavior, but also the most basic, material teleological principle of virtuous end-setting. Our next goal is to understand how this objective *end* of virtue acts also as a *telos* for virtuous end-setting generally, that is, how it acts to guide and structure one's virtuous end-setting overall. That is the task of the next chapter.

I.iv
A Deontological Deduction of the Obligatory Ends of Virtue

Introduction: The Establishment of an End as a Telos via Desire-Governance and End-Setting

Having deduced the proper objective and guiding telos of virtue for sensibly affected rational beings, we can now raise the question of how exactly this telos guides virtuous end-setting, with the goal of showing how a series of obligatory ends emerges from the reciprocally deontological-teleological principle of the Second Formulation of the Categorical Imperative. This chapter thus turns to telling the story of how this objective *end* of making persons as such one's end becomes the substantive, guiding *telos* it is meant to be: in this section, the objective end of respect for persons which we identified in I.iii is affirmed as the organizing telos of sensibly affected rational beings, the means by which such beings determine that more precise list of obligatory ends the setting and realization of which constitutes virtue. Kant suggests as much when, in discussion of the pursuit of moral perfection, he says that such pursuit is an entirely end-based one: "[A]s having to do with one's entire moral end, such [human] perfection consists objectively in fulfilling all one's duties and in attaining completely one's moral end with regard to oneself" (6:446/196).[1] In short, every obligatory end that is also a duty is thusly obligatory precisely because it is one objectively required end of action through the setting of which one seeks to affirm "one's entire moral end" of human perfection, that is, making persons as such—both oneself and others—one's end. All these obligatory ends will, in other words, be ends constitutive of

---

[1] In connecting the pursuit of virtue with the pursuit of human perfection, we thus, once again, place our own account in sympathy with Ward's (1971) account of "Kant's Teleological Ethics": "My thesis is that Kant's main ethical concern was with human perfection; while he rejected the Wolffian claim that one could define perfection independently of moral considerations, the categorical obligations of the moral law are, he believed, motiveless, arbitrary and absurd if they are not conceived as determining human perfection" (p. 337). Ward also notes: "It should be clear that Kant's ultimate concern in ethics was with human fulfilment in a harmoniously and constantly developing community; his religious doctrines are attempts to establish the possibility of such fulfilment, which uncertain in this life; and, without appreciation of that concern, the *Groundwork* must remain largely unintelligible" (p. 351).

the realization of this ultimate guiding end or telos of respect for persons taken as the pursuit and realization of moral perfection.[2]

Providing this account of how making persons as such one's end acts as a telos for end-setting is, however, a process more complex than simply to deduce the specific ends that emerge from this principle. We will indeed do just that, but we also need to tell a story of *how* the actual ordering and setting of such ends by this objective telos emerges in the self-governance of desire. We need, then, to explore the range of obligatory ends which this telos commands, but also to consider how this telos operates as the governing structure of one's inclinations and desires via these obligatory ends it sets. In so doing, we finally provide that story of reason-guided governance of desire that we asserted, in I.i, would be more satisfying than any mere governance of desire by desire.

This chapter is organized as follows. First, we consider how the objective obligatory end of respect for persons enters into one's desire-governance and end-setting, exploring the process by which the demand to make persons as such one's end establishes itself pervasively as the telos of one's end-setting. As we shall see, it is through acts of inner freedom expressed via the moral feeling of respect (which tracks the value of persons within our world of desire) that ends are set which express and constitute the value of this guiding telos. We can thus think of the self-constraint or governance of desire as what occurs through the establishment of obligatory ends set through one's capacity for inner freedom via the voice of one's moral-feeling-expressed experience of conscience. The result is that this telos of making persons as such one's end establishes itself as that value having governing authority over all one's desires.

We then respond to an objector who worries that respect for persons, like those self-elevated ruling second-order desires we considered in I.i, could provide only relativistic valuing and ordering of one's other desires, thereby failing to provide that evaluative distance upon those desires which would allow one to see them for what they really are. In response to this objector, we instead reaffirm that the proper, substantive, and organizing goal for the governance of our desires is a necessary and non-contingent goal beyond the mere satisfaction of desire, a goal which is itself established within the world of desire via the moral feeling of respect, a feeling which tracks the import of the value of persons and thus acts as a constraining voice of conscience throughout the entire process of one's end-settings. In accepting this objective telos for virtue which expresses itself through this feeling in the world of desire, one thus accepts that all one's choices governing

---

[2] Indeed, once we get to Part II, we shall discover that this substantive organizing telos of making persons as such one's end guides agents toward the pleasurable exercise of the free aptitude for virtue (viz., happiness rationally conceived) and also toward the pursuit of those pragmatic ends meant to constitute happiness empirically conceived. This telos thus becomes the means by which *all* one's end-setting, both moral and pragmatic, is structured, and by which one achieves happiness, both rationally and empirically conceived.

the constraint and cultivation of desire must be in agreement with this non-negotiable, absolute, objective, and exception-less demand to respect persons. One thus acquires, through appeal to this necessary principle of governance, a new proper evaluative distance upon one's now merely relativistically valuable desires, a distance that promises more success in governing them. The absolute value of persons becomes the end point for all my desires and the reason that explains why I govern them as I do: in everything that I do, I must respect persons. In affirming the centrality of personhood as the guiding telos of self-governance, we thus provide a more satisfying and more morally robust means by which to understand how self-governance constructs, affirms, and upholds valuable persons: respect for persons is revealed as the singular absolute value which provides proper evaluative distance upon all other desires and the merely relative values they represent.

We then turn to consideration of the exact nature of the obligatory ends which emerge in this process of desire-governance by the objective telos of respect for persons, focusing in particular upon aspects of Kant's discussion of obligatory ends which help us to further our continuing exploration of Deontological Eudaemonism as it will emerge in Part II. First, we reconsider the role that the First Formulation of the Categorical Imperative plays in conjunction with the Second to deduce that obligatory end toward others called the duty of beneficence, showing that although the First Formulation is unable on its own to generate the needed contradictions of one's maxim via a universalization test, more general reflection upon the importance of universalizability as one aspect of the nature of any end in which one makes persons as such one's end proves to be an important moral psychological tool of attentiveness, one which allows, for example, a more perspicuous expression of the nature of obligatory ends to others, including more clarity specifically about the obligatory end of beneficence.[3]

We then turn to consideration of two aspects of Kant's person-centered catalog of duties—the very category of duties to self and the interesting duty to cultivate the feeling of sympathy—to anticipate the usefulness of just these moral points in our forthcoming Part II discussion of Deontological Eudaemonism proper, that is, the usefulness of these ideas for the pursuit of pleasurable proper functioning overall, including the pursuit of happiness, empirically conceived. That Kant accepts the very category of duties to self reveals that the tool of the objective telos of making persons as such one's end is one which can be applied appropriately to oneself and to the needs of that self, a tool for assuring proper evaluative distance upon oneself and one's needs, an evaluative distance that will prove valuable not only for the pursuit of virtue but also for the pursuit of happiness

---

[3] In claiming the value of the First Formulation for purposes of attentiveness, we thus place ourselves in limited agreement with Timmons (2017), who suggests that the First Formulation is more valuable for furthering moral psychological purposes than for grounding normative purposes.

empirically conceived, thus leading to the overall pleasurable proper functioning of the sensibly affected rational being.

We then consider the duty to cultivate sympathetic feelings, an aspect in the development of virtue which is not only the establishment of a distinctive obligatory end but also the establishment of a model generally for how to appeal to the objective demand to make persons as such my end as a guide for the cultivation of feelings generally, a model which will prove helpful not only in the establishment of other natural feelings that can be elevated as components of virtue but also in the forthcoming Part II discussion of how one's feelings can be organized in the pursuit of happiness, empirically conceived. We thereby affirm that Kant's Deontological Teleology can indeed guide the governance of human lives through appeal to the capacity for inner freedom to establish these obligatory ends that are also duties, all guided by one's own rational law which demands that, in all end-setting, one be guided by the telos of respect for persons. What emerges through all of these discussions is an outline of what the well-self-governed virtuous person looks like.

Ultimately, then, we affirm Deontological Teleology as an approach to the virtuous self-governance of desire which elevates the world of desire beyond itself and beyond the pursuit of happiness through appeal to a rational principle of respect for persons. Such appeal to a strictly necessary rational principle to order the governance of desires introduces an absolute value which provides the proper evaluative perspective from which to assess all other desires, values, and ends, ultimately providing that point of view from which one can see and organize all one's desires and end-setting in a properly moralized light.

I. Desire-Governance via a Moral-Feeling-Expressed Experience of Conscience

Desire-Governance via a Moral-Feeling-Expressed Experience of Conscience

And so, before considering the precise catalog of objective ends which emerges through application of the telos of making persons as such one's end, we need first to consider *how* the objective end of respect for persons takes up this governing role in the organization of one's end-setting, thus becoming the substantive organizing telos of end-setting generally. Such a task returns us to the question of the nature of the proper self-governance of desire, first explored in I.i. But with this rationally authorized telos of respect for persons now in hand, we can return to consideration of such self-governance with the proper governing tool needed for that governance. Let us first pause to remind ourselves where we have been in consideration of self-governance so as to appreciate the larger context within which we introduce this new tool of self-governing, the objective telos of making persons as such my end.

Our discussion of self-governance began in I.i, where we saw that a Kantian approach to self-governance must reject mere desire-based governance of desire (those Frankfurtian second-order desires-cum-volitions) in favor of a rational and legitimate governor more capable than desire of raising ourselves to true personhood. In order to affirm this rational and legitimate governor, we needed also, however, to affirm the very possibility of the rational setting of obligatory ends within a system of *a priori* morality, a task that was accomplished in I.ii. Previous to our affirmation of this new category of obligatory ends, one might have thought of end-setting and desire-governance as essentially identical: the only way to set ends was by appeal to desires or inclinations, and so, the very act of end-setting would be the act of establishing inclination-based ends as governing rules in my person overall. End-setting here would simply be the task of using my rational choice to determine which inclinations I prioritize and pursue. We saw, in I.i, though, just how incomplete, fraught, and obsessive the pursuit of a governed life can be on this desire-only model.

But now, with the establishment of the obligatory end of making persons as such one's end, we have a new means for setting ends generally: by appeal to reason alone, ends can be set that are not simply the prioritizing and elevating of a particular desire or inclination. Instead, as we saw in I.iii, it is through appeal to the materialized version of the Second Formulation of the Categorical Imperative that we set material obligatory ends, without appeal to anything besides reason, and especially without appeal to inclinations. The rational demand to make persons as such my end thus provides material, and not merely formal, guidance in the setting of precise obligatory ends.

Indeed, via appeal to the objective end of respect for persons now taken as a guiding telos for one's end-setting generally, not only can we set ends entirely "*a priori* independently of inclinations" (6:381/146); further, ends can now be set that even require the *constraint* (that is, the refusal of fulfillment) of any and all inclinations and desires. When we engage in the setting of obligatory ends, we thus simultaneously engage in the governance of desire from the perspective of reason, that governance of desires of which we spoke in I.i which "scorns" the thought that desires could govern themselves (6:396/158) precisely because there is a more legitimate governor of those desires. Whereas desire-governance-only-by-desire resulted in incomplete, fraught, and morally problematic would-be "governed" "persons," or illicit forms of passionate self-governance in which an inclination subverts the governance proper to one's being, this desire-governance via the objective telos of one's being has both an axiological ordering power and governing authority that desires themselves lacked. Whereas desires could ground only a relatively valuable concern as a guiding principle, resulting in the warping or distorting of the nature all one's other desires which are governed by it, the absolute value of persons provides instead a more robust evaluative perspective from which to govern one's desires. And whereas passionate self-governance could not find a non-contingent and thus authoritative ground for its governance, the telos of respect for person provides just that, thereby introducing into desire-governance that value most apropos and authoritative to guide the life of a sensibly affected rational being.

There are now, however, a few further details about this new system of governance upon which we need to reflect. First, we need to explain in more detail exactly *how* the objective telos of respect for persons enters into one's world of desire so as to order it. And second, we need to consider precisely why this absolute, non-relative standard acts as a more adequate axiological guide in the governance of desires. I consider each of these points in turn.

So, first: when I assert that the obligatory end of respect for persons is established through reason alone and not through any appeal to inclination, I am not abandoning my previously argued claim that the moral feeling of respect plays a crucial moral epistemic role in revealing what reason demands categorically.[4] It is indeed, as we have seen, reason which affirms the objective end of the absolute value of persons and the objectivity of all obligatory ends proceeding from this telos. But this telos of respect for persons is, like any awareness I have of imperative demands, introduced to my moral consciousness *through* the moral feeling of respect. I have already discussed at length elsewhere how it is that this feeling, which has a distinctive noumenal and rational cause, acts as the means by which sensibly affected rational beings become aware of categorical rational demands of morality and, further, is the affective space within which one experiences one's moral consciousness generally.[5] In these previous discussions, we saw the establishment of the validity of the Categorical Imperative itself emerging in specific phenomenological experiences of the moral feeling of respect wherein one encounters a conflict between happiness and moral demands. But because this feeling has a special noumenal and rational source, phenomenological reflection upon it allowed us to ground claims about the rational, noumenal source and ground of those categorical moral demands which our phenomenological experience of the moral feeling of respect revealed to us.

We need now, however, to move from mere consciousness of moral demands via this feeling toward appreciation of how this same feeling is operative in the establishment of respect for persons as the telos and governor in one's world of desire. In describing the end-setting process of the would-be virtuous person, this

---

[4] See Grenberg (2013a).
[5] See Grenberg (2013a, especially chapters 6–9) where I discuss the moral epistemology of becoming aware of the Categorical Imperative. See also Grenberg (2018), where I argue further that moral feeling establishes the contours of one's moral consciousness, much as the Transcendental Unity of Apperception establishes the contours of consciousness generally.

same *feeling* enters into our realm of desire as a sort of quasi-*desire*, that is, not just as a feeling but as a feeling pointed toward influencing one's end-setting.

I call the moral feeling of respect a "quasi-desire" for a couple reasons. First, on the one hand, I call it a "desire" because it is a feeling that acts more like a desire in that it is action-focused.[6] But this desire status is only "quasi" because, although it is a feeling that operates on the same action-focused level with empirical desires, it is not itself an empirical desire. An empirical desire is something in one's practical consciousness that marks or identifies to one's practical consciousness a *lack* of something that needs to be fulfilled. The moral feeling of respect is not a desire in this sense. To the contrary, it is a feeling that points one toward a *capacity* for reason-giving one has that resides in a part of the self distinct from but related to one's empirical, desiring self. And because it is a feeling that points back to and is indeed caused by one's rational capacity for reason-giving, we confirm a second sense in which it is not empirical.

The moral feeling of respect is thus a rather special quasi-desire, one which, because of its rational cause, reliably tracks the noumenally based, necessary, and rational command to make persons as such my end. Every other inclination or desire I experience is based upon some empirical need I have. But the moral feeling of respect, far from being based in a need, is a feeling grounded in an awareness of myself as a truly rational agent with reasons for action grounded in the absolute value of persons, reasons which demand that I constrain, guide, and cultivate my other needs and desires in line with the demands of reason.[7]

What does it mean, though, to appeal to this quasi-desire in the process of end-setting and self-governance? In short, this feeling constitutes a sort of voice of conscience which reminds me of my most basic moral obligation to respect persons and thus helps me to govern and order my inclinations and desires accordingly. As Kant reminds us, conscience is simply "practical reason holding the human being's duty before him" (6:400/160). And the way that conscience works is "to affect moral feeling by its act" (6:400/160). That is, practical reason, which confirms the absolute value of persons and the constraints this absolute value

---

[6] See Grenberg (2001) for my extended defense of the idea that, while one must draw a technical distinction between feeling and desire for Kant, one can nonetheless identify a specifically practical feeling that, like desire, is pointed toward choice and action.

[7] There are disagreements amongst Kant interpreters about how best to understand both the nature and the role of this moral feeling of respect. Some interpreters accept the rational demand to respect persons but don't think there is or needs to be a desire or feeling which tracks this moral demand. These are what Richard McCarty (2009) has called the Intellectualist (as opposed to the Affectivist) interpreters of moral feeling. Reath (1989) is the primary representative of the Intellectualist school. McCarty, Patrick Frierson (2014), Ware (2014), and myself (2005, 2013, 2018, amongst others) represent the Affectivist school, viz. those who assert that one's awareness of and/or motivation to act upon the moral law involves some sort of appeal to the moral feeling of respect, *qua* affect. I have, more precisely, argued previously (in Grenberg 2013a) that the moral feeling of respect is a feeling which plays an epistemic role in helping one become aware of the categorical nature of moral demands and which has a distinctive causal provenance that allows it to play this role successfully: it is caused by our free, rational, autonomous, and moral selves. In this forthcoming chapter, I expand that epistemic role into a practical deliberative role akin to the presence of conscience in one's moral consciousness.

places upon our end-setting, *announces* these constraints to one's consciousness via the moral feeling of respect, that feeling which "make[s] us aware of the *constraint* present in the thought of duty" (6:399/160, emphasis added). And so, when I am contemplating which of my inclinations to set as ends, this moral feeling of respect acts as a sort of gate-keeper, reminding me internally through a feeling of conscience that, whatever inclinations I hope to realize, I must respect persons while realizing those inclination-based ends; and, further, that I must positively set ends which make concern for persons (both myself and others) central to my end-setting

In this latter setting of obligatory ends via appeal to the moral feeling of respect which acts as a constant marker within the world of desire reminding us of our non-relative, absolutely necessary moral obligations, we thus enter the realm of what Kant calls "inner freedom," that is, the exercise of one's freely and rationally grounded laws in an activity of "self-constraint not by means of other inclinations but by pure practical reason" (6:396/158). In other words, pure practical reason, through its influence on our sensible world of desire via the moral feeling of respect, is now put to work in the actual shaping of one's end-setting. This feeling becomes the tool by which reason actually constrains one's inclinations and desires so as to set those ends most appropriate to the realization of this overall end or telos of respecting persons.

This constraint and governing of one's inclinations and desires is, furthermore, accomplished specifically through the free and autonomous setting of ends. We enter here the explicit realm of duties of virtue, duties which, unlike duties of right, require the internal constraint to and establishment of precise ends of action, the setting of which is accomplishable only by oneself instead of by some external constraint. We thus enter the realm of the establishment of duties of virtue via the self-constraining power of inner freedom: "This extension beyond the concept of a duty of right [viz., in which our exercise of freedom moves from outer freedom to inner freedom] takes place through *ends* being laid down" (6:396/158). The establishment of these obligatory ends is thus a free act of self-constraint, the constraint, that is, of one's various desires and inclinations which would otherwise themselves compete to be taken up as ends utilized in the governance of oneself. As Kant puts the point: "[I]n the imperative that prescribes a duty of virtue there is added not only the concept of self-constraint but that of an end, not one that we have but one that we ought to have, one that pure practical reason therefore has within itself" (6:396/158). With this self-constraint of inclinations via appeal to this objectively existing end, we do, in other words, find that "[virtue] commands and accompanies its command with a moral constraint (a constraint possible in accordance with laws of inner freedom)" (6:405/164).[8] When I set an obligatory end, I thus set a positive end inspired by my moral-feeling-expressed experience

---

[8] We see in this quote also a nice reaffirmation of the existent nature of the end by which practical reason guides itself, a point first affirmed at 4:437/49.

of conscience which reminds me that I must make persons as such my end. And that obligatory end both furthers my realization of respect for persons in some precise way and simultaneously constrains me from acting on those desires and inclinations that would be in conflict with the realization of this higher end that has been identified as the objectively necessary telos of my being. We can thus think of the self-constraint or governance of *desire* as what occurs through the establishment of obligatory *ends* set through one's capacity for *inner freedom* via the voice of one's *moral-feeling-expressed experience of conscience*. This corralling, guidance, constraint, and ordering of desires and inclinations is just part and parcel of what it is to set obligatory ends and slowly thereby to become a virtuous person.

We thus most fully affirm the nature of self-governance with this proper objective telos of self-governance in hand: the governing of my affects and passions is accomplished via the legitimate authority of the telos of respect for persons most appropriate to my being in general and most apt for organizing and governing my desires overall. Via this telos, which acts upon my world of desire by inspiring a moral-feeling-expressed experience of conscience, I set all those obligatory ends which realize, express, and constitute this general rational demand to respect persons. And each of the obligatory ends that emerges from the telos of respect for persons, when set via inner freedom (instead of simply via inclination as simply pragmatic ends are set), acts to constrain, guide, and cultivate my inclinations generally in line with the order and reason of this objective and rationally grounded telos. Every one of the obligatory ends or duties of virtue that I set is, in other words, in addition to being one way in which I make persons my end, also a way that I constrain, guide, and cultivate the expression and choice of my desires: I govern my desires through the setting of this most general end of respecting persons, a general end which informs all subsidiary end-setting and desire-governance. *This* is legitimate and authoritative self-governance!

Is Respect for Persons Any Better than Self-Elevated Ruling Desires?

Before turning to consideration of the nature of some of these obligatory ends that emerge through this process, I want at this point to address the concerns of an objector. One might argue that a rational principle like the absolute demand to value and respect persons is subject to just the same criticisms that we saw in our I.i discussion of self-governance via passionate second-order desires. That is, if my ruling desire, perspective, or point of view is a concern for the value of persons, isn't it true that I am constrained only to evaluate other things relatively, for what import and value they have in relation to that ruling perspective of the value of persons, thereby warping or misconstruing the value of other things as they are in themselves?

This objector is, to a certain extent, correct: in governing my life in accordance with the objective telos of respect for persons, I will evaluate everything in my life in light of this value. But there is a difference here from any contingently elevated desire that would seek to operate similarly: respect for persons is a perspective which starts from admission of an *absolute* value. It thus makes *sense—is right* or proper—that everything else evaluated in light of this absolute value *would* find its value relative to this guiding value. That is just what it means to introduce an absolute value into one's governance structure: an absolute value governs absolutely. It provides a firm axiological point of view from which every other thing *should* be evaluated. When we replace the lens of contingent or naturalistically determined desire with an absolute valuing of persons (a respect for persons that has its marker or token to be found within the realm of desire), we thus find a point of view both more *capable* of and more *legitimate* for the evaluation and ordering of my desires. We have, in other words, found something truly capable of giving us proper *evaluative distance* on the relentlessly value-relative world of desire, a point of view that now gives me a purchase upon how to order that world. Instead of warping, misconstruing, or obfuscating the nature and value of those other desires, this point of view thus does just the opposite: it reveals them for what they really are, viz. reveals them all *as* merely relatively valuable things. From the perspective of desire, I can only judge all desires as related to some other desire, placing one desire instead of others in a ruling position and judging all other desires from that artificial place-holder. But when I claim a governing quasi-desire with a special, non-desire-based provenance pointing back to a non-contingent, necessary, and universally valid absolute value, then I can place the whole series of my desires in a new perspective, and can now, for the first time, value that series as one—but only one—thing that is true about me. I thus reject the self-absorption—what we might now call the "desire-fetishism"—of a naturalistic model of self-governance. It is no longer the case that the only concern I have in governing myself is to satisfy all my desires. I *do* have a concern to satisfy my desires, but I now also have a perspective from which I recognize that I am more than a desire-satisfaction machine. I am also a being who has the capacity to recognize, legislate, and execute strict moral demands grounded in the absolute value of persons.

We thus accept the idea that this ruling quasi-desire of respect for persons is indeed an appropriate and authoritative point of view from which to evaluate every one of my other desires and to set all of my ends appropriately in light of this guiding value. I will speak at greater length, in Part II of this book, about how we can still, on this picture, make sense of the *non*-moral value of things. That is, while we will not claim a thoroughly moralized conception of value, we shall see, nonetheless, that even the non-moral value of things can be appreciated properly only from this moralizing perspective.

For the present, though, we can confirm that, in addition to whatever desires I have, I thus now have a basis for understanding that *persons*—including myself—have value *independent of* desire. It is true and interesting—and a bit ironic—that on my reading of Kant's system of sensibly affected rational beings, we learn of this aspect of ourselves that is beyond desire only in the way that it *affects* and indeed truly *elevates* our very capacity for desire. That is, on my reading of Kant, we encounter this beyond-desire part of ourselves only via the natural-cum-phenomenological world of desire and the moral-feeling-expressed experience of conscience.

As such, one can perhaps appreciate more fully how important it is for our account to call this feeling only a "quasi"-desire: although this feeling is indeed playing the role of a desire in terms of guiding our end-setting, it is not a feeling that marks a lack or need within me to be fulfilled. Rather it marks a capacity or strength within me. Ironically, then, it is a quasi-desire that helps me recognize myself as something more than a desire-satisfaction machine. And, indeed, this irony is precisely the beauty of Kant's approach to the self-governance of desire: I learn that I am more than a desire machine through reflection upon an odd, special-provenance quasi-desire which points me beyond itself and, indeed, beyond the realm of desire entirely to something more deeply, pervasively true about me and about all humans. I am a sensibly affected being, and need to be concerned with the status and satisfaction of my desires. But within that very need for desire-satisfaction, I discover something that raises me above the pursuit of desire-satisfaction: I am a sensibly affected *rational* being.

A Footnote on Vice

Now that we can envision the possibility of evaluating desire from the introduction of this non-desire-based rational demand which nonetheless expresses itself in the world of desire, we can, furthermore, understand more powerfully than we were able to in I.i that desire just isn't the right sort of tool for the ultimate evaluation and governance of desires. Indeed, once we accept that respect for the absolute value of persons can be tracked within our world of desire as described above, we are able to appreciate just how inadequate any merely self-elevated garden-variety second-order desire is for governing one's life. Whereas the moral feeling of respect and the general demand to make persons as such one's end give one a point of view from which to view and evaluate the entire series of one's desires, every other desire in the series is merely that: something within the series of desires trying, but failing, to gain that distance from the other desires that would justify that original desire in some ruling position. Indeed, it is only now that we know making persons as such one's end is a better, more authoritative governor of our desires that we can really see the passionate governance of desires discussed in I.i as not only incomplete but also vicious. Let's explore this new territory.

We saw in I.i that one can choose to elevate an inclination into what Kant calls a passion, essentially an inclination that is given governing authority over one's desires in a way very similar to Frankfurt's appeal to second-order desires-cum-volitions. There is, however, a large difference between just any desire taking on this governance role and one's true, objective telos of one's person playing that role. Both apparently innocuous and apparently bad inclinations are equally problematic when elevated into second-order ruling passions. For, whatever passion I choose, it promises to be a state grounded solely in an inclination. As such, this state cannot provide that evaluative distance on my desires that we saw respect for persons could provide, an evaluative distance grounded in a more legitimate governing source and thus more adequate for the complete ordering of my person. Indeed, the establishment of passion-based governance will assure, eventually, that I care more about something than I do about morality. Whether it is the anger which, when taken up as a passion, becomes a constitutional hatred which guides my life,[9] or my desire for cheesecake which becomes an overall dietary and life principle, leading me to fail to care for myself properly, the choice of a desire, or inclination-cum-passion assures a disastrous and vicious outcome of desire-governance, one ultimately injurious of persons.

Indeed, from this height of desire-informed absolute value, passionate second-order desires can be seen as the truly *mutinous* things they are: on Kant's model of desire-governance via one's telos of making persons as such one's end, we acknowledge that there is something *else* within one's person that is better able than mere desires to evaluate all desires truly for what they are. We *should* be evaluating our desires according to the extent to which they are compatible with the worth of and respect for persons. But when we try to govern ourselves by something less capable of that governance, we mutinously reject this more worthy perspective, this more worthy part of ourselves. This is the source of egregious self-centeredness in the governance of one's desires. For, as we have just seen, one really interesting distinction to make between moral feeling and any garden-variety desire is that whereas the latter are based in need, the former is based not in need but in capacity. As such, to place what turns out inevitably simply to be one of one's needs in the role of governance is to privilege an egregiously need-based self-centeredness in one's governance in preference to an obviously preferable capacity-based ground. And this *self*-centeredness of a desire-based model of self-governance is furthermore the direct rejection of a *persons*-centered model of self-governance. *This* is the heart of the vicious failure of passionate desire-based

---

[9] "A *passion* is a sensible desire that has become a lasting inclination (e.g., *hatred*, as opposed to anger)" (6:408/166).

self-governance: I put satisfaction of my needs and desires above concern for respecting persons. Passions are, by definition, mutinous and vicious, an explicit rejection of one's proper authority in favor of a self-absorbed and egregiously self-interested conception of governing oneself.

With the establishment of a passion, one's response to incompleteness in the governance of one's desire-fulfillment gets taken to a new level: I passionately *reject* the very fact of personhood as a value (a value the importance of which nonetheless continues to resound internally in the world of my desires via my moral-feeling-expressed experience of conscience), and instead insistently pursue a governance of myself that would realize happiness, empirically conceived, on its own terms (viz., only within and guided by a need-based desire, with no appeal to a perspective from outside the world of desire to guide that process). I thereby take an imbalanced and incomplete thing and try, from my further imbalanced tendency to make everything about *me* in the first place (viz., from my sole interest in desire-satisfaction), to make that natural pursuit of fulfillment of desire complete. But I instead end up only institutionalizing its inherent empirical incompleteness as not only an imbalanced but now also *vicious* way of being (and "vicious" because the natural imbalance of a being concerned only with desire-fulfillment is a being who chooses everything in light of her own interests, someone who has put concern for herself above concern for morality). The limited resources of *natural* self-governance are thus revealed as being susceptible to influence and ultimately corruption by our *rational* tendency toward preferring ourselves, that is, by our tendency toward evil. Our natural pursuit of desire-fulfillment—while not vicious or evil in itself—is thus ripe or fertile (because self-absorbed) ground wherein our rational but now evil propensity to place ourselves above morality situates itself, expresses itself and finds its home.[10]

This perspective on the viciousness of a passionate life thus also further affirms the failure of Frankfurtian whole-heartedness in a passionate self-governance: once we accept that everyone has a voice of conscience within their series of desires reminding them of the need to make persons as such one's end, we find that it is impossible, by definition, for the vicious person to be whole-hearted. The vicious person must always fight that part of her that knows that there is something more important than the desire which she has made the most important, authoritative thing in her self-governance. Every effort to extirpate or quell this voice will, in the end, come back to haunt a person in one way or another, whether

---

[10] As Kant notes: "[A] propensity to an affect...does not enter into kinship with vice so readily as does a passion...The calm with which one gives oneself up to [a passion] permits reflection and allows the mind to form principles upon it and so, if inclination lights upon something contrary to the law, to brood upon it, to get it rooted deeply, and so to take up what is evil (as something premeditated) into its maxim. And the evil is then *properly* evil, that is, a true *vice*" (6:408/166).

it be through insomnia, madness, or just a vague sense of dissatisfaction.[11] As Kant notes, conscience:

> is not something that [the human being] (voluntarily) makes, but something incorporated in his being. It follows him like his shadow when he plans to escape. He can indeed stun himself or put himself to sleep by pleasures and distractions, but he cannot help coming to himself or waking up from time to time; and when he does, he hears at once its fearful voice. He can at most, in extreme depravity, bring himself to *heed* it no longer, but he still cannot help *hearing* it. (6:438/189)[12]

We thus accept the telos of making persons as such one's end as that tool for self-governance of desire most capable of providing the evaluative distance necessary for that governance overall. Indeed, it is that evaluative point of view which identifies one's governance as moving toward virtue instead of plunging into vice. Because this telos is the legitimate authority for governing the world of desire and because it thereby establishes that point of view from which to appreciate the merely relative value of all other values, any effort to place some merely relativistically valuable desire or value instead of it in a ruling position of one's soul cannot be understood as anything but seditious mutiny. In the governance of my desires, I claim a telos beyond desire-fulfillment, thereby assuring a governance of desire that is not mere self-absorption. And I accomplish this virtuous governance of desire via the setting of obligatory ends by means of my capacity for inner freedom which orders and constrains my desires in accordance with this telos, helping make all my end-setting constitutive of the realization of it.

II. A Dedication of Obligatory Ends

Introductory Thoughts on Deducing Obligatory Ends

We are finally at the point where we can consider the precise content of the obligatory ends that emerge from application of the objective end of making persons as such one's end, affirming the status of that end as the genuine telos of end-setting and

---

[11] Dostoevsky is particularly good at bringing such internal crises of conscience to life. Ivan's struggles in the *Brothers Karamazov* (2002) and Rascalnikov's struggles in *Crime and Punishment* (1993) come particularly to mind.
[12] I thus find myself in general agreement with Timmermann's (2006, 2016) discussions of conscience which also emphasize the impossibility of removing conscience from one's consciousness. I disagree strongly with him, however, on his (2006) suggestion that conscience is operative only in the realm of duties of right. The location of Kant's most extensive discussions of conscience squarely within the depths of the Doctrine of Virtue should be enough at least to make one hesitant about constraining its force to matters of duties of right.

desire-governance. As we know, when one claims respect for persons as the ultimate telos of one's desire-governance, one not only agrees to limit one's end-setting so as to assure that one does not thereby treat persons merely as means; beyond that, one chooses to make persons, generally, one's end: persons become that for the sake of which one acts. In other words, one makes persons' concerns, needs, and hopes the content and center of one's end-setting. As Kant notes, "a human being is under obligation to regard himself, as well as every other human being, as his end" (6:410/168). As such, I must "*do* that by which one makes oneself and others one's end" (6:410/168, emphasis added). The general injunction to respect persons thus needs to be realized in specific obligatory ends: we must *make* persons as such (and not just in general) *our* ends, our concern, our responsibility. This deduction of obligatory ends is thus simply an effort to do what is demanded by our general telos of respecting persons. These ends fill in the blanks, or make more particular, of this general demand to make persons as such (myself and others) one's end.

Furthermore, since these obligatory ends are to be deduced through appeal to this new, materialized version of the Formula of Humanity (and not simply through one's own personal, arbitrary preferences), we can also confirm the objectivity of the ends that emerge. These ends will, in other words, be "ends that it can be a *universal* law for *everyone* to have" (6:395/157, emphases added), or ends that all rational beings must set as ends.[13] That we are obligated to the precise ends we consider here—i.e., respect for oneself, and beneficence or sympathy toward others—is grounded in the absolute value of persons as ends-in-themselves first affirmed in the *Groundwork*: persons are that objective end, appeal to which raises otherwise would-be subjective ends like sympathetically helping someone into the realm of objectively necessary and universalizable ends. By taking this objective telos of respect for persons as our ground and telos, we thus also assure that the specific, person-centered obligatory ends of action which emerge from it and which constitute the realization of this telos are thereby raised from relativity and subjectivity into absolutely necessary, objectively valid, non-relative, and non-subjective ends. We affirm thereby that the telos of making persons as such one's end is a truly legitimate governor of all end-setting, a governing principle with objective authority for all sensibly affected rational beings.

The result of the deduction of these more precise obligatory ends is a genuinely person-centered catalog of virtues: a whole series of specific, material obligatory ends or duties of virtues which constitute the myriad ways of being respectful

---

[13] The appeal here to the universalizability of obligatory ends is the first helpful, if indirect, appeal to the materialized First Formulation, now not to deduce obligatory ends but merely to reflect with more depth on the status of the ends deduced: these person-centered ends are also universalizable! This tag-team Second and First Formulation approach to elaborating these ends is something which I'll discuss in more detail, below, when considering the deduction of the obligatory end of beneficence.

of persons, both myself and others. When I make a particular person my end, I make that person's concerns, needs, and hopes the center of my concern. I must, for example, refuse servility, be beneficent toward others, avoid gossiping about people, and express gratitude toward those who help me. In confirming these obligatory ends, we thus conclude Kant's search for the *a priori* establishment of ends, via reason itself and entirely independently of inclination: the setting of these obligatory ends is an autonomous and free act of end-setting, as confirmed in our I.ii discussion of the free and autonomous setting of obligatory ends, and the life of virtue is one of guiding one's end-setting and governing one's desires and inclinations generally through appeal to these rational, autonomously and freely set, but still obligatory ends. Ultimately, what emerges in taking respect for persons as the telos of self-governance is a catalog of virtues or obligatory ends specifically Kantian in nature: a *Kantian* catalog of virtues is revealed as a *person-centered* catalog of virtues.

But what are the precise ends toward which this telos points us? And how do we figure out exactly what ends to set? One expects at this point a series of further deductions: rational arguments that move us from the general demand to respect persons to these more specific obligatory ends. And, surely, Kant does exactly this in at least some of his discussions of obligatory ends. He deduces, for example, the need for the very category of duties to self (6:417ff/173ff). And he provides a deduction of the obligatory end of beneficence from the notion of universalizability (6:452ff/201ff). We shall consider especially this latter deduction of beneficence in due course.

Granting all this, we need to remember the looser kind of thing a specifically practical deduction is. We previously (in I.iii) understood the practical deduction of the telos of virtue itself as something accomplished via attentive reflection upon the already accepted fact of persons as existent ends: if we are going to respect the absolute value of persons, we mustn't be indifferent to their welfare and must instead make persons as such our end, our concern, our matter of choice. As we saw, then, Kant insisted that we could not realize the Second Formulation for what it is—a principle of end-setting grounded in the absolute value of persons—if we maintained an utter indifference toward persons: "it is not enough that [one] is not authorized to use either himself or others merely as means (since he could then still be indifferent to them); it is in itself his duty to make man as such his end" (6:395/157). When he introduces this demand to make persons as such one's end, he thus distinguishes this demand from a weaker demand in which we would be obligated only not to harm others. Simply not harming others, and remaining indifferent to their welfare and flourishing, fails to get to the heart of the point about the absolute value of persons: if some kind of being has absolute value, it is utterly inappropriate simply to ignore that being. Indifference to persons is thus a rationally inappropriate reaction to something of absolute value. Instead, as we have seen, the absolute value of persons demands of us that we positively set ends which further and affirm persons as existent ends with absolute value.

As we turn to deduction of particular obligatory ends, we can thus simply continue this attentive reflection on what it would mean to reject indifference to persons. This is a sort of common sense way of taking the demand to make persons my end as a guide for the setting of more precise obligatory ends. When we accept a materialized version of the Second Formulation as the telos of end-setting, we are accepting as our guiding value the fact that persons exist as sources of absolute value because they are free and rational beings, beings capable not just of reacting to stimuli but also of acting on reasons. Furthermore, we remind ourselves that we are deducing obligatory ends for *human* beings, or sensibly affected versions of these absolutely valuable rational beings.

One might argue that Kant's indifference argument appeals only to the absolute value of persons, but not to the notion that such persons are also needy. It is true that such appeal to neediness is not made explicitly there. But his appeal to the incoherence of indifference toward beings of absolute value does at least implicitly suggest that, were such beings to have needs, rejection of indifference would demand attentiveness to those needs. And although Kant does not explicitly appeal to such need as part of his indifference argument, one needn't do much work to make that implicit appeal explicit. One can, for example, grant that some rational beings—e.g., divine beings—are not simultaneously needy beings. We could, however, still make sense of what rejection of indifference would mean for such need-less absolutely valuable beings: they would be worthy of worship, not indifference. But other rational beings—i.e., sensibly affected rational beings—are, by the very appeal to the context of sensibility within which their rationality is expressed, also needy beings. Avoiding indifference for them would thus demand not worship but a willingness to be of assistance to them. So when, at one point, Kant describes sensibly affected rational beings succinctly as "rational beings with needs" (6:453/202), that is, rational beings who also find themselves dependent upon getting things from outside themselves in order to realize and flourish as the rational beings they are, we should take such appeal as an indirect reference to the demand to reject indifference to persons as rational beings, now specifically applied to sensibly affected rational beings.[14]

And so: since we must not be indifferent to absolute value; since a person's absolute value resides in her capacity to act freely for reasons; and since human beings are sensibly affected versions of these rational beings who are inevitably dependent upon sustenance from outside themselves in order to flourish, we can take both this capacity to act for reasons and this fact of the dependent nature within which this capacity realizes itself as guides for how exactly to reject

---

[14] I point the reader to Grenberg (2005, chapter 1), for a more complete discussion of the dependence of sensibly affected rational beings.

indifference and instead cultivate respect for *this* kind of being. In attending to this notion of persons as rational beings with needs, we thus intuitively fill in the blanks about what one would do to reject indifference toward such beings and instead affirm, support, and further them and their interests.

One might object at this point: although respect for persons, materially conceived, provides these just noted grounds for deducing individual obligatory ends, isn't even this materialized version of the demand to "respect persons" still rather abstract and formal? And isn't appeal to it therefore going to underdetermine exactly what we must do in particular situations? Is reason itself, even as amplified by these appeals to one's value being grounded in a capacity to act for reasons and to one's status specifically as a sensibly affected and therefore needy rational being, really going to fully determine our obligatory ends?

There is something to this objector's worry with which I can agree: pure reason is not going to tell me, for example, how exactly I should respect myself, or how exactly I should express sympathy for my friend's difficult situation. But, as we shall see below, reason alone does indeed ground at least general categories of obligatory ends. Indeed, we shall see that reason alone demands, e.g., that we respect ourselves and that we be beneficent toward those in need. Reason itself will allow me to look at a particular situation and identify the universal demands which visit upon that situation (e.g., ah, here I must be beneficent, or grateful, or self-respecting).

This means that "reason alone" does not determine obligatory ends abstractly, or entirely removed from actual decision-making situations, as if from some theoretical nowhere, but instead applies itself to particular situations, finding the specific obligatory ends which visit appropriately upon those individual situations and the needy rational beings we find within them. And although this application of reason is indeed via appeal to specific situations, the result of such application is universal, i.e. an obligatory end in the form of: "in these kinds of situations, I should do this kind of thing."[15]

The general category of obligatory ends thereby deduced will not, however, instruct us with precisely demanded specific actions as if via a mere algorithmic process. Instead, we affirm that the application of judgment—a sort of Kantian version of Aristotelian phronesis, viz. a capacity to apply one's principles to the concrete circumstances in which one finds oneself—is necessary to bring even this material version of the law to the actual guiding of action and character. This is, in fact, just what it means to recognizes obligatory ends as being duties of "wide" instead of "narrow" obligation (6:390/163). In all cases of duties of virtue,

---

[15] It is not, however, my intention here to provide a full deduction of all obligatory ends of virtue. Instead, I focus on a couple examples of how such deduction can successfully emerge from the application of reason alone to particular situations.

one will, in other words, discover there is latitude (literally, playroom or *Spielraum*) in how exactly one fulfills one's obligatory ends:

> for if the law can prescribe only the maxim of actions, not actions themselves, this is a sign that it leaves a playroom (*latitudo*) for free choice in following (complying with) the law, that is, that the law cannot specify precisely in what way one is to act and how much one is to do by the action for an end that is also a duty. (6:390/163).

That this playroom is an appeal to phronesis (that is, to good careful judgment in relation to particulars) and not just to some lawless space for doing whatever one wishes when the demands of reason come to the limit of their instruction is affirmed when Kant quickly goes on to note that "a wide duty is not to be taken as permission to make exceptions to the maxim of actions" (6:390/163), that is, is not to be taken as an opportunity to refrain from fulfilling the duty or to fulfill it in some willy-nilly inadequate way. In appealing to room for play, Kant instead is indirectly appealing to the need that an agent has to consider carefully the particulars of the situation in which she finds herself in order to allow those particulars to inform her judgment about how best to bring fulfillment of this duty to action, here and now. Here, then, not practical reason as such, but appeal to these particulars is what does the work of determining how specifically to fulfill an obligatory end.

Let us therefore take Kant's rejection of indifference to persons as a further general guide as we reflect upon how to set specific ends in light of the absolute value of persons who are free and rational choosing beings but who also are dependent and have needs. We will not, in the forthcoming discussion, provide a complete account of the person-centered catalog of duties of virtue that emerges from such reflections; that is a happy task for another time.[16] Instead, after briefly laying out the general structure of this catalog of virtues (noting that it is split into categories of duties to self and duties to others, and then that this latter category is split into duties of love and duties of respect), we will focus on the particular elements of this catalog of virtues which point toward our forthcoming Part II story of Deontological Eudaemonism. First, we will consider the establishment of the duty of beneficence, a discussion that allows us to revisit the question, set aside in I.iii, of the role of the First Formulation and universalizability in the deduction of the ends of virtue. Second, we shall turn to two further aspects of Kant's catalog of virtues—the fact that he affirms the category of virtuous duties to self and the fact that he affirms the demand to cultivate the feeling of sympathy for the sake of virtue—both of which, in different ways, point us toward our forthcoming

---

[16] It is my fervent hope that, at some happy point in the future, I will provide just exactly this complete list, relying also on characters in the novels of Jane Austen to help illustrate and articulate the nature of these states. For hints of what such an account would look like, see Grenberg (2015 and 2017).

Part II discussion of eudaemonism proper, viz. toward the idea that the desire-governance accomplished via the objective telos of respect for persons is a proper guide not only for virtue but for the proper functioning of sensibly affected rational beings generally, including their concern for happiness, both rationally and empirically conceived. The fact that virtuous duties to self is a meaningful category and, further, that the telos of respect for persons is a proper point of view from which not only to constrain but also to cultivate feeling—both of these points reveal that this telos of taking persons as such as my end, this tool of *virtue*, is also a tool inherently appropriate for being applied to oneself and one's feelings, thus preparing us for that principle to also become a tool for the pursuit of happiness empirically conceived. Let us turn to these discussions.

Duties of Love, Not Just of Respect

The most basic division of obligatory ends which Kant establishes is a division between duties to self and duties to others. We will, later in this chapter, consider the importance of his introduction of the very category of duties to self for our story of Deontological Eudaemonism. We begin, however, with consideration of the latter category of duties to others.

One interesting result of deducing obligatory ends in relation to others from the general objective telos of making persons as such one's end is that, within this division of duties to others, Kant introduces a further sub-division of duties of love and duties of respect. With all the discussion we have had thus far of one's relationship to persons generally being one of *respect*, one might reasonably have expected *not* to discover duties of *love* as such in this list. Kant himself, at times, makes a sharp distinction between love and respect, even claiming that "there can be no direct duty to love, but [that] *instead* [one must]…do that by which one makes oneself and others one's end" (6:410/168, emphasis added). In putting the point this way, Kant thus makes it seem that any would-be duty to love is even directly *opposed* to the telos of making persons one's end: *instead* of enjoining oneself to a direct duty to love, one should focus only on the respectful task of making oneself and others one's end.

And yet, to assume this to be Kant's meaning here would be wrong. When Kant says that making other persons one's end involves "no direct duty to love," he is not simply eschewing duties of love. His point here is the more limited one that duty cannot command us to *feel* love for others and, further, that such a feeling of love as such is not the proper way to conceive of our most basic relationship to those moral laws which constitute our duties, nor to those persons whom we seek to make our ends. Such a merely feeling-based connection to persons would first of all be merely feeling and not a practical, act-based relation. It would, in other words, not be a way of making persons my end at all, because it would involve no making or doing, but only feeling. Second, this particular feeling of love would not be the proper feeling for conceiving of my obligation to other persons. It would instead ground what Kant elsewhere calls a "moral enthusiasm,"[17] a self-deceived confidence that one is more whole-hearted in one's relationship to one's obligatory ends than in fact any human being could be. Such a merely feeling-based enthusiasm at the very basis of our connection with persons would thus subvert instead of realize the very telos toward which one is pointed (viz., *respect for persons*).

But all this does not mean that one's telos of respect for persons does not direct us to act in a *practical* loving way toward others. The general demand to make persons my end, a demand we have been describing generally as a demand to *respect* others, actually issues not only in specific duties of respect (as, for example, not to gossip about others, or to hold others in contempt) but also in a demand to *love* others *practically*. As Kant notes: "Since the love of human beings (philanthropy) we are thinking of here is practical love, not the love that is delight in them, it must be taken as active benevolence, and so as having to do with the maxim of actions" (6:450/199). So, when guided by the telos of respect for persons, we love persons not just via a wishful loving feeling toward them with no end or purpose in sight, but rather, in a way that has an actual effect in their lives: this practical, loving dimension of one's duties is just another way of describing what it means really to *make* persons one's end.[18]

One can, in fact, find in the distinction between duties of love and duties of respect a parallel way of expressing what we saw earlier as the more narrow and the more expansive ways in which to conceive of the Second Formulation of the Categorical Imperative. Recall that this formulation can, on the one hand, be understood merely as placing permissibility constraints upon one's actions; but that, by the time we get to the Doctrine of Virtue, Kant also explicitly argues that it must be taken more positively as a positive command to make persons one's end. But this distinction between a mere negative limit on one's choice and a positive command to take up persons as such as the matter of one's choice is now, in the Doctrine of Virtue, simply described in other terms as the distinction between duties of respect and duties of love to others:

> The duty of love for one's neighbor can, accordingly, also be expressed as the duty to make others' ends my own (provided only that these are not immoral). The duty of respect for my neighbor is contained in the maxim not to degrade any other to a mere means to my ends (not to demand that another throw himself away in order to slave for my end). (6:450/199)

---

[17] See, e.g., 5:85–86/73.
[18] For more reflection on the nature of practical love, see Grenberg (2014 and 2013b).

Put this way, it seems that the truly and fully virtuous way to act toward others, a mode of acting in which I go beyond what duties of right and externally constrainable acts demand of me, is to take up duties of love toward others. As Kant puts the point: "Performing [duties of love] is *meritorious* (in relation to others); but performing [duties of respect] is fulfilling a duty that is owed" (6:448/198). This positive and meritorious quality of duties of love is the reason why, as above, Kant is even willing to *equate* the taking up of such duties of love with the more general obligation and telos of making persons as such one's end, now specified to our concern for other persons (as opposed to myself as a person). As in the general deduction of the telos of making persons as such one's end that was discussed in I.iii, were practical reason here to demand only that I not injure others, and not also that I positively seek to enhance their lives, we would not be taking up the fullest virtuous attitude that is demanded toward a being of absolute value. To fulfill duties of love is thus the ultimate and complete—perhaps even the most characteristically and definitionally appropriate—way of fulfilling one's general telos of making persons as such one's end specifically in relation to other persons, thereby avoiding being merely indifferent to them.

Let us conclude this chapter by turning to some highlights of Kant's discussion of more precise obligatory ends (both duties to others and duties to self) which emerge from the objective telos of making persons as such one's end, and the rejection of indifference which grounds it. The purpose of these reflections is two-fold: they will help us, first, to appreciate how the objective end of making persons as such one's end acts as a telos to guide further end-setting; and, second, they begin to point us toward the contours of our forthcoming Part II consideration of Deontological Eudaemonism.

A. Duties to Others: Beneficence

The Relationship of the First and Second Formulations in any Forthcoming Deduction of the Duty of Beneficence

Having deduced the materialized *Second* Formulation as the telos of virtuous desire-governance and end-setting via the rejection of indifference, we now, as we approach the deduction of specific obligatory ends from this general telos of making persons as such one's end, have a better perspective from which to consider the question of what a materialized version of the *First* Formulation can and cannot do in such specific deductions. We will look at the particular duty of love that Kant calls the duty of beneficence to make sense of this reintroduction of concern for the First Formulation.

Let us begin by recalling our earlier discussion of the First Formulation: the materialized version of the First Formula of the Categorical Imperative was able to tell us that obligatory ends, whatever their content, must be ends that everyone can set. This formulation gave us general guidance, and a constraint that any answer to the question of what our most general obligatory end is would have to meet. But it was not able to reveal the content of that end. We thus, in I.iii, set aside this formulation as inadequate in itself to deducing the actual matter or content of our most basic obligatory end or telos and turned instead to the more material Second Formulation and its central notion of the existence of persons as ends-in-themselves to affirm that indifference to such beings had to be rejected and that, therefore, we must take persons as such as our objective end or telos.

And yet, to be true to Kant's very first introduction of the First Formulation of the Categorical Imperative back in the *Groundwork*, and to be true to the tersely stated articulation of the two materialized versions of the Categorical Imperative in the Doctrine of Virtue with which we began our discussion (again, in I.iii), we need now to think further about ways of bringing this essentially formal First Formulation of the Categorical Imperative back into the conversation about how to deduce obligatory ends. What we shall discover in consideration of the deduction of the duty of beneficence is that while the First Formulation cannot on its own ground the content of obligatory end-setting, it can work *together* with the Second Formulation in one deduction as a tool for moral psychological attentive reflection upon the complete nature of the objective telos of virtue revealed through the Second Formulation. A closer look at Kant's text suggests that Kant himself finds appeal to the First Formulation in conjunction with this already completed deduction of the general objective telos of making persons one's end to be valuable.[19] Let us turn to interpretation of this text.

Let's begin by reminding ourselves of the terse way that Kant introduces the materialized versions of both the First and Second Formulations. When Kant introduced the materialized First Formulation (viz., the idea that one must "act in accordance with a maxim of ends that it can be a universal law for everyone to have" (6:395/157)), he did not go on to explore what it meant to seek the universalizability of this new materialized thing, a "maxim of ends." Instead, he went on immediately to say: "In accordance with this principle [viz., the supreme principle of the doctrine of virtue which he is revealing here] a human being is an end for himself as well as for others" (6:395/157). The rapidity of his movement, in his pursuit of the supreme principle of virtue, from the universalizability of a maxim of ends to the idea of humans as existent ends is striking and, at least initially, curious. One might have expected him to reflect first on what it would mean to universalize a maxim of ends, distinguishing that process from the more familiar process of universalizing a maxim as such. Instead, to make sense of this "maxim

---

[19] In making this move, I place myself in general sympathy with Timmons' (2017) approach to understanding the First Formulation, one in which he asserts that a "formal constraint" reading of the First Formulation works not as a "decision procedure," but instead, more broadly, in "the overall economy of Kant's ethics."

of ends," he turns to that more obviously material Second Formulation idea of existent ends to articulate the "end" in question. So, at this point, he has not yet articulated exactly what he means by a materialized First Formulation; but it seems, in virtue of the contiguity of his brief introduction of a materialized First Formulation and his immediate appeal to a materialized Second Formulation, that Kant is seeking somehow to integrate the two formulations together into one supreme principle of virtue: both the formal claim that any end must be an end that holds as a universal law for everyone to have and the material claim that this end is "persons" toward whom we shouldn't be indifferent must somehow be brought together in the pursuit of an understanding of the complete supreme material (that is, end-focused) principle of virtue.

And although this move to merge the formulations might seem curious at first, upon reflection it makes sense: as we've already considered, it is difficult to conceive of how the First Formulation, on its own, could have any matter or end to it at all. Instead, it can only bring a formal constraint to what any end could be. At best, its own "matter" is just a formalized version of what that more material end of persons as such is: to claim persons as such as an end is to claim an end that can hold as a universal law of all persons. The notion of those ends which could be universally set by all rational beings is thus just another, more formal, way of describing that fully materialized version of the matter of the Categorical Imperative as stated in its Second Formulation: an end which could be universally set by all rational beings is just the rigorously formal way of articulating that end of persons as such. It is, in fact, hard to envision what else one could do to bring genuine matter or content to the First Formulation, other than to appeal in this way to the matter of its sibling, the Second Formulation. Hence the quick move Kant makes here from the materialized First Formulation to the materialized Second Formulation.

But this very point—that the First Formulation simply states the constraints of the objective telos of all end-setting first identified via the Second Formulation, but now in strictly formal terms—might just be an important moral reminder or guide as one pursues the explicit deduction or particularization of the more precise obligatory ends that follow from admission of the objective telos of making persons as such one's end. Let us then take this terse merging of the two formulations as a guide for further reflection. Perhaps, at least in the realm of virtue, the First Formulation is not *meant* to operate on its own. Perhaps, to the contrary, it is meant to affirm the formal constraints always present and attendant upon the obligatory ends we affirm and deduce from a more material, less formal source: the Second Formulation, that formulation that has already been identified back in the *Groundwork* as providing the "matter" or "end" toward which the Categorical Imperative points (4:436/43). It is in consideration of Kant's discussion of the deduction of the duty of beneficence that we can further explore such a possibility. Let's turn, then, to that discussion.

The Deduction of the Duty of Beneficence

That we have to deduce anything at all here in relation to the duty of beneficence might, once again, be a perplexing thought: if we have already deduced a strong notion of the Second Formulation in which one makes persons as such one's end the general and objective telos of all end-setting, and if (as we affirmed above) making *other* persons as such one's end is essentially equivalent to being beneficent to them, haven't we already deduced a duty of beneficence when we deduced that stronger, more positive command of the Second Formulation as our guiding telos of end-setting?

There is something to this objection: like any particular obligatory end meant to be constitutive of one's telos of making persons one's end, confirming a duty of beneficence is not so much the establishment of a further duty beyond that original telos as it is one particular way in which that very telos is realized. We are not trying to deduce further duties *beyond* that telos, but only to make more precise, particular, and perspicuous the duties that *comprise* or are *constitutive of* that telos. It would thus be tempting simply to say that the telos of making persons one's end, when particularized as the question of how to make *other* persons one's end, simply *is* the duty of love called beneficence, and leave it at that.

And yet Kant himself seems to need to say something more than this. As he introduces his discussion of beneficence, he notes: "It is not obvious that any such law [of beneficence] is to be found in reason. On the contrary, the maxim 'Everyone for himself, God (fortune) for us all' seems to be the most natural one" (6:452/201). This language almost exactly parallels in meaning a move he made in the *Groundwork*, in his first consideration of the challenges of deducing a duty of beneficence.[20] It seems, in repeating himself here in the Doctrine of Virtue, it is almost as if Kant himself has forgotten that he has already introduced something beyond his *Groundwork* discussion of such things, viz. his decisive rejection of indifference toward others as a morally tolerable stance. For surely that argument is a direct response to this objector, in either her *Groundwork* or Doctrine of Virtue guise: this maxim of "everyone for himself, God for us all" is, indeed, the very instantiation of just that indifference which he has already shown to be incompatible with respect for the absolute value of persons. And so when, despite the presence of that newer argument not found in the *Groundwork*, we still find the Kant of the Doctrine of Virtue anticipating the same sort of skeptical response to the suggestion that there really is duty of beneficence, it seems there is something in the air of the late 18th century which demands of him that he do something to

---

[20] There, he considered someone who would say, when confronting persons "whom he could very well help" who "have to contend with great hardships": "What is it to me? Let each be as happy as heaven wills or as he can make himself; I shall take nothing from him nor even envy him; only I do no care to contribute anything to his welfare or to his assistance in need!" (4:423/33).

underscore the argument already made, a further consideration or fuller articulation of the reasons we must reject such indifference.

The interesting thing Kant now does, as if to provide further ammunition for his point, is to appeal to the First Formulation of the Categorical Imperative to defend a duty of beneficence. This is a distinctive moment in the Doctrine of Virtue. He has not run a contradiction-generating universalizability test as such anywhere else in the Doctrine of Virtue, and he will not do another after this one. It is certainly the case that, elsewhere in the Doctrine of Virtue, he considers potential contradictions in our understanding of things, as for example when he worries that the very category of duties to self might involve an internal contradiction (6:417/173). But this is not appeal to contradiction in the sense of applying the First Formulation universalizability test of maxims. His appeal to the First Formulation here is singular, and seems motivated by the hope of providing more than one argument to defend a particularly contentious claim. He has already deduced a rejection of indifference to all persons, including other persons, when he deduced the general telos of making persons as such one's end. But now, in implicit response to someone who would say "Oh, c'mon, doesn't it really make more sense for every person simply to be concerned for themselves?" he provides the rejoinder of a second argument. Let's look at it.

In this deduction, Kant seems first simply to be applying the First Formula universalizability test in order to deduce the obligatory end of beneficence. But, in fact, closer investigation of this argument reveals that, much like his merging of First and Second Formula concerns in that earlier deduction, he either intentionally or unintentionally appeals to conclusions of our Second Formulation deduction as part and parcel of his First Formulation universalizability test. Here is that brief argument:

> To be beneficent, that is, to promote according to one's means the happiness of others in need, without hoping for something in return, is everyone's duty. For everyone who finds himself in need wishes to be helped by others. But if he lets his maxim of being unwilling to assist others in turn when they are in need become public, that is, makes this a universal permissive law, then everyone would likewise deny him assistance when he himself is in need, or at least would be authorized to deny it. Hence the maxim of self-interest would conflict with itself if it were made a universal law, that is, it is contrary to duty. Consequently, the maxim of common interest, of beneficence toward those in need, is a universal duty of human beings, just because they are to be considered fellowmen, that is, rational beings with needs, united by nature in one dwelling place so that they can help one another. (6:453/202)

Kant clearly begins here by appealing to universalizability constraints: the maxim of self-interest is presented as something that contradicts itself upon universalization.

Were I to set as an end the intention not to help others, I would not get the help I need myself in the world of the universalized maxim.

The question of whether this is an application specifically of a *materialized* version of the First Formulation is, however, an interesting one. Recall that the materialized version of that formulation was one in which universalization was meant to be brought to the level of ends. Instead of simply seeking a contradiction in one's maxim, one would thus need to seek a contradiction in one's "maxim of ends," a notion which, in that earlier section, went unexplained. Can his application of the First Formulation here help us make sense of what contradiction in such a "maxim of ends" would be? The end in question here would of course be one of setting the *end* of being beneficent, not just making it my *maxim* to be beneficent. Interestingly, though, no language of a maxim of ends, or even just simply of ends or end-setting appears in this argument. To the contrary, it is a straightforward application of the *Groundwork* universalizability test to maxims, one which mirrors almost exactly what Kant had already done in the fourth example of the First Formulation in the *Groundwork*.[21] The questions thus arise: are we really looking for contradictions in a maxim of *ends* or in *end-setting* in this Doctrine of Virtue version of the argument instead of (or in addition to) contradictions in *maxim-making*? Is there any way in which the "*maxim* of self-interest" (emphasis added) could be conceived as a maxim of the *end* of self-interest, and the "*maxim* of common interest" (emphasis added) as a maxim of the *end* of common interest?

I am tempted to believe that the answers to these questions are: no, or at least that, to the extent that these maxims would appeal to ends, they are not doing anything differently than what one would do in seeking to universalize maxims in the traditional, *Groundwork* sense. In trying to apply the materialized First Formulation, Kant runs into just the same roadblock he encountered when he first introduced it: a merely formal version of the Categorical Imperative cannot speak to precise ends. Then, he had introduced the language of a "maxim of ends," but did nothing to explain it. Now we learn that we cannot perform a universalizability test that generates a contradiction specifically within a maxim of ends that would be distinct in any way from a universalizability test that generates a contradiction in a maxim *simpliciter*.[22]

---

[21] The only real difference we see there is that Kant introduces language of the impossibility of this maxim holding as "a law of nature": "[A]lthough it is possible that a universal law of nature could very well subsist in accordance with such a maxim, it is still impossible to will that such a principle hold everywhere as a law of nature. For a will that decided this would conflict with itself, since many cases could occur in which one would need the love and sympathy of others and in which, by such a law of nature arisen from his own will, he would rob himself of all hope of the assistance he wishes for himself" (4:423/33).

[22] The issue becomes only more complex when one recalls that many interpreters agree with Korsgaard's (1996c) practical contradiction interpretation of the First Formulation, one in which the end or purpose of one's maxim must be understood in order to generate a contradiction.

Given all this, it is difficult to conceive of how one would do a universalizability test specifically of a maxim of ends, or if one did, how that would be any different from a universalizability test of maxims. Universalization seems already to be a test made for maxims which have ends or purposes. In any event, it does not seem that Kant himself tries to do anything different with his application of the universalizability test here. Having introduced a new, materialized version of the First Formulation, in his first (and only) application of the First Formula specifically for the purposes of virtue, he reverts to his original maxim-assessment form of it.

Indeed, looking at the generation of the contradiction in the Doctrine of Virtue presentation of it, it seems simply to replicate the structure and the problems that this same argument revealed in the *Groundwork*. That is: it seems that in order to generate a contradiction in the universalization of the maxim of self-interest, one must appeal to a thick and contestable notion of humanity: the idea that all persons will hope for help themselves. My refusal to help others generates a contradiction only if I assume in my maxim that I myself have needs which I hope will be fulfilled by others. If I didn't, then we would find no contradiction in the world of the universalized maxim: I would fail to help others, and others would fail to help me, and that would be the end of the story. For the contradiction to work, we must thus assume that the maxim of self-interest is one in which I intend to deny the help to others that I in fact hope to receive for myself. And, indeed, this is exactly the assumption found in both the *Groundwork* and the Doctrine of Virtue versions of this argument. One might assume, then, that Kant's argument for grounding a duty of beneficence through the First Formulation simply fails twice: he is trying to generate a contradiction only through formal appeal to universalizability, but in both versions of this argument, he illicitly sneaks in a thick notion of what all persons must want to generate the contradiction.[23]

But there is another way to read what Kant is doing, at least in the Doctrine of Virtue version of this argument. Remember, Kant has a tool in the Doctrine of Virtue he lacked in the *Groundwork*: an argument affirming the incoherence of indifference toward beings of absolute value. How might this fact make a difference for this argument for beneficence? Let's explore.

The thick conception of persons to which he appeals in the beneficence argument is simply, as Kant himself goes on to summarize, a description of persons as

---

[23] We thus revisit here a new version of the same problem we saw in Korsgaard's (1996c) rejection of Paton's Teleological Contradiction reading of the First Formulation. Korsgaard rejected Paton's interpretation precisely on the basis that such a reading needed to assume purposes for all humanity which she believes simply do not obtain. There, we considered the problem in relation to the question of suicide: in order to generate a contradiction in the suicide's maxim, one had to assume there being a purpose to living. Here, the problem we encounter is a similar one: in order to generate a contradiction in the maxim of self-interest, one has to assume that every human being wants help from others when she is in need. This too is a thick, purpose-laden conception of humanity. As we shall see in the forthcoming argument, I am once again more willing than Korsgaard to welcome such purposes into our interpretation of the First Formulation.

"rational beings with needs." It is just such needy beings who would indeed make the critical assumption that would generate the contradiction, viz. the assumption that all such persons would themselves want help from others. By definition, a being who identifies herself as a being in need would (apart from motivated cases of self-deception) be the sort of being to seek relief of that need from others: "For everyone who finds himself in need wishes to be helped by others." But, crucially for Kant's Doctrine of Virtue argument, to think of humans as rational beings with needs is just another way of describing an aspect of the notion of persons implicit in the materialized Second Formulation Kant has already deduced, the notion of persons as sensibly affected rational beings. One could thus, instead of suggesting that Kant illicitly introduces this thick notion of persons, say that he implicitly appeals to a conclusion for which he has already argued previously: Kant's argument for beneficence, when it appeals to "rational beings with needs" to complete its defense of the deduction of beneficence as an obligatory end, involves implicit appeal to the nature of absolutely valuable *sensibly affected* rational beings, a notion which has already been defended and implemented in his deduction of the objective telos of making persons as such one's end by appeal to the incoherence of mere indifference toward such beings. But such appeal is now legitimate in a way it was not in the *Groundwork*, legitimate because Kant has now already defended this notion of persons to which he appeals by other means, viz. by appeal to the Second Formulation's material notion of persons as ends-in-themselves.[24]

So: in order to generate the contradiction he wants, Kant needs to appeal to that thick conception of persons. This point is generally agreed and admitted. But, unlike those who would suggest that such appeal is illicit, we suggest that he already has a philosophical defense for just that thick conception of persons: why not appeal to it? The answer some would give to that question is that the First Formulation, if it is to work as it should, must not appeal to such material assumptions at all, defended or undefended. This formulation is meant to give us, by merely formal rational means, the tools necessary for deducing our duties. To admit appeal to some more material conception of persons to make the contradiction work thus seems to be a simple admission of the failure of this particular argument, or perhaps of the entire First Formulation procedure.

But, once again, one might conceive of things differently here. It is true that the First Formulation, in the way conceived above, cannot work on its own. But might it be doing something else that is valuable? We've already noted, at the beginning of this discussion, that it seemed that Kant didn't really need further

---

[24] One might argue that Kant's indifference argument appealed only to the absolute value of persons but not to the notion that such persons are also "needy." It is true that such appeal to neediness is not made explicitly there. But, as we saw above, his appeal to the incoherence of indifference toward beings of absolute value does at least implicitly suggest that at least some of them are the kind of beings who would find themselves in need.

deduction of the duty of beneficence in the first place; he had already accomplished as much in his Second Formulation argument for the incompatibility of indifference with respect for beings of absolute worth. So it could be that Kant sought out the First Formulation here not so much to provide an argument from a ground-zero starting point to prove beneficence as, instead, to provide a further way of appreciating or conceiving more deeply of something that we've already accepted. Granted that we accept indifference to persons is intolerable, how can we appreciate the contours of this intolerability? The First Formulation has tools to help us think about the incoherence of refusing aid to others in need, so Kant appeals to it. He uses it, in other words, to think more attentively and perspicuously about the state of rational beings with needs. Envisioning a world in which such beings refuse assistance to each other paints a clearer picture of the first rejection of indifference point: these rational beings with needs, once we accept that this is what they are, would find themselves in an incoherent and indefensible state were they to try to be indifferent to the state of others. Appeal to the First Formulation contradiction test is thus a means for attending more carefully to the demand already accepted that we must make persons as such our ends. Part of what this means, now specifically for our relationship to other persons, is that we must adopt a "maxim of common interest,...of beneficence toward those in need." Why? "[J]ust because they are to be considered fellowmen, that is, rational beings with needs, united by nature in one dwelling place so that they can help one another" (6:453/202). On this reading, the First Formulation is not so much a tool for proving or deducing a further duty as it is a means for highlighting, clarifying, paying attention to, or making more perspicuous the more precise nature of a duty already deduced.[25]

Even if we accept this most sympathetic reading of Kant's use of the First Formulation (as, indeed, I do), it seems, nonetheless, that, in trying to apply this formulation through a universalizability test, the original difficulty in even conceiving of a materialized First Formulation first encountered when he simply introduced the notion persists. Having asserted this materialized formulation as a

---

[25] It is on this point that I would favorably compare my own account of the First Formulation with Timmons' (2017) discussion of the same. According to Timmons: "rather than serving as a decision procedure..., the tests associated with FUL can serve to help foreground a conflict in one's practical deliberations between morality and self-interest." My position also, retrospectively, affirms from a new perspective the middle position I took earlier in Part I between Herman's (2010) and Formosa's (2014) readings of the question of the relationship between the First and Second Formulations of the Categorical Imperative. Herman finds these formulations equivalent, but Formosa takes the Formula of Humanity to be self-standing and more useful for practical application without appeal to the First Formulation, appeal to which would threaten contradictory outcomes for precise moral questions. I, however, take a middle road, agreeing with Formosa that the Formula of Humanity is best understood as basic and self-standing (thus putting myself into agreement also with Wood and Guyer on this point). But instead of rejecting the First Formulation as simply contradictory and counter-productive for the application of the Categorical Imperative, I find a positive, if subsidiary, moral psychological purpose of attentiveness for it.

means for seeking to universalize a maxim of ends, when push comes to shove, Kant cannot conceive of a specifically end-focused way of applying the contradiction test of that formula that genuinely issues in confirmation, on its own, of a specific content or obligatory end. This formula thus continues to reveal itself as too formal on its own to guide us in the establishment of an obligatory end. In order truly to derive the duty to beneficence, it is necessary to assume first the material existential fact of the nature and value of rational beings already deduced in the more general deduction of the overall objective telos of all end-setting, and then to rely upon universalizability as a tool of attentiveness for appreciating more precisely what that telos demands. To deduce specific obligatory ends, he must, that is, appeal indirectly to the Second Formulation to get epistemic access to that material "maxim of ends" he seeks.

One can, however, flip even this point in a more optimistic way: if, on the one hand, the First Formulation cannot deduce a specific end or content of duty on its own, on the other hand, and simultaneously, the Second Formulation actually *needs* the tools of the First Formulation—and especially its contradiction test—to help move itself forward: the indifference argument may essentially prove the need for beneficence, but it is the appeal to the non-universalizability of indifference to such beings that really brings the point home. I am a rational being with needs, but what exactly can and cannot hold universally in the treatment of such beings? Application of the universalizability test affirms the same claim but in a more precise way: we cannot envision a world in which rational beings with needs reasonably and on principle refuse help to other rational beings with needs.

What then does this mean for the usefulness of the First Formulation in identifying the obligatory ends of virtue? I would suggest that the First Formulation—especially once its relationship to the materialized Second Formulation is affirmed—can indeed play an important if still formal role in the articulation of obligatory ends. That is: its appeal to the notion of universalizability as such is what assures one can maintain an awareness of and commitment to the formal constraint of universalizability even as one pursues the material demands of the law which take center stage in his account of virtue. Kant is seeking to bring even this most formal of all formulations of the Categorical Imperative to the matter of choice, that is, to the determination of ends that are also duties. Although we needed to deduce the nature of obligatory ends generally through appeal to the Second Formulation, the First Formulation can still play its role of assessing the deduced individual ends so as to affirm their adherence to the formal criterion of universalizability.

With this further role for the First Formulation affirmed, we clarify the best role for the First Formulation in the pursuit of virtue: the First Formulation has not helped us to produce, deduce, or identify the material objective telos that guides the constraint of one's inclinations and the setting of one's ends overall. But this materialized version of the First Formulation *does* work well when it has matter from somewhere *else* than itself to work upon. It is better, that is, at helping one keep in one's mind's eye the formal constraints on any obligatory end or telos of virtue, than it is in producing from itself any specific material ends of virtue. There *is* a formal description of ends in play here in the First Formulation, viz. the notion of an end that can be set without contradiction, or an end that must be set universally by all persons. And although this merely formal conception of an end does not lead to a new kind of universalizability test, or get us on its own to any actual end or matter of choice that would constitute the telos of virtue, it is nonetheless very important as a constraining reminder for the quality that all obligatory ends as such must share.[26] What Kant did here for beneficence could, then, be done, certainly, for any duty of love (like sympathy or gratitude), but perhaps also for any obligatory end as such.

It thus seems that, to the extent one does appeal to this formulation in the determination of ends, it is not to provide a basis actually to deduce specific obligatory ends, but instead to keep one's eye on the formal concerns of morality, even as one determines those matters that should inform our material end-setting. That, it seems, is what Kant seeks when he describes a universalizability formula that now appeals to material ends: "act in accordance with a maxim of ends that it can be a universal law for everyone to have" (6:395/157). Even as you enter the material world of ends, make sure to stay true to the merely formal form of your ends.

B. Duties to Self: A Transition to Deontological Eudaemonism

The Very Category of Duties to Self

Let us shift gears now, and consider other aspects of Kant's deduction of obligatory ends which begin to move us toward an appreciation of how his distinctive objective telos of making persons as such one's end, and the distinctive person-centered catalog of virtues which emerges from and is constitutive of this telos, are in fact the tools most appropriate not simply for virtuous self-governance of desires but also for a euadaemonistic realization of one's person generally. For, recall that our just completed story of Deontological Teleology is offered as a central grounding for a larger goal of affirming Kant's Deontological Eudaemonism, an account in which the most successful pursuit of pleasurable proper functioning and happiness is grounded in appeal to that which is necessary or demanded for the kind of being that one is. All of our Part I discussion has been focused on

---

[26] I thus disagree with Wood's (2008) suggestion that, because of its utterly formal nature, the First Formulation can do absolutely nothing in the deduction of ends. To the contrary, although it can provide no direct derivation of duties, it is helpful in the ways we have suggested here, in providing indirect support for expanding upon our understanding of precise obligatory ends.

articulating what is necessary or demanded for sensibly affected rational beings: such are the fruits of our consideration of Kant's Deontological Teleology. But all of the forthcoming Part II discussion in this book is devoted to consideration of the eudaemonistic completion of these teleological commitments. So, now, as we approach the close of our discussion of Deontological Teleology, its objective telos, and the virtuous obligatory ends which constitute it, it will be helpful to focus on some moments in that catalog of obligatory ends or duties of virtue which point us helpfully toward its ultimate eudaemonistic conclusion.

One distinctive quality of Kant's persons-centered catalog of virtue is the idea that the objective telos of making persons as such my end instructs me on ends to set not only for the sake of other persons but also for the sake of myself as a person. Persons-centered virtue affirms, in other words, the very category of duties to self. Morality demands not only that we take the right attitudes and act in the right way toward other persons; it demands the very same toward ourselves.

One can, via the general injunction to make persons as such one's end, envision the sorts of things to which a rational being is obligated in regard to herself, in light of the absolute value of persons generally. In regard to herself, a free and rational choosing being who is also dependent and has needs would, first, take her own person as an end by respecting herself, not presenting herself in a servile fashion or tolerating others treating her with contempt. Further, one committed to the absolute value of rational beings and, implicitly, to the crucial communicative powers of that reason such beings possess would not use those rational powers to obfuscate or hide her purposes, that is, use them to lie. Nor would someone who considered herself absolutely valuable allow herself or her body to be used merely as a means for someone else's pleasure.

There is much—very much—that could be said about all these obligatory ends; for indeed, what the duty of beneficence does for duties to others these ends do for duties to self: they all serve to particularize and thereby constitute what it means to take persons as such—now the person in oneself—as one's end. But consideration of such matters is not the intent of this current discussion. Rather, I stand back from all these specific obligatory ends to self so as to reflect more generally on the import of an objective telos of one's end-setting that acts naturally, without any need for tinkering or adjustment, as a guide simultaneously for treating oneself and others properly. Were this not the case, that is, were Kant's project of morality and virtue one which conceived of such morality as emerging only when one encounters other persons in a social context, one might worry that its tools would be inappropriate to the pursuit of a eudaemonistic union of one's pursuit of virtue and happiness. That is: the inevitably and properly self-focused eudaemonistic pursuit of one's own pleasurable proper functioning generally, including a concern for one's own happiness, is itself a project which demands tools tuned to being used for the sake of and in regard to oneself. But if virtue were only about acting properly in my relations with other persons, it would not be a very good tool for these self-focused and self-enhancing purposes. It would indeed be rather limited in its ability to act as a tool for helping a person to become *herself*.

But, happily, Kant's conception of morality and virtue is not one that focuses exclusively upon one's interactions with other persons. To the contrary, it is one which possesses qualities which make it particularly apropos as a guide to thinking coherently about oneself and one's own pursuit of self-realization. For example, from our discussion of such things earlier in this chapter, we already know one particular self-focused role the telos of making persons as such one's end plays in the pursuit of virtue: it provides a perspective or evaluative distance upon oneself, and especially upon the merely relative value of the objects of one's desires. The absolute value of persons as the basis of this telos is, as we saw earlier in this chapter, the grounding and unchanging perspective point from which to evaluate everything else in the series of one's desires so as to order and govern those desires appropriately for the sake of virtue. But the very fact that this tool of virtue helps us to craft ourselves axiologically in this way means that this same tool can be of assistance in person-building generally, beyond the crucial virtuous demand to set the obligatory ends we've been considering. The very fact that the telos of sensibly affected rational beings is self-directed in this way (viz., is pointed toward the self as one of its proper objects) assures that this tool will be applicable not just for recognizing all one's obligatory ends but also for realizing that pleasurable proper functioning and happiness of one's whole self that is distinctive of a eudaemonistic approach to virtue. Indeed, as we shall see in Part II, one's ability to set and pursue non-moral ends and projects for the sake of happiness, empirically conceived, will not only be enhanced through appeal to this same objective telos of end-setting. Further, those non-moral ends set in pursuit of happiness, properly construed, will themselves, just like the realization of the obligatory ends we've been discussing here, be elevated and become more fully themselves in virtue of being made constitutive elements of the realization of this same objective telos of making persons as such one's end.

The Epistemic and Moral Psychological Priority of Duties to Self

Our goal for now, though, is the previous one of exploring the specifically self-focused use of the objective telos of making persons as such one's end. One interesting point in Kant's discussion of such things is that, beyond admitting such self-focused obligatory ends, he even suggests that there is something basic about these duties to self, making them a condition for duties to others. When he introduces the idea that "a human Being has Duties to Himself," Kant goes on to reflect:

> For suppose there were no such duties: then there would be no duties whatsoever, and so no external duties either.—For I can recognize that I am under obligation to others only insofar as I at the same time put myself under obligation,

since the law by virtue of which I regard myself as being under obligation proceeds in every case from my own practical reason; and in being constrained by my own reason, I am also the one constraining myself. (6:417–418/173)

There are a variety of ways in which one can take this claim; and, indeed, interpreters have.[27] I would suggest, however, that the best way to take Kant's argument here is as a combined metaphysical and moral psychological claim about the grounding of any and all duties.[28] Let's consider each of these points in turn.

First, Kant is making a metaphysical claim about the autonomous grounding of any obligation. As he notes, the law that grounds both duties to others and duties to self "proceeds in *every* case from my *own* practical reason." So, whether it is a duty to others or duty to self that emerges, the ground of that duty comes from me. And so, in all cases of duty, it is I that is putting myself under obligation. It is just that, sometimes, I put myself under obligation to myself and, other times, I put myself under obligation to others.

Kant's claim, though, is that duties to self which emerge from this self-imposition of duties are, in some way, more basic than duties to others: "for suppose there were no such duties: then there would be no duties whatsoever, and so no external duties either." But why is this the case? If all our duties are legislated autonomously, shouldn't we be able to legislate them in any order we see fit? Shouldn't it be as possible to legislate autonomously first toward others and then toward myself?

It seems, though, that there is a moral psychological fact at the basis of this metaphysical claim that all duties are legislated autonomously, a fact which requires that *legislation* of duties to self be, if not prior, then at least *simultaneous* with *recognition* of duties to others. As Kant puts the point: "I can *recognize* that I am under obligation to others only insofar as I *at the same time put* myself under obligation" (emphases added). His point here seems to be that although it may be,

---

[27] I am particularly sympathetic to M. Paton (1990) and her articulation of the import and priority of the category of duties to self for making sense of the central project of pursuing human perfection as the goal of Kant's ethics. In seeking to make sense of what Kant can mean when he says that "duties to self tak[e] precedence over duties to others," she suggests "that in some sense they are to be regarded as having greater importance in our endeavour to make sense of morality and to account for the possibility of morality as being other than prudence or even social concern. Thus, Kant would not be concerned with grading duties..., but with ordering at a higher level, such that duties to self are seen by him as laying the very foundations of morality by realizing a value without which morality could not exist" (p. 229). Paton also helpfully points to historical 20th-century reflections on the topic, including Singer's (1959) rejection of the very notion of a category of duties to self as incoherent, and Hart's (1958) rejoinder that rejecting duties to self makes sense only if one accepts an overly legalistic way of thinking about what ethics is, one which assumes a necessary reciprocity of duties and rights. One can also view Darwall (2006) as speaking to this question of priority of duties to self and other, but he seems to envision the opposite priority, viz. the priority of duties to others over duties to self.

[28] In so doing, I seek to expand upon Paton's (1990) suggestion that "duties to self...lay the very foundations of morality by realizing a value without which morality could not exist" (p. 229), a value which I identify here as autonomous legislation of duties.

objectively speaking, that I am always already obligated to both myself and others, I am not capable of *recognizing* the fact of obligation to *others* within my moral consciousness unless and until I actually put *myself* under obligation, that is, unless and until I actively obligate myself. Indeed, this recognition of duties to others and the putting of myself under obligation is something that occurs *simultaneously* in my moral consciousness: I must "*put* myself" under obligation "at the same time" as I "*recognize* that I am under obligation to others." Kant seems to take this simultaneity as an inevitable and unavoidable moral psychological fact.

Why would that be the case though? Why could I not *recognize* my obligation to others *previous* to *putting* myself under obligation? Darwall (2006) has suggested something similar to this in his second personal account of obligation: for him, it is in encountering the demands that others legitimately place upon me that I come to terms with the very notion of obligation as such. Indeed, one way of reading his appeal to a second-person grounding of obligation is to see it exactly as the flip of what Kant has said here, viz. that I cannot *put* myself under obligation to myself unless and until I *recognize* my obligation to others!

I have argued about the respective priority of appeal to such second- and first-personal points of view at length elsewhere.[29] For our current purposes, I simply re-emphasize the idea that there inevitably needs to be a first-personal taking up of one's obligations ("putting oneself under obligation") in order to recognize the very notion of obligation as such. This first-personal element is indispensable to obligation. This much I have argued before. But now Kant takes the point further: not only must I first-personally recognize obligation as such; I must, even when I recognize my obligation to others, be simultaneously appreciating that obligation to others as having a common source with my obligations to myself: both kinds of obligation are grounded autonomously in my own capacity for self-legislation.

But one still wonders why Kant demands this simultaneity: why is it necessary? It seems Kant wants to emphasize even further the very notion of obligation as a state in which *I* put *myself* under obligation. To think of it otherwise—e.g., to think that a genuine obligation could emerge thoroughly and only from outside myself—is to misunderstand the very notion of obligation as an autonomously imposed thing. Envisioning obligation as externally imposed would, thus, undermine the very notion of freedom, and inner freedom, we have been struggling to maintain as we move into the realm of the setting of obligatory ends.

If all this is true, then it seems that there is something very important, moral psychologically speaking, about that case in which I put myself under obligation *to* myself. It is only when I recognize myself as a moral being capable both of obligating and being obligated (all within one act of practical reason!) that I truly understand, from the inside as it were, the nature and import of obligation as

---

[29] See Grenberg (2013a, especially chapter 9).

such. I do not appreciate the inadequacy of external legislation until I see clearly and experience myself as engaging in this thoroughly internal legislation. And were I incapable of such legislation by myself to myself—"suppose there were no such duties"—then I couldn't really appreciate what it is to be a fully autonomous legislator as such. But the happy fact that one's practical reason works so thoroughly well—so completely and internally—prevents this counter-factual from occurring: we *can* envision true obligation to others because, regardless of any limits in my appreciation of the status of other persons as such, I know within *myself* that I can both obligate and be obligated. At every moment that I recognize my obligation to others, there is thus an underlying internal moment of me recognizing my autonomous capacity to put myself under obligation to myself. In obligating myself to others, I simply extend that internal, autonomous capacity to apply to a broader scope of beings as the target of my obligations.

Furthermore, in this experience of obligating myself, I encounter what it means to have obligations to rational beings as such. I am, after all, a rational being, and so when I encounter an obligation to myself, I encounter "both sides" as it were to what it is to have an obligation to a rational being. It is thus in experiencing myself as an obligated agent who obligated herself that I can truly appreciate that my own reason obligates me to rational beings as such. And it is only in experiencing myself *as* a rational being that I can confirm the fullness of my moral state.

The Evaluative Distance of Moral Self-Cognition

This focus on the primacy of duties to self can, furthermore, be taken to a deeper moral psychological level in a way that points us toward the import of Kant's virtue theory for our forthcoming Part II discussion of Deontological Eudaemonism. We have been saying from the beginning of this chapter that appeal to the telos of making persons as such one's end is something that provides evaluative distance upon the governance of one's desires. But if that is true and if, as we've just been suggesting, there is something moral psychologically prior in the experience of putting oneself under obligation via appeal to this telos, then one can also say that Kant's virtue theory is inherently built to provide persons with a duty-guided capacity for taking a proper evaluative distance upon oneself generally.

I have discussed elsewhere the centrality of self-knowledge in duties to oneself.[30] As Kant puts the point: to "*know* (scrutinize, fathom) *yourself*...in terms of your moral perfection in relation to your duty" is "the First Command of All Duties to Oneself" (6:441/191). In such classification of the duty of self-knowledge, we see yet another point at which duties to self take priority in obligating ourselves generally. First, we saw that we could not even recognize duties to others unless we also simultaneously put ourselves under obligation. But now we see that the

---

[30] See, e.g., Grenberg (2005, especially chapter 8, and also 2015).

"first" duty of all duties to self is to know yourself and where you stand in relation to your duties generally. Once again, a morally appropriate self-focus is at the heart of Kant's virtue theory.

Why is it that virtue is as self-focused as this for Kant? Why, in particular, do we need to know ourselves at all? Why not just do the right thing and be done with it? The answer, in short, to all these questions is that human beings are the sort of beings with a tendency to get things wrong about themselves, in either an accidental or a motivated way, and thus to be very much in *need* of taking that evaluative distance upon themselves which the duty of self-knowledge permits. We want to think well of ourselves; but, conversely, we're frightened that we aren't very good, or very worthy, or that others are better than us. And these tensions and uncertainties lead us to all sorts of misconstruals of ourselves which have the potential to create obstacles to our pursuit of virtue.[31] The first thing to do then, in trying to become virtuous is to, well, clean house! Look at yourself, figure out what you're seeing clearly about yourself and what you're lying to yourself about. Enter, that is, that "[m]oral cognition of oneself, which seeks to penetrate into the depths (the abyss) of one's heart which are quite difficult to fathom [and which] is the beginning of all human wisdom" (4:441/191). In the language we have been using, find a way to take an objective evaluative distance upon yourself.

The result of pursuing the duty to self of moral self-cognition is thus what we've been describing as taking a proper evaluative distance upon oneself. Through this self-cognition, we will be in a better state for looking at ourselves and valuing things within us as they should be valued. On the one hand, this means we'll be less prone to that self-hatred that can arise when one obsesses upon one's failings or weaknesses. As Kant puts it, "moral cognition of oneself will... dispel *fanatical* contempt for oneself as a human being (for the whole human race), since this contradicts itself" (6:441/191). The contradiction to be found and dispelled here is pretty clear once we remember that the law guiding this moral self-cognition is a law demanding that we take persons as such as our end. Surely, recognizing oneself as a being of absolute value requires one utterly to reject "fanatical contempt" for oneself. To gain knowledge about my moral condition—here, to remind myself that, whatever my failings and weaknesses, I am a being of absolute value—is thus one happy result of fulfilling this duty to self to know oneself. I am not saying such peace would be an easy state actually to achieve. But with the evaluative distance provided by the telos of making persons as such one's end, it becomes a possible outcome of the process.

On the flip side, the very same evaluative distance which rejects contempt for oneself also prevents one from reacting to one's fears and insecurities by putting on a mask of arrogance, essentially a contempt for others as a sort of defense

---

[31] And, indeed, as we shall see in Part II, to the pursuit of happiness as well.

mechanism for warding off contempt for oneself. As Kant puts it: "But such cognition will also counteract that egotistical self-esteem which takes mere wishes—wishes that, however ardent, always remain empty of deeds—for proof of a good heart" (6:441/191).

In short, pursuit of moral self-cognition provides one with that evaluative distance upon oneself which promises, as part and parcel of fulfilling one's obligatory ends toward oneself, that one will also develop a more stable relationship to oneself. As Kant summarizes the point, what emerges from the authentic pursuit of moral self-cognition is "[i]mpartiality in appraising oneself in comparison with the law, and sincerity in acknowledging to oneself one's inner moral worth or lack of worth" (6:441–442/191). I have, previously, described the acquisition of such impartiality and sincerity as an important aspect of the central virtue of humility that emerges in the pursuit of virtue generally.[32] I point the reader to that work for further consideration of such things. For now, though, we can affirm that knowing oneself and thereby taking the proper attitudes toward oneself is a concern at the heart of Kantian virtue. Sensibly affected rational beings are simply the sorts of beings who need to attend to themselves and get their own house in order even to have the bare possibility of becoming a moral person. And appeal to the absolute value of persons which grounds one's objective telos for self-governance gives one that evaluative distance on one's self necessary for the pursuit of virtue. Kantian virtue is indeed concerned with assuring proper attitudes and behavior in relation to other persons, but it is also simultaneously, and perhaps a bit more centrally or characteristically, a tool for knowing and becoming oneself.

The Tools of Virtue are the Tools of Happiness

It should thus not surprise us that the tools necessary for becoming virtuous will be the very ones which also help us to pursue happiness. Indeed, the pursuit of happiness seems just the next natural task to undertake when seeking to get one's own house in order; and the evaluative distance one gets on oneself in virtue of the absolute value of oneself and others as persons seems particularly promising for bringing a certain calm and equanimity to one's pursuit of happiness overall.[33]

That one might (and that some interpreters have, perhaps rather consistently!) thought otherwise—viz., that one might even be tempted simply to assume that the tools of virtue could not possibly be the tools of happiness—is perhaps attributable, in part, to Kant himself. His explicit rejection of eudaemonism,[34] his persistent rejection of happiness as a proper motive for morality, and his admittedly

---

[32] In Grenberg (2005, especially chapters 5 and 9).
[33] In affirming this, I am in deep sympathy with Holberg's (2018) similar claim that the tools of morality are also the tools of happiness. The work of Part II, and especially of II.iii, is an effort to take up and continue her excellent thoughts on this topic.
[34] A rejection which, in our Introductory Thoughts, we've shown to be misguided.

lamentable but equally persistent emphasis on examples which demand immense sacrifice and suffering from the person of virtue all encourage interpreters to draw a heavy line of distinction between the pursuit of morality and the pursuit of happiness. We will consider all such apparent obstacles to realizing the tools of virtue as the tools of happiness in Part II. For now, it is worth noting that these other discussions in which Kant appears to marginalize the import of happiness seem to have put blinders on many interpreters beyond what Kant ever intended in any of these moments at which he needs to keep happiness at bay for a specific philosophical or moral purpose. These blinders prevent interpreters from appreciating the point we have just made, viz. that the tools Kant presents for the pursuit of virtue, by helping one take a well-balanced evaluative perspective on oneself and especially one's desires, seem particularly well-built for helping one realize happiness and well-being generally.

This equal applicability of the tools of virtue to the pursuit of happiness is, of course, also what Aristotle sought to accomplish in his *Nicomachean Ethics*: indeed, for him, to seek one's virtue simply was to seek one's proper functioning overall and thus also to seek that pleasurable happiness which emerges in the experience of oneself as functioning properly. We shall in Part II consider at much greater length, especially in light of Kant's particular constraints upon the relationship of happiness and morality with which Aristotle did not have to contend, just exactly how, through his project of Deontological Eudaemonism, Kant joins Aristotle in the affirmation of a unified conception of proper functioning that integrates the realization of both virtue and happiness conceived rationally as a pleasure which visits upon the successful exercise of virtue. For now, I want only to indicate one advantage the project of Deontological Eudaemonism has in that pursuit which is, at best, a vexed question for Aristotle.

One perennial challenge Aristotelian virtue theory faces is that the central focus upon oneself and one's proper functioning as the ultimate objective telos of virtue threatens to be an *excessively* self-focused project, a project that actually wears away and waters down what should be a more centrally other-oriented pursuit of morality. For Aristotle, it is not clear whether the project of eudaemonism is a problematically self-aggrandizing project: is the pursuit of eudaemonism about being a moral person, or is it simply about celebrating one's own strength and nobility?

But this same problem is not to be found in Deontological Eudaemonism. To the contrary, the objective telos of respect for persons promises, as we have already seen, to provide just that evaluative distance necessary for the sake of governing one's desires properly so as to realize in one's person the right attitude toward persons generally, including oneself. It might be that on a certain interpretation of Aristotle—perhaps one that focused centrally upon how acting for the sake of the noble is the motive that must guide one's pursuit of virtue—one could alleviate Aristotle's problems in a similar direction. But even that principle for Aristotle is a notoriously vague one, itself subject to being read as a nobility narrowly construed as the excellence of oneself. And so challenges for Aristotle's eudaemonism remain that do not exist for Kant's.

Indeed, for Kant, it is exquisitely clear, almost obvious, that the proper functioning of a sensibly affected rational being could not collapse into simple self-aggrandizement. Our current appeal to the demand to make persons as such one's end, along with the demand this telos places upon persons to admit and realize obligatory ends toward oneself, makes that point clearly enough: a pursuit of virtue focused only narrowly and self-conceitedly on realizing one's own happiness could not realize the demands of *this* telos. And I point readers to my earlier writing which discussed the centrality of humility amongst Kant's duties of virtue to appreciate in more depth the particularly non-self-centered nature of Kant's theory of virtue.[35]

Our general point for now, though, is that the same telos of end-setting meant to guide virtue promises also and simultaneously to guide a non-self-aggrandizing pursuit of proper functioning more generally. The objective telos of virtue, properly attended to, is a tool most appropriate for just that reflection on oneself that will assure both the realization of moral demands and the pleasurable proper functioning of one's person overall, including the pursuit of happiness, empirically conceived. It is the very fact that a person-centered morality emphasizes duties to self—finding, that is, the proper evaluative distance from which to assess what is demanded of oneself in one's relation to oneself—that assures simultaneously that one will have tools to bring proper evaluative distance to oneself as one pursues happiness. Kant's appeal to duties to self is thus a happy harbinger of things to come in the governance of one's person. The tool most central to the realization of virtue—the objective telos of one's being—is one which is properly built not simply to assure that we treat other people properly, but also to bring about within oneself the pleasurable proper functioning of one's being. The first step in that proper functioning of self is the realization of obligatory ends toward oneself. But the capacity of this tool to govern one's desires from the right axiological perspective so as to assure a proper attitude toward oneself does not end there. Rather, as we shall see in Part II, the tools of virtue are, simultaneously, the tools of happiness. It will thus be in continuing to attend to what is objectively demanded of sensibly affected rational beings in realizing their telos of making persons as such one's end that these beings will find themselves best positioned to become properly functioning and happy sensibly affected rational beings.

---

[35] See Grenberg (2005). For further helpful reflections specifically on the nature of self-conceit for Kant, see Engstrom (2010); Moran (2014); and Ware (2015, 2014, and 2009).

C. Another Duty to Others: Sympathy

There is a final aspect of Kant's discussion of obligatory ends which reveals that discussion as being particularly applicable to the eudaemonistic realization of proper functioning. We have already seen that applying the telos of respect for persons to the governance of one's desires and end-setting makes that telos a tool whereby one begins to acquire an evaluative distance upon oneself, one's feelings, desires, interests, and pursuits generally. But there is one specific obligatory end, now an obligatory end toward others, which promises a similar sort of basis for helping to bring one's emotional house in order: Kant's claim that the cultivation of the feeling of sympathy is, generally, a duty. Consideration of this obligation to cultivate the feeling of sympathy not only will allow us to appreciate the importance of this particular feeling for the development of virtue but also will reveal a model generally for guiding the proper cultivation of feelings for both virtue and happiness. Once again, then, we shall discover that the tools of virtue promise also to be tools of happiness: pursuing virtue helps us to cultivate our feelings in ways that promise to be valuable not only for constituting one's state of virtue but also for moving one toward a more stable and satisfying state of happiness. The same means by which we cultivate feelings so as to make sure they are in line with respect for persons will be the means by which we cultivate feelings so as to help manage the many challenges and obstacles that can arise in the pursuit of happiness, thereby helping to assure an increase in that happiness.

And so, a further point of interest amongst Kant's set of obligatory ends which are established as duties of love is that, although a duty of love is not, most generally, a duty to feel in certain ways, one of these duties—the duty of sympathy—is indeed a duty at least to *cultivate* a certain kind of feeling:

> [I]t is a duty to sympathize actively in [others'] fate; and to this end it is therefore an indirect duty to cultivate the compassionate natural (aesthetic) feelings in us, and to make use of them as so many means to sympathy based on moral principles and the feeling appropriate to them.   (6:457/205)

There has been much said in recent years about the nature and import of this directive to cultivate sympathy. I am particularly sympathetic to those like Fahmy (2015) who emphasize the active quality of sympathy itself, viz. the idea that feeling sympathy can be an active state with a positive outcome for the other for whom I sympathize, even apart from any more substantive end achieved.

I do not intend here to challenge any of this literature; to the contrary, I am appreciative of the work Fahmy and others have done to unpack the import of this section of Kant's writing. But I am, for now, more interested in a general point that emerges when one welcomes this demand to cultivate the feeling of sympathy into the catalog of person-centered virtues. In introducing this virtue, Kant introduces what is essentially a new *kind* of obligatory end. For although all obligatory ends involve the governance—i.e., at least the constraint—of *desire*, no other obligatory end which Kant introduces—other than the general demand to attend to and cultivate the moral feeling of respect itself[36]—involves the active and positive cultivation of *feeling* as the very end to be pursued in the developing virtue, nor even the positive cultivation of feelings that might *indirectly* support some other virtuous end.

Let's dwell on this point for a moment. Recall that the establishment of a virtue via inner freedom involves both self-constraint and the laying down or establishment of an end: "[I]n the imperative that prescribes a *duty of virtue* there is added not only the concept of self-constraint but [also] that of an end, not an end that we have but one that we ought to have, one that pure practical reason therefore has within itself" (6:396/158). As such, every obligatory end indirectly involves self-constraint, and it is reasonable to infer therefore that the setting of every obligatory end involves a demand to constrain one's *feelings*. But such indirect appeal to the constraint of one's feelings does not obviously involve the simultaneous *cultivation* of those feelings which might support or enhance the setting of the obligatory end. That is, such cultivation, while perhaps useful or even recommended, does not seem to be *commanded* as such by these obligatory ends. Indeed, no other obligatory end Kant has considered involves a feeling component as part and parcel of the very end commanded. Even the duty of beneficence we considered above, another duty of love itself closely associated with the duty of love to cultivate sympathy, does not itself involve a demand specifically to cultivate feelings in relation to one's good-doing. But, with the introduction of the obligatory end to cultivate the feeling of sympathy, we have just that: a positive command to cultivate a feeling as an end constitutive of one's telos to make persons as such one's end. It is, therefore, distinctive and interesting that Kant introduces an obligatory end that specifically demands the cultivation of feeling.

It is, furthermore, interesting for our emerging story of self-governance that there is at least one obligatory end in accordance with which—in addition to

---

[36] See 6:399–400/160: "Obligation with regard to moral feeling can be only to cultivate it and to strengthen it through wonder at its inscrutable source." And the demand to cultivate this feeling is a distinctive case: the demand to cultivate respect isn't a demand to cultivate a feeling as a new obligatory end as such. The feeling of respect is, rather, as we've been discussing, the affective and desiring point of view established as one's conscience, that point of view *from* which one cultivates other feelings and *from* which one sets other obligatory ends. The demand to cultivate it is thus something different from a command to cultivate a naturally occurring feeling within us, like sympathy. When we cultivate moral feeling, we are reminding ourselves of the very source of morality and obligatory ends generally, reminding ourselves about something basic in our constitution as sensibly affected rational beings. (See Grenberg 2018 for more reflection on this point.) One could even say that the experience of the moral feeling of respect is the lens through which one cultivates other feelings: through the experience of this feeling, I am reminded of the demand to make persons as such my end, and so have an affective mark in relation to which I cultivate and enhance other parts of my affective experience, making those other feelings further now-recruited and elevated markers of my life-guiding telos to respect persons generally.

being an end for the sake of which one *constrains* one's contrary feelings, desires, and inclinations—one also includes a positive command to *cultivate* a particular set of feelings, desires, and inclinations. What exactly is the difference here? What does it mean to engage in that "self-constraint" involved in "governing" a desire and how does that differ from a self-constraint "cultivating" a feeling related to that desire? Surely, constraint involves constraining the active experience of one's feelings in relation to the desire (i.e., when I'm actually feeling the problematic feeling, I should be aware of that fact and then do my best to not let the experience of that feeling overcome me or take over my thoughts and actions). But, beyond that, it seems one must also do one's best to discourage oneself from actively feeling those feelings which would encourage one to pursue the end or goal of the desire in the first place, perhaps by trying to distract oneself from attending to that feeling and instead coaxing the focus of one's attention toward other things. But constraint probably also involves constraint beyond the constraint of *feeling* as such: it would also involve guiding one's *mind* so as not to dwell upon or attend to that end or goal of the desire itself. A successfully constrained desire would thus be a state in which one rarely or never felt those feelings which would encourage the desire and in which one rarely or never thought or dwelt upon the object, end, or goal of the desire.

Given this account of "constraint," the "cultivation" of feelings would thus be essentially the reverse of all these constraining activities: when I'm actively experiencing the feeling, I should make myself conscious of that fact, and then encourage and attend to the feeling itself, thinking more about the good reasons for experiencing it as I do and seeking opportunities to connect the feeling with particular ends or actions by which I could further the ways in which I make persons as such my end.[37]

---

[37] Implicit in this discussion is a distinction between feeling and desire which we've not needed previously, but which may be helpfully distinguished now. What is the difference between a feeling and a desire? I have previously (in Grenberg 2001) suggested that, although there is a technical difference between practical feeling and practical desire (because they are mental states belonging to different faculties, and further, because one (the feeling) is at least the partial cause of the other (the desire)), one can think of them informally as nearly identical: both feeling and desire are felt states pointed toward an object. For our current purposes, though, there is at least one further clarification of the distinction between them to be made: a feeling is simply a sensible "blip" on one's affective radar screen pointed toward some object (essentially what Kant would call an "affect"—6:407–409/166–167), whereas a desire (which would usually also involve such a sensible blip, or, more likely, many of them) is something more than a sensible blip which comes and then is gone. Beyond that, and more centrally, a desire is an established intentional state aimed at bringing something about. So, if I were to have a mere feeling, it would, like one of Kant's affects, simply come and then go, a sort of cloud passing over the sky of my practical consciousness. But if I have a desire and were I simply to allow it to operate unchaperoned, it wouldn't just come and go. Beyond that, it would lead me to begin to *do* things toward realizing that intentional state, end, or goal at which it is aimed. It is true that feelings are also intentional, i.e. they are pointed at objects. But to be pointed at an object in this way doesn't necessarily involve any extended-in-time experience of the feeling, nor any intent to *pursue* the object toward which one is pointed. So one could have an intentional feeling aimed at an object without that feeling being aimed at bringing something about in relation to that object. To the extent that one's feeling becomes more persistent temporally, thereby turning itself into something which points one toward

When reason commands a specific obligatory end to sympathize with others, it is to such acts of positive cultivation it enjoins us. Kant even emphasizes here that the feeling in need of cultivation is the "natural" feeling of sympathy in us, maybe even the sort of feeling of sympathy that arises coincidentally without us thinking about it. The task of cultivation thus involves taking what already happens naturally (and perhaps even unconsciously) in us, without any particular explanation or reason, and bringing such feeling into the realm of what is rationally and dutifully commanded of us. One consciously and actively reflects upon the feeling, encouraging it and enhancing it through reference to the general demand to respect persons. That is: I am enjoined to respect persons as free and choosing beings with needs, and part of what this means is that I should cultivate my natural tendency to sympathize with persons who are facing particular challenges to the realization of their free end-setting, helping that natural sympathy to become yet another expression and tool of my own end of making persons as such my end. Simply to feel in concert with them when they are feeling challenged is, in itself, a virtuous and respectful thing to do, a way of feeling that is partially constitutive of my general telos to make persons as such my end.

Furthermore, this demand to cultivate positively a particular feeling or desire from the point of view of duty is a particularly good example of what we have been describing generally as the "elevation" of feelings and desires which can occur within the process of self-governance. We have been saying generally that in the self-governance of desire, we need to understand desire or inclination—and, by implication, the feelings associated with that desire—as being put to the service of something larger than simply the fulfillment of a lack or need which one experiences: I, and persons generally, are not simply desire-satisfaction machines; instead, even our desires can be enjoined in service of a vocation higher than themselves. That one governs oneself and one's desires by the objective telos of respect for persons is the most general way to think of this elevation: by guiding all one's desires via appeal to the singular demand to respect persons, those desires, and their associated lacks, needs, and feelings, are organized and structured by appeal to a goal beyond themselves. Now, though, when the cultivation of the feeling of sympathy itself becomes morally *obligatory*, we can speak more precisely of a particular set of feelings that are put in the service of that higher rational and moral demand to respect persons. I am, in other words, enjoined to cultivate the sympathy I *feel* via the reasons I *understand* so as to elevate that natural feeling into being an assistant to one's rational self. When I cultivate my feelings of sympathy from the perspective of making persons my end, I regularly remind myself about the good reasons there are to feel sympathy for persons

---

doing something, we can say, to that extent, a feeling is becoming a desire. In making this distinction, I bring further reflection to the question of the difference between practical feeling and practical desire than I did in my 2001 consideration of such matters.

generally. So I continue to feel that natural feeling, but it is now a natural feeling that has a goal or purpose beyond itself: it is a natural feeling pointed not simply (or perhaps at all?) toward relief of the discomfort or pain I feel about another's situation, but also (or instead?) toward a rational goal, indeed, pointed toward the ultimate rational end and telos of my whole person. I can now say in a way that would not really have made sense or been appropriate before that there is something *right* about feeling this feeling: sympathy is appropriate precisely because it is one way I make persons as such my end. Feeling sympathy for persons is thus just another way of accomplishing such end-setting.[38]

This positive command to cultivate feeling from the point of view of duty does, furthermore, do something to expand our appreciation generally of what the self-governance of desire from the perspective of the defining telos of one's being can be: in setting those ends which are constitutive of this telos, I am not only in the business of constraining myself; I am also in the business of elevating parts of myself toward this higher, all-encompassing purpose. As one pursues this telos, it is of course inevitable that one will need to constrain feelings and desires inappropriate to it. But by introducing a natural feeling which, when elevated, can be constitutive of this telos, Kant introduces a more optimistic picture of the potential for the harmonization of the sensible and rational aspects of sensibly affected rational beings.

Furthermore, this demand to cultivate a particular feeling from the moral perspective of respect for persons provides a model for the practical cultivation of feeling generally. This can be said, in the first instance, about feelings one might have a moral obligation to cultivate. Kant himself speaks only of sympathy in this regard. But it seems the notion can be expanded to other feelings without injury to the moral structure of virtue Kant is envisioning here. Might not one take up certain experiences of anger, for example, from the perspective of respect for persons and thus understand that anger as justified moral indignation? Or take up even one's feeling of love for a person, or one's fear of doing something disreputable, again from this moral perspective, thus elevating these merely naturally occurring feelings into the service of morality? It is not clear to me that there is any reason within Kant's account of virtue that would prevent such expansion of the cultivation of this natural feelings model Kant himself introduces in the sympathy case.

Indeed, we can go even further: if virtue provides tools for the cultivation of natural feelings from the proper axiological perspective—that is, if virtue is the sort of thing that can act as a tool in the virtuous cultivation of one's feelings—surely this tool can also be a tool for the pursuit of happiness! That is: part of what one must do in the pursuit of happiness is to come to terms with one's feelings, to

---

[38] Fahmy (2015) would add that, because feeling in the right ways at the right time is a conscious and active thing to do, it is also something for which we can be blame-worthy or praise-worthy.

find ways to order oneself such that one is prepared for their experience. But the virtuous person will already know how to do that sort of thing: she's been doing it all along! On this score, the pursuit of happiness is thus not a different kind of thing from the pursuit of virtue: both involve reflection upon and cultivation of one's feelings from an appropriate evaluative distance. So, once again, the tools of virtue promise to become tools for the pursuit of happiness.

We thus see that Kant's particular approach to person-centered virtue is just the kind of thing to provide tools for making sense of a eudaemonistic approach to self-governance, an approach in which one's pursuit of virtue points naturally toward the pursuit of pleasurable proper functioning, including happiness, empirically conceived. What both the obligatory ends of duties to self and the obligatory end of cultivating the natural feeling of sympathy have in common is that both are examples of how the objective demand to make persons as such my end issues in obligations about the ordering of my *subjective* state in light of that demand: from the perspective of making persons my end, I begin to develop aspects of my internal moral consciousness—a perspective on my status as a moral agent and a more elevated way of experiencing my feelings of sympathy— pointed toward, consistent with, and indeed constitutive of the realization of that objective end. As we turn to our upcoming Part II discussion of the proper subjective telos of virtue as being also the proper subjective telos of the pursuit of happiness generally, we do so with these valuable tools in hand.

I.v
Objections to Deontological Teleology Considered

Introduction

There are a variety of concerns that one could raise about our just-completed defense of making persons as such one's end as the proper objective telos of virtue. Even if one were to accept the I.ii claim that deontology and teleology can be understood as reciprocal notions, one might still balk at the I.iii claim that the telos of making persons as such is the proper organizing telos of virtue, or the I.iv claim that this telos is the best point of view from which to organize one's end-setting generally.

We thus complete our Part I reflections on Deontological Teleology by considering a series of objections to it, all of which in one way or another challenge the idea that making persons as such one's end could be the proper telos of all end-setting. First, we'll consider an objector who insists that happiness must be the guiding telos for any truly eudaemonistic theory, and that this objective, rational, and strictly necessary telos of making persons as such one's end is thus not the proper telos for the governance of desire but instead a foreign intruder into that world of desire. We'll then turn to an objector who worries that respect for persons is too heavy-handed and moralistic a telos for organizing one's desires generally, especially one's non-moral desires. We'll conclude by considering an objector who worries that making persons the center of one's end-setting threatens to undermine proper attentiveness to non-person beings of value including animals and the environment. While each of these objectors will give us an opportunity to clarify various aspects of our account, we shall also discover the reasons they are generally mistaken. We thus conclude by affirming that Deontological Teleology introduces a substantive guiding telos for human existence which raises us above being mere desire-fulfillment machines, but also integrates a valuing of both non-human being and the non-moral pursuit of happiness (a topic which we will consider at much greater length in Part II).

Here is a brief summary of objections I will consider, all taken as slightly different twists on the general suggestion that respect for persons is not a proper goal of eudaemonism or desire-governance:

(1) Respect for persons is the wrong sort of goal for eudaemonism: any telos of a truly eudaemonistic system of self-governance has to be happiness. Eudaemonia is the pursuit of well-being, and to assert the structuring endpoint of eudaemonia as anything other than happiness is non-sensical.

(2) Respect for persons is the wrong sort of goal for desire-governance: this reason-based telos is not a realization of one's desires, but only a foreign invader into desire-governance, an organizing goal not proper to the world of desire.

(3) Respect for persons is the wrong sort of goal for desire-governance: it doesn't make sense to organize *all* one's desires—especially one's non-moral desires—via the moral demand of respect for persons. To do so is to introduce an excessively moralized conception of self-governance, one which illicitly rejects and constrains truly legitimate and thoroughly personal projects and concerns.

(4) Respect for persons is the wrong sort of goal for a complete and truly moral desire-governance: one cannot properly make sense of a moral response to non-human beings of value—either animals or the environment—with so egregious a persons-centered grounding of morality.

I consider each of these objections in turn, below, with a particular focus on (4).

I. Objections

Happiness, Not Respect, as a More Proper Telos?

One of the strongest reactions one might have to our defense of Deontological Teleology is that this is a teleology that would ground a eudaemonism whose central telos is not happiness as such. But does this make sense? Can one really speak of a eudaemonism or well-being which is not *centrally* concerned with happiness?

It is true that in claiming a non-naturalistic ground for the self-governance of desire, we are subordinating the satisfaction of desires generally, and thus the pursuit of happiness empirically conceived, to a higher, non-desire-based telos. And in thusly subordinating happiness as the sum of desire-satisfaction to this higher goal, one thereby rejects the idea that the perfect or complete realization of one's empirical pursuit of happiness is the ultimate telos of one's being. We must certainly grant to our objector here that such happiness empirically conceived—viz., the total realization of all my empirical desires—will not be realized in the life of the virtuous person. Happiness, as guided and limited by one's moral self, although (as we shall see in Part II) more *fully* realized through appeal to deontology, also can never be *completely* realized in this world. All of this will be considered in more depth in II.iii.[1]

We can at this point, however, respond a bit more to this objector, at least in general terms. As we have already seen, something has *happened* to our pursuit of happiness empirically conceived in the claiming of a deontologically informed telos for the governing of our desires: this pursuit of happiness acquires a new order and stability through being guided and limited now not by merely empirical rules but by exceptionless moral rules. I am indeed still interested in the fulfillment of my desires, but I am no longer utterly and blindly absorbed in that project; as such, any actual fulfillment of my desires will not collapse into mere self-absorption or what we earlier called a desire-fulfillment fetish. What this means is that happiness—understood specifically as simple desire-fulfillment—really *does* need to take a back seat here. It is too *low* a goal for describing the flourishing of a sensibly affected rational being. The forthcoming account of Deontological Eudaemonism, by offering an evaluative distance and perspective on happiness and the pursuit of desire-satisfaction that would not have been possible without the prioritization of morality over happiness, thus rejects the notion of self-governance as mere desire fetish, viz. the idea that all we are is desire-seeking beings and that all at which we could aim as the goal of one's governance and flourishing is the satisfaction of all our desires. We thus abandon happiness as the objective telos of one's person in the name of a *higher* telos.

But once we abandon that addiction to desire-fulfillment, we find ourselves on a more stable and, indeed (perhaps ironically!), *more satisfying* ground than what could be accomplished only within the world of desire. We abandon happiness empirically conceived as the complete telos of a sensibly affected rational being. But we do not reject the idea that pleasure, including the pleasure of desire-fulfillment, is an important part of a flourishing human life (like a certain sort of Stoic would do, one who says that once you have morality, you do, by that very fact, have happiness too). Kant emphatically rejects the idea that all we are is desire-satisfaction machines; but he also emphatically rejects the idea that all we are is moral rational beings. We are most centrally and essentially moral beings, but we are moral rational beings *in* a sensible world of desire; and there is thus something crucial, when articulating the most proper telos for this complex being, about understanding one's telos, and thus also the pursuit of *flourishing* and *satisfaction* of one's person *overall*, in a way that is true to one's being overall, both one's rational and one's sensible sides. In making happiness as desire-fulfillment a subordinate goal of the properly functioning person of virtue, we thus actually

---

[1] It is an interesting question whether happiness as the completion of that empirical series which are my desires is fully realized in another world, viz. via the Highest Good. But even there, it seems not *all* one's desires are realized, but only the ones consistent with your accomplishments of virtue.

make the realization of happiness and the higher integrity and proper functioning of one's person overall *more* possible. The eudaemonist dream of pleasurable proper functioning is not abandoned but elevated in the world of Deontological Eudaemonism. We will explore all this in much more depth in Part II.

Reason as Foreign Invader to World of Desire?

There is a rejoinder our objector might make at this point: it is not the demand to respect persons but instead happiness empirically conceived—viz., the *complete* satisfaction of all my desires—that is the *true* objective telos at least of my *desiring* self. Any appeal to respect for persons as the telos of desire, says this objector, is thus not the *proper* goal of desire, but instead a foreign *intruder* into it, a goal which would order my world of desire improperly, not on its *own* grounds but instead by being altered, coerced, and forced to become something that, on its own grounds, it was not meant to become. It just makes no sense to claim a telos for something that is external to the things to be governed, viz. a non-desire-based telos to govern desires.

This objector would be right were human beings merely and purely sensible beings: were I only a sensible being, then the proper goal for the realization of my being would simply be the fulfillment of all my desires. But when we speak of human beings, we are speaking not of sensible beings full-stop (e.g., a platypus), but of sensibly affected rational beings, and this changes things. One *could* argue that, for sensibly affected rational beings, one's sensible side has its own telos and one's rational side has its own telos. But this would make for an inherently conflicted and divided being: one part of me would be seeking realization in one direction, and another part of me in another. Such a being could never acquire *integrity* of person as such.

Of course, some would say that Kant accepts just such a divided model of the self.[2] But my suggestion to you, introduced when (in I.i and I.iv) we identified the moral feeling of respect as providing an affective marker of rational demands within the world of desire, is that, in accepting the notion that respect for persons expresses itself thusly *in* the world of desire, Kant implicitly rejects just this notion of sensibly affected rational beings being at odds with themselves. Instead of this divided picture, he envisions a more integrated notion of a sensibly affected rational being, one in which rationality and sensibility meet each other and integrate.

How can this meeting of reason and sensibility be understood? Sensibility, on its own, would properly seek only the fulfillment of all its desires. Yet, as we have

---

[2] Wood (2000) comes closest to arguing for such a stance. We will consider his position at greater length in Part II.

seen in I.i, sensibility, on its own, can never realize its own completeness. In conjunction with rationality, though, it has the hope of a new, and higher, sort of self-realization; it can become something more than it could be on its own. When rationality and sensibility meet, the very nature of sensibility itself is now *properly* elevated beyond itself. And Kant's vision of the governance of desire is thus based on the notion that desire is *meant* to go beyond itself: for sensibly affected rational beings, desires are meant to be more than themselves.

There are complexities, though, in this marriage of reason and sense. On Kant's story, the root of evil as self-absorption is found not in our sensible selves, but in our rational selves gone wrong: in our rationally grounded propensity to prefer oneself over any other object or person of value.[3] In other words, the very same part of ourselves that can elevate our world of desire could instead deflate or demote it. And, furthermore, because, as we've seen, desires themselves have a certain self-focus (viz., they want only to satisfy themselves), they provide particularly fertile ground for the realization of just this radically evil rational propensity to value oneself excessively relative to everything else of value. There are thus *tensions* not only between one's rational and sensible selves but also within the very nature of rationality itself, that need to be managed, tensions which threaten to rip the sensibly affected rational being into pieces. But the nature and quality of the moral feeling of respect itself—that moment in the world of desire that tracks the rational imperative to respect persons—expresses the way in which one affectively recognizes and manages these tensions so as to avoid so tragic a conclusion: it is a feeling which combines a negative affective experience of the constraint of one's rogue inclinations along with a positive affective experience of self-exultation in oneself as an autonomous and rational moral being. As Kant puts the point:

> This idea of personality, awakening respect by setting before our eyes the sublimity of our nature (in its vocation) while at the same time showing us the lack of accord of our conduct with respect to it and thus striking down self-conceit, is natural even to the most common human reason and is easily observed.   (5:87/74)

We will need, eventually, to consider the extent to which these tensions inherent to the lives of sensibly affected rational beings do or do not characterize the subjective experience of the life of a virtuous person. This will, indeed, be a central concern of Part II of this book. For now, we emphasize that, whatever these tensions are, they do not prevent us from welcoming this rational demand to respect persons as the proper telos of desire for sensibly affected rational beings.

---

[3] See 6:36/58–59, where Kant notes that although the human being is "dependent on the incentive of his sensuous nature because of his equally innocent natural predisposition," once one rationally chooses to "make...[those] incentives of self-love and their inclinations the condition of compliance with the moral law" one has turned that innocent disposition into a "radical propensity to evil."

Indeed, through the introduction of a rationally grounded quasi-desire-cum-telos concerned with respecting persons situated into the very world of desire itself, Kant envisions how the very *opposite* of a failure of the integrity of such beings is possible: instead of submitting to an inherently conflicted life with sense and reason in constant battle with each other, and instead of utilizing one's flawed rationality to pull sensibility into service for the realization of a life of self-absorption, one can instead utilize one's genuine rational appreciation for the absolute value of persons as a means of pulling one's sensible self upward into one's morally rational self, thereby realizing "the sublimity of our nature (in its vocation)" (5:87/74).

On a longer metaphysical story, in which I will not engage here, I think one can even argue that this resolution of sensibility to reason is simply one articulation of the resolution of nature to freedom, now expressed in the theater of one's own moral consciousness. This resolution of sense and reason is, then, just one expression of how the true telos of the world of *nature* overall, and not just of *our* (human) sensible and natural selves, is pointed toward a higher rational goal (and I would send you to the *Critique of Judgment* to investigate such happy possibilities). But for now I will make only the weaker moral psychological claim that it is possible for the proper objective telos of one's sensible self and of the world of desire with which it is concerned to be so oriented and elevated. Kant's appeal to the moral feeling of respect provides us with a model for thinking about what this resolution of nature and freedom looks like within the moral consciousness of a sensibly affected being. The result is the hope for a sensibly affected being to acquire integrity of person, to be the sort of being aimed at one overarching telos of her whole sensibly affected and rational person.

Respect for Persons is an Overly Moralized Telos of Humanity?

There is another version of our original objection which provides a more moral psychological, and less metaphysical, twist on this same worry: do we really want to accept the idea that the substantive and organizing goal of *all* one's desires is to respect persons? Don't I have goals beyond, before, or just separate from my need to respect persons? What about cello-playing, or downhill skiing? Am I really being true and fair to these desires and pursuits when, in order to govern them, I submit them heavy-handedly to a moralized conception of respect for persons?

I recognize these worries about the overmoralization of self-governance, and yet, ultimately, remain committed to the idea that all our goals are indeed moralized to a certain extent. We shall see as our story of eudaemonism unfolds in Part II that I do admit a non-moral conception of value. But given the ultimate "sublim[e]" "vocation" (5:87/74) of the sensibly affected rational being, even that non-moral value cannot fully realize itself unless and until it is put in its proper order in relation to an absolute moral value. In the end, for Deontological Eudaemonism, all our values and all our goals are part of the story of what it means to be a virtuous person. In some meaningful sense, then, the *fullest* telos of my desire, e.g. to become a better cellist, really *is* to respect persons, both myself and others. That activity—itself independent of moral demands—cannot become what it most fully can be unless it is guided by moral demands. That is, my cello-playing—something in which I engage simply as an opportunity to enjoy myself—becomes also an effort to realize my absolute value, as a person, and to enhance my respect for other valuable persons as well. That simple enjoyment realizes itself best when it has been educated by the refusal of self-absorption which its integration within a context of respect for persons assures. I'll discuss this point at much greater length when we address the nature of non-moral value in our discussion of happiness empirically conceived in II.iii.

II. A Further Objection: A Persons-Centered Telos Fails to Respect Non-Human Beings?

A Duty to and a Duty in Regard to: Direct and Indirect Duties

There is a final reason one might consider making persons as such one's end an inappropriate telos for either virtue or proper functioning more generally: one might argue that a persons-centered conception of eudaemonism has no basis for the proper valuing of non-animal beings or entities like animals or the natural environment generally.

It is not my intent here to provide a thorough-going defense of how a Kantian can manage a range of questions in animal and environmental ethics. But I shall provide an overview of how such a defense should proceed, indicating at least some general directions a Kantian can move to ground a robust moral concern for the value of non-human beings through an unapologetically persons-centered account of morality. Let us turn to that discussion.

A perennial topic of discussion in the literature about Kant and non-human beings is his claim in the Doctrine of Virtue that it is impossible to have duties to animals or divine beings because one cannot have duties to a non-human being:

> As far as reason alone can judge, a human being has duties only to human beings (himself and others), since his duty to any subject is moral constraint by that subject's will. Hence the constraining (binding) subject must, first, be a person; and this person must, second, be given as an object of experience, since the human being is to strive for the end of this person's will and this can happen only in a relation to each other of two beings that exist... But from all our

experience we know of no being other than a human being that would be capable of obligation (active or passive). A human being can therefore have no duty to any beings other than human beings. (6:442/206-207, emphases removed)

According to Kant's argument here, since duty involves a rationally grounded constraint of a will, such duties can, properly speaking, be applied only to beings who in fact have rational wills, viz. to persons. As such, animals and the environment, lacking wills, are not appropriate subjects of obligation. They are simply not the type of being that can obligate or be obligated.[4] Furthermore, we can have duties only to persons whom we can actually experience as existing, and to persons who strive for not-yet-realized ends. As such, although there might exist persons with wills other than human beings (as, for example, angels or God), we cannot speak of having duties to these other kinds of persons, since we do not encounter them in experience and we cannot conceive of them as having not-yet-realized ends. Human beings are thus the only kind of persons to whom we can have obligations.

And so, when Kant goes on to consider our moral relationship to animals and the environment, he does not speak specifically of obligations *to* these non-human beings, but instead of obligations *to oneself* but *in regard to* animals and the environment. And any thought to the contrary that we would in fact have duties directly to animals is based on a misunderstanding (or "amphiboly") about the nature of duties themselves:

> [I]f [the human being] thinks he has such duties [to non-human beings], it is because of an amphiboly in his concepts of reflection, and his supposed duty to other beings is only a duty to himself. He is led to this misunderstanding by mistaking his duty *with regard to* other beings for a duty *to* those beings.
> (6:442/207, emphases removed and added)[5]

---

[4] Note that this does not prevent animals from doing things that have moral import; it only asserts that we cannot *obligate* animals to do things like save someone's life or be sympathetic to another being's suffering. They may in fact do such things, but we cannot obligate them to do so, nor can they obligate themselves. This also means that animals themselves cannot impose obligations upon us. Again, care is demanded in assessing this claim. This does not mean that we have no obligations in relation to animals, nor that we consider animals to be utterly valueless except insofar as they serve our purposes; it simply means that the *source* of those obligations does not come from the animals themselves. Rather, these obligations in regard to animals and the environment, as with all duties for Kant, must come, as we shall see, from *ourselves*.

[5] Broadie and Pybus (1974) provide a helpful gloss on what an "amphiboly" is: "When [Kant] tells us that to suppose we have duties to beings other than man is to be guilty of an amphiboly, what he means is that such a supposition is based on the false assumption that beings which lack a faculty of reason are subject to a priori principles of morality; or, to put it more briefly, it is based on the false assumption that beings which do not have a noumenal self, do" (Broadie/Pybus 1974, 379). For such amphibolies to apply also to our misunderstanding of would-be duties to divine beings (beings which obviously *do* have rational wills), we must add the possibility of an amphiboly based on the false assumption that we have actual access to the existent will of a divine being.

To make sense of Kant's position on how to value non-human beings, we thus need to understand this notion of having a duty *to* oneself, but *in regard to* another being or thing. The tendency in the literature has been to understand this notion as being something similar to what Kant, elsewhere, calls "indirect" duties.[6] Indeed, the equivalence of these notions is something that goes back far in the literature. For example, O'Neill (1998b) seems simply to collapse the two notions (viz., indirect duties and duties with regard to something): "[Kant] allows for indirect duties 'with regard to' [animals] which afford welfare but not rights, and can allow for indirect duties 'with regard to' abstract and dispersed aspects of nature, such as biodiversity, species and habitats" (O'Neill 1998b, 211).

Assumption of such equivalence goes back as far as Broadie and Pybus (1974) who, in affirming the equivalence of "duties in regard to" something and "indirect" duties, also affirm that an indirect duty is "indirect" in that establishment and fulfillment of the object of any such duty stands in a means-end relation to a further, more basic, and direct object of duty:

> Kant uses two phrases in a technical sense in talking about the two kinds of duties. First, he speaks about having a duty to something, when the something is being regarded in its capacity as an end-in-itself. Secondly, he speaks about having a duty with regard to something, when the something is being regarded as a means to an end... Sometimes, instead of speaking of duties to [Kant] speaks of direct duties, and instead of speaking of duties with regard to he speaks of indirect duties. (Broadie and Pybus 1974, 379)

If this equivalence of "duties in regard to" and "indirect duties" is true, though, then saying that we have duties "in regard to" animals means that, although non-human beings have some value, it is not absolute but instead a value relative to and subordinate to some other human value the realization of which is the ultimate concern for establishment and fulfillment of the duty in regard to the animal. Humans are the only ones with the absolute value of personhood, and so we must understand animals as having always and only instrumental value in relation to human purposes. That is: we have only indirect, and no straightforwardly direct, duty toward animals.

One might, at this point, very understandably find this way of conceiving of our duties to animals to be inadequate really for appreciating their true value. It seems that, in providing no grounds for direct duties to animals, we have no basis for directly or intrinsically rejecting, e.g., the prolonged suffering of animals. Kantians thus fall short in grounding moral obligations to non-human beings.

---

[6] For a recent example, see Rocha (2015) whose argument in defense of some limited rationality for non-human beings starts from the assumption that we want to move from having a merely indirect duty in regard to such beings toward establishing direct duties toward them.

I would, however, suggest that the assumption of an equivalence between "duties with regard to" and "indirect duties" in the means-end relationship suggested above is a false assumption, and that we can articulate a meaning for "duties with regard to" that is more satisfactory for addressing the problematic case of our moral obligations in relation to non-human beings. Let's explore these ideas.

A More Satisfying Notion of Duties in Regard to

First, let's get clear on this notion we ultimately want to reject of an indirect duty as something we must do that is an instrumental means to some more basic and unfounded duty, the latter duty of which acts to ground or give reason for the former duty. Kant suggests in the *Groundwork*,[7] for example, that we have an indirect duty to pursue our happiness because realization of such happiness will help strengthen our motivation to morality. This duty is "indirect" in that the furtherance of our own happiness is not itself (to use Kant's Doctrine of Virtue language) "an end that is also a duty," but instead is a pursuit that assures a mental state which helps us to hold fast to our commitments to fulfilling other duties: "for discontent with one's state, in a press of cares and amidst unsatisfied wants, might easily become a great *temptation to the transgression of duty*." So, realizing one's happiness is a duty, but an indirect one; that is, its status as a duty is dependent upon some more basic duty to the completion of which it stands in a means-end relation. It is a duty for me to pursue my happiness because doing so allows me to be more successful in fulfilling duties which are themselves directly commanded (viz., duties the command of which does not itself rest upon some further duty to which it would stand in a further means-end relation). Conversely, an "indirect" duty involves just exactly this means-end relation: the satisfaction of one's own happiness is a duty (and thus is "valuable") only insofar as that internal state of happiness acts as a means via which to fulfill our explicit and directly obligatory ends. On this model, the object of one's indirect duty (viz., one's happiness) can thus have only instrumental worth in relation to absolute worth of doing one's duty: my happiness becomes a valuable thing here because realizing it will help me be more willing to pursue the demands of morality.

At times, Kant does appeal to indirectness in this sense when explaining what it means to have a duty "in regard to" something. He notes, for example, that a duty in regard to animals to not treat them cruelly finds its ground in being an instrumental means toward realizing a specifically human goal: "With regard to the animate but nonrational part of creation, violent and cruel treatment of animals...dulls his shared feeling of their suffering *and so weakens and gradually*

---

[7] See 4:399/67.

uproots a natural predisposition that is very serviceable to morality in one's relations with other human beings" (6:443/07, emphasis added).[8] Here, it seems that the reason we shouldn't mistreat animals has nothing to do with the animals themselves, but is, instead, that such mistreatment will ultimately make us less kind to human beings. On the basis of this text, having duties "in regard to" non-human beings is thus simply another way of saying that we have an indirect duty to treat non-human beings in certain ways: we are enjoined to act in certain ways toward these beings merely as a means ultimately to assuring that we treat human beings appropriately. And in terms of the value we attribute to such non-human beings, we would value them only insofar as they further our own ends in some way, in this case, insofar as treating non-human beings well cultivates our predisposition or sensitivity to the suffering of other humans, a disposition the cultivation of which would assure more of an ease and success in fulfilling my moral obligations to other persons.

It seems then, on this account, that the Kantian cannot attribute any value to animals in themselves, and can appeal only to their merely relative and instrumental worth. As such, one could understandably worry that Kantians leave no room for appreciating animals themselves as individual forms of life, or as beings with whom we might have important on-going relationships. If all this follows, a conclusion something like Skidmore's (2001) would indeed follow. According to him, Kant's account of duties in regard to non-human beings sanctions—perhaps even demands of us—that we become "*indifferent* to animal suffering without in any way losing the appropriate concern for human suffering" (emphasis added). Having no explicit concern for the value of non-human beings as such, one could cultivate and morally sanction "a complex ability to rid [oneself] of moral concerns directed toward creatures that do not deserve them" (Skidmore 2001, 6). Ironically, we would thus be affirming an attitude toward animals precisely the converse of what we have just seen in recent chapters argued by Kant for persons: we cannot tolerate indifference toward persons, but we can sanction or even demand such indifference toward non-human life. Indeed, we are justified in treating non-human beings as *mere* means. There is nothing valuable about non-human life in and of itself. If only we could get rid of this pesky, merely empirical connection between human suffering and animal suffering, we could be relieved even of the merely indirect duty to refrain from hurting animals!

But Kant's description of our duties in regard to animals as having this indirect and merely instrumental role in relation to our own moral purposes is not the end of the story in terms of understanding what it means to have a duty *to* oneself

---

[8] He even makes the point twice: "A propensity to wanton destruction of what is beautiful in inanimate nature... is opposed to a human being's duty to himself; for it weakens or uproots that feeling in him which, though not of itself moral, is still a disposition of sensibility that greatly promotes morality or at least prepares the way for it; the disposition, namely, to love something (e.g., beautiful crystal formations the indescribably beauty of plants) even apart from any intention to use it" (6:663/207).

but *in regard to* something else. It is true that I do not and cannot have a duty *to* non-human beings as such. But I *do* have obligations with regard to non-human beings that are not indirect in this egregious sense of reducing the value of the object of my regard to the status of a mere means. Let's envision a different meaning of having duties "in regard to" something which retains the notion of there being something "indirect" about such duties but which avoids the means-end indirectness just discussed and instead leads us toward a more satisfying conclusion about the nature of our obligations in regard to non-human beings and the relationship of such duties to our direct obligations to ourselves.

To begin, we first underscore Kant's original point: Kant draws this distinction between a duty "to" and a duty "in regard to" because all obligation to something is directed appropriately only to a being with a will that can be obligated. Because duties are about binding someone's will, they can be directed only toward beings who actually have a will that can be thusly bound. But this raises a new question: does this mean by definition that we have moral relationships only with beings who have wills? Or do we need simply to conceive differently of the moral relationship a being with a will has to a being without one (or to a being whose will is inaccessible)? In what I argue here, I take the latter route: although we do not and cannot stand in a relationship of direct obligation as such to non-human beings, we can nonetheless speak in a meaningful and satisfactory way about the moral relationships we have and must cultivate with such beings. Our question thus becomes: *how* can we make sense of our moral relationship to beings which do not have wills, or whose wills we cannot access?[9] Whatever moral relationship

---

[9] One could go a different way at this point to remedy the situation: instead of seeking a more satisfactory story of one's indirect moral relationship to beings without wills (the story I go on to tell here), one could explore whether in fact there actually *are* some non-human beings who have wills in the requisite sense and could thus be the focus of direct moral obligation. Perhaps some sentient animal beings—e.g., dolphins, primates, parrots—could meet the criterion of personhood, viz. the capacity to act for reasons, and thereby be welcomed into the realm of those beings capable of obligation. Rocha's (2015) work is a good example of seeking to move in such directions. Korsgaard (2018) takes a sort of middle-of-the-road approach, claiming that animals are not fully rational beings, but are sentient beings who can be conscious of themselves and for whom things therefore "matter," i.e. for whom things can be good or bad. Although, as we'll see, I too am sympathetic to the idea that animals are sentient beings, I am not willing to go as far as Korsgaard in suggesting that such a status would also give animals a basis from which to make direct moral claims upon us. And I am generally sympathetic with Wood (1998b) who takes an earlier version of Korsgaard's ideas on animals to task in an extended footnote which I find worth of repeating here: "My Kantian defence of duties regarding animals must be distinguished from the one offered by Christine Korsgaard in *The Sources of Normativity* (New York: Cambridge University Press, 1996), pp. 152-160. Her argument is more Kantian than mine, in that it (in effect, though not in so many words) accepts the personification principle, but then attempts to argue that animals (though not plants) should count as persons (or, as Korsgaard puts it, being an animal is 'a way of being someone', p. 156). She does so by grounding the value of personhood (as Kant does in his argument at G 4:428-429) on the fact that persons value themselves, and then by asserting (in what seems to me a brazenly paradoxical way) that animals do indeed value themselves. '[Pleasure and pain] are expressive of the value that an animal places on itself. It sounds funny to say that an animal places value on itself, because for us that is an exercise of reflection, so it sounds as if it means that the animal thinks itself to be of value. Of course I don't mean that, I am just talking about the kind of thing that it is. As Aristotle said, it is its own end. Valuing itself just is its nature. To say that life is a

one has to a being who does not have a will, it has to be a different relationship than a relationship of direct obligation.[10] And I would suggest that Kant's own

---

value is almost a tautology. Since a living thing is a thing for which the preservation of identity is imperative, life is a form of morality' (p. 152). For only a few brief sentences, this provides a lot to disagree with. To start near the end: 'Almost' implies close proximity, but the claim that life is a value-taken in any of the many senses which that assertion has been given by those who have made it and thought it importantly true-is far from tautologous. Second, life cannot literally be an imperative for any being incapable of comprehending or acting on imperatives. But among living things, only rational beings are capable of this. Perhaps life is 'imperative' for living things in some less literal sense-as by meaning that their life processes are purposively directed at survival before any other end which may be ascribed to them. But it is not clear how that fact can play a role in the kind of argument through which Kant attempts to show that rational nature is the sole end in itself, since that argument depends on being able to set ends according to reason, not on being able to exhibit natural purposiveness in general. Thirdly, Kant does agree with Aristotle in thinking that a living thing is its own end when he says that its purposiveness is inner rather than external (KU 5:366–369, 372–376). Neither one of them thought that living things 'value themselves' in any sense those words can reasonably be made to bear. (If being its own end or being internally purposive is enough for having a 'nature' that values itself, then plants clearly have that nature as much as animals do. Being conscious-which is Korsgaard's criterion for distinguishing 'being someone' from not 'being someone'-is relevant only if it is possible to be conscious of being someone and of valuing the someone that one is; but Korsgaard admits that animals are no more capable of this than plants. What Korsgaard does seem to hold is that an animal becomes 'someone' through having states (of pleasure and pain) which express its valuation of itself. But it seems clear that even in human beings, if pleasure and pain express valuation of something, it is not of oneself but only of the condition one is in. Why should we think they express more than this in the case of animals (who are not literally capable of valuing themselves as distinct from valuing their states, as human beings are)? Finally, it is not important for Kant's argument even about human beings that self-valuation should be reflective, but it is important that beings said to value themselves have the capacity to acknowledge this value reflectively, and hence that they are capable of acting in a way that can be interpreted as committing themselves to thinking of themselves as valuable. Because animals are not capable of such reflection, they are not capable of such behaviour or such commitment" (Wood 1998b, n11). I agree with Wood's criticisms of Korsgaard, but am more sympathetic than Wood with efforts more generally to envision *some* animals as possessing *some* rational capacities. That is not, however, the route I take here. Instead, as I have said, we need to understand Kant's distinction between an obligation to and an obligation in regard to something in a more satisfactory way, thereby telling a story of indirect duties that does not fall into the trap of being merely instrumentally valuable duties.

[10] In taking this route, I place myself in some sympathy with Wood (1998b), who suggests that Kant was wrong to claim what he calls the "personification principle," the thought that all direct duties must be duties to persons. But whereas I accept that point and then seek other ways to establish moral relationships with non-persons, Wood criticizes Kant for the very establishment of this restriction: "[W]here Kant goes wrong regarding his theoretical defence of our duties regarding nonrational nature is...in accepting what I have called the personification principle. This principle says that rational nature is respected only by respecting humanity in someone's person, hence that every duty must be understood as a duty to a person or persons" (Wood 1998b, 196). Interestingly though, although I disagree with Wood on the question of whether Kant was right or wrong in accepting this principle, we are very much in agreement on the question of what granting moral concern for beings beyond human beings can mean for Kantian morality. In particular, his appeal to the idea that we can appreciate the natural world as an expression of the divine being is very much in agreement with my forthcoming account: "Now it may seem self-evident that to respect or honour rational nature is always to honour it in the person of some rational being; it may even seem nonsensical or contradictory to think that we could honour rational nature in a being which does not have rational nature. But consider, for example, the ways theistic religions honour the supreme perfection, goodness and power of God. It is not the case that they honour God only in actions which have God alone as their object. On the contrary, all theistic religions hold that it is essential to worship of God that we behave in certain ways toward beings other than God, because these beings stand in certain salient relations God, such as being his creatures or being made in his image. These relations to God which make our conduct toward them expressive of our love for and devotion to God...I [thus] argue, a logocentric ethics,

thoughts urge us in this direction. When, just before asserting the means-end relationship of such things noted above, Kant also says things like "the violent and cruel treatment of animals is...*intimately opposed* to man's duty to himself" (MM443/238). he is indeed suggesting something more than the idea that treating animals properly is a mere and disposable means toward the fulfillment of essentially distinct, unrelated, and already existing duties to myself which have nothing to do in themselves with animals. To the contrary, he is suggesting a deeper, more "intimate" moral relationship between my treatment of animals and a duty to myself. Let us explore this new territory.

First, then, I find it particularly interesting that, whatever Kant is saying about having a duty "in regard to" animals, he does, from the very beginning of his discussion, parallel that moral relationship to animals with our moral relationship to divine beings. The relationship of these two categories of concern are set up from the very beginning of his discussion when, as we have already seen, Kant notes the constraints upon what sort of being can be involved in a "binding" relationship of direct obligation: "[T]he constraining (binding) subject must, *first*, be a person; and this person must, *second*, be given as an object of experience" (6:442/207). The first of these constraints limits us to having direct obligations only to persons with wills (and so not to animals), and the second limits us to having direct obligations only to persons we encounter in experience (and so not to divine persons). Kant goes on to speak of the duty we have in regard to divine beings as "the duty 'of recognizing all our duties as...divine commands'" (6:443/208). Given that these are the categories of moral relationships we need to determine at this point, it would be very odd if Kant were to go on to say that all such beings excluded from a relationship of direct obligation could have no value in their own right and could relate to us only in the indirect sense of being a mere means toward the fulfillment of direct obligations. Saying that at this point would lead to the unfortunate conclusion that, like animals and the environment, divine beings have only instrumental value as means to our own ends. Surely, that is not what Kant wants to say about divine beings! And surely he must be saying something else here. Reflection on this parallel between our duties in regard to these two rather different examples of non-human beings (viz., animals/the environment, on the one hand, and divine beings on the other) can thus help us to conceive more adequately of what it means to have a duty "in regard to" such beings while avoiding this problematic means-end relationship.

What we shall discover is a new sense of what it means for us to have "indirect" duties. We need to retain this language of "indirect" to understand what it means

which grounds all duties on the value of humanity or rational nature, should not be committed to the personification principle. It should hold that honouring rational nature as an end in itself sometimes requires us to behave with respect toward nonrational beings if they bear the right relations to rational nature. Such relations, I will argue, include having rational nature only potentially, or virtually, or having had it in the past, or having parts of it or necessary conditions of it" (Wood 1998b), 197).

to have a duty "in regard to" such beings because, as just noted, we know, by definition that we cannot have a "direct" relationship of obligation to such beings. Such direct obligations are possible only in relation to human persons. But we will avoid the problematic notion that this "indirect" moral relationship with such beings is a merely instrumental relationship in which we take them as mere means toward the end of realizing our direct duties. In so doing, we broaden the categories for what it means to be in a "moral relationship" with something: in addition to establishing moral relationships of obligations with human beings, we are enjoined to establish moral relationships with non-human beings via appeal to our own and particularly interesting capacity to obligate *ourselves* (viz., the capacity simultaneously to be both the obligating and obligated being) *to* such non-human beings.[11]

This appeal to self-obligation is admittedly also an "indirect" way of understanding such obligations. But it is indirect in a new way: because, in seeking to establish a moral relationship with either animals or God, I turn to an obligation not to them but to myself, I must speak of this as an indirect way of grounding my moral relationship with those beings. My moral relationship to the object of regard is "indirect" in the sense that, while the object with which I am seeking a *moral* relation is something outside of any possible *obligation* relation with me (because it has no will, or has a will essentially inaccessible or imperceptible by me), I nonetheless ground a moral relationship with that object "indirectly" via indirect appeal to myself and my capacity to ground an obligation to myself (viz., via my capacity to be both the constraining will and the constrained will in an obligation relation). But in introducing this new sense of the indirect establishment of moral relationships, we expand upon the nature and kind of moral relationships human beings can have with beings which, on their own, are not capable of the human moral relationship of obligation.

---

[11] I'll be focusing here on how this structure of an indirect obligation to myself in regard to other beings plays itself out in our relationship to animals, the environment, and divine beings. But this same structure of obligating myself with regard to other beings plays itself out also in Kant's understanding of the duty not to lie. Interestingly, in his Doctrine of Virtue discussion of this duty, Kant identifies not lying as a duty to *oneself*, even when my choice to lie or not lie is directed toward (viz., is done "in regard to") *other* persons. Now, this case is not perfectly identical to the case of animals and divine beings. In speaking of a duty to myself but in regard to other humans, we are not dealing with beings toward whom we are incapable of direct obligation. And, indeed, Kant confirms that, in addition to not lying being a duty to myself, it is also, on other grounds, a duty to others. Nonetheless, his appeal to not lying as a duty to self but in regard to others replicates just the structure of "indirectness" we assert here in relation to non-human beings. This duty not to lie which, though (at least in some cases) directed at our relations with other persons, is also considered, at its basis, to be a duty to oneself. An interesting interaction between Rascalnikov and Sonja in Dostoevsky's *Crime and Punishment* illustrates the point not only for lying but also for murder. When Rascalnikov finally confesses his crime of murder to Sonja, her immediate response is: "What have you done to *yourself?*" This comment is not a callous disregard for the value of the person he killed, but a deep insight into the nature of all moral obligations.

On this new picture of conceiving our moral relationship to non-human beings via self-obligation, one can even say that I affirm and realize the moral status of the world of non-human beings. Some reflection on the varying status of humans and non-human beings vis à vis morality will help to make the point. So, in one sense, we have to say that morality is in the world because humans are in the world: the existence of human beings in the world is the reason that moral questions can be formed and answered. We are the ones amongst all things in the world of nature who can think, speak, choose, and act in explicitly moral terms. But this doesn't mean that we thereby exclude from the moral world other beings who are not capable of such explicitly rational and verbalized moral activity. To the contrary, I instead grieve my inability to establish a direct moral relationship of obligation with these non-human beings. There is a loss here: the very same moral capacities that I respect and celebrate are subject to a limitation that I grieve. But, in the face of that loss, we find a back-door way of affirming the moral value of the whole world, including the non-human beings involved in it.

We need to be careful here: it is not so much that I take a world that was previously only natural and "moralize" it (i.e., make it something it inherently was not). In establishing a moral relationship with these beings, I am not bringing to them something they didn't already have. Rather, in light of my own incapacity to recognize their moral status directly in the way that I do with human beings, I instead, through appeal to my own capacity to obligate myself to act in certain ways, make explicit to myself an implicit rationality and morality that is already inherent in the world of nature. The lives of animals and the existence of the natural world are simply further expressions of the rationality of the universe, even though they themselves are not rational beings as such (viz., beings who act for reasons in the rigorous sense we attribute to human beings).

We can make this broad appeal to the rationality of the natural world because, as Kantians, we know from the *Critique of Judgment* that Kant himself seeks to resolve the mechanism of nature to the realization of teleological purposes, thereby conceiving of all of nature as being enlivened by rational purposes which pure practical reason seeks to realize. This is that further and ultimate resolution of nature and freedom of which we briefly spoke earlier in this chapter, a resolution of these apparently opposed forces, now on the scale not just of all persons, but all of reality. As such, the natural world itself is an expression of rationality itself. Non-human beings and things may not consciously verbalize and rationalize or make arguments about morality, but the natural world *exists* and thereby *expresses* itself as both rational and moral. In affirming an obligation to myself in regard to these non-human beings and things, I thus make explicit to myself a rational and moral relationship to these beings which has always existed implicitly in the fact that I share the same world with these beings, but which I could access in no other more "direct" way. In short, by appeal to self-obligation, I make the otherwise imperceptible rationality of nature and divinity perceptible and tangible to myself.[12]

In short, by establishing an obligation in regard to non-human beings indirectly through appeal to my capacity for self-obligation, my will *stands in* on behalf of the being whose will is either non-existent or inaccessible. I act on behalf of that being to establish a moral relationship in regard to a being with whom it is impossible for me to establish a direct relationship of obligation (because it either lacks a will or has a will imperceptible by and thus inaccessible to me). In doing so, I admit that the duty I have in regard to such beings is "indirect" in the sense that I had to travel through a duty to myself to identify and affirm my moral relationship in regard to this other being.[13]

A Non-Egregious Anthropocentric Affirmation of the Intrinsic Value of Animals and the Environment

One might object at this point: even if this explanation of duties in regard to non-human beings does not involve a merely *instrumental* appeal to the value of such beings, is it not still an egregiously *anthropocentric* way of grounding our appreciation for these beings? Why should we have to make sense of our obligations to animals by thinking so much about ourselves? It seems, relatedly, in appealing to self-obligation to address our problem, we've made it only that much more difficult to access the value of these beings *in themselves*.

Our response to this objector has two prongs: on the one hand, our account is both unavoidably and unapologetically anthropocentric. First: given the limits of

---

[12] This is the clearest point in this argument at which I admit that I am providing only an outline. Though I appeal to this background of a rational and moral world of nature to ground my argument, I will not pursue the textual defense of those claims here. I will instead hope for a happy time in the future when I engage in a deep discussion of aesthetic experience and teleology as discussed in the *Critique of Judgment* so as to ground these claims. Two places I would look in the former, aesthetic category include considering Kant's discussion of "beauty as a symbol of morality" and also his characterization of the dynamic sublime. Both these notions provide rich grounds for the claim that the natural world is a rational and moral one.

[13] We can push the point further and remind our readers that we have already affirmed that recognition of *all* duties requires previous appeal to one's capacity to have and fulfill duties to oneself ("for I can recognize that I am under obligation to others only insofar as I at the same time put myself under obligation, since the law by virtue of which I regard myself as being under obligation proceeds in every case from my own practical reason" (MM417-418/214)). The particular challenge of affirming this undergirding structure of self-obligation underlying other-obligation in relation specifically to animals, the environment, and divine beings is that, in these cases, I am trying to establish a moral relationship to something that, despite its intrinsic *value*, does not have a will, or a will perceptible by me. I must thus, in these cases, appeal to myself and the capacity of my own will to bind itself to expand the realm of duties as a sort of stand-in for the lack of such direct relationship to another's will. But in so doing, I am simply relying on that previous grounding relationship of duties to self which undergirds all duties to others, including to those others whom I can indeed directly obligate.

human reason, this appeal to self-obligation is the only way humans can affirm our moral relationships with animals. But, second: the value of animals which emerges through appeal to self-obligation is not only not that merely instrumental and disposable value we saw in previous interpretations of indirect duties but, instead, an affirmation of the *intrinsic value* of these beings. So, while our account is anthropocentric in the sense of requiring appeal to self-obligation, it is not egregiously anthropocentric. Our appeal succeeds (perhaps ironically) in affirming the *intrinsic* worth of non-human beings with appeal to *self*, but in a non-egocentric way. Let's explore each of these points in turn.

First, the story we have told about grounding duties to non-human beings indirectly through appeal to self-obligation, now that we have separated it from the earlier more problematic conception of "indirectness," *is* an appeal to the self, but it is not an *egoistic* appeal to the self. We appeal to the self not because humans are the most important thing in the world, but because the limits in the moral capacities and vision of merely sensibly affected rational beings prevents us from establishing these moral relationships in any more direct manner. Animals are an expression of the rational and moral universe, but they do not always wear this fact on their sleeves. Nor can they explain it to us. In Kant's language (which, ironically, he uses to explain the inaccessibility of the divine will, but I believe the point can be made in relation to the natural world as well), the moral and rational depths of the natural world are inaccessible to us by our usual means of perception. As such, we appeal—creatively I think—to our moral (and aesthetic) capacities to enter into an appreciation of the status and worth of non-human beings. So, when I say to myself: "I owe it to myself to treat animals and the environment with respect," I am not saying "I owe it to myself to use animals and the environment always only for my own purposes." Instead, I am saying: "I owe it to myself to treat animals and the environment with respect so as to affirm and establish within my person/character in the only way I can an abiding appreciation for the value these beings have as part of the one rational and moral world that we share."[14]

As such, we can say further that, despite the self-reference involved in confirming the value of these beings, the value that is recognized is intrinsic, and not merely instrumental, worth. It is true that, like the obligation in regard to these beings itself, this worth is also accessed "indirectly," i.e., via self-obligation. But such indirect appeal does not prevent me from affirming the worth of these beings that emerges in this process as intrinsic to them. That is: I am not, in the first instance, saying that these beings have only instrumental worth as a means toward the realization of some already existent duty to myself that has no connection as such

---

[14] As such, the intrinsic value we identify here is grounded in the point, discussed in the previous section, that the lives of animals and the existence of nature itself are expressions of the rationality of the universe, even if they themselves are not rational beings who act for reasons in the rigorous sense.

to these natural or divine beings. To the contrary, in affirming my obligations in regard to them, I am *heightening* my appreciation for the value of these beings *in themselves*. Indeed, with Kant, we welcome the idea that in affirming indirect obligations to these beings, we make explicit our appreciation for the *intrinsic* value of that being with whom I have established this moral relationship. As Kant puts the point, the "disposition" we establish in ourselves through the taking up of this indirect obligation to non-human beings is "the disposition, namely, to *love* something (e.g., beautiful crystal formations, the indescribable beauty of plants) *even apart from any intention to use it*" (6:443/207, emphases added). That is to say: in this moral relationship I have with these non-human beings, I value these beings "intrinsically." They are beings I now have a way of appreciating morally in and of themselves instead of appreciating them only for what they can be or do for me. It is not that my loving appreciation for such beings acts merely as a means to assure that I love human beings. It may indeed help with that as well. But in the first instance that loving appreciation is simply that: a loving appreciation for the existence and nature of this non-human being I encounter, whether that being is a small grey cat, a crystal formation, or the Divine Being itself. And the obligations I have to myself to treat these beings in certain ways (e.g., not to kick the cat, not to destroy the crystal formations by building a chemical plant upon them, or bowing down to and worshipping the majesty of a supreme being through reference to whom I understand my own fulfillment of moral obligations as a form of such worship) are all obligations I place on myself in light of a deep and loving appreciation for the intrinsic worth of these non-human members of the moral world.

Affirmation of this intrinsic value is thus, once again, accomplished in a non-egoistic, non-egregiously anthropocentric way. We do appeal indirectly to ourselves to affirm that intrinsic value, but that is just to say that we affirm the intrinsic value of animals, the environment or the divine through appeal to the only ways in which humans *can* relate morally to such beings. Lacking a capacity directly to obligate such beings, it is through our moral activity of self-obligation that we establish a deeper and moral relationship with non-human beings. And it is through my own moral capacities that I thereby affirm the intrinsically valuable rational and moral nature of the world around me. What assures that this appeal to self is a non-egoistic one though is the fact that appreciation of the value of this being need not involve any appeal to what this being could be for me and my own ends or purposes. Indeed, that is just what it means to say that I appreciate its "intrinsic" worth instead of seeking some "instrumental" worth for the same being.

We need, however, to distinguish this intrinsic worth from absolute worth. To say that something has intrinsic worth is to say that it has worth apart from any other purpose or end toward which that thing might act as a means. But to say that something has absolute worth is to say that the worth is one that cannot be placed on a scale which compares its worth relatively to other things with worth. No matter what the situation or with what or whom one is interacting, absolute worth remains as a marker in accordance with which one must always treat that being never simply as a means but always at the same time as an end.

And, even granting everything we've said thus far about the intrinsic worth of animals and the environment, we cannot say that these particular non-human beings also have absolute worth. For it remains the case that, for Kant, the only beings who have absolute worth (and the dignity that comes with it) are rational beings, beings who can act for reasons. This does not, however, mean that rational beings are the only beings who have worth in and of themselves. To the contrary, anything in the natural world can be appreciated intrinsically for the expression of the rational and moral world that it is. The case is different, of course, for those non-human beings who are divine beings. These beings are both intrinsically and absolutely valuable, but we ground the latter point of absolute worth through appeal to the claim that these beings (unlike animals and the environment) are also rational beings, beings who act for reasons.

This means that there are differences in the ways we determine our obligations in relation to animals and the environment on the one hand, and our obligations in relation to divine beings on the other.

The former, not having absolute worth, can indeed be used as means for our ends. We need, however, once again, to be careful here. We are not saying that animals can be used indiscriminately for our purposes. But we are saying that they can be used for our purposes in a way that we would not use other human (or divine) beings for our purposes. As such, animals and things in the natural world have *both* intrinsic worth and instrumental worth. That is, we can, in addition to appreciating them for what they are in themselves, also seek to use them for our purposes. We thus needn't retreat from the idea that, at least sometimes, animals and the environment can legitimately serve human purposes and are thus instrumentally valuable toward those purposes. And although, unlike humans upon whom we rely instrumentally for our ends, we have no moral constraint emerging directly from the Second Formulation of the Categorical Imperative that would demand that we simultaneously treat animals at the same time as an end, we can nonetheless speak of moral constraints upon the ways we use these beings for our purposes.

I am, in saying this, defending a certain cautious anthropocentrism in our account: we cannot be cavalier in our treatment of animals, but we can use animals for certain of our purposes as long as we maintain a simultaneous respect for them. Most centrally, affirmation of the intrinsic value of these same beings inspires caution and respect in determining how and when to rely upon them as means to our ends. Further, appeal to the intrinsic value of these beings can also become the basis for limiting the ways in which use animals, and, indeed, the precise purposes to which we put them.

Even once we grant all these ideas, there will still be lots of arguments to be had about how to resolve specific cases of conflict between humans and nature/animals and about the limits on how and when humans can use animals and nature for their own purposes. A Kantian account will not take the radical position that animals or nature could *never* be used for human purposes. But it would insist upon grounding the reasonable instrumental use of animal and nature within a broader respect for animals and nature as part of a rationally informed and teleologically guided world. We make sense of the proper moral response to animals within a larger world view wherein nature and freedom are united, and wherein the sensible world of nature, in itself, is never just sensible, but is also rationally oriented toward a telos. I am not, however, going to enter into such discussions here, only point out that Kantians have tools for engaging in those difficult discussions well and responsibly.

A Return to and Re-Visioning of Kant's Instrumental Appeal to the Usefulness of Nature for Our Purposes

Even Kant's instrumental appeal to the value of animals—viz., that if we treat them cruelly, we'll also be more inclined to treat human beings cruelly—can be revisited at this point from a more sympathetic perspective. On Kant's account, violent and cruel treatment of animals isn't prohibited simply because such actions prevent us from achieving something we want. Rather, it is prohibited because I can't engage in such activity and remain truly human; this is because such activities would reveal that I lack a "disposition of sensibility" (6:443/207) which Kant considers essential to being human, that disposition to love something in itself just discussed.

The need for such a sensible disposition further encourages us to suggest that part of what it means to be human is to treat animals and all of nature with *respect*. If we can't respect or love animals, or the environment, Kant worries about whether we can respect or love *at all*. The connection between sensitivity to animals and sensitivity to humans is thus not just an instrumental one—if I want the one I have to engage in the other—but instead one which reveals and affirms our connectedness to all living, sentient beings. Similarly, our treatment of animals is a symptom of whether or not we have taken up the obligation to animals and nature which our own nature imposes upon us. Our respect for animals is a respect for life itself.

And so: persons who treat animals badly don't just have questionable characters; beyond that, they have abandoned their own humanity. I cannot respect human beings unless I have a concern and care for sentient beings generally. I cannot kick dogs and still respect persons. This is not merely an instrumental concern (viz., that I treat animals respectfully only instrumentally for the purposes of assuring that I treat persons respectfully). Rather, *integral* to and constitutive of being respectful of *persons* is the idea that I must be respectful of sentient beings generally.

Indeed, as we've already seen, even we are trying simply to be respectful of human beings, we are being respectful of *sensibly affected* rational beings, rational beings with the needs and dependencies that a sensible nature introduces to their existence. The kind of rational being whom we are seeking to respect is one who is, simultaneously, "dependent on the incentive of his sensuous nature" (6:36/58). As such, even for humans, being respectful of human beings as rational beings includes attending to their sensible needs (e.g., that they have enough food, are warm enough, etc.).

But if we add to this point the further point already noted that, for Kant, "nature" is not reducible to a world of push-and-pull mechanistic causes, but itself has a rational telos, then we have a basis for reminding ourselves that all sentient beings share the same rational and moral world. Nature is a world infused with rationality and a rational purpose. Along with persons, then, nature too, must be treated respectfully. If all of this is true, then our indirect obligation to treat sentient beings with respect is something more integral to our very capacity to respect persons than any merely means-end relationship would suggest. To claim no inherent relationship between sensitivity to animals and sensitivity to humans would be akin to claiming that our lying to others had nothing to do with the retention of our dignity as speaking and communicating beings.[15]

Conclusion of Part I

The ultimate conclusion of Part I is thus achieved: a teleologically guided concern for persons becomes the focus of virtue for Kant. To act virtuously is to act in a way that one makes human beings as such one's end: one treats all persons,

---

[15] Here is one brief example of how one might apply such ideas to specific cases: could we, for example, ever justify causing pain to animals toward the end of achieving some human purpose? Kant would, I think, argue that in certain cases—i.e., in cases where human suffering outweighs animal suffering—we *can* use animals for our own purposes, that is, as means to an end. But this does not mean that we are given license to desensitize ourselves to their suffering or to treat them in a cavalier way. Indeed, it is precisely with an awareness of their potential for suffering (and of the link between sensitivity to that and sensitivity to human suffering) that we are *required*, even in using them for our purposes, to treat animals with respect. In this case, "respect" means to minimize their suffering to the greatest extent possible, and also to make sure that one engages in such activities only for weighty human purposes. It is only in the service of relieving significant human suffering that we can begin to defend a need to utilize animals in a way that might cause them pain. And it is precisely because of an awareness of this link between animal suffering and human suffering that we use animals for our purposes only with great caution, and perhaps even a certain amount of regret. It is our sensitivity to suffering—both human and animal—that guides us here. Instead of denying or ignoring the fact that we may cause suffering, it is in respectful awareness of the possibility of animal suffering (along with the fact of great human suffering) that we take great care to limit the ways in which we use animals. Awareness of the potential for human suffering will grant us reason for using animals for the purpose of medical research; but awareness of animal suffering will demand that we do so only for the best of reasons—i.e., relieving human suffering—and with continued respect for animals, i.e. without causing undue pain to them.

including oneself, with the respect that the absolute value of persons as ends-in-themselves demands. Through reflection upon the centrality of ends in the Doctrine of Virtue that could not be affirmed in the *Groundwork*, we affirm that the materialized, end-based Humanity Formulation of the Categorical Imperative is that conception of duty or lawfulness which is the proper governor for virtuous end-setting. Objectors of various sorts who worried that the notion of a telos was not appropriate to Kantian deontological virtue are thus proven wrong. To the contrary, *ends*—both the telos of making persons as such one's end and the obligatory ends of virtue which constitute the realization of this telos—are at the heart of a Kantian virtue guided by pure practical reason.

It is, perhaps, Kant's own refusal of the language of eudaemonism even within the very text of the Doctrine of Virtue itself that makes Kantians hesitant to claim the eudaemonistic language of "telos" for this central defining end of virtue. But now that we have grounded textually the role this objective telos of respect for persons plays in affirming and grounding those obligatory ends which constitute its realization; and, further, now that we affirm that deontology and teleology are reciprocally related to each other in the exercise of pure practical reason, it makes good sense to accept respect for persons as the objective telos of virtue, a telos which guides the governance of one's desires via the free setting of obligatory ends or duties of virtue. Indeed, the introduction of a term like "telos" to orient the pursuit of virtue is a welcome way of highlighting the deeply Kantian notion that pure practical reason expresses itself through the reciprocal relationship of deontological principles and guiding ends, a reciprocal relationship which we have confirmed in these recent chapters.

We turn now to our ultimate claim in the affirmation of Deontological Eudaemonism: consideration of how just this same telos of making persons as such one's end serves generally as the ground for one's subjective telos, viz. for achieving that internal state of person most appropriate to the pursuit of one's objective obligatory ends of virtue, a pleasurable internal state of proper functioning of which not only virtue but also the reasonable pursuit of one's happiness, empirically conceived, is constitutive. Let us turn to this ultimate discussion of Kant's Deontological Eudaemonism.

PART II
DEONTOLOGICAL EUDAEMONISM
The Subjective Telos of Virtue

II.i
Apathy, Moderation, Excitement
The Herculean Work of Virtue

Introduction: The Subjective Telos of Virtue

We have now completed our defense of the objective telos of virtue, revealing pure practical reason as reciprocally both deontological and teleological in nature. But, as we noted in I.i, this objective telos finds its subjective and supervening counterpart in an internal state of person most appropriate to the realization of that objective telos. Such a subjective state is, really just a characterization of what it is like from the inside to be a person of virtue: what her internal experience is like. We have already encountered hints of this subjective flip-side of one's objective pursuit of the telos of making persons as such one's end when we saw the establishment of obligatory ends constitutive of this objective telos of virtue which themselves involve the establishment of some sort of internal, subjective state (e.g., the state of knowing oneself, or the state of experiencing a more highly cultivated natural feeling of sympathy).

In this Part II, we dwell at length upon the development and resulting nature of this subjective side of virtuous self-governance in order to reveal how the teleological structures of Kant's ethics considered in Part I play themselves out in the pursuit of their ultimate eudaemonistic conclusion: the resolution, through the hard work of the practice of virtue, of the conflict between morality and happiness which initially characterizes one's moral consciousness into the pleasurable exercise of the aptitude for virtue, a state which constitutes a form of happiness rationally conceived but also establishes the most reliable point of view from which successfully to pursue happiness empirically conceived. We thus place Kant's Deontological Teleology within a broader picture of his Deontological Eudaemonism: the height of the exercise of one's aptitude for virtue yields a life in which the exercise of that virtue is pleasurable and the previous conflict between happiness and morality which characterized one's moral consciousness is resolved into that pursuit of happiness most satisfying and successful for a sensibly affected rational being. Although even the fully virtuous person must retain a vigilance about the bare possibility of succumbing to her propensity for evil, and even though circumstances outside of one's control might prevent a perfect coincidence of virtue and happiness empirically conceived, the person who achieves and maintains this aptitude for virtue has the promise of a life in which her virtue forms the center of her pleasurable properly functioning life, a life within which virtue and happiness are resolved toward each other to the highest extent possible for a sensibly affected rational being.[1]

Such reflection is particularly important in light of the fact that Kant is most often thought to be distinctively *non*-eudaemonistic: he is thought to envision a virtuous life of conflict and constraint, not of harmony and flourishing. Part II of this book is thus devoted to offering a more accurate picture of the subjective flourishing of the virtuous sensibly affected rational being, one in which, while this person is prepared to tolerate and manage unavoidable suffering, suffering and sacrifice as such are not integral to her life of virtue. Instead, the moderation and cultivation of a variety of natural states and feelings in agreement with her telos of making persons as such her end, and the resulting aptitude for the exercise of virtue which such cultivation brings, lead to a state characterized by the pleasurable experience of happiness, both rationally and sensibly conceived. It is true that even the fully virtuous person will need to maintain a vigilance about the bare possibility of her propensity to radical evil subverting her pleasurable life of virtue; and it is true that circumstances outside her control might similarly undermine full happiness empirically conceived. But granting both these caveats, we can nonetheless assert confidently for Kant that the moral life is a pleasurable life.

We shall, furthermore, in telling this story discover just how valuable it is for the pursuit of happiness that the virtuous person's desires acquired a goal beyond themselves via the moral feeling of respect: it is precisely because the virtuous person, through a moral-feeling-of-respect-guided capacity for what we shall call moral apathy and moral excitement, introduces this higher telos of making persons as such one's end into the process of desire-governance that one's desires are no longer so obsessively concerned only with themselves. And it is only because of this elevation of desire to a goal beyond itself that the hope of a higher integrity, harmony, proper functioning, and flourishing for one's being overall can be envisioned. In short, appeal to the telos of making persons as such one's end allows us to conceive of the proper functioning, happiness, and flourishing of a sensibly affected rational being in a new, less self-absorbed light. One pursues desire-satisfaction only to the extent that it is compatible with and expressive of the demand to make persons as such one's end. *That* will be the most satisfying thing for one's person overall, because it will be a state in line with one's whole person, not just with the narrow, self-absorbed concerns of one's desiring self.

---

[1] I thus place myself in deep sympathy in particular with Watson (1983) who asserts that "[t]he capacity to unite one's ends into a 'system' in accordance with reason requires the moral point of view" (p. 79). This achievement of eudaemonia which we will explore for the rest of this book is just that unified system of one's whole self, guided by the moral point of view.

This chapter is organized as follows. We begin our account of the subjective telos of virtue by taking on the caricature of the Kantian virtuous person as one sentenced to a life of sacrifice, suffering, and misery. We note, in fact, that Kant does rather regularly emphasize the potential suffering of the virtuous person. But, instead of taking such suffering and sacrifice as constitutive of the subjective state of the virtuous person or as a subjective telos toward which one should point the cultivation of one's person, we understand Kant's references to virtuous suffering as a pedagogical effort to help young students of virtue appreciate the impressively selfless and strong state that virtue is. We then, in a move that stands in sympathy with Forman's (2016) account of Kant's moderate cynicism, understand the capacity to manage such sacrifice and suffering as what we shall call morally apathetic toleration of sacrifice, a capacity via which one moderates one's felt attachments through appeal to one's experience of moral feeling and the absolute value of persons toward which that feeling points. In such apathetic moderation, one is now able to take a proper evaluative distance upon one's felt attachments and recognize them as the merely relatively valuable things they are, making the toleration of the loss of those objects to which one is affectively attached that much more manageable.[2]

We turn then to a broader consideration of this same ability to cultivate one's felt attachments by suggesting that the very same tools for apathetic moderation of one's affects are the tools for their governance generally, including not only their constraint and moderation but also their excitement and invigoration as guided by one's virtuous objective telos of making persons as such one's end. In so doing, we turn to the details of how best to govern one's felt attachments via the exercise of inner freedom, a process in which one relies upon contemplation of the power of one's moral feeling of respect and also upon the repeated practice of virtue to accomplish the constraint, cultivation, and governance of one's felt attachments generally. Reviewing the details of this process helps us to clarify just what Kant means by virtue requiring hard work and strength, indeed, strength of Herculean proportions. But this conflicted Herculean battle for virtue is not the end of the story. The product of all this hard work of governance is what, in the next chapter, we shall identify as an "aptitude" for virtue, a state of alacrity and ease in the exercise of virtue which constitutes the proper functioning of the

---

[2] As Forman puts the point: "the best chance we have for approximating happiness in this life lies in our willingness to do without (but not in actively denying ourselves) all the luxuries that have come to seem like necessities in our corrupt era...[T]his moderate Cynic prescription for happiness stands in harmony with virtue as Kant depicts it" (Forman 2016, 78). And: "[P]rudence itself—when understood in the proper, moderate Cynic way—limits my ambitions in a way that allows the end of happiness to be in harmony with the end of virtue" (p. 103). Forman thus relates this cynicism specifically to the pursuit of happiness, empirically conceived. That is a topic we'll consider explicitly in II.iii. But in II.ii, I will distinguish myself from Forman when I suggest that although I agree with him that "any authentic moral demands are wholly distinct from the demands of prudence" as such (p. 75), there is one sense of "happiness"—as unimpeded activity—which is indeed identical with the exercise of virtue.

sensibly affected rational being, a state which simultaneously integrates a new eudaemonistic conception not only of virtue but also of happiness, now rationally instead of merely empirically conceived.

I. Step One: Moral Apathetic Toleration of Sacrifice

Let's begin with the virtuous person's capacity to tolerate sacrifices. I know: this doesn't seem a very promising start for a story of eudaemonism. But it is a very popular thing to do to present the Kantian virtuous person in a sort of caricature wherein she needs always to constrain herself to do her duty and wherein she thus always suffers and hates what she has to do. We need, therefore, to take on this caricature head-on. In so doing, we shall discover the positive reasons that Kant emphasizes the suffering of the virtuous person so much; and, in making meaningful room for the need for sacrifices within a flourishing life, Deontological Eudaemonism will not only reveal one of its distinctive advantages (viz., its capacity over other virtue theories to provide a valuable means for the successful toleration of necessary suffering) but also allow us to establish a central capacity of the virtuous person—the moral-feeling-guided capacity for moral apathy—which not only helps the virtuous person tolerate suffering but, more importantly, acts as a guide for the development of a positive subjective state supervening on the exercise of virtue, a state characterized by regular experiences of pleasure, love, and cheerfulness in that exercise.

So: Kant regularly emphasizes that the person of virtue may have to make sacrifices. One thinks immediately of his Gallows Man example wherein the would-be free and virtuous person faces the possibility of needing to sacrifice his very life to maintain his moral integrity.[3] Here is a long, but helpful passage—presented as what one should present to a young student of virtue—which characterizes essentially this same Gallows Man's strength to tolerate sacrifices:

> One tells [the student] the story of an honest man whom someone wants to induce to join the calumniators of an innocent but otherwise powerless person (say, Anne Boleyn, accused by Henry VIII of England). He is offered gain[:]...great gifts or high rank; he rejects them. This will produce mere approval and applause in the listener's soul, because it is *gain* [which is rejected]. Now threats of *loss* begin. Among these calumniators are his best friends, who now refuse him their friendship; close relatives, who threaten to disinherit him (he is not wealthy); powerful people, who can pursue and hurt him in all places and circumstances; a prince who threatens him with loss of freedom and even of life itself. But, so

---

[3] See 5:30/27–28.

that the measure of suffering may be full and he may also feel the pain that only a morally good heart can feel very deeply, represent his family, threatened with extreme distress and poverty, as *imploring him to yield* and himself, though upright, yet with a heart not hard or insensible either to compassion or to his own distress; represent him at a moment when he wishes that he had never lived to see the day that exposed him to such unutterable pain and yet remains firm in his resolution to be truthful, without wavering or even doubting; then my young listener will be raised step by step from mere approval to admiration, from that to amazement, and finally to the greatest veneration and a lively wish that he himself could be such a man (though certainly not in such circumstances).

(5:155–157/128–129, all emphases except of 'imploring' added)

This man has acquired what we described in I.iv as the virtuous state of inner freedom, a virtue in which one constrains one's inclinations and guides one's end-setting by the moral demand to make persons as such one's end. And one can, through this particular example of its realization, see why Kant calls this same virtue "virtue as *strength*": the "strength of resolution in a human being as a being endowed with freedom, hence his strength insofar as he is in *control* of himself (in his senses) and so in the state of *health* proper to a human being" (6:384/148, first emphasis added). Virtue as inner freedom, or virtue as strength, is a capacity to control and shape one's inclinations, a capacity which constitutes the overall state of health of a sensibly affected rational being. And in this example, such strength is put to particularly impressive use: the strength of inner freedom allows this man to manage the worst of injuries to his person, but to remain firm in his refusal to lie in a way that would assure grave injury to persons.

But in the plight of our Gallows Man, this strength of virtue is deployed in a very particular way: as the strength to *tolerate sacrifices*. In mere constraint of inclinations, I prevent satisfaction of a desire in accordance with freely chosen principles (e.g., I allow myself a slice of cheesecake; but, out of concern for my health, I constrain myself from eating two slices every evening). But in *sacrifice*, I constrain a desire that, all other things being equal, I would *not* freely choose to constrain. Through appeal to higher values—here, respecting persons through honesty and a refusal to condone the injury of persons—our hero chooses to deny himself fulfillment of desires *very* important to him (his welfare, his freedom, or even his life). He thus reveals himself as a *very* strong person, someone particularly capable of tolerating the loss of things of value, things necessary not only for a happy life but simply for a life free of suffering. Through appeal to his life-guiding principle of respecting persons, he is strong in the face of the need to sacrifice the satisfaction of inclinations he would otherwise, reasonably, be very inclined, to satisfy.

A comparison with Stoic Eudaemonism will help us appreciate the nature of this state of toleration. Despite his admiration of Stoicism, Kant is *not* being Stoic in affirming the virtuous person's capacity to tolerate sacrifice. A Stoic would encourage not *toleration of* but *indifference to* such losses. My favorite example of such indifference is Epictetus' encouragement for one to care about the death of one's spouse no more than one would care about the breakage of a nice jug.[4] When I am thusly indifferent, I deny value to anything beyond virtue: as long as I am virtuous, what concern could I possibly have for the loss of such valueless things as you(, darling)?

But Kant distinguishes both the *attitude* of the virtuous person and the account of *value* underlying it from Stoic indifference. And it should not surprise us that Kant rejects indifference as a morally valuable attitude. Recall, after all, that his very deduction of the objective telos of making persons as such one's end required the rejection of indifference toward persons, since such indifference is incompatible with the absolute worth of persons. Here, that same rejection of indifference in the name of the absolute value of persons takes a new twist. His rejection of indifference to persons leads him also to reject indifference toward the value of other things persons might value through their inclinations and desires for these things. These things might not have the absolute value of persons themselves; but they do not lack value entirely. Indeed, Kant understands here, implicitly, that the satisfaction of a person overall will involve being able to get some of these merely relatively valuable things into one's life.[5]

Kant thus embraces not indifference, but "apathy" as the means for managing the loss of these things of relative value, seeking to rehabilitate this notion of apathy through the new terminology of "moral apathy," a state of being able to tolerate sacrifices of relatively valuable things while rejecting indifference to the value of the things sacrificed via the cultivation of one's feelings from the evaluative distance which is provided by one's experience of the moral feeling of respect:

> The word "apathy" has fallen into disrepute, as if it meant lack of feeling and so subjective *indifference* with respect to objects of choice;... This misunderstanding can be prevented by giving the name "moral apathy" to that absence of affects which is to be *distinguished from indifference* because in cases of moral apathy feelings arising from sensible impressions *lose their influence* on moral feeling only because respect for the law is more powerful than all such feelings together.   (6:408/166–167, emphases added)

Kant clarifies here what happens to one's experience of feelings and desires once one has claimed a telos for them beyond desire. It is not that I no longer have any

---

[4] "If you are fond of a jug, say you are fond of a jug; then you will not be disturbed if it be broken. If you kiss your child or your wife, say to yourself that you are kissing a human being, for then if death strikes it you will not be disturbed." See Epictetus (1916).

[5] I am thus in sympathy with Watson (1983) who similarly affirms the import of non-moral value for Kant. We shall discuss this point at greater length later in this chapter.

"feelings arising from sensible impressions." I do have them, because they are appropriate responses to things of value in the world. But the strength of such feelings is *moderated* by appeal to my experience of the moral feeling of respect and the value of persons of which that feeling reminds me: while I admit that things tied to my "sensible impression" have value, I recognize the *relativity* of their value in the face of my *absolute* demand to respect persons. And so, although I recognize the value of sacrificed things, I do not suffer *strong* feelings in my attachment to them, "because respect for the law is more powerful than all such feelings together." The moral feeling of respect, with its objective correlate of the absolute value of persons, thus helps me gain perspective on, and therefore control of, my affective life generally. I know what is most important, and instead of feeling constantly conflicted or bereft about what I have lost, I feel the power of the value of respecting persons pervading the core of my emotional life. The value of what I have lost can even—*usually*—be seen as *small* in this *larger* picture of value. A life that involves sacrifice can thus still be understood as a *healthy* (and, to a certain extent, as long as one avoids tragic situations[6]), even a *flourishing* life.

We call this capacity to moderate one's feelings in the face of sacrifices through appeal to the moral feeling of respect "morally apathetic toleration of sacrifice." It is worth noting that, in so doing, we confirm a second crucial role for this central feeling in the development of virtue. We first, in Part I, appealed to it as constituting the affective side of one's conscience, the voice reminding one of the absolute value of persons and the resulting demand to make persons as such one's end. In this new, moral apathetic role, moral feeling is essentially doing the same thing: reminding oneself internally and affectively of the value of persons. But now that reminder emerges within the virtuous task of moderating one's felt attachment to objects of desire in the face of the need to tolerate suffering.

We saw a hint of this flip-side of the work of constraining one's feelings when we discussed the work of inner freedom earlier, in I.iv. There we confirmed that the work of inner freedom to establish obligatory ends occurs simultaneously with the activity of self-constraint of one's inclinations. That is, the same activity of inner freedom, while doing the work of establishing and confirming the obligatory ends constitutive of one's objective telos to make persons as such one's end is also doing the internal and subjective self-constraining work of getting one's feelings and inclinations—one's felt attachments—in order relative to those obligatory ends. And so, the same rationally guided affective force which establishes obligatory ends simultaneously acts as the self-constraining force for one's feelings and inclinations. What we learn through this moral apathy passage, though, is more detail about the nature of that self-constraint: moral feeling accomplishes such constraint not simply by being a thug—viz., by being bigger and stronger

---

[6] A topic to which I'll return at the very end of this chapter.

than these other feelings and thus holding them captive—but instead by bringing a capacity for evaluative distance to one's experience of felt attachment. It is through evaluative appeal to the higher, absolute value of persons that those things connected to one's sensible feelings are found to have a lesser, relative value, and the strength of those feelings reduces thereby.

Morally apathetic toleration of sacrifice is a very important tool in the toolbox of the virtuous person. It is a capacity which provides one with the proper evaluative distance upon all things of value and which thereby allows one to *tolerate incompleteness* in the fulfillment of desire by weakening the strength of the feelings connected to one's unfulfilled desires. Such capacity is, furthermore, at the heart of our emerging non-naturalistic story of a non-self-absorbed self-governance of desire to replace the inevitably self-absorbed naturalistic self-governance of desire-by-desire. *Respecting* my person does not mean *indulging* my desires. Seeing something more valuable in myself and others, out of respect for myself and others, I learn instead to tolerate failures of desire-satisfaction. I have become a stronger, less self-absorbed person.[7]

This capacity to tolerate sacrifice through appeal to moral-feeling-guided moral apathy is, furthermore, a necessary moral psychological tool for establishing the foundations of a life of healthy proper functioning for the sensibly affected rational being. For, recall: sensibly affected rational beings—whom, as we've seen, Kant describes as "rational beings with *needs*"[8]—are, by definition, dependent, needy, and vulnerable beings. These are being inherently subject to loss. But if I am a kind of being who is subject to loss, and have no tools for managing loss, I'm not really able to function properly *as the kind of being I am*. One must thus *welcome* the strength to tolerate sacrifices as an important part of the *healthy* and *properly functioning* sensibly affected rational being. The moral-feeling-guided moral apathy with which the virtuous person regulates her emotions is precisely what allows her to function as the kind of being she is. For precisely this reason, such functioning is experienced by the virtuous person as a *healthy* state of *tranquility* even as she manages the ebbs and flows of an unpredictable natural world: "The true strength of virtue is a tranquil mind with a considered and firm resolution to put the law of virtue into practice. *That* is the state of *health* in the moral life" (6:409/167, first emphasis added).

Moral apathetic toleration of sacrifice is thus a particular capacity of the healthy, well-functioning, well-governed virtuous person, one which importantly distinguishes Kant's brand of eudaemonism from a Stoic one which would

---

[7] I am thus in deep sympathy with Forman's (2016) claim that Kant adopts "the Cynic view that the virtuous disposition is the one in which our non-moral needs can be easily satisfied since they are the simple needs of nature" (Forman 2016, 103). In establishing a regimen whereby I dissolve intense and excessive attachments to objects of desire, I become a person more able to tolerate loss and suffering should it arise.

[8] 6:453/202.

manage loss by refusing value to anything but virtue. Kant rejects the idea that the suffering the virtuous person experiences is only apparent suffering. Instead, because he accepts that human beings are rational beings with needs for things of genuine albeit rational value, and are therefore inherently subject to loss and suffering, he *grants* that there will be suffering in the life even of the virtuous person, but then affirms an aspect of precisely the proper and virtuous exercise of one's being that gives these vulnerable beings the tools to manage suffering well.

The Pedagogical Power of Examples of Sacrifice

Now, Kant focuses an *awful* lot on this capacity for morally apathetic toleration of sacrifice. The Gallows Man example is an example to which he returns repeatedly, especially in his lamentably brief discussions of proper moral education, both toward the end of the second *Critique* and at the very end of the Doctrine of Virtue. In both these places, Kant dwells on how important it is for new students of virtue to *observe* such capacity for toleration of sacrifice and also to *envision themselves* as capable of the same sort of strength.

Such consistent appeal to this theme of excellence in one's capacity for morally apathetic toleration of sacrifice and suffering shows that Kant believes the willingness to look the need for sacrifice right in the eye is an important and defining aspect of the life of the well-governed virtuous person. It shows, indeed, that Kant's brand of eudaemonism is distinctive in the way it admits the inevitability of suffering even in the life of virtue. But the centrality of such examples can also unintentionally encourage a false impression of what virtue, overall, is for Kant. One might start to get the idea, for example, that one should characterize the subjective experience of virtue *overall* as this bare toleration of sacrifice, even perhaps that the very goal or telos of virtue should include a *welcoming*, even a *pursuit*, of suffering so as to confirm one's capacity to tolerate it. But none of this is the case for Deontological Eudaemonism. Moral apathetic toleration of sacrifice *is* a particular capacity of the healthy, well-functioning, well-governed virtuous person, one which importantly distinguishes Kant's brand of eudaemonism from Stoics who would manage loss by refusing value to anything but virtue. But the virtuous person does not seek out or encourage such opportunities for sacrifice; and, surely, although the capacity to manage sacrifice and suffering does constitute one aspect of the subjective telos of virtue, actual sacrifice or suffering is not itself a *goal* or *telos* of virtue as such! Sacrifice or suffering is thus neither an objective nor a subjective telos of virtue.

We will, shortly, turn to our central question of what exactly that subjective telos of virtue is. But first, let us consider: why *does* Kant return so repeatedly to these examples of sacrifice? The answer to this question is related to an already very familiar interpretation and defense of Kant's moral theory. Barbara Herman

(1993b) has compellingly (and, for those of us committed to the study of Kant as a virtue theorist, seminally and foundationally) argued in her interpretation of *Groundwork I* that Kant's claim that the Friend of Humanity's acts of kindness to others have moral worth for the "first time" only once his actions are accomplished without sympathy—this claim is *not* an argument for rejecting sympathy as part of the life of the virtuous person, or even for insisting that one has moral worth only when one acts contrary to some opposing inclination. To the contrary, Kant's interest in presenting this example of the Friend of Humanity is to focus on those cases in which one's capacity to act out of the motive of duty is most *perspicuous*, when it is most possible for us to see clearly that the only viable motive for this person is the motive of duty. Such perspicuity is best assured when all one's inclination-based motives point one in the entirely opposite direction to that of doing one's duty, and this is exactly what the Friend of Humanity example presents. When I do my duty despite the fact that all my inclinations are screaming at me to do otherwise, it is pretty clear that my only motive can be the motive of duty itself.

There is a similar point to be made about Kant' regular references to Gallows-Man-like examples of suffering. I've already mentioned that Kant utilizes this example most frequently when he is engaged in questions of how to educate young persons into a life of virtue. When thinking about moral education, though, one needs to be centrally concerned with just this question of how to present the strength of virtue in its best—that is, its most *perspicuous*—light. And this is just the pedagogical purpose to which Kant regularly puts the examples of Gallows-Man-like toleration of suffering. His concern in these sections is, indeed, precisely identical to his concern in the *Groundwork I* motive of duty discussion: to show off in its clearest light both the very possibility of and the exact nature of virtue. The passage we considered above already reveals just these pedagogical concerns. His pedagogical purpose, he says, as he introduces his 10-year-old student to someone who is forced to endure increasing sacrifices in the name of "his resolution to be truthful, without wavering or even doubting" (5:156/128–129), is to assure that his young student can *see* the motives or incentives of morality in their "purity," and that in seeing such strength and purity this student will be motivated himself to pursue virtue even as he hopes fervently that he will not need himself to prove his own virtue "in such circumstances" (5:156/129). What is meant to be highlighted here, then, is not so much the *sacrifices* of virtue as such, but instead the exceeding *strength* of someone who possesses this thing called virtue.

Here, though, is Kant's best statement of his purpose in making such examples of suffering central in one's moral pedagogy:

[M]orality must have more power over the human heart the more *purely* it is presented. From this it follows that if the law of morals and the image of holiness and virtue are to exercise any influence at all on our soul, they can do so only insofar as they are laid to heart in their purity as incentives, unmixed with any view to one's welfare, *for it is in **suffering** that they **show** themselves most excellently*...I maintain, further, that even in that admired action, if the motive from which it was done was esteem for one's duty, then it is just this respect for the law that straightaway *has the greatest force on the mind of a spectator*, and not, say, any pretension to inner magnanimity and a noble cast of mind; consequently duty, not merit, must have not only the most determinate influence on the mind but, *when it is represented in the correct **light** of its inviolability, the most **penetrating** influence as well.* (5:156–157/129, all emphases added)

One can, that is, most clearly *see* what it is to *be* a virtuous person—and especially see how *strong* that thing called virtue is—when one looks at the virtuous person's strong capacity to accept, manage, and tolerate sacrifice. Kant's focus on sacrifice is thus a pedagogical effort to show how to make the strength of virtue *perspicuous*, especially to young students of virtue, whom he thinks need both to *observe* this capacity for moral apathetic toleration and to *envision themselves* as capable of the same strength.

The strength of Kant's conviction here that dutifulness itself has the potential to be the most motivating of examples is striking and worthy of further reflection. What is it that "has the greatest force on the mind of a spectator"? Not "any pretension to inner magnanimity and a noble cast of mind"—that is, not anything suggesting of the "merit" of one's person—but only "esteem for one's duty" and "respect for the law," *if* "represented in the correct light of its inviolability," will have the required effect on the mind of an attentive young student.

An implicit rejection of at least one aspect of Aristotelian eudaemonism lingers in the contrast Kant draws here. It is, I believe, generally agreed that Kant never read much Aristotle.[9] But a sort of common conception of what Aristotelianism is was surely in the air in Kant's late 18th-century Prussian world. The first hint of how this air of Aristotelianism influenced Kant's thinking on virtue was highlighted at the very beginning of our discussion, in the Introductory Thoughts, when we considered Kant's mistaken assumptions about the nature of euadaemonism generally. There, we saw that he essentially mistook eudaemonism for either a crass hedonism or a very basic form of act utilitarianism. Now we see another assumption Kant makes about Aristotelianism: Aristotelian virtue would be motivated by a "pretension to inner magnanimity and a noble cast of mind," a motive which seeks to emphasize one's own "merit" in the performance of impressive virtuous acts, perhaps even at the expense of morality itself. It is clear that Kant's worry here is that Aristotelian virtue is an overly self-absorbed conception of virtue. For Kant, were one to think of virtue as the pursuit of magnanimity and

---

[9] See, e.g., Kuehn (2001).

nobility, one would be entirely caught up with the question of one's own merit, and not at all concerned to adopt a more proper relationship of oneself to the demands of virtue, a relationship in which one understands the laws of morality as something to which one is bound by duty, not by the promise of impressive merit or glory for oneself.

I am not going to dwell here on the question of whether this is an appropriate interpretation of Aristotle. As we've already mentioned in passing in Part I, there is an interesting interpretive debate to consider in Aristotelian virtue theory about whether the realization of a life of eudaemonism really is problematically self-centered. I suspect, though, that there are Aristotelian resources upon which one could call to defend Aristotle himself from such accusations. It is not, however, the goal of this book to provide such defense of Aristotle in the face of Kant's easy assumptions about what Aristotelian virtue theory is. What we should take from Kant's assumptions here for the purposes of our current reflections is the likelihood that there was a certain received view of such things on the streets of Königsberg in the late 18th century: Kant was very unimpressed by the Aristotle who was spoken of there, an Aristotle whose notion of virtue seemed to reduce to the egregious valorizing of the most pretentious, self-satisfied pursuers of honor and glory for themselves instead of presenting anything truly virtuous. Kant was therefore worried about an egregious self-centeredness that could so easily emerge even from the inevitable and proper need to center upon the improvement of oneself in the pursuit of virtue. And his emphasis upon the notion of duty, and especially upon how impressive it is to be able to hold to one's duty even in the worst of circumstances, is one intended precisely to undermine the would-be self-centeredness of virtue and to counteract any undue emphasis upon the self in pursuit of virtue through appeal to an impressively selfless and dutiful virtuous person.

When the student of virtue is presented with this picture of the suffering dutiful person, this example is "laid to heart in [its] purity as incentive..., unmixed with any view to one's welfare." In other words, for Kant, it is precisely the *selflessness* of duty that has the potential to impress a spectator who views such a person. Furthermore, "it is in suffering that [persons of virtue] show themselves most excellently." That is: examples of suffering not only reveal the selflessness of the person of virtue but reveal that in such selflessness one finds an extraordinary *excellence*. Selflessness is not a wimpy, servile state, one which would suggest subservience or submissiveness to others, but instead is a state of excellence and strength. This is not, however, a strength grounded in self-aggrandizement. Instead, it is the strength of dutiful virtue itself. So, instead of being concerned with merit or self-centered pursuit of nobility or magnanimity so as to affirm herself, the student of virtue should thus admire and seek to emulate the excellent and selfless strength of the person of true, dutiful virtue.

Kant reveals a certain optimism here, an optimism about the potential of humans really not only to admire but also to hope to emulate the quality of genuine selflessness presented in the person of virtue facing suffering. There is no sense here of seeking to flatter the student of virtue, trying to appeal to her baser self-centered instincts to bootstrap herself into a more pure form of virtue. Virtue will, rather, demand that its students learn to love what is truly selfless. And so, Kant may be optimistic that such examples really are the ones that "have not only the most determinate influence on the mind but, *when it is represented in the correct **light** of its inviolability, the most **penetrating** influence as well.*" To see the strength and excellence of true selflessness is indeed an awe-inspiring thing, but does such awe inspire *emulation*? Does one really want to become such a person? Or do humans really, secretly, prefer a more self-centered life in which everyone is impressed with one's own merit, and not with one's willingness to set aside concerns of one's self? Kant's taking up of these examples of suffering to the extent that he does reveals that he is taking the optimistic view of human nature: if one is honest with oneself, and if the strength and excellence of virtue can be presented perspicuously, then humans recognize morality within themselves as the strongest thing within one's toolbox of self-construction, and claim themselves as the sort of being motivated to rise above their sensible selves and commit to something higher: the value of persons generally.

Granting all this—and, indeed, granting even this impressive pedagogical power to these examples of sacrifice in the name of duty—is not, however, to say that the subjective telos of virtue is best characterized as a grim life of sacrifice and suffering. It is not even the *usual* subjective experience of the person of virtue as such, but only the subjective quality of a virtuous person who finds himself in the most dire and unwanted of circumstances, circumstances which, admittedly, also reveal the quality of her virtue most perspicuously: she has the tool of moral-feeling-guided moral apathy to face them. And even as the virtuous person *cultivates* this moral apathetic toleration of suffering when and if the need for it arises, this does not mean that the virtuous person *aims* at suffering or that the life of the virtuous person is best characterized as this grim toleration of the worst of sacrifices. It just means that, when adverse circumstances arise, the virtuous person is ready for them. Furthermore, as we've already noted, a person capable of this moral apathetic toleration of suffering is someone who is particularly *healthy*, functioning properly as a dependent sensibly affected rational being should: she is most capable of managing the very fact of her sensible dependence and the vulnerability that fact brings to her being.

II. Step Two: Governing One's Felt Attachments in the Herculean Pursuit of the Subjective Telos of Virtue

Moral Apathy and Moral Enlivening

Having dealt with this improper caricature of the Kantian virtuous person as seeking out conflict, pain, and suffering, we can finally turn, more positively, toward the question of how best to characterize the proper subjective telos of virtue. One might think that we need to look entirely elsewhere than one's moral-feeling-guided capacity for moral apathy in the managing of loss and sacrifice to find that pleasurable subjective state which would positively complement the objective pursuit of virtue's end, the end of making persons as such one's end. But, in fact, it is this very same capacity for moral apathy—a capacity to evaluate and moderate felt attachments to things of relative value, all guided by the moral feeling of respect which points affectively toward the absolute value of persons and the resulting objective telos of making persons as such one's end—it is this very same capacity to which we can look to make sense of that capacity which guides the construction of one's complete and pleasurable subjective telos of virtue. For, in fact, when there are no adverse circumstances to manage, that same moral apathetic capacity to moderate felt attachments so as to tolerate loss and sacrifices exercises itself in other ways in the governing and organization of the affective life of the virtuous person.[10]

For, remember: this capacity for moral apathy is, at its heart, a capacity to manage one's felt attachments to relatively valuable things via the evaluative distance one gains on them through appeal to the absolute value of persons. It thus makes sense to expect that this same capacity, in more favorable circumstances, could also guide one's affective life more generally, helping to reduce one's felt attachment to things for reasons other than the need to tolerate sacrifice, or even helping to *increase* one's felt attachments to relatively valuable things—and indeed to absolutely valuable persons!—for moral purposes. When circumstances do not demand her to sacrifice things, the virtuous person's use of moral-feeling informed evaluation of her felt attachments is thus a means not only for the moderation of one's felt attachments, leading to moral apathy, but also for the elevation and strengthening of one's felt attachments, leading to what one might call moral excitement, the correlative or flip-side of moral-feeling informed moral apathy.[11] This dual-sided capacity to evaluate and regulate one's felt attachments to relatively

---

[10] In so doing, we move beyond Forman's (2016) claim that Kant's moderate Cynicism is limited to the negative task of reducing our felt attachments, though hopefully in a way with which Forman could be sympathetic.

[11] I don't think "excitement" is the right word here, but I'm not sure the English language provides us with a better one for what I am describing here. There is a long history in Western philosophy of appeal to apathy. It is a word used to describe a variety of ways in which one might moderate, calm, or lower the strength of one's feelings; and Kant's use of the term is just another effort in this long history. But we have no similar history of appealing to a state which results from the enhancing, strengthening, and heightened expression of feeling, and thus no succinct word to describe such activity. What, after all, should one call this state which is the correlative flip-side of moral apathy? It is, essentially, the same capacity to use the moral feeling of respect and the absolute value of persons to bring proper evaluative distance to all feeling-based, sensibly experienced desires or inclinations. But when proper evaluative distance on one's feelings encourages their strengthening and enhancement instead of their moderation and weakening, it doesn't seem right to call that a capacity for *apathy* as such. Rather, we call it now a capacity for morally appropriate strengthening of feeling resulting not in apathy but in excitement, that is, in a state of heightened and strengthened feelings.

valuable things and to absolutely valuable persons thus presents itself as a crucial tool in the exercise of virtue and especially in the development of a subjective state of person correlative to and supportive of that exercise of virtue. This capacity is, in other words, the means by which one realizes one's subjective telos of virtue, that internal state of person which supervenes upon and supports the development of one's objective telos of making persons as such one's end so as to heighten one's capacity to realize just that objective telos.[12]

Indeed, once we expand moral apathy in this way—welcoming it not only as a tool for apathetic moderation of feeling but also as a tool for the excited enhancement, strengthening, and cultivation of feeling—we can see that, in essence, it is *the* tool of the work of inner freedom. Recall, from our I.iv discussion of such things, that the realization of inner freedom in one's person has two sides: both the setting of obligatory ends and the simultaneous constraint of one's inclinations and feelings (and, indeed, that one realizes the former setting of obligatory ends *through* application of the latter constraint). The goal of such inner freedom was to assure "*ends* being laid down" (6:396/158). But this setting of ends comes about via constraint of inclinations, a "self-constraint not by means of other inclinations but by pure practical reason" (6:396/158). As such, the extension of practical reason to the realm of virtue "takes place through *ends* being laid down" (6:396/158), ends whose setting depends upon this free act of self-constraint, the constraint, that is, of one's various desires and inclinations which would themselves compete to be taken up as ends utilized in the governance of oneself.

As such, the notion of inner freedom has two sides: "there is added not only the concept of self-constraint but that of an end, not one that we have but one that we ought to have, one that pure practical reason therefore has within itself" (6:396/158). We saw also, however, that such *constraint* of inclinations for the sake of setting obligatory ends could also involve the *cultivation* of feelings supportive of obligatory ends; that is exactly what went on in affirming the cultivation of the natural feeling of sympathy as an obligatory end. And now we can confirm that this work of inner freedom to freely and autonomously set obligatory ends constitutive of virtue occurs via the tools of moral apathy and moral excitement: the moderation and excitement of one's feelings as informed by the evaluative distance one gains on them through the governing moral feeling of respect and its objective telos of making persons as such one's end.

---

[12] We shall even see, in II.iii, how this same capacity can help increase and decrease one's felt attachments in the name of the pursuit of happiness, empirically conceived, not just in the pursuit of virtue. A capacity to manage one's felt attachments to relatively valuable things would, indeed, be an exceedingly valuable capacity to engage toward the pursuit of happiness. One could, for example, use it to nurture an ability to set aside short-term desire-satisfaction in the pursuit of some particularly desired relatively valuable thing which requires long-term commitments (like becoming a better musician or acquiring a degree in philosophy).

In our I.iv discussion of such things, we were emphasizing the end-setting side of this work of inner freedom: how inner freedom sets obligatory ends constitutive of our objective telos of making persons as such one's end, not leaving such end-setting simply to one's discretion. By such means, we confirmed, amongst others, the obligatory end to cultivate one's natural feelings of sympathy. But now we revisit that same setting of obligatory ends via inner freedom focusing on the internal subjective process by which one's inclinations are constrained and one's feelings are cultivated, all in the service of the setting of obligatory ends: it is through application of the moral feeling of respect to one's felt attachments—and especially through appeal to the absolute value of persons toward which this feeling points—that one can look at all one's affective life—both the inclinations that need to be constrained and the feelings, like the natural feeling of sympathy, which need to be strengthened—and evaluate all such feelings from this new and higher evaluative perspective of an absolute value which grounds the objective telos of one's being.

Let's look, in particular, at what this means for the natural feeling of sympathy. In alliance with the moral feeling of respect, the natural feeling of sympathy is encouraged to strengthen itself, to become stronger, through this very alliance with morality which its connection to the moral feeling of respect offers. As Kant puts the point, through its connection to good moral reasons, one discovers "so many means to sympathy based on moral principles and the feeling appropriate to them" (6:457/205). In other words, we have a whole new variety of moral grounds from which to cultivate our previously only naturally (and thus coincidentally) occurring feeling of sympathy. Through this conscious moral cultivation of sympathy via the moral feeling of respect, one's natural sympathy thus becomes "the capacity and the will to share in others' feelings" (6:456/204), a new means by which one consciously, voluntarily, and intentionally makes other persons as such one's own end. We thus not only affirm that the cultivation of sympathy is something objectively demanded but now also understand the subjective process of cultivating the state of one's feelings so as to execute that demand. By tying the feeling of sympathy to those good reasons to strengthen its expression which the moral feeling of respect identifies and encourages, this natural feeling is elevated and heightened. Indeed, through this alliance with the moral feeling of respect, it finds support within one's very moral consciousness for expressing and realizing itself in new ways, finding ways to become most fully itself. It is now still a natural feeling, but a natural feeling which takes on rational and moral form and expression: it is no longer merely coincidental that one experiences it, and the mode in which it expresses itself when it arises assures that such expression of sympathy occurs only and insofar as such expression would support one's virtuous setting and realizing of obligatory ends.

What we see, then, through appeal to moral apathy and moral excitement as the tools of inner freedom, is that this governor of inner freedom who sets obligatory ends through self-constraint is indeed a gentle governor, one who pursues even her constraining work in the subtlest of ways. First, as we've just seen in the cultivation of the natural feeling of sympathy, this gentle form of governance involves not just constraint but also cultivation of one's felt attachments: our governor uses the very same capacity for evaluative and affective education of feelings which led to apathetic moderation of one's felt attachments in tension with virtue now also to enhance and strengthen those natural feelings, like sympathy, supportive of virtue. Furthermore, in either case of apathetic moderation or moral excitement of felt attachment, she doesn't do her work simply by leaving those felt attachments as they are and either putting them in jail or letting them roam free (i.e., by either constraining them in the thuggish way of simply preventing a very strong feeling from realizing itself in end-setting and action, or by allowing a supportive feeling simply to have free reign in one's person). Instead, she *reasons* with her feelings! That is, she provides an evaluative basis of absolute value, itself expressed in the language of these feelings (i.e., affectively, in the form of the moral feeling of respect), an evaluative basis which, in the case of apathy, leads those feelings *themselves* to express themselves more moderately—or, in some cases, no longer at all—in light of the affectively expressed reasons inherent to moral feeling; and which, in the case of excitement, leads those feelings to express themselves not only more intensely but also more intelligently, with a clearer sense of *why* expression of that feeling is a *good* expression of feeling for the sake of one's being.

Moral feeling as a tool of governance is thus a combined rational-evaluative and affectively expressed tool, not simply a direct and bludgeoning constraint of a very strong feeling that needs harshly to be prevented from realizing itself in action, or a simple affirmation and encouragement of a feeling simply to continue on as it has been, but instead an affectively expressed moderation or heightening of one's feelings encouraged by the evaluative perspective which moral feeling (and its connection to our objective telos of making persons as such one's end) provides: rogue feelings are affectively educated into becoming more moderate (and perhaps eventually dissipating); and fresh-faced, supportive—but perhaps still naïve and unreflective—natural feelings are affectively educated into becoming more fully and more strongly what they can be.

Practicing the Constraint and Cultivation of Felt Attachments

We can thus now speak of inner freedom as a general capacity of the virtuous person to evaluate and educate one's feelings through affective appeal to the telos of making persons as such one's end. One gets the sense here, though, that this work of inner freedom in the managing of one's felt attachments is not just a one-shot deal in which one presses a button and changes a feeling, but rather a slow process over time in which one gently develops, moderates, strengthens, and enhances the expression of one's felt attachments. And, indeed, this is just what Kant confirms: this capacity of inner freedom needs to be constantly applied and exercised through what Kant calls the *practice* of virtue as guided by attentiveness to one's guiding law:

> For while the capacity (*facultas*) to overcome all opposing sensible impulses can and must be simply presupposed in man on account of his freedom, yet this capacity as strength (*robur*) is something he must acquire; and the way to acquire it is to enhance the moral incentive (the thought of the law), both by contemplating the dignity of the pure rational law in us (*contemplation*) and by practicing virtue (*exercitio*). (6:397/158–159)

The first step of this application of one's capacity for inner freedom—"contemplation of the dignity of the law"—is a contemplation achieved through what I have previously described as attentiveness to the moral feeling of respect,[13] that same moral feeling of respect which will eventually be doing the affective and evaluative moderation and excitement of one's felt attachments generally, attentiveness to which morally excites or enlivens the expression of that governing feeling itself: "Obligation with regard to moral feeling can be only to cultivate it and to strengthen it through wonder at its inscrutable source" (6:399–400/160). Contemplation of the dignity of the moral law occurs, that is, through attending to one's experience of the feeling and thereby increasing the strength of that moral feeling itself, that very feeling which provides "consciousness of obligation" by "mak[ing] us aware of the constraint present in the thought of duty" (6:399/160).

But then, once one has this moral feeling of respect clearly and strongly at the center of one's moral consciousness, utilizing it as a tool for remembering the nature of the moral law—remembering, that is, that the telos of one's being is to make persons as such one's end—one then turns to "*practicing* virtue" (emphasis added). Part of what is meant by such practice is, of course, to seek to act in way that realize the obligatory ends one has set for oneself. But, as we have seen, the correlative subjective side of such virtuous end-setting and realization also involves the constraint and cultivation of one's felt attachments, that is, all the "practices" of applying the moral feeling of respect as the governor of one's felt attachments through moral apathy and moral excitement, in the ways we've been describing. In the case of the need for sacrifice, that governance helps one to moderate one's feelings: slowly, over time, through the "practic[e]" of virtue, one

---

[13] See Grenberg (2013, chapter 3).

reduces the strength of certain feelings which attach one to relatively valuable things because one realizes that, although those things are valuable, making persons as such one's end is more important. In the case of encountering natural feelings generally opposed to the ends of virtue, one's governance operates in a similar moderating fashion. In both cases, we call the resulting state a state of moral apathy, that is, a state in which the strength of one's feelings has been lessened and moderated. But when one's natural feelings are in agreement with and supportive of the ends of virtue, that same evaluative and affective governance works in the opposite direction: slowly, over time, through the practice of virtue, one educates and thereby increases the strength of certain feelings which attach one either to relatively valuable things or to absolutely valuable persons because one realizes that these feelings enhance one's ability to make persons as such one's end. One thus practices the use of the very same evaluative capacity previously pointed toward a moderating, apathetic outcome also to heighten, enhance, and intensify those feelings supportive of morality. The governance of my affects through inner freedom is no longer simple constraint of those feelings and inclinations opposed to the pursuit of virtue, but also moderation of those feelings opposed to it and, finally, enhancement, enlivenment, and cultivation of those feelings and inclinations in agreement with it.

The result of all this repeated practice of the training of one's felt attachments is that one becomes a person who feels natural emotions only in telos-bound ways: one's natural emotions opposed to making persons as such one's end are moderated or extinguished and one's natural emotions supportive of making persons as such one's end are heightened, increased, and excited. And, in the rare case one does feel a strong natural emotion inappropriately, one recognizes it as such and constrains oneself from grounding maxims on such emotions. In the even rarer case that one might try to establish a particular felt attachment as the overall governor of one's person—viz., were one to try to establish one's inclination as a passion—our virtuous person recognizes that as well and does the harder psychological work of fighting against the mutinous and rebellious passion.

Overall, then, we can reject the mistaken notion that a virtuous life would be an unfelt one, lacking in strong feelings. Rather, the same capacity for moderating one's felt attachments in tension with one's committed moral goals can also serve to heighten those felt attachments which are supportive of one's moral purposes; and the same practice which encourages the moderation and/or elimination of some feelings can be applied for the strengthening, heightening, and excitement of others. There is, then, an effect that the moral feeling of respect has on one's emotional life overall: this sensible feeling which tracks and is caused by the objective telos of making persons as such one's end becomes the rationally informed affective basis from which one constructs a vigorous and lively affective life in line with the telos of one's being.

Subduing Affects

We want, ultimately, to focus on the ways in which Kant himself encourages the moral excitement, that is, the cultivation and strengthening of feelings for moral purposes. But let us begin by reflecting at greater length upon the first process of apathy, or moderation of feeling. We have previously (in I.i) identified two kinds of feelings in need of guidance: affects and passions, and have elsewhere (in I.iv) considered some of the challenges of governing exactly these sorts of felt attachments. But this structure of specific kinds of inclinations—affect and passions—can, furthermore, be very helpful to us as we make further sense of exactly how it is, through inner freedom's moral-feeling-guided tool of moral apathy, one moderates one's feelings. In particular, the difference which Kant describes in these affective states helps us to clarify the exact nature of that control of them required to achieve inner freedom's goal. As Kant helpfully summarizes, one must "*subdue*[e] one's affects" but must "*govern*...one's passions" (6:407/166, first emphasis added). Let's explore, then, the differences in the work of inner freedom upon each of these kinds of felt attachments.

So, first: how does one subdue an affect? As we have seen in I.i, an affect is something that makes proper reflection on a matter difficult or impossible: "Affects belong to feeling insofar as, preceding reflection, it makes this impossible or more difficult" (6:407/166). That is, when overtaken by an affect, one loses one's *composure*. The goal here thus needs to be to *regain* one's composure, which is precisely what is suggested in Kant's parenthetical Latin reference to the kind of constraint necessary for affects: "being one's own *master* in a given case (*animus sui compos*)" (6:407/166). But the pursuit of such composure is made even more difficult in that the experience of an affect comes as a "surprise" (7:252/150). One isn't expecting such an emotional flutter to come upon oneself; it simply visits when it will.

But before considering *how* one accomplishes this composure in the face of a disconcerting surprise affect, we should ask the previous question, though, of in what exactly this sought-for composure would consist: is Kant saying that one who subdues her affects is no longer subject to them at all? Or is he saying that one who subdues her affects experiences them but has learned not to allow herself to be carried away by that flutter of emotion? Does keeping one's composure (dictionary definition: "the state or feeling of being calm and in control of oneself," "serene, self-controlled state of mind"), mean that one has affects but is able to keep them in their place, or that one simply is no longer subject to them?

Textually, things are ambiguous on this point. In the *Anthropology*, Kant explicitly *defines* an affect *as* a *loss* of composure: "Affect is surprise through sensation, by means of which the mind's composure (animus sui compos) is suspended" (7:252/150). Such a definition thus implies that when one experiences an affect, one simply cannot be composed; one is necessarily under its sway. This suggests that the person of inner freedom, as the person of composure, would not experience any affects at all (since the bare experience of an affect would, simultaneously, be the loss of composure). And yet there seems something too strong about this utter identification of affect with loss of composure. Surely there is moral psychological space in between someone having no affects at all and someone losing her composure through the experience of an affect. Here is that middle space: if one has the mastery and composure of inner freedom, one might still experience affects (one needs, it seems, to grant this, since at least the bare emergence of an affect is, by definition, a "surprise" or something out of one's control), but would be better at *managing* these surprises when they do show up. One may need to admit that, because affects are "surprises," even the person of inner freedom cannot *entirely* control when and how they show up. One might be able to act in ways that discourage such surprise affects, but even the most composed person will sometimes encounter one. Composure would thus be realized not in fully preventing ever having an affect in the first place, but in being able to manage one when it does arise.

As such, it seems best to define composure as *both* the *infrequency* of surprise affects but also as the ability to manage these affects when they do arise unexpectedly. So, to be "composed" is, first, to be in that state which we've been calling apathy, but now understood strictly as a state of mind characterized not just by the moderation of feeling, but by "an *absence* of affects" (6:408/167, emphasis added). And, yet, we also grant that one can still be composed when an affect *does* unexpectedly arise. To be "composed" when an affect comes upon one as a surprise would mean to experience the affect but to manage it in such a way as to minimize the extent to which that affect throws one into confusion or prevents proper reflection. As Kant puts it, for the composed person experiencing an affect, "reason says, through the concept of virtue, that one should *get hold of* oneself" (6:408/166) while the flutter of the affect passes through one's mind. The composed person is the person capable of doing just that: getting a hold of oneself.[14]

How, then, does one accomplish this composure which constitutes the subduing of one's affects? We've already seen that, the acquisition of virtue on any level— including the pursuit of that strength necessary for coming to terms with one's felt attachments—comes about through two activities: contemplation of the dignity of the law and the practice of virtue. Kant thus provides us with two tools— *contemplation* and *practice*—to utilize in both the subduing of affects and the governing of passions, both of which are pointed toward "enhanc[ing] the moral incentive (the thought of the law)" (6:397/158). Let's consider each of these tools

---

[14] P.G. Wodehouse's (1991) character Jeeves is perhaps the paradigmatic example of a person of composure. Jeeves, I suspect, experiences very strong affects when he observes various of the indiscretions in which his lord, Bertie, engages. But the only evidence of those internal affects we observe is the slightest raising of an eyebrow. He does, in other words, maintain composure even as he suffers that flutter of an affect.

in turn in relation, first, to our current question of how to subdue of affects, and then in relation to the more challenging task of governing of passions.

Affects, by their very fleeting nature, are best managed simply through suffering them at the moment they arise, preventing any immediate action upon them, and then (after they are gone) reflecting on why and how they emerged. This might seem like a simple and straight-forward process: I simply acquire an ability to manage whatever emotions come along. And yet such a capacity is not something simply to be assumed as present in a person. Someone who isn't good, e.g., at counting to ten before expressing one's anger to another person, cannot simply, on a dime, acquire the ability to manage such affects with composure. Indeed, learning to subdue affects is rarely an easy process. Surprising affective experiences often reveal hopes, desires, or fears of which one had not previously been consciously aware, some of which might be disturbing, others of which might encourage a rash and sudden response. The affect is a strong experience and one needs a strong response to it in order to acquire composure in relation to it. One needs, then, to acquire a certain sternness of purpose, a strong willingness unflinchingly to look clearly in the face at whatever an affect presents or highlights in one's felt consciousness. If I do not acquire this strength to look at my affects, I will never acquire composure. I will instead be subject to these surprises again and again. I might even begin to look like someone hunted by affects which chase me. To subdue an affect, I mustn't let it chase me. I must be brave enough to see it coming, to stare it down as it approaches, to calmly suffer it while it passes, then to reflect upon what the very experience of that affect does or doesn't mean for my person overall.

It is in just this context that Kant's first tool of contemplating the dignity of the moral law via the moral feeling of respect comes into play. To be able to appreciate how such contemplation operates specifically in the subduing of affects, we need, however, first to remind ourselves of, and expand upon, what exactly this contemplation of the dignity of the law is. To contemplate the dignity of the law is, first and foremost, an act of attentiveness. Contemplation involves *turning* your attention to the presence of the law in your moral consciousness and then *paying* attention to it, paying attention in particular to the hold that law has on one's moral consciousness, feeling its power and authority over your person. It is the law that provides us the most adequate and authoritative ground—the most "dignified" ground for rational beings—for structuring one's end-setting and person. And it is in paying attention to its presence within us that this authoritative ground will have the most capacity to influence that end-setting in the way that the realization of one's inner freedom would demand.

The particular strength of this reflection on the dignity of the law is revealed in how such honest reflection upon the law can cast down the pretensions of other parts of our soul seeking to dislodge its authority. By honestly contemplating the dignity of the law in my felt experience of the moral feeling of respect, I focus my attention on that felt clarity of vision in which the law simply presents itself to me as the proper, true basis of all end-setting. In short, I'm focusing my conscious reflection upon the absolute value of persons and the dignity inherent in such value.

How, then, does contemplation of or attentiveness to the dignity of the law help me in subduing my affects? If I am going to acquire an ability unflinchingly to encounter various and sundry surprise affects, some of which have the potential to disturb, intimidate, or confuse me, I need something upon which to rely for *strength*. And this is exactly what previous contemplation of the dignity of the moral law via the moral feeling of respect will provide me in the face of an affect: a strong *affective* point of view from which to suffer that new affect. If I have previously had a genuine, first-personal, affective recognition of just how powerful and dignified that law which is my own is, I know that I have a strong place to stand and from which to defend myself when unexpected affects wash up on my shores. The previous affective experience of the dignity of the law has allowed me actually to experience the categorical demands of virtue *as* categorical.[15] But in so doing, my other felt attachments pale in comparison because I now have a central, strong, and safe affective space from which to manage them. Just as Odysseus demands of his crew that they lash him to the mast as their boat passes the tempting voices of the Sirens, we too can lash ourselves to the law that we know guides our moral voyages. In so doing, one creates what I've been calling "evaluative distance" upon one's affect: a safe psychological and affective space from which to observe the flutter of the affect which is indeed still going on within me. There is, in other words, simultaneously, *another* part of me—my recollection of my previous moral-feeling-guided reflections upon the dignity of the law—that is *not* fluttering while the affect continues its fluttering. It is from that safe, non-fluttering space that I identify this affect, experience it, and understand it for what it is.

This attentiveness to the dignity of the law which allows us the strength to suffer our experience of an affect is, however, only the first step in subduing an affect. Having encountered or suffered a surprise affect bravely, from the safe viewing point of morality, I need, post-affect, to prepare for the potential for future surprises. We are thus led to the second of Kant's tools or admonitions for how to accomplish virtue. After reflection on the dignity of the moral law has given us that strength necessary to suffer the experience of the affect, we then need to turn to "the practice of virtue" to manage the future. What is important about identifying and reflecting upon these surprises when they show up is that one thereby has the hope of being more prepared for the possibility of future surprises. And it is through the repeated *practice* of virtue—here, through the repeated practice of

---

[15] I argue as much in Grenberg (2013a, chapters 1 and 7–9).

managing my affects better in the future—that I become even more strong and composed in the face of them.

But what exactly would such practice mean in the context of affect management? An example will help here. If one unexpectedly discovers the experience of fear while on a plane, it would make sense to expect that next time one is on a plane, the surprise affect of fear will show up again. But when one *expects* its arrival, that is, when one *expects* to feel the flutter the next time one flies, it is no longer a surprise. It is, indeed, something for which one can plan and thereby learn even better how to control. Perhaps I will learn meditation techniques. Perhaps I will bring calming music with me to listen to while I fly. And so on. By *practicing* my management of affects, I am "practic[ing] *virtue.*" That is, through repeated attention to the experience of my affect, I develop a *strength* in relation to my experience of that affect. If I do this over and over, my composure grows and my fear recedes. I have, that is, "subdue[d]" my affect of fear through contemplation of the dignity of the law and then the practice of virtue.

One is also, through this process of practicing one's reaction to affects, thereby more on guard about the dangerous potential surreptitiously to turn this affect into a passion. I am less likely to discover at some point in the future that I have secretly turned a passing affect into an established passion if I have not allowed that affect to wander around my consciousness un-mentored, without a chaperone. Unchaperoned affects threaten to become mutinous passions. The affect of anger is a good example here. It might turn out that unchaperoned surprise anger has an unnoticed positive effect for me: perhaps expression of it makes me feel powerful, even happy. Harsh expression of anger does, after all, give one a way to put down others who have been annoying. It would thus be very tempting were I to have unconsciously gotten in the habit of using anger to improve my mood, to decide, eventually, consciously, and calmly to integrate this anger into my way of being with persons I dislike. That is, perhaps, one moral psychological story of how anger becomes the "hatred" of which Kant speaks: "A *passion* is a sensible *desire* that has become a lasting inclination (e.g., *hatred*, as opposed to anger)" (6:408/166). But chaperoned affects have less psychological space for such surreptitious mutinous plotting. That is, if I reflect upon the past affect, understand its genesis, and especially understand any temptations I might have to allow the affect to provide a basis for further action or accomplishments, then I have subverted the possibility of such integration of an affect into a passion from occurring self-deceptively or less than straight-forwardly. I am composed now, and have a plan for how to be composed in the future.

Governing Passions

Despite our best efforts, it is likely that a passion will arise. Passions, however, because they are more long-lasting and more firmly entrenched than affects, also require more stern governing control. Kant says one must "*govern* passions," thereby "*ruling* oneself" (6:407/166, emphases added). Such ruling is, furthermore, glossed in Latin as an "imperium in semetipsum" or an *absolute* power over oneself. Indeed, the Latin phrase "imperium," referred, in ancient Rome, to "the supreme power held by consuls or emperors to command and administer specifically in *military* affairs".[16] When passions are around, we need to get even more stern, strong, and serious about controlling ourselves than we already did with affects, and this precisely because the establishment of a passion threatens a quasi-rational mutiny of the true governing ruler of one's soul, one's objective telos of making persons as such one's end. As we have seen in our discussion of such things in both I.i and I.iv, passions are not just passing episodes, like affects. Beyond that, the establishment of a passion is the establishment of a new ruling order in one's soul. It is a genuine overthrow of the authority of one's proper governing telos in favor of the authority of one's passion. These mutinous passions must therefore be captured and defeated much as a seditious plotter would be captured and defeated. That is, they must be governed in the way that anyone administering military affairs facing a potential mutiny would need to govern them: use one's legitimate authority to defeat and then contain or imprison (and perhaps ultimately destroy?) the would-be mutineer.

Now I know I've been describing the governor of inner freedom as a gentle governor, so the use of such harsh military language may seem in tension with the picture we've been drawing. It is certainly true that the ultimate effects on one's moral consciousness of successfully governing a passion will be more dramatic, and the process of getting there more intense. But, as we shall see below, even this more intense process occurs via the gentle moral psychological tools of inner freedom: that process via which one combats rogue emotions not just thuggishly by pushing them out of the way, but evaluatively by educating them to a higher purpose. It is just that the education of passion is the education of the most recalcitrant student in the class, one not very interested in being educated. Let's explore this process.

The difference between controlling affects and controlling passions is the difference between controlling the bare experience of feeling as compared to controlling what one has (perhaps surreptitiously) *done* with one's feelings in the establishment of one's end-setting and self-governance. That is, in a passion, I have already made a decision that the experience of the affect and/or its object is something *important* to me. I have claimed it as my own in a way that the mere passing affect cannot (yet) be said to be my own. I haven't chosen the affect, but I have chosen the passion. I have explicitly placed that inclination as the basis of my maxim of choice. And I've not only chosen the passion as one thing amongst

---

[16] See www.dictionary.com.

others; I have also, as we saw in I.i, chosen it as a ruling component in my soul. I brood on this passion; it is rooted deeply in me.

An already established passion thus presents a particular challenge in self-governance: how do I govern something I've already so subversively made central to my end-setting and character? One needs, ultimately, to de-maxim-ize or de-incorporate the inclination at the basis of one's passion. That is, I have to un-*choose* this inclination and the ends it grounds. But how does one do this? In the first instance, one must become more aware of just how much influence the experience of a particular inclination has already had on one's end-setting process. I realize that a particularly strong affective experience (because surely every passion started out as a mere, passing affective experience) has gotten a hold of me. More precisely, *I* have latched on to *it*. Previously, it was just something that passed over me, an affect. But the experience of that affect led me to reflect upon something in myself that I wanted or needed so much that I was willing, either consciously or surreptitiously, to give up proper governance of my soul in order to realize that thing. Governing a passion, then, involves *detaching* my rational choice from that intensely felt inclination which is currently acting as a ground of my end-setting. If I don't find a way to detach the inclination from my end-setting, thereby removing the identification I have made between myself and this inclination, this passion will still operate on me.

But this is no small thing to accomplish! If I have really allowed a certain inclination to become so deeply entrenched in my end-setting and self-governance, there will be a mighty civil war when I try to extricate it from my person. The experience will be something akin to the "revolution" in character Kant describes when one overturns one's meta-maxim of radical evil in favor of one's meta-maxim of the moral disposition.[17] Indeed, if a passion really is a deeply entrenched aspect of one's end-setting, one which has become a ruling passion, then nothing less than this revolution of character in which I overturn the passion and make the objective telos of my being my authoritative, ruling, and guiding "passion" will be adequate. What would this process of revolution—though, really, not a *revolution* but the *re-establishment* of the original legitimate authority in the soul—look like?

Recalling Kant's two-pronged process for establishing inner freedom—viz., contemplating the dignity of the law and practicing virtue—will help us again here. First, recall that Kant says the goal of this contemplation of the law and practice of virtue must be to strengthen one's moral incentive: "the way to acquire [the strength of virtue] is to enhance the moral incentive (the thought of the

---

[17] See especially 6:47/67–68: "[T]hat a human being should become not merely *legally* good, but *morally* good (pleasing to God) i.e., virtuous according to the intelligible character [of virtue]...cannot be effected through gradual *reform* but must rather be effected through a *revolution* in the disposition of the human being (a transition to the maxim of holiness of disposition). And so a 'new man' can come about only through a kind of rebirth, as it were a new creation...and a change of heart."

law...)" (6:397/158). In the case at hand, this means that, to govern one's passions, one needs first to strengthen the forces of the *legitimate* authority that will oppose these seditious plotters. That is, one needs to strengthen one's motivations which take one's objective telos of making persons as such one's end, instead of this rogue passion, as one's ruling "passion" or governor. But how does one do that?

First, as with the subduing of an affect, one again begins by contemplating the dignity of the law. This initial act of attentiveness is, if anything, even more important for the governing of passions than for the subduing of affects. This is because, essentially, the acquisition of a passion is by definition a previous *failure* of this attentiveness; as such, detaching oneself from a passion will have to involve, in the first instance, coming to terms with this imbalance in attentiveness: the passion has led one to focus one's thoughts only on some things and not on others. To restore governing control of one's person, though, one needs to have one's attention regularly and constitutionally focused on the authority of the moral law itself. This attentiveness to the moral law is what has been lost in the passion-formation stage, and is what needs to be regained to govern the passion.

It is from this perspective that we can thus, once again, appreciate Kant's admonition to "contemplat[e]...the dignity of the pure rational law." What we see here is a corrective for one's failures in attentiveness first introduced by the establishment of a passion. If a passion is a failure in attentiveness, correction of it must involve, first, improving one's attention to things of value that really matter and that really have ultimate authority in the organization of one's soul: one must put one's loves or passions in the right place.[18] For Deontological Eudaemonism, that means contemplating the authoritative dignity of the law, viz. contemplating affectively, through appeal to the moral feeling of respect, how the absolute value of persons grounds in me a telos of making persons as such my end. And everything that we saw such attentiveness doing for the managing of affects is operative again here: my attention to the telos of my being establishes in me that safe and strong space from which I approach the management of my emotional life generally, not only my affects but now also my entrenched passions.

This will, however, be a more difficult thing to accomplish if one's passions are already established. If I really have already established a mutinous ruling order in myself, my habits of attentiveness will be guided by my passion. It will, therefore, be *painful* to place my attention elsewhere, especially to place my attention in a place that will reveal my perfidy and corruption! Contemplation of the dignity of the law requiring that I make persons as such my end will, after all, make my own passion pale in comparison. My hatred of persons who get in my way may feel

---

[18] Putting it this way reminds me of Augustine's *Confessions* (1993): for Augustine, getting one's loves and passions in the right place meant learning to love God more than sex and honor, and learning to love all such merely finite and contingent things only in God. For Kant, of course, we're seeing that such organization of one's loves and passions means, in the first instance, contemplating the dignity of the law.

good to me as I climb to the top of the corporate ladder. But in comparison with the dignity and absolute value of all persons, my hatred looks like a pitiful, spiteful, mean, tiny, meaningless thing. This is no fun to experience. Forcing myself to look clearly at the dignity of the law is therefore, in itself, one's first genuine moral *accomplishment*. I have already, that is, begun to dislodge the mutinous conspirators when I welcome them into the clear light of day provided by the light of the dignity of the law.

But there is more to be said here about this first step in the dislodging of passions. We need to consider more precisely how exactly it is that attentiveness to and contemplation of the dignity of the law allow one to move, moral psychologically, from obsession and fixation upon one's passions to the true and focused path of realizing virtue. Most centrally, this increase in focus on the proper object of attentiveness (viz., the law, as expressed via moral feeling) allows one to loosen up that process of reflection leading to choice and end-setting and—importantly for our purposes in reflecting upon how to govern a passion—to *dislodge* that process of reflection which led to the choice of one's firmly lodged passion in the first place. Because one has contemplated the true authority of the guiding objective telos of one's person, one is now in a better position from which to assess the worthiness or otherwise of one's already incorporated inclinations as passions. One might even envision here that in this new process of reflection, grounded in a more firmly established attentiveness to the moral law, the scales fall from one's eyes, and one sees oneself and one's choices and ends for what they really are: a corruption or warping of one's soul. One can, that is, *see*, *feel*, and *sense* the corruption of oneself. One can see one's bad choices as *bad* choices, choices in need of being changed. This is just what one needs to change oneself, to engage in that revolution of person which is the relinquishment of one's passion: I need to *see* the horror of myself and therefore *want* to establish a new structure of soul in order to engage in a new, more proper task of end-setting and self-governance. Such successful reflection on one's choice of a passion seems a necessary step toward governing (and, eventually, eliminating) that passion. In order to hope to engage in new, virtuous practices, one must first honestly reflect on the good *reasons* to *not* let one's original passion-established inclination become a ground of one's end-setting. And it is contemplation of the power and authority of the moral law via attentiveness to one's experience of the moral feeling of respect which again provides that new, safe psychological space and evaluative distance from which to do exactly that (viz., to reflect on the good reasons to reject one's passion).

The Herculean Effort of Virtue

We should pause at this point really to appreciate how arduous the pursuit of virtue is. Breaking down steps in a theory of action can, at times, seem a dry and analytical task, but one must emphasize that this dull catalog of steps in a theory of action in fact tracks an existential, life-changing event as well as a painful and arduous process. One does discover in this process what I've been calling a safe and strong psychological space from which one engages in this task of self-renovation, but this doesn't mean that this is an easy or pleasant experience in which to engage. I have been describing the governor of virtue as a gentle governor, but such gentleness is required largely because the work of attaining virtue is exceedingly painful and difficult. Indeed, Kant himself reminds us that this first of all duties to self, viz. to know oneself, is most often experienced as "the descent into the hell of self-cognition" or an effort "to penetrate into the depths (the abyss) of one's heart" (6:441/191). And facing oneself honestly in this way takes an immense amount of strength and courage.

With this articulation of reason's existential and life-changing task of subduing affects and governing passions in the name of one's rational commitment to respect for persons in hand, we can thus appreciate why it is that Kant frequently speaks of the pursuit of virtue as an internal *battle* within oneself. One good example of his reliance on battle imagery to explain the pursuit of virtue is, early in the Doctrine of Virtue, when Kant envisions the struggle for virtue through reference to "the beautiful fable [which] places Hercules between virtue and sensible pleasure" (6:380n/145n). In this fable (much depicted artistically in the centuries since its first mention by the 5th-century-BC sophist Prodicus of Ceos[19]), Hercules is pointed by Virtue (*Arete*) herself to the rough, hard path of virtue but is simultaneously encouraged and coaxed by Pleasure (*Hedone*) herself to choose instead the easy path of pleasure.

That Kant considers this image an apt one for thinking about our own pursuit of virtue is meaningful and instructive: it is an image that helps us appreciate the situation of the sensibly affected rational being. Part of the point of Kant's appeal to this fable is to emphasize the precarious position in which the choosing and would-be moral person finds herself. We are beings on the precipice between virtue and vice. We are capable of seeing the heights of virtue, but subject to the temptations of a self-centered and vicious life grounded only in pleasure and desire-satisfaction. The former is arduous and hard; the latter appears luxurious and easy. But in addition to vividly depicting the precariousness of the human situation, this fable also depicts the potential *strength* of the person facing this choice. This is *Hercules* after all (not Cupid!) who is facing this decision. Implicitly, then, Kant's suggestion is that the strength of virtue, if chosen, could be a strength of Herculean proportions, entirely capable of vanquishing so paltry an opponent as pleasure or mere desire-satisfaction.

---

[19] As reported in Xenophon (1923): 2.1.21–34 = Prodicus 84 B 2 Diels-Kranz (II313f).

This image of Hercules at the crossroad is the ultimate guiding image for appreciating that, for Kant, success in the acquisition of virtue would be the establishment of a strong state of *self-governance* which emerges via an internal battle within oneself between one's rational appreciation of the need to make persons as such one's end as *the* guiding value of one's life and one's pursuit of pleasure expressed through one's felt attachments (affects, inclinations, and passions). That is: virtue is that state in which I not only do what is good and right but also, and most centrally, in which I control, govern, coax, and cultivate those parts of me tempted to go astray through excessive concern for self-centered pursuit of pleasure, all resulting in an overall ordering of oneself best understood as a state of legitimate governance of (all of) oneself.

It must be admitted that appeal to internal battles isn't a popular way of construing Kantian virtue these days. To the contrary, it has been popular in recent years to emphasize that Kant's account of virtue is *not* about battles.[20] I do not entirely disagree with these ideas in themselves: I agree, for example, that incorporation of incentives into maxims (instead of direct causal influence of inclinations on choice) is the best way to think about Kant's theory of free action; and I believe (as Part II of this book will go on emphatically to assert and defend) that there is more to virtue than *simply* struggling to constrain strong countervailing desires; virtue is, ultimately, a story of how one learns to function smoothly, pleasurably, and properly as the kind of being one is, expressing a complete integrity in one's person. And yet there is still something very important, given Kant's account of human nature, about the idea that the pursuit of virtue involves a *battle* wherein strong affects, inclinations, and passions are the combatants which reason and virtue face. Kant does, after all, conceive of virtue as "fortitude" (6:380/146) or "strength" (6:384/148); but virtue needs to be strong precisely because its job is, in part, to *battle* against and constrain opposing forces.

Indeed, Kant regularly characterizes the pursuit of virtue as this Herculean battle between, on the one hand, one's true moral nature which knows and accepts the demand of making persons as such one's end which one's status as a free, rational, and moral being places upon one's life; and, on the other hand, the

---

[20] For example, Hensen's (1979) "battle citation" account of virtue—in which the height of moral accomplishment is merely success in the battle to prevent strong but immoral desires from becoming operative in action—has been found to be an inadequate conception of virtue. On his account, even the best of us only get "battle citations" for being able to control or contain strong countervailing desires, preventing them from becoming operative in action (as opposed to being more the Aristotelian virtuous person who has no countervailing things to control). But it has been argued that virtue needs to be understood more positively than this and, further, that the image of battle fails aptly to characterize the true nature of Kant's theory of action in which reasons instead of physical forces do the choosing. It has thus been argued that moral motivation is not best characterized as a battle in which one's moral motives are stronger in some quasi-mechanistic or quasi-physical way than one's non-moral motives; instead, we must speak only of the strength of reasons or maxims (which have incorporated various inclinations or incentives) competing with each other. See, e.g., Reath (1989) and Allison (1990). Battle references in Kantian virtue have thus been found problematic from a variety of angles.

temptations one has to give in to a life governed by pleasure and desire-satisfaction. He says, for example, that "[i]mpulses of nature...involve obstacles within man's mind to his fulfillment of duty and (sometimes powerful) forces opposing it" (6:380/145). Indeed, he even explicitly suggests that natural inclinations themselves have some role, in concert with the power of one's rational choice, in those vicious choices we make to place desire-satisfaction above morality, in encouraging us, that is, "to *rebel* against the law" (6:383/148, emphasis added), or to engage in a subversive, mutinous challenge to that law's legitimate authority. As interpreters of Kant, we thus need to be committed to making sense of Kant's meaning when he appeals so regularly to battle imagery in the pursuit of virtue. We should thus welcome the idea that the pursuit of virtue involves an internal battle, and that this battle, for sensibly affected rational beings, occurs both on the level of reason and on the level of natural inclinations.

We need, however, to reflect more thoroughly on the background question that lurks here: if the pursuit of virtue does indeed involve a battle between the rational demand to make persons as such one's end and the lure of instead following a self-centered life of desire-satisfaction, what precise role do the competing affects, inclinations, and passions play in this battle? If Kant's theory of action really is a rational theory of action in which the battle for the determining grounds of choice is a battle amongst competing reasons, not amongst competing mechanistic forces, how can we make sense of sensible affects, inclinations, and passions having any stature or place to stand in the battle at all?

If we can answer this question, we'll be providing an understanding of Kant's theory of action that sets it in a better light in relation to our common experience of what it is to be a choosing being. We humans are indeed capable of rational choice, but it is hard to deny that such choice can be influenced by the strength of our inclinations: our desires, needs, and inclinations make demands on us. They clamor for our attention. They address us, coax us, plead with us. But we need—and, fortunately, have the potential for—strength in the face of these demands of our sensible nature. The question for humanity is, thus, the very question that Hercules faces: will we choose in the name of the arduous path of virtue, thus claiming our bastion of strength as free and rational beings, thereby creating a strength of character by which we are not unduly susceptible to the lures of the easy path of pleasure and vice? Or will we reject the strength of virtue in the name of the ease of pleasure and simple desire-satisfaction which will, all too easily, become the principled and passionate life of vice?

Although I will not provide a complete theory of action here, I have argued previously[21] that this story of how inclinations have influence on rational choice can be told via appeal to *attentiveness*: it may be that the strength of an inclination

---

[21] See Grenberg (2013a).

as such is not what determines my choice, but the fact that I take up one inclination instead of another as the basis for my reasons for action is explainable by the fact that one inclination is more insistently and continually present in my mind's eye while others fade into the background. After all, it is simply implausible to assume that all my desires present themselves as equally possible grounds for incorporation and that the question of which will be incorporated is based only on the strength of reasons and not at all on the strength of the underlying inclinations or incentives. Indeed, if this were the case, we would never do anything but the right thing, because, on the basis of reasons alone, moral reasons inevitably prove to be strongest. We must, therefore, tell a story, within the construct of a theory of action centered on incorporation, about how the varying strengths of desires still play their role in choice and thus provide the grounds of this internal battle.

And so an appeal to attentiveness resolves our problem: simply stated, strong inclinations attract more of my mental gaze than weak ones. Some desires are paltry and passing, while others clamor incessantly for attention. And of course I'll be more inclined to choose to incorporate the more demanding inclinations: the squeaky wheel gets the grease! Ultimately, we will be more moved to choose those things that demand and captivate our attention; and, conversely, we don't even have the opportunity or chance to choose something of which we are not aware. For all our insistence, then, that Kant's account of virtue is not just about battles, we must thus admit that the strength of our inclinations competing for attention has *some* impact on our capacity to choose, even as we grant that choice ultimately depends not directly on that strength but most centrally upon our free capacity to incorporate or not incorporate those inclinations into our maxims. The *strength* of an inclination influences *where* my mind's eye directs itself and makes it that much more likely that I will choose in the direction of that stronger inclination. I can only make choices about the objects to which I attend, and those objects which grab my attention are the more plausible candidates for choice.

The influence of attentiveness on choice indeed helps us understand why, as we have already seen, Kant considers "enhanc[ing] the moral *incentive* (the thought of the law)...by contemplating the dignity of the pure rational law in us (*contemplatione*)" (6:397/158–159) to be the first step in the pursuit of virtue. We need to find ways to make sure that we regularly—even habitually—focus our attention on moral incentives, motivations, and reasons for action so as to strengthen their potential for influence upon our choosing selves. When this incentive is present and lively in one's moral consciousness, it becomes that much more reliably the basis of one's choice of ends. It is only in attending to the power and force of reasons to place respect for persons at the absolute center of my life that I will successfully choose to set those ends which guide my life autocratically by that demand.

In the end, then, the battle for virtue is best construed as a battle in the City of Reason which takes place on the Field of Inclinations. These inclinations are so many potential combatants conscriptable to armies of ends which are under the command of either virtue or self-interest, a sort of battle in the setting of ends, a battle between ends one might set grounded in inclinations and desire-satisfaction, and ends one must set on a fully *a priori* basis:

> For since the sensible inclinations of human beings tempt them [viz., human beings] to ends (the matter of choice) that can be contrary to duty, lawgiving reason can in turn check their influence only by a moral end set up against the ends of inclination, an end that must therefore be given *a priori*, independently of inclinations. (6:380–381/146)

The question of what ends we set is, however, influenced by what grounds for ends we entertain: we will only set ends based on things to which we attend! The image of Hercules sitting at the crossroads, between "virtue and sensible pleasure" (6:380n/145n), is thus a metaphor for the battle for attentiveness which precedes the actual choice of ends one sets—virtuous or vicious—in the effort to govern one's life and action.[22]

We thus now have a vision of the Herculean effort required to become a new person. Really to look oneself in the mirror, with no flinching or blinking—now, not only in the face of passing affects but in the face of the small-minded, passionate person whom I have chosen to make myself—demands an immense, Herculean strength. Indeed, one hopes for Herculean strength as one prepares to face those strongest of opponents, one's own self-constructed demons.

Practicing One's Way Out of Passions

Let us envision, though, that this painful process of self-reflection has occurred: I look at myself, and know that I need to reject my passions and build a new structure of my soul. But again, *how*, ultimately, does one actually change one's previous choices and ends, and thus oneself? The answer here, once again, as with managing affects, is to turn to new and repeated *practices*. Reflection on how the "practice of virtue" is important in the governance of passions can furthermore, beyond clarifying the nature of that governance, allow us also to appreciate more

---

[22] Importantly, when Kant discusses the Herculean dilemma, he notes that, whatever freedom is, it is not a conception of freedom adequate for explaining *why* one would choose pleasure-based pragmatic ends over moral ends or vice versa. Rather, the image of Hercules caught between sensuous inclinations and virtue shows instead that we simply cannot explain why one chooses one or the other: for, when we want to give *reasons* for the free choice of one or the other, our effort to describe the freedom of this choice collapses into apparent causal determination: "for we can explain what happens only by deriving it from a cause in accordance with laws of nature, and in so doing we would not be thinking of choice as free" (6:380n/145n).

deeply the meaning of Kant's appeal to this second tool of "practices" in the establishment of virtue generally. When we apply the need to practice virtue in the process of seeking the governance of our passions, one can really see Kant encouraging something that seems rather Aristotelian in nature: Kant is indeed, in encouraging us to practice virtue to acquire virtue, telling us that quasi-Aristotelean habitual action or practice that would start to urge one's choices in the direction of new end-setting (and would, regularly, consistently, constitutionally discourage the re-connection of one's old inclination to a maxim and/or end) is what is necessary firmly to establish one's virtue as strength. That is, one begins, as Aristotle would put it, to act as the virtuous person would act: even if you are not yet that person of virtue, pretend that you are. You are in fact still the person committed to soul-warping passions. The strong things in your soul have been the embedded experiences of strong inclinations made into a way of being. But now you start acting as the virtuous person would act. That is, you start acting as if you actually had that strength to control your affects and passions that the truly virtuous person in fact already possesses. You are acting, repeatedly, as a practice, in the way that the virtuous person would act. What this means for a Kantian is that one acts with a clear sense of the dignity of the law (that object of contemplation acquired in the first step of moral transformation) firmly established in one's mind: one repeatedly reminds oneself to make persons as such one's end, and starts to set ends and act in ways that realize this telos. All of this is done as a sort of corrective to the fact that you've previously been acting as the vicious person does act, and you now need to get to know new ways of acting. Practice is the only way to accomplish that. And, eventually, one wakes up one morning and finds it is an easy thing to do, this new habit of acting for the sake of persons.

We thus have a clearer sense of how to enact Kant's admonition to govern one's passions. In order to govern and rule a passion, one needs to think more carefully and morally about one's choices. But to do that, one needs first to do the hard work of contemplation and attentiveness: that is, to turn our attention back to something that has more value than this inclination upon which I have lavished so much of my rational reflection, and reflection upon which will allow me to engage in further, more satisfying because more thoroughly rational, consideration of how to respond to and what to do with the inclination at the basis of my passion. Passions are failures of attentiveness and contemplation, and can be governed ultimately only by new studies in attentiveness and contemplation followed by better reflection with better starting points and ending in the establishment of new practices or ways of acting that form the new person. It is only because I'm finally looking at the big picture of value more clearly, honestly, and perceptively that I can de-maximize old choices, claim new ones, and thus do something to change the structure and disposition of my soul.

Conclusion

But as I have been emphasizing repeatedly in this chapter, a life of struggle and conflict is not the end of the story of a life of virtue for Kant! We have rejected the idea that this caricature of the Kantian virtuous person as one riddled with conflict and suffering is the height of virtue. Instead, the experience of conflict and Herculean struggle reflects the work of *becoming* virtuous: it is the work of inner freedom in guiding our capacity to tolerate suffering as well as in governing, heightening, and exciting/invigorating our felt life in accordance with the demands of morality so as to resolve our internal conflicts.

We thus turn in the next chapter to the product of all this hard work of self-governance of one's felt attachments and to what is really the true and accurate ideal characterization of the subjective state of virtue for Kant's fully virtuous person: a free aptitude for virtue which is experienced as pleasure in the virtually unimpeded activity of one's will. Kant describes such an aptitude for virtue as both "a facility in acting" and "a subjective perfection of choice [Willkür]" (6:407/165). What we shall see in the coming chapter is that, through repeated practice of my Herculean battle to constrain and cultivate my felt attachments as described in this chapter, the fully virtuous person exits this state of battle and conflict, and instead acquires a particular alacrity and ease in the exercise of her free choice, an alacrity and ease which, since it constitutes the most proper functioning of her capacity for choice, is something she experiences pleasurably. And in welcoming this notion of the pleasurable exercise of an aptitude for virtue, we thereby simultaneously welcome a rational, non-empirical notion of happiness for Kant which is identical with that hard-won virtue. Let us turn to that discussion, a discussion which constitutes the heart of Kant's Deontological Eudaemonism.

II.ii
Happiness, Rationally Conceived
Pleasure in the Virtually Unimpeded Activity of a Free Aptitude for Virtue

Introduction

In this chapter, we step back from the suffering, challenges, and Herculean hard work of self-governance to appreciate the fruits of all this labor: a subjective state which supervenes immediately upon the exercise of one's aptitude for virtue understood as happiness, rationally instead of empirically conceived, a state which constitutes the heart of Kant's Deontological Eudaemonism. As we have already seen back in I.i, happiness empirically conceived consists in the sum of pleasures that result from the achievement or fulfillment of something that one has lacked, a lack that is expressed in the mental state of a desire. But happiness rationally conceived, as we shall see in this chapter, consists in the virtuous person's experience of non-felt pleasure in the virtually unimpeded exercise of the activity of her rational will and choice, an experience, that is, of having what Kant calls a "free aptitude" for virtue. Such pleasure is not so much a felt twinge which confirms desire-satisfaction, but instead an expression of the harmony, facility, and ease with which the fully virtuous person succeeds in being just the kind of being she was meant to be, an experience of her negative freedom combined with an experience of the ease with which she exercises her rational will (or *Wille*, since her choice, or *Willkür*, is entirely in conformity with that will). And although this is not a pure experience of positive freedom as such (only a purely rational and non-sensible being could have such an experience), the experience of a free aptitude for virtue is the height or full excellence of what a sensibly affected rational being can accomplish. Further, this pleasurable and virtually unimpeded activity of one's will, which is essentially the fullest expression of inner freedom, is so central to one's being that it deserves the moniker of happiness, rationally or intellectually conceived. We thus welcome a rational, non-empirical notion of happiness for Kant which is identical with the realization of full virtue and which constitutes the heart of one's subjective telos of virtue. This is Kant's Deontological Eudaemonism.

We have already seen, in the previous chapter, the arduous process of ordering one's felt attachments via one's commitment to making persons as such one's end. What we explore in this chapter is the end-point of that process: the establishment of an aptitude for virtue within which one experiences that exercise as pleasant. In the first instance, this pleasure is simply the flip-side of the exercise of virtue itself: when one experiences oneself as functioning properly as the kind of being one is, the experience of this virtually unimpeded activity is itself pleasant and, indeed, pleasant in a way that Kant himself describes as "intellectual contentment of oneself." Virtue and pleasure are so closely identified here that, once we show that state to be essential identical to Aristotle's conception of unimpeded activity, we shall be entitled to describe these fruits of the hard work of the pursuit of virtue as "happiness."[1] We thus affirm a vision of the proper functioning of the sensibly affected rational being which promises, except for in the most tragic of contingently unavoidable circumstances, to be a pleasant life of happiness, rationally conceived.

This chapter is organized as follows. We begin with a review of the current state of the literature on the eudaemonistic or non-eudaemonistic relationship of morality and happiness for Kant, a discussion wherein we identify a range of interpreters with whom we will be engaging for the rest of Part II. We then turn to an interpretation of Aristotle's notion of pleasure as unimpeded activity, a notion that will serve for the rest of this chapter as an interpretive lens through which to understand and interpret Kant's ideas. We then turn to a careful reading and consideration of Kant's notion of "aptitude," relying upon the Aristotelian notion of happiness as unimpeded activity to help unpack the import of Kant's claims, showing ultimately that an aptitude for virtue is experienced both as a felt negative freedom from external constraint and also as a pleasurable facility or ease concomitant with the activity of virtue itself. In so doing, we position our account of this pleasure sympathetically with Zuckert's (2002) account of non-felt aesthetic pleasure as an expression of the harmony of one's faculties, but identify a new, practical example of such pleasure: a practical version of the harmony of the faculties one finds in Kant's *Critique of Judgment* discussion of aesthetic pleasure, now found in the harmony of one's practical faculties of will and choice.

In affirming this non-felt form of pleasure, we thereby reject Elizondo's (2014) suggestion that there is a purely intellectual *feeling* of pleasure for Kant, akin to Aristotle's notion of pleasure in unimpeded activity. Although we agree with Elizondo that a rational pleasure exists for Kant, we reject Elizondo's suggestion that such pleasure consists in a purely active feeling. Because feeling as such for Kant definitionally involves a moment of passivity, we instead understand the rational pleasure that is equivalent with the exercise of virtue to be a non-felt

---

[1] In so doing, I, on the one hand, place my reading of Kant in sympathetic comparison with Annas' (2011, 1995) reading of Aristotle and, on the other, distinguish myself from Forman's (2016) reading of Kant as a "moderate cynic" who must entirely eschew any identity of virtue and happiness. For, once we welcome happiness as unimpeded activity, in addition to the more familiar notion of happiness empirically conceived as desire-fulfillment, we can admit the former though not the latter as being identical with the exercise of full virtue as such.

pleasurable experience of the harmony, facility, and ease with which one experiences the alignment of one's rational will with one's choice. And because this is pleasure in not just any activity but in that activity which defines who the sensibly affected rational being is, we call that pleasure not just intellectual contentment, but intellectual or rational happiness as such.

We conclude this chapter by articulating and responding to a series of would-be objectors to the picture of Deontological Eudaemonism we have just completed. First, we address an objector who would assert that taking pleasure in moral activity undermines the very notion of the moral law expressing itself as an imperative, in response to whom we argue that it is not pleasure but self-conceit that would so undermine one's proper relationship to the law. We then consider a related objection: if the person exercising the aptitude for virtue really experiences no hindrances, is the moral law really still an imperative for her? To affirm that even the fully virtuous person experiences the law as an imperative, we note two important caveats to the assertion of a pleasurable experience of virtue: on the one hand, because of the inextirpable propensity to evil, even the fully virtuous agent must experience her pleasure alongside an attitude of humble vigilance which she brings to her exercise of virtue; and, on the other, we grant that extreme experiences of suffering outside of one's control have the potential to undermine the otherwise necessary coincidence of virtue and intellectual or rational happiness.

We conclude by addressing a final objector who would assert that these demands for vigilance and the admission of the mere possibility of the collapse of pleasure because of uncontrollable circumstances mean that there is not a perfect coincidence or identity of happiness and virtue and hence no true "eudaemonism" to be found in Kant's system. In response to this objector, I note that were one to insist upon so strict an identity between virtue and happiness, one which did not allow for these exceptions, we would be seeking a eudaemonism inappropriate for human existence.

Let us turn to our discussion of Kant's Deontological Eudaemonism.

I. Review of Secondary Literature

Twenty-first-century interpretive literature on Kant and eudaemonism began with Allen Wood's (2000) consideration of the topic. Wood describes what he calls Kant's "distinctively modern" and distinctively divided notion of humanity, a picture of the human being in which there is a strong and ineffaceable opposition between morality and happiness. This disunified picture of the human being has, perhaps ironically, encouraged efforts to efface or moderate the strong opposition Wood has asserted. I quote him at length so as to set up the terms of the opposition as he sees them:

Kant agrees, of course, that our real self is the rational self. But his theory reflects a distinctively modern conception of humanity, because he recognizes that the human self is inevitably disunited, conflicted, self-alienated, in a deeper sense than any of the ancient theories could admit...Kant's view is...that the self is in conflict with itself because the *whole* self *simultaneously* takes two conflicting standpoints. One standpoint is the "natural-social" standpoint, expressed through my natural inclinations as they appear under conditions of social life. The other is the moral or rational standpoint, expressed through my lawgiving reason.

(Wood 2000, 264–265)

Wood goes on to describe these two essentially opposed "standpoints" of the human being at greater length:

[T]he eudaimonistic standpoint [emerging from the "natural-social standpoint"] is originally the standpoint from which each human being seeks superiority over others. By contrast, the standpoint of morality or reason is one from which the worth of all rational beings is *equal*. From this standpoint, human beings are required to respect every rational person as having the dignity of an end in itself...Human nature is therefore caught in a fundamental struggle between the natural-social standpoint, whose principle is one's own happiness, and the pure rational standpoint, whose principle is the moral law.

(Wood 2000, 272)

By locating one's "eudaimonistic" pursuit of happiness within the "comparative-competitive" standpoint of the "natural-social" world (a standpoint which he elsewhere emphasizes is also at the center of his distinctive version of Kant's radical evil[2]), Wood asserts that the pursuit of happiness is essentially the opposite of the pursuit of morality: in seeking happiness, I operate in immoral comparative-competitive ways, but in pursuing morality I eschew such comparative-competitiveness, seeking instead a life affirming the equality of persons as guided by my "real self" whose pursuit, sadly for the would-be unity of this being, are inevitably and intrinsically opposed to those pursuits that would elevate one's well-being in the first sense. Indeed, by asserting that the very pursuit of happiness is inherently comparative-competitive, Wood sees that pursuit, essentially, as evil; for Wood, "the desire for happiness is neither so natural nor so innocent as eudaimonists would like to pretend" (Wood 2000, 271).

Responses to Wood's point of view that have emerged in the literature find the distinction in standpoints he has set up to be overly harsh. The effort has thus been to interpret Kant in ways that soften this harsh distinction between the

---

[2] See Wood (1999). See also Grenberg (2010b) for my rejection of his interpretation of the social dimensions of Kant's conception of radical evil.

pursuit of happiness and the pursuit of morality as Wood has set up. Forman (2016), for example, laments that "[Wood's] conclusion that the pursuit of happiness as such is grounded in a delusory self-conceit [and thus] seems to rule out the possibility of a morally benign form of happiness" (Forman 2016, 91n34). He goes on to articulate a conception of Kant's "Moderate Cynicism" which conceives of a more harmonious relationship between morality and happiness in Kant's writings.[3]

I agree with Forman that it is too extreme to think that there is no "morally benign form of happiness" for Kant. With him, it is my conviction that we can discover in Kant's texts a conception of happiness that is compatible with virtue. Most recent literature on such things[4] focuses, however, on seeking a harmonious relationship of virtue with what I have been calling happiness empirically conceived, viz. happiness conceived as the sum of desire-fulfillment. I am not uninterested in that question, but it is not until II.iii that we will address it. This is because there is a previous and related question we must consider first: the question of whether and to what extent Kant conceives of a notion of happiness which is not simply an expression of the success we've had in satisfying our sensible lacks and desires, but is instead more integral to the exercise of virtue itself. That is the topic of concern for this current chapter. What we shall see in the forthcoming account of this chapter is that, taking Annas' (1995, 2011) interpretation of the Aristotelian notion of happiness as pleasure in the unimpeded exercise of one's proper function as an interpretive lens, we unearth and understand a notion in Kant's writings that is very similar: pleasure in the virtually unimpeded exercise of one's free aptitude for virtue. The attainment of virtue is indeed a struggle, and at times a painful one, as we have seen in the previous chapter confirming that Herculean task. But the fruits of those hard efforts are equally strong: an intense rational pleasure in the virtuous life one has built for oneself.

---

[3] See also Holberg (2018): "In contrast to eudaimonism, Kant argues that moral reasoning and prudential reasoning are two distinct uses of practical reason, each with its own standard for good action. Despite Kant's commitment to the ineradicable potential for fundamental conflict between these types of practical reasoning, I argue that once we shift to consideration of a *developmental* narrative of these faculties, we see that virtuous moral reasoning is able to substantively influence prudential reasoning, while prudential reason should be responsive to such influence. Further, Kant indicates the integration of virtue as a commitment concerning practical priorities, and so too what should and should not agree with the agent, is beneficial for prudential reasoning by prudential reasoning's own standards. Although Kant's ethical system breaks from eudaimonism in significant ways, it retains the eudaimonist claim that virtuously-informed pursuits of happiness are not only better for virtue, but also better for happiness" (Holberg 2018, 1). And although he does not use the language of eudaemonism in making the point, and would have to be taken anachronistically as a response to Wood, Watson's (1983) discussion of morality as the best point of view from which to pursue a unified life is another important interpreter who wants to insist upon a more unified conception of the self than what Wood offers. I will consider both Holberg's and Watson's claims at greater length in II.iii.

[4] See especially Forman (2016), as well as Holberg (2018) and Wike (1994). Watson (1983), though less recent, fits into this group as well.

Concern with this new question leads us, therefore, to a series of new engagements with current interpreters. First, in claiming this notion of happiness as virtually unimpeded activity, I distinguish my account of eudaemonism from Forman's "Moderate Cynical" reading of Kant. I had previously (in II.i) found common ground with Forman's moderate cynicism: we both find that a capacity to moderate one's felt attachments is an important means by which to bring the pursuit of morality and the pursuit of happiness into harmony with each other. But in making his claims, Forman considers only the notion of happiness, empirically conceived. As such, despite the healthy harmony he claims between virtue and happiness, he must also adhere to a strict distinction between them.[5] I agree with Forman that a distinction must be made between virtue and empirical conceptions of happiness as desire-satisfaction; the refusal to conflate virtue and happiness empirically conceived in a quasi-Stoic fashion is a center-piece of Kant's understanding of morality, and something that clearly distinguishes Kant from Stoicism. But in welcoming a non-empirical conception of happiness for Kant, we broaden the playing field and find a notion of happiness identical with the exercise of virtue. To this extent, then, Kant will have his Stoic moment: it is not necessary to maintain a strong distinction between virtue and happiness conceived as the pleasurable virtually unimpeded activity of those dispositions most proper to one's being. To the contrary, the new notion of happiness identified in this chapter simply is the subjective experience of the exercise of virtue. The only distinction we will need to make between Kant and Aristotle on this point is that, because for Kant we admit an inextirpable propensity for evil, we must also accept that such exercise is virtually and not perfectly unimpeded.

Another interpreter of interest to us is Wike (1994), who, unlike Forman, has considered the possibility of a rational and moral conception of happiness in Kant at some length. She notes that we can identify at least three different moral "analogues" to happiness empirically conceived: moral happiness, self-contentment, and bliss. But having articulated these moral analogs to happiness, Wike goes on to set them aside as not genuinely "happiness" as such:

> Happiness... is a contentment that has a sensible cause, the satisfaction of inclinations. Since Kant gives an account of happiness as involving a sensible state of

---

[5] For Forman, the harmony of morality and happiness is just that: a harmony established between two essentially distinct parts of ourselves: "Kant's account of happiness shows that the requirements for morality are in many ways harmonious with the requirements for prudence, even revolving around the same set of ideals involving the extirpation of passions through self-mastery and hence independence or freedom. And this is enough for us to establish that the pessimistic scenario does not hold and thus that the demands of morality do not require me to abandon my hopes for happiness in this life. We are entitled to this hope not because morality allows me wide latitude in pursuit of my private ends, but rather because prudence itself—when understood in the proper, moderate Cynic way—limits my ambitions in a way that allows the end of happiness to be in harmony with the end of virtue" (Forman 2016, 103).

affairs... and since his attempts to identify happiness with an intelligible or moral state of affairs are heavily qualified and often denied..., it follows that happiness concerns a person's condition in the sensible world. Happiness is not moral happiness, self-contentment, or bliss. Strictly speaking, moral happiness, self-contentment, and bliss ought not 'stand under the name of' happiness nor should they 'be called' happiness. (Wike 1994, 23–24)

In short, because we need to understand happiness as the sensible and empirical notion of the satisfaction of lacks and desires, and because she takes Kant himself to be skeptical of the non-empirical conceptions of happiness he presents, Wike asserts we must not honor these other states of contentment with the moniker of "happiness."

Curiously, this insistence on rejecting the language of happiness puts Wike in sympathy, at least on this point, with Wood's (2000) rather more extreme understanding of such matters. Recall that Wood strongly emphasizes a distinction in standpoints between one's rational self and one's happiness-pursuing self. As such Wood too, like Wike, emphasizes that, whatever these "moral analogues" of happiness we encounter in Kant's writings are, they are a far cry from happiness:

> Kant wants to consider the "contentment" people feel when they are conscious of having done their duty as entirely distinct from their happiness, forming not the smallest part of it (*Morals*, 6:387; *Practical Reason*, 5:38, 88, 117, 156). He criticizes the ancients for identifying the two kinds of goods, and the moderns for confusing them (*Practical Reason*, 5:64–5). (Wood 2000, 263)

Both Wike and Wood thus express a strong predilection toward rejecting the language of "happiness" for any state of contentment that is not an expression of one's sensible self.

But in so doing, they only exacerbate the picture of a sensibly affected rational being at odds with herself. Even if we don't accept Wood's extreme view that happiness is inherently evil, to assume that satisfaction in one's sensible self needs to be a wholly distinct and different thing than satisfaction in one's rational self, and that the latter (if it exists) doesn't even deserve the moniker of happiness—this point of view can only provide a foundation for building a human being at odds with herself. Wood and Wike are certainly right that the rational states of contentment which Kant articulates differ in significant ways from happiness empirically conceived. But I would (and will!) argue that this is exactly the point! That is: we should be glad to see Kant conceiving of ways in which our rational as well as our sensible selves can participate in well-being or flourishing. That it would be a different thing to describe such well-being on the level of one's rational self makes sense. But such differences needn't demand of us that we stop calling the well-being or flourishing of one's rational self "happiness," nor that we stop exploring the possibilities for resolving these varying states of contentment with each other into an integrated conception of the state of well-being of the sensibly affected rational being overall. To the contrary, claiming the language of happiness for both sensible and rational states of satisfaction, even as we admit the differences among them, underscores the importance of pursuing a holistic conception of well-being for human beings and, indeed, opens up possibilities for effacing that rational-sensible divide which Wood so strongly asserted, exploring instead the possibility that, although such states are different in nature, they can be resolved to each other in an overall account of the proper functioning of the sensibly affected rational being. My forthcoming account does just that: it shows that we have tools in Kant's texts for understanding a rational or intellectual notion of happiness. My own account focuses particularly on the notion of "self-contentment" that Wike rejects, showing what I think is better translated as "intellectual contentment of oneself" to be essentially identical to what Aristotle calls pleasurable unimpeded activity. In providing such an account, and thereby rejecting Wike's suggestion that we cannot really speak of a rational and non-sensible notion of happiness for Kant, we simultaneously and decisively reject Wood's insistence upon a strict divide in standpoints for such beings, a divide which would assure that they be condemned to a life that is "*inevitably* disunited, conflicted, self-alienated" (Wood 2000, 264, emphasis added).

The forthcoming account is thus one most in sympathy with Watson's (1983) efforts to show that, Kant's account of the relationship of morality and happiness, we must welcome a sort of unity of one's contentments overall. According to Watson:

> [T]o live a life appropriate to a human being is to organize and pursue the satisfaction of one's needs and interests under the discipline of practical reason. To live under that discipline is to be virtuous; to succeed to a significant degree in one's pursuits is to fare well. One's contentment with one's life on the whole will properly depend upon both of these factors. And happiness consists in such contentment. Therefore, happiness has an eminent place in Kant's theory of value. (Watson 1983, 94)

For Watson, then, in order to assure that the human being has "contentment with one's life on whole" and not just a part of it, one needs contentment both in the virtuous exercise of one's "discipline of practical reason" and contentment in "the satisfaction of one's needs and interests." In other words, contentment is to be sought on both sides of this moral/non-moral divide. Watson himself does not use the language of "happiness" to describe this "contentment" on the moral side. Nonetheless, I take his position to be more in line with my own, i.e. more willing than either Wike or Wood to conceive of that broader contentment as something like "happiness": "contentment" with one's moral state is something that, unified with contentment with one's success in pursuing fulfillment of one's needs and interests leads to an overall "contentment with one's life on the whole." In my pursuit of a conception of happiness rationally conceived which is essentially identical to Aristotle's conception of happiness as unimpeded activity, I too seek a more unified conception of contentment or well-being for the sensibly affected rational being.

One interpreter who has already made some progress in exploring the possibility of a notion of pleasure in Kant equivalent to Aristotle's conception of pleasure in unimpeded activity is Elizondo (2014). Elizondo interprets a passage in Kant's *Critique of Judgment* so as to lead us to the notion that "there is a kind of pleasure that is nothing but the phenomenological manifestation of self-directed, self-maintaining activity" (Elizondo 2014, 435). He also suggests that such self-directed and self-maintaining activity could reasonably be associated with Aristotle's notion of proper functioning:

> [This intellectual] pleasure turns out to be something like the feeling of a faculty's proper functioning. Put this way, the Kantian account of pleasure can begin to look very similar to the Aristotelian account (Aristotle 2000, VII, 11–14). If so, then it should be no surprise that Kant and Aristotle have similar views on the pleasantness of moral activity. (Elizondo 2014, 435n13)

Finally, Elizondo (2016) pushes the point further and suggests that we can conceive also of an explicitly intellectual notion not of "happiness" as such, but of "well-being" or "self-contentment" as arising from such purely intellectual pleasure:

> [T]he Kantian account of well-being is not exhausted by the Kantian account of happiness. Well-being is a genus with two species: one sensible—happiness—and one intellectual—self-contentment. Thus while morality, as rational activity, can only be extrinsically related to happiness, it can be intrinsically related to self-contentment and thereby to well-being. (Elizondo 2016, 8)

I am in general sympathy with the trajectory of Elizondo's account, especially with his all-too-brief suggestion that the notion of pleasure as "the phenomenological manifestation of self-directed, self-maintaining activity" is both a Kantian and an Aristotelian notion; and also with the related notion that we can speak of an account of well-being—or what I eventually will be happy to call "happiness"— that is guided by an intellectual notion of self-contentment and thus has an "intrinsic" relationship to morality and virtue. I will however depart from Elizondo's (2014) suggestions that this intellectual *pleasure* is a purely intellectual *feeling* as such, showing his reading of a passage from the third *Critique* which he takes to be essential to his account to be fundamentally mistaken. On my account, all feelings, including the distinctive moral feeling of respect, are sensible feelings. As such, I argue that the rational pleasure of unimpeded activity for Kant, involves not a pure, non-sensible feeling (something that just doesn't exist for Kant) but instead, first of all, a sensible feeling of negative freedom which emerges when the external pressures that had been impinging upon one's rational will are removed. Then, that feeling of negative freedom associates itself with the resulting experience of ease or facility in the way one exercises one's will, an ease which points one toward appreciation of where one's negative freedom came from (viz., from one's positive freedom as a rational being, now expressed in the perfect alignment of one's choice (*Willkür*) with one's will (*Wille*)). The pleasure that pervades the experience of the person with a free aptitude for virtue is thus not the experience of a purely intellectual, non-sensible feeling but instead a combination of these two moments of the sensible feeling of negative freedom and the pleasing consciousness of the harmony, ease, and alacrity with which one performs an activity that is central and indeed definitional to one's very being. In insisting that this pleasure is non-felt pleasure, I thus place myself in sympathetic agreement with Zuckert's (2002) account of pleasure, expanding her notion of the non-felt aesthetic pleasure in the harmony of one's faculties to a practical version of the same, a non-felt practical pleasure in the harmony of one's practical faculties of will and choice.

Let us turn toward these discussions.

II. A Kantian Story of the Pleasure of Unimpeded Activity in the Free Aptitude for Virtue

An Aristotelian Interpretive Lens

First, let's think about the Aristotelian notion of proper functioning and the related notion of the experience of pleasure in the unimpeded activity of one's proper function so as to have in hand an interpretive lens to bring to the reading of those parts of Kant's texts which point us toward similar notions.

To have a "proper" function is to have some sort of activity or purpose that is definitional or descriptive of one's being. And Aristotle asserts that humans do indeed have just such a function:

> [I]t may be held that the good of man resides in the function of man, if he has a function. Are we then to suppose that, while the carpenter and the shoemaker have definite functions or businesses belonging to them, man as such has none, and is not designed by nature to fulfil any function? Must we not rather assume that, just as the eye, the hand, the foot and each of the various members of the

body manifestly has a certain function of its own, so a human being also has a certain function over and above all the functions of his particular members?

(*NE* I.7, 11–12)

Aristotle's notion of a function proper to being human as such defines that activity that is most central to and distinctive of being human: in order to be good at being a human being, I need to be good at this function or activity that is "proper" or apropos to my being. To be able to identify such a function is, furthermore, quite valuable since, once one knows the kind of activity that is proper to one's being, one can take the excellent exercise of that activity as a teleological guide both for how that being should act and for how that being realizes well-being or flourishing.

Aristotle then, later in the *Nicomachaen Ethics*, associates the exercise or activity of one's proper function with a distinctive sort of pleasure. According to him, this "pleasure is...called activity of the natural state" and is "unimpeded" (1153a13). In other words, Aristotle suggests that any activity that is proper to one's being, precisely because it expresses the "natural" state of that being, is best described as an intrinsically *pleasurable* activity.

Furthermore, to any who would suggest that pleasure is the sort of thing that, by its very nature, confuses, upsets, or disarranges one's state, he suggests to the contrary that "[n]either practical wisdom nor any [natural] state of being is impeded by the pleasure arising from it; it is *foreign* pleasures that impede, for the pleasures arising from thinking and learning will make us think and learn all the more" (1153b12, emphasis added). Aristotle makes an important distinction here between kinds of pleasures: there are pleasures which arise from some source that is foreign (that is, external) to one's activity and those that arise from a source that is natural and proper to one's activity (and thus have an internal source). It is only the former pleasures—pleasures that arise from the fulfillment of a lack expressed as a desire for some object external to me, but which also dissipate when that external object is no longer present, leading to fears, tribulations, and anxiety about whether the would-be object of desire will be present or not—which threaten to upset, disrupt, or confuse one's activity. And they confuse the activity precisely because they introduce pleasures (or lack of pleasure) foreign to the activity itself, complicating and confusing the exercise of that activity itself. The latter pleasures, to the contrary, precisely because they are simply an outgrowth or expression of the pure unimpeded natural activity itself can only be understood to heighten and intensify the exercise of the activity of which they are an expression.

Indeed, Aristotle even suggests that such internal activity- or "disposition"-related pleasures, when taken as a sum of all activities natural to one's being, can be understood as that distinctive pleasure called "happiness" (*eudaemonia*): "if each disposition has unimpeded activities," then "the activity (if unimpeded) of *all* our dispositions or that of some one of them is happiness" (1153f3, emphasis added).[6] In other words, the pleasure one experiences which is natural to one's activity is so important that it deserves the title not just of any pleasure but of that distinctive pleasure that is happiness (*eudaemonia*) as such.

Julia Annas' gloss on this notion of happiness or eudaemonia as unimpeded activity is particularly helpful for our purposes. According to Annas, the pleasure of which Aristotle speaks as the sign of virtue is not pleasure in the fulfillment of a desire or in the acquisition of something one previously had lacked, but instead "precisely the pleasure that marks absence of conflict and struggle" (Annas 1995, 93). Furthermore, for Annas' Aristotle, the pleasure expressed in this state, or "the enjoyment of virtuous activity does *not* consist in felt twinges of pleasure" but instead "in the *way* the activity is done" (Annas 2011, 76, emphases added), that is, in the way one experiences or engages in the relevant activity. As such, happiness as unimpeded activity is "a matter of the performance [or activity] being ready and in harmony with the person's other goals and commitments" (p. 76).

Annas suggests, furthermore, that this notion of the pleasure in unimpeded activity is "something we recognize every day in ourselves and others" (pp. 79–80). That is, we can just tell when someone is "in the groove," acting in a way that comes naturally, with ease, and as it should be. The pleasure involved in unimpeded virtuous activity for Aristotle is thus a matter of performing that activity in harmony with one's virtuous character, and this pleasure is to be distinguished from the pleasure or positive feelings one has as the result of the satisfaction of a desire, or some previous lack of something.

Annas' distinction in kinds of pleasure is very important for our forthcoming account. Essentially, Annas provides us with a category of "pleasure" that is not a mere "twinge" of desire-fulfillment, viz. a feeling connected to the success one has in achieving something that one had previously lacked. Instead, via her

---

[6] Aristotle's equivocation here on whether eudaemonia is constituted by a cluster of dispositions or by a single defining natural disposition is an indication of a tension internal to his own account of eudaemonia: does one's most natural activity consist in the activities in which we shape a whole range of emotions toward the mean, all pointed to one's engagement with the political world of which one is a part, or does it consist in the singular, higher, and more solitary activity of contemplation? This problem for Aristotle's account of eudaemonia will not haunt Kant, since he is not concerned to defend contemplation or any analog to it as a complete practical pursuit. The closest he would come to such a thing is his insistence that one contemplate and attend to the way that the moral feeling of respect operates upon our consciousness: "Obligation with regard to moral feeling can be only to cultivate it and to strengthen it through wonder at its inscrutable source" (6:399–400/171). Such "wonder" or contemplation is not, however, an end-in-itself but an activity whereby one assures the fulfillment of the ultimate telos of making persons as such one's end. Other than that, when Kant speaks of whether virtue is one or many, it is without the Aristotelian worry that one end of virtue might point one in a direction opposite to the other. Instead, he speaks of the qualities of numerous and distinct individual virtues only in the context of speaking of how that cluster of individual virtues constitutes or articulates one overall pursuit of virtue for the sake of virtue: "To think of several virtues (as one unavoidably does) is nothing other than to think of the various moral objects to which the will is led by the one principle of virtue" (6:406/176).

interpretation of Aristotle, she introduces a "pleasure" that is not a "feeling" in the usual (nor indeed in the Kantian) sense of the term. Instead of being constituted by a twinge of feeling, this pleasure is more positively and deeply rooted in the way one engages in an activity that is unimpeded: as long as I am doing this activity in a way that is truly unimpeded, this pleasure will be stably and reliably present as the way in which I experience the ease and appropriateness of this activity. It is upon this new definition of pleasure that I will rely when I go on to describe pleasure in one's exercise of the aptitude for virtue as "non-felt."

A Free Aptitude for Virtue

We want now to explore Kant's notion of a free "aptitude" (*fertigkeit*) for virtue that emerges as the prize of self-governance, for it is in just this notion that we shall ground a conception of happiness, rationally conceived along the lines of Aristotle's idea of a happiness grounded in the pleasure one takes in unimpeded activity that is proper to our nature. Our goal in the forthcoming sections is thus to interpret this notion of aptitude even while keeping in the back of our mind this just-completed Aristotelian story of pleasure as unimpeded activity. The result will be an appreciation of a distinctively Kantian version of the same notion, one which while pointing toward a rational notion of happiness that affirms the power of our free and rational natures, nonetheless also clings insistently to a transcendentally ideal mode of expression and access to such claims, a mode which remains respectful of the unavoidable limits and finitude of sensibly affected rational beings. Let us engage in that analysis.

And so, first: we have seen in the previous chapter (II.i), that a crucial step in the virtuous management of one's felt attachments—of one's affects, passions, inclinations, and desires generally—is engaging in repeated practices which slowly, over time, educate those felt attachments in accordance with the evaluative and affective guidance of the moral feeling of respect, practices which work to realize inner freedom within one's person.

But Kant famously and repeatedly warns us that getting into repeated habits is exactly what one does *not* want in the pursuit of virtue. And the precise reason we should avoid habits is that they threaten the loss of one's freedom instead of promising its realization:

> [M]oral maxims, unlike technical ones, cannot be based on habit [*Gewohnheit*] (since this belongs to the natural constitution of the will's determination); on the contrary, if the practice of virtue were to become a habit the subject would suffer loss of that freedom in adopting his maxims which distinguishes an action done from duty.   (6:409/167, translation slightly amended)

Habit seems the antithesis of virtue, the very loss of freedom and, with that, of any strong and free virtue we would claim for ourselves. Because habitual action finds its ground in "the natural constitution of the will's determination" instead of the rational constitution of that same will, habitual action is, essentially, a causally determined action. And yet, for all his worries about the problems of appealing to an unthinking, merely naturally or causally based conception of habit, Kant has indeed insisted, as we saw in II.i, that "practice"—a repeated choice and end-setting that looks an awful lot like a habit—is indeed the way to establish an ordering of one's felt attachments consistent with and constitutive of virtue.

How to resolve this apparent contradiction? In the passage above, it is clear that Kant's condemnation of habit is based on his worry that habits are grounded in one's "natural constitution," and that relying only on one's natural constitution in the determination of one's will guarantees the loss of our freedom of choice and end-setting.[7] How, then, to assure that the practices we pursue in the management of our felt attachments, and ultimately in our pursuit of virtue, *are* compatible with freedom? What prevents this practice of virtue from descending into some merely sensible or "natural constitution of the will's determination"?

In short, we simply need to reaffirm at this point that such practices are guided by the moral feeling of respect and thus by the free and rational cause that brings this quasi-desire into the sensible world: this feeling itself is a marker in our affective lives for the governing rational will at the basis of inner freedom. The result of such moral-feeling-guided governing work of inner freedom is thus not what Kant calls a mere *habitual* way of choosing or acting (that would be the unfree route), but instead a free "*aptitude*" (*fertigkeit*) in acting (6:407/165). Kant describes such an aptitude for virtue as both "a facility in acting" and "a subjective perfection of choice [Willkür]" (6:407/165). In other words, through my evaluative and affective constraint and cultivation of my felt attachments, now realized in repeated practice, I acquire a particular alacrity and ease in the exercise of my free choice, an alacrity and ease which constitutes the "perfection," and thus the most *proper* functioning of, that capacity for choice.

It is worth noting here that we are already beginning to see a hint of the compatibility of this notion of aptitude with Aristotle's appeal to the pleasure of unimpeded activity: both notions appeal to the ease or alacrity in the *way* in which one engages in the activity that emerges when external impediments to that activity are removed. Indeed, as Annas has emphasized, the pleasure of such unimpeded activity is not so much an experience of a twinge of felt pleasure, but instead an experience of the way or mode in which one does the activity, viz. as unimpeded. And when Kant suggests that an aptitude for virtue is "a *facility* in acting"

---

[7] Kant is using the idea of "nature" here in a different sense than Aristotle did, above. He is not (yet) speaking of what is most natural and proper to us, but is instead appealing to our natural or sensible, as opposed to our rational, being.

(6:407/165, emphasis added), he is suggesting the very same thing: someone who has an aptitude for virtue (viz., someone who has eliminated the external impediments to her fully rational activity) exercises virtue in a certain "way," i.e., easily and with a certain facility (because unimpeded). Her exercise of her rational will is, in other words, something that is experienced by her as going naturally and smoothly, in the way that it was meant to be done: this is the "way" she engages in that activity. We will eventually explore at much greater length in exactly what this way of doing an activity consists, but we need first to complete our account of aptitude so as to present that fuller account more successfully and precisely.

So, first, there are some textual complexities about the nature of an aptitude that we need to resolve. Although an aptitude is a facility in the operation of one's faculty for choice (or *Willkür*) brought about through the repeated activity we've been describing, really to understand the formation of such an aptitude, we need to trace this facility in *choice* (or *Willkür*) back to one's legislating *will* (or *Wille*). The question we are asking here is this: what *exactly* is it in us that is accomplishing this control and cultivation of felt attachments which results in this facility for acting that Kant calls the free aptitude of choice?

It is tempting to think that one's capacity for choice (or *Willkür*) is doing all the work here. This is, after all, the capacity at work in any decision an agent makes, including decisions about the cultivation of her affective state. Crucially, though, in order for this *facility* in choosing not to reduce to mere, blind habit, and to be truly an inner expression *of freedom*, it is something that needs to issue from the very depths of one's legislating self. After all, it would be very possible to establish, through repeated activity, a certain ease or facility in choosing that had very little to do with the establishment of freedom in one's capacity for choice. The more that I let my husband make me martinis, the easier it is for me to choose every evening to have a martini before dinner. It used to be hard for me to decide whether to have so strong a drink as a martini, but there is now an ease or facility in making this choice that wasn't there before. I have developed an aptitude for choosing martinis. But this can't be quite what Kant means when he says the virtuous person has a *free* aptitude for virtue.

One could suggest instead (and Kant himself does suggest at one point) that an "aptitude is *not* a property of choice but of the will" (6:407/165, emphasis added). But this too cannot be quite what he means. Surely he means that an aptitude is not *merely* a property of choice but is *also* simultaneously a property of the will. After all, Kant has already told us that an aptitude is "a facility in *acting*" and "a subjective *perfection* of the *faculty of choice* [*Willkür*] " (6:407/165, emphases added). It thus makes no sense to say that "this aptitude is *not* a property of choice" (6:407/165): if an aptitude were not a *property* of our faculty of choice, it could not be a *perfection* of our faculty of choice!

But in order for an aptitude to be a *free* aptitude, it needs to be something more than simply a product of choice. Such an aptitude will indeed still be a facility, or ease in the operation, of my choice, or *Willkür*, developed through the repeated exercise of that choice; but it will also need to be a choice that springs more deeply than simply from my conscious capacity (or even my unconscious tendency) to choose to get into a habit. It must, in other words, be an expression specifically of my free, autonomous will, or *Wille*. As Kant puts it:

> [N]ot every such facility [i.e., aptitude] is a free aptitude (*habitus libertatis*); for if it is a habit (*assuetudo*), that is, a uniformity in action that has become a necessity through frequent repetition, it is not one that proceeds from freedom, and therefore not a moral aptitude. Hence virtue cannot be defined as an aptitude for free action in conformity with law unless there is added "to determine oneself to act through the thought of the law," *and then this aptitude is not a property of choice but of the will, which is a faculty of desire that, in **adopting** a rule, also **gives** it as a universal law*. Only such an aptitude can be counted as virtue.
>
> (6:407/165, italicized and bolded emphases added)

Kant's point here is not immediately clear. First of all, as we've already noted, when he says that an "aptitude is not a property of choice but of the will," he must surely mean that an aptitude is not *merely* a property of choice but is *also* simultaneously and more deeply a property of the will.

But in what exactly does this simultaneity consist? His point here is that, when one acquires an aptitude, one's capacity for choice has so perfectly taken on the laws of one's will that it is as if one's *Willkür* simply has become one's *Wille*. That is, an aptitude is the thorough, perfect expression in one's capacity for *choice* of the demands of law legislated in and by one's *will*; or, as Kant puts the point at the end of this quote, to say that an aptitude is a property of the will, is to say that it is a property of the "faculty of desire that, in *adopting* (i.e., choosing) a rule, also *gives* it (i.e., legislates it) as a universal law." In short, when one has a free aptitude, one's *Willkür* or actual choice is perfectly in line with one's *Wille*, or universal self-legislation of the moral law: rational legislation (or "giving") of the law is perfectly in line with choice (or "adopting") of that law in guiding one's actions.

It is, furthermore, this perfect symmetry of *Wille* and *Willkür* which allows us to say of one's *Willkür*—and also of the felt attachments moderated and cultivated by that *Willkür*—that it is perfectly *free*. Because one's choices in the evaluation and cultivation of one's felt attachments are always guided by, and indeed at one with, one's autonomous will, all these choices are indeed both negatively and positively free, in the senses we discussed such notions in Part I. As such, this aptitude or facility of the *Wille/Willkür* simply *is* the successful acquisition of what we have been calling the "inner freedom" of the *Wille/Willkür*: having legislated a law to ourselves through our own wills, we now execute that law and its freedom by expressing its demands within the choices we make and even in the state of one's felt attachments.

When one repeatedly practices virtue, one is thus in the business of developing not a mere habit, nor even a mere aptitude, but instead a *free* aptitude for choice in one's will which becomes established in the ordering of one's felt attachments and ultimately in the setting of one's ends. Through repeated conscious choices to constrain one's affects, inclinations, and passions in accordance with the moral law grounded in one's will—for us, the telos of making persons as such one's end—one develops a facility for realizing just those morally informed choices of end-setting associated with one's objective telos. Virtue as strength, which is in fact just another way to describe this free aptitude, is thus "a constraint possible in accordance with the law of inner freedom" (6:405/164) and thereby *deserves* to be called a free aptitude instead of a mere habit. It is a governance of one's choice and of one's felt attachments in accordance with one's own objective telos, guiding all of oneself toward those ends that are also duties which constitute that objective telos of making persons as such one's end. As a result, the moral demand to respect persons perfectly pervades one's capacity for choice: one's *Willkür* simply becomes an expression of that freedom and autonomy legislated by one's *Wille*.

But Kant's language suggests that this unified state of *Wille/Willkür* pervades one's whole person even more completely than just this proper ordering of one's rational will. Indeed, in the true spirit of the discussion of such things we saw in I.i, inner freedom is established in and pervades absolutely all of one's person. According to Kant, the ultimate prize of this self-governance is that one acquires a particular *Gemutsart* or "frame of mind" through the continual control and cultivation of one's felt attachments (one's affects, inclinations, and passions), and ultimately one's ends and choices. Having just concluded his claim that we need to subdue our affects and govern our passions, Kant thus says: "In these two states [viz., subduing of affects and governing of passions] one's frame of mind *Gemutsart* (*indoles*) is noble (*erecta*); in the opposite case it is mean (*indoles abiecta, serva*)" (6:407/166, emphasis added, translation slightly modified). The battle for self-governance is thus the battle to acquire either a noble or a mean frame of mind in one's person.

Gemutsart is, however, a difficult word to translate. Gregor uses the terminology of "character"; I have opted for "frame of mind." But one wishes for a phrase even more broad than that. "Frame of mind" is apt, as long as we are willing to construe "mind" broadly enough to include metaphorical reference to the state of one's "heart" or even one's "soul." Translation difficulties aside, the crucial point to appreciate is that a virtuous aptitude springs from the rational will, but expresses itself and resides not just as a state of one's rational will but, more broadly, as a state or disposition of one's whole person. On the basis of this appeal to the *Gemutsart* of the virtuous person, it is thus even appropriate to speak of the person of inner freedom as having her *heart* in the right place, or as being a good-*souled* person.[8] Through my chosen strong constraint of my affects, inclinations, and passions, I acquire a facility—an alacrity and ease—in the exercise of my free choice, and an integrity and tranquility in my whole person, all of which constitutes the most perfect realization of what that capacity for choice and my person should be. I have become who I was meant to be as a free and rational being.

Kant speaks in striking and strong language about what the exercise of choice is like for this person who possesses a free aptitude for virtue grounded in inner freedom. This person not only has the capacity to choose autonomously (all rational persons have that); beyond that, the *ease* or *facility* with which the person of inner freedom chooses becomes the distinctive quality of his character or disposition. He is "in possession of himself" (6:405/164) and therefore reliably and unchangingly chooses in line with the moral demand to make persons as such one's end. Kant even says that the person of inner freedom "cannot lose his virtue" (6:405/164). For such a person, it is not so much "as if a human being possesses virtue but rather as if virtue possesses him; for in the former case it would look as if he still had a choice (for which he would need yet another virtue" (6:406/165).

This is a particularly strong reading of what happens when choice perfectly aligns with one's autonomous will. A return to Kant's battle image of Hercules at the crossroads, first considered in II.i, helps us make our point here. In that image, we saw humanity at a crossroads, a point of choice, trying to decide whether or not to pursue the path of virtue. Hercules, in this depiction, has not yet made the choice of virtue. If he had, the temptation of the easy path would not be quite so perspicuous as it is usually depicted in artistic realizations of this dilemma. It is, after all, a *di*-lemma, that is, a proposal for action with two possible outcomes (and, indeed, a dilemma that, as we have seen, expresses itself as a *battle* for control of one's soul). That he sees the need for a choice here is precisely what reveals that Hercules does not yet have the virtuous aptitude of the person of inner freedom: he is still attentive to those inclinations which present themselves as plausible grounds for choice and even as plausible grounds for the governing authority of the soul. But for the person who has acquired that aptitude for virtue grounded in inner freedom, the battle is won: the path not chosen recedes so far into the background of one's mind (that is, it is so little an object of attentiveness) that it is as if there were no other path to consider. Hercules is no longer at the crossroads; he is not even marching up the hard mountain of virtue. He is, rather, at the peak of the mountain of virtue with the clear view of himself and his duties

---

[8] And, indeed, Caygill (1995) notes that Kant's use of the term is not dissimilar to medieval ideas of a disposition. With such context for the word, *Gemut* thus refers to "a stable disposition of the soul which conditions the exercise of *all* its faculties," including feeling, heart, soul, and mind" (Gilson, 1955, emphasis added). I thus take up this language of "stable disposition" to describe what is created in the virtuous person when she has a free aptitude for choice.

that such a singular vision of himself allows. For such a faculty of choice, the only real option is clear. For the person with an aptitude for virtue—a person who is entirely in control of her affects, inclinations, and passions—what began as a battle completes itself in ease, alacrity, composure, and tranquility: "The true strength of virtue is a *tranquil mind* with a considered and firm resolution to put the law of virtue into practice. That is the state of *health* in the moral life" (6:409/167).

A Free Aptitude for Virtue is the Experience of Unimpeded Activity

This appeal to a free aptitude for virtue—that is, to a facility, alacrity, or ease in the exercise of the will which expresses itself as the tranquil and healthy state of the virtuous person—is a particularly important moment for Kant. In welcoming a notion of the ease with which the fully virtuous person exercises her capacity for choice as if it were simply her objectively determined will, it becomes clear that Kant's fully virtuous person is one who experiences what Aristotle would call the unimpeded exercise of one's proper function. Let's explore this comparison in more depth.

First, I am particularly struck at this point by the similarity of the language Kant uses to describe the person who has a free aptitude, and the language Annas has used to describe Aristotelian pleasure in unimpeded activity. Recall, first of all, that, for Annas' Aristotle, the pleasure in unimpeded activity "does *not* consist in felt twinges of pleasure" (Annas 2011, 76) that one would experience in the fulfillment of a desire, but instead is "precisely the pleasure that marks absence of conflict and struggle" (Annas 1995, 93), and, as such, is a state of "being ready and in harmony with the person's other goals and commitments" (Annas 2011, 76).

And but for the "pleasure" word, we can say exactly all these things of our Hercules who is no longer at the crossroads. First, the ease or facility he is experiencing "does *not* consist in felt twinges of pleasure" (Annas 2011, 76). To the contrary, as Kant reminds us (and as we discussed in II.i), the best way to describe the felt state of the virtuous person is that she is in a state of "moral apathy." Kant says we should: "giv[e] the name '*moral apathy*' to that absence of affects which is to be distinguished from indifference because in cases of moral apathy feelings arising from sensible impressions lose their influence on moral feeling only because respect for the law is more powerful than all such feelings together" (6:408/178). It seems, then, that the felt twinges of pleasure, empirically conceived, are absent for the person who has this free aptitude.

Furthermore, given that he is in this moral apathetic state, Hercules' facility or ease in exercising virtue is indeed well-described as one that "marks absence of conflict and struggle." Or, more positively put, the way in which he experiences his free aptitude is as "being ready and in harmony with [his] other goals and commitments." Because he has removed all obstacles to virtue through his governance of his affects and passions as discussed in II.i, he does not experience the exercise of his choice as guided by his rational will to be a difficult thing.[9] To the contrary, he experiences his choice as occurring with a certain ease, alacrity, or facility. And so, because Kant describes this state as one of facility or ease, we can also agree with Annas and Aristotle too that, whatever it is like to be in this state, it involves an experience of "the *way* the activity is done" (Annas 2011, 76, emphases added). That is, Hercules experiences the exercise of virtue unimpededly, as something he accomplishes with facility and ease: that is just the "*way*" he does this activity—easily—and that ease characterizes the heart of his experience of himself.

It is thus interesting and worthy of note that at no point in this Doctrine of Virtue discussion of free aptitude does Kant appeal to the idea of this state being "pleasant" or "pleasurable" as such. This is curious. It is, after all, odd that the state replicates absolutely every other aspect of the Aristotelian notion of the experience of unimpeded activity but does not come to the Aristotelian conclusion that such unimpeded activity, by definition, would have to be experienced as pleasant. Kant does not (at least in these passages in the Doctrine of Virtue) speak of this person as feeling "pleasure" as such. Instead, she is described as "tranquil," and, instead of having the experience of any positive pleasure as such, is merely experiencing an apathetic absence of those empirical (what Aristotle would call "foreign") pleasures that would threaten to introduce conflict and turmoil to her state.

This is, therefore, a question worthy of further consideration. We need to reflect at greater length upon the question of whether, through appeal to other of his texts, Kant would be willing to grant that this state of unimpeded activity which he attributes to the person who has the free aptitude for virtue is also a pleasant state, albeit not pleasant in the sense of experiencing felt twinges of empirical pleasure as desire-fulfillment. Could there be a pleasure for Kant that is simply an expression of the unimpeded way one experiences the very exercise of free virtue? And could one, on the basis of such pleasure affirm a distinctive intellectual or rational notion of happiness for Kant? In taking on this question, we come not just to questions about the nature of pleasure and happiness, but we return also to questions about the precise nature of freedom and, even more, to the heart of Kant's commitment to Transcendental Idealism, viz. to the idea that we are beings who engage with the world from both the rational and the sensible perspectives. What we shall discover in these explorations is that Kant can indeed welcome the Aristotelian notion that the unimpeded exercise of one's choice,

---

[9] We will, later in this chapter, note a slight caveat to this point: because no sensibly affected being could ever remove at least the bare possibility of taking up her propensity to evil, we need ultimately to understand this state in which every empirical inclination is calmed as only "virtually" unimpeded. This unavoidable admission will not introduce conflict, but only vigilance, into the disposition of the person with a free aptitude for virtue.

when it is in full agreement with one's will, is indeed an experience of pleasure, now not pleasure empirically conceived as desire-fulfillment but pleasure rationally conceived as intellectual contentment of oneself. Let us turn to that discussion.

III. A Transcendentally Ideal Defense of the Nature of the Pleasure One Takes in the Unimpeded Activity of Virtue

A Reluctant Rejection of Elizondo

We thus need to make sense of whether and to what extent Kant can welcome a new rational sense of pleasure and happiness as part of his story of the virtuous person's experience of unimpeded activity. As we noted earlier, something similar to just this has been suggested recently by Elizondo (2014), a commentator who has argued strongly for the notion that a purely rational feeling of pleasure does indeed exist for Kant. Here, I thus take Elizondo's reflections as a springboard for entering into my own account. Although I both admire and feel tempted by Elizondo's reflections, ultimately, I distinguish my own account of rational pleasure and happiness from his so as to preserve, even as we welcome experiences which affirm the activity of our truly and purely rational selves, Kant's abiding commitment to Transcendental Idealism and the limits of knowledge which such idealism places on the epistemic experiences of the sensibly affected rational being.

So, as we've already briefly seen, according to Elizondo, Kant does indeed defend a notion of a felt, but purely rational and intellectual pleasure. To review: Elizondo characterizes his project as rejecting the common assumption that "rationalists must reject the attractive Aristotelian thought that moral activity is by nature pleasant" (Elizondo 2014, 425). He then goes on to provide a detailed analysis of a key moment in Kant's *Critique of Judgment* to argue that implicit in such ideas we do indeed find a moment of pure felt intellectual pleasure for Kant, a notion that he argues can be brought to Kant's moral philosophy via the notion of the determination of the will as a good will. Whereas, "in the aesthetic case," this felt moment is found in "the free play of the cognitive faculties,... in the moral case, [it is] the determination of the will by law" (Elizondo 2014, 433). His conclusion is thus that "moral activity is by nature pleasant because at least some pleasures are by nature rational" (Elizondo 2014, 425).

Elizondo summarizes his own conclusions thusly:

> The state of mind of a subject who is engaged in self-directed, self-maintaining activity is identical to pleasure, because what it is like to be in that state is pleasant. If this is right, then it seems that we have found what we are looking for: a

pleasure that is intellectual rather than sensible because it expresses our activity rather than merely being a response to it.   (Elizondo 2014, 433)[10]

For Elizondo then, we can identify in Kant's works appeal to a pleasure that is simply the expression of activity itself—viz., of the "self-directed" and "self-maintaining" activity of either aesthetic experience or morality. As such, this pleasure is not a passive pleasure in response to and an effect of something else, but instead a purely intellectual active feeling of pleasure which is simply an expression of rational activity itself.

The temptation, for our purposes, of signing on to Elizondo's account here is clear. Elizondo asserts what is essentially an active instead of a passive feeling: whereas most feelings are a passive reaction to the attainment or loss of something external to oneself, this active feeling which Elizondo identifies is just the way it feels to experience one's own properly functioning rational activity. And this seems to be something just like the pleasure that would attend upon the unimpeded activity of the person with a free aptitude for virtue, in line with Annas' understanding of a similar state in Aristotle. Although one would need to introduce some fine-tuning and clarification to Elizondo's suggestion that this pleasurable feeling occurs in *every* "determination of the will," it seems one could, with only a little tweaking, bring his account into at least compatibility with our own.[11]

So, yes, there is much by which to be tempted in Elizondo's account. But ultimately, although we welcome the general trajectory of his pursuit of a pleasure identical with intellectual activity, we must, in the name of Transcendental Idealism, reject his particular account of such things. Because Kant is committed to Transcendental Idealism—and especially to the notion that sensibly affected rational beings achieve both knowledge and action via a combination of reason and sensibility—he must pursue a more indirect (and therefore a slightly more complex) story of the pleasure that supervenes upon the exercise of the fully virtuous will than what Elizondo suggests. I depart in particular from Elizondo's suggestion that the feeling he points out from Kant's *Critique of Judgment* discussion is in fact an example of Kant welcoming a non-sensible feeling which is

---

[10] Importantly for our understanding of his position, Elizondo also insists that this "pleasure" is "feeling" as such, since he describes his conclusion as "admit[ing] that the feeling of pleasure, at least, is intrinsic to moral agency" (Elizondo 2014, 426). I thus take it to be something like what Annas had been calling a "twinge," now not in response to desire-fulfillment, but instead a twinge expressing one's self-directed and self-maintaining activity.

[11] Most crucially, we'd have to assert that this pleasure does not supervene upon just any "determination of the will" but only upon such determination within the person who has come to great facility in such determinations, viz. the person who has acquired an aptitude of virtue as we have been describing it. If Elizondo is willing to grant that only such virtuous determination of the will is the sort of activity which can be intrinsically pleasant in the way he describes—and that "the good will" is just a stand-in for our language of "the fully virtuous person"—then we are perhaps not too far from each other at least in terms of understanding the kind of activity upon which pleasure could supervene.

identical with intellectual activity. Although we will be able in our forthcoming discussion of such things to identify a pleasure identical with the successful exercise of the rational will, this pleasure will, first of all, not be a feeling (or, in Annas' language, a "twinge") as such (since all feeling is sensible for Kant); and, second, will bear upon itself the marks of the finitude of the sensibly affected agent who experiences it.

I turn at this point to my own positive account of such things, engaging with and distinguishing myself from Elizondo's position as I go.

Pleasure and Freedom

Before considering our more adequate notion of pleasure attending upon the exercise of a free aptitude for virtue, there is a previous, but central and guiding, point we need to appreciate: whatever account we come to here, it must, first and foremost, be a pleasure related to freedom. For Kant, the unimpeded activity of virtue is, at its heart, a state of freedom, and any pleasure attendant upon such activity must be concomitant with an expression of that freedom. This appeal to freedom raises an interesting at least apparent disanalogy between Aristotle and Kant on the nature of unimpeded activity. Aristotle does not speak of "freedom" as such when he speaks of the pleasure of unimpeded activity; as such, many interpreters, historically, have assumed that he is not committed to the notion. I take it to be an interesting question of Aristotle interpretation, though, whether, despite him not speaking of the notion of "freedom" in so many words, we could, through appeal to his notion of pleasure as unimpeded activity, in fact identify Aristotle's abiding concern for freedom. But, alas, I leave that more complete project of Aristotle interpretation for another time.

Nonetheless, it is my suspicion that if Aristotle did appeal to a notion of freedom implicit in the experience of unimpeded activity, it would, in the first instance, be an experience of what Kant calls "negative freedom." Indeed, that is just what the "unimpeded" part of "unimpeded activity" seems to suggest: a freedom from external constraints that Kant calls negative freedom.[12] The "activity" part of "unimpeded activity" would thus, respectively, be an experience of what Kant calls "positive freedom" or of a will being causality or law unto itself.[13] Drawing these connection between unimpeded activity and freedom in these two senses points us in some new directions: it points us, that is, toward consideration

---

[12] Kant describes negative freedom as "that property of... [a rational] causality, as it can be efficient independently of alien causes determining it" (4:446/56).

[13] Or, as Kant describes it "a causality according to immutable laws, but of a special kind" (4:4446/56), viz. according to rational instead of natural laws of causality and thus a case of "autonomy, the property of the will of being a law to itself" (4:447/56).

of how Kant's discussions of negative and positive freedom inform our understanding of what it is like to experience the free aptitude for virtue.

And so, the question now becomes one of whether or not Kant's account of a free aptitude integrates the idea that the finite sensibly affected rational being can indeed have a pleasurable experience of both negative and positive freedom. The stakes are high here: it is, most basically, the question of whether Kant is a thoroughgoing Transcendental Idealist or not. That is, we are asking whether or not he believes that there is some human experience—viz., a pure experience of the activity of positive freedom—that raises such beings above the normal constraints that sensibility places on rationality, and that thus sets aside for practical purposes the usual limits of reason which demand that concepts without intuitions are empty and intuitions without concepts are blind. Elizondo has suggested that we can indeed find a notion in Kant of pure, non-sensible, and purely intellectual feeling, a feeling that is not at all sensible but only a purely intellectual feeling of pleasure in activity. I feel sorely tempted to follow him down that alluring route. But I am hesitant as well. If he is right, then this is the first time that Kant abandons his grounding in Transcendental Idealism and, with that, his commitment to the notion of a human being as a truly finite, because truly and intrinsically sensibly affected, being.

In the end, however tempting Elizondo's suggestion is, I just cannot go down this route; that is, I cannot accept, even at the very height of virtue, that Kant would suggest that the virtuous person escapes or "shuffles off the mortal coil"[14] of her sensibility. The structural costs of such a reading are just too great. It would be as much as to say that the fully virtuous person is no longer really a sensibly affected rational being, and that is too much to say. And so, however tempting it is to accept Elizondo's account of a pure felt but non-sensible experience of positive freedom, we cannot do so.

In the forthcoming account, I thus articulate a different story of the contours of a phenomenological experience of what it is like to be a person with a free aptitude for virtue. This account is a furtherance of the phenomenology of obligation I provided in Grenberg (2013a). There, I identified the phenomenological experience of obligation in the experience of conflict between happiness and morality, and argued specifically that it is impossible for sensibly affected beings to have a direct phenomenological experience of positive freedom.[15] I still hold to these claims here. But now we are seeking to understand the phenomenological experience of someone on the other side of a lot of hard work of virtue, all that hard work we described in II.i as the governance of one's felt attachments, the

---

[14] "Devoutly to be wish'd. To die, to sleep; To sleep, perchance to dream—For in that sleep of death what dreams may come, When we have shuffled off this mortal coil, Must give us pause, there's the respect, That makes calamity of so long life" (Shakespeare 2009).
[15] In Grenberg (2013a, especially chapters 5 and 10).

governance and ultimate dissolution of the impediments that had threatened the would-be virtuous person's pursuit of that inner freedom of virtue. What we shall discover in this new phenomenological account is that although we must reject any pure experience of positive freedom as such, the person who has an aptitude for virtue does experience both a felt experience of negative freedom (i.e., of being unimpeded) and a non-felt but still pleasurable experience of the ease or facility with which she exercises her rational will, an ease identified not as a pure experience of positive freedom but instead as the combined rational and sensible state of having brought her choice into perfect alignment with her will. Of course, because this experience attends only upon the activity of one who has achieved the heights of virtue, not all sensibly affected beings will have this experience. But when one does achieve these heights, we can say, although one still does not experience pure positive freedom as such (doing so would demand that I remove myself entirely from my sensible nature), one has nonetheless, because of the utter alignment and identification of one's *Willkür* with one's *Wille*, achieved an experience of what it is like for specifically sensibly affected rational beings to reach the height of excellence in the rational activity of positive freedom. This pleasurable dispositional expression of the power of her purely rational activity of positive freedom is thus the ultimate example of a sensibly affected rational being acting excellently in accord with her most proper function. As such, this is a state that is most appropriately described as happiness, intellectually or rationally conceived.

The Felt Pleasure of Negative Freedom

And so, we need to tell a story of the status of rational pleasure and happiness more in agreement with Kant's Transcendental Idealist commitments than what Elizondo's account provides. Let us return, then, to the notion of the unimpeded activity of the free aptitude for virtue, and explore, through appeal to our new perspective on such activity as free activity, how to make sense of what it is like to experience the rational activity of someone with a free aptitude for virtue.

First, and most obviously, as we have been saying, the activity of the person of aptitude is *unimpeded* activity. As Aristotle had noted, the only thing that could impede or interrupt the pleasure of an activity that is proper to one's being is to have that activity disrupted by some foreign or external force. But what we have been doing in our II.i discussion of the governance of one's felt attachments is showing how the person of virtue eliminates just exactly those sorts of external impediments. Indeed, Aristotle's language of "unimpeded" is simply another way of speaking of what, for Kant, emerges when the affects and passions discussed in II.i were removed, moderated, and excited via the activity of inner freedom. These rogue affects and passions were the "external impediments" (i.e., impediments external to the will) which were making the exercise of virtue unpleasant, or, when it was pleasant, making it pleasant in a way that left the agent as a prisoner of fortune, because such pleasure depended upon the external object of one's desire being present. These impediments of ungoverned affects and passions are what threatened to step into the exercise of one's proper activity of choice and pervert and corrupt it into something it was not naturally meant to be. But now that those impediments have been cleared by the exercise of my rational will, we have the experience of activity that is, in Aristotle's language, genuinely *unimpeded*, i.e. there is nothing in its way.[16]

We can, furthermore, identify a specifically *felt* pleasure which Kant associates with such an experience of the removal of external impediments: it is the sensibly felt pleasure of negative freedom. I've discussed this feeling previously,[17] noting that Kant understands it as part and parcel of the common phenomenological experience of being a sensibly affected rational being. Kant describes this experience which "the commonest understanding" calls "feeling" as one related to "representations which come to us involuntarily (as do those of the senses)" (4:450–451/56). As such, in this feeling, I experience "representations given us from somewhere else and in which we are passive" (4:451/56). To experience negative freedom, though, is to experience oneself as being removed from the constraints these representations coming from somewhere else would normally impose; in Kant's language, it is a feeling of being "efficient independently of alien causes determining [the will]" (4:446/52). In my previous writing on such things, I found a paradigmatic example of this feeling of negative freedom in the thrill a small child feels as she chases seagulls on a beach, not being constrained by anything around her (especially her mother!). It is fair to say now, though, that the person who has a free aptitude for virtue, precisely because her exercise of virtue is unimpeded in the same way that the child's running across the beach is unimpeded, similarly experiences the exercise of her virtue with this same sensible felt pleasure of negative freedom.

It is worth taking a moment to distinguish this feeling of negative freedom from the moral feeling of respect upon which the virtuous agent depended to do her work of self-governance. The feeling of respect is not a feeling of negative freedom at all. To the contrary, it is a dual feeling of constraint and exultation, both aspects of which emerge from the experience of one's will being objectively determined by—that is, obligated by—rational principles. As Kant puts it, this

---

[16] There is a caveat to this point that we'll discuss later in this chapter: because a sensibly affected being can never extirpate the bare possibility of being tempted to place concern for self above moral demands, the unimpeded activity here will be "virtually" unimpeded: the fully virtuous person does not experience live opposition to the demands of virtue in specific affects or passions, but instead maintains a vigilant and humble awareness that one always could choose to acquire such opposition.

[17] As part of my discussion of the failure of the argument of *Groundwork III* in Grenberg (2013a, chapter 5).

feeling expresses "an unavoidable constraint put on all inclinations though only by one's own reason" (5:80/69). But this feeling also "contains something elevating, and the subjective effect on feeling, inasmuch as pure practical reason is the sole cause of it, can thus be called *self-approbation* with reference to pure practical reason, inasmuch as he cognized himself as determined to it solely by the law" (5:80–81/69). But the feeling of negative freedom is, as we've just noted, a feeling of *not* being constrained by anything external to oneself. The constraint one experiences in the moral feeling of respect is thus exactly what is *lifted* when the virtuous person acquires a free aptitude for virtue: because this person has governed her affects and passions so as to acquire the state of what, in II.i, we called moral apathy, she has no live affects or passions in need of constraint. This is not to say that the person of virtue will never again feel the negative aspect of moral feeling. We will in fact discuss at length later in this chapter her need for humble vigilance about the possibility of her affects and passions getting out of order and thus needing further constraint. But when one is experiencing the free aptitude for virtue, that need for constraint is not present. Instead of feeling the negative aspect of moral feeling, this agent thus experiences the thrill of not being constrained that is precisely the experience of a feeling of negative freedom.[18]

But this cannot be the end of the story of how to describe what it is like to experience the exercise of a free aptitude for virtue. To experience negative freedom is indeed an exhilarating experience, and it is a part of what the person with an aptitude for virtue experiences; but it does not *fully* characterize what that person experiences. The experience of negative freedom is, simply, an experience of having no constraints.

But the person experiencing an aptitude for virtue is not only experiencing being free from external constraints. She is also, as we have seen, experiencing more positively "a *facility* in acting" (6:407/165), that is, an *ease* or alacrity in the exercise of her will. Indeed, this facility is the product or fruit of her previous labors: she has carefully cultivated over time and through hard work a particular skill in the exercise of her will. Her experience of such activity thus is not *just* an experience of an exuberant celebration of the removal of constraints. In

---

[18] One might worry that this feeling is a mere "twinge" in Annas' sense, though here instead of the twinge being associated with desire-fulfillment, it is a twinge associated with removal of obstacles. But that is not quite right, for it is not a twinge at all. A twinge is a more unstable experience of feeling, one dependent upon the fulfillment of a desire. But here we have (admittedly) a feeling, but not a feeling dependent on fulfillment of desire. It is instead a feeling of having impediments removed: what had previously been constraining a person is no longer constraining her. And it is no longer constraining her because of an intense activity of cultivation of her felt attachments in which she has engaged. So this is not a twinge of feeling connected to desire-fulfillment but instead a sensible feeling marking the removal of these obstacles which one's own activity has accomplished. It is entirely possible though that, in individual cases, an experience of the feeling of negative freedom could be linked with twinges of feeling related to desire-fulfillment (e.g., that "because I am unimpeded here, I have the hope of getting what I want!").

addition to that, she is experiencing herself as exercising a cultivated skill. The seagull-chasing child does not experience anything like *that*!

We thus need to go beyond affirmation of the felt pleasure of negative freedom in our story of the experience of the person with an aptitude for virtue by exploring in more depth in just exactly what this facility for acting consists. And the examples of ease and alacrity I go on to discuss here (playing the cello, Mr. Grewgious' virtuous expression of sympathy, the Knight of Faith) all seek to emphasize, in one way or another, that we're dealing here with persons who bring a particular cultivated skill to bear upon the exercise of their activities (musical prowess, a deeply engrained sense of moral responsibility, or a deeply engrained ability to be happy, faithful, and trusting in the face of logical paradox), and who thereby, in addition to not being constrained externally, also experience an ease in the exercise of the skill they have developed.

The Impossibility of a Non-Sensible Feeling of Pleasure in Positive Freedom

But telling the story of this experience becomes more complex at this point. I've suggested before[19] that although one can have a felt phenomenological experience of negative freedom, one cannot have a phenomenological and sensible feeling of positive freedom as such. The reason for this is that while an experience of positive freedom would have to be an experience of thoroughly pure rational or intellectual activity, feeling as such for Kant is inevitably passive and sensible: the activity of positive freedom and the experience of a feeling are thus mutually contradictory phenomena. But it is on exactly this point that Elizondo and I disagree, because he believes there *is* such a category of purely intellectual feeling for Kant. So, I pause at this point to reflect more on exactly why we need to reject the very notion of an active, intellectual, and non-sensible feeling of positive freedom.

For, as it turns out, Elizondo's textual defense for this idea that there could be a non-sensible, non-passive, and thus thoroughly active feeling of pleasure for Kant is thin, at best. In support of his position, he quotes the third *Critique* where Kant says that "'the state of mind of a will determined by something…is in itself already a feeling of pleasure and is identical with it, thus it does not follow from it as an effect'" (5:222, as quoted by Elizondo 2014, 429). He then uses this passage to suggest that Kant is defending the existence of a non-sensible feeling, a feeling, that is, which is not a passive, sensible experience but instead one identical with pure activity itself:

---

[19] In Grenberg (2013a), especially chapter 5 on the argument of *Groundwork III* and also chapter 10 on freedom.

> That there is a kind of pleasure that is not an effect on the subject but is identical with (the consciousness of) a certain psychological activity is very suggestive. For, it indicates that, his many categorical claims about feeling and sensibility notwithstanding, Kant at least sometimes countenances the possibility of a pleasure that bears no constitutive connection to sensibility.
>
> (Elizondo 2014, 430)

Elizondo's point here seems to be, first, that since (according to the cited quote) this feeling of pleasure is not the cause of the related state of mind, it is thus instead simply identical with that state of mind (that is, with the determination of a will). So far, so good. But Elizondo then concludes, because of this identity of the state of mind (or determination of will) with this feeling of pleasure, that we have found "a pleasure that is intellectual rather than sensible because it expresses our activity rather than merely being a response to it" (Elizondo 2014, 433) That is, for Elizondo, we have found a feeling that is not an effect of some other cause but is instead entirely identical with and simply an expression of an active state of mind of the will. We have, in other words, found a purely active, non-sensible feeling.

But this is a misreading of this passage. What Elizondo fails to notice here is that the "state" in question (viz., the one Kant has just said is identical with a feeling of pleasure) is a "state of mind of a will *determined by something*" (emphases added)! That is: the entire state being discussed, the state which is said to be identical to the feeling of pleasure, is a state that has itself been "determined"—that is, caused—by "something" else, and is thus not itself a full state of activity but instead the passive effect of whatever that cause is. As an effect of some other cause, this feeling/state combination is thus as much a passive expression of sensibility as any other feeling or state of a sensibly affected rational being.

Furthermore, closer attention to this passage reveals that the "something" which is the cause of this dual state/feeling is either "the idea of the moral" or "a causality that rests on a supersensible characteristic of the subject, namely, freedom" (5:222/67). Here is a larger excerpt from the section from which this passage is extracted which reveals this:

> It is true that in the *Critique of Practical Reason* we did actually derive a priori *from universal moral concepts* the feeling of respect (a special and peculiar modification of the feeling of pleasure and displeasure which does seem to differ somehow from both the pleasure and the displeasure we get from empirical objects). But there we were also able to go beyond the bounds of experience and appeal to *a causality that rests on a supersensible characteristic of the subject, namely, freedom.* And yet, even there, *what we derived from the idea of the moral, as the cause*, was actually not this feeling, but merely the determination of the will, except that the state of mind of a will determined by something or other is in itself already a feeling of pleasure and is identical with it. Hence the

determination of the will [by the moral law] does not [in turn] come about as an effect from the feeling of pleasure, [with that feeling being produced by the concept of the moral]. (5:222/67, emphases added and removed)[20]

What Kant is trying to avoid in this passage is any assumption that the genesis of the determination of the will in question has to go through a two-step causal process. One might think this determination of the will occurs in this manner:

Idea of the moral/Freedom → moral feeling of respect → determination of the will

On this picture, our "supersensible" notion of the moral expressed as freedom would be the supersensible cause of a sensible feeling, and then that sensible feeling would itself act as a further cause which now determines the will.

Kant rejects this causal story. Instead, he affirms the following:

Idea of the moral/Freedom →
$$\begin{array}{c}\text{Moral feeling of respect} \\ || \\ \text{Determination of the will}\end{array}$$

That is, the causal force of the idea of the moral expressed as supersensible freedom causes one effect that is simultaneously a feeling of pleasure (and displeasure for that matter) and a determination of the will.

In this passage, Kant thus simply does not appeal to a non-sensible feeling that is not the effect of a cause, not at all. To the contrary, he is doing exactly that: he is explaining a state/feeling combination that is the effect of a supersensible cause. Indeed, he is telling the distinctive causal story of what happens to one's very sensible "feeling of pleasure and displeasure" (presented here as being, really, a sensible faculty to be determined) when it is determined by a special "supersensible" cause instead of by "empirical objects." Elizondo's conclusions that we have here "a pleasure that bears no constitutive connection to sensibility" (Elizondo 2014, 430) and that he has identified "a pleasure that is intellectual rather than sensible because it expresses our activity rather than merely being a response to it" (p. 433) are thus simply false. To the contrary, in this passage, Kant describes precisely a feeling that is a response to rational activity, that is, a feeling which is the sensible effect of a previous rational cause, not a description of any feeling of pleasure internal or intrinsic to the activity of reason itself. Indeed, the genesis of the feeling that is described here is entirely in accord with my own story of the

---

[20] I would suggest here that Kant is talking about an intellectual and objective determination of the will by my rational self. Elizondo suggests that Kant eschews appeal to such causal stories to explain the moral feeling of respect in particular, since to tell a causal story would be to assert an empirical cause of the feeling. But I've argued at length elsewhere (Grenberg 2018) that we need instead to explore the murky metaphysical territory of an intellectual cause with an empirical effect in order to understand the genesis of the moral feeling of respect.

genesis of the moral feeling of respect as a sensible feeling with an intelligible cause,[21] just exactly the story of feeling beyond which Elizondo claims he will move in this article.[22]

We thus firmly reassert the idea that there is no such thing as active, non-sensible feeling for Kant. Such a thing would, indeed, be a contradiction in terms: an active thing that is passively received. Such a point is confirmed in Kant's most complete discussion of such things, early in the *Metaphysics of Morals*. There, even when he speaks of the most intellectual of intellectual feelings—what he calls "a sense-free inclination"—he insists that even this inclination is the passive effect of a previous active cause: "an inclination of this sort would not be the cause but rather the effect of this pure interest of reason, and we could call it a sense-free inclination" (6:213/15, emphases removed).[23]

Given all of this, we can also reaffirm our rejection of any would-be sensible feeling of positive freedom. The feeling of positive freedom, were one to have it, would have to be a feeling of thoroughgoing activity, with no passivity involved. But, by definition, a feeling is something passively experienced, something that is caused by something else. As such, for Kant, feeling is not the kind of thing that can express or be identical with a state of pure activity of positive freedom.[24] There is thus no such thing as a sensible feeling of positive freedom.

We have already affirmed as much in previous writings, instead articulating one indirect mode of access to positive freedom of which Kant speaks: Kant speaks not of the felt experience of positive freedom, but instead of how, via

---

[21] See especially Grenberg (2018) for a full account of this "special and peculiar modification of the feeling of pleasure and displeasure which does seem to differ somehow from both the pleasure and the displeasure we get from empirical objects" (5:222). As I describe there, what is "special and peculiar" about this feeling is not that it is a non-sensible feeling. Rather, it is sensible feeling that instead of being caused by "empirical objects" (5:222) has a "special and peculiar" cause, viz. the "causality that rests on a supersensible characteristic of the subject, namely, freedom" (5:222).

[22] Elizondo notes: "Kant is often taken to be...a clear proponent of the kind of rationalism I am trying to move away from—one according to which moral feelings are, at best, empirical effects of a rational cause" (Elizondo 2014, 427) He thus implies there is something unsatisfying about limiting the category of "feeling" to such passively experienced feelings.

[23] It is perplexing, then, that Kant calls this a "sense-free" inclination. His real point is that this is an inclination that does not have a sensible *cause*. For even the moral feeling of respect has a sensible component, and is thus passive in this sense. I have suggested as much in Grenberg (2013a and 2018). Moral feeling is a sensible (and therefore passively felt) feeling, but it is also a sensible feeling with a distinctive causal history: it has a rational, and therefore active, cause. It is for this reason that we have, in this work, been calling that feeling a "quasi"-desire ("quasi" because while it is a sensible feeling, it is not fully sensible in the way all other feelings are). When Elizondo suggests, in passing, that he wants his account of intellectual pleasure to be more than "empirical effects of a rational cause" (Elizondo 2014, 427), I can only envision that he had to be thinking, at least indirectly, of my work. Alas, he did not say as much.

[24] I am not denying here the identity Kant asserted in the *Critique of Judgment* passage that Elizondo quoted. There, Kant is simply asserting that there is an identity between a state of the will and a feeling of pleasure. But it is still the case for that state/feeling identity that the whole complex is itself a passive effect of a previous cause. I am not denying that a feeling could be identical with a state in just this sense. All I am denying is that a sensible feeling could be identical specifically with a state of pure activity like the activity of positive freedom.

appeal to one's conflicted phenomenological experience of categorical obligation, one can indirectly *infer* to understanding oneself as positively free.[25] I still hold firmly to this claim that it is impossible to have a *sensible* (and thus passive) feeling of *positive* (and thus active) freedom as such. This does not, however, mean that we must abandon the Aristotelian hope of a pleasure that is identical with the exercise of a free aptitude for virtue. Instead, as sensibly affected beings, we must make some other, more indirect, approach to our appreciation of ourselves as positively free, one which appeals not to a purely rational, non-sensible feeling, but instead, following Annas' lead, to a non-felt but still pleasurable way in which one experiences one's activity. Let's explore that territory in more detail.

A Phenomenological Experience of Ease in the Exercise a Free Aptitude for Virtue

So, we turn, finally, to our main question at hand: can we somehow affirm that the state of unimpeded activity which Kant attributes to the person who has the free aptitude for virtue is also a *pleasant* state, albeit not pleasant in the sense of experiencing felt twinges of empirical pleasure as desire-fulfillment? Could there be a pleasure for Kant that is not a feeling as such but on the basis of which we could ground a distinctive intellectual or rational notion of happiness?

It is perhaps odd, even ironic, to seek a *pleasure* that is not a *feeling*; but this irony is something imposed upon us by Kant's strict terminology. As we have seen, a feeling is an inherently passive experience: it is a sensible "shiver" or "twinge" that is always caused by something else (even when that something else isn't a heteronomous empirical object but instead, as in the case of the moral feeling of respect, one's supersensible self acting on one's sensible self). So, when we ask the question we are asking now—viz., the question of what it is "like" to experience the *activity* of virtue—the language of feeling as such is out of order: we cannot, common sense ways of speaking of such things notwithstanding, talk about what activity "*feels* like." Nonetheless, there is surely *something* it is "like" to experience the activity of virtue, and that is what we seek to understand in this section.

In seeking this non-felt notion of pleasure, we take a cue from and place ourselves in sympathetic interpretive agreement with Zuckert's (2002) claim that we can find a "formal" and "intentional" notion of pleasure in Kant's writings. The

---

[25] And this is exactly what I did in Grenberg (2013a, chapter 10), when I argued that awareness of oneself as positively *free* is something to which one *infers* from a felt phenomenological experience of *obligation*. In the forthcoming account, I go beyond this and suggest that, for the fully virtuous person, she can also even more confidently infer her status as positively free through appeal to the phenomenological experience of ease she has in the activity of virtue.

forthcoming account is particularly in agreement with Zuckert's suggestion that, for Kant, pleasure can be "formal": "[P]leasure is distinct in kind from sensations, which are, Kant claims, the 'material' or 'real' in perceptual experience (Sec.39, p. 291). Unlike sensations, pleasure is a formal state, or (more properly) a consciousness of a formal, temporal relation among other states or presentations" (p. 240). In accordance with this general definition of it, pleasure as such is not necessarily a feeling. For Zuckert, only pleasure in what is agreeable (or, in our on-going language, pleasure in desire-fulfillment) is attached to a sensible feeling; and, thusly, "understood as a temporally-extended and -located sensory state[,] seems to be a paradigmatically empirical phenomenon" (p. 240).

In contrast to this empirical expression of a specifically felt pleasure, pleasure as such is more formally defined. It is, at its heart, a "consciousness of a formal, temporal relation among other states" of one's person (Zuckert 2002, 240). One might say (and Zuckert herself eventually does) that this formal pleasure is a recognition of the "harmony" of those states toward which the pleasure is directed, and is an intentional attitude toward those harmonious states such that one seeks to perpetuate their harmonious existence: "Pleasure is a mental state in which a presentation is in harmony with itself, which is the basis either for merely preserving this state itself...or for producing the object of this presentation" (p. 246). Of particular interest for our purposes is Zuckert's suggestion here that pleasure in this formal sense is a reaction to and an interest in perpetuating the continuation of a state of *harmony* in one's other mental states. As we shall see in the forthcoming discussion, pleasure in the unimpeded activity of virtue, understood as the perfect alignment of one's Wille with one's Willkür, is just such an example of formal pleasure directed at the harmony of one's other states.

Interestingly though, the pleasure we identify here will fall between the cracks of the kinds of formal pleasures Zuckert herself identifies. For her, as noted above, we find two categories: a pleasure which provides the basis "for merely preserving this [harmonious] state" and another pointed toward "producing the object of this presentation." And, for Zuckert: "On the first alternative, the judgment about the given presentation is an aesthetic judgment of reflection; on the second, a pathological aesthetic judgment or a practical judgment. (FI VIII, pp. 230–232)" (Zuckert 2002, 246). In short, Zuckert suggests a pleasure meant simply to perpetuate the relevant state is an aesthetic pleasure or judgment, and a pleasure meant to produce the object(s) toward which the pleasure is directed is a practical judgment.

Our state of non-felt pleasure, however, covers aspects of both these kinds of pleasure identified by Zuckert: pleasure in the harmonious state of one's Wille and Willkür which constitutes one's unimpeded activity is indeed a state the agent wants to perpetuate, and the pleasure one takes in that harmonious state is indeed the means for such perpetuation. Because it is a pleasant state, I seek to remain in that state. Obviously, though, this is a practical and not a merely aesthetic state of pleasure; that is, one's pleasure is directed toward a state of harmony which itself is concerned with the successful realization of virtuous character and realization of obligatory ends in the world. But this is not a practical pleasure in the sense of it being a pleasure toward the production of a not-yet-existent object (as, say, an anticipated pleasure in getting a bite of the cheesecake I just baked would be). Rather, it is a practical pleasure in that the harmonious states toward which it points are states of the practical *faculties* of the acting agent (viz., her *Wille* and *Willkür*).

As such, we welcome a new kind of formal pleasure beyond the kind which Zuckert identifies. Zuckert herself has suggested that this formal pleasure pointed simply toward the continuance of a harmony in one's states is something that Kant does not identify until the *Critique of Judgment*. But, as we shall see, Kant's appeal to this non-felt pleasure in the harmony of one's *Wille* and *Willkür*, though not fully articulated until the third *Critique*, finds an earlier nascent form in the *Critique of Practical Reason*, earlier than the third *Critique* discussion. I hope, though, Zuckert could find this discovery earlier in Kant's corpus of a pleasure in the form he perhaps most fully articulates not until the third *Critique* a friendly amendment to her account.

And so, what we shall see in our forthcoming account, with assistance from Aristotle and Annas, and as has already been hinted in our first interpretive review of Kant's discussion of an aptitude, is that we can introduce a space not for a sensible feeling of positive freedom, but instead for a distinctive non-felt rational pleasure in the *way* the fully virtuous person experiences the exercise of virtue, an experience of the unimpeded activity of her *Wille* and *Willkür* from which this person can confidently infer her power of positive freedom. This will not be an experience of positive freedom as such, but instead an experience of her full virtue: the perfect alignment of her choice with the rational demands of her own autonomously legislated will. This is, furthermore, a pleasure in the *harmony*, *ease*, and *alacrity* with which one performs one's proper function: the way a person of full virtue phenomenologically experiences the exercise of her virtue is *harmoniously*, with ease and facility and so is, simply, pleasant. We are not saying here that the activity *causes* a feeling of pleasure in our sensible selves (though this is a further claim that could be made and that is compatible with what we are saying here). Rather, the ease or facility with which one engages in the activity of virtue is simply and inherently pleasant in itself: doing something with ease is an intrinsically pleasant experience.

It is in just such a vein that we should understand Kant's claims, already noted, that this person with an aptitude for virtue has a *"facility"* in acting" (6:407/165, emphasis added) and is therefore in a state of "tranquility" or "health."[26] Furthermore,

---

[26] "The true strength of virtue is a *tranquil mind* with a considered and firm resolution to put the law of virtue into practice. That is the state of *health* in the moral life" (6:409/167).

this is not just *any* pleasurable activity, but a pleasurable activity that is central and definitional to the kind of being who one is. As such, when a sensibly affected being successfully acquires a free aptitude for virtue, she is exercising, well and completely, that activity most proper to her being, and so can be described as being *happy*, intellectually or rationally speaking.

Phenomenological Images of Harmony, Ease, and Alacrity

This appeal to a non-felt rational pleasure in the way one engages in an activity may seem an abstract and mysterious notion to some, but I hope to dispel that notion. For, to the contrary, with Annas, we suggest that it is indeed a very familiar kind of experience. To appreciate that as being the case, and to further appreciate the nature of the pleasurable experience of facility thereby, let us first, before further confirming the existence of this pleasurable state in Kant's texts, appeal to a variety of examples that approximate what Kant means by the experience of ease or facility in the exercise of an activity, examples which bring to life the brief discussion he has provided of that aptitude in the Doctrine of Virtue.

First, as I write this sentence, I can confirm today as a writing day in which the ideas are simply flowing unobstructedly. There is an ease or facility to my writing today. This is not the experience of the unimpeded activity of virtue, but it is an analogous experience of unimpeded activity, and furthermore, one that is experienced *pleasantly*. But it is not happy or pleasant in the sense of experiencing a separate strong feeling of, say, joy. Rather, we say not that I am experiencing a passive feeling of joy in response to the attainment of something I previously lacked, but instead that I am experiencing a pleasure that is simply concomitant with the activity of writing itself.

Indeed, if I did experience a separate strong feeling of joy, such a feeling would probably kick me *out* of the ease of the writing groove I'd gotten into. That's because this separate feeling would point me toward some object or state of affairs external to and outside of the realm of action in which I was so intensely engaging when I was writing. To say that there is something pleasurable about the activity *without* such appeal to an object external to the activity is thus a helpful way of clarifying just what it means to say that the pleasure I experience is *internal to* or *concomitant with*, the activity itself: instead of pointing me toward something I desire outside of the activity itself, the pleasure I experience points me only all the more intensely toward the continuance and furtherance of that activity itself.[27] It is a pleasure which encourages the self-perpetuation of an activity,

---

[27] I've just had a fly repeatedly land on my arm as I try to write this and am reminded of how distracting it is to experience a feeling pointing me toward something outside my activity when I am so pleasantly in the midst of my activity!

instead of a pleasure which threatens to distract one from continuation of the activity at hand.[28]

And so we discover what it is "like" to engage well in the activity of virtue: it is pleasant. The important point to appreciate here is that this is an active pleasure, not a passive, sensibly felt pleasure. In other words, it is a pleasure experienced as part and parcel of *doing* something, not a pleasure I feel passively as a response to *getting* something. It is for this reason that we must also say that, for Kant, this pleasure is not a sensible feeling as such, because, for him, feeling (all feeling) is a passive experience. So the pleasure we reveal here is not a *feeling*, but instead an experience of the *way* in which one engages in the unobstructed rational activity of one's will: easily, with an expert facility.

Playing music is another good example of a kind of activity that has its own active pleasure, but which can be disrupted by even a good passive pleasure. If when I'm playing my cello really really well for my teacher—when I'm "in the groove" and simply taken up in the activity of producing music—if, in the midst of this, I have the thought (and the accompanying pleasure) that my teacher is going to be really impressed that I was able to do this... well, then the moment is lost and I am no longer in that pleasurable groove of activity. I'd probably make a mistake in my playing at that point. I would surely no longer experience the production of my music as easy and flowing in the way that it had previous to me having that thought which introduced passive, externally focused pleasures into my internal active pleasure.[29]

Pleasure in the Ease of Virtuous Activity

The examples I've considered thus far are all mere analogs of the state we're most interested in, because they are all examples of being in the groove for non-moral activities. But we can also illustrate what it would be like to be in the groove of virtue. The character of Mr. Grewgious from Charles Dickens' *The Mystery of Edwin Drood* is an excellent example of someone capable of being in the groove of virtue.

Mr. Grewgious is an older man living in London who is the legal guardian of a young woman named Rosa whose mother, now deceased, was someone whom Grewgious had quietly loved but to whom he had never expressed his affections. Rosa goes to a boarding school in a small town some distance from London.

---

[28] This is something Elizondo has described as a "self-directed [and] self-maintaining" (Elizondo 2014, 433) activity. So, although I disagree with him about whether there is a non-sensible feeling which supervenes upon rational activity, I am in concert with him about the idea that something like a self-directed and self-maintaining activity can exist for Kant.

[29] I would thus suggest that the way this pleasure feels is not unlike what a psychologist calls a "flow" experience. See https://en.wikipedia.org/wiki/Flow_(psychology)

While at school, she is sexually threatened by an older man in the community who is the uncle of the eponymous Edwin Drood, a man who himself has recently been found murdered. In a sudden fit of decision, Rosa comes to London on her own to seek Mr. Grewgious' protection.

Here is how Dickens describes her arrival at Mr. Grewgious' lodgings in London:

> Guided by the painted name of Mr. Grewgious, she went upstairs and softly tapped and tapped several times. But no one answering, and Mr. Grewgious's door-handle yielding to her touch, she went in, and saw her guardian sitting on a windowseat at an open window, with a shaded lamp placed far from him on a table in a corner.
>
> Rosa drew nearer to him in the twilight of the room. He saw her, and he said in an under-tone: "Good Heaven!"

Rosa fell upon his neck, with tears, and then he said, returning her embrace:

> "My child, my child! I thought you were your mother! But what, what, what," he added, soothingly, "has happened? My dear, what has brought you here? Who has brought you here?"
>
> "No one, I came alone."
>
> "Lord bless me!" ejaculated Mr. Grewgious. "Came alone! Why didn't you write to me to come and fetch you?"
>
> "I had no time. I took a sudden resolution. Poor, poor Eddy!"
>
> "Ah, poor fellow, poor fellow!"
>
> "His uncle has made love to me. I cannot bear it," said Rosa, at once with a burst of tears, and a stamp of her little foot; "I shudder with horror of him, and I have come to you to protect me and all of us from him, if you will?"
>
> "I will!" cried Mr. Grewgious, with a sudden rush of amazing energy. "Damn him!
> > Confound his politics!
> > Frustrate his knavish tricks!
> > On Thee his hopes to fix?
> > > Damn him again!" (Dickens 1974, 236)

What we emphasize in this exchange between Rosa and Mr. Grewgious is the extraordinary facility and ease with which the latter steps up to become Rosa's protector. He is an older man living quietly by himself, far away from his charge. But when she shows up with her request, unexpected and unannounced, clearly in a way that is going to significantly disrupt his quiet life, Mr. Grewgious pauses not even for a moment before whole-heartedly promising to protect her, finding himself spontaneously appealing to words from the second verse of the British

National Anthem as he does so.[30] The situation Rosa presents to him is not a pleasant one, but it is with alacrity and ease that Mr. Grewgious takes up his duty to her, and even we the readers experience that moment of virtuous activity in him as pleasant: it is so obviously the right thing to do and his ability at the drop of a hat to know and do the right thing reveals the ease, alacrity, and even the pleasure with which he takes up his duty to his charge.

There is another, final example of this kind of pleasure in the way one engages in an activity that I find helpful for making sense specifically of the moral version of this state of facility or ease. Kierkegaard, in *Fear and Trembling*, distinguishes between the Knight of Infinite Resignation and the Knight of Faith in a way that suggests that the Knight of Faith has this ease or alacrity in the way he pursues not a life of virtue but a life of faith, an ease or alacrity that is just exactly what his counterpart, the Knight of Infinite Resignation, lacks. Kierkegaard's Knight of Faith is someone who has found an elegant and smooth way to accept and live a paradox that reason cannot resolve. He can at once believe in the promise of an infinite world of an afterlife but not thereby abandon his conviction that he will get everything for which he hopes in this finite world. His facility or ease in smoothly and effortlessly living a life that demands affirmation of this paradox of finitude and infinitude is something that Kierkegaard himself describes with particular eloquence and facility. I quote him at length to make the point:

> [The Knight of Faith] drains in infinite resignation the deep sorrow of existence, he knows the bliss of infinity, he has felt the pain of renouncing everything, whatever is most precious in the world, and yet to him finitude tastes just as good as to one who has never known anything higher, for his remaining in the finite bore no trace of a stunted, anxious training, and still he has this sense of being secure to take pleasure in it, as though it were the most certain thing of all. And yet, and yet the whole earthly form he presents is a new creation on the strength of the absurd. He resigned everything infinitely, and then took everything back on the strength of the absurd. He is continually making the movement of infinity, but he makes it with such accuracy and poise that he is continually getting finitude out of it, and not for a second would one suspect anything else. *It is said that the dancer's hardest task is to leap straight into a*

---

[30] The words of the verse are:
> O Lord our God arise,
> Scatter our enemies,
> And make them fall!
> Confound their politics,
> Frustrate their knavish tricks,
> On Thee our hopes we fix,
> God save us all!

from https://lyricsondemand.com/n/nationalanthemlyrics/britiannationalanthemlyrics.html

definite position, so that not for a second does he have to catch at the position but stands there in it in the leap itself. Perhaps no dancer can do it—but that knight does it. The mass of humans live disheartened lives of earthly sorrow and joy, these are the sitters-out who will not join in the dance. The knights of infinity are dancers too and they have elevation. They make the upward movement and fall down again, and this too is no unhappy pastime, nor ungracious to behold. But when they come down they cannot assume the position straightaway, they waver an instant and the wavering shows they are nevertheless strangers in the world. This may be more or less evident, depending on their skill, but even the most skilled of these knights cannot hide the vacillation. One doesn't need to see them in the air, one only has to see them the moment they come and have come to earth to recognize them. But to be able to land in just that way, and in the same second to look as though one was up and walking, *to transform the leap in life to a gait, to express the sublime in the pedestrian absolutely*—that is something only the knight of faith can do—and it is the one and only marvel.

(Kierkegaard 2003, 69–70, emphases added)

Kierkegaard's image here of the most adept and skilled dancer is very helpful to us for our own purpose of understanding the experience of facility in the exercise of virtue. The crucial point that distinguishes the Knight of Faith from the Knight of Infinite Resignation—viz., that the former manages the difficult balance of the infinite and the finite while the latter achieves smoothness in his life only by relinquishing the finite for the sake of the infinite and therefore looks awkward in the finite world—is exactly the final point we need to clarify our understanding of the Kantian person with a free aptitude for virtue. The person who has an ease in her exercise of virtue does not accomplish that ease by abandoning or ignoring her sensible self ("shuffling off her mortal coil"), but instead by putting that sensible self in perfect order in accordance with her rational self. She, like the Knight of Faith, is the dancer who can "transform the leap in life to a gait [or]...express the sublime in the pedestrian absolutely." That is: just as the Knight of Faith manages the paradox of infinity and finitude, the person of with an aptitude for virtue manages the paradox of being a sensibly affected rational being with perfect ease and alacrity. She does not abandon one part of herself for the sake of realizing the other, but brings the two sides of herself into perfect alignment or harmony: she is a wonderful dancer! For, as we have been saying, for the person with a free aptitude for virtue, it is as if her *Willkür* has simply become her *Wille*. She has accomplished that "marvel[ous]" movement from a sublime leap through the rational air to her earth-bound, sensible, and pedestrian gait, all with a perfect ease or smoothness that anyone whose affects and passions are not in the same perfect order as hers lacks. Indeed, one can even envision Mr. Grewgious as making this elegant leap of virtue: his unhesitating defense of principles of morality in a messy and gritty world exhibits a similar ease.

Are we saying, then, that the pleasure with which the person of virtue experiences her exercise of virtue is, simply, a pleasurable experience of positive freedom? This isn't quite the way to understand what is going on here. To experience positive freedom as such, our sensibly affected being would have to abandon her sensibility. She would become the Knight of Infinite Resignation instead of the Knight of Faith, a knight who solves the paradox of a paradoxical existence by eliminating one term of the paradox. But that is not what is happening for the person with a free aptitude for virtue. Instead, something even more "marvel[ous]" than that is accomplished here: instead of shuffling off her mortal coils in a pure experience of intellectual activity, she assures that her sensibility and her rationality are so perfectly coinciding with each other that she experiences and exhibits her sensible-rational activity *as if it were* perfectly rational activity. Even then, though, she experiences that rational activity as only a sensibly affected rational being can, viz. as the perfectly smooth and elegant coincidence of two apparently distinct and opposed parts of herself. She thus does have a *sort* of experience of positive freedom, but it is not a *pure* experience of that supersensible activity. Instead, it is an experience of what the supersensible activity of positive freedom looks like when it is done fully and well from the perspective of a sensibly affected rational being. At most, we could say that she gains a *glimpse* of what pure rational activity would be like for a being who was only and purely rational. But she gains that glimpse only from the perspective of one who does the rational activity thing *as* sensibly affected, and then is able to infer for herself, post-experience, that she has positive freedom.

We can now characterize the overall phenomenological experience of the person who has a free aptitude for virtue. Rational pleasure in unimpeded activity, for Kant, involves, first of all, a sensible feeling of negative freedom which emerges when the external pressures that had been impinging upon one's rational will are removed. Second, that feeling of negative freedom associates itself with the ease or facility in the way one experiences the perfect coincidence of one's choice with one's free and autonomously legislating will, an ease which is experienced pleasurably, and which thereby points the virtuous agent toward appreciation of where her negative freedom came from in the first place (viz., from her positive freedom as a rational being). The pleasure that pervades the experience of the person with a free aptitude for virtue is thus not the experience of a purely intellectual, nonsensible feeling but instead an experience of how one's sensible choice is perfectly in sync with one's rational will, an experience really of one's prowess in the exercise of that rational activity proper to a sensibly affected rational being, that activity which is central to and indeed definitional of her very being.[31]

---

[31] We thus re-emphasize the fact that the feeling of negative freedom is a sensible feeling while the pleasure in the ease of the exercise of virtue is not. The reason negative freedom is sensibly felt while this ease is not is that the former, because it is defined "negatively" (viz., as freedom from something,

With this story of the pleasurable ease with which one experiences a free aptitude for virtue, we thus welcome something very, but not exactly, like what Elizondo was seeking, viz. "a pleasure that is intellectual rather than sensible because it expresses our activity rather than merely being a response to it" (Elizondo 2014, 433) Importantly though, although the pleasure we affirm here is indeed identical with the experience of the exercise of the free aptitude of virtue, it is, as we have seen, neither a sensible feeling nor a purely intellectual activity. Instead, it is a mode of experiencing oneself as a sensibly affected rational being who has brought her *Wille* and *Willkür* into perfect alignment. And so although this is a pleasure that is identical with the experience of an unobstructed activity, it is not an expression of absolutely pure intellectual activity, but instead an expression of how a sensibly affected rational agent experiences her intellectual activity when it stands in perfect alignment with her sensibly affected self.[32]

Further, because we affirm this pleasure through appeal to the notion of the facility in action of the virtuous person in the unimpeded exercise of her will, we distinguish this pleasure from the moral feeling of respect. First, moral feeling is, well, a sensible feeling, whereas this pleasure is a non-felt harmony of one's rational faculties. Further, moral feeling involves a conflict that this pleasure does not: in moral feeling, the negative side of the feeling expresses the experience of the constraint of inclinations which oppose morality; but the experience of pleasure of which we speak here involves no conflict or obstruction. Indeed, it is precisely because the fully virtuous person experiences no active opposition within herself to her commitment to morality that this new pleasurable experience of ease or facility emerges.

There is more we can say to distinguish the pleasure integral to the exercise of an aptitude for virtue that distinguishes it from moral feeling. The pleasure of an aptitude for virtue is a pleasure identical with engagement in the activity of virtue itself. But the moral feeling of respect is a sensible feeling one experiences as a result of recognizing one's status as an obligated rational being. Even—and perhaps even especially—the non-virtuous person can experience this moral feeling of respect. Indeed, *every* sensibly affected rational being experiences moral feeling: it is simply the mode by which one becomes aware of one's status as an

---

from some constraint of things external to me), still involves a reference *to* those external things (those are the things that are not impeding me!). Hence, even while being a form of freedom, it is not an experience of pure activity but instead involves a moment of passivity in relation to my escape from determination by things external to me. Sensibility, and thus feeling, is thereby engaged here, because that is the mode by which one's sensible self expresses itself: through feeling.

[32] Elizondo is right, however, to have suspected that the aesthetic experience could point us toward these same sorts of notions affirming the promise of our intellectual and supersensible home and heritage. But that is just to say that we need *aesthetic* experience (viz., an experience inextricably linked with our *sensible* natures) to access these rational truths about ourselves. That is the only possible, and necessarily indirect route, we must take to an appreciation of our supersensible and free selves. As sensibly affected rational beings, we must access the truths of our rational nature indirectly, *via* sensibility.

obligated being. But not every sensibly affected being experiences the pleasure of ease in the unobstructed exercise of an aptitude for virtue. This experience is possible only, of course, for someone who has successfully done the hard governance work of virtue, the work we described in II.i. Moral feeling is, furthermore, as we have already discussed, the effect of a rational cause (the moral law imposing itself on one's will), and not something concomitant with the exercise of the unobstructed activity itself. But ease or facility in the activity of virtue does not "cause" a separate pleasure as such; it just *is* pleasurable in itself to engage in this activity of virtue with ease and facility. And so the pleasure of which we speak here is not a sensible feeling of pleasure experienced passively, but instead one way of describing the activity itself: this activity simply is, in itself, pleasant.

I would also distinguish this feeling from the sort of feeling that Cohen (2018) identifies as "theoretical reason's feelings that...[are] affective manifestations of reason's activity" (p. 10). According to her, one can, through investigation of Kant's "What is Orientation in Thinking?," identify a feeling related to theoretical pursuits that is parallel to the moral feeling in practical pursuits. What makes this feeling essentially a theoretical parallel to the moral feeling of respect is that, like that practical feeling, this feeling of reason has two opposing components:

> the activity of speculative reason is the cause of two distinct feelings: a positive one, the pleasure of systematization, and a negative one, the feeling of reason's need...Insofar as the feeling of reason's need is a negatively valenced feeling, it triggers a desire to dispose of it and thus of what has cause it, namely the gap between reason's ideal for cognition and its current state. (p. 15).

This is a fascinating discovery and another interesting feeling to add to the catalog of feelings we find described in Kant's works. But this feeling of reason is rather different from the pleasure in the exercise of the aptitude of virtue we describe here. First, as noted above, Cohen's theoretical feeling is more similar to moral feeling than to a pleasure that attends the exercise of an aptitude for virtue, especially in that it (like moral feeling) is a feeling composed of both positive and negative parts. But again, the non-felt experience of pleasure in the ease and facility with which one exercises one's aptitude for virtue has nothing dual or oppositional about it. To the contrary, it is a pleasure that emerges precisely because one is in harmony with oneself, experiencing no opposition or impediments to one's exercise of virtue. Further, reason's feeling, as Cohen understands it, is not identical to the activity of the exercise of speculative reason, but instead a sensible feeling caused by that activity: "the activity of speculative reason is the *cause* of two distinct feelings" (Cohen 2018, 15, emphasis added) It is certainly true that these are feelings that "*manifest* the state of the subject's mental agency" (p. 14, emphasis added), but they are sensible feelings distinct from that mental agency itself whereas the non-felt pleasure we describe here is identical with its underlying rational activity.

We affirm once again, however, that this pleasure we have defined is very much in accord with Zuckert's (2002) identification of formal pleasures that are not merely empirical twinges tied to desire-fulfillment (or, in Zuckert's third *Critique* language, that are not merely pleasures in the agreeable). The pleasure in the exercise of one's aptitude for virtue is pleasure pointed at the harmony that has been established between one's faculties of will and choice, a harmony which is furthered, encouraged, or perpetuated by that very experience of pleasure in it and is thus a practical version of that formal aesthetic pleasure which Zuckert identifies as an expression of the harmony of one's intellectual faculties.

Pleasure in the Ease of Virtuous Activity is an Analog of Happiness

There is a final, but crucial, point to appreciate about this pleasurable activity of virtue: because the activity in question is an activity most proper to my being, the pleasure which supervenes upon it is not just any pleasure, but something the experience of which we can identify as happiness, rationally conceived. In so doing, we reaffirm the move first made by Aristotle when he suggested that if the pleasurable activity in question is one that is natural to and definitional of one's being, then we can understand that pleasure to be the distinctive pleasure called "happiness" (*eudaemonia*): "if each disposition has unimpeded activities," then "the activity (if unimpeded) of *all* our dispositions or that of some one of them is happiness"(1153f3, emphasis added). In other words, when the pleasurable activity in which one engages so excellently is an activity so natural and central to one's very being, that pleasurable activity itself deserves the title of happiness (*eudaemonia*) as such, happiness in the sense of a state that expresses the excellent realization of one's proper function.

One might think that Kant himself could not make this move: because he so insistently, and narrowly, conceives of happiness as desire-fulfillment, it would seem he'd heartily reject even a glimmer of calling this pleasurable ease of virtue "happiness." To a certain extent, this is true: he does not use the explicit language of happiness (*Gluckseligkeit*) for any such state. And yet, interestingly, he does not *heartily* reject the word. Instead, although he ultimately calls this state "contentment" instead of "happiness," he nonetheless affirms that this non-felt satisfaction with oneself that supervenes upon the activity of virtue can at least be called an "*analogue* of happiness" (5:117/98, emphasis added).

I quote at length a passage from Kant that is absolutely crucial for confirming his commitment to a eudaemonistic conception of this moral analog to happiness, a non-felt pleasure or contentment that is identical with the exercise of virtue:

Have we not, however, a word that does not denote enjoyment, as the word happiness does, but that nevertheless indicates a satisfaction with one's existence, an analogue of happiness that must necessarily accompany consciousness of virtue? Yes! This word is contentment of oneself, which in its strict meaning always designates only a negative satisfaction with one's existence, in which one is conscious of needing nothing. Freedom, and the consciousness of freedom as an ability to follow the moral law with an unyielding disposition, is independence from the inclinations, at least as motives determining (even if not as affecting) our desire, and so far as I am conscious of this freedom in following my moral maxims, it is the sole source of an unchangeable contentment, necessarily combined with it and resting on no special feeling, and this can be called intellectual contentment. Aesthetic contentment (improperly so called), which rests on satisfaction of the inclinations, however refined they may be made out to be, can never be adequate to what is thought about contentment.

(5:117–118/98, translation slightly modified)

This is an important moment for Kant. Although he does not say it in so many words, what he is identifying here is, essentially a non-felt experience of pleasure, just what we have, from Aristotelian inspirations, been interpreting his appeal to facility in the exercise of the free aptitude of virtue to be. The contentment of which he speaks "rest[s] on no special feeling"—in our[33] language, it is not a sensible feeling—but is nonetheless a state of "contentment of oneself" (*Selbstzufriedenheit*). Contentment of oneself is thus new language for describing what it is like pleasurably to experience the exercise of a free aptitude for virtue.

I have chosen, however, to alter the standard English translation of the word "Selbstzufriedenheit." The Cambridge translation of *Selbstzufriedenheit* is "contentment *with* oneself," but such language misses Kant's point here. To be content *with* oneself would suggest that, posterior to one's exercise of virtue, one steps back from that activity and is pleased with oneself. But that would be a sensible feeling of self-contentment, one of those "foreign" feelings that pulls one out of engagement in the pleasurable activity of virtue itself. One can appeal to such feelings related to virtue; and, elsewhere, Kant does.[34] But that is *not* what Kant is saying here. To the contrary, he very precisely distinguishes the contentment he is articulating from any merely "[a]esthetic contentment" that involves sensible feelings.[35] What he is articulating here, then, is a "contentment *of* oneself," that is, a non-felt contentment that comes built-in with the very exercise of virtue, in just

---

[33] And Zuckert's (2002).
[34] See, for example, 5:38/35: "I certainly do not deny that frequent practice in conformity with this determining ground [of the moral law] can finally produce subjectively a feeling of satisfaction with oneself; on the contrary to establish and to cultivate this feeling, which alone deserves to be called moral feeling strictly speaking, itself belongs to duty."
[35] Or what Zuckert has identified in the third *Critique* as pleasure in the agreeable.

the sense we have been suggesting in this chapter. What he has just done here, then, is to perfectly articulate a pleasurable state of proper functioning. And so, although Kant is only willing to go so far as to call this state an "analogue" of happiness, we coax him just that much further down the eudaemonistic path and say that what he has done here is to give us an account of intellectual, rational, or moral *happiness* to complement his empirical account of the same.

Furthermore, dwelling upon this passage at greater length confirms just the combined experience of negative freedom and pleasurable ease which we have articulated above. Kant describes this contentment as "the consciousness of freedom as an ability to follow the moral law with an unyielding disposition," and such appeal to the "unyielding" nature of one's disposition is just another way of describing that harmony of *Wille* and *Willkür* we described in one's aptitude for virtue. Further, Kant notes that, in one sense, this contentment is "only a negative satisfaction": one is conscious of an "independence from inclinations," and thus conscious of "needing nothing." One is conscious, in other words, of negative freedom, here, of having no dependence on alien causes or the inclinations that would connect us to such causes.

Beyond that, though, Kant also suggests that one finds in this passage a glimmer of positive freedom: "*so far as I am* conscious of this freedom in following my moral maxims, it is the sole source of an unchangeable contentment, necessarily combined with it [i.e., with the awareness of one's independence from inclinations] and resting on no special feeling, and this can be called intellectual contentment" (emphasis added). In appealing to having some limited consciousness of "freedom in following my moral maxims" (or what he described just previously as a consciousness of one's ability "to follow the moral law with an unyielding disposition"), Kant thereby appeals (at least indirectly) to consciousness of *positive* freedom. For indeed, this freedom "in following my moral maxims" is a freedom *to* do something from myself instead of merely a freedom *from* constraint by alien causes, and is thus freedom in its positive sense. Kant speaks, though, not of having full consciousness of this positive freedom but instead suggests that it is only "[in] so far as I am" conscious of this freedom that I can speak of being content. That is: we do not have complete consciousness or felt experience of positive freedom as such but only the awareness of the ease I experience in "following my moral maxims" with an "unyielding" ease which assures me in the existence of that freedom. We have, in other words, found in this text a state of contentment that is identical with the exercise of positive freedom as expressed in the way that only a sensibly affected rational being can experience it. We have, that is, a notion of intellectual or rational contentment that we now call happiness, intellectually or rationally conceived.

Furthermore, by insisting that this contentment of self involves a pleasure that "rest[s] on no special feeling," we reconfirm our earlier agreement with Zuckert (2002) that we can discover a contentment or pleasure that is non-felt. What we have here with this contentment of self is a formal, non-felt, pleasurable state pointed toward the harmony of one's practical faculties of will and choice which constitutes the pleasure of happiness, rationally conceived.

To-may-to, To-mah-to?

I have in this interpretation of Kant's appeal to contentment of self as an "analogue to happiness" been seeing his use of this phrase as an indication of a rather positive and encouraging association Kant wants to assert between these two states, one which encourages us to find a deep similarity between contentment of oneself and happiness empirically conceived. On this optimistic reading of his use of the phrase, one would thus take his appeal to it as an indication that we really should be ok with calling this contentment of self a new "happiness" of a sort, since it is so very similar to the state that we are already familiar with and which we call "happiness": it is an "anologue" of it!

One could, however, argue that when Kant calls this contentment of self an "analogue" to happiness, we should read this appeal more negatively, viz. that contentment of self is *merely* an *analog* to happiness and so not the real thing. In other words, one might read that appeal more pessimistically as Kant's effort to drive a wedge between this contentment of self and anything that *really* deserves the moniker of "happiness," and thus as an indication that we should studiously reject the temptation to call this contentment of self "happiness."[36]

There are a few things to say to this objector. First, it is significant to me that Kant is willing even to breathe the word "happiness" in the phrase "analogue of happiness." If he were really intent on driving a wedge between contentment of self and happiness empirically conceived, it seems to me he'd have been much more wary even of using the word in this contextualized sense.

But suppose, for the sake of argument, that Kant really does want to insist here that we not use the word "happiness" in any context to describe this contentment of self (even though I don't accept this since, clearly, he *is* willing to use the word to refer to contentment of self when he says of that contentment that it is an "analogue of happiness"). If this is what he's getting at here, then when he insists on calling this contentment of self *merely* an analog of happiness and not a new form of happiness as such, I am convinced that he would have to be thinking of the word "happiness" in its most narrowly construed sense as applying only to the sum of one's feelings of desire-satisfaction. So maybe he would reject the idea that one can be "happy" in the exercise of virtue in this strict sense of understanding "happiness" as "desire-fulfillment." My reading of this contentment as a form of

---

[36] I thank an anonymous reader from Oxford University Press for raising this concern.

happiness is, however, entirely in agreement with the need to drive *that* wedge between it and happiness.

But if I then asked Kant whether there is a state that expresses contentment or satisfaction or pleasure in the very exercise of one's moral aptitude for virtue, I suspect he'd heartily agree. So maybe the only disagreement he and I would have at this point is of whether we should open up the word "happiness" to a broader set of meanings. Maybe in his consciousness "happiness" is just so tightly associated with the "desire-satisfaction" meaning that he recoils from using the term even for states very different from that state of satisfaction which nonetheless express a state of satisfaction in the agent. At this point, though, our disagreement becomes a merely nominal one: it is not that we disagree about whether there are a range of states of satisfaction that properly visit upon the human being and are indicative of that being's proper functioning; it is just that we disagree about what words best describe these states. So Kant heartily confirms that there is a state of contentment for sensibly affected rational beings tied specifically to their unimpeded exercise of the aptitude for virtue. I just want to say to him that because, like happiness empirically conceived, this state of contentment of oneself is a state of satisfaction that speaks of a satisfaction constitutional and definitional of what it is to be a properly functioning human being—that for this reason, this state deserves to be given the name of a "happiness" of some sort. Both these states are not just any passing satisfaction, but rather deep satisfactions which help confirm that this being in question is functioning in a way proper to her being: one describes a state of complete desire-satisfaction and the other describes a state of internal harmony of one's practical rational faculties.[37]

And so, to be clear: I am not asserting that the pleasure of the exercise of an aptitude for virtue is happiness in *exactly* the same sense that the sum of desire-fulfillment is happiness. What I am saying is that this pleasure in the exercise of virtue is so fully an expression of what is right and proper to one's being that it is as important to one's satisfaction overall as a human being that one experience this form of contentment as that one experiences that form of contentment that is pleasure in the sum of the fulfillment of one's desires. In insisting on using the same word for these kinds of states, I thus seek to move us closer to a more

---

[37] I am here perhaps relying implicitly upon Watson's (1983) line of argument when he compellingly shows that, despite the myriad ways pursuit of it can go wrong and become an enemy of virtue, happiness is not something that we should wish we could extricate from a human life, but is instead part and parcel of a well-lived human life. As Watson puts the point: "A good life for us as human beings—as finite, rational creatures with needs—simply could not be a life that failed to meet our basic needs and interests... [S]uch a fate would prompt the judgment that their existence as finite rational beings is lacking in something significantly good" (Watson 1983, 93). Further: "Kant's position is that human beings necessarily will care significantly about the fulfillment of their natural needs and desires. Even if we were perfect in virtue, our contentment with our lives on the whole would depend upon fortune. When things go very badly (and virtue does not preclude this), we will not be happy. While [moral] self-contentment is not irrelevant to happiness—not excluded by definition—it is simply insufficient to provide us with contentment with our lives on the whole" (p. 93).

unified conception of what it is to be "satisfied" overall, as a sensibly affected rational being. Happiness empirically conceived is not the only game in town as a candidate for such satisfactions. In pushing the import of reading Kant in a way that affirms such unity, I thus once again affirm my deep sympathy with Watson (1983) who, almost forty years ago now, affirmed that we need to seek a unity overall in the state of contentment that one experiences. And my insistence on calling this contentment of oneself "happiness" is just another effort to emphasize that unity of forms of satisfaction with which Kant is concerned. To again quote the conclusion of Watson's work:

> [T]o live a life appropriate to a human being is to organize and pursue the satisfaction of one's needs and interests under the discipline of practical reason. To live under that discipline is to be virtuous; to succeed to a significant degree in one's pursuits is to fare well. One's contentment with one's life on the whole will properly depend upon both of these factors. And happiness consists in such contentment. Therefore, happiness has an eminent place in Kant's theory of value. (Watson 1983, 94)

I'll admit that even Watson doesn't want to call the moral half of this contentment "happiness." His larger goal is to show that happiness empirically conceived is as important a state of satisfaction as any state of satisfaction with explicitly moral content or object. But at this point, I challenge both him and Kant: if we all agree that the human being can experience states of satisfaction that are central to the proper functioning of the kind of being she is, and if we agree that one of these kinds of states is found in desire-satisfaction and the other is found in the excellent harmonious functioning of one's rational will and capacity for choice, why not call these both happinesses, just of different sorts?[38]

Objections to the Assertion of a Pleasurable Life of Virtue

I want to pause here, as there are other objections one might raise to the story I'm presenting. Isn't this pleasurable exercise of virtue simply *Schwärmerei*, that moral enthusiasm in which I take precisely the *wrong* relationship to the law, assuming that I am more capable than in fact I am in fulfilling it, and ignoring the inextirpable parts of my being in need of constraint for the sake of it? For, as Kant reminds us,

---

[38] I will return to the questions of the "unity" of these different modes of satisfaction with one's state, and also to the commitment to a claim of genuine non-moral value that comes with this hope of unity, toward the end of II.iii.

it is always necessary for [the dutiful person] to base the disposition of his maxims on moral *necessitation*, *not* on ready fidelity but on respect, which demands compliance with the law even though this is done *reluctantly*; *not* on love, which is not anxious about any inner refusal of the will toward the law. (5:84/71–72)

To love the law—or to take pleasure in one's fulfillment of it—seems to be in conflict with respecting it. Respect is reluctant, but pleasure or love would not be reluctant, or "anxious," or even *aware* of, any internal opposition to the law. But it is just this *respect* for the law, and *not* love for it, that must be the proper motive of the virtuous person. The moral *law* is a moral *imperative*, a relationship to that law which assumes the identification within oneself of inextirpable "subjective limitations and hindrances" (4:397/10) to its fulfillment. But the person of virtue exercising her aptitude for virtue pleasurably seems to lack all such hindrances.

One surely does have to avoid enthusiasm. But enthusiasm is *not* defined as taking pleasure in the exercise of virtue. Enthusiasm is when I become *arrogant* and *self-conceited* about my capacity to fulfill the demands of duty, turning the point of duty *away* from the law and *toward* celebratory self-aggrandizement. When Kant talks about enthusiasm, he thus tends to associate it not with love or pleasure, but with attitudes of nobility, sublimity, or magnanimity, all of which, as we saw in our discussion of moral pedagogy in II.i, he takes to imply arrogance. Here is one example of such discussions, one which very clearly mirrors the language of magnanimity and merit which we saw the student of virtue being taught to avoid:

> By exhortation to actions as noble, sublime, and magnanimous, minds are attuned to nothing but moral enthusiasm and exaggerated self-conceit; by such exhortations they are led into the delusion that it is not duty—that is, respect for the law…—which constitutes the determining ground of their actions and which always humbles them inasmuch as they observe the law, but that it is as if those actions are expected from them, not from duty but as bare merit.
> (5:84–85/72)

The lesson we took in moral education from II.i re-emerges here as a general admonition to the would-be virtuous person, young or old: to avoid moral enthusiasm, focus on respect for the law, not vain, self-centered hopes for nobility or magnanimity of person. Once again, then, Kant worries that these quasi-Aristotelian exhortations to nobility and magnanimity in a life of virtue get at just the wrong point: they encourage a sort of self-absorbed way of taking up duty, turning the point of duty away from concern for the law and making it more an opportunity for celebratory self-aggrandizement. Kant's fascination with Gallows-Man-style examples of strong toleration of sacrifice can, once again, be put into proper relief here: in appealing to the strength of persons who sacrifice things for the sake of virtue, we find a way of displaying how admirable and selfless the strength of virtue is *without* doing anything to engage that self-absorption or self-conceit that would be virtue's biggest enemy and downfall.

Such self-conceit does not, however, result from taking pleasure in the life of virtue. It comes instead when one *stops* respecting the *law* and instead focuses only on being very impressed with *oneself*. One thus needn't worry that Kant's concerns about enthusiasm do anything to make the life of virtue incompatible with pleasure. Such assumptions are just wrong.

To say that I take pleasure in the life of virtue is thus entirely compatible with the idea that I accept the proper relationship of myself to the law as one of respect and, with that, an admission that the law is authorized to *constrain* any subjective hindrances within me which oppose it. Pleasure in the exercise of virtue is not a replacement for the need respectfully to do one's duty; such pleasure is, rather, the frame of mind within which one experiences the height of successful respectful adherence to the law.

Conclusions on Pleasure and Happiness

We thus accept, even at the height of virtue, an indirect and transcendentally ideal route to appreciation of one's positive freedom. This experience of ease or facility at the heart of one's happiness, rationally conceived, is not a pure out-of-body experience of rationality and positive freedom as such, but instead a pleasurable experience of the height of what is possible for a sensibly affected being: an experience of the unyielding facility, alacrity, and ease expressed in the perfect alignment of one's *Wille* and *Willkür*.

To preserve Kant's Transcendentally Ideal commitments, we thus reject the idea that the virtuous person literally pulls herself out of her sensible self and experiences herself always and only as a rational being. That is simply not possible. Indeed, it is not even desirable. This is just the point of the parallel we drew with Kierkegaard's Knight of Faith: the alacrity and ease with which the Knight manages finitude and infinitude is a marvelous and elegant feat of holding together two sides of a paradox. He does not abandon the finite world for the sake of the infinite. To the contrary, that is what the lesser Knight of Infinite Resignation does. In Kierkegaard's words (well, Johannes de Climicus'), what the Knight of Infinite Resignation does "is a bagatelle," or a simple game to play. To abandon one's finite and sensible self for a purely infinite and rational self is, in the end, something very simple and not very interesting! The harder thing is to live so coherent, elegant, and marvelous a life while holding seamlessly together such apparently discordant elements: the finite and the infinite, for Kierkegaard; or the sensible and the rational, for Kant.

What *is* possible then—and marvelous—for the person who experiences the free aptitude for virtue is that her felt sensible experience of negative freedom, along with her experience of ease in the perfect alignment of her *Wille* and *Willkür* culminate in a pleasurable and happy experience of the exercise of virtue. Our fully virtuous person has successfully removed impediments to virtue: that is the negative freedom part. But as she continues, day-in and day-out, to act free from impediments, she experiences the *naturalness*, the *rightness*, the *pleasure* of being the kind of being she was meant to be. This is not just the sensible pleasure of being free from something else, but, more profoundly, the pleasure of being most fully and excellently oneself: one experiences the proper activity of one's person as just exactly what one was meant to do and be. One thus realizes the ultimate telos of one's being, and we call this state happiness, rationally or intellectually conceived.

In reflecting upon this necessarily indirect route to a notion of happiness, rationally conceived, I am reminded of Kant's admonition in the introduction to the *Critique of Pure Reason* (an admonition that remained intact and in the same form in both the A and B editions of the *Critique*), an admonition to avoid the admittedly splendid excesses, temptations, and blandishments of pure rationalism. His admonition takes the form of an analogy between the aspirations of the human spirit for knowing and a dove. Having just reflected on how mathematics "gives us a splendid example of how far we can go with a priori cognition independently of experience" (A4/B8), he goes on to reflect:

> Captivated by such a proof of the power of reason, the drive for expansion sees no bounds. The light dove, in free flight cutting through the air the resistance of which it feels, could get the idea that it could do even better in airless space. Likewise, Plato abandoned the world of the senses because it set such narrow limits for the understanding, and dared to go beyond it on the wings of the ideas, in the empty space of pure understanding. He did not notice that he made no headway by his efforts, for he had no resistance, no support, as it were, by which he could stiffen himself, and to which he could apply his powers in order to put his understanding into motion. (A5/B8–9)

In retrospect, Elizondo's effort to identify a thoroughly rational feeling and a thoroughly non-sensible experience of pleasure in rational activity falls victim to the dove admonition: this dove needs air resistance (viz., some sort of appeal to sensibility) in order to fly (i.e., in order to access knowledge). In practical terms, that resistance can be found only in the connection of one's rational self with one's sensibly affected will. I thus distinguish my account from Elizondo's in that while he welcomes the notion of an explicitly and thoroughly intellectual feeling and activity, I instead welcome a virtuous person who finds her pleasure by seeking "resistance" in the need to bring her sensible self into alignment with her rational will. This is a more indirect way of getting to the pleasure of the activity of the virtuous will: it is not a pure experience of that will itself but instead an experience of the alignment of the rational and sensible parts of herself, an alignment which is experienced in the ease or facility with which one exercises virtue. By finding "resistance" in the need to govern and align one's sensible self as part of the story of accomplishing this ease of activity, we identify that pleasurable experience of virtue simultaneously attendant to the constraints of Transcendental Idealism, and possible for a specifically sensibly affected rational being.

In telling this story about the happiness one finds in the pleasurable exercise of the free aptitude for virtue—all while rejecting any would-be sense-free pure rational feeling of positive freedom itself—we thus underscore, even as we welcome a rational notion of happiness, Kant's enduring commitment to Transcendental Idealism, viz. to the idea that we are beings who engage with the world from both the rational and the sensible perspectives.

IV. Caveat #1 to Happiness: Virtually Unimpeded Activity

Aristotle Problems

One might, however, challenge this picture of the pleasant life of virtue from another direction: does the virtuous person thusly described *have* any subjective hindrances to virtue which need constraining? This is a vexed question because if she *does*, then it's hard to envision the life of virtue as a life of pleasure; but if she *doesn't*, we've lost our grip on the distinctively Kantian conception of morality as an imperative which assumes constraint at its core. Underlying this worry is another distinction traditionally made between Kantian and Aristotelian conceptions of virtue beyond the contrast between duty and magnanimity we noted earlier: Aristotle is thought traditionally to accept the idea that one could attain a state of *perfect* virtue in which one has absolutely no obstacles to its pursuit, but Kant is thought traditionally to accept the idea that virtuous fulfillment of duty *always* involves constraint of *something* within oneself opposed to the law. But where are we now with this distinction, since we admit the possibility of a human being with an aptitude for virtue whose will and choice so perfectly mirror each other as we've suggested above? Aren't we saying that the person who has realized inner freedom in her person as an aptitude for virtue no longer has any obstacles to virtue? Have we thereby lost the sense of Kantian morality as an imperative?

This is a fair worry, and one that needs to be addressed. What we shall see is that although the person of complete inner freedom has really left behind the internal conflict and dilemma of Hercules at the crossroads, she must still nonetheless maintain a humble vigilance in her continued pursuit of virtue, a vigilance that the perfect Aristotelian person of virtue would reject as unnecessary. This need for vigilance is grounded in the consideration that one must remember that virtue is always in progress precisely because changing circumstances in an empirical world always provide the conditions for one's ever-present bare propensity for evil to raise its head and express itself. Ultimately, it is not so much the presence of would-be rogue inclinations as such, but the underlying non-inclination-based rational propensity to evil that is always present (and in potential need of constraint) that explains why even the fully virtuous person of inner freedom needs to maintain an attitude of humble vigilance, and needs to accept the ever-present possibility of finding something within herself in need of constraint. We thus affirm this pleasurable exercise of an aptitude for virtue even as we maintain a distinction between such aptitude and Aristotle's would-be perfect virtuous person. Let us reflect on these ideas further.

The first point to appreciate, then, is that although our free and virtuous Hercules at the top of the mountain of virtue has realized a perfect mirroring of his will and choice, he cannot thereby say that he is done with his pursuit of virtue. To the contrary, Kant reminds us both that virtue is *always* in progress and that it always, in a certain sense, must start from the *beginning*:

> Virtue is always in progress and yet always starts from the beginning.—It is always in progress because, considered *objectively*, it is an ideal and unattainable, while yet constant approximation to it is a duty. That it always starts from the beginning has a *subjective* basis in human nature, which is affected by inclinations because of which virtue can never settle down in peace and quiet with its maxims adopted once and for all but, if it is not rising, is unavoidably sinking.
>
> (6:409/167)

Kant makes two distinct points here, one "objective" and one "subjective." Let us consider each in turn.

First, Kant says that one is always in the process of pursuing virtue because it is an unattainable ideal the pursuit of which must always be understood as a mere approximation of that ideal. On the face of it, this claim is in contradiction with Kant's suggestion, noted earlier, that the person of virtue achieves a perfect symmetry of her will and choice within which she stops understanding herself as even needing to choose between two alternatives.[39] Hasn't this person actually *attained* what Kant is here calling an *un*attainable ideal of virtue? In what possible sense could we say that our Hercules has *not* fully attained virtue? Otherwise stated: in

---

[39] See especially that the person of inner freedom "cannot lose his virtue" (6:405/164), and further, that, for such a person, it is not so much "as if a human being possesses virtue but rather as if virtue possesses him; for in the former case [him possessing virtue] *it would look as if he still had a choice* (for which he would need yet another virtue" (6:406/165, emphasis added).

what possible sense could we say that our Hercules still has within himself *obstacles* to the perfect harmony of his will and choice?

It is at this point that we need to emphasize that the person of virtue is still a being subject to radical evil. Kant himself does not always emphasize this point in the Doctrine of Virtue as much as I think he should. But when we put his Doctrine of Virtue reflections on virtue together with his more extensive *Religion* discussion of radical evil, the following picture emerges. It may well be that the person of virtue has all her current felt attachments—her affects, inclinations, and passions—in order; she has acquired a rational control of her sensible self. But the very condition for the possibility of evil does not lie in our sensible inclinations. The propensity to evil is, as we noted earlier, a mutinous plotter within the City of Reason itself.[40] As such, we must admit that, even when all one's felt attachments are in order, there is still within even the most virtuous of persons the bare possibility that she will choose to take up one of her passing affects or inclinations in a way that places concerns for self above her respect for morality. Humans are, in other words, *always* tempted to prefer the self to other persons and objects of value. This, I would suggest, is the "objective" point that Kant is making when he says that virtue, as an ideal, is unattainable. To say that virtue is an unattainable ideal is simply to say that it is impossible for a state of virtue ever to be such that it contains absolutely no potential opposition to it. Even if one's affects, passions, and inclinations are in order, we must accept at the heart of human nature a bare tendency to prefer oneself.

This objective fact of one's propensity to evil is, furthermore, tied to the second "subjective," claim that Kant makes: we humans are always subject to inclinations. More precisely, we humans, simply because of the natural, physical, and sensible world within which we find ourselves, are *always* subject to affects, or surprise inclinations. The variability and unpredictability of the sensible, physical world in which we live assures that we will always encounter changes in circumstances and experiences. But that means we will also always encounter *new* opportunities—ways we hadn't previously considered—to take up inclinations in a way counter to the moral law. We have, in II.i, indeed said that the person of inner freedom is the person of composure, and such composure is expressed as "moral apathy," that is as "the *absence* of affects" (6:408/166–167, emphasis added) that would oppose her objective telos of making persons as such her end. But given that the human being is, in part, a sensible being in a sensible world, there is no avoiding the possibility that even the most composed person will, through surprise engagement with something new in the messy empirical world, be *affected*. That is, there is no avoiding the possibility of new and unexpected affects even in the person of composure.

---

[40] I have argued this point at greater length in Grenberg (2010a).

We discussed this point in II.i, when we first thought about the subduing of one's affects and considered what it meant, really, to be composed. Then, we came to the conclusion that composure involves generally the absence of surprising affects but also the occasional possibility of needing to manage a surprise affect without letting it disrupt one's reflections. That is, the person of composure has the ability to get a hold of herself when the odd, unexpected affect (caused not by her own bad choices but simply by new circumstances which arise in the natural world within which she finds herself) does arise. The import of this point for our overall account of virtue now reveals itself: Kant's conviction is that the life of a being who is at least partly sensible or natural cannot be said to have absolutely clean lines or borders around it. One's rationality does do the work of ordering one's soul. But one's soul finds itself in a natural world, a world within which one cannot make oneself into an absolute and complete whole.[41] As such, even the most virtuous of person finds herself in a world within which she must expect the unexpected, that is, within which she must expect to experience new and various affects in relation to new and constantly changing circumstances.

But when we put this subjective fact together with the previous objective one (viz., that all humans have a tendency toward radical evil), then the reason that we must accept that Kantian virtue is not absolutely perfect and never-changing Aristotelian virtue becomes clear: a combination of the inevitable experience of new inclinations (or old ones now within new and more tempting circumstances) with one's radically evil tendency to place concerns for one's own happiness above all else leads to the ever-present possibility that one will take up one of these surprise inclinations in a way that undermines the work of virtue that led you to the mountaintop. In other words, one can indeed topple from that mountain of virtue, perhaps making a rather dramatic fall to the bottom where one finds Hedone waiting hopefully again at that same crossroads one had long ago left behind.

So, while all one's inclinations are in order, one's propensity to evil still exists. And this propensity is not something that *could* be extirpated. One's inclinations can be constrained, calmed, cultivated. I can even get to the point where I do not generally experience affects, as such, but only calmer emotional moments. But one's bare tendency to prefer the self and its pursuit of happiness to morality is something always potentially ready to strike, seeking to reclaim one's inclinations for its own purposes, and returning us to that exhausting affect-filled and passion-guided world of the vicious. As a result, even the fully virtuous person must welcome a constant vigilance in her life. Or, as Kant puts the point: "human morality *in its highest stage* can still be nothing more than virtue, even if it be entirely pure (quite free from the influence of any incentive other than that of duty)" (6:383/148, emphasis added). If one does not maintain vigilance in the ways that new

---

[41] This point takes us back to our I.i rejection of happiness empirically conceived as the proper telos for a human life. The natural world is, inherently, a messy world.

circumstances and experiences in life tempt one's ever-present propensity to prefer oneself to all else, then even a perfect aptitude for virtue can easily, and will eventually, be lost.

One can thus now appreciate, in a new context, Kant's claim that "if [virtue] is not rising, [it] is unavoidably sinking" (6:409/167). His worry here is that even the person of perfect virtue could, through inattentive engagement in the empirical world, wake up one morning and find that her aptitude for free action has already descended or decomposed into mere, and unvirtuous, habits. If one does not constantly do the work of virtue—that is, that contemplation of the dignity of the law and that practice of virtuous choice of which we spoke in II.i—then we can be assured that it will lose its hold on one's person: "[I]f the practice of virtue were to become a habit [instead of remain an aptitude] the subject would suffer that loss of freedom in adopting his maxims which distinguishes an action done from duty" (6:409/167). It would not be hard at all, unthinkingly, simply to fall back into non-virtuous habits, leaving our carefully cultivated aptitude for virtue behind.[42]

We must thus accept that even the virtuous person no longer at the crossroads may need, at times, at least to remind herself of her previous choice of virtue over self-aggrandizement. This should not lead us, however, to assume that the work of virtue has been for naught. The crucial thing to remember is that, with one's aptitude for virtue in place, one is well-situated to continue to pursue virtue even in the face of unexpected and surprising turns of fortune and affects. Without this aptitude "[virtue] is neither armed for all situations nor adequately secured

---

[42] I make this same point at greater length, and in response to Stephen Enstrom, in Grenberg (2010a, 168–169): "Although Engstrom suggests that Kantian virtue is more similar to Aristotle's virtue than continence, things aren't so straightforward. There is a parallel to be drawn between the apathy of the Kantian virtuous person and the unconflicted state of the Aristotelian virtuous person. But there is also a similarity to be admitted between Kantian virtue and Aristotelian continence: for both, something in the person is in tension with the 'right' way to go, and thus needs to be constrained. For Kant, the thing in need of constraint is not (as it is for Aristotle) natural inclinations themselves, but rather something at the heart of reason itself (not just that part of the rational soul meant to obey reason, but that part of the rational soul that gives reasons). The state of conflict for the Kantian virtuous person is thus somewhat different from that of the Aristotelian continent person. Consider: the person who admits an inextirpable conflict between reason operating properly and reason tempted toward rationalization could, at the very same time, have developed a state of her feelings in accord with reason operating properly. She could, that is, be beyond Aristotelian continence. Her conflict is not one of reason versus inclinations; it is a conflict within reason itself. Often, though not always, one's feelings will express the unruly side of one's freedom. But when one has trained one's feelings toward virtue, then the Kantian virtuous person has gone beyond continence even as she admits something in her that could tempt her astray. Her house is in order, but a potential threat remains. She is thus not the person of 'complete excellence' in the Aristotelian sense, since this would be a state in which one has no fear of internal, mutinous factions. But Kant cannot accept this ideal: humans are not 'finite holy beings (who could never be tempted to violate duty)' (MS 6:383). Indeed, were such beings to exist, 'there would be [for them] no doctrine of virtue but only a doctrine of morals.' We humans can only take holiness as a regulative 'ideal (to which one must continually approximate),' not as an attainable goal. All of this is, however, just as it should be. This state of strength in the face of an inextirpable enemy is that state of virtue most appropriate to *human* beings, not the Aristotelian dream of a divine (Kant would say 'holy') state."

against the changes that new temptations could bring about" (6:384/148). But of course, *with* this aptitude, one *is* armed for all situations and *is* adequately secured against the changes that new temptations could bring about! One experiences even new temptations and new, unexpected situations *with composure*.[43]

As such, unlike what one might be tempted to say of Aristotle's fully virtuous person, Kant's fully virtuous person must always maintain a certain vigilance, since: "human morality in its highest stage can still be nothing more than virtue, *even if it be entirely pure* (quite free from the influence of any incentive other than that of duty)" (6:383/148, emphasis added). Even at its height, virtue as strength (achieved through inner freedom as a free aptitude in the exercise of one's rational will) is virtue *as strength*, that is, not the perfect blemish-less virtue of Aristotle, or a state in which it is not even possible to think about doing something wrong, but instead a *strength* to *oppose* would-be vicious inclinations and dispositions.

Humble Vigilance in the Pursuit of Virtue

Let's explore the nature of this state of vigilance in more detail. We had started this discussion with the worry of an irresolvable dilemma: if the virtuous person *does* have opposing inclinations to constrain, then it is hard to envision the life of virtue as a life of pleasure; but if she *doesn't* have opposing inclinations to constrain, we've lost our grip on the distinctively Kantian conception of morality as an imperative which assumes constraint at its core. Our appeal to vigilance in the exercise of one's aptitude for virtue provides us, however, with a happy middle position which refuses both horns of this dilemma. A life characterized by *constant* constraint of rebellious temptations wouldn't be consistent with a life of pleasure. But pleasure *can* sit entirely, uh, happily with a *certain* amount of internal opposition to law. It is not necessary that one be Aristotle's absolutely perfect magnanimous man of virtue in order to take pleasure in virtue. To affirm such

---

[43] What we see here in this person of composure is something very similar to what Alasdair MacIntyre (1981) has called the virtue of "constancy." For MacIntyre, the person who is constant remains the same person she is even as circumstances shift and flow. Whatever changes occur—and whatever new temptations are revealed in those new and unexpected situations—she remains the same person that she is, committed to the same values and able to rely upon the same cultivated and therefore calm emotional reactions to counteract any new and would-be rogue inclinations. But the solidity in the person of inner freedom with an aptitude for virtue who really has only one path—one live option—even in the face of new circumstances is just this person of constancy. MacIntyre identifies constancy as a central virtue especially in the characters in Jane Austen's books. Virtue demands constancy in the world of Austen's heroines because Austen's world is one in which many things are changing in her society, and her virtuous person needs to be someone for whom certain things remain firm and unchanging amidst all that social flux. But the language of inner freedom accomplishes that same task, and does so in a way that confirms Austen's concern for virtues of all sorts are tied to related notions of freedom and duty.

compatibility of virtue and pleasure, the internal opposition to virtue must, admittedly, be rather *slim*. But with the picture of the person of virtue we have just drawn, we can affirm just this: the virtuous person, while *recognizing* some internal opposition to respecting the law, has also done an awful lot to *minimize* that internal opposition—she has, after all, removed all affects and passions in opposition to her rational will—and thus, generally, takes pleasure in the exercise of virtue.

Reflection upon the overall moral psychological structure of the virtuous person as compared to that of the vicious person will make this point. To do so, we must, once again, place the idea of the virtuous person as presented in the Doctrine of Virtue alongside the person of radical evil as presented in the *Religion*. Once we do so, we see that the choice and end-setting by which one pursues virtue is guided, as with any and all of one's choices, by a meta-maxim which either places pursuit of desire-fulfillment above respect for morality, or viceversa.[44] The virtuous person has chosen the latter option, and we have understood this choice as the abandonment of any self-absorbed pursuit of desire-fulfillment in the name of making one's objective telos of making persons as such one's end the center of one's life. The opposite choice, of the vicious person, would be the story of a mutinous self-governance guided by an inclination that has been illicitly raised into a ruling passion.

On this picture, the virtuous person has her sensibly grounded felt attachments in perspective via appeal to her objective telos of making persons as such her end; her previously unwieldy and tumultuous experience of strong and contrary affects and passions has been moderated. She has become the person of moral tranquility. The fully virtuous person with an aptitude for virtue might even have *all* her affects, passions, and inclinations in this well-chaperoned state: she has no *active* or *present* inclinations to constrain as such. Nonetheless, such a person still has an inextirpable propensity to evil present in her moral consciousness. This propensity is best understood as the ever-present temptation (on some level) to collapse back into that self-absorption that is a passion-ruled life. That is just what it means to say that human beings are subject to radical evil at the basis of their choice and end-setting. Even when I commit to placing concern for persons above desire-fulfillment, and even when that commitment has pervaded my world of desire, this bare temptation to return to that self-absorbed state still exists within me.

To say that this is a bare *propensity* instead of the guiding *principle* of one's self-governance gets across, though, just how different the internal lives of the

---

[44] In the *Religion*, Kant notes two possible meta-maxims: placing concern for self-love above the law, or placing concern for the law above self-love: "[T]he difference, whether the human being is good or evil, must not lie in the difference between the incentives that he incorporates into his maxim (not in the material of the maxim) but in their subordination (in the form of the maxim): which of the two he makes the condition of the other" (6:36/59).

virtuous and vicious persons are. The vicious person has insured a rather high level of conflict within herself: both her propensity to evil and the governance of her inclinations are in concerted opposition to her inextirpable voice of conscience reminding her of the absolute value of persons. And Kant is quite emphatic about the reliability and staying power of that voice of conscience, even in someone thoroughly taken up by a mutinous ruling passion:

> Every human being has a conscience and finds himself observed, threatened, and, in general, kept in awe (respect coupled with fear) by an internal judge; and this authority watching over the law in him is not something that he himself (voluntarily) makes, but something incorporated in his being. It follows him like his shadow when he plans to escape. He can indeed stun himself or put himself to sleep by pleasures and distractions, but he cannot help coming to himself or waking up from time to time; and when he does, he hears at once its fearful voice. He can at most, in extreme depravity, bring himself to heed it no longer, but he still cannot help hearing it. (6:438/189)

This persistence of the voice of conscience in the vicious person really is just further affirmation of the idea that the telos of making persons as such one's end is the objective telos of one's being. What we are meant to be is built into our persons, "incorporated in [one's] being." So one might choose to guide oneself in all sorts of ways that set this telos aside. But, given that it is simply a built-in expression of who one is, the voice of conscience which tracks the nature of one's being will not go away. Rather, "it follows [one] like [one's] shadow." We can thus envision what the subjective experience of the vicious person would be like: it will be somewhat akin to a civil war in which mutinous forces are in constant battle with legitimate ones. One claims an illicit governance structure, but the depths of one's being rebels against that choice.[45]

Even someone who is not fully vicious but is still struggling to acquire virtue would also face a relatively high level of internal conflict. She might not have to

---

[45] I thus diverge at this point from Forman (2016), who accepts the idea that the vicious person *could* be unbothered by her conscience: "Kant thus considers it a refutation of the eudaimonist's attempt to unite virtue and happiness to point out that the virtuous man suffers especially acute pangs of conscience, giving him a 'gloomy air,' while the wicked man is 'often in full enjoyment of his happiness' since 'the greater the villain, the less does conscience plague him' (VMo-MronII, 29:623; cf. *KpV* 5:38.18–22 and *TP* 8:283n.29–35).20 And Kant makes essentially the same point against those who defend God's justice by claiming that the wicked are punished by their own consciences: it is a delusion to think that the workings of conscience provide for the harmony between virtue and happiness that would be needed to find justice in this world ('Theodicee,' 8:261)" (Forman 2016, 86). Although I agree that the pangs of conscience the vicious person experiences may not be adequate for establishing divine justice, and can even agree that the pang of conscience in a virtuous person may have a particular edge to it because of her keener attentiveness to the demands of morality, Kant's Doctrine of Virtue insistence that no one can escape the pangs of conscience is, I think, something that puts especially the *Lectures on Ethics* comments to which Forman appeals in perspective.

fight a mutinous attitude of principled objection to the moral law; but she could still very easily have a whole range of inclinations counter to the law which demand regular and active constraint and attention.

But the virtuous person has ordered all her desires in accordance with her conscience-driven demand to make persons as such her end. Both her life-guiding principle *and* the state of her affects, passions, and inclinations are in agreement with her conscience at the depth of her being. The *only* thing in her opposed to this order is the bare temptation to revert to self-absorption, an opposition to the law which, while still present, has been reduced to the merest of logical points. This is, of course, a logical point to which one needs occasionally to *attend*. But this is just our point: such attentiveness to that barest of logical points in the face of changing circumstances and affects is precisely what "vigilance" about the state of one's virtue is. New opportunities for self-absorption could trigger a revolution in one's self-governance, allowing self-conceit to become the ruling principle of one's soul. The virtuous person thus welcomes vigilance into her life to manage such possibilities.

But *vigilance*, thusly defined, is not *conflict*. Indeed, to the contrary, this vigilance is yet another particularly valuable tool within the moral psychology of the virtuous person for helping to assure that one maintains that *humility* which prevents one's pleasure in a virtuous life from becoming a problematic enthusiasm for morality which thinks it can be perfect, noble, and magnanimous and thus trips over itself into self-absorption. Enthusiasm, as we have seen, assumes arrogance. And it is the temptation toward precisely such arrogance-based enthusiasm—just exactly that enthusiasm against which the young student of virtue was warned and which we discussed in II.i—which provides a particularly tricky and surreptitious way in which self-absorption can re-emerge from the very heart of virtue: when one begins to take excessive pride in one's realization of virtue and thus presents oneself as the ultimate and noble arbiter and expression of virtue, then one's virtue has descended into vice. But *love* of virtue *rejects* this arrogance, and instead *humbly* embraces vigilance.

Kant's suspicion of a noble and magnanimous cast of mind thus leads to humility at the heart of virtue. It might seem more attractive to seek a conception of virtue grounded in nobility, but such nobility all too easily casts one back toward a self-absorbed and vicious instead of a person-centered, vigilant, and virtuous state of mind. One must thus reject nobility and cling instead to humble vigilance.[46]

But a life of humble vigilance is entirely compatible with a pleasurable life of virtue. Kant even suggests, at the very end of his ethical ascetics that is, that the

---

[46] I have written previously at great length (in Grenberg 2005) about the centrality of humility for Kantian virtue. This affirmation that the avoidance of arrogance is not just one virtue amongst others but, more than that, an attitude at the absolute center of pursuit of any and all other states of virtue is a final affirmation of the claim made there about the centrality of this virtue.

heart of one's education into virtue, not only that, beyond pleasure, even an attendant *cheerfulness* in the exercise of virtue is *compatible* with virtue but also that one would not be fully virtuous unless this were the quality of one's subjective experience: "[T]he training (discipline) that a human being practices on himself can become meritorious and exemplary *only* through the cheerfulness that accompanies it" (6:485/228, emphasis added). Fortunately, though, Kant also seems to find such cheerfulness not something that must be produced or pursued, but instead something that simply emerges as the supervening subjective expression of the state of virtue: "For who should have more cause to be cheerful and not even find it a duty to put himself in a cheerful state of mind and to make it his habit, than someone who is conscious of no intentional transgression, and who is secured against a downfall into it?" (6:485/227) It is, in other words, precisely the person who has acquired an aptitude for virtue informed by humble vigilance—someone who has "secured against a downfall" into transgressions—who will, simply, find herself one day to be a cheerful person engaged in the pleasurable exercise of virtue, without even having tried consciously to get herself into the habit of cheerfulness as such.

Indeed, given the reduction of conflict within the virtuous person which we've described—and especially the removal of all affects, passions, and inclinations that would be in opposition to her virtue—one can even say that the fully virtuous person's pleasurable exercise of the aptitude for virtue, free of conflict though vigilant of the possibility of self-conceited temptations to take hold, is a good overall Kantian description of that state of "unimpeded activity" which Aristotle defines as eudaemonia. The only possible impediment is the merely logical possibility that she could, in the future, and in the face of new and changing circumstances, choose to indulge her propensity for evil. We thus admit that while her activity of virtue is not *perfectly* unimpeded, it is *virtually* unimpeded.

One might worry that it is too strong to say that the activity of virtue is virtually unimpeded. Can one really speak of virtue as *strength* if it is not *actively* engaged in restraining or constraining some strong opponent? It is important to remember here that, for Kant, the presence of an opponent of virtue is what makes the strength of virtue *perspicuous*. As Kant notes: we "hav[e] no way to measure the degree of a strength except by the magnitude of the obstacles it could overcome (in us, these are inclinations)" (6:397/158). But the presence of an opponent does not *define* the strength of virtue as such. To assume that would be "to mistake the subjective conditions by which we assess the magnitude for the objective conditions of the magnitude itself" (6:397/158). The strength of virtue can thus be defined positively and objectively as the established commitment expressed throughout one's end-setting to make persons as such one's end, and this requires no appeal to an opponent, even as we admit that *perceiving* this strength would indeed require such an opponent.

We do, of course, admit though that, unlike Aristotle's dream of a perfectly virtuous person who experiences absolutely nothing within herself contrary to virtue, the Kantian virtuous person is never perfect: she always has *something* within her at least *potentially* in conflict with her virtue. Does this mean, though, that Kant is not a *eudaemonist*? If we admit that all sensibly affected rational beings have something inextirpable within them opposed to morality, is it impossible for that kind of being to function properly, and thereby unite her exercise of virtue and experience of pleasure? The assumption that a properly functioning life would have to be a *perfect* life in order to be a *pleasurable* life is, however, far too quick an assumption to make. We have just told a story of Kant's virtuous person in whom these subjective hindrances ensconced in one's propensity toward evil are so minimal and well-managed that one's subjective experience of being a person of virtue is not one of conflict, sullenness, and reluctance, but instead one in which—even as she maintains a humble vigilance about her inextirpable tendency toward self-absorption—the person of virtue generally experiences her life as one of healthiness, tranquility, pleasure, and cheerfulness. Even the admission of an inextirpable propensity toward evil self-absorption thus does nothing to undermine our claim that Kant's virtue theory is eudaemonistic.

V. Caveat #2 to Happiness: A Postscript on Suffering in the Life of Virtue

I've noted in passing, though, that there is a caveat to the claim that a supervenience relationship obtains between successful exercise of virtue which realizes one's objective telos and a positive and pleasurable subjective state in the experience of such exercise that expresses and facilitates realization of that objective telos. Now is finally the time to address this caveat: given the context of unpredictable nature within which one pursues a life of virtue, what would otherwise be a necessary connection between these two objective and subjective poles of virtue will not always obtain. That is: the pleasure I take in exercising my aptitude for virtue[47] might be vitiated by external circumstances outside of my control. The assurance of taking pleasure in virtue is thus not a *strictly* necessary outcome of pursuing the life of virtue.

One might be tempted to think otherwise. For example, one might say that while pleasure in being *virtuous* has a *necessary* connection to the exercise of virtue, non-moral pleasures related only to happiness and not to virtue do not have this necessary connection, and this is precisely because they are more susceptible to the vicissitudes of fortune than the pleasure I take in virtue. However tempting

---

[47] And the pleasure I take in non-moral end-setting and activities related to happiness as well, but that is a topic for II.iii.

such a suggestion might be to some, this just isn't quite right for making sense of Deontological Eudaemonism; and it is, indeed, another quality of Deontological Eudaemonsim that distinguishes it from Stoicism. The Stoic believes that the only thing of value is virtue and that when one has this virtue nothing else can injure or tarnish it. There is a sort of self-sufficiency to the Stoic person of virtue that protects her entirely from injury, and even allows her to enjoy or take pleasure in her virtue even in the worst of circumstances. But as we saw in II.i, this self-sufficiency comes at a cost: the utter rejection of value to anything except the successful exercise of virtue. Kant, to the contrary, thinks that in Gallows-Man-like circumstances the pleasure of the exercise of virtue *can* be lost; and, as we'll see in II.iii, he also thinks that in the pursuit of virtue, all *sorts* of pleasures related to one's pursuit of happiness can be lost. That is, both moral *and* non-moral pleasures are equally susceptible to being undermined by forces outside oneself and by circumstances external to one's control. We will consider what this means for moral pleasures and the exercise of virtue here, a discussion which returns us to the earlier question of the relationship of virtue and suffering; we will then turn in the next chapter to consideration of the extent to which the exercise of virtue is compatible with the pursuit of happiness empirically conceived.

We begin, then, by reflecting on the extent to which toleration of the sacrifice of external goods is consistent with an overall pleasurable and flourishing life. We have said, in II.i, that the person of virtue has a particular capacity for managing the need to sacrifice: this is her moral apathetic capacity for toleration of sacrifice. This strong internal state is the central means for managing the obstacles presented to the would-be virtuous person by the external world. Are there *limits*, though, to this toleration, limits such that the sacrifices demanded in a virtuous life could eclipse, or even destroy, the pleasure meant to supervene upon its exercise? Just how *much* suffering and sacrifice can a pleasurable life of virtue tolerate? Stated conversely, to just what extent is it necessary to enjoy one's proper functioning in order to say that this *proper* function is *eu*-daemonism, that is, a good and pleasurable functioning or flourishing? An awful lot of things *can*, from the perspective of a greater value, eventually look small, even meaningless, in comparison to upholding one's values. But it also seems too much to say that the person of virtue could look at absolutely *every* sacrifice with such nonchalance. To determine the limits of toleration, and to determine thereby the extent to which things external to the person of virtue could undermine the pleasure in, love for, and cheerfulness about a life of virtue, let's think about such sacrifices in terms of the value of the thing lost relative to one's overall structure of valuing.

One does undoubtedly experience a certain amount of the need for sacrifice on the way to virtue. I do after all have to give up—i.e., sacrifice—those passionately held desires which previously sought to be mutinous and take over my self-governance. Even if these are things to be given up that *should* be given up, it is reasonable to think of giving them up as a sacrifice of sorts.[48] One can thus happily admit even very *difficult* sacrifices into a life that we will eventually call a pleasant and flourishing, properly functioning life. These are the sacrifices that one needs to make of those loves-cum-passions that stand in the way of becoming virtuous, things that, on the other side of one's acquisition of virtue, will not be felt as strongly as losses.

There *are* more problematic sacrifices, though, ones which do *not* seem to promise to be perceived by the emerging virtuous person as no great loss, as a loss that isn't really a loss once one's moral house is in order, or as a loss worth it for the sake of something greater. For example, what if (because of the unlucky, unpredictable natural world) I must sacrifice the possibility of satisfying a desire to do something particularly important and particularly good for the affirmation of respect for persons? Only I was in the position of trying to save the life of a drowning person, but I failed. Or I observe a government which systematically injures, insults, and degrades a certain category of person, but can do nothing to stop such abuses. Does my telos of making persons as such my end do anything to help me tolerate *that* sort of failed desire, viz. a desire positively connected to the realization of my ultimate telos in life? Or is this something that will haunt my pleasurable exercise of the life of virtue for the rest of my life? There are no easy answers to these questions.

Ultimately, though, the most problematic examples of sacrifice are of the sort which the Gallows-Man example highlights, the sort which take away things absolutely central to a stable life. The Gallows Man, to maintain his virtue, has to sacrifice his happy way of being, his connection to his family and friends, his assurance of a financially secure life, and even, perhaps, his very *life* in the name of morality. And one can reasonably worry that such sacrifices demanded of a life of virtue are, well, *in*tolerable. Such sacrifices force us to push the question of just how much suffering is too much suffering for the maintenance of a properly functioning and flourishing life of virtue. At what point must one say that one has to sacrifice so much of who one really is that it no longer makes sense to look at the virtue accomplished as *pleasurable*, or indeed even as a state of truly *proper* functioning of this person? If I sacrifice a part of myself that really does *not* prove virtually meaningless from the perspective of my most central value of making persons as such my end, can I still be said to be functioning well as the kind of being I am?

The story of managing sacrifices we have just considered shows that one can indeed maintain oneself as an integral whole even as one sacrifices an awful lot in oneself. We'll need to admit a limit here, though. If the Gallows Man gives up his *life* for the sake of honesty and integrity of person, we might admire him, but he is

---

[48] I think here of Augustine's (1993) struggles to let go of sex, honor, and an obsession with the theater as good examples of this kind of sacrifice.

also *losing* that person of absolute value who had this strength and moral integrity. Remaining alive but being forced to do something thoroughly in opposition to one's most basic moral principle of making persons as such one's end is another tragic example of the loss of integrity and proper functioning of the virtuous person.[49] It is in these sorts of examples that we must admit that the sacrifices and suffering demanded by virtue become insuperable obstacles to the realization of a pleasant and flourishing life of virtue. When one's sacrifice involves being killed, or being forced to act egregiously in opposition to one's life-guiding telos of making persons as such one's end, it becomes impossible to envision taking pleasure in one's life; it is even hard to say—despite the fact that one has done everything humanly possible to realize a life of virtue—that one is functioning as one should as the kind of being one is.

It may thus be that circumstances of a particular person's life are such that the sacrifices demanded for the sake of virtue cannot be tolerated pleasurably and cheerfully. But on this point, Kant is no worse off than Aristotle. Aristotle had to admit that the "fate of Priam" (the King of Troy, who sees his entire life destroyed by invading Greeks[50]) can undermine that pleasure that should supervene upon a life of virtue. Similarly, Kant has to admit that it might be too much to say that the Gallows Man, when he goes to that gallows for refusing to tell a lie, goes off *cheerfully* whistling. We *admire* him, we are able palpably to appreciate the strength of his virtue, but we don't expect him to be cheerful.

But all of this is just to say that both Aristotle and Kant have to admit that the dream of pleasure supervening upon a flourishing, properly functioning life of virtue has its limits in the face of what Aristotle would call unrealized external goods and what Kant would call the sacrifice of things with moral and non-moral value. While this is difficult, and sometimes tragic, it is not a point that makes Kant any less a *eudaemonist* than Aristotle. It is just to admit that when we accept that there is value to things both in and beyond virtue we make ourselves vulnerable to the loss or failure of those valuable things. Such vulnerability is, in any event, I would assert, preferable to retreating to the Stoic alternative of indifference, that is, to the rejection of value to those things lost.

One must emphasize, though, that such examples are extreme, even tragic, examples. It is not impossible for any of us to have to face Gallows-Man-like situations (situations in which I am called upon to find a way to tolerate apparently intolerable sacrifices). But these examples are at the extreme of virtue. While they may be the best examples for showing the ultimate excellence and strength of virtue, they do not, in themselves, define the normal subjective experience of the person of virtue. The admission of the need to manage sacrifices well into the

---

[49] I think here of cases of persons being forced to kill other persons, or of being forced to treat other persons in degrading ways.
[50] See Aristotle (1962, book I, chapters 9–10).

realm of what is demanded of the virtuous person does not, in itself, prevent Kant's system of virtue from being a eudaemonist one. Nor does it prevent him from asserting that the life of a virtuous person is best characterized as a pleasurable life in which one is committed to the cheerful exercise of one's duties. To the contrary, his willingness to reflect as much as he does on the potential for suffering in a life of virtue has given us a deeper sense of the moral psychological tools upon which one can and must rely to maintain as much balance, order, integrity, and healthiness as possible, even in the worst of circumstances.

Indeed, in comparison with Aristotle, Kant has done *more* to help us think about how the person of virtue manages these vicissitudes of fortune. Aristotle admits their existence, and briefly suggests that the person of virtue will be best situated to manage them; but Kant picks the ball up at that point and dwells at greater length upon *how* to live a flourishing life even in the midst of suffering. In so doing, Kant has given us an account of virtue more viable for an imperfect world, a world of cruel nature, vicious persons, and unjust states, a world which does not promise to adhere to the principles of morality and justice. Aristotle himself suggests that a perfectly virtuous person could only exist and exercise her virtue within a perfectly just society. But Kant coaxes us toward the possibility that the best of virtuous persons could solidly maintain her virtue even in the worst of states, the worst of natural disasters, or the worst treachery of a friend.[51]

Indeed, for Kant, in the end, the life of virtue does not *promise* pleasure. What it promises is that—*whatever* the circumstances of one's life—one will function in

---

[51] I think in fact the question of where Aristotle stands on this point is a vexed one. The most obvious textual guides on this point in the *Nicomachean Ethics* reveal that Aristotle himself struggles with the question, going back and forth about whether he must ultimately admit that a truly virtuous person could be laid low by fortune. In I.9, Aristotle says simply of Priam that "[w]hen a man has met a fate such as his and has come to a wretched end, no one calls him happy" (Aristotle, 1100a, 8–9). But a chapter later, he hedges his bets on this straightforward claim, saying that "no supremely happy man can ever become miserable…; but even so, supreme happiness will not be his if a fate such as Priam's befalls him. And yet, he will not be fickle and changeable; he will not be dislodged from his happiness easily by any misfortune that comes along, but only by great and numerous disasters such as will make it impossible for him to become happy again in a short time" (Aristotle, 1100b, 33–34; 1101a, 7–12). Perhaps the best thing to say based on these texts is that Priam is not "supremely" happy but still maintains his virtue and is not miserable because his virtue allows him to remain unchangeable. But other texts, especially at 1097b, 7–12 and in the *Politics*, suggest that even his virtue is in danger, since the fully virtuous person is one who operates within a fully virtuous household and society (which, obviously, Priam cannot): Priam has lost his society, so though he remains individually virtuous, he is no longer, because of circumstances outside of his control (the loss of his city), able to exercise his virtue fully. In the end, I am tempted to say that Priam retains both virtue and happiness on some level but not on the highest level possible. There is, however, much disagreement on this point in the literature, but I will not engage with that here. This ambiguity in Aristotle's texts on the question of just how much the loss of external goods impacts the life of the virtuous person is precisely what leads to the whole movement in Greek and Roman philosophy toward Stoicism (viz., the clean resolution of the problem via the rejection of non-moral value). My main point is that Kant is less ambiguous on this question: as we have seen, he wants unequivocally to assert that virtue is meant to hold up unscathed even in the face of treachery of friends, or the loss of civil society, and that one can even therewith maintain a certain level of happiness, at least happiness rationally conceived. I thank an anonymous reader from Oxford University Press for raising questions about the status of Priam for Aristotle.

the best and most pleasurable way possible for those circumstances, even if sometimes "the most pleasurable" means "the most capable of managing suffering." I am reminded here of a particularly apt quote from the Chinese philosopher, Wang Yang-ming. Wang speaks of virtue as involving what he calls a "Pure Heaven Pattern," a form or essence which realizes itself in *whatever* circumstances it finds itself. And so:

> If one wants this mind to remain Pure Heaven Pattern, one must apply effort *wherever* Pattern is manifested... If it is manifested while living in wealth and honor, or poverty and humble circumstances, then one must study how to preserve Heavenly Pattern while living in wealth and honor, or poverty and humble circumstances. If it is manifested while living in difficulty and deprivation, or among barbarians, then one must study how to preserve Heavenly Pattern while living in difficulty and deprivation, or among barbarians. (Ming 2014, 272)

In other words, the particular strength of virtue—our "Heavenly Pattern" or ordering of our person—is its capacity to remain itself, whatever the circumstances in which one finds oneself, what we earlier described as the constancy of virtue. One can even hope that the cheerfulness and pleasure that visit upon virtue in less oppressive circumstances could still find their way to be expressed in the midst of these more oppressive circumstances. Kant's virtuous person has the moral psychological means to live a pleasurable, happy life even in the face of the need to tolerate sacrifice. One mustn't underplay just how crucial such an ability is in today's society!

In the end, Deontological Eudaemonism challenges us in a way that Aristotelian eudaemonism does not: it challenges us to envision a properly *functioning*—and even a *pleasurable* and *flourishing*—life of virtue which involves *sacrifices* in the name of virtue. When I give things up for the sake of the thing that is most important to my being, I am indeed functioning well as the kind of being that I am; I am flourishing! One can even envision this virtuous life involving sacrifice as being a pleasurable life, one characterized by a dispositional cheerfulness in the performance of one's duties.

We have considered two caveats to this claim that the life of virtue is a life of pleasure. On the one hand, we admit that extreme failure in the realization of external goods can undermine the pleasure of virtue. On the other, we admitted in the previous section that, unlike Aristotle's dream of the perfect virtuous person, our virtuous person must maintain a calm, humble vigilance about a slim though ever-present possibility of temptation to revert to self-absorption. The pleasure of virtue can be marred by the loss of external goods, and the pleasure of virtue sits side by side with a humble vigilance that keeps one's temptation to self-absorption at bay. But in both these admissions, Kant's virtue theory either matches or exceeds Aristotle's. In the former, he is no worse off than Aristotle (for both must admit the possibility of tragic loss of external goods outside one's control). And in the latter, he is more honest and true to humanity than Aristotle (since in admitting a need for humble vigilance, he clings to the more plausible view of human nature that one is always at least a little tempted toward self-absorption). So, when it comes to *external* subversion of the life of virtue, Kant is no worse off than Aristotle. And when it comes to admission of the potential for *internal* conflict in the life of virtue, Kant is just a bit more honest than Aristotle about what is true for humans. The very fact that virtue involves sacrifice and subjective hindrances to virtue does not, in other words, prevent us from understanding Kant's theory of virtue as eudaemonistic. Indeed, one might find his a preferable and more honest story of eudaemonism in virtue of his honest willingness to integrate the need for sacrifice and vigilance into a pleasurable life of virtue. On Kant's model of self-governance, one in which the pursuit of happiness empirically conceived is demoted to a secondary goal of governance, we discover a model of self-governance most appropriate to free and rational but sensibly affected beings.

Let us allow one last objector to enter the scene: don't these demands for vigilance and the admission of the mere possibility of the collapse of pleasure because of uncontrollable circumstances surely mean that there is not a perfect coincidence or identity of happiness and virtue, and hence no true "eudaemonism" to be found in Kant's system? In response to this objector, I note that were one to insist upon so strict an identity between virtue and happiness, one which did not allow for these exceptions, we would be seeking a eudaemonism inappropriate for human existence. The most rigorous of Stoics would be the only possible story of eudaemonism, but the most rigorous of Stoic lives would not be a genuine human life which both admitted and welcomed the facts of non-moral value, human need, and finitude. The most satisfying account of eudaemonism for human beings is one, like Kant's, that integrates within the general identity of virtue and happiness rationally conceived, the possibility of its loss.

Conclusion

We thus affirm our establishment of our first step in Kant's Deontological Eudaemonism: there is, at least for the fully virtuous person who has acquired a free aptitude for virtue, a pleasure in unimpeded activity that is identical with the exercise of that virtue. We thus reject Wood's suggestion that the final word in Kant's moral theory would be a picture of a human being who has two standpoints at odds with each other and thus is a kind of being intrinsically at odds with herself.[52] To the contrary, a human being who is at odds with herself in the

---

[52] "Kant's view is...that the self is in conflict with itself because the *whole self simultaneously* takes two conflicting standpoints. One standpoint is the 'natural-social' standpoint, expressed through my natural inclinations as they appear under conditions of social life. The other is the moral or rational

way Wood describes is simply a human being who has not done the hard work of virtue. Human beings do have two standpoints which threaten to tear them apart; but, at the end of the day, Kant does not accept that divided picture as all the human being can hope for as a result of her own activity of virtue. To the contrary, it is the very activity of virtue itself that heals that wound of human nature, gently bringing one's sensible self into agreement with the governance of one's rational self.

We are finally at the point where we can turn our gaze to the second, and final, step in our story of Deontological Eudaemonism: consideration of the extent to which happiness, empirically conceived, can be in harmony with a life of virtue. It is to this task that we turn in the next and concluding chapter.

---

standpoint, expressed through my lawgiving reason" (Wood 2000, 264–265). And: "[T]he eudaimonistic standpoint [emerging from the 'natural-social standpoint'] is originally the standpoint from which each human being seeks superiority over others. By contrast, the standpoint of morality or reason is one from which the worth of all rational beings is *equal.* From this standpoint, human beings are required to respect every rational person as having the dignity of an end in itself...Human nature is therefore caught in a fundamental struggle between the natural-social standpoint, whose principle is one's own happiness, and the pure rational standpoint, whose principle is the moral law" (Wood 2000, 272).

II.iii
Happiness, Empirically Conceived
The Virtuous, Non-Self-Absorbed Pursuit of Desire-Fulfillment

Introduction

We confirmed in the last chapter a conception of happiness, rationally conceived, which is identical with the exercise of a free aptitude for virtue. But in all this discussion of the pleasure one experiences in the exercise of virtue, we've not yet gotten to the fullest account of the life of pleasure that the virtuous person can expect. Indeed, if Kant thought that the pleasure one takes in the exercise of the free aptitude for virtue were the only kind of pleasure for which the virtuous person could hope, then he wouldn't be anything more than a Stoic Eudaemonist, i.e. someone whose conception of flourishing is construed so narrowly that the pleasure one takes in being moral is sufficient to constitute happiness, full stop. But Kant's conception of human flourishing is more expansive than this: in addition to the pleasure one takes in being virtuous, the virtuous person has the hope, through use of the same tools she uses to realize her subjective telos of virtue, of also maximizing her pleasure overall, including the pleasure of desire-fulfillment, in all sorts of non-moral activities like bird-watching, cello-playing, good joke-telling, relationships, travel, etc. We now need, therefore, to consider the relationship of happiness empirically conceived as the summation of all one's desire-fulfillment to the account of virtue we've just completed, and then to consider the relationship between this happiness empirically conceived and that happiness rationally conceived as the pleasurable exercise of the aptitude for virtue which we discussed in the previous chapter.

Now, Kant himself doesn't reflect as much upon how the virtuous person pursues happiness empirically conceived as he does upon how the virtuous person manages sacrifices. Indeed, Kant scholars often at this point turn away from an account of the pursuit of happiness in *this* life and toward Kant's discussion of the Highest Good, his story of the promise of *another* life in which the accounts of virtue and happiness are settled properly and justly. I do not want to deny anything about this story; I am, in fact, very much a proponent of settling the accounts of virtue and happiness in the afterlife in this satisfying and just way. Nonetheless, completion of our story of Deontological Eudaemonism demands that we maintain our focus on self-governance in this life. And we can indeed find guidance in Kant's texts for thinking about how best to pursue happiness, empirically conceived, in this life.

This story of the pursuit of empirical happiness will not, however, be entirely distinct from our just completed discussion of both the pursuit and the realization of virtue. Rather, what we shall discover in this forthcoming story of the virtuous person's pursuit of happiness, empirically conceived, is that the objective telos of one's being, the demand to make persons as such one's end, provides guidance not only in the exercise of virtue but also in the pursuit of empirical happiness. This shouldn't surprise us. We've already seen, with the introduction of this objective, material, and non-negotiable telos of making persons as such one's end to the governance of one's desires overall, that the virtuous person subjectively experiences the interesting new fact that, because her desires now have a goal beyond themselves (i.e., the realization of this objective telos), they are no longer simply absorbed in themselves. What we learn in this chapter is that this same reorientation of desire guides not only the process of desire-*governance* but now also desire-*satisfaction*. That is: the admission of a non-desire-based telos for one's desires allows one to pursue the most complete fulfillment of one's desires overall—that is, empirical happiness—from a new, more satisfactory, because less self-absorbed, perspective. Indeed, the very same tool that gave one the evaluative distance upon oneself necessary for tolerating sacrifices and taking pleasure in virtue can provide that evaluative distance necessary for managing one's pursuit of happiness as desire-fulfillment, resulting in the most balanced, satisfying, and non-self-absorbed realization of happiness possible. This happy outcome occurs, furthermore, precisely because this virtue-guided pursuit of empirical happiness is grounded in a clear commitment to just those values most proper to sensibly affected rational beings. In short, the most successful fulfillment of desire overall is achieved through a continuing realization of the objective telos of making persons as such one's end.

All such guidance of desire-fulfillment via one's objective telos of making persons as such one's end does mean, though, that the subjective experience of empirical happiness as such, while not rejected as an interest of desire-governance, is also no longer its primary goal. And yet, in submitting to this higher goal of making persons as such one's end, our interest in desire-satisfaction is not abandoned but instead elevated: it is now pursued in a less self-absorbed way, via guidance by and governance of that primary person-centered telos of making persons as such our end. As such, even as we grant that the realization of happiness empirically conceived becomes a secondary goal of self-governance, we also ultimately achieve on this model of Deontological Eudaemonism a more satisfying fulfillment of desires than any non-naturalistic effort at the same (viz., than any effort at desire-fulfillment solely from within the realm of desire itself, without any appeal to a non-contingent, non-desire-based guide) could accomplish: the non-negotiable and exception-less way in which the goal of making persons as such one's end is integrated into the activity of seeking empirical happiness brings a new order and stability to the subjective experience of the pursuit of desire-fulfillment, introducing an objective goal for the organization and realization of that desire-fulfillment which is more proper to the kind of being one is overall. The subjective experience of the pursuit of desire-fulfillment is thus going to be more satisfying overall because it will be more in line with one's *whole* person, and not just with the narrow, self-absorbed concerns of one's desiring self. I want now to satisfy my desires within the context of assuring that all my desire-realization is compatible with and expressive of the value of persons. *That* will be the *most* satisfying thing for my person overall.

We will thus, through this account of virtue-guided pursuit of happiness, affirm the most complete notion of the proper functioning and flourishing of sensibly affected rational beings. Indeed, once we welcome not only the pleasure of the exercise of virtue but also the pleasure of desire-fulfillment generally within the scope of guidance by one's objective telos of making persons as such one's end, the result is the complete acquisition of Deontological Eudaemonia: a properly functioning, flourishing, and well-lived life in light of what is necessary for and demanded of sensibly affected rational beings. A life guided by a deontological—that is, a necessary and exception-less—telos is not a life unconcerned with happiness. It is, rather, a life in which one realizes a less self-absorbed happiness which is simultaneously a central component of the most authentic and genuine realization of the proper functioning for the kind of being one is. Although this achievement of happiness empirically conceived cannot be considered utterly identical with virtue (as its counterpart, happiness rationally conceived, can), and there will thus be moments when the pursuit of virtue will involve an injury to my happiness, empirically conceived, we ultimately discover nonetheless a reliable unity of the contentments or satisfactions of the sensibly affected rational being, including both the happiness rationally conceived as discussed in the previous chapter and the pursuit of happiness empirically conceived discussed here, now unified into an overall state of satisfaction for sensibly affected rational beings precisely because both these states are most successfully realized from the same singular, moral, and virtuous point of view of making persons as such one's end.

This chapter is organized as follows. In Section I, we begin with a brief consideration of recent work in Kant studies which seeks to resolve the moral life with the pursuit of happiness, empirically conceived, and confirm our own reflections as a more precise continuation of both Forman's (2016) and Holberg's (2018) efforts to reject the overly harsh distinction between moral and prudential reasoning suggested by Kohl (2017). In so doing, we confirm as our own the goal articulated by Watson as early as 1983 that it is both possible and preferable to seek a unified conception of human satisfactions for the sensibly affected rational being.

In Section II, we consider first, in light of Kant's already articulated skepticism about the ability of reason to guide desire-fulfillment, the apparent oddity of relying upon reason at all in the pursuit of happiness, empirically conceived. But by distinguishing reason working simply on desire's own territory from reason bringing its own tools to the incompletable world of desire, we show reason is indeed the right tool to bring to this next level of self-governance. We turn then to an extended discussion of Kant's introduction of the duty to develop one's natural capacities for pragmatic purposes to serve as the basis for making sense of how the virtuous person pursues happiness. By pursuing pragmatic end-setting under the auspices of yet again affirming one's objective telos of making persons as such one's end, the very pursuit of happiness as desire-fulfillment is elevated into a higher task, pointed toward one's life-guiding telos. Indeed, the heightening and intensifying of one's felt attachments to one's pragmatic pursuits accomplished in this orientation of one's desire-fulfillment is simply another example of the process of moral excitement we considered in II.i.

In Section III, we then look in more detail at what it looks like to fulfill this duty of developing one's capacities with pragmatic purposes but for a moral end. First, we affirm the intimate intertwining of virtue and happiness empirically conceived both in the integration of absolute moral and relative non-moral value assessment, and in the felt experience of so doing, confirming along the way Watson's (1983) insistence that there is a robust notion of non-moral value to be found in Kant's practical philosophy. The picture of the happy virtuous person we draw thus emerges as an intimate and complete interweaving of concern for relative non-moral and absolute moral value on the one hand, and the integrated expression of natural and moral feelings on the other, all in the pursuit of happiness: in a marriage of pragmatic interests and moral concern, one's previously merely relatively valuable pursuits take on a new value in light of their ability to contribute to one's telos overall of making persons as such one's end; and one's natural pleasure in pursing these ends is tied to the moral pleasure of affirming one's identity as a free setter of ends. Happiness empirically conceived is thus confirmed fully and thoroughly as a project within the purview of the virtuous person's telos of making persons as such one's end, and not simply as a distinct part of oneself, distant from and unrelated to that life-guiding telos. Although unavoidable circumstances external to oneself may lead at times to situations where the pursuit of virtue results in injury to one's happiness empirically conceived, in this virtuous pursuit of happiness, we discover a stable and reliable marriage both of relative non-moral and absolute moral value on the one hand, and a thoroughgoing intertwining of one's pragmatic and moral felt attachments on the other.

We thereby affirm an interpretive sympathy with a variety of extant literature on this topic. With Watson, we affirm the existence of a robust conception of non-moral value, a commitment which firmly/decidedly distinguishes him from any would-be Stoic account of happiness or eudaemonism. Also with Watson, we confirm the possibility of the pursuit of a unified life of contentment for the sensibly affected rational being, confirming his assertion that "to live a life appropriate to a human being is to organize and pursue the satisfaction of one's needs and interests under the discipline of practical reason," leading to a "contentment with one's life as a whole" (Watson 1983, 94). Although Deontological Eudaemonism cannot affirm a perfect identity of virtue with happiness empirically conceived and must thus tolerate the fact that (in extreme circumstances) virtue and happiness empirically conceived can come apart, we can nonetheless affirm a stable unity of a life in which all of one's person and all of one's satisfactions are guided by the single goal of making persons as such one's end. Deontological Eudaemonism thus assures a reliable (and, at times, extraordinarily joyous!) unity of one's person.

Further, with Holberg (2018), we confirm that, in fact, the pursuit of virtue is the *best* way to pursue happiness successfully, since the very tools of virtue, considered both objectively and subjectively act also as tools for the pursuit of happiness: virtue helps both to heighten and focus one's objective capacity for good judgment about the relative ordering of things of non-moral value, and, subjectively, provides an evaluative perspective, akin to the one which assured moral apathy and moral excitement in the pursuit of virtue, which allows one to shape and guide one's feelings in relation to that pragmatic end-setting meant to encourage the best development of happiness. In so doing, we affirm that the tools of virtue are simultaneously the tools of happiness empirically conceived, that the pursuit of happiness rationally conceived and happiness empirically conceived are both guided by a singular life-guiding telos of making persons as such one's end, and our story of Deontological Eudaemonism is complete.

I. Recent Literature on the Relationship of Morality and Happiness, Empirically Conceived

The object of our concern in this chapter is the question of whether and to what extent one can harmonize the exercise of virtue with the pursuit of happiness, empirically conceived. This is a topic that has also occupied the thoughts of some recent commentators. We have already, earlier in Part II, noted, for example, the work of Forman (2016), who challenges Wood's notion of a necessarily disunified self, and defends instead the notion that we can affirm an alignment between virtue and happiness, one grounded in a confidence that "virtue is a state that allows for the satisfaction of non-moral desires" (Forman 2016, 86n20). For Forman, "Kant's own prescription for approximating happiness in this life is one that...depict[s] the end of happiness as standing in harmony with the end of virtue" (p. 82). Forman's project is thus, most centrally, one of defending the idea that the distinct ends of morality and happiness are not directly at odds with each other, and that it is indeed therefore reasonable for the finite moral agent to hope for the realization of happiness through the "Cynical" means of moderating one's excessive desires.

In II.ii, we found reason to distinguish ourselves from Forman. Forman insists that "Kant's own view is not that virtue is equivalent to...worldly happiness" (Forman 2016, 86n20).[1] But we pushed him then on the question of whether one can identify a different, non-empirical, but still this-worldly, notion of happiness which is indeed equivalent to, or identical with, virtue. Having found that notion of happiness, rationally conceived, in the previous chapter, we continue to distinguish ourselves from Forman thusly. Nonetheless, we also heartily agree with Forman's suggestion that one makes the pursuit of happiness, empirically conceived, more possible when one acquires the virtuous person's "Cynical" ability to moderate her affects and passions. In this chapter, we continue our sympathetic agreement with Forman's suggestion that the ends of morality and happiness are compatible. Indeed, we seek only to push his point further, even to the suggestion that—absent tragic circumstances that would undermine it—the virtuous life will also be the happy life, empirically conceived, because the very same tools that promote virtue also promote happiness, empirically conceived.

In pushing the point that the tools of virtue are the tools of happiness, we also place ourselves in sympathetic agreement with Holberg (2018). Because her account of Kant's "quasi-eudaemonism" is so much in the spirit of my own forthcoming account, I provide an extended consideration of her ideas which will, simultaneously, act as an introduction to my own account of the virtuous pursuit of happiness, empirically conceived.

So, according to Holberg, "[a]lthough Kant's ethical system breaks from eudaimonism in significant ways, it retains the eudaimonist claim that virtuously-informed pursuits of happiness are not only better for virtue, but also better for happiness" (Holberg 2018, 1). In making this claim, Holberg first rejects Kohl's (2017) overly harsh distinction between reasoning about morality and reasoning about happiness. According to Kohl, reasoning about the pursuit of happiness, because it is concerned only with maximal pleasure and not with value as such, is not really *practical* reason at all, but only theoretical reasoning. In opposition to this claim, Holberg suggests that the account of prudential reasoning upon which Kohl relies to make this claim is impoverished:

> To explain why Kant characterizes prudential reasoning as an exercise of theoretical reason, Kohl (2017) *downplays* the way that judgments of which pleasures to

---

[1] Forman's insistence upon the non-identity of virtue and happiness depends, of course, upon conceiving of happiness empirically as desire-fulfillment: "The key point to note here is that for Kant, unlike for the Stoics, our happiness *always depends on something other than our virtuous activity*, namely on the satisfaction of non-moral desires. This marks an essential difference between the physical good (happiness) and the moral good" (Forman 2016, 85).

prefer to be [what is] maximally pleasurable reflect what the agent does *value* [but also *wants* to value/enjoy better]. For example, making New Year's resolutions is usually an exercise of prudential reason: this judgment about what will be maximally pleasurable for an improved me over the long haul often does not straightforwardly reflect what I currently find maximally agreeable. Kohl's argument that prudential reasoning, as the determination of what would be maximally agreeable for me, makes sense of Kant's characterization of this as an exercise of theoretical reason, but the possibility of better and worse conceptions of happiness held by better and worse versions of me, emergent from practical choices I will have made, complicates the account of happiness-seeking as a theoretical endeavor.
(Holberg 2018, 7n13)

Essentially, Holberg rejects Kohl's idea that the pursuit of happiness is only a theoretical endeavor because such pursuit is intrinsically concerned with notions of what is "better and worse," that is, with notions of value.

Holberg then goes on to provide an account of how the pursuits of morality and happiness are in fact more intertwined than what Kohl had suggested. She ultimately, however, describes Kant as only a "*quasi*-eudaemonist," since, for her, the distinction between "moral reasoning and prudential reasoning [as] two distinct uses of practical reason, each with its own standard for good action" (p. 1) still demands of us that we reject the explicitly eudaemonistic claim that happiness is the goal or end-point of morality: "The eudaemonist defends a unity of practical reason in a very strong sense: The total coherence of moral goodness and happiness means that when aiming at one, you are aiming at the other" (Holberg 2018, 2). Because we cannot say that in aiming at virtue, we aim simultaneously at happiness, empirically conceived, we must thus, according to Holberg, admit that Kant is only a "quasi"-eudaemonist, and not a strict eudaemonist as such.

Here, then, is one way that Holberg describes Kant's quasi-eudaemonistic point of view:

Despite Kant's commitment to the ineradicable potential for fundamental conflict between these types of practical reasoning, I argue that once we shift to consideration of a *developmental* narrative of these faculties, we see that virtuous moral reasoning is able to substantively influence prudential reasoning, while prudential reason should be responsive to such influence... Although Kant's ethical system breaks from eudaimonism in significant ways, it retains the eudaimonist claim that virtuously-informed pursuits of happiness are not only better for virtue, but also better for happiness. (p. 1)

Holberg goes on to describe this "developmental" account as promoting what she calls "an intrapsychic functional unity" (Holberg 2018, 3) between virtue and happiness. In other words, although we must grant a strict distinction between the standards of moral and prudential reasoning, once we look at how such reasonings work in practice, we find that they are mutually compatible and, indeed, mutually dependent upon each other. Holberg describes three "intrapsychic" ways in which the tools of virtue are valuable in the pursuit of happiness: "virtue fosters the development of skill, roots out the passions, and facilitates our understanding and ability to utilize others...[T]hese are good, useful capacities according to the normative standards of each [i.e., of both virtue and happiness]" (Holberg 2018, 13).

She suggests, furthermore, that virtue has a unifying or totalizing effect upon happiness, an effect prudential reasoning could not accomplish on its own merits:

> Because of the totalizing ambition of virtue, its concern with the whole of the agent's life, virtue proffers an answer as to how the determination of happiness should proceed: what ends should be prioritized and what should be agreeable (or not)... [V]irtue yields a more tightly constrained, yet still formal prescription for how an agent should conceive of her happiness, supplying shape to the amorphous target of happiness" (Holberg 2018, 15).

In Holberg's summative language, virtue has a "transformative effect upon the agreeable" (Holberg 2018, 20), helping the virtuous person to cultivate new targets for her desires and to order those new desires in a more coherent way so as to accomplish a more stable realization of happiness.

Although I must depart from Holberg in one important way, I'm generally and deeply sympathetic with her project. The main point of distinction between us is, perhaps, obvious: because I've already argued, in II.ii, that Kant is indeed a wholehearted eudaemonist at least in relation to happiness intellectually or rationally conceived, I must reject Holberg's idea that Kant is only a "quasi-eudaemonist." For Holberg, the standard for conforming with complete, non-quasi, eudaemonism is indeed strict: "The total coherence of moral goodness and happiness means that when aiming at one, you are aiming at the other" (Holberg 2018, 2). But on our II.ii account of such things, we meet that high standard: there is indeed a meaningful notion of happiness, rationally conceived, at which we aim simultaneously with our pursuit of virtue.[2]

---

[2] I wonder, though, whether Holberg might be sympathetic with the story of happiness, rationally conceived, that I provided in II.ii. On the one hand, she seems to reject such notions: "Within ancient eudaimonist theories, virtue is simultaneously thought of as moral perfection and the pleasurable fulfillment of one's natural function. Because Kant assumes a metaphysical divide between the moral and natural orders, a different account of virtue is needed (*MdS* 6:482).16 Virtue cannot be a habit, understood as a sensible disposition acquired through the repeated performance of a certain kind of action, because moral worth requires reason subjecting itself to its own law (*MdS* 6:409). Nor is virtue pleasure in doing the right thing, for pleasure lies beyond the province of the will" (Holberg 2018, 9). But her suggestion that the thing that essentially distinguishes virtue and happiness is that the latter is

Nonetheless, we still need to face the question of whether a notion of happiness empirically conceived can as seamlessly be resolved with the pursuit of virtue. And on this score, I am in deep sympathy with the moves Holberg has made. I particularly appreciate the way she has set up her project in opposition to Kohl's account, one which I agree involves an overly harsh distinction between reasoning about morality and reasoning about happiness. I am also deeply sympathetic with her positive suggestions about the developmental and intrapsychic ways in which virtue enhances and guides the pursuit of happiness, agreeing with her that prudential reasoning, on its own merits, is too messy a process to issue in a coherent notion of desire-fulfillment.[3] With Holberg, I seek, versus Kohl, to affirm the lines of continuity between prudential and moral reasoning. Indeed, I consider my own forthcoming account to be a furthering of her general suggestion that the tools of virtue are simultaneously the best tools for the pursuit of happiness.

My own articulation of this symmetry will focus, however, on an important point in Kant's account of virtue upon which Holberg has not focused: the idea that Kant identifies an obligatory end of virtue with pragmatic content. And, because the pursuit of any obligatory end on our account involves orientation and direction specifically by the guiding objective telos of making persons as such one's end, our account of how the virtuous person realizes this obligatory end with pragmatic content will need to be informed and shaped by that most basic and orienting telos of virtue. What results is a thoroughly moralized account of happiness, one which I take to be in general agreement with Holberg's account of a happiness achieved through appeal to an organizing principle of virtue.

But, in so doing, both Holberg and I implicitly take our lead from Watson (1983), who asserted almost forty years ago that "[t]he capacity to unite one's ends [including those pragmatic ends constitutive of happiness empirically conceived] into a 'system' in accordance with reason requires the moral point of view" (p. 79), since "the life devoted [merely] to inclination" would lead us only "on a futile search for significance among the various ends of inclinations" (p. 90). It is Watson, then, who first laid down this basic expectation that if we are going to hope for some sort of coherent pursuit of happiness, it must be done from the moral point of view.

---

grounded in sensibility and thus in what effects can be brought about in oneself instead of in what activity one can engage in, hints that, if one *could* affirm a more active conception of pleasure and happiness as we did in II.ii, she might be sympathetic to the identity of morality and happiness at least to that extent: "Because happiness (roughly, a sense of agreeable satisfaction that persists in time) is grounded in sensibility as 'an effect and not an activity of the will,' success in the pursuit of happiness can never fully align with successful realization of virtue's aim of good willing (*GMS* 4:400)" (Holberg 2018, 2).

[3] Indeed, her discussion of such things is very much in line with our own I.i discussion of the unwieldy nature of happiness, empirically conceived.

What emerges in my furthering of his project, below, is a practical guide for taking the concern to make persons as such one's end as a principle by which to pursue happiness, empirically conceived. Let us turn to that account.[4]

II. An Obligatory End with a Pragmatic Purpose: The Virtuous Pursuit of Happiness

Introduction: Is Moral Reason the Appropriate Tool for Pursuing Happiness?

We want ultimately, then, to make sense of the virtuous pursuit of happiness. But a previous question immediately presents itself: there is something very odd for Kant about the very notion that happiness—most broadly construed as the pursuit of *pleasure*—could be sought *virtuously* through appeal to our capacity for *rationality*. The oddness of the thought stems from Kant's own emphatic separation of happiness from morality and reason in many of his works. For example, in the *Groundwork*, the pursuit of the supreme principle of morality demanded that we set aside heteronomous and anthropological groundings of morality generally, and groundings of morality in the pursuit of happiness in particular. Here is Kant's perhaps strongest statement of the point, a passage which we considered in our Introductory Thoughts when we showed that Kant's purported rejection of eudaemonism in fact reduced essentially to a rejection of hedonism, and especially to a rejection of any empirical and heteronomous effort to ground moral principles:

> *Empirical principles* are not fit to be the foundation of moral laws at all... Yet the principle of one's own happiness is the most objectionable [of empirical principles], not merely because it is false, and [because] experience contradicts the pretense that being well always tallies with behaving well,... but [more centrally] because it underpins morality with incentives that rather undermine it and annihilate all its sublimity, since they put motives to virtue and those to vice in the same class and only teach us to improve our calculations, but totally and entirely extinguish the specific difference between the two.
>
> (4:442/53, translation slightly modified)

Clearly, then, the pursuit of happiness cannot be taken as a non-heteronomous basis for grounding the supreme principle of morality. Such a stance does not,

---

[4] For the sake of efficiency, I will, for the rest of this chapter, understand "happiness" to refer to "happiness, empirically conceived." If I appeal to happiness, rationally or intellectually conceived, I will identify it as such.

however, prevent us from considering the possibility that the reverse—viz., that morality and moral reasoning could be taken as a guide for the pursuit of happiness—might make sense.

But there is another point in the *Groundwork* at which Kant more clearly draws a line between happiness and morality, perhaps making one worry that the tools of morality in fact are inappropriate for the pursuit of happiness. As we also saw earlier, Kant argues that it would be a really bad idea to try to use reason to guide one's happiness, since it is so badly adapted to the task and in fact itself has a higher telos than the mere satisfaction of desire (viz., the realization of a good will), a telos toward which it is most properly adapted and which it is more capable of realizing. Indeed, we relied on just this passage in our I.i discussion of such things to defend the idea that desire-based governance of desire was inadequate:

> In actual fact, we do find that the more a cultivated reason engages with the purpose of enjoying life and with happiness, so much the further does a human being stray from true contentment; and from this there arises in many, and indeed in those who are most experienced in its use, if only they are sincere enough to admit it, a certain degree of *misology*, i.e., hatred of reason, since after calculating all the advantages they derive[,]...they still find that they have in fact just brought more hardship upon their shoulders than they have gained in happiness, and that because of this they eventually envy, rather than disdain, the more common run of people, who are closer to the guidance of mere natural instinct, and who do not allow their reason much influence on their behavior.
> (4:395/396/11)

We asserted in I.i, on the basis of this text, that humans are simply not very good at rationally calculating what will make them happy, and that the rough-around-the-edges empirical world within which humans pursue happiness is a particularly fraught place to hope for reason to be successful in so incompletable a task.

This text does, then, raise a serious question about our current task: having argued that reason is not apt for guiding the pursuit of happiness, it seems very odd—even contradictory—to say now that one's rational telos of making persons as such one's end is going to do the work of guiding one toward happiness! If the reason which grounds morality isn't *good* at doing anything to organize the pursuit of one's desires so as to realize happiness, shouldn't that moral rationality simply sit on the side-lines when it comes to pursuing happiness? That is, shouldn't it simply apply its permissibility constraints to one's pursuit of happiness—setting the boundaries for what sorts of desires and associated pleasures are in and out of bounds for a virtuous life—and then let one's desiring self carry on with the task of organizing the fulfillment of one's desires as best one can? Isn't it wrong, on the one hand, and just futile on the other to try to use moral reasoning to guide happiness?

Interestingly, as we shall see, this is not the direction in which Kant moves. Why his eventual introduction of the telos of one's being—the effort to make persons as such one's end—as the perspective from which to order one's pursuit of happiness makes sense, though—particularly in light of this *Groundwork* suggestion that reason is incapable of such things—is a point worthy of reflection. Is Kant simply contradicting himself when, on the one hand, he asserts that reason is incapable of guiding the pursuit of happiness and, on the other, that the virtuous person must take the moral rational telos of making persons as such one's end as her guide for pursuing happiness?

The crucial distinction we need to make here in order to relieve this tension is a distinction in how reason operates vis à vis one's desires. On the one hand, reason could try to guide desire-fulfillment entirely on desire's own territory, that is, try to realize a completed series in the empirical world by using desires themselves as empirical governing principles. This is just the task Kant revealed as futile in the *Groundwork* and which we affirmed as both futile and vicious in I.i. But reason, now in its guise as the governor of a virtuous person, could guide desire-fulfillment in a different way: instead of trying to order desires within the foreign territory of desire by its own merely empirical rules (the futile task just noted), the virtuous person can bring reason's own rule to this foreign territory of empirical desires, thereby elevating the incompletable empirical series of one's desires beyond itself to a higher goal, and putting the pursuit of desire-fulfillment in the service of the realization of the objective telos of one's being.[5]

In so doing, reason does not now assert that the previously incompletable empirical series of one's desires is completable. To the contrary, reason, in the person of the virtuous person, admits and tolerates such incompleteness, but now places that incompleteness within a higher, more realizable, and more apt goal for sensibly affected rational beings: the realization of the demand to make persons as such one's end. And reason is indeed capable of just this kind of ordering: it is not able to complete an incompletable empirical series, but it is entirely capable of organizing one's desires in light of objective demands of reason, like the demand to make persons as such one's end, an organization that is concerned not simply with the constraint of desire, nor even just with the cultivation of desires supportive of one's moral goals, but now also with the cultivation of morally permissible desires supportive of one's pursuit of happiness. It is to an understanding of exactly this task that we now turn.

---

[5] It is with just this move that I place myself in sympathy with Holberg's (2018) suggestion that virtue has a "totalizing ambition" (p. 15) which it brings to the pursuit of happiness.

The Moral Pursuit of Happiness: A Marriage of Nature and Freedom

We thus assert that happiness can be pursued virtuously, viz. that moral reasoning does have something to contribute to the realization and fulfillment of one's desires overall. One might think that, even in the Doctrine of Virtue, Kant would set aside any and all such concerns in the name of this previous goal we've been considering, viz. the goal of affirming those obligatory ends the virtuous realization of which would constitute one's objective telos of making persons as such one's end. But, interestingly, in the very heart of his articulation of the obligatory ends of virtue, we find one of these ends to be very clearly connected to those pragmatic concerns more traditionally pursued under the aegis of happiness. This obligatory end is the duty to self which, under the category of "Imperfect Duties to Himself (with Regard to His End)," Kant describes as the "Human Being's Duty to Himself to Develop and Increase His Natural Perfection, That Is, for a *Pragmatic* Purpose" (6:444/194, emphasis added).[6]

This is a curious, surprising, perhaps even confusing kind of duty to introduce. What could it possibly mean to fulfill an *obligatory* end for a *pragmatic* purpose other than to set that end for the *wrong* reasons? That is: isn't it required that anything obligatory be done, as was described by Kant in the *Groundwork*, in accordance with "the motive of duty"?[7] Shouldn't the obligatory end of developing and increasing one's natural perfection be done for the moral and virtuous purpose of making persons as such one's end, and *not* for an inclination-based pragmatic purpose of any sort? Indeed, were one to attempt to fulfill a duty of virtue for a pragmatic purpose, would one not undermine the virtue of one's act thereby?

These are exactly the questions we need to explore in making sense of this new obligatory end. In so doing, we shall affirm a new connection between the pursuit of virtue and the pursuit of happiness, one in which the latter is itself taken up in the former's project of realizing the objective telos of one's being. Let us therefore

---

[6] Holberg (2018) does, very briefly, consider a similar move, though she limits the import of Kant's introduction of a duty to pursue pragmatic ends to the import of acquiring a skill. Here is the entirety of her discussion of this point: "Firstly, virtue as respect for rational will obliges us to 'procur[e] and promot[e] the *capacity* to realize all sorts of possible ends,' and so the development of skill (*MdS* 6:392): [A human being] has a duty to diminish his ignorance by instruction and to correct his errors. And it is not merely that technically practical reason *counsels* him to do this as a means to his further purposes (of art); morally, practical reason *commands* it absolutely and makes this end his duty so that he may be worthy of the humanity that dwells within him. (*MdS* 6:387) Skill can be developed independently of virtue. But because 'prudence presupposes skillfulness' as 'the faculty of using one's skillfulness effectively,' prudential reasoning benefits from virtue, which commits additional weight to the aim of developing skill (*Päd.* 9:455). Conversely, an agent's skill can be put in service of ends prescribed by the moral law" (Holberg 2018, 14).

[7] As Kant notes, for a maxim to have "moral content" it must be focused on grounding an action "not from inclination but *from duty*" (4:398/11).

explore more carefully this integration of pragmatic purposes and free end-setting so as to appreciate how this pragmatic purpose can indeed be integrated into the objective telos guiding one's being without undermining the moral character of one's activity.

To begin: one must admit that there is no mention of "happiness" (*Glückseligkeit*) as such in this entire passage. Nonetheless, there are two points about just the very titles of this section, and then several moments within the section itself, which reveal this particular duty to self as being centrally concerned to bring the pursuit of happiness under the aegis of one's life-guiding objective telos of making persons one's end. First, the general category with which Kant is concerned here, under which the duty to develop one's natural perfections is situated, is duties to oneself "with regard to [one's] *end*" (capitals removed, emphasis added). This is "end" in the singular here, not the plural. In other words, Kant is talking about *the* end of one's pursuit of virtue, indeed of one's life, an end he eventually describes in the first passage of this section (on increasing one's natural perfections) as "the end of [one's] existence" (6:445/194), and in the next passage of this section (on increasing one's moral perfections) as "the end of humanity in our own person" (6:447/197). Surely, the end he intends here is what we have been describing as the telos of one's being, that end of making persons as such one's end, that end which will eventually move oneself and all rational beings toward that Kingdom of Ends wherein all persons act for the sake of the absolute value of persons. Now, it is certainly the case that *all* our obligatory ends are meant to be realized "with regard" to this end. But in this specific sub-category of imperfect obligatory ends to oneself (and nowhere else!), Kant marks the point explicitly: these imperfect duties to oneself to cultivate one's perfections, both natural and moral, are duties centrally and explicitly identified as ends one should set for oneself in light of the ultimate end of one's existence.

Second, the first particular duty he introduces in this sub-category of imperfect duties to oneself in regard to one's end is one which speaks of a duty, or obligatory end, to increase one's "*natural* perfections... for a *pragmatic* purpose" (6:444/194, capitals removed, emphases added). What exactly does this mean? What does this duty demand of the would-be virtuous person? In short, this duty to develop one's natural powers and abilities for a pragmatic purpose is an integration of one's natural, instinctual, and desiring self with one's free, choosing, moral, and virtuous self so as to strengthen, improve, and elevate the former in light of the latter.[8] One has a variety of natural capacities; but to leave these natural capacities to themselves, that is, to demand of them *only* that they be put to the service of one's

---

[8] And it is with just exactly this move that we conclusively reject Wood's (2000) suggestion that conflict between two standpoints in a sensibly affected rational being cannot be effaced. To the contrary, Kant suggests here that it is precisely the task of the virtuous person to integrate her sensible self and concerns under the auspices of her moral self. This is what I have been calling the "elevation" of the sensible toward the rational.

"natural needs" would be to demand too little of them, or of oneself: "Even supposing that he could be satisfied with the innate scope of his capacities for his natural needs, his reason must first show him, by principles, that this meager scope of his capacities is satisfactory" (6:444/194, emphasis removed).

But, in fact, what one discovers in holding one's natural needs and capacities to this principled test is that one can and must demand more of oneself and one's natural capacities than what one's natural needs demand of those capacities: "for, as a being capable of ends (of making objects his ends), he must owe the use of his powers not merely to natural instinct but rather to the freedom by which he determines their scope" (6:444/194). One must, in other words, when determining the proper scope of one's capacities, look at one's natural capacities through the lens of being a free and choosing being and not just as ways to unthinkingly and instinctively satisfy one's natural instincts. Indeed, Kant suggests that a person "owes" something to her natural capacities in light of the fact that these natural capacities express themselves within a person who also has a free end-setting capacity. The natural capacities of an unfree being could be left to themselves and to the natural needs which inspire them. But the natural capacities of a sensibly affected rational being deserve more than this. These natural capacities need to be introduced to one's capacity to set ends freely. Indeed, increasing one's natural capacities beyond the extent to which such capacities satisfy one's merely natural instincts and needs through appeal to the ways in which one's free capacity to set ends can push those natural capacities further is precisely the way to pay this debt to one's natural self. Now, these natural capacities are elevated by being put in the service not only of satisfying one's natural needs, but also by placing that satisfaction of natural needs within the context of one's free end-setting, making them a further expression of that absolutely valuable capacity. The possible "scope" (6:444/194) of the influence of these capacities is thus widened.

What exactly does it mean, though, to widen the "scope" of one's capacities? In short, one uses one's natural capacities not only for the realization of natural needs but also for the purposes of free end-setting. To do this, one needs first to identify consciously to oneself that one has these natural capacities. Then one *consciously* (instead of merely instinctively) *exercises* these capacities so as to improve one's ability to use them. That is, one no longer simply unthinkingly and instinctively utilizes a natural capacity to fulfill a natural need as instigated by a natural instinct, and then lets that natural capacity lay dormant when no pressing natural need is calling it into service. Instead, one consciously takes up that capacity, actively seeking new ways to exercise and realize it, ways that take it beyond the original natural needs to which the capacity was originally targeted. Through all of this, not only is the scope of that capacity increased (viz., one applies it to more situations and needs, and now not just to needs but, further, to desires and ends), but one also thereby gets better at exercising this capacity. Better in what sense? Surely one at least gets better at using these capacities to fulfill the original natural needs to which they are targeted, enhancing and heightening one's facility to engage in the capacity in question. One gets better at this capacity, that is, in that one's regular exercise of it, like any repeated exercise, leads to an ease or facility in that use. It is this combination of an increased facility in the exercise and an increased scope in the application of one's capacity that, together, constitute that capacity's cultivation.[9]

An example of how natural capacities are increased beyond their ability to satisfy merely natural instincts may help here. One has, for example, a natural instinct for eating food, and also a natural capacity to produce things that satiate that hunger. When one's natural instinct to eat kicks in, one seeks out food to satisfy it. But this obligatory end would encourage one to focus upon that capacity to produce food and, in accordance with one's pleasures and preferences, become even *better* at making food that is worthy of being eaten and enjoyable to eat. One might engage in such activities even when one's own natural instinct for food does not kick in. You might start to cook for other people, or take particular care in what and how you cook for yourself so as to make it attractive and enjoyable to eat. You might even become a professional chef. What had previously been something that one just did naturally thus becomes something upon which one consciously and rationally focuses, thereby cultivating, increasing, and developing that original natural capacity and increasing the scope of ends to which the capacity is applied. I get better at making food and take even more pleasure in doing so precisely because I've brought that natural ability under the guidance of my capacity for free end-setting.[10]

What makes this cultivation of natural capacities really interesting for our purposes though is that, while the capacities themselves have a pragmatic purpose of some sort—e.g., satisfying one's hunger, or helping others to do so—the cultivation of these capacities is done with a moral goal in sight. The ultimate goal of all this cultivation of one's natural capacities, through this widening of the scope of one's capacity and the further cultivation of that capacity, all under the aegis of one's free end-setting capacity, is not just to realize these pragmatic purposes but, furthermore, to elevate one's natural and pragmatic self toward one's moral self. In Kant's words, the person who successfully engages in such cultivation thereby becomes "in a pragmatic respect a human being equal to the end of his existence" (6:445/194). One will, that is, guide and cultivate one's pragmatic end-setting—the cultivation and realization of all sorts of capacities, talents, and perfections—in a way that makes those natural capacities worthy of being part of a being whose end it is to make persons as such one's end. One is, in other words,

---

[9] Holberg (2018) describes something similar to this in her appeal to the development of "skills."
[10] We'll discuss the nature of such cultivation at much greater length later in this chapter when I shift the example in question to one of playing the cello.

exercising these natural capacities in a way that is respectful of oneself as a person: I have made persons as such—here, my own person as such—my end in this very particular way. In so doing, the increased facility I have for exercising this capacity becomes part of that free aptitude for virtue discussed in II.ii. Instead of letting one's natural capacities remain unused, or used only when one's natural instincts urge one to utilize them, one actively recognizes these natural capacities for what they are in themselves and for what they could be not just for the satisfaction of natural instincts but also for the realization of one's free end-setting generally. One thus cultivates these capacities toward new and broader ends and increases one's facility in the exercise of such capacities thereby. I have fulfilled a duty to myself, specifically the duty toward realizing the moral end of making oneself worthy of the humanity within oneself.

This cultivation of one's natural capacities in light of one's free capacity to set ends is, however, still done for a *pragmatic* purpose. What this means is that, in cultivating one's capacities, one is not just doing what reason demands, but is also following one's pragmatic preferences and pleasures in deciding what exact capacity to cultivate and how to cultivate it. That is, the demand to make persons as such my end does not itself demand of me specifically that I become a cook, a cellist, a fashion model, or a spy. Rather, what I decide to cultivate depends entirely upon my pragmatic concerns (as limited by permissibility constraints that treating persons as ends and never merely as means would demand). Kant had earlier, in a general introduction to increasing one's own perfections as an obligatory end, noted how it is that reason leaves room for such pragmatic considerations within an obligatory end:

> No rational principle prescribes specifically how far one should go in cultivating one's capacities (in enlarging or correcting one's capacity for understanding, i.e., in acquiring knowledge or skill). Then too, the different situations in which human beings may find themselves make a man's choice of the occupation of which he should cultivate his talents very much a matter for him to decide as he chooses. (6:392/154–155)

A "rational principle"—that is, the rational demand to make persons as such my end—thus demands that I cultivate my capacities. But deciding which capacities to cultivate is determined not by an obligatory reason dictated from one's rational will but by more quotidian and pragmatic concerns already present in the agent. Here, Kant suggests such decisions simply depend upon the "situation" in which one finds oneself.

Back in the main section discussing such things, he suggests further that the choice of what capacities to cultivate can depend also upon what *pleases* a person and what one is *good* at doing. As Kant puts the point:

> Which of these natural perfections should take precedence, and in what proportion one against the other it may be a human being's duty to himself to make these natural perfection his end, are *matters left for him to choose in accordance with his own rational reflection about what sort of life he would **like** to lead and whether he has the **powers** necessary for it* (e.g., whether it should be a trade, commerce, or a learned profession). (6:445/195, all emphases added)

In cultivating one's capacities toward the moral end of making oneself worthy of the humanity within oneself, one thus relies upon pragmatic thoughts and urges about "what sort of life [one] would *like* to lead" and about what one happens, naturally, to be good at doing, in choosing one's activities. These considerations are "pragmatic" in that they are guided not by the duty of making persons as such my end, but instead simply by what happens to make me happy. And so: one reflects on what one finds naturally pleasing and enjoyable in life, and brings those pleasures within the scope of one's free and rational pursuit of one's ultimate objective telos of making persons as such one's end, here, acting in such a way as to make one's own life and activities worthy of the person one is.

I thus choose to describe fulfillment of this duty to increase one's natural capacities for pragmatic purposes as a "marriage" of freedom and nature: in the fulfillment of this duty, one marries, or harmoniously connects, those many natural abilities in which one takes pleasure (and which therefore constitute a central aspect of one's pursuit of happiness) with one's rational capacity for end-setting. And in the exercise of this free capacity for end-setting toward whatever natural capacity is cultivated, one not only continues to enjoy whatever natural capacity is being enhanced—e.g., one's capacity to make and one's natural instinct to consume food—but one also further exercises and further enjoys that natural capacity via its connection to one's virtuous capacity for free choice, recognizing that ability to set ends—even when applied merely for pragmatic purposes—as something that expresses one's value as a person capable of setting ends. My sensible self is thereby elevated into the world of my rational self, and this is a happy marriage indeed.

By expanding one's end-setting capacity beyond obligatory ends as such and toward the obligatory cultivation of pragmatic purposes in this marriage of nature and freedom, one thereby affirms the absolute value of one's person in a new way: as an able *pragmatic* end-setter. As Kant puts the point:

> [I]t is a command of morally practical reason and a duty of a human being to himself to cultivate his capacities (some among them more than others, insofar as people have different ends), and to be in a *pragmatic* respect a human being equal to the *end* of his existence. (6:445/194, emphases added)

The Increase of Pragmatic and Moral Pleasures

There is, furthermore, an important affective side to this taking up of one's pragmatic purposes under the auspices of one's objective telos of making persons as such one's end. Because it is our pragmatic purposes, along with the felt attachments related to such purposes, that we are cultivating here, the cultivation of this end also involves the cultivation and elevation of all one's felt attachments related to this end by appeal to one's objective telos of making persons as such one's end. We've already seen such elevation in I.iv, in Kant's affirmation of the cultivation of natural feelings like sympathy for moral purposes. Here, that same sort of elevation occurs, now in relation to all one's natural desires, instincts, and feelings, in a sort of marriage between those natural states, on the one hand, and one's free capacity to set ends as guided by the objective telos of one's being on the other.

This elevation of one's natural felt attachments into the circle of one's moral identity as an end-setter provides, in fact, a particularly important way of attending to, celebrating, and integrating one's experience of the moral feeling of respect in one's interior affective life. We have already seen (in II.i) that it is through appeal to moral feeling that one guides the cultivation of one's affects and passions, leading to an apathetic moderation of those feelings counter to the law and a moral enlivening or excitement of those supportive of the law. This latter moral enlivening of feelings is, however, rather particularly emphasized in this obligation to cultivate one's capacities for a pragmatic purpose. When one brings even one's pleasures in the pragmatic pursuit of quotidian tasks under the auspices of one's moral self, one can celebrate the pleasure one takes in such things in a new way. And such enhancement of one's pleasures, like any moral enlivening of one's felt attachments, occurs precisely through the moral feeling of respect, a feeling which itself has its positive felt moments akin to pleasures.

Here is one way Kant describes this positive side of this moral feeling which is going to do the work of morally enlivening or exciting one's natural feelings:

> [S]o little *displeasure* is there in [the moral feeling of respect] that, once one has laid self-conceit aside and allowed practical influence to that respect, one can in turn never get enough of contemplating the majesty of this law, and the soul believe itself elevated in proportion as it sees the holy elevated above itself and its frail nature. (5:77–78/67)

What Kant describes here is that the positive aspect of moral feeling is simply the joy of seeing one's "soul...elevated above itself and its frail nature." That is, in being reminded of what is "holy" in oneself—one's absolute value as a free and rational being—one feels a particular joy in celebrating who one is.

But such joy in seeing oneself rise above one's merely natural self is also precisely the affective point of view from which one cultivates and elevates those felt attachments related to one's natural self and one's pragmatic pursuits. Indeed, the connection of this positive aspect of moral feeling to the precise obligatory end of cultivating one's natural capacities is particularly evident in Kant's discussion of the former. In this same passage on moral feeling, Kant immediately turns to presenting the "industry in cultivating" one's "native talent" as the paradigmatic example of how this positive pleasure-like side of the moral feeling of respect is expressed. Here, though, Kant emphasizes how one can experience this positive feeling more as admiration for *others* who have cultivated their talents than as a joy in *oneself*. He notes though that this admiration of others "is not mere admiration" precisely because it is in fact an admiration of their presumed moral merits in pursuing the cultivation of their capacities. Here is how he articulates the point:

> No doubt, great talents and activity proportioned to them can also produce respect or a feeling analogous to it, and it is also quite proper to offer it; and then it seems as if admiration were the same as that feeling. But if one looks more closely one will note that, since it always remains uncertain how much was contributed to someone's competence by native talent and how much by his industry in cultivating it, reason represents it to us as presumably the fruits of cultivation and so as merit, and this noticeably reduces our self-conceit and either casts a reproach on us or imposes on us the following of such an example in the way suitable to us.   (5:78/6)

Kant struggles here to distinguish *admiration* for another's talents from *respect* for that person generally, since the two feelings are very similar. Indeed, their similarity is only heightened when the admiration for another's talents is based in an assumption of the meritorious—and virtuous—cultivation of those talents. That is: when one sees a great talent in someone else, reason encourages us to assume that such talent was indeed the product of cultivation, a product of the free endsetting personhood of this person, something worthy of moral praise. The result is an affective experience within oneself not just of admiration, but of morally tempered admiration, an admiration accomplished in tandem with one's moral feeling of respect for that person simply as a person.

Kant then goes on to suggest in this passage that such moral admiration for another can have a rebound effect upon oneself, resulting in the same sort of moral admiration for oneself as the pleasant result of one's efforts at self-cultivation of one's natural capacities. Indeed, to see others' talents in such a moralizing light does something to help our own pursuit of the cultivation of our capacities and the internal affective response we have to such cultivation: to remind oneself that others deserve one's admiration precisely because of their industrious and meritorious pursuit of the realization of their capacities discourages oneself from descending into a sort of "self-conceit" that could easily attach to one's admiration of oneself for one's own talents. That is: when I see someone whom I reasonably take to have done an awful lot to cultivate her natural talents, I am humbled. I think about how I could be accomplishing the same myself, but also about how whatever admiration I might feel tempted to feel for myself must be guided and tempered by that same moral feeling of respect which reminds me that the pleasure I can take in my talents rests in my willingness to cultivate those talents from my own valuable capacity as a free end-setting person. And so, when I do accomplish things or increase my talents, I can indeed take pleasure or morally tempered admiration in myself and my accomplishments, but precisely *as* cultivated accomplishments, something I worked hard to bring to its fullest expression, and something I was able to bring about precisely because of the humanity in my person, that is, the part of me I share with all others, the part of me capable of free end-setting. I admire, in other words, "the holy" in me that has helped me bring this natural capacity beyond "itself and its frail nature." And, in so doing, I can take something like pleasure in my accomplishments without descending into a self-conceit that would encourage me to dwell too much, or in the wrong way, upon my own merits.

And so, although Kant does not use the explicit language of "happiness" in his Doctrine of Virtue discussion of this cultivation of natural capacities for a pragmatic purpose, nor in this second *Critique* reflection upon the joys of self-cultivation, his overall point is clear: even the pursuit of pragmatically desirable ends (the pleasurable realization of which would constitute a portion of one's happiness) should be pursued in a way most worthy of the kind of being one is. And, in assuring that these ends are taken up in this way, one enhances the enjoyment of the pursuit of such ends. One shouldn't pursue happiness in a slavish or piggish way, but only in a way worthy of the kind of being who has as "the end of his existence" something higher than happiness, viz. "the end of humanity in our own person" (6:447/197). This is just where one's pragmatic interests meet and are elevated by one's moral self: to be worthy of myself as a free and rational choosing being, even my natural, pragmatic pursuits and pleasures need to be brought under the aegis of my objective telos of making persons as such my end, here, making myself and especially my pursuit of happiness through the cultivation of my natural capacities, pleasures, and interests my end.[11]

---

[11] It should be obvious from this whole discussion that Kohl (2017) is proven wrong. He asserted a harsh distinction between moral and pragmatic reasoning, suggesting that the latter should be understood as merely theoretical reasoning because it was not really concerned with judgments of value as such. But in this discussion, we have seen Kant moving in a direction entirely opposite to that would-be opposition: we see in these texts so obvious an integration of moral and pragmatic thinking that Kohl's effort to drive a wedge between the two must simply be rejected.

Initial Objections Answered

We return, then, to our original worry that cultivating one's natural capacities for a pragmatic purpose threatened to undermine the moral and virtuous quality of one's end-setting. Where are we at with this question now? Have we abandoned virtuous and moral motivation through the setting of this obligatory end with a pragmatic purpose? Pretty clearly here the answer is no. To say that one is developing one's abilities for a pragmatic purpose is not to say that the ultimate reason I cultivate my capacities is to increase my happiness or to achieve some self-interested advantage. That is not Kant's meaning here. To the contrary, what we've seen is that the capacities on which I am focusing are those intended for pragmatic purposes, capacities the realization of which will constitute a part of my happiness: cooking, or cello-playing, or wittiness. But when I am cultivating these capacities which have pragmatic purposes, I am doing so as guided by a larger, explicit, and ultimate purpose or motive of affirming the humanity in my person, affirming, that is, "the end of [one's] existence" (6:445/194), that end of making persons as such one's end. And so: one way of affirming one's humanity is to welcome even one's natural, pragmatic purposes and thus one's pursuit of happiness into the realm of something which expresses one's humanity as a free and rational being. One's ultimate purpose is to affirm one's humanity; but here, one affirms one's humanity by taking up one's pragmatic interests and thus one's pursuit of happiness in this new, morally sanctioned way. Even my pragmatic interests and pleasures thus become morally informed and become a further means by which I realize my telos of making persons my end.

So, we affirm that it would be wrong—or at least lacking in virtue—to take the promise of pleasure in the cultivation of my natural capacities as the ultimate and only motive for why I pursue this, or any, obligatory end. But that is not what is going on here in Kant's affirmation of an obligatory end with a pragmatic purpose. Rather, we affirm this obligatory end of developing one's natural capacities as yet another way that the virtuous person realizes her objective telos to make persons as such her end. Her motive here remains squarely within what can reasonably be described as acting from the motive of duty: a respect for the law which demands respect for persons. But when it comes to this particular obligatory end of "Developing and Increasing [One's] Natural Perfection...for a Pragmatic Purpose" (6:444/194), it makes sense, as part of the process, to look at one's "*natural* perfections" and one's pragmatic concerns and pleasures to decide how exactly to pursue the virtuous task at hand.

Indeed, finding those things in which I take pleasure and which I thus am naturally motivated to pursue seems exactly the *right* way of narrowing down what precise thing to do to enhance one's natural perfections, a task which, as we've seen, Kant emphasizes is not commanded by virtue and is instead chosen at the discretion of the person seeking the end. Indeed, if "no rational principle prescribes specifically how far one should go" (6:392/154–155) in such cultivation, it seems the *only* other route one *could* take is this pragmatic, natural, sensible, and circumstantial one: find the activities which excite your feelings and which are present and available to you (or could be made present and available to you), and rely upon guidance from all this to establish your projects of cultivation and development. We thus affirm a duty of virtue which realizes itself in part through the pursuit of happiness, without having the motivation for such realization undermined by heteronomous motives.

One might even be so convinced at this point that the pursuit of these pragmatic ends is indeed done for a moral motive that one might raise precisely the opposite objection: is this development of natural capacities for a pragmatic purpose really about the pursuit of *happiness* at all? Is it not, in fact, just another example of exercising *virtue*, viz. yet another example of virtuous obligatory end-setting, now by establishing and realizing the end of increasing one's natural perfections as an expression of one's objective telos of making persons as such one's end?

There is no doubt that the pursuit of this end is, as we have seen, centrally concerned with virtue. And yet the point we have been making is that this end is concerned with *both* happiness and virtue; this is a *marriage* of nature and freedom, happiness and virtue. This is an important point. In the establishment of this obligatory end, Kant is welcoming one's pursuit of happiness *within* one's pursuit of virtue, and not simply as something else one does outside of virtue but within the permissibility constraints marked out by moral demands. There is, furthermore, a value claim underlying this integration of pragmatic pursuits within virtue: in the establishment of this duty, Kant is emphatically *not* making the Stoic suggestion that the only thing that matters in life is the pursuit of virtue. Indeed, this is the whole point of cultivating capacities which themselves have specifically "*pragmatic* purpose[s]" (6:444/194, capitals removed, emphasis added). In affirming the value of cultivating just these sorts of capacities, Kant thus simultaneously affirms the value of natural capacities and instincts which have their own natural, pragmatic, and non-moral needs, felt attachments, interests, and ends. Kant's main point, of course, is to emphasize that the pursuit of such things, and the happiness that comes with such pursuit, finds its most proper ordering and cultivation from a moral perspective. But such a point does not undermine the fact that pragmatic pursuits and their objects have a non-moral value of their own.[12]

---

[12] We thus affirm Watson's (1983) argument that there is a robust conception of non-moral value in Kant's works. As he notes: "Kant's position is that human beings necessarily will care significantly about the fulfillment of their natural needs and desires. Even if we were perfect in virtue, our contentment with our lives on the whole would depend upon fortune. When things go very badly (and virtue does not preclude this), we will not be happy. While [moral] self-contentment is not irrelevant to happiness—not excluded by definition—it is simply insufficient to provide us with contentment with our lives on the whole" (Watson 1983, 93). And then later: "A good life for us as human beings—as finite, rational creatures with needs—simply could not be a life that failed to meet our basic needs and

This is a true *marriage* of virtue and happiness! This particular way of increasing one's happiness—viz., via the moral elevation and enhancement of one's natural pleasures and perfections—is an intimate intertwining of moral and pragmatic elements: because I am elevating natural capacities and the felt attachments related to the exercise of those capacities, such enhancement will inevitably increase my happiness; this is its pragmatic element. But, by connecting this pursuit of happiness with my free capacity to set ends, I am pursuing that happiness under the aegis of my objective telos of making persons as such my end; this is the moral element.

III. A Picture of the Virtuous Pursuit of Happiness

A. The Complete Marriage of Virtue and Happiness

The Complete Marriage of Virtue and Happiness: An Objection Considered
Let's explore just how far one can take this intimate marriage of happiness and virtue, as guided by the obligatory end to cultivate one's natural capacities with pragmatic purposes. The main question to ask at this point is this: is it the case that *any* activity constitutive of one's happiness is required to have this dual moral/pragmatic structure, or is there a pursuit of happiness that occurs outside the auspices of one's moral concern to make persons as such one's end? Surely, we can admit that Kant will demand, at minimum, a permissibility constraint upon the pursuit of any activity meant to be constitutive of one's happiness: whether having a G&T[13] here and now in this way conflicts with other ends I have prioritized in my virtuous end-setting will always present the possibility of a relevant constraint to my pursuit of happiness. But does pursuit of one's objective telos demand more than that in one's pursuit of happiness? We've told a story in Part I in which the command of the Second Formulation of the Categorical Imperative takes us beyond permissibility constraints. It introduces also the positive command to reject indifference to persons and thereby sets the positive task of making persons as such my end. The question now, though, is just how thoroughly that command should pervade one's existence. Is this so much an objective telos of my existence that we would admit that *everything* I do—even everything I do in relation to increasing my *happiness*—*m*ust be brought under its purview? When I'm just enjoying a G&T on the porch, is the pleasure I'm taking there

---

interests" (p. 93). In short, satisfaction with one's virtue is not an adequate satisfaction, on its own, for a truly human life. We humans also need the assurance of the satisfaction of at least some of our needs and interests. An assertion of non-moral value—the value of the objects of our needs and interests—is thus affirmed. I shall discuss the nature of this moral value in greater depth in the next section of this chapter.

[13] For teetotalers, that's a "gin and tonic."

(and the value I attribute to the experience) merely pragmatic, or does even this simple pleasure somehow need to be made constitutive of the objective telos of my being?

There are certainly ways in which one *could* understand such simple pleasures as having deeper import. Why, for example, do I enjoy sitting on the porch with a drink? In part, I do it just to relax. But in part such opportunity for relaxation also allows me to discover myself—my cares, my relationships, my joys, my worries— more deeply and successfully than what only a busy world of work would allow. So even a simple pleasure like drinking a cocktail has the potential to be connected with the identity-building end of the affirmation of oneself as a person. Our question, though, is this: *must* this be the case? Am I doing something wrong, or at least failing to do something meritorious and virtuous, if I fail to integrate *all* my pleasures into the story of building an identity for myself as a being of absolute value? Some may worry that this would be just too heavy-handed a conception of happiness. We can admit that some examples of drinking a G&T can be meaningfully integrated into larger, moral, and identity-constituting end-setting activities. But isn't it too heavy handed to say that *all* the pleasure I might take in drinking a G&T is related to some further end, that is, to some end beyond the obvious end of taking pleasure in the drinking of it? Will integrating my objective telos of making persons as such my end demand even that I take up each experience of pleasure in my drinking of a G&T into that telos, making the pleasure I take in such drinking an expression of my valuing of persons?

My suggestion is that Kant would answer, emphatically "yes!," and, further, that we should welcome this move. Deontological Eudaemonism is indeed a call for a strong commitment to the moralization of one's life. One *would* be failing to realize one's virtue if some aspect of one's pursuit of pleasure and happiness could not be brought within the guidance and aegis of one's objective telos. Indeed, this is just exactly what it means to say that the demand to make persons as such my end is the *telos*—*t*hat is, the ultimate and organizing end—of my being: it is the end toward which everything in me is pointed and the end therefore which orders and structures everything in me.

Another Objection Considered

I realize that some may consider this moralization of happiness a problematic, heavy-handed move, essentially an overmoralization of one's life. I believe, though, that the best argument against such objectors is to provide a picture of the life of a person engaged in this virtuous pursuit of happiness: by providing such a picture, one can see the attractiveness of such a life, and avoid misguided caricatures of it. For the rest of this chapter, we will thus respond to this objector by exploring the thoroughgoing marriage of virtue and happiness in greater depth.

I want first, though, to consider another sort of objector, one who would suggest that, in the account we have provided here, happiness is presented only as something that is the product of one's end-setting. But, in fact, so this objector continues, happiness is not simply a project of end-setting; it is, on the one hand, something broader and, on the other, something more serendipitous and coincidental than the project of end-setting. Even if some of one's happiness is the product of one's conscious activity and thus integratable within one's projects of moral end-setting, sometimes happiness comes upon a person unexpectedly and unexplained, not as a result of any direct end-setting, and certainly not from that direct end-setting in which I make happiness as such my end. Indeed, it seems that making happiness as such one's end is a recipe for disaster, not happiness.

This objector raises legitimate concerns. It is certainly true that our account of happiness emphasizes a happiness attainable through end-setting. And were Kant's account of happiness overall concerned only with that happiness which is achievable through end-setting, he would be missing something. We can, however, affirm the import of realizing happiness through the setting of ends while simultaneously admitting that at least some aspects of one's happiness are not a product of such end-setting and, indeed, are not in the control of the end-setter. Let's dwell on the ways in which this can be the case.[14]

First, we can affirm that, on the model we have just described, "happiness" as such is not the explicit content of the end one pursues. In pursuing the end of cultivating one's natural capacities for a pragmatic purpose, one does not say: "I am going to pursue happiness." Rather, one says: "I am going to pursue the expression of this or that natural capacity because I enjoy it and because getting better at it will make me a better person." What one trusts in the process of engaging in and losing oneself in the pursuit of these ends, though, is that an increased pleasure will result. And when one does this with the whole series of one's most compelling natural capacities, the sum of those pleasures simply will be "happiness." So, in this process we have been describing, happiness is not something directly sought as an end, but rather something that supervenes upon the setting and realization of ends whose content themselves is not "happiness" as such but only "something that I naturally enjoy."[15]

Second, end-setting is a necessary, though not sufficient, aspect of one's happiness. After all, if one didn't set ends at all, it is unlikely one would be happy. A couch-potato plan for happiness is guaranteed to fail as a plan to satisfy beings who are by nature end-setters; for such beings, this seems more a rejection of

---

[14] It is an interesting question to ask whether, in his second *Critique* discussion of the Highest Good, Kant is indirectly or implicitly encouraging us to envision a conception of happiness tied explicitly and only to end-setting. That is: if I am worthy only of that happiness justified by my successful realization of virtue, then, in this ultimate settling of the books, do we need to understand happiness itself as always and only related to end-setting? If this is true, then my suggestion here that some legitimate happiness is unrelated to end-setting would need to be revised. I will, however, set this question aside for another time.

[15] We will explore the import of pursuing happiness in just this way at greater length later in this chapter.

one's nature and a plan for depression than a plan for happiness. So the activity of end-setting—having some sort of impetus or inclination to *do* things—is not *un*related to the pursuit of happiness and, indeed, seems central to it. After all, every *pursuit* of pleasure as such is related to end-setting: if I'm *pursuing* a pleasure, that very pursuit is best understood as an *end* that I've set in relation to that pleasure which I am trying to realize. This is almost a tautological claim.

But here is the problem: is every *experience* of pleasure related to my happiness something I *pursue* and therefore something intrinsically related to end-setting in this way? The clear answer here has to be: no. Pleasure is something that can come unexpectedly upon oneself, unbidden, as for example when one suddenly and unexpectedly sees a bird or flower that is beautiful.

So in our discussion of the pursuit of happiness under the aegis of one's objective telos of making persons as such one's end, we are indeed implicitly assuming that the happiness to be thusly integrated is that happiness which is pursued through the setting of ends which would satisfy one's desires and increase one's pleasures (keeping in mind the indirect way in which this is accomplished, viz. that I set ends not with the explicit content of "happiness" but with the explicit content of "this is something I enjoy"). But we can admit, simultaneously, that not all experiences of pleasure in part constitutive of our happiness are related to end-setting in this way. As we've said, some pleasure just arrives, unbidden: the surprise appearance of a beautiful bird on one's bird feeder, the early spring blooming of a flower. And if there is anything here in these experiences of unbidden pleasures that needs to come under the purview of one's objective telos, it is going to be something a little different than any direct duty to cultivate those pleasures. One might, instead, try to set one's ends generally in a way that makes one the sort of person more prepared for or disposed to welcome the serendipity and spontaneity of such unexpected pleasures (and, conversely, that makes one the sort of person prepared or disposed to reject and restrain the experience and pursuit of those unbidden pleasures which promise conflict with one's objective telos). It would certainly, in any case, not be impossible to do the opposite: to set ends in a way that makes a person *unwilling* to take pleasure in unexpected things, or *unable* to realize the value of (and therefore the worthiness of taking pleasure in) something that just appears before oneself (e.g., a bird, butterfly, or flower...); or to set ends in a way that did *not* prepare one to *reject* illicit unbidden pleasures.

Indeed, once we realize this possibility of being either good or not good at welcoming unexpected pleasures properly, it becomes clear that there is something potentially blameworthy (and thus, conversely, potentially praiseworthy) about the way in which one manages unexpected pleasures. Some happiness comes upon us unbidden. Even here, though, it is possible, and incumbent upon us—or at least meritorious of us—to become the sort of person prepared to welcome the unbidden pleasures the world has to offer in the right way. Indeed, if we are going to welcome the complete integration of one's person under the aegis of one's objective telos of making persons as such one's end, becoming a person who is disposed to welcome unbidden pleasures properly, as both limited and encouraged by that life-guiding telos, is simply another aspect of pursuing happiness virtuously.

We can thus welcome this indirect end-setting of the development of such a disposition as yet another means by which the virtuous person indirectly pursues happiness without assuming that all pleasures are themselves the result of explicit end-setting: some pleasures come unbidden, but the virtuous person is the person who knows how to make the best of unbidden pleasures![16]

B. Values and Pleasures

The Intertwining of Pragmatic and Moral Pleasure, and of Relative Non-Moral and Absolute Moral Values

Having affirmed this moral demand to pursue the pleasures that constitute one's happiness in an elevating way—that is, in a way that affirms oneself as a free end-setter and thus as a being of absolute value—let us now explore this process in more detail: what is it like when one takes up the cultivation of a natural capacity, thereby elevating one's pragmatic interests and pleasures into something constitutive of one's virtuous and moral telos of making persons as such one's end? What we shall discover is that this marriage of pragmatic interests and virtue is, essentially, the story of the virtuous pursuit of happiness. And in this virtuous pursuit of happiness, we discover a marriage both of relative non-moral and absolute moral value, on the one hand, and of pragmatic and moral felt attachments on the other.

First, then, we shall encounter the interrelation of relative and absolute value within the life of a virtuous person: all pursuit of things of relative non-moral value is guided by the absolute moral value of persons. That absolute value thus provides the evaluative distance necessary for the most satisfying pursuit of those things of relative value, the acquisition of which would constitute one's happiness, an evaluative distance which properly places these things of relative value in proper relation to the purpose of one's being overall. And then, second, we discover an intertwining of one's felt attachments related to pragmatic purposes and

---

[16] There is work one could do here to connect such a disposition to Kant's discussions of the need for an aesthetic appreciation of nature. He speaks, for example, of the importance of a "disposition...to love something (e.g. beautiful crystal formations, the indescribably beauty of plants) even apart from any intention to use it" as valuable for "promoting morality" (6:443/207). But such a disposition could also be understood as valuable for promoting happiness. Such connections are even more tantalizing to explore once we remember, as we saw in II.ii, that the pleasure one takes in the unimpeded exercise of one's aptitude for virtue is strikingly similar in form to aesthetic pleasure. In taking up the aesthetic experience of beauty, one thus brings the harmony of one's practical faculties to a higher level by connecting it with the harmony of one's intellectual and perceptual faculties.

one's ultimate and organizing felt attachment, the moral feeling of respect, an intertwining in which one acquires that affective state both most satisfying and most stable and reliable for the continuing pursuit of happiness in the face of the vicissitudes of fortune. Let us turn to this consideration of the virtuous pursuit of happiness, a story of the intimate interaction of pleasure in relatively valuable things and pleasure in affirming and enhancing the absolute value of persons that emerges when one marries the moral demand to make persons as such one's end with one's pragmatic interest in being happy through one's end-settings.

To appreciate the marriage of relative non-moral and absolute moral value in the virtuous person's pursuit of happiness, and the intertwining of pragmatic and moral felt attachments associated with this marriage, let's first step back and reflect upon the hierarchy of value that has been emerging in our account of virtue overall. In II.i, and II.ii, we saw Kant appeal to moral apathetic toleration of sacrifice, to moral enlivening and excitement of one's felt attachments, and, ultimately, to a non-felt pleasure in the exercise of one's free aptitude for virtue to describe the subjective state of the person of virtue. We now, through this just-affirmed obligatory end of developing one's natural capacities for a pragmatic purpose, also see him welcoming the pleasurable cultivation and excitement of natural instincts, natural capacities, and pragmatic concerns into this sphere of the subjective experience of the exercise and pursuit of that objective telos which constitutes virtue. But underlying all these points—admitting genuine loss in suffering, welcoming the pleasure one takes in virtue, integrating the pleasure one takes in pragmatic pursuits—underlying, that is, all these points as part of the subjective state of the virtuous person, we find grounding assumptions about the nature of value. We discover, in particular, a basis for Kant's rejection of a Stoic conception of valuing, and especially a rejection of the Stoic idea that the only thing of value is the exercise of virtue. Instead, in all of these moments constituting the subjective experience of a person exercising virtue, we see Kant's insistence upon the value of things beyond the absolute moral value of persons within the life of virtue. Let's reflect further on the story of value implicit in these discussions.[17]

On the account of virtue we've developed, anything of value needs to be assessed in light of the absolute moral value of persons. This does not, however, mean that nothing else has value, only that every other thing will have only relative non-moral value, a value assessed relative to and in light of this absolute

---

[17] As already noted, I take the forthcoming account to be in sympathy with Watson (1983), whose account of the importance of happiness in the moral life is predicated upon the previous assumption that there are things of value to the virtuous person beyond her virtue: "Kant's position is that human beings necessarily will care significantly about the fulfillment of their natural needs and desires. Even if we were perfect in virtue, our contentment with our lives on the whole would depend upon fortune. When things go very badly (and virtue does not preclude this), we will not be happy. While self-contentment is not irrelevant to happiness—not excluded by definition—it is simply insufficient to provide us with contentment with our lives on the whole" (p. 93).

moral value of persons. Our first application of this point was in II.i, where we saw Kant reject Stoic indifference, that refusal of attribution of value to anything but virtue. When the virtuous person faces loss, instead of becoming indifferent to those things lost, she is able to moderate her felt attachments through appeal to the moral feeling of respect. As a result, the virtuous person continues to realize the value of what she has lost, but can regulate her felt attachments to those things since she also realizes that their relative non-moral value pales in comparison to the absolute moral value of persons. This decrease in felt attachment is thus pegged to proper assessment (or reassessment) of the value of the thing lost: unlike the Stoic prioritization of virtue as the only thing of value, Kant rejects the idea that everything else loses all value in the face of the absolute value of persons, and instead suggests that a proper virtuous attitude *is* to realize the value, but merely the *relative* value of everything else.[18] One's felt experience of moral feeling is, then, that affective means which helps the person of virtue to experience her felt attachments to other things less precisely because she realizes all else is in fact less valuable than the absolute value of persons.

We then, in II.i, saw the moral excitement or enlivening of one's felt attachments as the correlative capacity for heightening those felt attachments which are supportive of virtue. Such enlivening or excitement is, furthermore, like the moral moderation of one's feelings, tagged to an underlying story of value: one's feeling of, e.g., natural sympathy increases when one is able to cultivate that sympathy from the moral concern to make persons as such one's end. In so doing, the value of being sympathetic is heightened: it is no longer simply a coincidental natural response, but now also a cultivated moral one. There is, however, a slightly different story to tell of the interweaving of relative and absolute value here. In the case of apathetic toleration of loss, something of relative value is confirmed as being *merely* of relative value and so one's felt attachment to it decreases in light of the recognition of something else of absolute value. But here, in the case of moral excitement, something of relative non-moral value (e.g., one's natural sympathies) is *confirmed* as a relatively valuable thing (viz., that it is a valuable thing to connect naturally with other persons and their needs), but it is no longer *simply* a relatively valuable thing and feeling. Rather, it is now also welcomed as a further affective affirmation (alongside and in conjunction with the moral feeling of respect) of the absolute moral value of persons. What had previously been of merely relative non-moral value in one's affective life (viz., one's natural affective

---

[18] Again, we are in agreement with Watson (1983) here: "Kant would have to reject the Stoic's first premise instead. He would have to deny that the only thing worth caring significantly about is virtue. Otherwise the discontent of the virtuous person would not be consonant with the correct judgment of value. This denial is perhaps implicit in Kant's complaint that the Stoics 'not only exaggerated the moral capacity of man' (in thinking people capable of holiness) but 'refused to recognize the second component of the highest good, i. e., happiness, as a special object of human desire' (2,131[127])" (p. 93).

tendency to be concerned about other persons and their needs) now takes on at least the reflected glow of absolute moral value through its cultivation in cooperation with the moral feeling of respect. It remains a natural feeling, and a heightened, excited, and enlivened natural feeling; but it is now also a natural feeling with a moral purpose and a moral expression.

Finally, with this chapter's introduction of the obligatory end of cultivating one's natural capacities, we welcome pragmatic interests, and natural instincts, and the felt attachments related to them, as further positive expressions of this life-orienting telos of making persons as such one's end. What does this mean, though, about the nature of value implicit in such pursuits? The model to apply here is more like the account of moral excitement just articulated: the things one values relatively and the feelings connected to that valuing are affirmed for what they are, but are also brought into communion with the absolute moral value of one's person and the feelings connected to that value.

Consider, for example, the value I find in playing the cello. Cello-playing is an activity which has relative, non-moral values and natural feelings attached to it: when I play the cello, I'm simply enjoying myself through the sounds I produce and through the pride I feel in being the one producing them. These things are valuable to me, and the motives I have for engaging in this activity are pragmatic, non-moral, and pleasure-based motivations.

But my playing of the cello, like all my desires, goals, and activities, must be assessed via my non-negotiable commitment to making persons as such my end. This is, initially, simply a permissibility constraint: I mustn't pursue cello-playing in any way that would violate respect for persons. One shouldn't assume, however, that this mere permissibility constraint is an easy thing to accomplish. Most any professional musician can tell stories of how one's capacities as a musician can be weaponized as tools to humiliate, insult, and injure others. Or, an aspiring but struggling musician could tell stories of the temptation to see her failing efforts to become a good cello-player as a basis upon which she begins to deprecate and even hate herself. All of these would be examples of taking up one's natural capacity for musicianship in a way that fails to meet the permissibility constraints of one's life-guiding objective telos of making persons as such—oneself and others—one's end. Instead of connecting that capacity with a pragmatic purpose to my moral goals, I violate those moral demands through its exercise either by injuring and disrespecting others or by injuring and disrespecting myself.

But beyond these permissibility constraints, my cello-playing also must be taken up positively into my telos of making persons as such my end, assuring that the non-moral value of the activity becomes enhanced via its connection to the affirmation of the absolute moral value of persons: playing the cello thus becomes one of the ways I affirm respect for myself, through the fulfillment of the duty of perfecting my natural capacities. And it might even (if I get good enough at it to play truly dulcet tones!) become one of the ways for me respectfully to enhance the happiness of others.[19]

What, then, is the implicit story of value we are telling when we welcome the integration of the cultivation of natural capacities with pragmatic purposes into one's expression of one's life-guiding telos of making persons as such one's end? We begin, of course, with something of relative non-moral value that simply pleases me: it is a valuable thing to produce music, and I enjoy doing it. But it is precisely because this activity pleases me that it then becomes the basis for my choice of how to express the rationally demanded duty to cultivate my natural capacities. I am not obligated to play the cello, but through appeal to the specifics of my own situation, opportunities, interests, likes, and dislikes, I decide that it is through this activity that I will satisfy the rational demand to cultivate my capacities. If the activity of cello-playing didn't make me happy (i.e., if I didn't take pleasure in the activity as such), then I wouldn't choose it as a way of enjoying myself, much less as a way of fulfilling my obligatory end to develop my natural capacities.

But when I do make this activity that I enjoy a piece of how I make persons as such my end (viz., when I welcome it, by developing my natural ability to play the cello and thereby broadening the scope of the applicability of this natural ability as one way in which I respect myself as a being of absolute moral value), that natural, non-moral enjoyment of things of relative value is elevated by its new relationship to the absolute moral value of persons via the duty of the cultivation of natural capacities with which it is now associated. In so doing, both the *value* of what I am doing is enhanced (because this *relatively* valuable thing of cello-playing is now connected with enhancing the life of an *absolutely* valuable being), and the *pleasure* I take in the activity is heightened (because the *natural* pleasure in cello-playing is connected to the *moral* pleasure of affirming and becoming myself through the cultivation of my natural perfections: in addition to just enjoying playing the cello, I also take pleasure in seeing that activity as an expression of my worth and identity as a person). I acquire, in other words, that admiration for myself tempered by my moral commitments in a way that prevents such admiration from descending into self-conceit. When one takes up one's natural pleasures as guided by this obligatory end of increasing one's natural capacities (itself an end constitutive of one's objective telos of making persons as such one's end), one thus not only elevates the value of what one is doing (connecting a thing of relative non-moral value with someone of absolute moral value) but also increases the pleasure in doing the activity (since the pleasure of that activity is

---

[19] My efforts to learn to play the cello have actually had an influence on my understanding of, and thus my respect and sympathy for, my own philosophy students' struggle to take on a new activity which they've never done before. Struggling even to *play* "Row, Row, Row Your Boat" without sounding like I'm strangling chickens reminds me of my need to be gentle and supportive of my students as they struggle to take up a brand new activity of their own, as for example understanding the argument of Descartes' *Second Meditation*.

now connected with the further pleasure of becoming more fully oneself and affirming one's value as a person). Now I'm motivated to play the cello not only because I enjoy it but also because I realize I am affirming my own capacities and identity as a free and end-setting being: I take pleasure not only in the fact that what I am doing is fun but also in the fact that I'm using my freedom to take a natural thing in me and elevate it as an expression of my personhood. Having begun by elevating my natural capacity into a moral obligation, I come out the other end with an integration of my concern for things of relative value and my ultimate commitment to persons of absolute value, and with an increase in my pleasures overall. Otherwise stated: in making my pragmatic pursuit of cello-playing a duty, I find a virtuous way of becoming happier!

It is worth underscoring the point that the kinds and levels of both value and pleasure involved in this cultivation of one's capacities here are dual. One considers it a valuable thing to be able to produce pleasing music, and one takes pleasure in the exercise of one's natural capacity toward satiation of one's natural instinct to do so. But one also now considers it a valuable thing—an absolutely and life-guiding valuable thing—to affirm persons as such, and one thus takes a further pleasure in elevating these natural capacities and instincts precisely from the perspective of one's absolute value as a person (viz., via one's capacity for free end-setting). It is, in other words, even more *valuable* and more *enjoyable* to do what one naturally loves when one can become better at that thing through the application of one's free capacity for end-setting which makes that natural capacity a part of one's person overall. It is a *pleasing* thing to bring one's pragmatic concerns within the circle of one's moral self. This story of the integration of the natural capacity for musicianship within one's pursuit of virtue thus provides a model for pursuing happiness generally: seeking to bring all of oneself, all one's pleasurable pursuits, within the circle of oneself as a free, end-setting being of absolute value is, simply, the story of the virtuous pursuit of happiness.

Consider one more example of the way in which relatively valuable things and the pleasure one takes in them can be enhanced through relationship of those things to the absolute moral value of persons so as to pursue happiness appropriately to one's situation and opportunities. My father was an intelligent, witty, and sympathetic person who had a thoroughly debilitating illness preventing him from walking, or even being able to sit up in a chair. Indeed, he lost the capacity to do most anything that is typically associated with making one's life pleasurable. But even as he lay in a hospital bed for ten years unable to move, and barely able to talk, he could occasionally make jokes. He even made jokes about when and how he would die: when he told my mother not to buy flowers for their wedding anniversary, but instead for his funeral, and she (after trying to coax him into refusing the idea that he was near death) responded by asking what kind of flowers he'd like, his response was "Dandelions!" That he could make jokes about such things in his condition—that he could care about *anything* in his condition, and that he could care about using his mind and his wittiness excellently even though he had lost most every quality of a well-lived life typically construed—speaks volumes to me about the potential for a person to regulate and enliven the weight of relative values and pleasures therein in light of the absolute moral value of persons so as to increase one's happiness. My father was able, even in this condition, to continue caring for himself and others: to continue valuing things like a loving, joking relationship with his wife and developing his own characteristic capacity for wittiness. He was, furthermore, able to heighten or excite the value both of wittiness and of flowers in a way particularly expressive of his person: the dandelions we threw on his grave before placing dirt over the top of his coffin had become heightened in value in relationship to his personhood. They were still only objects of relative non-moral value; but in their association with the well-lived life of a person who had suffered much but who still found ways to enhance his happiness and virtue, their worth was elevated beyond themselves. They weren't just weeds anymore. They were also an expression of my father's love, wittiness, and strength of character, an expression of his ability to increase his natural capacity for jokes through his free choice, an example of his ability to act lovingly toward my mother even in the most difficult of circumstances. In Kant's language, my father found a capacity, the cultivation of which was appropriate within the constraints of his circumstances, by which he affirmed his worth as a person: he valued and enjoyed his natural capacity for being witty, and cultivated that capacity in the name of his own person and in the name of his love for his family, showing that he was capable of a gentle wit even in the most difficult of circumstances. This too, then, is an example of how the virtuous person pursues happiness.

One has to admit, of course, that one hopes that one's own life will not be limited to these sorts of expressions of virtue and happiness. My father's life, and his happiness, had their limits. One can even ask: is this happy enough to count as a life of happiness and virtue? It is certainly true that one can envision lives—especially lives of happiness empirically conceived—that are somewhat more robust than his. But, on the other hand, both my father and my mother also repeatedly insisted to us that "*My* life is not a tragedy; *our* lives are not a tragedy!" My father could have succumbed to his condition, losing concern for anything of value in his life, wanting instead to kill himself: *that* would have been the tragedy. But he didn't. He instead found a way within the very constrained circumstances that life threw at him to become the best and happiest person he could be. I shall take his example as a model for the rest of my life.

There is a further objection one could raise to this example: in an episode of injury to happiness empirically conceived so intense as this, isn't there also an injury to his happiness rationally conceived? That is: mustn't we now admit that his difficult physical state becomes an impediment to his exercise of virtue and that even though he acts virtuously, he lacks the true ease, harmony, or facility which we've attributed to one who has a genuine aptitude for virtue?

In response to this objector, one needs to recall the particular capacity of the person of virtue in remaining herself even as she manages suffering. Indeed, one might say that virtue has something like a Teflon coating: you can spatter things at it, but they wipe off pretty easily. All of which is to say: for my father, there will be a blip of impediment as he or any virtuous person manages the next difficult thing that comes down the path. Call them bumps in the road of an otherwise harmonious road of virtue. But the underlying state of virtue already established is one that is particularly made to manage suffering in the strongest possible way. This was the whole point of our initial II.i discussion of such things. So I envision that when my father had to take on yet another reduction in his physical functioning, he did indeed experience an initial impediment, blip, or bump. But once the new loss or suffering is integrated into one's person overall—understanding that loss as lesser, reducing one's affective response to it in light of one's overall capacity to remember the absolute value of persons—he returned to a smoother state. One can perhaps wish not to have to be this person of virtue, one whose virtue is tested so regularly and intensely by negative experiences which injure one's happiness empirically conceived. But, with Kant, I suggest that such persons stand as a testament to the power of what virtue can be. My father, amidst all these injuries to his person, was happy, rationally conceived. He even managed a healthy dose of happiness empirically conceived.

I should emphasize here that what we have just described my father doing is *not* an example of Stoicism. He did not say to himself that the loss of his mobility or of his speech, etc., was not a valuable thing. Instead, he placed the immense value of such activities in perspective relative to his and others' absolute worth as a person. Such reflection allowed him to manage the loss of things with relative non-moral worth with strength and equilibrium. It is such return to a stable state of equilibrium that allowed him, instead of losing himself in self-pity, to make jokes: "I can't walk or talk now, but I still have my wittiness!!" My father thus brought moral value to that merely pragmatic activity of wittiness precisely because the wittiness he displayed put into such extraordinary relief the power of his capacity for free choice.

Note, too, that his and all these stories of the integration of happiness and virtue are not stories of *dissolving* relative non-moral value into absolute moral value. My cello-playing still has a value distinct from the moral value it acquires through such guidance. Furthermore, the pleasure I take in playing my cello is not reducible to the moral pleasure I take in the ways that this activity points me toward virtue. Once integrated into a life governed by respect for persons, the activity of cello-playing has its moral goals and moral pleasures. Nonetheless, engaging in this activity also has a value and pleasure not reducible to moral value or moral pleasure. Rather, non-moral values and pleasures are themselves enhanced, heightened, and elevated through relationship to one's life-guiding demand to respect persons.

To put the point conversely: this elevation of non-moral values and pleasures does not turn them into values and pleasures concerned *only* with absolute moral value. Rather, they remain pleasures attached to things of relative value. But that relative value is heightened both in itself and also in relation to the fact of absolute moral value which guides one's life. Indeed, to call the value which pervades my pursuit of activities constitutive of my happiness "relative" in the first place is just another way of saying that I affirm the value of that activity *in light of* the *absolute value of persons*: I assess the value of this activity *relative* to that absolute and non-relative value. And yet, this *is* a valuable and pleasurable activity in its *own* right: I want a life in which I experience the pleasure of being a good cello-player, just for itself. Virtue did not demand of me that I become a cello-player; virtue demands of me that I make persons as such my end and that I cultivate my capacities. And so I look at myself and the many things that please or fulfill me, and find my own distinctive ways of affirming the demands of virtue even as I simultaneously enjoy myself and become myself. I find a virtuous way to pursue my non-moral pleasures, pursuing the relative value of a whole range of things not specifically demanded by virtue. When we say that Kant is concerned with happiness beyond pleasure in the life of virtue, it is to such pleasures, activities, and values that we point: for a virtuous person to flourish, she needs a happiness that includes taking pleasure in these identity-constituting and non-morally valuable things.

The Virtuous Pursuit of Happiness Is the Non-Self-Absorbed Pursuit of Happiness

A crucial point to appreciate about this virtuous pursuit of happiness is that this pursuit assures the fulfillment of one's desires in a less self-absorbed way than what one would typically think of the pursuit of happiness as involving. As we've just seen, the virtuous person evaluates and organizes everything she does in accordance with her life-guiding telos of making persons as such one's end, both constraining herself from actions which violate that demand and attaching to all her activities a moral value of making persons as such one's end which informs and enhances their original non-moral value and the pleasure one takes in that relatively valuable thing. But this means her desires are no longer simply about themselves. Indeed, the fullest telos of any desire the fulfillment of which would be constitutive of my happiness (like my desire to become a cellist, or my father's desire to be witty) thus really is a telos beyond itself, a telos of making persons as such one's end. Those activities, themselves independent of moral demands, cannot become what they most fully can be, value- or pleasure-wise, unless they are guided by moral demands which connect them both to the realization of oneself as a person and to the enhancement of one's respect for other valuable persons. The simple enjoyment of cello-playing or joke-telling thus realizes itself best when it has been educated by the refusal of self-absorption which its integration within a context of making persons as such one's end assures.

My suggestion here is, then, that the best and most successful pursuit of happiness is a non-self-absorbed pursuit of happiness. This is not easy. Desire—and especially not-yet-fulfilled desire—is the kind of thing that can turn a person in on herself, making her oblivious of the true nature of values in the world around her. Instead of taking an evaluative distance upon one's pursuit of happiness in the way that appeal to absolute value allows, one could instead become absorbed in oneself, in what one lacks, and in the drive to fulfill that desire. The effect of such self-absorption is not pretty. It would be something like that egregiously hurtful and insulting use of one's musicianship mentioned earlier: people for whom the pleasure of being the best cellist (or of believing one is the best cellist) causes them to be injurious and insulting toward others who would dare to think they could play together or consider themselves equal with that person musically. Instead of tethering one's pursuit of happiness to respect for persons, one thus weaponizes that pursuit into something injurious to persons. One can pursue happiness in this way, but my suggestion is that, inevitably, this is going to be not only an immoral pursuit but also a less successful pursuit of happiness.[20]

This capacity to enhance relative non-moral values and the pleasure one takes in them through connection to moral values is, thus, just another example of the capacity for *moral excitement* at work, that flip-side of the virtuous person's moral apathetic capacity for toleration (viz., her capacity to downplay non-moral values when she needs to sacrifice something) which we discussed in II.i. Whether it is to heighten or to moderate value, appeal to the demand to make persons as such one's end acts as a regulator of one's relative non-moral values and pleasures. The only unchanging, absolute standard of value is the value of persons, and everything else—absolutely *everything* else—becomes regulated through appeal to this firm point.

C. The Virtuous Pursuit of Happiness

Introduction

What these examples of cello-playing and wittiness reveal is the nature of the intimate interweaving of moral and pragmatic concerns in the virtuous pursuit of happiness, both value- and affect-related. Let us further explore each side of this moral pursuit of happiness—viz., the marriage of relative and absolute value (and the evaluative distance one gains on the value of one's pragmatic pursuits thereby), on the one hand, and the intimate intertwining of pragmatic and moral pleasures

---

[20] This claim that the virtuous pursuit of happiness is the most successful pursuit of happiness is something to which I'll return at greater length in our final discussions of virtue and happiness, below, in Section II.

(from the perspective of the same evaluative distance) on the other—so as to tell a complete story of the virtuous pursuit of happiness.

We can, indeed, understand each side of this virtuous pursuit of happiness as a description of different kinds of tools the virtuous person brings to the pursuit of happiness, both objective and subjective tools of self-cultivation. First, on the objective side, the virtuous person brings the non-negotiable demand to make persons as such one's end to her pursuit of happiness so as to provide focus and guidance about how precisely to value things of relative non-moral value and thereby to help her decide how best to pursue the realization of non-moral, relatively valuable things in her life. Second, on the subjective side, the affective ground of virtue which we have identified as a moderating and regulating of all one's felt attachments through the moral feeling of respect (resulting in moral apathy, moral excitement, health, tranquility, pleasure, and cheerfulness in the exercise of virtue) and the pleasurable experience of the exercise of one's aptitude for virtue which emerges as the fruit of all this hard work, serve as a strong affective point of view from which to further stabilize, regularize, and manage one's affective experience of the pursuit of happiness so as to help the person of virtue internally manage the vicissitudes of fortune. Let's consider each of these points in turn.

To summarize briefly what we shall see in the forthcoming: first, we shall see that the objective demand to make persons as such one's end becomes a meta-rule for implementation of the rules of prudence, thereby not only *constraining* one's pursuit of happiness (so as to assure that it is respectful of all one's person, both rational and sensible) but, more importantly, also *enhancing* one's ability to evaluate one's pragmatic options (so as to see more clearly the value of things that really have the potential to make one fulfilled overall). In other words, once again, the absolute value of persons provides the virtuous person with a distinctive evaluative distance on her desires, an evaluative distance which allows her to assess things of relative value from the perspective of that thing of absolute value which defines one's being, thereby assuring that one pursues things of relative value in the most attentive, properly construed, and therefore successful way possible.

Then we shall see that, subjectively, this experience of the pursuit of happiness from the perspective of virtue provides the virtuous person with the strongest point of view from which to take on the challenges inevitably presented by one's pursuit of happiness. One's state of moral apathetic tranquility, excitement, pleasure, and cheerfulness with which one pursues virtue in fact provides a strong subjective point of view from which to manage the vicissitudes of fortune—both the ups and the downs of it—which visit upon one's pursuit of happiness. For the virtuous person, when things go well, she doesn't let it go to her head; and when things go ill, she doesn't collapse in despair. Her experience of the ups and downs of fortune evens out a bit, and her experience of being happy increases thereby. Overall, then, both objectively—in terms of value assessment—and subjectively—in terms of her subjective felt experience—the virtuous person does not misconstrue her pursuit of happiness, but instead is most able to appreciate the proper value of things and to subjectively enjoy that value most appropriately. And in this even-handed approach to it, the sun of happiness rises!

The Objective Tools of Virtue for Pursuit of Happiness

First, then, the virtuous person's commitment to the objective, non-negotiable value of making persons as such one's end provides the virtuous person with the perspective from which to assess the proper relative value of things she is considering pursuing. This guidance does not, however, take the form of a categorical demand to take up some particular natural capacity instead of another; for, indeed, we have already confirmed that

> [w]hich...natural perfection...should take precedence, and in what proportion one against the other it may be a human being's duty to himself to make these natural perfections his end, are *matters left for him to choose in accordance with his own rational reflection about what sort of life he would* like *to lead.*
> (6:445/195, emphases added)

That is, one's objective telos of making persons as such one's end does not require one to take up any particular natural capacity. This determination depends, as we have seen, upon one's pragmatic interests and pleasures. Nonetheless, the categorical demand to make persons as such one's end can guide and inform these non-categorically demanded choices about how to pursue relatively valuable activities in one's life. Most centrally, by evaluating everything of relative value from the perspective of the absolute value of persons, one is better able to understand those things of relative value for what they are. One is thereby more able to choose appropriately because one's choice of values and activities is not corrupted by egregious misvaluings grounded in one's own temptations to value things only from an excessively self-absorbed and self-conceited point of view. In short, the objective non-negotiable demand to make persons as such my end, by evening out one's valuing of and ultimate desire for things of relative value, provides a focus and guide for valuing relatively valuable things and the pleasures one takes in them for what they really are. Someone who knows that there is something about herself more important than desire-fulfillment is going to approach her assessment of things she desires and the fulfillment those desires differently than someone who has no such distance from which to put the whole pursuit of happiness into perspective. Affirmation of a value beyond desire-satisfaction thus enables her to assess the value of the things she desires from the more stable, non-self-absorbed position of granting the absolute value of persons. Whatever she pursues, she knows that *none* of these things are more important than respecting and valuing persons; and she knows that *all* of them gain more import and value in light of their connection to the absolute value of persons.

What exact sort of focus does the virtuous person bring to the objective side of desire-management, when she remembers that anything she pursues is not as important as respecting persons? Most centrally, she does not *mis*value things. The virtuous person will, as she assesses the objects of her desires, be better able to appreciate the true value of things she pursues in the hopes of being happy. She won't under- or overestimate (or even simply misconstrue) their value because of some filter, lens bias, or self-absorption which warps her appreciation for what value a thing really has. She will not, for example, be able, like Epictetus, to treat her husband like a broken jug (viz., she will not be able to *under*estimate the value of persons in the assessment of the value of any persons connected to her happiness). *Over*estimate is, however, the more likely excess that gets avoided in the virtuous pursuit of happiness. St. Augustine's struggles with his desires, as described in his *Confessions*, come to mind here as good examples of the sort of overestimated misconstrual of values that goes on all too easily in the pursuit of happiness. As Augustine describes it, it wasn't just that he *liked*, e.g., sex. Beyond that, he put so much *value* upon sexual activity that he took it to be the center of what made him stable and whole as a person. He thus could not imagine himself living without sex: to do so was akin to the death of himself. Gus wasn't appreciating the relative value of sex from the perspective of the proper, absolutely valuable thing (for him, God). Instead, he gave to sex an absolute value it did not deserve, the pursuit of which made his life miserable.

A virtuous person committed to the absolute value of persons generally just couldn't pursue desire-fulfillment in this way. She would look at sexual relations as an exceedingly valuable thing, but not the most important identity-constituting and governing thing in her life. Or, to return to my cello-playing example: however important an activity music-making might become for the virtuous person, she would never get to the point of valuing it over absolutely everything else. It could get very, very high in her ordering of her values, but would never mutinously overtake the value that guides all values (viz., the absolute value of persons) such that it could easily become a weapon for attacking and insulting persons. Sex and cello-playing, like other things with relative value, are thus always appreciated from the perspective of that absolute value of persons which grounds one's pursuit of virtue, even as one makes choices about pursuing such things in their own right. The virtuous person thus has an enhanced value-assessment perspective from which to pursue happiness, one which assures that things of relative value are not misconstrued as things of absolute and life-governing value.

Another way to conceive of this enhanced value-assessment perspective of the virtuous person is to say that her pursuit of happiness no longer occurs *solely* via what Kant calls "counsels of prudence."[21] "Counsels of prudence" or "empirical counsels" are indeed rules which, in the absence of categorical rational demands that would order specific things to pursue toward happiness, help to guide one's decision about what sorts of things to pursue toward the realization of one's happiness. "One cannot...act on determinate principles for the sake of being happy, but only on empirical counsels, for example, of a regimen, frugality, courtesy, reserve and so forth, which experience teaches are most conducive to well-being on the average" (4:418/29). These counsels, then, are rules which, when there is no command to determine one's choice, help one to think about what is and is not in one's self-interest, both short- and long-term.

Furthermore, precisely because these are rules that do not command categorically, they are rules the application of which require a very particular pragmatic rational skill, a "*skill* in the choice of means to one's own happiness" (4:416/29, emphasis added). Such skill is required in the use of counsels of prudence because, as we've seen in I.i, the end of happiness is not determinate enough to establish in itself an analytic and necessary relationship between that end and the means to it. As we saw earlier, such completeness and determinacy in the pursuit of happiness is impossible:

> [I]mperatives of prudence cannot, to speak precisely, command at all, that is, present actions objectively as practically necessary;...that the problem of determining surely and universally which action would promote the happiness of a rational being is completely insoluble, so that there can be no imperative with respect to it that would, in the strict sense, command him to do what would make him happy; for happiness is not an ideal of reason but of imagination, resting merely upon empirical grounds, which it is futile to expect should determine an action by which the totality of a series of results in fact infinite would be attained. (4:418–419/29)

As such, instead of following fully categorical rules which would require no judgment in their application (since such rules would command, with no room for discretion), one needs instead skill in assessing, applying, and following these rules or counsels of prudence.

One appeals to these counsels of prudence as a sort of rule-of-thumb kind of advice about which kinds of pursuits generally promise more happiness overall. But this means that these rules have lots of fudge room in their application. And in a complex life with potentially conflicting self-interests, some of us are better,

---

[21] In connecting rules of prudence with a guiding rule of morality, as we go on to do here, we take up and expand upon Holberg's (2018) original suggestion, versus Kohl (2017) discussed earlier, that prudential and moral reasoning are more intimately intertwined than Kohl asserts them to be.

and others worse, at "tak[ing] care of one's advantage" (4:417n/28n). Being prudent in the pursuit of happiness is, in other words, a "skill" to be acquired (4:416/29).

Our claim, though, is that the virtuous person knows *best* how to utilize rules of prudence, that is, becomes most *skilled* in their deployment.[22] Why would this be? It is not because she takes the pursuit of her advantage to the highest quasi-categorical level possible, but precisely for the opposite reason: because these rules of prudence are *not* the last word in the ordering of a life pursuing happiness, she places them within the higher life-guiding context of her objective telos of making persons as such one's end. This is just that same evaluative distance upon one's desires of which we have been speaking: this global perspective of an abiding respect for persons assures that realization of one's self-interest will never become the overall life-guiding, passionate, second-order desire of one's life. But this is just as much as to say that my utilization of rules of prudence become beholden to a higher rule, the rule of making persons as such one's end.

We need to be careful in understanding this relationship of counsels of prudence and the "rule" of one's objective telos of making persons as such one's end. Counsels of prudence are still "counsels" and not "commands" here, viz. it is not that, through connection to my telos of respecting persons that they now order one's choices via either analytic or synthetic categorical necessity. And yet, these counsels are both clarified and enhanced through appeal to my objective telos of making persons as such my end. First, in virtue of this telos, rules of prudence now have a sort of rim or perimeter beyond which they will not go, certain permissibility constraints which exclude some moves within the application of counsels of prudence that, in terms only of the goals of prudence, would be allowed. Within that perimeter, one's generally reliable counsels for increasing one's happiness thus rest on the protective cushion of one's categorical demand to respect persons.

I describe these permissibility constraints as a "cushion" because the virtuous person would not think of these constraints just as unfortunate and uncomfortable borders. What these limits are doing is assuring that one's pursuit of happiness *fits* into one's flourishing *overall*, fits into one's existence as a sensibly affected,

---

[22] In so arguing, we place ourselves in sympathy with and seek to expand Holberg's (2018) similar claim: "Firstly, virtue as respect for rational will obliges us to 'procur[e] and promot[e] the *capacity* to realize all sorts of possible ends,' and so the development of skill (*MdS* 6:392): [A human being] has a duty to diminish his ignorance by instruction and to correct his errors. And it is not merely that technically practical reason *counsels* him to do this as a means to his further purposes (of art); morally, practical reason *commands* it absolutely and makes this end his duty so that he may be worthy of the humanity that dwells within him. (*MdS* 6:387) Skill can be developed independently of virtue. But because 'prudence presupposes skillfulness' as 'the faculty of using one's skillfulness effectively,' prudential reasoning benefits from virtue, which commits additional weight to the aim of developing skill (*Päd*. 9:455). Conversely, an agent's skill can be put in service of ends prescribed by the moral law" (Holberg 2018, 14).

rational, and moral being. They do prevent one from going in certain directions in pursuit of one's happiness, but they do so precisely as a way of reminding oneself who one is overall: I am not the kind of being—the kind of *person*—who would do *that*! Were one to realize desire-fulfillment in a way that did not respect these constraints and boundaries, ironically, one would not ultimately be functioning or flourishing well as the kind of being one is. Rather, one's flourishing would be lop-sided: I would realize myself as a sensible being (subject only to the demands of that part of myself unrelated to my rational and moral self) while rejecting or ignoring myself as a moral and rational being. And, believe me, there would be a moral psychological price to pay for this lop-sided realization of flourishing! As we saw in II.i, one's conscience would find its way to express itself, either directly (through 3 o'clock in the morning insomnia) or indirectly (through madness or violence). And one's integrity of person (including one's subjective pleasurable experience of being oneself) would quickly evaporate.

But the cushion or perimeter of morality put in place to inform one's deployment of counsels of prudence is not the end of the story of the guidance of prudence by virtue. Counsels of prudence also receive further structure, guidance, and focus from one's overall telos of making persons as such one's end. Indeed, one's capacity to deploy rules of prudence is in fact enhanced by connecting it to the tools of virtue, and new possibilities for their skilled deployment emerge. This meta-rule of the telos of my being guiding my implementation of counsels of prudence gives me a new, higher point of view from which to discriminate within myself *which* of my desires I am most compelled by and interested in, indeed, which desires the satisfaction of which will be most *fulfilling* to me overall as a person.

We need to be careful here, because, as we've already repeatedly noted, one's objective telos does not instruct the virtuous person categorically in what exact things she should pursue for the sake of her happiness; no rational principle can do that. But as we have also already noted, this rational telos does provide an evaluative distance and perspective upon all things of relative value, helping one to see the value of such things in the light of the absolute value of persons. And this means that this telos helps me to see the value of things as they are instead of as any excursion into self-absorption would encourage me to evaluate them.

How would this work? How would being committed to making persons as such my end help me in thinking about how I want to spend my leisure time, or about what does and does not please me generally? In short, as we've already noted above, when one thinks about the value of the objects of one's desire from the perspective of respecting persons, one is more able to see clearly the value of those things. But this also means that I am going to be able to see more clearly what things would and would not make me happy, overall, in the long term. Guiding counsels of prudence by the meta-rule of making persons as such my end thus helps me to see more clearly the value of things that really have the potential to make me, *all* of me, happy. Because I can see things of relative value clearly, for what they really are in the life of a sensibly affected rational being, I am better able to assess which things would—and which things wouldn't—be fulfilling to me as a person overall. This is not to say that my objective telos specifically instructs me in what activities to pursue; indeed, we have already confirmed that this is precisely what one's rational principles do not do. It is just that through appeal to the absolute value at the basis of my life-guiding telos, I am able to see all my possible capacities and activities more clearly for what they are, and for what potential they have to be satisfying. I won't, for example, be able to set my desire-fulfillment goals too low. It is not that I won't, once in a while, be glad to succumb to an evening of G&Ts, potato chips, and bad B movies, but rather that I won't be able to think of that as what makes me most happy. Out of respect for myself, I'll want to find ways of making myself happy that realize more parts of myself than that. And when I do succumb to these lower pleasures, my enjoyment of them will make all the more sense as a sort of balance to the quasi-demands I place upon myself to engage in the more disciplined pleasures of cello-playing or philosophy. The person who respects herself realizes that the aura of such low pleasures wears off quickly when they are the only things one demands of oneself. One takes all the more pleasure in doing nothing when one has pushed oneself first to accomplish something. And the person committed to making persons as such her end understands just exactly this point of the value of balancing kinds of pleasures in the skillful deployment of the rules of prudence.

Kant's list of empirical counsels is, in fact, a helpful summary of the kinds of more reflective and skillful ways of approaching happiness that would emerge from such guidance by an overall concern to respect persons. It is true that such counsels are what emerge, in the first instance, simply from experience in trying to realize happiness: "empirical counsels, for example, of a regimen, frugality, courtesy, reserve and so forth, which experience teaches are most conducive to well-being on the average" (4:418/29). But once one understands these counsels, review and application of them in light of one's meta-rule of making persons as such one's end heightens one's skill in such application and, indeed, elevates these rules of prudence toward a moral end. Courtesy, for example, is elevated to yet another way of making other persons as such one's end; or regimen and frugality become ways of making my own person as such my end. In so doing, one understands better the potential for what such states can be in the first place.

The Subjective Tools of Virtue for Pursuit of Happiness

We affirm, then, that the objective telos of respect for persons provides an objective ground and evaluative distance whereby the virtuous person can more adequately evaluate, assess, value, order, and pursue desire-fulfillment. The objective demand to make persons as such my end is a meta-rule in application of counsels of prudence, thereby both constraining one's pursuit of happiness (so as to assure that it is respectful of all one's person, both rational and sensible) and enhancing the proper perception of one's options in the pursuit of happiness (so as to help me see more clearly the value of things that really have the potential to make me feel fulfilled overall).

But someone who guides her life by the non-negotiable telos of making persons as such one's end also has that moral apathetic tranquility, moral excitement, pleasure, and cheerfulness in the exercise of virtue, and this aptitude for virtue provides a more stable *subjective* ground for realizing happiness than someone who has only naturalistic, desire-based tools for the governance and fulfillment of her desires. In particular, this pleasurable experience of the exercise of one's aptitude for virtue provides a strong subjective ground for managing the *vicissitudes of fortune*—both the ups *and* downs of it—which visit upon my pursuit of happiness.

How is it that one's subjective, affective experience of virtue accomplishes this? This is a new sort of evaluative distance, now an evaluative distance not on the relative value of the thing pursued but on the felt attachments one experiences as one pursues those things of relative value. Because the virtuous person knows that there is something more important than desire-fulfillment, she has developed a steady and stable affective life which we have been describing as the pleasurable experience of the person with a free aptitude for virtue. And from this subjective affective state, she is able not only objectively but also subjectively and affectively to pursue desire-fulfillment from a less frantic, addictive, or unsettled point of view than someone who lacked such perspective. She can find and pursue those things that make her happy without clinging to them so tightly as to feel herself incapable of living without them. As in the world of sacrifice (as discussed in II.i), when she loses something, or has to struggle very hard to get it, she has within her subjective state of virtue particular tools for managing such an internal sense of loss and struggle. She has, in other words, a tranquility of person girded by the confident belief that, even as she loses something or struggles to attain something, there is something more important she is succeeding in upholding and affirming. And when the virtuous person *is* successful in realizing her happiness, the pleasure and peacefulness that is the ground of her subjective experience of the activity of virtue becomes the stable context within which she enjoys her success in desire-fulfillment without allowing that success "to go to her head." Neither objectively—in terms of value assessment—nor subjectively—in terms of her subjective felt experience—does she misconstrue her pursuit of happiness.

The sort of relationship between virtue and happiness that I envision here is akin to what is suggested in Kipling's (1943) poem, "If." In one famous line of that poem, Kipling, speaking to his son, suggests that "When you can meet with triumph and disaster and treat those two imposters both the same," then "Yours is the earth and everything that's in it." That is, if one can acquire a balanced attitude toward both the successes and failures in one's life—in our language, if one can acquire the right attitude toward things of relative non-moral value—then one really has the potential securely and stably to have and hold everything in the world that really matters even as fortunes shift. When one finds things going well, one enjoys it but doesn't let it go to one's head; and when one finds things going ill, one doesn't collapse in despair or believe oneself destroyed by the experience. One's experience of the ups and downs of fortune thus evens out a bit, and one's overall experience of being happy increases thereby.

Indeed, this subjective support virtue provides in the pursuit of happiness is, really, simply a further deployment of the virtuous person's ability both to tolerate suffering and to excite and enliven her felt attachments supportive of virtue. The same perspective from which she appreciates something of value beyond desire which makes it more possible for her to tolerate suffering within the world of desire also acts to attenuate the inevitable ups and downs in her subjective experience of the pursuit of happiness. It is even the very same tool she would use to decide to put off certain short-term pleasures—e.g., having another martini tonight—in the name of long-term pleasures—e.g., of getting up tomorrow morning to perform well in a cello concert. The person of virtue, from that higher ground of recognizing the non-negotiable demand to make persons as such one's end, has the hope not only of tolerating necessary sacrifices of desires but also of pursuing desire-fulfillment in a more stable and therefore more tranquil way. She welcomes happily the pursuit of all those desires in agreement with her non-negotiable demand to respect persons, and manages calmly any disappointments or failures in her pursuits that come along. The result is that her pursuit of happiness is informed by the pleasure and moral apathetic tranquility of virtue, that ease and calmness grounded in the conviction that the pursuit of happiness is not all there is that is true or important about her. The virtuous person thus pursues happiness with a certain calmness, confidence, ease, stability, and strength in the management of her world of desire that would not be possible for a person lacking the life-guiding absolute value of respect for persons.

And we've already seen, conversely, that the virtuous activity of moral excitement can inform the pursuit of happiness: when I connect things like my cello-playing with my identity as a free end-setting person, my heart is elevated, my emotions intensified in a way that they could not be without such appeal.

We thus complete our story of what happens to happiness when, still within a eudaemonistic structure, we subordinate it to a larger telos of making persons as such one's end. The pursuit of happiness acquires a new order and stability through being guided by the exception-less telos of one's existence. I *am* interested in the fulfillment of my desires, but I am no longer self-*absorbed* in that project. What this means is that happiness, empirically conceived as simple desire-fulfillment, really does take a backseat. It is too low a goal for describing the flourishing of a sensibly affected rational being. Deontological Eudaemonism, by offering us a perspective on happiness and the pursuit of desire-satisfaction that would not have been possible without the prioritization of morality over happiness, thus rejects desire-fetishism, viz. the idea that all we are is desire-seeking beings and that all we could aim at as the goal of one's flourishing is the satisfaction of all our desires. We can thus abandon happiness as the primary telos of one's person in the name of a higher telos. And once we abandon that addiction to desire-fulfillment, we find ourselves on a more stable and, indeed (ironically!), *more satisfying* ground than what could be accomplished only within the world of desire. Happiness, empirically conceived, is no longer the complete telos of a sensibly affected rational being. It is not that such happiness is no longer at all important; but by being put in its proper order in relation to morality, the failures and remainders in one's pursuit of happiness are more manageable. I do not rise or fall as a person solely on the basis of whether I can satisfy my desires. Instead, my worth as a person shines through whether I succeed or fail.

But, simultaneously, we do not reject the idea that pragmatic pleasures, desire-fulfillment, and some sort of happiness are an important part of a human life. Kant emphatically rejects the idea that all we are is desire-satisfaction machines; but he also emphatically rejects the idea that all we are is moral rational beings. We are most centrally and essentially moral beings, but we are moral rational beings in a sensible world of desire, and it is thus crucial to pursue satisfaction of one's person overall, both rational and sensible. In making happiness as desire-fulfillment a subordinate goal of the well-functioning person of virtue, we thus actually make the realization of happiness and the higher integrity and well-functioning of one's person overall *more* possible. Ultimately, by being constrained, guided, and focused by the non-desire-based telos of making persons as such one's end and, with that, being grounded in and girded by the correlative subjective experience of apathy, excitement, health, tranquility, pleasure, and cheerfulness of the virtuous person, one's pursuit of happiness becomes a more stable (because less self-absorbed) thing. What emerges is a life of integrity: a strength and flourishing of one's entire person guided by one's non-negotiable commitment to the absolute value of persons.

Of course, as we've already seen in II.ii, it is true that the subjective enjoyment of virtue is subject to luck, and this is no less true of that subjective experience of virtue which constitutes one's happiness. But if the virtuous person ends up not being a happy person in this life, this will not be because of any obstacles to happiness set up by virtue but only because of external obstacles set up by cruel nature, vicious persons, or unjust societies, as discussed in II.ii. We can thus welcome the heightened capacity for happiness empirically conceived as integral to being a virtuous person in this world. While admitting the possibility of misfires due to circumstances outside of one's control, a *virtuous* life is also going to be a *happy* life.

D. Concluding Thoughts

The Distinction between Happiness and Virtue

There is, however, an important question that arises here once we affirm so emphatically the intimate interrelationship of virtue and happiness: given the story we have told about the integration of the cultivation of natural capacities for a pragmatic purpose into the pursuit of virtue, and given the just-asserted claim that the exercise of virtue leads to a state of proper functioning which encompasses both virtue and happiness, must we now say that virtue and happiness have become a single state?

Were this to be the case, it would be a problem; for, certainly, to be true to Kant's texts, we must maintain a distinction between at least happiness empirically conceived and virtue. Kant's paradigmatic example of the Gallows Man affirms this point in spades: the Gallows Man's great suffering as he strongly clings to the way of virtue reveals quite clearly that virtue and happiness can come apart; they thus must be different things. Furthermore, Kant's discussion of the Highest Good in the *Critique of Practical Reason* makes it clear that he himself is thinking of these states as two distinct things:

> [T]he maxims of virtue and those of one's own happiness are quite heterogeneous with respect to their supreme practical principle; and, even though they belong to one highest good, so as to make it possible, yet they are so far from coinciding that they greatly restrict and infringe upon each other in the same subject. (5:112/94)

There is thus more than ample evidence that Kant himself considered virtue and happiness to be two distinct states.

Has our account run afoul of Kant's intention then? It is certainly the case that we assert a deep and intimate interrelation between virtue and happiness empirically conceived. As we've suggested in our just completed discussion of the virtuous pursuit of pragmatic interests, virtue and happiness do indeed meet, or even marry, each other: when I am pursuing activities with pragmatically oriented purposes and pleasures, I am simultaneously taking those pragmatic pursuits and pleasures as partially constitutive of my objective telos of making persons as such my end.

Furthermore, one can't really say at this point that any of one's desires escape this net of virtue, viz. that one has a separate set of desires fulfilled that we now call "happiness" as distinct from these pragmatically oriented but virtuously realized pleasures which now constitute part of "virtue." To the contrary, one's objective telos is one's objective telos, and *all* of one's end-setting and *all* of one's desiring comes properly under its purview. By definition, were one to have desires not submitting to the purview of this telos, they would be rogue, mutinous desires. For the virtuous person, then, the realization of happiness (that is, the fulfillment of desires) *must* occur from within the realm of virtue, not separate from it.

Does this mean, though, that virtue and happiness empirically conceived are identical? That would be too quick a move to make. We have, after all, affirmed the possibility of that distinction between virtue and happiness empirically conceived that the Gallows Man's tragic example holds before us: as we saw in II.i, although the Gallows Man is virtuous, it does not make sense to call him empirically happy, as if he went off cheerfully whistling to said gallows.[23] He has done everything he can to order his natural desires within the purview of the demands of virtue, but sometimes extreme situations prevent the realization of virtue from issuing in that complete-enough fulfillment of one's natural desires that could meaningfully be called happiness.

But this is just the point that affirms a distinction between virtue and happiness: no matter how well one integrates one's person, one does, after all, have both natural desires to satisfy and moral imperatives to obey. These are two different things. The story we've told is one in which one seeks an integrity of person wherein one's natural desires and feelings are elevated, as far as is possible, into the life-guiding telos of making persons as such one's end. But even when this is accomplished as perfectly as is possible (indeed, even assuming, *per impossibile*, for the sake of argument, that one had absolutely perfectly realized all one's natural inclinations always and forever as being in service of one's moral ends), one would still need to make a distinction between happiness empirically conceived and virtue: the former is the sum of the fulfillment of all one's natural desires, and the latter is the strength to constrain, guide, and cultivate one's desires in the name of one's life-guiding objective telos of making persons as such one's end, which, at its height, issues in a pleasurable aptitude for the exercise of virtue. We have, of course, complicated things here by showing that one's natural desires can be put in the service of the realization of one's objective telos. But even in the most perfect realization of virtue, one can still at least speak of the same fulfillment of a desire from two points of view: on the one hand, such fulfillment is simply the realization of a natural desire, and this is happiness, empirically conceived; but, on the other, such fulfillment constitutes an aspect of one's telos of making persons as such one's end, and this is virtue. Ultimately, then, at least in the virtuous person, the very same fulfillment of desire plays these two distinct, but now virtuously related, roles. The subjective state which supervenes upon a life of virtue can be viewed from two points of view, one consisting of all those subjective states insofar as they are pointed to the realization of one's telos of

---

[23] Though we do assert it would still be possible for him to be happy, rationally conceived, as we discussed in II.ii.

making persons as such one's end, and the other consisting of all those states insofar as they are a realization or satisfaction of one's natural pleasures.

Happiness empirically conceived is thus indeed a part of virtue to the extent that it has been taken up and elevated as pointing toward one's objective telos of making persons as such one's end. That is: when I cultivate my natural capacities from a virtuous perspective, my pleasure in engaging in those capacities increases. But we can call this same increase in pleasure an increase in "happiness" precisely because it is an increase in one's natural pleasures related to the realization of one's natural capacity with a pragmatic purpose. And yet, we can also speak of this increase in pleasure as a *moral* increase in pleasure. This is just what we admitted earlier in this chapter when we saw the role that the moral feeling of respect plays in elevating natural pleasures toward one's objective life-guiding telos. Even granting all this, though, these natural capacities and pleasures still are natural capacities and pleasures. And when I increase them and experience them, I'm increasing and experiencing happiness, empirically conceived. Indeed, as we've seen, such heightening of one's non-moral pleasures from the perspective of one's life-guiding objective telos is just another example of that capacity for moral excitement first noted in our I.iv discussion of how natural sympathies could be elevated toward moral purposes. What was done for natural sympathy there is now extended to all of one's natural inclinations. The integration of the pursuit of happiness within a life of virtue is thus not even really a different category or state from that general state of being able to regulate one's felt attachments in light of one's objective telos. What was done for sympathy then is done for the pursuit of happiness here.

One can even affirm the converse of this: one can, that is, look at one's heightened natural sympathy, now a moral sympathy, also as an increase in one's natural happiness. After all, this natural sympathy, even as it is elevated toward moral purposes, remains also a natural sympathy. And an increase in and satisfaction of one's natural felt attachments is a good example of an increase in happiness! Indeed, if the state of my natural desires is a more satisfying one in virtue of this elevation of sympathy into a moral role, one *must* admit that it is also an increase in my happiness.

For the virtuous person, then, happiness and virtue are distinct but internally related states: happiness is the overall fulfillment of one's natural desires, and virtue is the strength to organize one's desires toward one's objective telos of making persons as such one's end and to exercise one's will and choice in accordance with that end. But we can also affirm, simultaneously, that there is a deep and intimate interrelationship between these two states: even as we admit that happiness and virtue are distinct, we also affirm that, at least in the virtuous person, the one (happiness) becomes partially constitutive of the other (virtue).[24]

---

[24] Are we now in tension with Kant's claims about the relationship of virtue and happiness in a different way? The whole notion of the Highest Good suggests that the possible disconnect between

The Tools of Virtue Are the Tools of Happiness

In this account of the objective and subjective tools of virtue for the pursuit of happiness, we thus affirm a sort of reciprocity between virtue and happiness, empirically conceived. On the one hand, as we've already seen, happiness constitutes a part of one's state of virtue (since the increase in satisfaction that results from the cultivation of one's natural capacities acts, simultaneously, as a part of one's state of virtue in affirming the objective telos of one's existence). But, on the other hand, we can now also affirm the converse, viz. that virtue provides tools for the most satisfactory realization of one's happiness empirically conceived. The claim, then, is not only that the virtuous person is morally obligated to pursue her pragmatic end-setting and thus her happiness in accordance with her life-guiding telos of making persons as such her end; beyond that, we assert that virtue helps the virtuous person to become happy empirically. Indeed, we assert that the virtuous person is *best-situated* to pursue this happiness *successfully*, certainly better situated than anyone who did not appeal to this life-guiding tool. The virtuous pursuit of happiness will be more successful than the non-virtuous, or vicious, pursuit of happiness.

More precisely, virtue (the strength to order all oneself toward one's objective telos) facilitates the pursuit and realization of happiness (the most satisfying fulfillment of one's natural desires) from both these objective and subjective perspectives. Indeed, the very same things that constitute me as a virtuous person (viz., my objective telos of making persons as such my end, the affective expression of the pursuit of that telos in the moral feeling of respect, and the ease and pleasure with which I exercise my fully realized aptitude for virtue) provide me also with the best tools for becoming a happy person. The virtuous person appeals to these very states of virtue as tools that help her to craft her pursuit of the satisfaction of her desires in the most successful way possible. The higher happiness that results from such application of the tools of virtue is thus still a part of the subjective telos of virtue in that it is the outcome of the cultivation of natural capacities from a moral point of view and thus something we can anticipate will

---

virtue and happiness is so likely that in order to assure the justice of the virtuous person getting the happiness she deserves, we must appeal to the practical postulates of God and immortality. But can we still say at this point that happiness in proportion to virtue is something for which we need appeal beyond our own powers in this way? Or would realizing happiness so successfully in this world through the exercise of virtue vitiate the need for that practical argument for God and immortality? That is: is the argument for the Highest Good one that needs to assume a particularly strong distinction between virtue and happiness, one which I've just problematically effaced? We need to remember at this point that even if one is happy in this life, one might not have *all* the happiness one deserves. This is especially the case since, in the pursuit of virtue, we have already seen the virtuous person's capacity to *moderate* her desires so as to manage inevitable suffering and sacrifice. Kant's concern with appeal to the Highest Good is to make sure that such accounting is accomplished perfectly, in a way that no experience in the natural world could assure, and in a way that "gives back" what one gave up. This is why Kant is content to affirm that there is no absolute distinction between happiness and virtue, but only a coincidental divergence of them given the sensible status of finite rational beings: "that a virtuous disposition necessarily produces happiness is false not absolutely but only insofar as this disposition is regarded as the form of causality in the sensible world" (5:114/96).

be present in the well-functioning person of virtue, in just the ways we've described above with our cello-playing and wittiness examples. Nonetheless, this state is also an increase in our natural desires, that is, happiness.

There are a couple caveats we must make as we complete this story of the marriage of virtue and happiness. First, the happiness which realization of one's telos encourages cannot, of course, in itself be the *objective* telos of virtue, nor the *motive* for why I pursue virtue; that would be heteronomy. Instead, as we've seen, the virtuous pursuit of the cultivation of one's capacities provides a framework within which one can pursue one's pragmatic interests, and one's happiness generally, from a moral point of view, without descending into heteronomy, that is without taking the realization of such happiness as the reason for one's engagement in the cultivation of one's natural capacities. Furthermore, the experience of pleasure related to such pragmatic pursuits thusly integrated into one's effort to make persons as such one's end even constitutes part of the subjective experience of being a virtuous person; that is, it constitutes, in part, the *subjective telos* of virtue, that subjective state which supervenes upon the exercise of activities constituting the objective telos of virtue. So, we do indeed assert that this elevated subjective state, including the elevation of one's natural capacities with a pragmatic purpose and the pleasures related thereto, is an *outcome* of the pursuit of virtue; but this state is not the *reason* or motive for pursuing that virtue.

Another caveat to re-emphasize: when we say that the virtuous person will be the one to realize happiness most successfully, we must also admit the luck factor—Gallows-Man-like situations—and its potential to dislodge the otherwise reliable supervenience of happiness upon virtue.[25] Whether I am able to avoid the most pernicious and miserable of states as I insistently prioritize the demands of virtue will at times depend upon circumstances outside my control, and becoming virtuous does not make me any luckier than I was before in relation to these circumstantial possibilities. As such, we admit that one's virtuous pursuit of happiness is subject to being undermined by bad luck of all sorts, and it is possible for particularly egregious episodes of such bad luck to undermine the happiness that would otherwise supervene upon virtue. We have admitted as much already when, at the end of II.ii, we granted that we don't expect the Gallows Man to go cheerfully whistling to said gallows. Granting all this, though, we simultaneously affirm that virtue gives a person particular strengths and resources for maintaining happiness in the face of many if not most episodes of bad luck: my father's bad luck in having a horrible illness didn't prevent him from being happy. The

---

[25] This is just another way of affirming Kant's point that virtue cannot bring about happiness "absolutely," but only on the assumption of some non-sensible means of bringing the two into balance with each other: "that a virtuous disposition necessarily produces happiness is false not absolutely but only insofar as this disposition is regarded as the form of causality in the sensible world" (5:114/96). The vicissitudes of the empirical world are what stand in the way of a perfect realization of virtue and happiness, empirically conceived, in this natural world.

virtuous person is particularly capable of managing the vicissitudes of fortune as she seeks happiness. Episodes of bad luck that might subvert a non-virtuous person's pursuit of happiness will not undermine the virtuous person's pursuit thereof, or at least not fully undermine it. But, just as the virtuous person's pleasure in being virtuous can be vitiated by the bad luck of extraordinary suffering, so too can the virtuous person's pleasure in being happy be thusly vitiated.

We return, then, to our claim: just as we can expect moral apathetic tranquility, moral excitement, pleasure, and cheerfulness all to supervene upon the exercise of virtue, so too can we expect the pleasure of happiness, empirically conceived, to supervene upon such exercise. The tools of virtue are also the tools of happiness, so the *virtuous* person—the person who rejects self-absorption and guides her end-setting by the absolute, non-negotiable telos of making persons as such her end—will (subject to the limits of luck) also be the *happy* person. And the reason for this is that virtue provides, as we have seen, a higher, orienting, and non-self-absorbed evaluative point of view from which to seek the fulfillment of desires, thereby making one's pursuit of happiness the most *appropriate*, and therefore the most *satisfying*, one for the sensibly affected rational being one is. The exercise of virtue, that is, leads us to a state of proper functioning overall for the kind of being one is, and this proper functioning will express itself not only as the state of happiness rationally conceived discussed in II.ii but also as a state of happiness, empirically conceived.

In saying that heightened happiness follows upon realization of virtue, we are, furthermore, underscoring our previous claim that while the virtuous person does not *aim* at happiness, she nonetheless reliably *realizes* it. To say that it is in the pursuit of virtue that one will become most happy is very much in line with that common (albeit ironic) adage that the best way to achieve happiness is not to pursue it directly—not to make "the satisfaction of all my desires" the ultimate goal of one's life—but instead to aim at something else, and then trust that happiness will follow. Kant affirms this adage, but with particular concern to assure that the activity at which one aims is the realization of one's objective telos of making persons as such one's end: it is only when one recognizes something *more* important in the world than desire-fulfillment that one is *most* able to fulfill one's desires. The non-negotiable objective telos of making persons as such one's end—as well as the non-self-absorbed subjective telos of moral apathetic tranquility, moral excitement, cheerfulness, and pleasure all of which supervene upon a life guided by this objective telos—thus all become *tools* for desire-*fulfillment*, tools which promise a *higher* and *better* realization or fulfillment of desire overall than is possible in any vicious, or merely naturalistic, pursuit of the self-governance of desire. What results is a story of the pursuit of happiness that is not a tale of self-absorption.

One can, furthermore, say that once this virtue-guided happiness is realized, it has a sort of rebound effect on the virtuous state from which it came. That is, even as virtue facilitates the acquisition of happiness, the happiness thereby acquired turns around and itself facilitates and strengthens one's already extant virtuous realization of the objective telos of respecting persons. All of this is just to affirm Kant's own argument, in the *Groundwork*, for why the pursuit of happiness is an indirect duty: "To assure one's own happiness is a duty (at least indirectly); for, want of satisfaction with one's condition, under pressure from man anxieties and amid unsatisfied needs, could easily become a great *temptation to transgression of duty*" (4:399/12). Being a happy person, in other words, provides one with a strong point of view from which to further pursue a life of virtue, and reject the blandishments of a passion-governed life.

To affirm this facilitating role for happiness is, furthermore, another way in which we can see the realization of happiness as part and parcel of one's overall subjective telos of virtue: such happiness is a part of that subjective telos in that it is a subjective state in me that serves to facilitate my realization of my objective telos of virtue. The non-self-absorbed pursuit of happiness empirically conceived facilitates and enhances my life-guiding goal to make persons as such my end. We are not saying here that the desire for happiness supplants one's commitment to respecting persons as one's motive for virtue. But Kant regularly welcomes the idea that the realization of happiness is a piece of what is needed in the subjective state of the person of virtue so as to stabilize and situate that virtue firmly. It is from this perspective that he so strongly affirms the pursuit of happiness as an indirect duty for the person of virtue. This duty is indirect in that I am not obligated to be happy in itself. But the virtuous person is obligated to pursue a state of happiness in herself which then plays the facilitating role in supporting her pursuit of virtue which we have just described.

Coda on Non-Moral Value

I hope the picture I have drawn of the virtuous pursuit of happiness has done something to calm the concerns of that original objector I considered very early in this chapter, who worries that a pursuit of happiness entirely intertwined with the exercise of virtue would be too stifling. In this marriage of happiness and virtue which we assert, we discover the intensification and the elevation of happiness and one's natural self, not the rejection of it in the name of one's rational self.

I want, though, explicitly to consider the point of view of those who would continue to worry that such a conception of the complete moralization of happiness leaves no room for genuinely individual, idiosyncratic personal expressions of oneself and one's identity. I am considering here thinkers like Wolf (2012), Nehemas (2016), and others who claim that there are values to things personal that are distinct from moral values, and that may at times conflict with and even trump those moral values. For such thinkers, my thoroughly moralized account of the pursuit of happiness would thus be problematic, even opprobrious.

Is there anything further to say in response to such worries? I sometimes sense such thinkers as themselves experiencing a word like "duty" as a dirty word, a notion which is inherently problematic, something that is unduly constraining, and has no positive qualities: a "duty" simply tells me what I mustn't do, or perhaps it represents a story of the constraints I must place upon my action in light of the existence of other people, constraints to which (but for these other people) I would have no internal compulsion or motivation to concede. On such a model, bringing one's entire pursuit of happiness under the purview of "duty" would indeed have a very different, and bitter, flavor than what I have suggested here. Such a constraint on happiness would, in essence, prevent one from becoming oneself, and so would be an utterly inappropriate and contradictory point of view from which to explore and discover oneself more positively and expansively. Someone who thinks of duty in this narrow way would thus indeed have much more reason to make as much room as Wolf and Nehemas do for the realm of the pristinely personal.

I am, indeed, very sympathetic to the worry that moral theories can all too easily become unconcerned with the pursuit of personal identity. And I thus sympathize with the concern that motivates these positions: a heavy-handed moralizing of one's self which did not allow one truly to realize who one was would be a position to reject. But the story we have told here is a different story than this. Ours is a broader and more capacious definition of duty than the one which these thinkers assume as their enemy, one which goes beyond the notion of "right" thinly conceived, and which connects itself with a robust conception of value and flourishing. For us, duty itself is grounded in a notion of what is best and proper for the realization of one's truest identity as a person. Furthermore, the pursuit of that higher person, self, or soul has been shown to be one in which one's idiosyncratic loves and concerns can be affirmed and elevated, not rejected or merely restrained. I offer, then, an olive branch to these thinkers: to the extent that you can welcome this broader conception of duty, and the teleological pursuit of the good within which it is established, perhaps you can also welcome the thorough moralization of the pursuit of happiness which I offer as less egregious than you might previously have thought it to be?

Conclusion

Our review of the subjective telos of Deontological Eudaemonism thus reveals that, even as he emphatically rejects the idea that all we are is desire-satisfaction machines, Kant also emphatically rejects the idea that all we are is moral rational beings. We *are* most centrally and essentially moral rational beings, but we are moral rational beings *in* a sensible world of desire, and it is thus most proper to pursue satisfaction of one's person overall, both rationally and sensibly. In making happiness as desire-fulfillment a subordinate goal of the well-functioning person of virtue, Kant thereby makes this higher integrity and well-functioning aspect of one's person overall more possible than it would be otherwise. Being guided by the non-desire-based goal of making persons as such one's end, and being grounded in and girded by the correlative pleasurable experience of the exercise of virtue, along with the moral apathetic tranquility and cheerfulness which come with it, one's pursuit of happiness, empirically conceived, becomes a more stable (because less self-absorbed) thing than it would be otherwise. What emerges is a life of integrity: a strength and flourishing of one's entire person guided by the non-negotiable commitment to making persons as such one's end. Although this achievement of happiness empirically conceived cannot be considered identical with virtue (as its counterpart, happiness rationally conceived, can), and there will thus be moments when the pursuit of virtue will involve an injury to one's happiness empirically conceived, we ultimately discover nonetheless a reliable unity of the contentments or satisfactions of the sensibly affected rational being, including both the happiness rationally conceived discussed in the previous chapter and the pursuit of happiness empirically conceived discussed here, now unified into an overall state of satisfaction for sensibly affected rational beings. This unity is assured precisely because both these states are most successfully realized from the same singular moral and virtuous point of view of making persons as such one's end.

I thus submit to you that we can make sense of a eudaemonism in which the telos of a properly functioning life is something more broadly construed than happiness, empirically conceived. That Kant is interested in pursuing that dream of a well-ordered, proper functioning, and flourishing beyond happiness conceived of as desire-fulfillment is, furthermore, what affirms his system as fully and distinctively both deontological and eudaemonistic. It is not that Kant isn't interested in happiness, empirically conceived. It is just Kant's conviction that such integrity—to be truly "proper" to one's being—needs to look beyond happiness as desire-fulfillment: that is too low and too unstable a goal for absolutely valuable, sensibly affected rational beings. We are more than that, and should aim, as the teleological goal of our pursuit of virtue, at realizing the non-negotiable goal of making persons as such our end, which, when properly established, assures pleasure in the ease of one's aptitude for virtue, as well as the health, apathy, cheerfulness, and pleasure which come with it as the best possible perspective on realizing our non-moral desires within the changeable world of happiness, empirically conceived. The ultimate result is the integrity of one's person overall, both morally and sensibly. This is Kant's Deontological Eudaemonism.

Bibliography

Kant Texts

Kants gesammelte Schriften, hrsg. von der Preußischen Akademie der Wissenschaften zu Berlin. 29 vols. Berlin: Walter de Gruyter, 1902–1983.
I will use the Cambridge University Press English translations of the following of Kant's works:
Critique of Practical Reason, trans. Mary. Gregor, 1997.
Groundwork of the Metaphysics of Morals, trans. Mary Gregor and Jens Timmermann, 2012.
The Metaphysics of Morals, trans. Mary Gregor, 1998.
Religion Within the Limits of Reason Alone, trans. Allen Wood and George di Giovanni, 1998.
I will also use the following translation of Kant's work:
Critique of Judgment, trans. Werner Pluhar, 1987.

Secondary Works

Allison, Henry. *Kant's Theory of Freedom*. Cambridge: Cambridge University Press, 1990.
Allison, Henry. "Kant's Practical Justification of Freedom," in *Kant on Practical Justification*. Oxford: Oxford University Press, 2013, pp. 284–299.
Annas, Julia. *The Morality of Happiness*. Oxford: Oxford University Press, 1995.
Annas, Julia. *Intelligent Virtue*. Oxford: Oxford University Press, 2011.
Aristotle. *Aristotles gesammelte Schriften*, hrsg. von der Preußischen Akademie der Wissenschaften zu Berlin, 1831.
Aristotle. *Nicomachean Ethics*, trans. Martin Ostwald. Indianapolis, IN: Bobbs-Merrill, 1962.
Augustine, St. *Confessions*, trans. F.J. Sheed. Indianapolis, IN: Hackett Publishing, 1993.
Baier, Kurt. "Radical Virtue Ethics," in *Midwest Studies in Philosophy*, Vol. XIII. Notre Dame: University of Notre Dame Press, 1988.
Baxley, Anne Margaret, *Kant's Theory of Virtue: The Value of Autocracy*. Cambridge: Cambridge University Press, 2010.
Beck, Lewis White. *A Commentary on Kant's* Critique of Practical Reason. Chicago, IL: University of Chicago Press, 1960.
Broadie, Alexander and Pybus, Elizabeth M. "Kant's Treatment of Animals," in *Philosophy*, 49(190) (Oct. 1974): 375–383.
Caygill, Howard. *A Kant Dictionary: Blackwell Reference on Kant*. London: Wiley-Blackwell, 1995.
Cohen, Alix. "Rational Feelings," in *Kant and the Faculty of Feeling*, ed. Kelly Sorensen and Diane Williamson. Cambridge: Cambridge University Press, 2018.
Cureton, Adam. "A Contractualist Reading of Kant's Proof of the Formula of Humanity," in *Kantian Review*, 18(3) (2013): 363–386.
Darwall, Stephen. *The Second Person Standpoint: Morality, Respect, and Accountability*. Cambridge, MA: Harvard University Press, 2006.

Dean, Richard. *The Value of Humanity in Kant's Moral Theory*. Oxford: Clarendon Press, 2006.

Dean, Richard. "The Formula of Humanity as an End in Itself," in *The Blackwell Guide to Kant's Ethics*, ed. Thomas E. Hill. London: Wiley-Blackwell, 2009, pp. 83–101.

Dean, Richard. "Humanity as an Idea, an Ideal and as End in Itself," in *Kantian Review*, 18(2) (2013): 171–195.

Denis, Lara. "Kant's Formula of the End in Itself," in *Philosophy Compass* 2(2) (2007): 244–257.

Denis, Lara. "Humanity, Obligation and the Good Will: An Argument Against Dean's Interpretation of Humanity," in *Kantian Review* 15(1) (2010): 118–141.

Dickens, Charles. *The Mystery of Edwin Drood*. New York: The Penguin English Library, 1974.

Dillon, Robin. "Toward a Feminist Conception of Self-Respect," in *Hypatia* 7(1) (1992): 52–69.

Dillon, Robin, ed. "Toward a Feminist Conception of Self-Respect," in *Dignity, Character and Self-Respect*. London: Routledge, 1995.

Dostoevsky, Fyodor. *Crime and Punishment*, trans. Richard Pevear and Larissa Volokhonsky. London: Vintage Classics, 1993.

Dostoevsky, Fyodor. *Brothers Karamazov*, trans. Richard Pevear and Larissa Volokhonsky. London: Farrar, Straus and Giroux, 2002.

Elizondo, E. Sonny. "More than a Feeling," in the *Canadian Journal of Philosophy*, 4(3–4) (Aug. 2014): 425–442.

Elizondo, E. Sonny. "Morality is Its Own Reward," in *Kantian Review*, 21(3) (Nov. 2016): 343–365.

Engstrom, Stephen. "The Inner Freedom of Virtue," in *Kant's Metaphysics of Morals: Interpretive Essays*, ed. Mark Timmons. Oxford: Oxford University Press, 2000.

Engstrom, Stephen. *The Form of Practical Knowledge: A Study of the Categorical Imperative*. Cambridge, MA: Harvard University Press, 2009.

Engstrom, Stephen. "The Triebfeder of Pure Practical Reason," in *Kant's Critique of Practical Reason: A Critical Guide*, ed. Andrews Reath and Jens Timmermann. Cambridge: Cambridge University Press, 2010, pp. 90–118.

Epictetus. "Enchiridion," in *The Discourses of Epictetus*, trans. P.E. Matheson. Oxford: Clarendon Press, 1916), section 3. Accessed at http://www.sacred-texts.com/cla/dep/dep102.htm.

Esser, Andrea. "The Inner Court of Conscience, Moral Self-Knowledge, and the Proper Object of Duty (TL6:437–444)," in *Kant's "Tugendlehre": A Comprehensive Commentary*, ed. Andreas Trampota, Oliver Sensen, and Jens Timmermann. Berlin: De Gruyter, 2013, pp. 269–292.

Fahmy, Melissa. "Love's Reasons," in *Journal of Value Inquiry*, Vol 50, Iss 1 September 2015, pp. 153–168. DOI 10.1007/s10790-015-9504-y.

Fairbanks, Sandra Jane. *Kantian Moral Theory and the Destruction of the Self*. New York: Routledge Press, 2018. Originally published by Westview Press, 2000.

Forman, David. "Kant's Moderate Cynicism and the Harmony between Virtue and Worldly Happiness," in *The Journal of the History of Philosophy*, 54(1) (Jan. 2016): 75–109; http://muse.jhu.edu/journals/journal_of_the_history_of_philosophy.

Formosa, Paul. *Kantian Ethics, Dignity and Perfection*. Cambridge: Cambridge University Press, 2017.

Formosa, Paul. "Dignity and Respect: How to Apply Kant's Formula of Humanity," in *The Philosophical Forum*, 45(1) (2014): 49–68.

Frankfurt, Harry. "Freedom of Will and the Concept of a Person," in *Journal of Philosophy*, 68 (1971): 5–20 (republished in *The Importance of What We Care About*. Cambridge: Cambridge University Press, 1998).
Frankfurt, Harry. "Reply to Susan Wolf," in *Contours of Agency: Essays on Themes from Harry Frankfurt*, ed. Sara Buss and Lee Overton. Cambridge, MA: MIT Press (A Bradford Book), 2002.
Frankfurt, Harry. *The Reasons of Love*. Princeton, NJ: Princeton University Press, 2006.
Frierson, Patrick. *Kant's Empirical Psychology*. Cambridge: Cambridge University Press, 2014.
Gilson, Etienne. *History of Christian Philosophy in the Middle Ages*. London: Sheed and Ward, 1955.
Grenberg, Jeanine. "Feeling, Desire and Interest in Kant's Theory of Action," in *Kant-Studien: Philosophische Zeitschrift der Kant-Gesellschaft*, 92(2) (2001): 153–179.
Grenberg, Jeanine. *Kant and the Ethics of Humility: A Story of Dependence, Corruption, and Virtue*. Cambridge: Cambridge University Press, 2005.
Grenberg, Jeanine. "What Is the Enemy of Virtue?" for *Kant's* Metaphysics of Morals: A Critical Guide, ed. Lara Denis. Cambridge: Cambridge University Press, 2010a.
Grenberg, Jeanine. "The Social Dimensions of Kant's Conception of Radical Evil," in *Kant's Anatomy of Evil*, ed. Sharon Anderson-Gold and Pablo Muchnik. Cambridge: Cambridge University Press, 2010b.
Grenberg, Jeanine. *Kant's Defense of Common Moral Experience: A Phenomenological Account*, Cambridge: Cambridge University Press, 2013a.
Grenberg, Jeanine. "Love in the Lectures on Ethics," in *Kant's Lectures on Ethics: A Critical Guide*, ed. Lara Denis. Cambridge: Cambridge University Press, 2013b.
Grenberg, Jeanine. "All You nNeed Is Love?," in *Kant on Emotions and Value*, ed. Alix Cohen. London: Palgrave Publishers, 2014, pp. 210–223.
Grenberg, Jeanine. "Self-Deception and Self-Knowledge: Jane Austen's *Emma* as an Example of Kant's Notion of Self-Deception," in *Con-textos kantianos*, no. 2 (2015): 162–176. http://www.con-textoskantianos.net/index.php/revista/issue/view/7.
Grenberg, Jeanine. "The Inveterate Debtor as Arrogant, Conceited Ass and Servile, Sycophantic Flatterer: Kant and Austen on Failures in the Virtues of Self-Respect and Debt Management," in *Rethinking Kant*, ed. Pablo Muchnik and Oliver Thorndike. Cambridge: Cambridge University Press, 2017.
Grenberg, Jeanine. "The Practical, Cognitive Import of Feeling: A Phenomenological Account," in *Kant and the Faculty of Feeling*, ed. Kelly Sorensen and Diane Williamson. Cambridge: Cambridge University Press, 2018.
Grenberg, Jeanine, and Vinton, M. "Kant on Humanity," in the *Oxford Handbook of Kant*. Oxford: Oxford University Press, 2021.
Guyer, Paul. *Kant on Freedom, Law and Happiness*. Cambridge: Cambridge University Press, 2000.
Guyer, Paul. "Ends of Reason and Ends of Nature: The Place of Teleology in Kant's Ethics" in *Kant's System of Nature and Freedom: Selected Essays*. Oxford: Oxford University Press, 2002.
Hart, H.L.A. "Legal and Moral Obligation," in *Essays in Moral Philosophy*, ed. Abraham I. Melden. Washington, DC: University of Washington Press, 1958, pp. 82–107.
Henson, Richard G. "What Kant Might Have Said: Moral Worth and the Overdetermination Of Dutiful Action," *Philosophical Review* 88 (1979), pp. 39–54.
Herman, Barbara. "Leaving Deontology Behind," in *The Practice of Moral Judgment*. Cambridge, MA: Harvard University Press, 1993a.

Herman, Barbara. "On the Value of Acting from the Motive of Duty," in *The Practice of Moral Judgment*. Cambridge, MA: Harvard University Press, 1993b.
Herman, Barbara. "The Difference that Ends Make," *Perfecting Virtue: New Essays on Kantian Ethics and Virtue Ethics*, ed. Lawrence Jost and Julian Wuerth. Cambridge: Cambridge University Press, 2010, pp. 92–115.
Hill, Thomas, Jr. (1980), "Humanity as an End in Itself," *Ethics* 91/1: 84–99 (re-published in his *Dignity and Practical Reason in Kant's Moral Theory*. New York: Cornell University Press, 1992, pp. 38–57).
Holberg, Erika. Kant's Quasi-Eudaemonism," in *The Southern Journal of Philosophy*, 56(3) (2018): 1–16. ISSN 0038-4283, online ISSN 2041-6962. DOI:10.1111/sjp.12296.
Johnson, Robert. "Value and Autonomy in Kantian Ethics," in *Oxford Studies in Metaethics*, Vol. 2, ed. R. Shafer-Landau. New York: Oxford University Press, 2007, pp. 133–148.
Johnson, Robert. "Was Kant a Virtue Ethicist?," in *Kant's Ethics of Virtue*, ed. Monika Betzler. Berlin: DeGruyter, 2008, pp. 61–76.
Johnson, Robert, with Cureton, Adam. "Kant's Moral Philosophy," in *The Stanford Encyclopedia of Philosophy* (Spring edition), ed. Edward N. Zalta. Stanford, CA: Standford University Press, 2019. https://plato.stanford.edu/archives/spr2019/entries/kant-moral/.
Kerstein, Samuel J. *How to Treat Persons*. Oxford: Oxford University Press, 2013.
Kierkegaard, Soren. *Fear and Trembling*, ed. Alastair Hannay. London: Penguin Classics, 2003.
Kipling, Rudyard. "If," in *A Choice of Kipling's Verse*. New York: Charles Scribner and Sons Publishing, 1943. https://www.poetryfoundation.org/poems/46473/if-.
Kitcher, Patricia. "A Kantian Argument for the Formula of Humanity," in *Kant-Studien*, 108(2) (2017): 218–246.
Kohl, Markus. The Normativity of Prudence," in *Kant-Studien*, 108(4) (2017): 517–542.
Korsgaard, Christine. "Kant's Formula of Humanity," *Kant-Studien* 77 (1986): 194–197 (reprinted in *Creating the Kingdom of Ends*, New York: Cambridge University Press, 1996).
Korsgaard, Christine. *The Sources of Normativity*, ed. Onora O'Neill. Cambridge: Cambridge University Press, 1996a.
Korsgaard, Christine. "From Duty and for the Sake of the Noble," in *Aristotle, Kant and the Stoics: Rethinking Happiness and Duty*, ed. Stephen Engstrom and Jennifer Whiting. Cambridge: Cambridge University Press, 1996b.
Korsgaard, Christine. "Kant's Formula of Universal Law," in *Creating the Kingdom of Ends*. Cambridge: Cambridge University Press, 1996c.
Korsgaard, Christine. *Self-Constitution: Agency, Identity, and Integrity*. Oxford: Oxford University Press, 2009.
Korsgaard, Christine M. *Fellow Creatures: Our Obligations to the Other Animals*. Oxford: Oxford University Press, 2018.
Kuehn, Manfred. *Kant: A Biography*. Cambridge: Cambridge University Press, 2001.
Louden, Robert. "Kant's Virtue Ethics," in *Philosophy* 61 (1986): 473–489.
MacIntyre, Alasdair. *After Virtue*. South Bend, IN: University of Notre Dame Press, 1981.
MacIntyre, Alasdair. *Whose Justice? Which Rationality?* South Bend, IN: University of Notre Dame Press, 1988.
MacIntyre, Alasdair. *Three Rival Versions of Moral Inquiry: Encyclopaedia, Genealogy, and Tradition*. South Bend, IN: University of Notre Dame Press, 1994.
Makkreel, Rudolf. *Imagination and Interpretation in Kant: The Hermeneutical Import of the Critique of Judgment*. Chicago, IL: University of Chicago Press, 1995.
McCarty, Richard. *Kant's Theory of Action*. Oxford: Oxford University Press, 2009.

Moran, Kate. "Delusions of Virtue: Kant on Self-Conceit," in *Kantian Review*, 19(3) (2014): 419–447.
Morrisson, Iain. *Kant and the Role of Pleasure in Moral Action*. Athens, OH: Ohio University Press, 2008.
Murdoch, Iris. *Sovereignty of the Good*. London: Routledge, 1970.
Nehemas, Alexander. *On Friendship*. London: Basic Books, 2016.
O'Neill, Onora. "Kant's Virtues," in *How Should One Live?* Oxford: Clarendon Press, 1996.
O'Neill, Onora. *Towards Justice and Virtue*. Cambridge: Cambridge University Press, 1998a.
O'Neill, Onora. "Kant on Duties Regarding Nonrational Nature," in *Proceedings of the Aristotelian Society*, Supplementary Volumes, 72 (1998b): 189–228.
O'Neill, Onora. "A Kantian Approach to World Hunger," in *Disputed Moral Issues: A Reader*, ed. M. Timmons. Oxford: Oxford University Press, 2007.
Paton, H.J. *The Categorical Imperative: A Study in Kant's Moral Philosophy*. Chicago, IL: University of Chicago Press, 1948 (republished 1962, 1971).
Paton, Margaret. "A Reconsideration of Kant's Treatment of Duties to Oneself," in *The Philosophical Quarterly (1950–)*, 40(159) (Apr. 1990): 222–233.
Potter, Nelson T. Jr. "Maxims in Kant's Moral Philosophy," in *Philosophia*, 23(1–4) (1994): 59–90.
Reath, Andrews. "Kant's Theory of Moral Sensibility: Respect for the Moral Law and the Influence of Inclination," *Kant-Studien*, 80 (1989): 284–302.
Reath, Andrews. "Legislating the Moral Law," in *Nöus*, 28(4) (1994): 435–464.
Reath, Andrews. "Formal Approaches to Kant's Formula of Humanity," in *Kant on Practical Justification*. Oxford: Oxford University Press, 2013, pp. 201–228.
Rocha, James. "Kantian Respect for Minimally Rational Animals," in *Social Theory and Practice*, 41(2) (April 2015): 309–327.
Rossi, Philip J. *The Ethical Commonwealth in History: Peace-Making as the Moral Vocation of Humanity*. Cambridge: Cambridge Elements series of Cambridge University Press, 2019.
Rudd, Anthony. *Self, Value and Narrative: A Kierkegaardian Approach*. Oxford: Oxford University Press, 2012a.
Rudd, Anthony. "Kierkegaard's Platonism and the Reasons of Love," in *Love Reason and Will: Kierkegaard After Frankfurt*, ed. John Davenport and Anthony Rudd. London: Bloomsbury Press, 2012b.
Schneewind, Jerome. "Kant and Stoic Ethics," in *Aristotle, Kant, and the Stoics: Rethinking Happiness and Duty*, ed. Stephen Engstrom and Jennifer Whiting. Cambridge: Cambridge University Press, 1996, pp. 285–301.
Seneca. *The Stoic Philosophy of Seneca*, trans. Moses Hadas. Garden City, NY: Doubleday, 1958.
Shakespeare, William. *Hamlet*. Oxford: Oxford University Press, 2009.
Sherman, Nancy. *Making a Necessity of Virtue: Kant and Aristotle on Virtue*. Cambridge: Cambridge University Press, 1997.
Singer, M.G. "'Duties to Oneself," in *Ethics*, LXIX (1959): 202–205.
Skidmore, J. "Duties to Animals: The Failure of Kant's Moral Theory," in *Journal of Value Inquiry*, 35(4) (2001): 541–559.
Spinoza, Benedict. *Ethics*, trans. Samuel Shirley. Indianapolis, IN: Hackett Publishing, 1992.
Timmermann, Jens. "Kant on Conscience, 'Indirect' Duty, and Moral Error," in *International Philosophical Quarterly* 46(3) (2006): 293–308.
Timmermann, Jens. "What's Wrong with Deontology?" in *Proceedings of the Aristotelian Society*, CXV(1) (1 April 2015): part 1, pp. 75–92. doi: 10.1111/j.1467-9264.2015.00385.x.

Timmermann, Jens. "*Quod dubitas, ne feceris*—Kant on Using Conscience as a Guide," in *Studi Kantiani*, 29 (2016): 163–168. https://doi.org/10.19272/201602901010.
Timmons, Mark. "The Practical and Philosophical Significance of Kant's Universality Formulations of the Categorical Imperative," in *Significance and System: Essays on Kant's Ethics*. Oxford: Oxford University Press, 2017 (also published in Oxford Scholarship Online: April 2017, DOI: 10.1093/acprof:oso/9780190203368.001.0001).
Velkley, Richard. *Freedom and the End of Reason*. Chicago, IL: University of Chicago Press, 1989.
Wang Yang-ming. "From *A Record For Practice*," in *Readings in Later Chinese Philosophy*, ed. Justin Tiwald and Brian Van Norden. Indianapolis, IN: Hackett Publishing, 2014.
Ward, Keith. "Kant's Teleological Ethics," in *The Philosophical Quarterly*, 21(85) (Oct. 1971): 337–351.
Ward, Keith. *The Development of Kant's View of Ethics*. Oxford: Wiley-Blackwell, 1972 (republished 2019).
Ware, Owen. "The Duty of Self-Knowledge," in *Philosophy and Phenomenological Research*, LXXIX(3) (2009): 671–697.
Ware, Owen. "Kant on Moral Sensibility and Moral Motivation," in *Journal of the History of Philosophy*, 52 (2014): 727–746.
Ware, Owen. "Accessing the Moral Law through Feeling," in *Kantian Review*, 20(2) (2015): 301–311.
Watson, Gary. "Kant on Happiness in the Moral Life," in *Philosophy Research Archives*, 9 (1983): 79–108.
Wike, Victoria S. *Kant on Happiness in Ethics*. New York: SUNY Press, 1994.
Williams, Bernard. *Ethics and the Limits of Philosophy*. London: Fontana Press, 1985.
Wodehouse, P.G. *The Jeeves Omnibus*. London: Hutchinson Publishers, 1991.
Wolf, Susan. "The True, the Good and the Loveable: Frankfurt's Avoidance of Objectivity," in *Contours of Agency: Essays on Themes from Harry Frankfurt*, ed. Sara Buss and Lee Overton. Cambridge, MA: MIT Press (A Bradford Book), 2002, pp. 227–244.
Wolf, Susan. "The Meanings of Lives," in *Introduction to Philosophy: Classical and Contemporary Readings* (6th edition), ed. John Perry et al. Oxford: Oxford University Press, 2012.
Wood, Allen. "Kant's Historical Materialism," in *Autonomy and Community: Readings in Contemporary Kantian Social Philosophy*, ed. Jane Kneller and Sidney Axinn. Albany, NY: SUNY Press, 1998a.
Wood, Allen. "Kant on Duties Regarding Nonrational Nature," in *Proceedings of the Aristotelian Society*, Supplementary Volumes, 72 (1998b): 189–228.
Wood, Allen. *Kant's Ethical Thought*. Cambridge: Cambridge University Press, 1999.
Wood, Allen. "Kant versus Eudaimonism," in *Kant's Legacy: Essays in Honor of Lewis White Beck*, ed. Cicovacki Predrag. Rochester, NY: University of Rochester Press, 2000, pp. 261–282.
Wood, Allen. *Kantian Ethics*. Cambridge: Cambridge University Press, 2008.
Wood, Allen. *Kant's Moral Religion*. Ithaca, NY: Cornell University Press, 2009.
Wood, Allen. *Kant and Religion*. Cambridge: Cambridge University Press, 2020.
Wood, Allen with Schönecker, D. *Immanuel Kant's Groundwork for the Metaphysics of Morals: A Commentary*. Cambridge, MA: Harvard University Press, 2015.
Xenophon. *Memorabilia*, in *Xenophon in Seven Volumes*, Vol. 4, trans. Edgar Cardew Marchant. London: William Heinemann, Ltd., 1923.
Zuckert, Rachel. "A New Look at Kant's Theory of Pleasure," in *Journal of Aesthetics and Art Criticism*, 60(3) (2002): 239–252.

Index

For the benefit of digital users, indexed terms that span two pages (e.g., 52–53) may, on occasion, appear on only one of those pages.

activity, virtually unimpeded 280–5, 291–4, 298–304; *see also* proper function
affect
 as a loss of composure 264–5
 in contrast to passion 48, 268–9
 see also passion; composure
Allison, Henry 19n.18, 40n.2, 49n.8, 51–2, 90n.26, 113–15, 119, 168n.28, 274n.20
animals
 as beings of value 235–40
 duties to 225–35
Annas, Julia 12, 24–5, 281n.1, 284, 291–4, 298–302, 306n.18, 310–11, 313–14
anthropocentrism 235–8; *see also* persons; animals
apathy, *see* moral apathy
aptitude for virtue, *see* virtue
Aristotle 280–305, 331–47
attentiveness 50–4, 271–2, 275–8; *see also* passion
attitude 166–7, 210–12
Augustine 271n.18, 343n.48, 388
Austen, Jane 336n.43
autonomy 206–8
 of legislation 127–8
 see also freedom

Baier, Kurt 94n.34
Baxley, A.M. 1–2
Beck, L.W. 77n.3
beneficence, duty of 193–205
Bentham, Jeremy 2–4

Categorical Imperative 6
 equivalence of the formulations 21, 89–90, 168
 see also First Formulation; Second Formulation
causality, natural 37
 as an incomplete series 37
 see also Third Antinomy
Caygill, Howard 297n.8
coercion, *see* freedom

cognitions, pure and empirical 35–6
Cohen, Alix 321–2
composure 48, 264–6, 333–6; *see also* affect
conscience 65, 173–85
consequentialism 2–3, 86n.19; *see also* utilitarianism
constructivism 20, 90n.27, 92n.30, 153n.15, 157n.19, 168–9
contemplation
 of the dignity of the law 262
 as a means of subduing affects 265–7
contentment 24–8, 280–9
 as an analogue to happiness 322–6
 see also happiness
counsels
 of prudence 388–93
 of reason 40–1
Cureton, Adam 90nn.26–7, 153n.15, 168n.28
Cynicism, Moderate 23–4, 69–70, 247, 283–5

Darwall, Stephen 207
Dean, Richard 82nn.11–12, 89n.25, 90n.27, 153n.15, 168n.27
deduction, practical 140,
 of obligatory ends 138–40
Denis, Lara 82n.11, 85n.17, 89n.25, 90n.28
deontology 1–4
 as the doctrine of right 2, 79–80
 as the science of duty 3–4, 16
 as reciprocal with teleology 87–9, 144, 161–3
desire
 empirical 35
 Frankfurtian second-order 41–65
 governance of 33–5, 60–5
 satisfaction 181–2, 273–5
Dickens, Charles 315–16
dignity, *see* contemplation
Dillon, Robin 85
Doctrine of Right 102, 117
Doctrine of Virtue 4, 19–20, 75–6
Dostoevsky, Fyodor 185n.11, 233n.11
Dutiful Maxim Test 117–18; *see also* maxim

duty
    direct and indirect 225–9
    motive of 81, 253–4, 361, 370
    narrow and wide 189–90
    of love and of respect 191–3
    of right and virtue 165–6
    perfect and imperfect 20
    to others 190–3
    to self 203–8

Elizondo, E.S. 288–9, 300–10
end
    as the matter of choice 20
    independently existing 155–6, 167–9
    in-itself 89–94
    obligatory, rational, objective 119–30
    pragmatic, empirical, subjective 108–19
    that is also a duty 126–7
    to be effected 155–6, 169–71
Engstrom, Stephen 1n.1, 90n.26, 168n.28, 212n.35, 335n.42
environment 225–6, 232–9
Epictetus 249–50, 388
Eudaemonism 4–9; *see also* happiness
evaluative distance 208–13
evil 59–60
    propensity for radical 285, 331–2, 340
    see also self-absorption
excitement, *see* moral excitement

Fahmy, Melissa 110n.44, 154n.17, 213–14, 217n.38
feeling, *see* moral feeling
felt attachments 257–63
First Formulation
    materialized version of (end-based) 144–6, 193, 199, 202–3
    practical contradiction interpretation 77, 198n.22
    teleological contradiction interpretation, 76–7, 149n.10, 199n.23
    universalization test 21, 145–6, 174
    see also Categorical Imperative; Maxim
Forman, David 69–71, 284–5, 353–4
Formosa, Paul 20, 89nn.25–8, 91, 96–7, 153nn.15–17, 168nn.27–9, 201n.25
Formula of Humanity (FH), *see* Second Formulation
Formula of Universal Law (FUL), *see* First Formulation
Frankfurt, Harry 41–9
freedom
    as incorporation 19–20, 33–4
    inner 48, 126–9, 259–66
    negative 302–7
    of end-setting 106–8
    positive 126–9
    see also autonomy; Incorporation Thesis
Friend of Humanity 253–4
Frierson, Patrick 62–3, 178n.7

Gallows Man 23–4, 248–9, 253, 343–4, 396–7, 400–1
God 61, 231n.10
Guyer, Paul 19n.16, 80nn.7–9, 81–3, 90n.27, 153n.15, 201n.25

habit 292–6
happiness; *see also* pleasure; Eudaimonism
    empirically conceived as desire-satisfaction 11–28
    rationally, non-empirically conceived as pleasurable proper functioning 280, 324–5
    relationship to morality/virtue 353–4, 358, 361–6
Hart, H.L.A. 206n.27
hedonism 1, 255–6, 358
Hegel, G.W.F. 121, 146
Hercules at the crossroads 24, 274, 297–8, 331–2
Herman, Barbara 12n.10, 20–1, 73, 80–2, 91–7
heteronomy 6–9
Highest Good 69–70, 310n.24, 349–50, 396
Hill, Thomas Jr. 90n.28
Holberg, Erica 11n.8, 24–8, 284n.3, 354–7
humanity
    not an abstract entity 83–6
    see also persons; rational nature
humility 339
hypothetical imperative 100, 104, 119, 123–4

impulse, sensuous 108–12
inclination 47–52
incentive 112–14; *see also* Incorporation Thesis
indifference
    rejection of 159–60
    to persons 187–93
Incorporation Thesis; *see also* freedom; incentive
    as applying to ends 112–16
    as applying to maxims 51–2
integrity 56–7, 221–4, 343–4, 390–8, 403–4
intuition, sensible 138

Johnson, Robert 75n.2, 80n.7, 99n.38, 151n.13

Kerstein, S.J. 153n.15
Kierkegaard, Søren 317–18, 329
Kingdom of Ends 78, 149–50, 362
Kipling, Rudyard 393–4

Knight of Faith 307, 317–19, 329
Knight of Infinite Resignation 317–19, 329
Kohl, Markus 1–2, 8n.6, 24–7, 301n.11, 310n.21, 351–7
Korsgaard, Christine 22, 77–9, 90nn.26–7, 93n.32, 145n.8, 149n.10, 151n.12, 153n.15, 165n.22, 168nn.27–8, 199n.23, 230n.9
Kuehn, Manfred 255n.9

legislation, *see* autonomy
Louden, Robert 1–2

MacIntyre, Alasdair 336n.43
Makkreel, Rudolf 78n.4
maxim
  empirical 112–21
  end/object/matter of 101–7
  form of 97–100, 121, 124–5, 131–2, 144–5
  moral 121–2, 144–5, 324
  see also First Formulation; Dutiful Maxim Test
McCarty, Richard 19–20, 62–3, 178n.7
Metaphysics 68, 78–9, 164–5, 206–7
moderation of feeling, *see* moral apathy
moral apathy 248–64, 298
moral consciousness 29, 177, 224
moral excitement 258–64
moral feeling
  affectivist vs. intellectualist interpretation 62–3, 178n.7
  of respect as a quasi-desire 61–3, 177–9
moral law, *see* Categorical Imperative
moral motivation
  hedonistic 5–6, 9
  desire-based 9
moral principles
  rationally, not empirically grounded 36–7, 44, 59–60
  unconditional 7–8
moral psychology 205–8
Moran, Kate 212n.35
Morrisson, Iain 119
motivation, *see* moral motivation
Murdoch, Iris 14n.13

natural capacities 362–81, 396–400
necessity 35–9

obligation 205–9
obligatory end, *see* end
Odysseus 267
O'Neill, Onora 1–2, 22, 45n.5, 227
order
  of being 163–5
  of knowing 163–5

passion 49; *see also* affect; attentiveness
  in contrast to affect 48–9, 268–9
  as mutinous and vicious 183–4
  governance of 18
Paton, H.J. 21–2, 76–7, 149n.10, 199n.23
Paton, Margaret 206nn.27–8
persons
  as absolutely valuable 20, 62–3
  as ends-in-themselves 74, 94, 98, 168, 186, 199–200
  as sensibly affected rational beings 61
  as the objective telos of self-governance 83–4, 241
  see also rational nature; humanity
phenomenological
  experience 140–1
  method 28–9
phronesis 189–90
pleasure
  non-moral 341–2
  moral 341–2, 380–1, 383–6
  aesthetic 24–5, 281, 312, 322
Potter, N.T. 19n.18, 114
practical reason, *see* reason
Priam 18–19, 71, 344–5
principles, *see* moral principles
proper function 9–13, 289–90; *see also* activity, virtually unimpeded
pure reason, *see* reason

rational nature
  as an end-in-itself 89–95
  see also persons; humanity
rational self 61–2, 286–7
rationalism 330
Rawls, John 78
realism 55
reason
  counsels of 40–1
  prudential 284n.3, 354–7
  pure practical 78, 130–4
  pure theoretical 354–5
Reath, Andrews 62–3, 75n.2, 80n.7, 90nn.26–7, 99n.38, 151n.13, 153n.15, 168nn.27–8, 178n.7, 274n.20,
respect
  for persons 61–7, 175–82
  for oneself 186
  see also moral feeling
Rocha, James 22, 227n.6, 230n.9
Rossi, P.J. 78n.4, 79, 131n.56, 152n.14
Rousseau, Jean-Jacques 69–70

sacrifice, *see* toleration
Schneewind, Jerome 75n.2, 80n.7, 99n.38, 151n.13
Second Formulation
 as a negative principle 155–8
 as a positive principle 152–5
 materialized, end-based version of 135–7, 141–8
 see also Categorical Imperative
self-absorption, *see* evil
self-conceit 212, 328–9
self-constraint, *see* self-governance
self-governance
 of desire by desire 35, 43–51
 of desire by the moral feeling of respect 34
 Frankfurtian account of 40–9
 as an internal battle 273–6
selflessness 256–7
Shakespeare 303n.14
Singer, M.G. 206n.27
Skidmore, James 22, 229
Stoicism 12–13, 249–50, 285, 341–2, 383
suffering, *see* toleration
supervenience
 as conditionally necessary 18–19, 71
 as the relationship between the subjective and objective telos of virtue 67–71
sympathy, feeling of 213–18

teleology
 as reciprocal with deontology 86–9
 as the study of the good 79–80
 as a reading of Kant 86–8
telos
 not happiness empirically conceived 18
 of respecting persons 61–7
 objective 63–5
 of self-governance 64
 subjective 65–71
Timmermann, Jens 2–4, 185n.12
Timmons, Mark 21, 145n.8, 174n.3, 194n.19, 201n.25
Third Antinomy 37; *see also* causality
toleration
 of sacrifice and suffering 247–57

Transcendental
 Aesthetic 123
 Idealism 299–304, 330–1
 Unity of Apperception 177n.5

utilitarianism 1–2, 5–6, 255–6; *see also* consequentialism

value
 absolute moral in contrast to relative non-moral 376–85
Velkley, Richard 78n.4
vice 49, 182–5, 275
vigilance 331–2, 334–41
virtue
 aptitude for 280–4, 288–341
 as strength 128–30, 249, 296, 336
 battle for 247–8, 276–7
 catalog of 186–7, 190–1, 203–4, 213–14
 practice of 261–8
 relationship to happiness 395
virtue ethics 15, 69–70, 91–6, 132–3
 radical 93–4

Wang Yang-ming 345–6
Ward, Keith 19n.17, 77n.3, 78–9, 80n.8, 88–9, 96–7, 135–6, 172n.1
Ware, Owen 62–3, 178n.7, 212n.35
Watson, Gary 24–8, 287–8, 326–7, 351–3, 357
Wike, V.S. 19n.17, 80n.8, 87–8, 285–8
will
 free 99–100, 103–4, 127–8
 good 149–50, 156–7
 rational 7–11
Williams, Bernard 81–2, 85
Wodehouse, P.G. 48n.6, 265n.14
Wolf, Susan 402–3
Wood, Allen 21–2, 24–5, 81–4, 86–7, 282–8, 347–8, 353–4

Xenophon 273n.19

Zuckert, Rachel 24–5, 281, 288–9, 311–13, 322, 323nn.33,35, 324–5